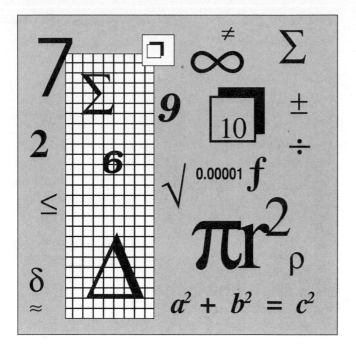

JAMES S. CANGELOSI
Utah State University

Teaching Mathematics in Secondary and Middle School

Research-Based Approaches

Merrill, an imprint of Macmillan Publishing Company
New York

Maxwell Macmillan Canada
Toronto

Maxwell Macmillan International
New York Oxford Singapore Sydney

Cover and text photos: Ted Hansen
Editor: Linda James Scharp
Developmental Editor: Kevin M. Davis
Production Editor: Mary M. Irvin
Art Coordinator: Lorraine Woost
Photo Editor: Gail Meese
Text Designer: Anne Flanagan
Cover Designer: Robert Vega
Production Buyer: Pamela D. Bennett

This book was set in Century Schoolbook and Helvetica
by Carlisle Communications, Ltd. and was printed and
bound by Semline. The cover was printed by Phoenix Color Corp.

Macmillan Publishing Company
866 Third Avenue
New York, NY 10022

Macmillan Publishing Company is part of the
Maxwell Communication Group of Companies.

Maxwell Macmillan Canada, Inc.
1200 Eglington Avenue East, Suite 200
Don Mills, Ontario M3C 3N1

Library of Congress Cataloging-in-Publication Data

Cangelosi, James S.

  Teaching mathematics in secondary and middle
  school: research-based approaches / James S.
  Cangelosi

    p.   cm.

  Includes bibliographical references and index.

  ISBN 0-675-21324-X

  1. Mathematics--Study and teaching
  (Secondary)   I. Title.

QA11.C23 1992

510′.71′2--dc20

                                        91-7865
                                          CIP

Printing: 1 2 3 4 5 6 7 8 9
Year: 2 3 4 5

TO ALLISON

PREFACE

Contrary to popular belief, mathematics is a human endeavor in which otherwise ordinary people of all ages discover relations, invent methods, and solve problems posed by their own real worlds. New mathematics are discovered and invented every day, as shown in the case of Ms. Lowe's students' work with "Nortons" in the scenario beginning on page 15. As illustrated by 15-year-old Brenda in Vignette 4.1, creative applications of mathematics are not limited to the efforts of professional mathematicians and researchers working on extraordinary problems. Brenda and Ms. Lowe's students find mathematics exciting and relevant to their personal interests as they confidently use it to address problems. How do these students acquire such healthy attitudes about and abilities with mathematics? According to consistent findings of numerous research studies, students acquire these attitudes and abilities by experiencing (a) conceptualization lessons in which concepts are inducted and relations discovered, (b) direct instruction for gaining knowledge of conventions and facts and developing and polishing algorithmic skills, (c) comprehension lessons for learning how to communicate with and about mathematics, and (d) application lessons in which solutions to real-life problems are deduced (see, for example, Driscoll, 1982; NCTM, 1988–89; Suydam, 1989).

However, *most* students acquire a considerably different view of mathematics, perceiving it as a boring string of terms, symbols, facts, and algorithms, truly understood only by rare geniuses. In stark contrast to Brenda and Ms. Lowe's students, it is typical for students only to memorize mathematical content—never discovering, inventing, nor creatively applying it (Dossey, Mullis, Lindquist, & Chambers, 1988). The unhealthy attitudes and the inability to extend mathematics beyond what is memorized are perpetuated by the most dominant method of teaching mathematics in our schools from kindergarten through college: Typically, mathematics lessons begin with the teacher telling the students a fact or giving them the steps in an algorithm. The teacher then works a textbook example and assigns students to work exercises from the textbook to help them remember the fact or process. The lessons are void of experiences whereby students discover, invent, or apply mathematics to problems they find meaningful (Jesunathadas, 1990).

For at least the past century, mathematics education specialists have encouraged teachers to practice the research-based approaches rather than the more commonly-practiced approaches. The recent widespread dissemination and support for the National Council of Teachers of Mathematics' (NCTM) plan for school mathematics curricula reform as articulated in *Curriculum and Evaluation Standards for School Mathematics* (NCTM, 1989) promises to bring typically practiced mathematics teaching in line with the research-based approaches. *Professional Standards for Teaching Mathematics* (NCTM, in press) represents a unified effort of exemplary mathematics teachers, mathematics education specialists, mathematicians, and educators to spell out what mathematics teachers must be able to do to take advantage of the research-based approaches and teach in harmony with the recommendations of the *Curriculum and Evaluation Standards for School Mathematics* (NCTM, 1989).

Teaching Mathematics in Secondary and Middle School: Research-Based Approaches is designed to help you, as a secondary or middle school mathematics teacher, successfully utilize the research-based approaches so that your students eagerly learn to discover, invent, and apply mathematics to solve real-world problems. To succeed with the research-based approaches you must design and conduct conceptualization, direct instructional, comprehension, and application lessons in ways that motivate students' cooperation and make use of accurate assessments of their progress. This book integrates those aspects of mathematics instruction in nine chapters:

❏ Chapter 1, "$T_i(S)$ = L: A Set of Messy Functions," points out the complexities of teaching and demonstrates that whether students find mathematics mystifying or understandable depends largely on the approaches employed by their teachers.

❏ Chapter 2, "Developing Mathematics Curricula," discriminates between typical and research-based curricula and explains how you as a mathematics teacher can develop the curricula you consider appropriate for your secondary or middle school students.

❏ Chapter 3, "Defining Learning Goals," demonstrates how to define the mathematical content and learning levels upon which to focus your lessons.

❏ Chapter 4, "Research-Based Approaches to Designing Lessons," demonstrates how to sequence and design lessons that lead your students to achieve the mathematical learning goals you set for them.

❏ Chapter 5, "Managing Student Behavior," suggests and illustrates methods for establishing a classroom climate that is conducive to learning mathematics, gaining and maintaining students' cooperation in the classroom, and efficiently dealing with student off-task behaviors.

❏ Chapter 6, "Engaging Students in Learning Activities," demonstrates how to design, organize, and conduct different types of learning activities (e.g., interactive lecture sessions, questioning and discussion sessions, small task-group sessions, independent work sessions, and homework) in ways that motivate students to be attentive and to cooperate eagerly with you and with each other.

❏ Chapter 7, "Assessing Student Achievement," introduces fundamental measurement and evaluation principles and demonstrates how to develop and use tests that provide feedback for guidance in designing lessons and valid data for judging student progress.

❏ Chapter 8, "Theory into Practice: Casey Rudd, First Year Mathematics Teacher," affords you the opportunity to experience vicariously the thoughts, plans, classroom activities, decisions, disappointments, and successes of a high school mathematics teacher as he attempts to implement the suggestions from Chapters 1 through 7 of this text.

❏ Chapter 9, "Looking Ahead," is intended to stimulate your thinking about the current movement to reform the way mathematics is typically taught in schools and to reflect on your own professional role in that movement.

Teaching Mathematics in Secondary and Middle School: Research-Based Approaches is an unusual book in that it not only presents research-based principles for teaching mathematics, but also demonstrates each via realistic classroom-based examples and contrasts them with examples that violate the principle. Furthermore, it integrates topics (e.g., defining learning goals, designing lessons, motivating student cooperation, and evaluating achievement) throughout, using approximately 250 scenarios that follow teachers' thoughts, actions, and reactions as they design, organize, conduct, evaluate, and re-design lessons. The book is structured to use the same type of research-based teaching strategies that it suggests you use with your students. In other words, (a) the book uses inductive approaches with carefully orchestrated examples to lead you to discover principles, (b) it incorporates direct instructional strategies in the presentations to expose you to information and techniques, and (c) it uses deductive structures to lead you to apply the principles and techniques. Throughout, the text uses comprehension strategies to introduce technical terms and advanced organizers.

Such an approach means that some topics that are treated separately from one another in other mathematics teaching methods texts are integrated throughout this text. For example, there is no separate chapter or section on "motivating student interest in mathematics" nor one on "gender issues in mathematics." However, those two topics are inextricably meshed throughout all nine chapters as are accommodating multiple achievement levels within one classroom, teaching general mathematics, teaching algebra, teaching geometry, teaching discrete mathematics, teaching consumer mathematics, teaching calculus, teaching trigonometry, and the other topics included in the *Guide to Integrated Topics* that supplements the table of contents. As a further illustration of this guide, note that unlike some other mathematics methods or teaching resource books, there is no separate part of this book devoted to "mathematical activities." However, such activities are illustrated within the 250 scenarios exemplifying research-based teaching practices (see, for example, the scenario involving Fred and Lottie in Vignette 2.11, the example of Mr. Krebs' opening day lesson in Vignette 5.4, or Mr. Rudd's lesson plan on pages 273 through 277).

Each of the book's examples and scenarios reflects aspects of actual events, but they are presented herein with fictitious names, locations, and institutions. Circumstances, actions, and situations are likely to appear familiar to any reader acquainted with the realities of schools, but any similarities among names, locations, and institutions in these examples and vignettes are strictly coincidental.

I am particularly grateful to the numerous but proportionally rare mathematics teachers who have demonstrated that research-based approaches are practical in realistic classroom situations. They are the people who provided me with the bases for the examples, without which I could not have written a book that uses inductive and deductive teaching strategies. Research and development outcomes from the Underprepared Mathematics Teacher Assessment Project (Cangelosi, 1988b), sponsored by the U.S. Office of Education and the Mathematics Teacher Inservice Project (Cangelosi, 1989b), sponsored by the National Science Foundation, had a significant impact on this work. I am indebted to those two funding agencies as well as to the numerous researchers cited throughout this work.

Ken Stillwell, Northeast Missouri State University; Ed Dickey, University of South Carolina, Columbia; William K. Tomhave, Concordia College; Mary M. Lindquist, Columbus College; Katherine Pederson, Southern Illinois University; Jay Graening, University of Arkansas; Earl J. Zwick, Indiana State University; Mark Klespis (also did accuracy check), St. Xavier College; Sandra J. Olson, Winona State; Boyd Holton, West Virginia University; Virginia Horak, University of Arizona; William L. Merrill, Central Michigan University; Nancy A. Minix, Western Kentucky University; E. Alexander Norman, University of North Carolina–Charlotte; and Stephen F. West, SUNY College at Geneseo provided expert reviews of the manuscript. Credit for this work is shared with the many professionals of Macmillan Publishing, including Jeff Johnston, Mary Irvin, Kevin Davis, and Larry Woost. Linda Thompson used her extraordinary mathematical, pedagogical, and writing talents and energetically attended to details as she expertly copyedited the manuscript. To my best friend, Barb Rice, I extend by sincerest appreciation for her support and counsel.

TO THE PROFESSOR

The manuscript for *Teaching Mathematics in Secondary and Middle School: Research-Based Approaches* was field-tested in mathematics teaching methods courses for both preservice and inservice teachers at Utah State University. Besides providing extremely positive feedback on the content and presentation of the material, implications for effectively incorporating the text in such courses are suggested by the results of the trials:

❑ Although the first eight chapters are longer than those in typical textbooks, all nine chapters can efficiently be included in a three-semester or five-quarter hour course. The extended number of chapter pages is a function of the integrative way topics are presented and the use of inquiry strategies with ample classroom-based examples, not due to the number of topics.

❑ Utah State University's preservice program for middle and secondary school teachers includes separate courses in classroom management and in educational measurement and evaluation. However, both chapters 5 and 7, which deal with those two areas, are still critical components of the mathematics teaching methods course because those chapters emphasize specific applications for the mathematics classroom.

❑ One effective strategy is to assign sections of the book to be read prior to dealing with those sections' topics in class meetings and then to center class activities around the end-of-chapter "Self-Assessment Exercises" pertaining to those topics. Discussions on responses to the exercises seem to identify issues, principles, and techniques on which class activities should focus.

❑ Although achievement of objectives for most chapters depends on achievement of objectives for previous chapters, methods courses need not be designed to progress uniformly from chapter to chapter. The following appears to be an effective arrangement:

1. The initial one-sixth of the course is devoted to achieving the objectives for the first two chapters. The preservice or inservice teachers acquire fundamental background information and begin organizing their thoughts in ways that will help them creatively design courses,

teaching units, and instructional strategies during subsequent phases of the course.

2. Another one-sixth of the time is spent with Chapter 3. Participants learn to define goals for teaching units by formulating sequences of objectives that specify the mathematical content and learning levels for their students to achieve. Each participant begins to design her or his own course and one teaching unit for that course. By following the "Self Assessment Exercises" chapter by chapter, each preservice or inservice teacher will have designed a course, developed a teaching unit, planned a variety of lessons, and constructed a unit test by the time he or she completes Chapter 8.

3. Half the time is spent designing and refining lessons applying the research-based approaches of Chapter 4. This is the centerpiece of the course. However, as participants work on those lessons, they are also reading and completing self-assessment exercises for chapters 5 through 7 —fine-tuning their lessons in light of what they gain from those three chapters. During this phase of the course, participants share and critique course, unit, and lesson plans and try out ideas in videotaped microteaching episodes. Scenarios from those chapters are reread in class with the professor raising leading questions (e.g., relative to the scenario in Vignette 6.11, "Why do you suppose Ms. Cramer interrupted Simon with, 'Just *read* it from your paper'? How would you have handled it?"). Although participants are not assigned to read Chapter 8 during this phase of the course, examples (e.g., how Mr. Rudd went about developing the unit plans appearing in Exhibit 8.10, 8.32, 8.33, and 8.34) are interjected into class meetings as needed to stimulate ideas and clarify points.

4. Loose ends are pulled together in conjunction with Chapters 8 and 9 during the final one-sixth of the course. During this phase, participants relate their struggles in developing and refining their courses, units, lessons, and tests to Casey Rudd's.

As you try different organizational patterns and techniques in conducting your methods of teaching mathematics courses, consider collecting data relative to what is and what isn't effective. The results of your field tests might prove valuable to many other mathematics education specialists if you choose to share them via the professional literature.

GUIDE TO INTEGRATED TOPICS

AFFECTIVE-LEVEL TEACHING AND LEARNING

Explanations, ideas, and principles: pp. 65–66, 68, 79–82, 215–216.

Sample objectives: pp. 65–66, 69–70, 79–82, 215–216.

Sample lessons and learning activities: pp. 79–81, 248–256.

Sample tests and test items: pp. 215–216.

ALGEBRA AND PREALGEBRA

Sample teaching units: pp. 36, 38–39, 213, 260–287, 231–233.

Sample goals and objectives: pp. 37, 57–60, 65–70, 79–80, 85, 93, 102, 116–119, 157, 171, 204, 216–217, 220–222, 226–229, 260–262.

Sample lessons and learning activities

    Inquiry: pp. 7–8, 17–18, 22–23, 37–40, 44, 47, 49–53, 79–81, 85–92, 93–95, 102–103, 112–114, 116, 119–122, 171–175, 182–187, 192, 248–251, 260–287, 309–312.

    Direct: pp. 17, 22–23, 37–38, 45, 102–103, 126, 146, 157, 178–179, 188–189, 260–287.

Sample tests and test items: pp. 199, 204, 217, 220–222, 226–230, 329–331.

ALGORITHMS, MATHEMATICAL

Explanations, ideas, and principles: pp. 15, 63, 103, 108, 223–227.

Sample lessons and learning activities: pp. 17–18, 32–34, 37–38, 45, 49–50, 104–108, 177, 188–191, 260–290.

APPLICATION-LEVEL TEACHING AND LEARNING

Explanations, ideas, and principles: pp. 24–26, 39–40, 67, 74–79, 109–114, 175–177, 225–230.

Sample objectives: pp. 11, 37, 58–60, 65, 57, 69–70, 110, 112, 182, 202, 210, 216, 226–230, 260–262, 288–294.

Sample lessons and learning activities: pp. 7–8, 37–38, 110–114, 182 187, 193, 260–290, 309–312.

Sample tests and test items: pp. 199–200, 202, 210, 214, 226–230, 331.

ARITHMETIC

Sample lessons and learning activities: pp. 30–32, 84–85.

Sample tests and test items: pp. 29–30, 84–85, 199.

ATTITUDES ABOUT MATHEMATICS

Common misperceptions including cultural, ethnic, and sex biases about learning mathematics: pp. 6, 11–13, 18, 22, 30, 114–116, 255–257

Building healthy student attitudes: pp. 11–18, 79–82, 114–116, 125–151, 248–259.

CALCULATORS

Accessibility, uses, and selection: pp. 10, 31–34, 49–50.

Sample learning activities with calculators: pp. 49–50, 260–290.

CALCULUS AND PRECALCULUS

Sample teaching units: pp. 246–247, 290, 292–294.

Sample goals and objectives: pp. 66–68, 106, 116, 122, 292–294.

Sample lessons and learning activities

Inquiry: pp. 116, 246–247, 254–256, 292–294.

Direct: pp. 33–34, 105–108, 292–294.

Sample tests and test items: pp. 222.

CLASSROOMS

Organization, procedures, and arrangements: pp. 53–56, 131–135, 143–145, 241–248.

Selection and use of learning materials and equipment: pp. 40–53, 242–245.

Establishing a favorable climate for learning mathematics: pp. 127–151, 241–260.

COMPREHENSION-LEVEL TEACHING AND LEARNING

Explanations, ideas, and principles: pp. 66–67, 77–79, 98–103, 175–177, 220–223.

Sample objectives: pp. 58–60, 66–70, 99, 102, 204, 220–222, 260–262, 288–294.

Sample lessons and learning activities: pp. 99–103, 260–290.

Sample tests and test items: pp. 199, 204, 220–222, 330–331.

COMPUTERS AND COMPUTER SOFTWARE

Accessibility, uses, and selection: pp. 10, 44–48, 144–145

Examples of computers as teaching tools: pp. 44–48, 211–214, 260–290

Examples of computers as learning tools: pp. 48–49, 144–145, 260–290.

CONCEPTS, MATHEMATICAL

Explanations, ideas, and principles: pp. 60–63, 84–92, 98.

Sample lessons and learning activities: 83–92, 110–111, 167–169, 171–175, 191–192, 260–290.

CONCEPTUALIZATION-LEVEL TEACHING AND LEARNING

Explanations, ideas, and principles: pp. 60–63, 67, 77–79, 82–95, 175–177, 216–219.

Sample objectives: pp. 11, 37, 58–60, 67, 69–70, 85, 100, 171, 216, 260–262, 288–294.

Sample lessons and learning activities: pp. 3–5, 15, 22–23, 37–40, 47, 51–53, 85–95, 119–122, 158–161, 168–169, 171–175, 191–192, 260–290.

Sample tests and test items: pp. 202, 216–219, 330–331.

CONSTANTS, MATHEMATICAL: pp. 60–63.

CONSUMER MATHEMATICS

Sample teaching units: pp. 246, 290–291.

Sample goals and objectives: pp. 57, 59, 69–70, 228, 290–291.

Sample lessons and learning activities

Inquiry: pp. 252–253, 290–291.

Direct: pp. 290–291.

Sample tests and test items: pp. 214, 228–229.

CONVENTIONS, MATHEMATICAL

Explanations, ideas, and principles: pp. 13–16, 60, 64.

Sample lessons and learning activities: pp. 37–38, 157, 170, 260–290.

COOPERATIVE LEARNING

Explanations, ideas, and principles: pp. 53, 175, 180–187.

Sample lessons and learning activities: pp. 47, 85–95, 146, 178–187, 189–190, 260–290.

CREATIVITY-LEVEL TEACHING AND LEARNING

Explanations, ideas, and principles: pp. 67–68, 78–79, 114–116, 230–231.

Sample objectives: pp. 58–60, 67–70, 116, 230.

Sample lessons and learning activities: pp. 47, 116.

Sample tests and test items: pp. 67, 230–231.

CURRICULA, MATHEMATICS

Explanations, ideas, and principles: pp. 21–71, 73–79, 155–156, 297–299, 313–322.

Sample course designs and descriptions: pp. 36–40, 245–256, 301–307, 324–327.

Sample teaching units: pp. 36–38, 260–294, 329–331.

DISCRETE MATHEMATICS

Sample goals and objectives: pp. 59–60, 70, 79–80, 82, 85, 96, 112, 226–227.

Sample lessons and learning activities

Inquiry: pp. 79–81, 83, 85–92, 112–114, 158–161, 168–169, 175–177.

Direct: pp. 96–97, 158, 167–168, 177

Sample tests and test items: pp. 199, 226–228.

EVALUATING STUDENT ACHIEVEMENT

Explanations, ideas and principles: pp. 197–237.

Testing: pp. 48, 199–231, 279, 329–331.

Formative feedback: pp. 38, 147–148, 167, 172, 180, 187, 190–193, 197–198, 200–201, 215, 217, 231, 266–285.

Grading student achievement: pp. 38, 150, 178, 198, 200–201, 215, 217–218, 231–234, 285–287.

GAMES AND PUZZLES, MATHEMATICAL

Explanations, ideas, and principles: pp. 39, 104, 178–179.

Sample learning activities: pp. 39, 43–44, 146–147, 178–179.

GEOMETRY

Sample teaching units: pp. 246, 287–289.

Sample goals and objectives: pp. 11, 57–59, 66–67, 69–70, 110, 202, 204, 210, 218–220, 288–289.

Sample lessons and learning activities

Inquiry: pp. 3–5, 15, 51–53, 83, 110–111, 128–131, 191–192, 250–251, 288–289.

Direct: pp. 2–3, 105, 288–289.

Sample tests and test items: pp. 202, 204, 210, 218–220.

HISTORY OF MATHEMATICS

Explanations, ideas, and principles: pp. 12–16, 18–19, 43, 170.

Sample lessons and learning activities: pp. 96, 180–181, 192.

HOMEWORK

Explanations, ideas, and principles: pp. 9–10, 138, 150, 191–195.

Sample assignments and learning activities: pp. 33–34, 81, 83, 90–92, 96, 98, 126, 191–194, 248–252, 260–287.

INDEPENDENT WORK SESSIONS

Explanations, ideas, and principles: pp. 187–191.

Sample sessions: pp. 106–108, 136, 148, 248–252, 260–287.

INTEGRATING MATHEMATICS WITH OTHER SUBJECT AREAS: pp. 247–248, 287–290.

KNOWLEDGE-LEVEL LEARNING

Explanations, ideas, and principles: pp. 66, 76–79, 96–98, 103–108, 157, 177, 219–220.

Sample objectives: pp. 58–60, 66, 69–70, 96–97, 106, 157, 204, 216–217, 219, 223–225, 260–262, 288–294.

Sample lessons and learning activities: pp. 2–3, 17–18, 22–23, 37–38, 96–98, 106–108, 158, 167–168, 178–180, 188–191, 260–290.

Sample tests and test items: pp. 199, 202, 219–220, 223–225, 330–331.

LECTURE SESSIONS, INTERACTIVE

Explanations, ideas, and principles: pp. 156–167.

Sample sessions: 22–23, 51–53, 97–98, 106–108, 157–161, 260–287.

MEASUREMENT, MATHEMATICAL

Explanations, ideas, and principles: pp. 50–51, 63.

Sample lessons and learning activities: pp. 260–287.

NUMBER THEORY

Sample goals and objectives: pp. 58, 66, 99–100, 220–221, 230.

Sample lessons and learning activities

Inquiry: pp. 56, 39, 47, 83, 99–101.

Direct: pp. 99–101.

Sample tests and test items: pp. 205–206, 220–221, 230–231.

OBJECTIVES, LEARNING

Explanations, ideas, and principles: pp. 11–12, 36–37, 57–71, 78–79.

Sample objectives

Appreciation learning level: pp. 59–60, 65, 69–70, 79–80.

Willingness-to-try learning level: pp. 58–59, 65–66, 69–70, 82, 215–216.

Simple-knowledge learning level: pp. 58–60, 66, 69–70, 96–97, 157, 219, 260–262, 288–294.

Knowledge-of-a-process learning level: pp. 36–37, 58–60, 66, 69–70, 106, 199, 202, 216–217, 223–225, 260–262, 288–294.

Comprehension learning level: pp. 58–60, 66–67, 69–70, 85, 93, 171, 202, 216–219, 260–262, 288–294.

Conceptualization learning level: pp. 11, 37, 58–60, 67, 69–70, 85, 93, 171, 202, 216–219, 260–262, 288–294.

Application learning level: pp. 11, 37, 58–70, 67, 69–70, 108, 110, 112, 199–200, 202, 210, 214, 226–230, 260–262, 288–294.

Creativity learning level: pp. 58–59, 67, 69–70, 116, 230.

PARENTS, WORKING WITH: pp. 10, 139–143, 255–258.

PROBABILITY AND STATISTICS

Sample goals and objectives: pp. 58–60, 70, 79–80, 112, 226.

Sample lessons and learning activities

Inquiry: pp. 80–81, 112–114, 158–161, 168–169, 175–177, 226–228.

Direct: pp. 158, 167–168, 177, 179–180.

Sample tests and test items: pp. 199, 226–228.

PROBLEM SOLVING: pp. 7–9, 24–26, 30, 39–40, 44, 47, 74–78, 102–103, 109–110, 181–182, 225–231, 260–286, 298, 317–322, 329–331.

PROOFS: pp. 47, 64, 99–101, 205–206, 230–231.

QUESTIONING/DISCUSSION SESSIONS

Explanations, ideas, and principles: pp. 167–180.

Sample sessions: pp. 4–5, 22–23, 84–92, 99–103, 109–114, 116, 167–175, 260–287.

READING, LISTENING, SPEAKING, AND WRITING ABOUT MATHEMATICS: pp. 8, 16, 40–43, 64, 98–103, 220–223.

RELATIONS, MATHEMATICAL

Explanations, ideas, and principles: pp. 18, 60, 63–64, 92–95, 98.

Sample lessons and learning activities: pp. 2–6, 15, 22–24, 37–39, 47, 51–53, 79–82, 93–95, 97–102, 158–161, 171, 260–290.

SMALL TASK-GROUP SESSIONS

Explanations, ideas, and principles: pp. 180–187.

Sample sessions: pp. 93–95, 146, 180–185, 260–287.

***STANDARDS*, NATIONAL COUNCIL OF TEACHERS OF MATHEMATICS (NCTM):** pp. 10, 26–35, 38, 40, 43, 55–56, 64–65, 74, 115, 185, 199, 201, 235, 237, 246, 297–299, 313–322, 338.

STUDENTS

Differential aptitudes for learning mathematics: pp. 5–11, 75–78, 114–116.

Differential stages of achievement: pp. 5–11, 22, 29–34, 48, 180–182.

Special needs: pp. 9–11, 48.

Motivation for learning mathematics: pp. 6–12, 18–19, 24–27, 76–82, 127–131, 151–167.

Behavior Management: pp. 10–11, 51–53, 118–195, 205, 258–259.

TEACHERS, PROFESSIONAL

Professional conduct: pp. 141–143, 148–151, 239–241, 291, 294.

Beginning teachers of mathematics: pp. 6, 122, 239–296, 299.

Colleague assistance: pp. 42, 149–150, 243–245, 252, 260.

Instructional supervision: pp. 41–42, 241, 259–260, 290–294, 299.

Administrative supervision: pp. 241–260.

Professional organizations: pp. 42, 290–294, 298–299.

TECHNOLOGY IN THE CLASSROOM: pp. 4, 43–55, 128–131, 166, 289–290, 298, 317–322.

TEXTBOOKS, MATHEMATICS: pp. 7–8, 13, 38–41, 102–103, 207, 242–247, 260–290, 301–303.

TRIGONOMETRY

Sample goals and objectives: pp. 66, 97.

Sample lessons and learning activities
  Inquiry: pp. 109–110.
  Direct: pp. 9–10, 97–98, 179.

Sample tests and test items: pp. 199–200.

VARIABLES

Explanations, ideas, and principles: pp. 41, 50–51, 61.

Sample lessons and learning activities: pp. 83, 126–127, 171–175.

WRITING, SPEAKING, READING, AND LISTENING ABOUT MATHEMATICS: pp. 8, 16, 40–43, 64, 98–103, 220–223.

CONTENTS

CHAPTER 1
$T_i(S) = L$: A Set of Messy Functions   **1**

A SET OF TIDY FUNCTIONS (f_i)   1

TEACHING AS A SET OF FUNCTIONS (T_i)   2

STUDENTS AS AN INDEPENDENT VARIABLE (DOMAIN OF T_i)   5
Variations Among Students   5
Interest in Mathematics   6
Perception of Mathematics   6
Aptitude for Reasoning with Abstractions   6
Perception of What Is Important   7
Experiences Upon Which You Can Build   7
Prior Mathematical Learning   8
Communication Skills   8
Coursework in Other Academic Areas   8
Special Needs   9
Self-Confidence   9
Attitude Toward Learning   9
Study Skills   9
Use of Drugs   10
Home and Social Life   10
Time Available for Studying Mathematics   10
Access to Calculators, Computers, and Other Relevant Tools   10
Attitude Toward School   10

Classroom Citizenship   10
Personal Values   11

STUDENT LEARNING AS A DEPENDENT VARIABLE (RANGE OF T_i)   11
Achievement of Stated Objectives   11
Side Effects of Incidental Outcomes   11

THE MYSTIFICATION OF MATHEMATICS   12

DEMYSTIFYING MATHEMATICS   13
Human Discoveries and Human Inventions   13
    From Where Does Mathematics Come?
Teaching Comprehension of Mathematical Language   16
Integrating Topics   16

INVOLVING STUDENTS IN THE DISCOVERY/INVENTION PROCESS   18
Monitoring Your Own Attitudes   18

CHAPTER 2
Developing Mathematics Curricula   **21**
A Curriculum   21
Two Views   24
    Learn Mathematics to Learn More Mathematics ❑ Learn Mathematics to Solve Real-Life Problems

REAL-LIFE PROBLEMS 25

THE NATIONAL COUNCIL OF TEACHERS OF MATHEMATICS' (NCTM) STANDARDS 26

The Gap Between Research-Based Curricula and Typical Practice 26

Curriculum and Evaluation Standards for School Mathematics 28

MATHEMATICS CURRICULA OUTCOMES 29

Elementary School–Level Outcomes 29

Traditional Curriculum ❑ NCTM Standards–Based Curriculum

Middle School—and Junior High School—Level Outcomes 31

Traditional Curriculum ❑ NCTM Standards-Based Curriculum

High School–Level Outcomes 32

Traditional Curriculum ❑ NCTM Standards–Based Curriculum

COURSES 35

TEACHING UNITS 36

The Learning Goal 36

The Set of Specific Objectives that Defines the Learning Goal 36

The Planned Sequence of Lessons 37

Mechanisms for Monitoring Student Progress and Utilizing Feedback in the Design of Lessons 38

A Summative Evaluation of Student Achievement of the Learning Goal 38

APPROACHES TO DESIGNING COURSES 38

The Follow-a-Textbook Approach 38

The Contrived Problem-Solving Approach 39

The Real-World Problem-Solving Approach 39

Combining Approaches 40

SELECTION OF LEARNING MATERIALS, RESOURCES, EQUIPMENT, AND FACILITIES 40

Textbooks 40

Sources of Ideas on Teaching 41

Colleagues ❑ Professional Organizations ❑ School-District-Sponsored Resource Centers and Workshops ❑ Colleges, Universities, Foundations, and Research and

Development Centers ❑ Publishing Houses

Sources for Mathematical Topics 43

Sources for Mathematics History 43

Manipulatives and Concrete Models 43

Computers, Printers, and Computer Software 44

Uses

Computer-Assisted Instruction (CAI) 48

Accessibility ❑ Selection

Calculators 49

Measuring Instruments 50

Video and Audio 51

The Classroom Arrangements 53

CHAPTER 3
Defining Learning Goals   **57**

LEARNING GOAL 57

The Purpose of a Teaching Unit 57

The Need for Specificity 58

A SET OF OBJECTIVES 58

THE CONTENT SPECIFIED BY AN OBJECTIVE 60

The Need to Classify Content 60

Concept 60

Constant 62

Relation 63

Algorithm 63

Convention 64

Other Ways of Classifying Content 64

THE LEARNING LEVEL SPECIFIED BY AN OBJECTIVE 65

The Need to Classify Learning Levels 65

Learning Domains 65

Affective Objectives 65

Appreciation ❑ Willingness to Try

Knowledge-Level and Intellectual-Level Cognition 66

Knowledge-Level Cognitive Objectives 66

Simple Knowledge ❑ Knowledge of a Process

Intellectual-Level Cognitive Objectives 66

Comprehension ❑ Conceptualization ❑ Application ❑ Creativity

USING THE SCHEME FOR CLASSIFYING LEARNING LEVELS 68

CHAPTER 4
Research-Based Approaches to Designing Lessons   **73**

REQUISITES FOR LEARNING TO APPLY MATHEMATICS TO REAL-LIFE PROBLEM-SOLVING 74

Problem-Solving in the Real World 74

Requisite Attitudes, Skills, and Abilities 76

Requisite Learning Experiences 77

SEQUENCING THE OBJECTIVES OF A TEACHING UNIT 78

LEARNING ACTIVITIES FOR AFFECTIVE OBJECTIVES 79

Appreciation 79

Willingness to Try 82

LEARNING ACTIVITIES FOR CONCEPTUALIZATION-LEVEL OBJECTIVES 82

Challenging but Critical to Teach 82

Inductive Reasoning 83

Inductive Learning Activities 83

Conceptualizing Concepts 84

Concepts Attributes and Psychological Noise ❑ Incorporating the Seven Stages into a Concept Lesson

Conceptualizing Relations 92

Necessary Conditions and Psychological Noise for Relations ❑ A Seven-Stage Lesson for Conceptualizing a Relation

LEARNING ACTIVITIES FOR SIMPLE-KNOWLEDGE-LEVEL OBJECTIVES 96

Facilitating Reception and Retention through Direct Instruction 96

Exposition ❑ Explication ❑ Mnemonics ❑ Monitoring and Feedback ❑ Overlearning

A Five-Stage Lesson for a Simple-Knowledge Objective 97

LEARNING ACTIVITIES FOR COMPREHENSION-LEVEL OBJECTIVES 98

Comprehension of a Particular Message 98

Literal and Interpretive Understanding ❑ Designing Learning Activities for Literal Understanding ❑ Designing

Activities for Interpretative Understanding ❑ A Lesson for Comprehension of a Particular Message

Comprehension of a Communications Mode 101

LEARNING ACTIVITIES FOR KNOWLEDGE-OF-A-PROCESS OBJECTIVES 103

Processes, the Most Common Type of Content 103

Facilitation Process Skills through Direct Instruction 104

Analyze the Process ❑ Identify Any Prerequisite Skills of Abilities Students Might Need

A Nine-Stage Lesson for a Knowledge-of-a-Process Objective 105

LEARNING ACTIVITIES FOR APPLICATION-LEVEL OBJECTIVES 109

Problem-Solving 109

Deductive Reasoning 109

Facilitating Application-Level Learning 110

A Four-Stage Lesson for an Application Objective 112

LEARNING ACTIVITIES FOR DEVELOPING MATHEMATICAL CREATIVITY 114

Some Thoughts on Creativity 114

Preserving Creativity 115

Fostering Creativity 115

Synectics 116

A Lesson Designed to Foster Creativity 116

CHAPTER 5
Managing Student Behavior   **119**

A WELL-DESIGNED LESSON GONE AWRY 119

A TEACHER'S MOST PERPLEXING PROBLEM 122

ALLOCATED AND TRANSITION TIMES 122

STUDENT BEHAVIORS 124

On-Task Behavior 124

Engaged Behavior 124

Off-Task Behavior 124

Disruptive Behavior 124

Isolated Behavior 124

Behavior Pattern 124

TEACHING STUDENTS TO BE ON-TASK 125

Learned Behavior 125

Communicating Expectations 125

Reinforcing On-Task Behaviors 127

Planning for Students to Be On-Task 127

ESTABLISHING A FAVORABLE CLIMATE FOR LEARNING MATHEMATICS 127

Priority on the Business of Learning 127

A Businesslike Beginning 127

Preparation and Organization 131

Modeling Businesslike, Purposeful Behavior 132

Efficient Transitions 133

Taking Care of Administrative Chores ❏ Directing Students into Learning Activities ❏ Distributing Learning Materials ❏ Preparing Illustrations and Audiovisual Aids

A Comfortable, Nonthreatening Environment 135

COMMUNICATING EFFECTIVELY 135

Proximity and Body Language 135

Descriptive Versus Judgmental Communications 136

Supportive Versus Nonsupportive Replies 137

Assertive Versus Hostile or Passive Communications 138

Being Responsible for One's Own Conduct 139

Communicating with Parents 139

A Cooperative Partnership ❏ Teacher/Parent Conferences ❏ Written Communiques

Professional Confidences 141

Violations of Trust ❏ Privileged Information

ESTABLISHING RULES OF CONDUCT AND CLASSROOM PROCEDURES 143

Necessary Rules of Conduct 143

Procedures for Smoothly Operating Classrooms 144

Teaching Rules and Procedures to Students 145

DEALING WITH OFF-TASK BEHAVIORS 145

A Systematic Approach 145

Thirteen Suggestions 147

CONDUCTING ENGAGING LEARNING ACTIVITIES 151

**CHAPTER 6
Engaging Students in
Learning Activities   155**

INTEGRATING DIFFERENT TYPES OF LEARNING ACTIVITIES INTO LESSONS 155

The Traditional Approach 155

The Resurrection of an Eighteenth-Century Approach 156

The Suggested Research-Based Approach 156

ENGAGING STUDENTS IN LARGE-GROUP INTERACTIVE LECTURE SESSIONS 156

Appropriate Uses of Large-Group Interactive Lecture Sessions 156

Large-Group Sessions ❏ Lectures ❏ Interactions ❏ Interactive Lecture Sessions ❏ Direct Instructional Methods in Interactive Lecture Sessions ❏ Inquiry Instructional Methods in Interactive Lecture Sessions

Common Misuses of Large-Group Interactive Lecture Sessions 157

Two Contrasting Examples 158

Providing Directions 161

Initiating Student Engagement 161

Readiness to Listen ❏ Establishing Set

Maintaining Engagement in Large-Group Interactive Lecture Sessions 162

Using Formative Feedback 167

Achieving Closure

ENGAGING STUDENTS IN LARGE-GROUP INTELLECTUAL-LEVEL QUESTIONING/DISCUSSION SESSIONS 167

Intellectual-Level Questions 167

Appropriate Uses of Intellectual-Level Questioning/Discussion Sessions 169

Common Misuses of Intellectual-Level Questioning/Discussion Sessions 170

Initiating and Maintaining Student Engagement in Large-Group

Intellectual-Level Questioning/Discussion Sessions 172

Responding to Students' Questions 175

Student-Initiated Intellectual-Level Questions

ENGAGING STUDENTS IN LARGE-GROUP RECITATION SESSIONS 177

Knowledge-Level Questions 177

Appropriate Uses of Large-Group Recitation Sessions 177

Common Misuses of Large-Group Recitation Sessions 177

Initiating and Maintaining Student Engagement in Recitation Sessions 178

ENGAGING STUDENTS IN SMALL TASK-GROUP SESSIONS 180

Appropriate Uses of Small Task-Group Sessions 180

Peer Instruction Groups ❑ Practice Groups ❑ Interest or Achievement-Level Groups ❑ Problem-Solving Groups

Common Misuses of Small-Task-Group Sessions 182

Initiating and Maintaining Student Engagement in Small-Task-Group Sessions 185

ENGAGING STUDENTS IN INDEPENDENT WORK SESSIONS 187

Appropriate Uses of Independent Work Sessions 187

Common Misuses of Independent Work Sessions 188

Initiating and Maintaining Student Engagement in Independent Work Sessions 188

ENGAGING STUDENTS IN MEANINGFUL HOMEWORK 191

Appropriate Uses of Homework 191

Use of Homework as Preparation for Classroom Activities ❑ Use of Homework as an Extension of Classroom Activities ❑ Use of Homework as a Follow-Up to Classroom Activities

Common Misuses of Homework 193

Initiating and Maintaining Engagement in Homework Activities 194

**CHAPTER 7
Assessing Student Achievement 197**

DIFFICULT DECISIONS 197

Formative Evaluations 197

Summative Evaluations 198

COMMON MALPRACTICE 198

RESEARCH-BASED PRACTICE 198

MEASUREMENTS 199

EVALUATIONS 200

MEASUREMENT VALIDITY 202

Relevance to Student Achievement of the Stated Learning Goal 202

Pertinence of Items to the Content and Learning Levels of Objectives ❑ Emphasis on Objectives According to Relative Importance

Measurement Reliability 203

Internal Consistency ❑ Scorer Consistency

MEASUREMENT USABILITY 206

TYPES OF TESTS 207

Commercially Produced Tests 207

Standardized Tests 207

Teacher-Produced Tests 207

DESIGNING AND CONSTRUCTING TESTS 207

A Systematic Approach 207

The Haphazard Method ❑ The Research-Based Method

Clarify the Learning Goal 208

Develop a Test Blueprint 208

The Complexity of the Test Design ❑ Administration Time ❑ Scoring Time ❑ Types of Items ❑ Number of Items ❑ Difficulty of Items ❑ Estimate of the Maximum Number of Points on the Test ❑ Number of Points for Each Objective ❑ Method for Determining Cutoff Scores ❑ Test Outline

Obtain and Maintain Relevant Item Pools 211

The Advantages of Item Pools ❑ Desirable Characteristics of Item Pools ❑ Computerized Item Pools

Synthesize the Test 214

DEVELOPING ITEMS 214

ITEMS RELEVANT TO ACHIEVEMENT OF AFFECTIVE OBJECTIVES 215

A Matter of Choice, Not Ability or Skill 215

The Self-Report Approach 215

The Direct Observational Approach 215

ITEMS RELEVANT TO ACHIEVEMENT OF CONCEPTUALIZATION OBJECTIVES 216

Grouping Examples and Explaining Why 216

Items for Formative Feedback 217

Items for Tests Used to Make Summative Evaluations 217

Controlling the Difficulty Levels of Conceptualization Items 218

ITEMS RELEVANT TO ACHIEVEMENT OF SIMPLE-KNOWLEDGE OBJECTIVES 219

Stimulus-Response 219

Controlling the Difficulty Levels of Simple-Knowledge Items 220

ITEMS RELEVANT TO ACHIEVEMENT OF COMPREHENSION OBJECTIVES 220

Deriving Meaning from Expressions 220

    Comprehension-of-a-Message Items ❏ Comprehension-of-a-Communication-Mode Items

Novelty 221

Controlling the Difficulty Level of Comprehension Items 221

ITEMS RELEVANT TO ACHIEVEMENT OF KNOWLEDGE-OF-A-PROCESS OBJECTIVES 223

Emphasis on the Process, Not the Outcome 223

Error-Pattern Analysis 224

Controlling the Difficulty Levels of Knowledge-of-a-Process Items 225

ITEMS RELEVANT TO ACHIEVEMENT OF APPLICATION OBJECTIVES 225

Deciding How to Solve Problems 225

AVOIDING "GIVEAWAY" WORDS 226

Extraneous Data 228

Missing Data 228

Mixing Example and Nonexample Problems 229

Controlling the Difficulty Levels of Application Items 229

ITEMS RELEVANT TO MATHEMATICAL CREATIVITY 230

USING TEST RESULTS 231

Formative Feedback 231

Converting Test Scores to Grades 231

    Grading ❏ Traditional Percentage Method ❏ The Visual Inspection Method ❏ The Compromise Method ❏ Evaluating Instructional Effectiveness

**CHAPTER 8
Theory into Practice: Casey Rudd, First-Year Mathematics Teacher 239**

CASEY RUDD AND HIS FIRST TEACHING POSITION 239

Preservice Preparation 239

Selecting a Position at Malaker High School 240

The Assignment 240

    The Teaching Load ❏ Other Responsibilities

ORGANIZING FOR THE YEAR 241

The Situation as of July 15 241

Valuable Help from Colleagues 243

    Discovering the Computer Lab ❏ Discouraging Advice from Don Delaney ❏ Progressive but Pragmatic Advice from Vanessa Castillo

Planning and Organizing the Courses by Writing Syllabi 245

    First-Period Algebra I ❏ Third-Period Geometry ❏ Fourth-Period Geometry ❏ Fifth-Period Consumer Mathematics ❏ Sixth-Period Precalculus

Organizing the Classroom 247

Setting Up the System of Item Pool Files 247

Arrangements and Acquisitions 247

THE BEGINNING OF AN EVENTFUL SCHOOL YEAR 248

Opening Day 248

Learning from Experiences 251

    Becoming More Assertive ❏ Addressing Behavior-Management

Problems ❑ Benefiting from Instructional Supervision ❑ Preparing for Administrative Supervision

SAMPLE ALGEBRA I TEACHING UNIT 260

Designing a Unit on Factoring Polynomials 260

DAY-1: REVIEWING THE UNIT TEST ON POLYNOMIALS AND SETTING THE STAGE FOR THE UNIT ON FACTORING 263

Planning for Day 1 263

Day 1 266

Planning for Day 2 270

Day 2 and Planning for Day 3 272

Day 3 and Planning for Day 4 273

Day 4 and Planning for Day 5 273

Day 5 275

Planning for Day 6 279

Day 6 280

Reflecting on Day 6 and Planning for Day 7 284

Days 7 to 14 284

Day 7 ❑ Day 8 ❑ Day 9 ❑ The Weekend ❑ Day 10 ❑ Day 11 ❑ Day 12 ❑ Day 13 ❑ Day 14

Scoring and Interpreting the Test 285

Day 15 287

SAMPLE GEOMETRY TEACHING UNIT 287

SAMPLE CONSUMER MATHEMATICS TEACHING UNIT 287

SAMPLE PRECALCULUS TEACHING UNIT 290

INSERVICE OPPORTUNITIES AND THE NCTM CONFERENCE 290

WINDING DOWN THE SCHOOL YEAR AND ANTICIPATING NEXT YEAR 294

**CHAPTER 9
Looking Ahead 297**

A MIXED HISTORY 297

AN IMPENDING REFORMATION 297

YOUR ROLE 299

**APPENDIX A
Topics from the Table of Contents of a Prealgebra Textbook 301**

**APPENDIX B
Excerpt from *Mathematics Core Curriculum: Grades 7–12* Relative to the Teaching of Elementary Algebra 305**

Course Description 305

Core Standards for the Course 305

**APPENDIX C
"An Application of Quadratic Equations to Baseball" 309**

**APPENDIX D
List of Standards from *Curriculum and Evaluation Standards for School Mathematics* 313**

Curriculum Standards for Grades K–4 313

Standard 1: Mathematics as Problem Solving ❑ Standard 2: Mathematics as Communications ❑ Standard 3: Mathematics as Reasoning ❑ Standard 4: Mathematical Connections ❑ Standard 5: Estimation ❑ Standard 6: Number Sense and Numeration ❑ Standard 7: Concepts of Whole-Numbers Operations ❑ Standard 8: Whole Number Computation ❑ Standard 9: Geometry and Spatial Sense ❑ Standard 10: Measurement ❑ Standard 11: Statistics and Probability ❑ Standard 12: Fractions and Decimals ❑ Standard 13: Patterns and Relationships

Curriculum Standards for Grades 5–8 315

Standard 1: Mathematics as Problem-Solving ❑ Standard 2: Mathematics as Communications ❑ Standard 3: Mathematics as Reasoning ❑ Standard 4: Mathematical Connections ❑ Standard 5: Number and Number Relationships ❑ Standard 6: Number Systems and Number Theory ❑ Standard 7: Computation and Estimation ❑ Standard 8: Patterns and Functions ❑ Standard 9: Algebra ❑ Standard 10: Statistics ❑ Standard 11: Probability ❑ Standard 12: Geometry ❑ Standard 13: Measurement

Curriculum Standards for Grades 9–12 317

Standard 1: Mathematics as Problem-Solving ❑ Standard 2: Mathematics as Communication ❑

Standard 3: Mathematics as Reasoning ❏ Standard 4: Mathematical Connections ❏ Standard 5: Algebra ❏ Standard 6: Functions ❏ Standard 7: Geometry from a Synthetic Perspective ❏ Standard 8: Geometry from an Algebraic Perspective ❏ Standard 9: Trigonometry ❏ Standard 10: Statistics ❏ Standard 11: Probability ❏ Standard 12: Discrete Mathematics ❏ Standard 13: Conceptual Underpinnings of Calculus ❏ Standard 14: Mathematical Structure

Evaluation Standards   320

Standard 1: Alignment ❏ Standard 2: Multiple Sources of Information ❏ Standard 3: Appropriate Assessment Methods and Uses ❏ Standard 4: Mathematical Power ❏ Standard 5: Problem Solving ❏ Standard 6: Communication ❏ Standard 7: Reasoning ❏ Standard 8: Mathematical Concepts ❏ Standard 9: Mathematical Procedures ❏ Standard 10: Mathematical Disposition ❏ Standard 11: Indicators for Program Evaluation ❏ Standard 12: Curriculum and Instructional Resources ❏ Standard 13: Instruction ❏ Standard 14: Evaluation Team

APPENDIX E
Casey Rudd's Syllabus for His First-Period Algebra I Course   **323**
What Is This Course All About?   324
What Is Algebra?   324
Why Should You Learn Algebra?   324
Are You Ready to Learn Algebra?   324
With Whom Will You Be Working in This Course?   324
Where Will You Be Learning Algebra?   324
How Will You Be Expected to Behave in This Class?   325
What Materials Will You Need for Class?   325
What Will You Be Doing for This Class?   325
What Will You Learn from This Class?   326
How Will You Know When You've Learned Algebra?   326
How Will Your Grades for the Course Be Determined?   326

APPENDIX F
Test Casey Rudd Constructed for Unit 7 of His First-Period Algebra I Course   **329**

REFERENCES   **333**

INDEX   **341**

ABOUT THE AUTHOR   **347**

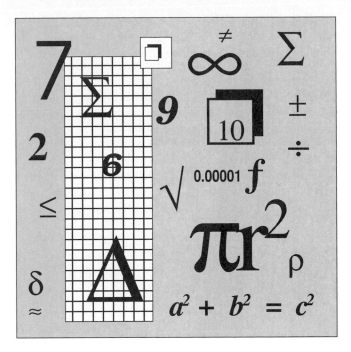

CHAPTER 1

$T_i(S) = L$: A Set of Messy Functions

This chapter suggests two things: that you view teaching as a set of functions you design and control, and that whether students find mathematics mystifying or understandable depends largely on how it is taught. The intent is to increase your awareness of the complexities of teaching. Subsequent chapters describe and illustrate ways of dealing with those complexities. Specifically, Chapter 1 is designed to help you:

1. Explain how students' perceptions of mathematics and abilities with mathematics are dependent on (a) the learning experiences provided by their teachers and (b) the individual characteristics the students bring to those experiences.
2. List student variables (e.g., aptitudes for abstract reasoning, prior experiences, and personal biases) that you will need to take into consideration whenever you design and execute teaching functions.
3. Explain why the most commonly practiced method of teaching mathematics leads students to perceive mathematics as a mysterious sequence of symbol and word meanings, facts, and algorithms to be memorized.
4. Explain the general differences between (a) the most commonly practiced method of teaching mathematics and (b) methods that lead students to perceive mathematics as a human pursuit that they can creatively apply to solve problems from their own real worlds.
5. Describe the difference between those aspects of mathematics that are discoveries and those that are inventions.

A SET OF TIDY FUNCTIONS (f_i)

Let x be a variable such that $x \in \{-3, -0.5, 0, 0.01, \sqrt{3}, 2\}$. Consider four functions of x, f_1, f_2, f_3, and f_4 defined as follows:

$$f_1(x) = 3x^2 - 8$$
$$f_2(x) = -10x^2 + 1$$
$$f_3(x) = x$$
$$f_4(x) = 3x$$

f_1, f_2, f_3, and f_4 are all well defined; the result of substituting each value of x in each function is completely predictable. Thus, you can make the following statements with certainty:

$$f_1(-3) = 19 \qquad f_2(-3) = -89$$
$$f_1(-0.5) = -7.25 \qquad f_2(-0.5) = -1.5$$
$$f_1(0) = -8 \qquad f_2(0) = 1$$
$$f_1(0.01) = -7.9997 \qquad f_2(0.01) = 0.999$$
$$f_1(\sqrt{3}) = 1 \qquad f_2(\sqrt{3}) = -29$$
$$f_1(2) = 4 \qquad f_2(2) = -39$$

$$f_3(-3) = -3 \qquad f_4(-3) = -9$$
$$f_3(-0.5) = -0.5 \qquad f_4(-0.5) = -1.5$$
$$f_3(0) = 0 \qquad f_4(0) = 0$$
$$f_3(0.01) = 0.01 \qquad f_4(0.01) = 0.03$$
$$f_3(\sqrt{3}) = \sqrt{3} \qquad f_4(\sqrt{3}) = 3\sqrt{3}$$
$$f_3(2) = 2 \qquad f_4(2) = 6$$

Furthermore, the following conclusions are indisputable:

❑ $f_i(-0.5) < 0$ for $i = 1, 2, 3, 4$.
❑ Substituting x in f_3 does not yield values different from x.
❑ $f_2(-0.5) = f_4(-0.5)$.
❑ $f_1(2) > f_2(2)$.
❑ The arithmetic mean of $f_3(x)$ is greater than the arithmetic mean of $f_2(x)$.
❑ The standard deviation of $f_2(x)$ is greater than the standard deviation of $f_3(x)$.
❑ The values of $f_i(-3)$ vary according to the value of i to a greater degree than do either $f_i(-0.5)$, $f_i(0)$, $f_i(0.01)$, $f_i(\sqrt{3})$, or $f_i(2)$.
❑ $f_i(\sqrt{3})$ is rational for $i = 1, 2$.
❑ $0 < f_i(0.01) < 1$ for $i = 2, 3, 4$.

f_i for $i = 1, 2, 3, 4$ is a set of *tidy* functions because

1. The characteristics of the domain (i.e., $\{-3, -.5, 0, .01, \sqrt{3}, 2\}$) are well understood. For example, (a) each element is a real number, (b) $-3 < -0.5 < 0 < 0.01 < \sqrt{3} < 2$, (c) each element, except for $\sqrt{3}$, can be expressed as the ratio of two integers, and (d) the square of each of these numbers, except for 0 and 0.01, is greater than the number.
2. The result of substituting each value of x in any one of these four functions is completely predictable; the outcome is certain.
3. The resulting range of each of these functions consists of real numbers that are as well understood as the domain. You understand why each result occurs (e.g., why substituting -3 for x in $f_1(x) = 3x^2 - 8$ yields 19).
4. Each of these functions can be consistently executed. For example, tripling the square of -3 and then subtracting 8 from that result always yields 19. Any other result can be traced back to a failure to follow the rules of f_1, not to some inherent changes in either x or $f_1(x)$.
5. The domain of these functions remains constant over time. You can be assured, for example, that since -3 is less than -0.5 today, -3 will be less than -0.5 tomorrow.

All functions are not as tidy as f_1, f_2, f_3, and f_4. Some are rather *messy* because

1. The characteristics of the domain are too complicated to be completely understood.
2. The result of submitting each value from the domain to such functions cannot be confidently predicted.
3. The resulting range of such functions cannot always be readily identified, nor can the impact of the functions always be explained.
4. The execution of such functions cannot necessarily be repeated at will.
5. The domain of such functions may vary with time.

Why would anyone choose to work with messy functions instead of tidy functions? You are in a position to answer that question because when you decided to be a teacher, you chose to join a profession of people who devote their time to designing and executing extremely *messy* functions.

TEACHING AS A SET OF FUNCTIONS (T_i)

Teaching is a set of functions, $T_1, T_2, T_3, \ldots, T_k$, with a domain, S, consisting of *students* and a range, L, comprising different types and levels of student *learning*. In other words, $T_i(S) = L$.

Just as the value of f_i depends on (1) which function is used (i.e., whether $i = 1, 2, 3$, or 4) and (2) which element of the domain is used (i.e., whether $x = -3, -0.5, 0, .01, \sqrt{3}$, or 2), so do *learning outcomes* (i.e., L) depend on (1) how teaching is designed and executed and (2) the *students*. Consider the following vignette.

❑ **VIGNETTE 1.1**
Ms. O'Farrell uses *direct* instructional methods (Arends 1988, 362–385; Joyce and Weil 1986, 317–336) almost exclusively to teach her students mathematics. She employs *directive strategies* (Beyer 1987, 99–105) in conducting virtually all her lessons by

1. First naming the skill the students are to acquire. "Today, we're going to learn how to graph linear equations using the slope and y-intercept.")
2. Explaining the skill and, with the aid of an overhead projector, listing each step in the process the students are to follow.
3. Demonstrating the skill with at least two examples.
4. Responding to students' questions about any of the steps.
5. Assigning exercises from the textbook for the students to begin in class and complete for homework.
6. Circulating among the students as they work on the exercises, responding to individual questions.
7. Checking on homework the next day, using the overhead projector to explain homework exercises with which students said they experienced difficulties.

8. Testing students' skills with the process.
9. Deciding to either reteach the skill or move to the next lesson.

Maxine and Ron are both 15-year-old students in one of Ms. O'Farrell's geometry classes. Maxine is motivated by a desire to maintain a high grade-point average, which she believes will help her obtain a college scholarship. Ron realizes that with his current grade-point average he has little chance of receiving a scholastic scholarship and, besides, "life after high school" seems like a lifetime from now. Although Ron would like to improve his grades, he's not motivated to work very hard on lessons *solely* for grades. He's willing to work only on lessons that appear to be relevant to the life he is living at the moment.

Following her direct instruction formula, Ms. O'Farrell opens a lesson by announcing to the class, "Today, we're going to learn how to compute the lateral surface area of a right cylinder." On an overhead transparency she draws and writes the following:

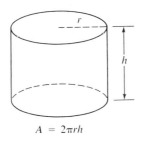

$$A = 2\pi rh$$

She explains, "As you can see by the formula, to find the lateral surface area of a right cylinder you multiply 2π times the radius of the base times the height. Here, let me work an example for you. Suppose the cylinder's height is 20 centimeters and. . . ."

Maxine assiduously follows the step-by-step explanation without bothering to think about why the area can be found by completing the prescribed multiplications or why anyone would ever want to compute the lateral surface area of a right cylinder. After completing the exercises Ms. O'Farrell assigned at the end of the lesson, Maxine has mastered the algorithm for computing the lateral surface area of a right cylinder.

Ron, on the other hand, fails to follow Ms. O'Farrell's explanation from the moment she writes out the formula. As she is working through the first example, he is busy thinking to himself, "Just what I wanted to know, lateral surface areas and right cylinders! I don't even know what a wrong cylinder is! Two-pi-r-h! Who thinks up this stuff? I'd better get this anyway; she's going to quiz us tomorrow." But Ron's heart isn't in the lesson and by the time he gets his mind-wandering under control and tries to follow the explanation, Ms. O'Farrell is midway through the presentation.

Ms. O'Farrell designed and executed a teaching function (T_1) with her students (S) that resulted in certain learning outcomes (L) by planning and conducting the lesson on lateral surface areas of right cylinders. The lesson's effects on Maxine were different from its effects on Ron. Because T_1 is a messy function, its effects are not completely predictable. On another day (e.g., one in which Maxine is distracted by an argument she had with a friend or in which by chance Ron realizes that the drums he loves to play are cylindrical), the responses of the two students to the lesson may be at odds with the aforementioned anecdote.

Although teaching functions are messy, research studies in the areas of mathematics education and cognitive science do provide us with a basis for predicting the learning outcomes of certain types of lessons. The type of instructional strategies Ms. O'Farrell employs tend to

1. Effectively lead self-motivated students (Maxine) to acquire knowledge-level skills in executing algorithms (Beyer 1987, 99–105; Good, Grouws, and Ebmeier 1983; Phye 1986).
2. Neglect both conceptual-level understanding of relationships (e.g., why $A = 2\pi rh$) and the ability to apply mathematics in real-world situations (Good 1984; Wadsworth 1979, 142–143; Linn 1986)
3. Leave the impression that mathematics is a magical "bag of tricks" that students memorize in school (Ball 1988a, 1988b; Cangelosi 1989a)
4. Be time-efficient in that explanations and discussions are relatively brief, but time-inefficient in that students are apt to forget the algorithm shortly after the test (Ellis and Hunt 1983, 61–171; Schoenfeld 1985, 358–360)

The teacher's instructional strategies in the following example deviate from Ms. O'Farrell's; consequently, the learning outcomes differ dramatically.

❑ **VIGNETTE 1.2**

Ms. Lowe uses *inquiry* instructional methods (Hunkins 1989, 157–167; Jacobsen, Eggen, and Kauchak 1989, 194–203; Joyce and Weil 1986, 25–69) almost exclusively to teach mathematics to her students. She employs *inductive* and *deductive* strategies (Beyer 1987, 31, 87–99; Quina 1989, 154–158) in conducting virtually all her lessons by

1. Initially confronting students with a perplexing problem. (As a lead-in to a lesson to discover how to graph linear equations using the slope and *y*-intercept, Ms. Lowe says, "Suppose you just took a job. You want to project how much you will have earned at any point in time after taking the job. How might you picture your predicted earnings from the job?")

2. Using open-ended questions to lead students to solve a problem.

3. Repeating the first two phases of the lessons with two or three more examples exemplifying the type of problem that can be solved by the mathematical process Ms. Lowe's lesson is designed to teach.

4. Engaging students in a question-and-discussion session designed to draw generalizations about the example problems they have just solved.

5. Engaging students in written exercises and discussion sessions designed to stimulate students to formulate a general method for solving any problem of this type in the future.

6. Summarizing the students' conclusions and explicitly stating the hypothesized solution formula.

7. Assigning exercises for homework in which students are directed to distinguish sample problems for which the formula is applicable from problems for which the formula does not lead to solutions.

8. Engaging students in a question-and-discussion session designed to stimulate students to use deductive reasoning to check the homework exercise.

9. Testing how well students can (a) explain why the formula works and (b) distinguish between problems to which the formula applies and problems to which it does not apply.

10. Deciding either to reteach or move to the next lesson.

In one of her geometry classes, Ms. Lowe begins a lesson on the lateral surface area of right cylinders by telling the students, "With the permission of Mr. Duke [the head custodian for the school], I've asked Izar and Elaine to bring in one of the trash barrels that are scattered about the school grounds." The two students, Izar and Elaine, stand the barrel up in the front of the classroom. (See Exhibit 1.1.) Ms. Lowe continues, "Mr. Duke tells me he plans to repaint all these barrels. He thought instead of using this drab gray again, he'd try to make them a bit more decorative this time. Yes, Parisa, you have the floor."

Parisa: What has this got to do with us?
Ms. Lowe: Mr. Duke thought you might have some ideas on what colors he should use. Yes, Izar?
Izar: Could we have pictures and stuff drawn on them?
Ms. Lowe: Mr. Duke said each of the three sections of the barrels could be a different color, but nothing fancier than that. He also said he'd let us choose the colors in exchange for providing him with an estimate of the amount of paint he has to buy. If he's going to use colors other than the gray he has now, it's going to be expensive and he doesn't want to buy more than he needs.

Further discussions lead the students to recognize the need to find the lateral surface area of the barrels. No one has a formula for computing it, but Ms. Lowe continues, "We may not know how to figure the area of this barrel, but

Exhibit 1.1
Elaine, Izar, and Ms. Lowe discovering a formula for computing surface areas of right cylinders.

there are some shapes with areas we can compute. Everyone, please write down on your worksheet three shapes for which we have area formulas. In the order I read your names, read your lists: Elaine, Mark, Eli, and Norton."

Elaine: Square, rectangle, triangle.
Mark: Rectangle, triangle, and any other polygon.
Eli: Same as theirs.
Ms. Lowe: Read them.
Eli: Rectangle, square, and triangle.
Norton: Rectangle is the only one I put.
Mark: But a square is a rectangle, so you didn't also need to list a square.
Ms. Lowe: Isn't that also true for that barrel?
Michelle: No, a barrel isn't a type of rectangle.
Ms. Lowe: I guess you're right; I was just thinking about the part of the barrel that needs painting.
Izar: Well we said only the outside needs to be painted.
Ms. Lowe: What if we just covered the barrel with colorful contact paper?
Michelle: That would never hold up.
Ms. Lowe: Yeah, I guess you're right. Seeing this butcher paper here gave me that idea. It seemed so simple just to wrap paper around the barrel. Too bad it wouldn't hold up!
Ebony: Ms. Lowe, could I try something with your butcher paper?

Ebony wraps a section of the paper around the barrel, cuts it, unwraps it, and then displays the rectangular-shaped sheet to the class. Eyes light up around the class as most of the students understand what Ebony demonstrated: The lateral surface area of the barrel is equivalent to the area of a rectangle whose dimensions can be obtained from the barrel.

The lesson continues, with Ms. Lowe playing upon Ebony's discovery to get the students to associate the circumference of the base of a right cylinder with a rectangle's width and the height of the cylinder with the rectangle's length. By the end of the day, virtually everyone in the class understands *why* the lateral surface area of a barrel is $2\pi rh$.

Learning activities that help the students apply the formula they discovered to different real-life problems are conducted over the next 2 days. Almost all the students gain an understanding of why the formula works and how to decide when to use it to solve real-life problems. However, some students do not respond well to the frustration of being confronted with a perplexing problem before being provided with the tools for solving it. Consequently, their attention during the first part of the lesson wavered, and they never felt confident that they ever had the "right" formula. Also, Ms. Lowe never provided enough practice exercises for all students to master completely the skill of computing with the algorithm.

The teaching function (T_2) that Ms. Lowe designed and executed had different effects on different students. T_2, like Ms. O'Farrell's T_1, is a messy function. But research findings do suggest that the type of instructional strategies Ms. Lowe employs tends to do the following:

1. Intrinsically motivate students to engage in mathematical learning activities (Ames and Ames 1984, 1985; Brophy 1986; Cangelosi 1988a, 130–138; Cangelosi 1990a, 21–27).
2. Effectively lead students to both conceptual-level and application-level understanding of relationships (Behle 1985; Cobb 1988; Romberg and Carpenter 1986; Wadsworth 1979, 142–143).
3. Neglect mastery of algorithmic skills (Beyer 1987, 124–137; Cooney, Davis, and Henderson 1983, 174–201; Good, Grouws, and Ebmeier 1983).
4. Leave students with the impression that mathematics is a doable endeavor, discovered and invented by ordinary humans for human purposes (Ball 1988a; Cangelosi 1989b).
5. Be time-inefficient in that explanations and discussions are relatively time-consuming but time-efficient in that students are apt to retain what they learn over an extended period of time (Joyce and Weil 1986, 23–158; Post and Cramer 1989).
6. Depend on the teacher's (a) creative use of examples, (b) understanding of his or her students as individuals, and (c) classroom management strategies (Arends 1988, 211–401; Berliner 1986; Cangelosi 1988a, 287–289; Leinhart and Greeno 1986; Shulman 1987).

Of course, as a teacher, you will need to design and execute your own teaching functions $(T_3, T_4, T_5, \ldots, T_k)$ that (1) combine the more effective features of both Ms. O'Farrell's and Ms. Lowe's approaches, (2) are appropriate for your unique set of students, and (3) match your unique personality and capabilities. Designing and executing successful teaching functions require you to utilize your expert understanding of your students, pedagogical principles, and mathematics as you carry out the following instructional responsibilities (Cangelosi 1991, 129–143; Leinhardt and Greeno 1986):

1. Organizing for teaching
2. Developing curricula
3. Determining learning goals
4. Designing lessons
5. Managing student behavior
6. Conducting lessons and engaging students in learning activities
7. Assessing student achievement

STUDENTS AS AN INDEPENDENT VARIABLE (DOMAIN OF T_i)
Variations Among Students

This book is intended to help you effectively integrate and perform the complex operations inherent in teaching functions. However, I began the book by introducing you to the algebraic functions, f_i for $i = 1, 2, 3, 4$ that combine some straightforward operations (e.g., squaring x, multiplying by 3, and subtracting 8) on a familiar domain, $\{-3, -.5, 0, .01, \sqrt{3}, 2\}$. Why begin with f_i when the focus is to be T_i?

The one thing I know about you is that you've chosen to make a profession out of teaching mathematics. Thus, I assumed that you are attracted to the field of mathematics. So, I began the book with a treatise on some familiar algebraic functions in an attempt to use your interest in mathematics to seduce you into thinking about how different instructional approaches influence students in various ways. You, too, need to play on the interests of *your* students to entice them into studying mathematics. But to do this, you need to learn from them what they consider important.

Students are the independent variable in your teaching functions; you have little, if any, say in who your students are. Of course, you exert some control when you decide on the school at which you will work (e.g., whether it is an urban junior high, a suburban middle school, or a rural high school) and you may even express a choice in the courses to which you are assigned (e.g., prealgebra, consumer mathematics, or advanced-placement calculus). Historically, however, beginning teachers' options are limited. Typically, first-year teachers plan on teaching only college-preparatory courses but are virtually always assigned at least some sections involving what many—but not all—teachers consider the more mundane aspects of mathematics.

The first thing to remember about your students is that each is a unique individual, unlike any other. They range in age from 11 (for the younger middle school students) to 20 (for the older high school students). Thus, most are adolescents. However, there is extreme variation among adolescents regarding factors that have an impact on how you should design and execute your teaching functions.

Interest in Mathematics

Adolescents' interest in mathematics ranges from obsessive avoidance to obsessive pursuit. Your students will come to you with a wide variety of interests within those two extremes. *Most* (over half) peoples' interest in mathematics deteriorates between the ages of 8 and 15 (Cangelosi 1984c; Dossey et al. 1988). Consequently, you can expect that most of the students arrive in your classroom with a distaste for the subject. This creates some tension between your interests and theirs. After all, you chose to pursue a career working with mathematics. Most students are not so inclined, at least not until they've benefited from your tutelage. One mathematics teacher's comment reflects the attitude held by some: "Mathematics is beautiful; everyone should enjoy it. I expect my students to like it." I also think mathematics is beautiful, but I also understand that beauty is in the eye of the beholder. If you expect your students to be interested in mathematics simply because you think they should be, you will be disillusioned and will probably fail to provide them with the type of experiences that can eventually build their interest.

Perception of Mathematics

One of the reasons most students' interest in mathematics seems to wane between the ages of 8 and 15 is that their view of mathematics narrows from a wide range of processes (e.g., quantifying, grouping, and ordering) considered an integral part of everyday life to an exacting, *school-based* skill involving manipulating symbols (e.g., numerals and geometric representations) (Schoenfeld 1988). Unfortunately, most mathematics teachers tend to view mathematics narrowly as a school-bound sequence of vocabulary and symbol meanings, rules, algorithms, and theorems that are not applicable to the outside-of-school interests of adolescents (Cangelosi 1989b).

Aptitude for Reasoning with Abstractions

Consider the following exchange as it occurred in Ms. Cook's prealgebra class.

❑ **VIGNETTE 1.3**

Ms. Cook: Is point three-three-three and so on [0.333...] rational or irrational?

Martin: Irrational.

Ms. Cook: Why?

Martin: Because the 3s go on forever; it's a nonterminating decimal.

Ms. Cook: Is $\frac{1}{3}$ rational or irrational?

Martin: Rational.

Ms. Cook: Why?

Martin: Because it's the ratio of two integers.

Ms. Cook: What's the decimal equivalent of $\frac{1}{3}$?

Martin: 0.333....

Ms. Cook: So, $\frac{1}{3} = 0.333....$

Martin: Yes.

Ms. Cook: But you said 0.333... is irrational and $\frac{1}{3}$ is rational! How can that be if they are equal?

Martin: I don't know; it just is.

Ms. Cook: But if x is a rational number and $x = y$, doesn't that mean y must also be a rational number?

Martin: Sure! That's the substitution principle.

Ms. Cook: Okay, then let $x = \frac{1}{3}$ and $y = 0.333....$ Is $\frac{1}{3}$ rational?

Martin: Yes.

Ms. Cook: Is $\frac{1}{3} = .333...$?

Martin: Yes.

Ms. Cook: Therefore, is .333... rational?

Martin: No, because it doesn't terminate.

Ms. Cook: Aggaahh!!!

Before Ms. Cook's frustration got the best of her, she attempted to lead Martin to recognize the contradiction in his statements. But her strategy depended on Martin being able to *reason with abstractions*. An *abstraction* is an intangible (e.g., a number, set, or function) that exists in the form of an idea (concept) rather than as a specific that can be empirically detected (smelled, seen, felt, tasted, or heard). Reasoning about intangibles that cannot be empirically sensed is an arduous process for some adolescents but presents virtually no difficulty for others. Because the study of relations among abstractions is paramount to mathematics, you will have to contend with this student variable.

The *formal operational stage* of Jean Piaget's *stages of cognitive development* (Santrock 1984, 135–156) is associated with students' abilities to reason with abstractions. Sometimes people try to convert a complex theory into a few simple rules for teaching practice. Piaget's theory for stages of cognitive development has suffered such an abuse via the oversimplification that students cannot reason with abstractions until they have matured from Piaget's *concrete operational* stage into the *formal operational* stage between the ages of 11 and 15. Consequently, some argue that students are incapable of learning so-called abstract subjects such as algebra prior to age 11 and perfectly capable of doing so after 15 (Engelmann 1977; Furth and Wachs 1974; Smedslund 1977). In truth, many children under the age of 11 successfully reason with abstractions (Baroody 1989; Kouba 1989), whereas some over 15 struggle terribly (Schoenfeld, 1985, pp. 11–45).

An oversimplified version of another theory, *left and right hemispheric learning* (Quina 1989, 425–431) suggests that students are either left-brain learners or right-brain learners. Supposedly, left-brain learners have an easier time with mathematics because they are better able to cope with the "cold" logic of abstract reasoning, whereas right-brain learners are more inclined to "warmer" aesthetic pursuits. In truth, mathematics is not the cold and exacting technical endeavor that some purport it to be. Mathematics includes both left-brain functions (e.g., logical thinking and calculations) and right-brain functions (e.g., sensory patterns and creativity). Thus, mathematics teaching needs to provide experiences that appeal to both sides of the brain for all students.

In Vignette 1.2, Ms. Lowe began the lesson with a concrete operational reasoning task that appealed to students' aesthetic and sensory inclinations by having the students empirically examine the barrel. In a subsequent stage of the lesson, students were challenged with an abstract reasoning task when they attempted to formulate a general rule for finding lateral surface areas of right cylinders.

Perception of What Is Important

Your students are more likely to work eagerly at mathematical tasks that they relate to things they consider important than on tasks that they perceive as irrelevant to their immediate interests (Brophy 1986). Thus, you need to capitalize on students' existing values to design lessons that focus on problems they consider important (Cangelosi 1988a, 130–138). But since what is important to one student is not necessarily important to another, how can such lessons be designed for any one group of students? This question is addressed in Chapters 4, 6, and 8.

Experiences Upon Which You Can Build

Different students bring different backgrounds to your classroom. Participating in sports, caring for younger children, repairing motors, raising gardens, doing carpentry work, working in stores, traveling, moving from residence to residence, purchasing an automobile, planning parties, engaging in debates, conducting experiments, taking surveys, operating cash registers, applying for jobs, serving in school clubs, dieting, doing charity work, caring for ill family members, cooking, programming computers, playing music, watching television, and raising animals are a small sampling of the types of student experiences to which you can relate mathematics. The variety can work in your favor as illustrated by the following example.

❑   **VIGNETTE 1.4**

Mr. Pepper thinks to himself as he plans a lesson on solving first-degree open sentences: "Before demonstrating methods for solving these algebraic sentences, I should first have them analyze some application-level problems. Let's see, what kind of word problems does the textbook offer? Looks like the right kind of problems but not very motivating for these ninth graders. I could rewrite them so the mathematics stays the same but the situations are more in line with their interests. Okay, the first one reads:

> An exotic tribe has a rule that the number of guards protecting the tribe must be at least one-tenth the number in the tribe less 50. According to this rule, how many tribespeople can be protected by 40 guards?

"Great! An exotic tribe—just what my students can identify with! What should I make this relate to? Something where one number depends on another. Phil has experience racing dirt bikes. Maybe I could do something with the relation between tire size and power instead of guards to tribespeople. Oh, I've got it! At least a dozen of the kids love to go to rock concerts. I'll change the guards to security people for a concert and the tribespeople become the concert goers. I've got to work this out. Okay, here's the problem:

> The number of security guards working at rock concerts depends on the number of people expected to be in attendance. One rule of thumb stipulates that the

number of security guards must be at least one-tenth of the number of concert goers less 50. According to this rule, how many people can attend a concert with 40 security guards?

"But I don't know if that rule is at all realistic. It doesn't make any more sense to me than the one for the exotic tribe. Oh, another brilliant idea! Naomi is always reading those rock magazines. I'll bet she could be our resource person for coming up with the rule. There's bound to be something about that in her magazines. This is perfect! Naomi hates math, but this time she can be the one to provide the formula we plug into the word problem.

"Okay, I'll make this next one relate to something different. Let's see. . . ."

Prior Mathematical Learning

Look at the first chapters of middle, junior high, and high school mathematics textbooks. Note how each book begins with remedial material that overlaps the content for three or four prior grades. Simple whole-number computational tasks (such as $138 + 48 = ?$ and $458 \times 9 = ?$) greet sixth-through eighth-grade mathematics and prealgebra students when they open their textbooks. Algebra textbooks begin with scores of exercises such as, "Find the value of $(12 - 8) + 3$" or "Show that each number is rational by naming it as a quotient of integers: $-13, 9.3, -\frac{4}{7}, \ldots, 0.06$."

Apparently, the authors of these texts recognize that having been exposed to mathematical topics in prior courses does not guarantee that those topics were learned by all students. Most of your students will lack some mathematical skill that is prerequisite to what you plan to teach them, but the gaps will vary from student to student. Furthermore, many students, although lacking some remedial skills, will have already acquired understanding of

some advanced topics that you are expecting to introduce to them.

Communication Skills

Mathematics lessons typically require students to *receive* messages (e.g., by *listening* to the teacher and to one another and *reading* explanations, examples, and directions appearing in textbooks, on visual classroom displays, worksheets, computer screens, and tests) and *send* messages (e.g., by *speaking, writing,* and *entering information in computers*). Schools typically provide students with extensive exposure to lessons targeting general communications skills (reading, writing, speaking, and listening) in language arts courses (such as English, spelling, and reading). However, communications skills in the language of mathematics are blatantly neglected, and many of your students will need you to provide remedial work in (1) the technical vocabulary of mathematics, (2) how mathematical language differs from conventional languages with respect to precision and structure, (3) how to comprehend mathematical text content, (4) how to read shorthand symbols, numerals, and formulas (e.g., English narratives normally appear in rectangular arrays to be read row by row from left to right, but as illustrated by Exhibit 1.2, mathematical communications are often meant to be read bottom-up, right to left, and diagonally), (5) how to structure and link precise, rigorous mathematical statements, (6) the rules for expressing mathematical arguments, and (7) illustrating mathematical relationships (Cobb 1988; Kane, Byrne, and Hater 1974; Roe, Stoodt, and Burns 1987, 246–262).

Coursework in Other Academic Areas

Real-life problem-solving applications of mathematics are most efficiently taught through mathematics lessons that are integrated with lessons from other

Exhibit 1.2
Reading mathematical expressions does not proceed in the usual left-to-right, top-to-bottom order.

The expression $\frac{7}{x} - (5 - 3x)^2$ is read in this order:

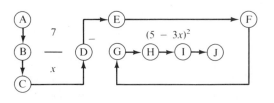

Begin at Ⓐ, reading "7," go down to Ⓑ to read "divide by"; then continue down to Ⓒ to read "x" and up to Ⓓ for "subtract." Go over to Ⓔ for "quantity of," up and over to Ⓕ for "square the quantity," down to Ⓖ for "5," right to Ⓗ to "subtract," right to Ⓘ to "three times," and right to Ⓙ for "x."

disciplines (e.g., social studies, language arts, physical education, and physics) (Callahan 1985; Romberg and Carpenter 1986). Integrated curriculum efforts, in which teachers from various disciplines (such as mathematics and social studies) coordinate their lessons so that students apply what they are learning in one class to a problem presented in another (Cangelosi 1988c), have proven successful. Although all your students will not necessarily be taking the same courses other than mathematics, some integration is still possible whenever you can find a willing collaborator among your colleagues from other disciplines (see, for example, the overall plan for lessons in Exhibit 8.32).

Special Needs

You can expect to have a few students mainstreamed into your classes whose special needs have been formally identified. Included among the labels are learning disabled, hearing impaired, hard of hearing, blind, visually handicapped, orthopedically impaired, behaviorally disordered, emotionally handicapped, gifted, and multihandicapped (Ryan and Cooper 1988, 211–218). Besides contending with these students' special needs, you can be assured that your so-called normal students also vary considerably in their abilities to hear, see, perform mental tasks, control their emotions, concentrate, and perform physical tasks. For example, it is estimated that at any one point in time, 25 percent of students with normal hearing are suffering a temporary hearing loss (e.g., because of an infection) serious enough to interfere with their ability to follow an oral presentation (Berg 1987, 22–38).

Self-Confidence

The amount of effort students are willing to invest in a mathematical task is dependent not only on the value they recognize in the task but also on their perception of the likelihood that they will successfully complete the task (Ames and Ames 1985). Problem solving, discovering relationships, proving theorems, analyzing situations, and interpreting mathematical communications are all cognitive tasks requiring students to work through perplexing moments. Those who are not confident in their own mathematical abilities tend to stop working on a task as soon as they become perplexed; more-confident students tolerate perplexity longer and are more likely to continue with the task.

Attitude Toward Learning

Some students view learning tasks as opportunities to acquire new abilities and skills. Others consider learning tasks as presenting competitive situations in which their existing abilities and skills are challenged. Unlike the latter group, the former are not burdened with the fear that their mistakes will be ridiculed, so they are willing to pursue even perplexing tasks and to learn from their mistakes.

Study Skills

Consider the following vignette.

❑   **VIGNETTE 1.5**

"Would you show us how to do number 7 from the homework assignment? I had trouble," Ruth asks Mr. Camparell. Mr. Camparell answers: "Please write it on the board and we'll think it through together." Ruth writes the following:

> When the angle of elevation of the sun is 27°, the shadow of a tree is 75 ft long. What is the height of the tree?

Mr. Camparell: Think aloud for us as you begin.
Ruth: First, I drew this picture.

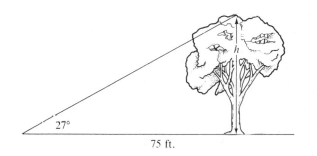

75 ft.

Mr. Camparell: Okay, so you've got the problem visualized very nicely. Where do we go from here?
Ruth: Let h equal the tree's height. So, here's what I did, but it didn't check with the answer in the back:

$$\frac{h}{75} = \sin 27°$$

$$\frac{h}{75} = 0.45399$$

$$h = 75(0.45399)$$

$$h \approx 34.05 \text{ ft}$$

Ruth: I used my calculator, so I don't know why it doesn't come out to be 38 feet like the back of the book.
Mr. Camparell: What is the sine of any angle?
Ruth: Opposite over adjacent.
Mr. Camparell: What is tangent?
Ruth: I don't remember.
Mr. Camparell: Ruth, your only difficulty is that you haven't memorized the six trigonometric functions, as you were told to do. The difficult part of problems like this is to visualize them and set up the opening sen-

tence. Obviously, you can do that. But just memorizing the functions is something anybody can do if they'll just put in the time. Now, study these functions so you'll know them by tomorrow.

Ruth may not have had the six trigonometric functions memorized because she never spent the time studying them. However, there may be another reason. Ruth may not know *how* to study efficiently. Although how to study is not formally taught in most schools, recent research studies indicate that it is a skill that varies widely among students and needs to be systematically learned (Weinstein, Goetz, and Alexander 1988).

Use of Drugs

Inadequate study skills, boredom, lack of confidence, fatigue, hyperactivity, and nonacademic interests are just some of the many factors hindering students' willingness to engage in mathematical learning activities. Being either high on or depressed from drugs at school or when trying to study is just one more factor that hinders students' academic work (Cangelosi 1990a, 64–66). That factor is given special attention herein, not because it is any more pervasive than others but because its influence seems to be increasing at an alarming rate (Elam 1989; Towers in press) and information on how to deal with students who abuse drugs has recently become available (see, for example, Cangelosi 1988a, 245–255; Rogers and McMillin 1989; Towers 1987).

Home and Social Life

Adolescents are under continual domestic and social pressures. The parenting of your students will range from supportive to neglectful, healthy to abusive, and constant to absent. For most students, peer acceptance is of paramount concern (Charles 1989, 70–87; Dreikurs 1968). Some have friends who encourage their pursuit of mathematics and cooperation with your efforts. Others may perceive that they risk acceptance of those whose friendship they value most by being studious and cooperative with you.

Although it is important that you understand the pressures and influences with which adolescents live, please keep two things in mind:

❑ Each student is a unique individual. Do not apply the aggregate results from demographics studies to judge individuals. For example, as a group, Japanese children tend to value academic activi-

ties more than western children (Allen 1988; Illinois Council of Teachers of Mathematics 1989), but that doesn't mean that any particular student from a Japanese family will be more motivated toward mathematics than a student of native American heritage. Nor will any one student living in an inner city housing project be any more inclined to abuse drugs than one from a suburb.

❑ Because students live with disadvantages (such as abusive parents), it does not mean that they cannot control their own behaviors nor should it imply that you should expect less from them (Cangelosi 1988a, 25–33; Glasser 1986).

Time Available for Studying Mathematics

Due to differences in the aforementioned factors (home and social life, special needs, and coursework in other academic areas), some students have more time than others to devote to your work with them. A student need not be excused from homework because she or he has a night job, but your awareness of the situation helps you better diagnose difficulties.

Access to Calculators, Computers, and Other Relevant Tools

Technological tools (such as, computers) are as necessary for mathematical work today as paper and pencils. Although the *Curriculum Standards for School Mathematics* (National Council of Teachers of Mathematics (NCTM) 1989, 8) emphasizes the necessity of all students to have access to computers and calculators, the availability of these tools varies tremendously from school to school and from home to home.

Attitude Toward School

Some of your students will greet you as their friend, expecting to benefit from the experiences you provide. Others arrive with little regard for how you might help them and view you as an authority figure who interferes with activities they would prefer to be doing.

Classroom Citizenship

Dealing with uncooperative, disruptive, and off-task student behaviors generally presents teachers, especially beginning teachers, with their most difficult challenges (Doyle 1986; Steere 1988, 5–9; Weber 1986). Classroom management strategies that work well with one student don't necessarily work well with others. Some students cooperate with one teacher but present discipline problems for another. How to elicit students' cooperation and keep them on-task and engaged in learning activities is the focus of Chapter 5 and is also dealt with throughout the text.

Personal Values

People who misunderstand the nature of mathematics often think of it as a cold, impersonal subject void of human values. But using mathematics to solve real-life problems raises emotional issues involving politics, human rights, ethics, environmental matters, civic responsibilities, family, and so on. Your students' personal values and beliefs will vary tremendously. You may value the pursuit of accurate information, whereas some of your students appreciate fantasy more than truth. This is a reality you must face and contend with as you design teaching functions.

STUDENT LEARNING AS A DEPENDENT VARIABLE (RANGE OF T_i)

Teaching functions lead to two types of student learning: (1) achievement of stated curriculum objectives and (2) side effects, or extraneous outcomes.

Achievement of Stated Objectives

Vignette 1.1 alludes to a lesson Ms. O'Farrell conducts for the purpose of teaching her students to *compute lateral surface areas of right cylinders*. Helping students to acquire that skill was the *objective* of the lesson. Vignette 1.2 relates a lesson in which Ms. Lowe attempts to help her students achieve two objectives:

1. Explain why the lateral surface area of a right cylinder equals $2\pi rh$.
2. Given a real-life problem, determine whether or not computing the lateral surface area of a right cylinder is applicable to solving that problem.

Lessons are designed for the purpose of helping students achieve learning objectives. Each learning objective specifies both a *mathematical content* and an *achievement level*. The mathematical content is the topic about which the student is to learn (e.g., definition of rational number, division of two rational numbers expressed in decimal form, graphs of quadratic relations, volume of spheres, proof by mathematical induction, conditional probabilities, convergent sequences, and derivatives of quadratic

functions). The achievement level is the cognitive or affective behavior students are to display with the content by achieving the objective. For example,

❏ The content of Ms. O'Farrell's lesson's objective was *lateral surface areas of right cylinders*. The achievement level was *remembering the steps in an algorithm* (which is classified as "knowledge of a process" (Chapter 3)).
❏ The content of Ms. Lowe's first objective was *lateral surface area of right cylinders*. The achievement level was *understanding why* (which is classified as "conceptualization" (Chapter 3)).
❏ The content of Ms. Lowe's second objective was *lateral surface area of right cylinders*. The achievement level was *discriminating between problems to which the content applies and those to which it does not* (which is classified as "application" (Chapter 3)).

How you should design a lesson depends on the type of learning objective you intend for your students to accomplish. The success of a lesson depends on how well students achieve its learning objective.

Side Effects or Incidental Outcomes

Besides achieving learning objectives, students are influenced in other, often unanticipated, ways by the experiences orchestrated by mathematics teachers. Some of these side effects or incidental outcomes are desirable; others are undesirable.

Desirable Effects. Consistently engaging in appropriately designed, research-based lessons leads students to (1) enjoy mathematics, (2) perceive mathematics as a useful tool that they can creatively apply for the enhancement of their own lives, (3) develop confidence in their own abilities to work through perplexing problems, (4) utilize systematic thought processes for decision making, (5) pursue careers in mathematically related fields, and (6) increase their opportunities for success both within and outside of school.

Undesirable Effects. Unfortunately, the type of teaching that dominates mathematics classrooms in today's schools (Jesunathadas 1990) tends to produce undesirable side effects, including leaving students with the impression that (1) mathematics is a boring sequence of technical vocabulary, rules, and algorithms to be memorized for the purpose of passing tests in school, (2) it is more important for males to succeed in mathematics than females, (3) only people with an exceptional aptitude for mathematics can creatively use mathematics, and (4) mathematics is a complex, mystifying subject that was handed down to us by some ancient mystics (e.g., from Greek mythology). (See Exhibit 1.3.)

THE MYSTIFICATION OF MATHEMATICS

Were you ever attending a social gathering when it became known that you plan to be a mathematics teacher? If so, you probably immediately heard comments such as, "Math?!! So, you're some kind of genius! I was never any good at math!" "Gosh, I avoid every math course possible!" "Math! How can you learn all that stuff? It's impossible for me!" "I can't imagine teaching math! How can you possibly learn to work all those problems? I can't even keep my checkbook straight!" "Really, mathematics? My roommate is smart too. He does math all the time; I think he's studying to be an accountant."

Why is mathematics commonly thought of as this mystifying subject that is virtually impossible to learn by most people? There are at least four contributing factors. First of all, mathematical vocabulary, symbols, concepts, relations, and algorithms are typically presented in school without reference to their origins. Without an understanding of who, why, when, and where a relation (such as the area of a circular region $= \pi r^2$) was discovered or a convention (such as $P!$, a shorthand notation for $P(P - 1)(P - 2)\ldots(1)$) was invented, mathematics is perceived as some sort of magic. Most students' exposure to the origins of mathematics is limited to either a passing mention of ancient Greeks (e.g., Euclid or Pythagoras) in a geometry course or captioned pictures inserted in a textbook or on a wall poster of a few of the "great *men* of mathematics" (e.g., Carl Friedrich Gauss) who lived many years ago. Students are likely to confuse the ancient Greek mathematicians with the mythical Greek gods they read about in language arts courses. The fact that mathematics is an alive, thriving area in which discoveries and inventions are occurring today by modern and otherwise ordinary people (not only men and not only geniuses) is lost.

Second, a glance through almost any mathematics textbook reveals shorthand notations and symbols that appear strange to the uninitiated. Exhibit 1.4 contains some examples. However, the meanings

Exhibit 1.3
Many people confuse the origins of mathematics with ancient mythology.

Exhibit 1.4
A sample of conventional
mathematical shorthand notations.

$\sqrt{a}$, or $a^{1/2}$ means "The nonnegative number whose square is a."

$A \cap B = \varnothing$ means "Sets A and B have no elements in common."

$\sum_{i=3}^{6}(i^2 - 4)$ means "$(3^2 - 4) + (4^2 - 4) + (5^2 - 4) + (6^2 - 4)$."

$\prod_{i=1}^{6}(6 + i)$ means "$(6 + 1)(6 + 2)(6 + 3)(6 + 4)(6 + 5)(6 + 6)$."

$\forall$ means "for each," or "for every."

$\exists$ means "there exist."

of any vocabulary, signs, or symbols are a mystery to anyone who has not learned the rules for translating them. Unless you are aware of certain rules and vocabulary of American Signed English, the sequence of gestures depicted in Exhibit 1.5 is beyond your comprehension. Those who are familiar with the language recognize the familiar message, "We are friends."

Similarly, the following shorthand expression is incomprehensible to those who are unaware of the rules for simplifying (or translating) it:

$$\int_{1}^{2}\left(2x^3 - \frac{3}{x^2}\right) dx$$

But as you learned from your study of calculus and as illustrated in Exhibit 1.6, the expression simply denotes the whole number 6. Note that the algorithm for simplifying this expression can be boiled down to nothing more than permutations of the four fundamental operations (addition, subtraction, multiplication, and division) with whole numbers. Most people do not think of adding, subtracting, multiplying, and dividing two whole numbers as difficult, but integrating a function is mystifying to them.

Third, the number of topics listed in the table of contents of most mathematics textbooks appears overwhelming. Examine the list from a prealgebra textbook (Brumfiel, Golden, and Heins 1986) that appears in Appendix A. At first glance, there appears to be a plethora of concepts to be learned. But a more careful examination reveals that only a few concepts are introduced and that much of the content involves different ways of expressing and relating those concepts. For example,

There are separate chapters on decimals, fractions, and percents. Typically, students perceive these three

topics as if each is a concept, unrelated to the other two (Cangelosi 1989b). However, in reality, decimals, fractions, and percents are simply three different ways of expressing *one* concept, namely, ratios.

Redundancy of expressions and multiple methods for reaching the same results are ubiquitous in mathematics. Virtually everything in the field of calculus revolves around only one concept, *limits*. Yet, a typical sequence of college calculus courses requires students to read between 750 and 1200 textbook pages.

Finally, relationships (e.g., the product of two negative integers is positive or $\pi = C/d$) are presented in the most commonly conducted type of mathematics lessons (e.g., Ms. O'Farrell's, Vignette 1.1) as facts without providing students with the experiences that lead them to understand why the relationships exist (Post and Cramer 1989).

DEMYSTIFYING MATHEMATICS
Human Discoveries and Human Inventions
From Where Does Mathematics Come?

Mathematics seems far less mystifying once one understands that it originates with mortal, mistake-prone human beings attempting to solve their problems and explain the world within which they live. For example;

❏ The Greek mathematician Archimedes (287 B.C.–212 B.C.) invented methods of experimenting with physical models for the purpose of discovering relationships. For example, to find the area or volume of a figure, he would cut up a model of the figure into a great number of thin parallel planar strips and hang the pieces at one end of a lever in such a way as to be in equilibrium with a figure

Exhibit 1.5
We are friends.

whose content and centroid are known. This *method of equilibrium* led to the discovery of relationships leading to some of today's familiar formulas (e.g., for surface area and volume of a sphere). To demonstrate the validity of formulas he discovered through equilibrium and other experimental methods, Archimedes invented the cumbersome, indirect *method of exhaustion* based upon ideas that centuries later became fundamental to the development of integral calculus. Much of Archimedes' work was motivated by the need to solve real-world problems of his times (e.g., the development of weaponry during the siege of his home state of Syracuse by Roman armies) (Aaboe 1964, 73–99; Eves 1983b, p. 83–95).

❏ Amundson (1969) provides the following account of the origins of expressing ratios as percents:

Percent has been used since the end of the fifteenth century in business problems such as computing interest, profit and taxes. However, the idea had its origin much earlier. When the Roman emperor Augustus levied a tax on all goods sold at auction, *centesima rerum venalium*, the rate was $\frac{1}{100}$. Other Roman taxes were $\frac{1}{20}$ on every freed slave and $\frac{1}{25}$ on every slave sold.

Exhibit 1.6
An algorithm for integrating a function reduces to four fundamental operations with whole numbers.

$$\int_1^2 \left(2x^3 - \frac{3}{x^2}\right) dx$$

$$= \int_1^2 (2x^3 - 3x^{-2}) \, dx$$

$$= 2\int_1^2 x^3 dx - 3\int_1^2 x^{-2} \, dx$$

$$= 2\left(\frac{x^4}{4}\right)\Big|_1^2 - 3\left(\frac{x^{-1}}{-1}\right)\Big|_1^2$$

$$= 2\left(\frac{16}{4} - \frac{1}{4}\right) - 3\left(\frac{2^{-1}}{-1} - \frac{1}{-1}\right)$$

$$= 2\left(4 - \frac{1}{4}\right) - 3\left(-\frac{1}{2} + 1\right)$$

$$= 6$$

Without recognizing percentages as such, they used fractions easily reduced to hundredths.

In the Middle Ages, as larger denominations of money came to be used, 100 became a common base for computation. Italian manuscripts of the fifteenth century contained such expressions as "20 p 100," "x p cento," and "vi p c°" to indicate 20 percent, 10 percent, and 6 percent. When commercial arithmetic appeared near the end of the century, use of percent was well established. For example, Giorgio Chiarino (1481) used "xx. per .c." for 20 percent and "viii in x perceto" for 8 to 10 percent. During the sixteenth and seventeenth century, percent was used freely for computing profit, loss, and interest.

The percent sign, %, has probably evolved from a symbol introduced in an anonymous Italian manuscript of 1425. Instead of "per 100," "P 100," or "P cento," which were common at that time, this author used "P ⚬̸." By about 1650, the ⚬̸ had become ⚬̸, so "per ⚬̸" was often used. Finally, the "per" was dropped, leaving ⚬̸ or %.

❑ In 1984, Narendra Karmarker formulated a new algorithm for linear programming that has the potential of obtaining the most efficient solutions for optimizing systems of thousands of equations in thousands of unknowns (Peterson 1988, 111–112)

❑ How to evaluate the validity and estimate the error of achievement and aptitude tests used in schools is a problem that has been pursued since 1845, when Horace Mann attempted to defend written examinations for groups of students (Strom 1969, 270–345). Developments in statistical and numerical analytic models for the purpose of assessing the validities and reliabilities of mental measurements have advanced from E. L. Thorndike's (1904) initial work and continue feverishly today (see, for example, Keeves 1988; Linn 1989a).

❑ In 1985, while exploring figures with the aid of a computer, Rob Stringer, a tenth grader, discovered a new theorem in Euclidean geometry for partitioning the interior of a triangle into five regions of equal area (Kidder 1985).

❑ Several days after Ms. Lowe conducted the lesson on lateral surface area of a right cylinder alluded to in Vignette 1.2, her students figured out how to compute the surface area of a fish bowl Norton brought to class. The shape is depicted in Exhibit 1.7. Over the course of the following week, they discovered relationships that they used to invent the following formula for estimating the surface area of any size figure with the shape of that fish bowl; they named the figure a "Norton":

$$\text{Area of a Norton} = 2\pi(2s^2 + 2sw - t^2)$$

where
s = the radius of one of the side-circled panels,
w = the width of one of the curved sides
t = the radius of the opening at the top

Exhibit 1.7
A Norton.

❑ Allison is working hard to earn and save enough money to buy a car in 2 years when she is 18. To help her determine the best buy for her needs, budget, and desires, she designs a mathematical function for assessing the value of car buys. Her function accepts a number of variables (e.g., size, gas mileage, age, looks, extra features, horsepower, and guarantee) weighted according to importance to her and yields a value-to-dollars ratio. She writes a computer program to execute the function.

Mathematical Discoveries. Concepts (e.g., areas of figures, whole numbers, ratios, angles, finite sets, circles, and irrational numbers) and relations (e.g., the ratio of the circumference of any circle to its diameter is a little greater than three; $x^2 < x$ if $0 < x < 1$; $17 \div 4 = 4.25$; $\lim_{x \to 3}(x^2-9)/(x-3)=6$) exist in our world. One goal of mathematics is to *discover* such concepts and relations so that we can better control our existence. Archimedes' discovery of a relation between the radius of a sphere and its volume provided him with insights he used in the design of weapons. Ms. Lowe's students discovered that they needed to make only three measurements to calculate the area of a Norton. Mathematical discoveries can be explained via logic and reasoning. From your study of Chapter 4, you will understand how a mathematical discovery should be taught differently than a mathematical invention.

Mathematical Inventions. Methods (e.g., step-by-step algorithmic procedures), conventions (e.g., criteria for a valid proof), and mathematical language are inventions. Archimedes invented his method of *equilibrium* for discovering relations about areas and volumes. Ms. Lowe's students discovered the relation *area of a Norton* $= 2\pi(2s^2 + 2sw - t^2)$ after inventing the name for any figure shaped like Norton's fish bowl. Generally speaking, invented methods and conventions, unlike discoveries, need to be memorized. Understanding why a method (e.g., an algorithm for using the quadratic formula to solve quadratic equations) works requires discovery and reasoning, but knowing how to execute it simply taxes the memory.

Teaching Comprehension of Mathematical Language

Communications within any specialty field (e.g., chemistry, carpentry, aeronautics, or mathematics) depend on three types of vocabulary:

1. *General*-usage terms consist of words and symbols with conventional meanings listed in standard dictionaries that are understood by people both within and outside the specialty. With respect to mathematics, *friend, horse,* and *red* are examples.
2. *Special*-usage terms consist of words and symbols from the general vocabulary whose meaning changes when used in the context of the discipline or specialty. With respect to mathematics, *field, union, derivative, imaginary,* and *power* are examples.
3. *Technical*-usage terms consist of words and symbols that have meaning only within the context of the discipline or specialty. With respect to mathematics, *cosine, polyhedron,* and *vector space* are examples.

Both special- and technical-usage terms hinder communications within any field (e.g., welding, electronics, football, or mathematics) until the contextual meaning of those terms is understood. Imagine how mystifying football would seem to anyone who had never been taught that a clip is neither something done with scissors nor a device that holds objects in place.

Besides its special and technical vocabulary, the nuances of reading mathematics need special attention if students are to derive meaning from their textbooks. Much of the mystery associated with mathematics evaporates when research-based methods for teaching comprehension of its language are incorporated in mathematical lessons (Kane, Byrne, and Hater 1974; Roe, Stoodt, and Burns 1986, 246–276). Strategies for teaching students to comprehend mathematical language are explained in Chapter 4.

Integrating Topics

The popularity of precision teaching, mastery learning, and direct instruction (Bowden 1991; Joyce and Weil 1986, 317–336) have encouraged topics to be taught in small, fragmented segments with easier skills preceding those more difficult to learn. The fifth chapter of the prealgebra text outlined in Appendix A, for example, deals with multiplication of fractions; the sixth chapter deals with addition of fractions. Presumably, multiplication is treated first because the algorithm is simpler than that for addition, in which one must bother with finding a common denominator. When the two are presented as unrelated algorithms, remembering one tends to interfere with—rather than enhance—the learning of the other (Chance 1988, 205–238). Consequently, the following error pattern is likely to emerge in representative samples of students' work (Ashlock 1990).

Seventh grader:

$$\frac{17}{10} + \frac{4}{7} = \frac{21}{17}$$

Ninth grader:

$$\frac{x+1}{x-1} + \frac{3}{x+7} = \frac{x+4}{2x+6}$$

If addition of fractions is treated first and then multiplication is presented simply as a special case of addition, students would be more likely to relate the two and then the learning of one would enhance the learning of the other. Methods for integrating topics so that students have fewer concepts with which to contend are explained and illustrated throughout this book. However, here is a brief example just to provide you with some semblance of the idea.

❑ **VIGNETTE 1.6**

Mr. Sanchez has just used direct instructional methods to develop his algebra students' skills in adding two polynomial fractions by the method used in the following example:

$$\frac{x-9}{4} + \frac{2x+3}{x-5} = \frac{(x-9)(x-5)}{(4)(x-5)} + \frac{(2x+3)(4)}{(4)(x-5)}$$

$$\frac{(x-9)(x-5) + (2x+3)(4)}{(4)(x-5)} = \frac{(x^2 - 14x + 45) + (8x + 12)}{4x - 20}$$

$$= \frac{x^2 - 6x + 57}{4x - 20}$$

Now, to introduce multiplication of polynomial fractions, he tells his class, "Consider *multiplying* these two numbers." He writes on the board:

$$\frac{2x-1}{x+3} \cdot \frac{4}{x-2}$$

He continues, "Since we already know how to add polynomial fractions, let's turn this into an addition problem. Multiplication is repeated addition, so we can write the following:"

$$\frac{2x-1}{x+3} \cdot \frac{4}{x-2}$$

$$\underbrace{\frac{2x-1}{x+3} + \frac{2x-1}{x+3} + \frac{2x-1}{x+3} + \cdots + \frac{2x-1}{x+3}}_{\frac{4}{x-2} \text{ times}}$$

Mr. Sanchez: But four over the quantity *x* minus two times doesn't make a lot of sense to everyone. So,

let's rework what we've done to this point with a constant in place of *x*. Pick an odd whole number for us, Gretchen.

Gretchen: Seven.

Mr. Sanchez adds to the illustration on the board:

$$\underbrace{\frac{2(7)-1}{7+3} + \frac{2(7)-1}{7+3} + \frac{2(7)-1}{7+3} + \cdots + \frac{2(7)-1}{7+3}}_{\frac{4}{7-2} \text{ times}}$$

$$\underbrace{\frac{13}{10} + \frac{13}{10} + \frac{13}{10} + \cdots + \frac{13}{10}}_{\frac{4}{5} \text{ times}}$$

Mr. Sanchez: I know what adding $\frac{13}{10}$ to itself four times means, but what in the world does adding $\frac{13}{10}$ to itself $\frac{4}{5}$ times mean? Cam-Loi?

Cam-Loi: You add $\frac{1}{5}$ of $\frac{13}{10}$ four times to itself.

Mr. Sanchez: Oh! So you mean, (as he writes):

$$\left(\frac{13}{10} \div 5\right) + \left(\frac{13}{10} \div 5\right) + \left(\frac{13}{10} \div 5\right) + \left(\frac{13}{10} \div 5\right)$$

$$= \frac{13}{50} + \frac{13}{50} + \frac{13}{50} + \frac{13}{50}$$

$$= \frac{(13 + 13 + 13 + 13)}{50} = \frac{(13)(4)}{50} = \frac{52}{50}$$

Mr. Sanchez: Plug 7 into our original polynomial fractions and see if the product comes out $\frac{52}{50}$.

Students verify the following at their places: Letting $x = 7$,

$$\frac{2x-1}{x+3} \cdot \frac{4}{x-2} = \frac{13}{10} \cdot \frac{4}{5} = \frac{52}{50}$$

Mr. Sanchez: Now, let's use the same process to work out an answer in variable form.

$$\frac{2x-1}{x+3} \cdot \frac{4}{x-2}$$

$$\underbrace{\frac{2x-1}{x+3} + \frac{2x-1}{x+3} + \frac{2x-1}{x+3} + \cdots + \frac{2x-1}{x+3}}_{\frac{4}{x-2} \text{ times}}$$

which is

$$\left[\frac{2x-1}{x+3} \div (x-2)\right](4)$$

or simply

$$\frac{(2x - 1)(4)}{(x + 3)(x - 2)} = \frac{8x - 4}{x^2 + x - 6}$$

Mr. Sanchez: By the way, what is $(8x - 4)/(x^2 + x - 6)$ if x is 7?

The lesson continues with the rule being specifically stated and practice exercises assigned.

_____

INVOLVING STUDENTS IN THE DISCOVERY/INVENTION PROCESS

Mr. Sanchez, like Ms. Lowe, did not simply tell students a rule (e.g., for multiplying polynomial fractions or for computing the lateral surface area of a right cylinder). Students need to engage in Archimedian-type reasoning if concepts, relations, rules, and algorithms are to appear intelligible rather than as some sort of "other-world" magic (Schoenfeld 1985, 1989). Most people who remember the following rules after being told them in school have no idea as to why they work:

❑ $\left(\dfrac{a}{b}\right) \times \left(\dfrac{c}{d}\right) = \dfrac{ac}{bd}$.

❑ The product of two negative integers is a positive integer.

❑ If a function f is integrable on the interval $[a, b]$ and is such that $D_x F(x) = f(x)$ for each $x \in (a, b)$, then

$$\int_a^b f(x)dx = F(b) - F(a)$$

Being required to memorize and then use rules that work for reasons that are not understood adds to the mystery of mathematics. In Vignette 2.4, Mr. Cocora's lesson leads his students to discover for themselves the rules for multiplying signed numbers. Such lessons tend to demystify mathematics.

Monitoring Your Own Attitudes

As long as mathematics is divorced from the present real worlds of students, mathematics remains couched in a language that is not specifically taught, and students do not discover and invent mathematics for themselves, mathematics will continue to be perceived as a boring, mystifying subject to be understood only by extraordinary people. As long as that perception is widespread, you and I can continue to enjoy reputations as "extraordinary people"

who know something most people don't. If the teaching functions you design and conduct for students are intended to perpetuate that myth, you will spend more time defending your mathematical expertise than enjoying your students' development into creative users of mathematics. To avoid that trap born of the insecurities we all suffer, routinely check your motives for teaching the way you do.

❑❑❑❑❑❑❑❑❑❑❑❑❑❑❑❑❑❑❑❑

SELF-ASSESSMENT EXERCISES

The self-assessment section for each chapter provides exercises to help you (1) evaluate your achievement of the chapter's objectives so that you can identify your areas of proficiency and the topics you need to review and (2) reinforce and extend what you've learned from the chapter. An ulterior purpose of these exercises is to encourage you to articulate your thoughts about mathematics and teaching mathematics in both writing and oral discourse. Understanding of mathematics is enhanced through such reading and writing activities (Cangelosi 1988c; Fennell and Ammon 1985; Nahrgang and Petersen 1986).

1. Observe a mathematics class with a colleague who is also either a preservice or in-service mathematics teacher. Independent of one another, you and your partner are to (a) select two students on whom you will focus your attention, (b) describe the activities within the classroom and the students' apparent involvement in those activities, and (c) assess, for each of the two students, how you think the activities affected his or her abilities with and attitudes about mathematics. Distinguish each student's achievement of objectives targeted by the teacher from side effects. Report your findings in writing and exchange your report with that of your partner. Compare the two reports and discuss observed differences in the two students that might have influenced them to respond differently to the learning activities.

2. Look over a mathematics textbook currently being used in a middle, junior high, or high school. Select any two topics and examine how the book presents each. Label aspects of each topic as to whether they originated as a discovery or invention. For example, here's how I labeled some aspects of two topics from the text whose table of contents appears in Appendix A:

   Topic Formula: perimeter

   ❑ The concept *perimeter* exists in nature and was discovered by people. The name for the concept, *perimeter*, is an invented convention.

❑ The following method of depicting the dimensions of a rectangle is an invention:

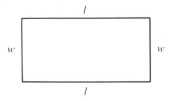

The concepts *rectangle, length,* and *width* are discoveries. Their names, *rectangle, length,* and *width,* are inventions.

❑ The relation $P = 2l + 2w$ is a discovery, but the expression of that relation is an invention.

Topic   Graphing equations

❑ The *Cartesian plane* is an invention for illustrating relations that are discovered.
❑ The *procedure for graphing a linear equation* is an invention.
❑ The fact that the graph of any equation that can be expressed as $Ax + By = C$ (where A, B, and C are real constants and x and y are real variables) is a line is a discovery.

Now, write a brief paragraph describing one way the two topics are related. For example, here's what I wrote for the two topics I chose:

The perimeter of a rectangle is dependent on two variables, length and width. One type of problem that the formula can be used to solve involves determining the possible dimensions of a rectangle with a given perimeter (e.g., in the case of fixed amount of fencing available for a garden). For such situations the perimeter formula is of the form $Ax + By = C$, where C is the given perimeter and $A = B = 2$. Thus, the possibilities for the length and width can be illustrated via the graph of a linear equation.

3. Interview an adolescent student, asking him or her the following questions:
   a. If it were not a required subject, would you choose to study mathematics? Why or why not?
   b. Is mathematics more or less interesting than other school subjects you take? Explain your answer.
   c. Is mathematics more or less difficult than other school subjects you take? Explain your answer.
   d. From where do you think the mathematics we study in school comes? Explain why you believe what you just told me.
   e. What's the most interesting thing about learning mathematics?
   f. What's the most boring thing about learning mathematics?
   g. What's the easiest thing about learning mathematics?
   h. What's the hardest thing about learning mathematics?
   i. How often and for what reasons do you ever use mathematics outside of school?
   j. Do you read your mathematics textbook any differently than you read any of your other textbooks? Explain.
   k. Do you have a routine for doing homework? Describe how and where you completed your last mathematics homework assignment.
   l. How many of your friends really like to do mathematics? How many of your friends really hate doing mathematics?
   m. What else would you like to add about your opinions of mathematics?
   Record the responses from the interview, and if you obtain the student's permission to share his or her answers, compare the responses you got with those of a colleague who completes this exercise with another student.

❑ ❑

TAKING WHAT YOU'VE LEARNED TO THE NEXT LEVEL

Take the following thoughts with you as you begin Chapter 2:

1. How you design and conduct teaching functions should depend on (a) what student outcomes you want to produce and (b) a complex of student variables.
2. The way you should teach is not necessarily the way you were taught nor the way most teachers teach mathematics to their students.

With those thoughts in mind, we turn our attention to recent curriculum reforms and issues affecting the selection of mathematical topics you will teach, the learning levels of the goals you establish for your students, your choice of resources, facilities, and learning materials, and how you organize courses.

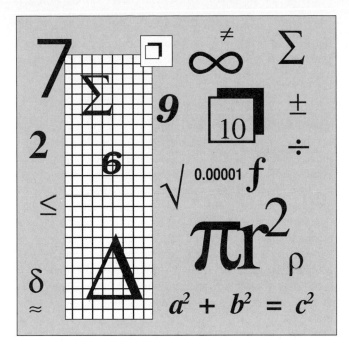

CHAPTER 2
Developing Mathematics Curricula

This chapter focuses attention on the teacher's impact on curricula, the discrepancy between typical and research-based mathematics curricula, and thoughts on how you might go about developing curricula. Specifically, Chapter 2 is designed to help you:

1. Define *curriculum* and *curriculum guidelines* and explain the relationship among school, course, mathematics, school-district, and state-level curricula.
2. Describe how teachers develop and control curricula as they design and conduct lessons.
3. Explain the differences between (a) a curriculum based on the view that students should learn mathematics for the purpose of being able to learn more mathematics and (b) a curriculum based on the view that students learn mathematics for the purpose of solving real-life problems.
4. Describe a mathematics curriculum that is based on the NCTM *Standards* and contrast it to a more traditionally based mathematics curriculum.
5. Define *teaching unit* and describe how a course is composed of a sequence of teaching units.
6. Explain how courses differ according to whether they are designed by (a) the following-a-textbook approach, (b) the contrived problem-solving approach, (c) the real-world problem-solving approach, or (d) a combination of these three approaches.
7. List types of learning materials, resources, equipment, and facilities needed to conduct a mathematics course and explain factors influencing their selection for your classroom.

A CURRICULUM

Many teachers, instructional supervisors, and school administrators perceive a *curriculum* as "the textbook series adopted, mandated state or local curriculum guides, and/or content and skills appearing on mandated tests" (Zumwalt 1989, 174). Definitions range from that very narrow view to the broad, all-encompassing view forwarded by Brubaker (1982, 2): ". . . curriculum is defined as *what persons experience in a setting*. This includes all the interactions among persons as well as the interactions between persons and their physical environment. . . ."

Herein, the meaning of *curriculum* falls between those two extremes (Cangelosi 1991, 135–136):

A *school curriculum* is a system of the planned experiences (e.g., coursework, school-sponsored social functions, and contacts with school-supported services (such as the library)) designed to educate students.

A *course curriculum* is a sequence of teaching units designed to provide students with experiences that help them achieve specified learning goals. A *teaching unit* consists of (a) a learning goal defined by a set of specific objectives, (b) a planned sequence of lessons, each consisting of learning activities designed to help students achieve specific objectives, (c) mechanisms for monitoring student progress and utilizing feedback on that progress to guide lessons, and (d) a summative evaluation of student achievement of the learning goal.

A *mathematics curriculum* is a sequence of mathematics courses, as well as any other school-sponsored functions for the purpose of furthering students' achievements with and attitudes about mathematics.

A *school-district curriculum* is the set of all the school curricula within that school district.

A *state-level curriculum* is the set of all school-district curricula within a state.

State-level, district-level, school-level, and mathematics *curricula guidelines* are articulated in documents stored in the files of virtually every school. The consistency between official curricula guidelines and actual school curricula varies considerably. Obviously, a school's curriculum can be no more in line with official guidelines than the composite of the course curricula developed by its teachers.

Because mathematics is widely misunderstood to be a linear sequence of skills to be mastered one at a time in a fixed order, some people think teaching mathematics is a matter of following a prescribed curriculum guideline or mathematics textbook. In reality, there are three reasons you must creatively develop curricula to succeed as a mathematics teacher. First of all, state-level and district-level curriculum guidelines typically list objectives for mathematics courses (see Appendix B for an excerpt from the Utah curriculum guidelines relative to elementary algebra) but leave the responsibility of designing lessons for achieving those objectives up to individual teachers. Textbooks present information and exercises on mathematical topics. However, each teacher needs to select, supplement, and organize text content so the objectives listed in curriculum guidelines are addressed and tailor lessons to the unique characteristics of that teacher's students.

Second, although understanding of one mathematical topic (e.g., solving first-degree equations) is requisite to the understanding of another topic (e.g., solving quadratic equations), there is no fixed linear sequence that is optimal for all groups of students. Effective teaching requires teachers who arrange topics in response to feedback on their students' progress, diagnoses of students' needs, and students' interests at any one time.

Third, the way you design and conduct lessons usually influences what your students learn about mathematics more than which mathematical topics are addressed in the lessons. Compare the following four examples.

❏ VIGNETTE 2.1

Mr. Jackson's algebra students have learned to solve quadratic equations by factoring, providing the left side of the equation in standard form can be factored easily (e.g., $x^2 - 6x - 16 = 0$). To teach them how to solve any quadratic equation (e.g., $3x^2 + 5x + 1 = 0$), he introduces the quadratic formula by displaying it on an overhead transparency and saying, "Here is a formula for finding the solutions of any quadratic equation. For example, suppose we want to solve for $3x^2 + 2x = 7$. Watch how much easier it is to use the formula than to try and factor the polynomial. First, we rewrite the equation in standard form, and then . . . ."

He continues, working through several examples and then assigning some exercises in which the students practice using the formula.

❏ VIGNETTE 2.2

Ms. Youklic's algebra students have learned to solve quadratic equations by factoring, providing the left side of the equation in standard form can be factored easily (e.g., $x^2 - 12x + 32 = 0$). She wants to teach them to solve any quadratic equation (e.g., $x^2 + 6x + 4 = 0$) using the quadratic formula. But instead of simply stating the quadratic formula, she introduces a real-world problem whose solution requires finding roots to quadratic equations. Because of some of her students' interest in baseball, she takes an idea from the *Mathematics Teacher* article (Eisner 1986) that appears in Appendix C and uses baseball-related situations to establish a need for solving quadratic equations. Most of the equations are not easily factored, so she leads them through the process by which they solve them by completing the square.

Using inductive questioning strategies (illustrated by Vignette 4.8) she has them generalize from their experiences completing the square and ultimately leads the students to discover the quadratic formula.

After agreeing to and articulating the formula, Ms. Youklic uses direct teaching strategies (illustrated by Vignette 4.17) to improve their algorithmic skills with the quadratic formula.

❏ VIGNETTE 2.3

Ms. Estrada tells her students, as she lists the rules for multiplying signed numbers on the chalkboard, "A positive times a positive is positive. A positive times a negative is negative. A negative times a positive is negative. A negative times a negative is positive. Zero times any number or any number times zero is zero. Do you understand?"

She directs them to complete a worksheet at their places and she circulates among them looking at their work, correcting errors, and individually responding to questions. She notices that Bonita's paper includes the following:

$(17)(10) = \underline{170}$ $(.3347)(0) = \underline{0}$ $(-4.1)(3) = \underline{-12.3}$

$(1/4)(-2/3) = \underline{-2/12}$ $(-20)(9) = \underline{-180}$ $(-5)(-10) = \underline{-50}$

$(0)(-19) = \underline{0}$ $(-11)(-1/17) = \underline{-11/17}$ $4\pi(8) = \underline{32\pi}$

Ms. Estrada: Bonita, what is -5 times -10?
Bonita: Minus 50, it's right here.
Ms. Estrada: But a negative times a negative is positive.
Bonita: Why?
Ms. Estrada: Because that's the rule. See, I have it listed on the board and it's right here on page 23 of the text.

❑ VIGNETTE 2.4

With an overhead projector, Mr. Cocora displays Exhibit 2.1 to his class and says, "A friend of mine works for the city's Traffic Control Department. She asked if I could help her solve a problem. I said yes, with your help. Here's the situation. The department wants to estimate when and where city traffic is likely to be congested. Part of the data they're collecting is at this observation post marked here on the screen. The post is located at Highway 30 right at the west edge of the city. She tells me most of the traffic entering from west of the city passes this observation point.

"Here's the deal. Using a radar gun, the observer measures the direction and rate in miles per hour of vehicles traveling on Highway 30. They want some rules for using this one observation to determine where the vehicle will be or was at any point in time. Do you think we can help?"

A discussion ensues in which the problem is clarified and Mr. Cocora explains that at traffic control, (1) travel into the city is coded as a *positive* ($+$) number of miles per hour, (2) travel out of the city is coded as a *negative* ($-$)

number of miles per hour, (3) locations to the city-side of the observation point (i.e., east) are coded *positive* ($+$), (4) locations to the west, outside of the city are coded *negative* ($-$), (5) time in the future is coded *positive* ($+$), and time in the past is coded *negative* ($-$).

Moving a toy car over the highway on the transparency, Mr. Cocora confronts the students with each of the following questions:

1. Where will a red Chevrolet that is headed into the city at 60 miles per hour be located 6 minutes from now?
2. Where will a dump truck that is headed out of the city at 60 miles per hour be located 6 minutes from now?
3. Where was the red Chevrolet 6 minutes ago?
4. Where was the dump truck 6 minutes ago?
5. Where is a green Toyota that is passing the observation point right now?
6. Where will a yellow van that is broken down and not moving in front of the observation point be in 5 minutes?

Mr. Cocora directs his class into small task groups that are to answer the six questions and then generalize rules for the Traffic Department to use. All the groups answer the questions by applying the relation *rate $\times$ time = distance* as follows:

1. $(+60)(+0.1) = +6$ (i.e., 6 miles east of the observation point)
2. $(-60)(+0.1) = -6$ (i.e., 6 miles west of the observation point)
3. $(+60)(-0.1) = -6$ (i.e., 6 miles west of the observation point)
4. $(-60)(-0.1) = +6$ (i.e., 6 miles east of the observation point)
5. $(?)(0) = 0$ (i.e., in front of the observation point)
6. $(0)(+5) = 0$ (i.e., in front of the observation point)

After further discussions led by Mr. Cocora, the students settle on rules for the Traffic Department that are tantamount to the usual rules for multiplying signed numbers.

The next day, Mr. Cocora restates the rules they devised in the more conventional textbook form. He then uses direct instructional techniques to help them remember the rules.

Both Mr. Jackson and Ms. Youklic taught lessons on the quadratic formula, so their students learned about a different mathematics topic than Ms. Estrada's and Mr. Cocora's students. However, Mr. Jackson's and Ms. Estrada's lessons were similar in that both their classes of students learned to think of mathematics as a set of rules to be memorized and used but not necessarily understood. Both Ms. Youklic's and Mr. Cocora's students experienced

Exhibit 2.1
Mr. Cocora's overhead transparency for his conceptual-level lesson on the rules for multiplying signed numbers.

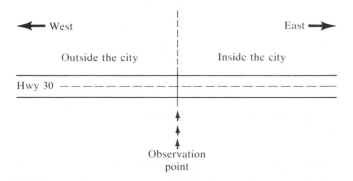

discovering and inventing mathematics. Thus, although according to a curriculum guideline or textbook section, Mr. Jackson and Ms. Youklic were "covering" the same topic, student outcomes were vastly different.

TWO VIEWS
Learn Mathematics to Learn More Mathematics

Over the past 20 years, I have asked hundreds of mathematics teachers and others who have been instrumental in the development of state-level and district-level mathematics curricula guidelines why students should learn mathematics. Virtually all the answers were given without hesitation and could hardly be contested. For example,

❏ "Mathematical literacy is a necessity in today's world. It's needed for everything from budgeting, to being a wise consumer, to holding down many jobs. The mathematically able have more options available to them. If we didn't teach mathematics, we would deny opportunities to individuals and fail to produce the brainpower society needs for scientific, sociological, and technological advancement."
❏ "Obviously, fundamental mathematical skills are needed as basic survival tools for life. Furthermore, the world is changing so rapidly, we don't know what kinds of problems today's children will be facing tomorrow. So above all, they need to be able to be systematic, logical problem solvers. Appropriate experiences with mathematics enhance that ability."

However, most of those I queried were much slower to respond to questions about why selected topics are included in mathematics curricula. For example,

❏ "Why do you teach sixth graders about primes?"
"Well, it's in all the textbooks I've ever seen. And, prime factorization is critical to finding least common multiples and greatest common divisors."
❏ "Why is there so much emphasis on associativity and commutativity of operations in the seventh-grade curriculum?"
"That's a good question. I guess students are expected to know that before they get into algebra."
❏ "I see volume formulas are included in the pre-algebra section of your curriculum guidebook. Why is that?"
"It's always been a part of our junior high math. I think it's because volume problems provide a lot

of nice applications of solving open sentences. We want to get these kids ready to learn how to solve equations."
❏ "Why do you spend so much time on factoring polynomials in algebra?"
"Well, the book really emphasizes it. And then, the students need it when they get into solving second-degree and higher equations and inequalities."
❏ "Why are compound interest formulas included in your consumer mathematics course?"
"Most everybody needs to understand banking and financing to survive today. Some of my students are in the process of buying a car. It's useful to them right now!"
❏ "What's the point of proving so many theorems in geometry?"
"I've wondered about that myself. There's some logic to be learned, but more importantly, I think they need to see how a mathematical system evolves."
❏ "Why do you include this 'application' section from the trigonometry book? Do your students really need to be able to find the angle of the shadow cast by flagpoles?"
"Very funny! There are two very good reasons. One, these kind of problems are on the standardized tests that they need to pass. Second, they'll need this stuff when they get into calculus."

After listening to hundreds of such comments, it is obvious that many teachers and other curriculum developers recognize intrinsic value in mathematics; thus, mathematics courses (except for consumer, business, and general mathematics courses) are viewed as preparation for subsequent courses. To many, the most honorable goal of precollege school mathematics is preparing students to pass calculus.

Mathematics curricula based on the goal of preparing students to learn more mathematics are justifiable in light of the following:

1. Generally speaking, the farther individuals advance in school mathematics, the greater the variety of occupational opportunities available to them (Steen 1987, 1988).
2. Society needs a mathematically literate citizenry and an increasing number of mathematicians, scientists, engineers, and other mathematically expert professionals (NCTM 1989, 3–5).

Learn Mathematics to Solve Real-Life Problems

Although the inclusion of mathematics in school curricula can be justified solely on the intrinsic merit of mathematics, research findings suggest that such a curriculum fails for three reasons:

1. Most students seem unable to transfer mathematical processes learned in isolation from situations they perceive as real life to solve problems dissimilar from example problems directly presented in lessons (Dossey et al. 1988, 8–13; Schoenfeld 1985).
2. Students are likely to retain algorithmic skills and knowledge of rules only as long as they continue to use them. Unless they've learned to apply them to solve problems from their own real world, they're hardly motivated to continue to use them once the skill has been tested and they have moved on to other lessons (Schoenfeld 1989). Hence, it is typical for a mathematical topic to be repeatedly cycled through curricula, being taught initially and then reviewed each time it is a prerequisite to another topic.
3. Most adolescents are simply not highly motivated to work toward goals whose benefits appear only to be long-range (Santrock 1984, 553–563). "Learn this now so you'll be able to pass calculus next year," seems reasonable to most 16-year-olds but pales as a motivator in comparison to immediate concerns.

These research-based findings have implications for mathematics curricula:

As new topics are introduced, students need to be provided with experiences that lead them to be able to apply their understanding of that topic to solve problems they consider to be real life and relate that topic to previously learned mathematical topics.

Adherence to this curriculum-design principle does not preclude teaching mathematics for the purpose of learning more mathematics, but it does rule out completely divorcing topics from students' real-life problems.

REAL-LIFE PROBLEMS

According to Merriam-Webster (1986, p. 1807), a *problem* is "an unsettled matter demanding solution or decision and requiring usually considerable thought or skill for its proper solution or decision : an issue marked by usually considerable difficulty, uncertainty, or doubt with regard to its proper settlement : a perplexing or puzzling question . . . a source usually of considerable difficulty, perplexity, or worry."

Because problems are associated with difficulty and perplexity, some people consider them distasteful. However, the existence of problems serves as a strong motivator for human endeavor. A perfectly satisfied person, one who feels no need to solve a problem, lacks the motivation to change and, thus, to learn (Cangelosi 1988a, 136).

Do not confuse *problems* with mathematical textbook exercises. Schoenfeld (1989, 87–88) states

For any student, a mathematical *problem* is a task (a) in which the student is interested and engaged and for which he wishes to obtain a resolution, and (b) for which the student does not have a readily accessible mathematical means by which to achieve the resolution.

As simple as this definition may seem, it has some significant consequences. First, it presumes that engagement is important in problem solving; a task isn't a problem for you until you've made it *your* problem. Second, it implies that tasks are not "problems" in and of themselves; whether or not a task is a problem for you depends on what you know. Third, most of the textbook and homework "problems" assigned to students are not problems according to this definition, but exercises. In most textbooks, the majority of practice tasks can be solved by direct application of procedures illustrated in the chapter — e.g., solving quadratic equations after you have been taught the quadratic formula, or a "moving trains" problem when the text has illustrated the specific procedures for solving "distance-rate-time" problems. In contrast, real problem solving confronts individuals with a difficulty. They know where they are, and where they want to get — but they have no ready means of getting there. Fourth, the majority of what has been called "problem solving" in the past decade — introducing "word problems" into the curriculum — is only a small part of problem solving.[1]

Who outside of school is ever moved to engage in mathematics unless she or he has a problem to solve? People have problems to solve whenever they have questions they want to answer. Before you are in a position to design mathematics lessons around problems students are interested in solving, you need to identify problems they perceive from their real worlds. Strategies for identifying such problems are illustrated in Chapter 4 (e.g., Mr. Polonia's approach and Ms. Smith's approach in Vignettes 4.3 and 4.9, respectively). Exhibit 2.2 contains a list of problems adolescent students identified as important to them. These problems were successfully incorporated into lessons relevant to mathematical topics included in middle, junior high, and high school curricula.

Exhibit 2.2
Problems identified as important by adolescents that have been incorporated into mathematics lessons.

Art and Aesthetics
❑ While thinking about how to sketch a picture: At what angles should I make these lines intersect to give the illusion I'm trying to create?
❑ In deciding how to decorate a room: What color combinations do people tend to associate with being happy?

Cooking
❑ While planning a meal: How should I expand this recipe so all my guests get enough to eat, but I don't have a lot of food left over?
❑ What, if any, functions can I formulate (and then write a computer program for) for relating recipe ingredients to output variables such as calories, fat content, nutrients, sweetness, and sourness?

Earning Money
❑ In considering a fund-raising class project: Would we net more money with a car wash, a bake sale, a "run for donations," used book sale, or "rent-a-teenager" offer?
❑ Is this offer to sell greeting cards I just received in the mail a good deal for me?

Electronics
❑ How can I efficiently interlink this cable television, videotape recorder, and computer?
❑ What, if any, functions can I formulate for maximizing amplification of this sound system while minimizing reverberations?

Employment
❑ Considering time on the job, travel, expenses, opportunity for advancement, security, and benefit from experiences, which of these three jobs should I take?
❑ Is my paycheck accurate, considering my hours and overtime?

Environmental Concerns
❑ What's the most efficient way for us to get our message across to the most influential people?
❑ In preparing for a field trip: How can we minimize our impact on the flora and fauna of the forest?

Family
❑ In response to her father's claim that she spends too much time listening to music and watching television and not enough time working on school work and doing chores: How much time do I usually spend a day on each of those four things?
❑ How can I help my brother manage his time better?

Friends
❑ Do people really care how their friends dress?
❑ What factors create friendships?

Gardening and Growing Plants
❑ What, if any, rules can I formulate (and then write a computer program for) to maximize the growth of beans as a function of soil composition, space, exposure to sun, moisture, etc.?
❑ What effects do varying amount and frequency of watering these types of plants have on their health?

Health
❑ What's the best exercise program for me?
❑ How should I change my diet?

Managing Money
❑ How should I go about saving enough money to buy a car when I'm 16?
❑ How should I budget my money?

Music
❑ Who is the hottest music group right now?
❑ Since I eventually want to work in a rock group, would I be better starting off learning to play the piano, guitar, or drums?

THE NATIONAL COUNCIL OF TEACHERS OF MATHEMATICS' (NCTM) STANDARDS
The Gap Between Research-Based Curricula and Typical Practice

In the early 1900s, experimental studies of teaching and learning (e.g., James 1890; Thorndike and Woodworth 1901) undermined the faculty psychology and formal discipline principles upon which the prevailing mathematics curricula of the day were based (Strom 1969). Unfortunately, a gap still exists between how mathematics is typically taught and how research-based principles indicate it should be

taught (Brophy 1986). Even in today's secondary schools, the most commonly practiced method of teaching mathematics follows a tiresome pattern (Jesunathadas 1990):

The teacher introduces a topic by stating a rule or definition and then demonstrating it on the chalkboard or on overhead transparencies with textbook examples. Students work on exercises at their seats as the teacher provides individual help to those experiencing difficulties with exercises. Similar exercises are completed for homework and checked as "right" or "wrong" in the beginning of the next class period. Homework exercises that were particularly trouble-

Parties
- ❑ How many people should we invite?
- ❑ What kind of food should we serve?

Personal Appearance
- ❑ What's the best way to treat pimples?
- ❑ How do different people respond to "muscular" women?

Personal Planning
- ❑ How should I budget my time?
- ❑ Would I be better off taking more college-prep or business courses in high school?

Pets and Raising Animals
- ❑ What kinds and numbers of fish can this aquarium support?
- ❑ Is the behavior modification I've started with my cat working?

Politics
- ❑ What strategies should we employ to get Allison elected to the student council?
- ❑ What can we do to sway people's thinking on this gun-control issue?

School Grades
- ❑ What's the relation between the amount of time I study and the grades I get?
- ❑ Is it best to "cram" the night before a test or spread test preparation out over a longer period of time?

School Subjects Other than Mathematics
- ❑ In response to a problem assigned in science class: How much does it cost to burn a light bulb?

- ❑ In response to a health and physical education assignment: How many push-ups would I need to do to burn 100 calories?

Social Issues
- ❑ Considering the composition of our school body with respect to ethnicity and gender, did ethnic or sex bias influence the outcome of the last school election?
- ❑ What can we do to discourage drug abuse in our school?

Sports and Games
- ❑ What kind of tennis racquet should I buy?
- ❑ What strategy (e.g., regarding lap times) should I use to minimize my time in the 1500-meter run?

Television, Movies, and Videos
- ❑ How does gun use in movies compare to gun use in real life?
- ❑ In what ways are people influenced by television commercials?

Travel
- ❑ What is the most efficient way for me to get from here to Tucson?
- ❑ In planning a class trip: Where should we plan to stop along the way?

Vehicles
- ❑ Which of these two skateboards is better for speed, control, and durability?
- ❑ Regarding a remote-control model car: How are speed, acceleration, maneuverability, and response time affected by battery power and distance between controller and car?

Source: Cangelosi 1989a, 1990c

some are worked out for the class either by the teacher or student volunteers.

Emphasis is almost entirely on algorithmic skills. Neither understanding of why rules and algorithms work nor applications to real-life problems are stressed. The teacher's expectations for all but a few students are very low. The pace of lessons is slow with plodding, repetitive exercises.

Research-based principles do not suggest that these expository, drill, and review lessons should be eliminated, but they should not continue to be the dominant form of instruction. Acquiring algorithmic

skills should not be the primary goal of school mathematics curricula.

Numerous curricula-reform efforts have attempted to bring the teaching of mathematics more in line with the research-based principles that indicate students need experiences discovering and inventing mathematics and utilizing mathematics to solve real-life problems (e.g., The 1908 Committee of Fifteen on the Geometry Syllabus (Kinney and Purdy 1952, 22–23), The Joint Commission to Study the Place of Mathematics in Secondary Education (NCTM 1940), The School Mathematics Study Group (Begle, 1958), *An Agenda for Action: Recom-*

mendations for School Mathematics of the 1980s (NCTM 1980), *Educating Americans for the 21st Century* (National Science Board Commission on Precollege Education in Mathematics, Science, and Technology 1983), *The Mathematical Sciences Curriculum K–12: What is Fundamental and What Is Not* (Conference Board of the Mathematical Sciences 1983a), *New Goals for Mathematical Sciences Education* (Conference Board of the Mathematical Sciences 1983b)).

One of the more promising and expansive curricula reform projects produced the *Curriculum and Evaluation Standards for School Mathematics* (NCTM 1989). This NCTM-sponsored document was developed with broad input from mathematics teachers, mathematics education specialists, cognitive scientists, mathematicians, and instructional supervisors and has been endorsed by scores of relevant professional associations (e.g., Mathematical Association of America, American Mathematical Society, School Science and Mathematics Association, and Association for Women in Mathematics). It has the potential of serving as a national-level mathematics curriculum guideline. It states (NCTM 1989, v, 1):

The *Standards* is a document designed to establish a broad framework to guide reform in school mathematics in the next decade. In it a vision is given of what the mathematics curriculum should include in terms of content priority and emphasis. The challenge we issue to all interested in the quality of school mathematics is to work collaboratively to use these curriculum and evaluation standards as the basis for change so that the teaching and learning of mathematics in our schools is improved. . . .

These standards are one facet of the mathematics education community's response to the call for reform in the teaching and learning of mathematics. They reflect and are an extension of the community's responses to those demands for change. Inherent in this document is a consensus that all students need to learn more, and often different, mathematics and that instruction in mathematics must be significantly revised.

As a function of NCTM's leadership in current efforts to reform school mathematics, the Commission on Standards in School Mathematics was established by the Board of Directors and charged with two tasks:

1. Create a coherent vision of what it means to be mathematically literate both in a world that relies on calculators and computers to carry out mathematical procedures and in a world where mathematics is rapidly growing and is extensively being applied to diverse fields.
2. Create a set of standards to guide the revision of the school mathematics curriculum and its associated evaluation toward this vision.

Curriculum and Evaluation Standards for School Mathematics

The 265-page document lists, explains, and illustrates

❏ Thirteen curriculum standards for grades K–4
❏ Thirteen curriculum standards for grades 5–8
❏ Fourteen curriculum standards for grades 9–12
❏ Fourteen evaluation standards

The following two types of standards are described:

Curriculum Standards. When a set of curricular standards is specified for school mathematics, it should be understood that the standards are value judgments based on a broad, coherent vision of schooling derived from several factors: societal goals, research on teaching and learning, and professional experience. Each standard starts with a statement of what mathematics the curriculum should include. This is followed by a description of the student activities associated with that mathematics and a discussion that includes instructional examples. (NCTM 1989, 7)

The Evaluation Standards. The evaluation standards are presented separately, not because evaluation should be separated from the curriculum but because planning for the gathering of evidence about student and program outcomes is different. The difference is most clearly illustrated in comparing the curriculum standards titled Connections and the evaluations standards titled Mathematical Power. Both deal with connections among concepts, procedures, and intellectual methods, but the curriculum standards are related to the instructional plan whereas the evaluation standards address the ways in which students integrate these connections intellectually so that they develop mathematical power. (NCTM 1989, 11)

Both the curriculum and evaluation standards are listed in Appendix D. However, without the explanations of student activities and the examples, the ideas behind each standard are lost. Thus, you should obtain your own personal copy of *Curriculum and Evaluation Standards for School Mathematics* from NCTM as a guide for developing curricula and designing lessons.

A curriculum developed with the *Standards* as a guide emphasizes the following far more than traditional mathematics curricula:

❏ Real-life problem solving
❏ Conceptualization of why rules and algorithms work
❏ Experiences with mathematical discovery and invention

❑ Integration across mathematical topics
❑ Use of calculators and computers
❑ Comprehension of the language of mathematics
❑ Writing and speaking about mathematics
❑ Testing for guiding instruction
❑ Testing for comprehension, conceptual, and application levels of learning

Furthermore, compared to traditional curricula, a *Standards*-based curriculum places somewhat less emphasis on the following:

❑ Word problems that do not reflect real-world situations
❑ Paper-and-pencil calculations
❑ Segregation of topics and subdisciplines of mathematics
❑ Memorization of formulas
❑ Verification by appeal to authority
❑ Mindless exercises
❑ Problems with one exact solution
❑ Testing at the knowledge cognitive level
❑ Testing solely for grades

The ideas, suggestions, and illustrations in this textbook will help you develop curricula and design and conduct lessons that are consistent with the *Standards*. This is important because lessons consistent with the *Standards* are consistent with research-based principles, and the *Standards* is the guide for state-of-the-art mathematics curricula of the 1990s and into the 21st century ("Emphasize Application of Math Skills," 1989; Holden 1989; Dossey 1987; "Use New Standards to Upgrade Math," 1989).

MATHEMATICS CURRICULA OUTCOMES
Elementary School–Level Outcomes

Traditional Curriculum
As a middle or secondary school mathematics teacher, you need to understand what your students experienced and achieved while in elementary school. After all, you are responsible for building upon those experiences and advancing those achievements. Of course, there are considerable differences among students on these two variables. Besides the differences among students in how they respond to similar experiences, the differences among teachers are also great. Some students will have enjoyed the benefits of effective teachers who provided them with enriching experiences discovering and inventing mathematics. But research suggests that most are not so fortunate.

Typically, students engage in activities with hands-on manipulatives counting, sorting, measuring, and naming objects in kindergarten and the beginning of first grade. But by second grade, such concrete activities are usually replaced almost entirely by skill-level drills for memorizing addition and subtraction facts. Some conceptual work in identifying geometric figures and fractions is included, but fluency with facts and algorithms involving the four fundamental operations are paramount through the fifth grade.

On the average—but with wide variation about this average—the impact of this traditional elementary school mathematics curricula on students is as follows:

❑ Most students exit fifth grade with an arsenal of memorized algorithms for adding, subtracting, multiplying, and dividing whole numbers and rational numbers expressed in decimal form. Their facility for manipulating numbers expressed as fractions is typically limited to one- and two-digit numerators and denominators whose prime factors are obvious to them. Computational skills with numbers expressed as percentages are emphasized by many teachers and ignored by many others. However, having topics accurately presented in textbooks and by teachers does not imply that most students learn them accurately. What is "covered" is not necessarily what is learned. Many students' arsenals of algorithms include memorized error patterns (Ashlock 1990; Ginsburg 1977, 79–149) that produce incorrect computational results. Analyze, for example, the following sample of Phil's work on a "review exercise" administered by his teacher on the first day of sixth grade:

$$
\begin{array}{r}
230 \\
\times\ 23 \\
\hline
690 \\
460 \\
\hline
5,290
\end{array}
\qquad
\begin{array}{r}
^{3\ 2\ 5}197 \\
\times\ 18 \\
\hline
40426 \\
197 \\
\hline
42,396
\end{array}
\qquad
\begin{array}{r}
^3 14 \\
+8 \\
\hline
322 \\
^{33} \\
\times 8 \\
\hline
404
\end{array}
\qquad
\begin{array}{r}
^{2\,1\ 2\,1}435 \\
\times\ 43 \\
\hline
1525 \\
2400 \\
\hline
25,525
\end{array}
$$

Phil faithfully follows the algorithm he remembers, not even bothered by the fact that the product he got for 197 and 18 is considerably larger than the one he got for 230 and 23. He is likely to continue this error pattern until a teacher diagnoses that he is adding carried digits one step too soon. (For instance, in the second exercise, he begins by thinking, "Eight times 7 is 56. Put down the 6 and carry 5. Five plus 9 is 14. Fourteen times 8 is. . . .") Although most of Phil's products are not even approximately correct, he correctly executes the vast majority of the steps in the algorithm; he simply executes one repeated step out of order. Typically, students' computational errors are not random.

❑ Students fail to detect their own error patterns because they have learned to execute algorithms faithfully with a myopic step-by-step view, never conceptualizing the whole process or bothering to predict a reasonable outcome (Schoenfeld 1989). The following example illustrates the phenomenon.

❑ **VIGNETTE 2.5**

For the purpose of stimulating discussion and giving him some insights about his students as they begin sixth grade, Mr. Stokes displays the following on the overhead screen and directs the class, "Simplify this:"

$$\frac{8.47 + 8.47 + 8.47 + 8.47}{4}$$

Without hesitation, 23 of the 26 students begin the process of adding 8.47 to itself four times and dividing the sum by four. One asks, "Can we use a calculator?" Another inquires about the number of decimal places Mr. Stokes wants in the answer.

Mr. Stokes asks, "Why did you go to all that trouble, when you could see that four of any number divided by four is the number?" Brad: "That's not the way we learned to do it." Molina: "Yeah, the rule is to simplify the numerator first and then. . . ."

_____

❑ Students are generally proficient in completing one-step skill-level tasks (e.g., recalling facts, associating names with figures, and executing the first step of an algorithm) alluded to in curriculum guidelines. However, there is a dramatic drop in proficiency for multistep tasks (e.g., working two-step word problems) ("U.S. Teens Lag Behind in Math, Science," 1989).

❑ Considering traditional curricula's distinctions among topics (e.g., percents and fractions, expanded notation and counting, graphs and word problems, and sets and ratios) and mathematical specialties (e.g., arithmetic, algebra, geometry, probability, statistics, and measurement), it is not surprising that most students fail to interrelate what they learn in one lesson to what they learn in other lessons.

❑ Most students have access to calculators at home but not in school (Dossey et al. 1988, 79). In general, students are able to use calculators for trivial tasks (e.g., checking answers to computational exercises) but use them neither to save time spent in computation nor in ways that take advantage

of special functions (e.g., Σ) or features such as memory storage (Kansky 1986).

❑ Only a small proportion of students appear to possess the conceptual understanding necessary to explain why (1) the algorithms they know work (e.g., why, when multiplying 84 by 3, one should first multiply 3 by 4 and then carry the 1 from the 12) or (2) relations they've memorized (e.g., area of rectangle = length × width) are facts ("U.S. Students again Rank near Bottom in Math and Science," 1989).

❑ Only a small proportion of students appear to possess the application-level understanding necessary to distinguish among appropriate and inappropriate mathematical procedures when confronted with a problem-solving task (Carpenter et al. 1988).

❑ By the time students enter sixth grade they tend to believe mathematics has little or nothing to do with real-life problem solving, mathematical tasks are completed either quickly or not at all, and only geniuses can be creative with mathematics (Schoenfeld 1985, 43).

❑ Although most students perceive mathematics to be composed mainly of rule memorization and do not expect to use mathematics outside the classroom, those with more favorable attitudes tend to be more skillful with mathematics and also learn mathematics at more sophisticated cognitive levels (e.g., conceptual and application levels) (Dossey et al. 1988, 11).

NCTM Standards–Based Curriculum

In response to the question, "What in the *Standards* is new compared with current practice?" NCTM's 1988–1990 president, Shirley Frye (1989a, 7; 1989b, 316) states

These new major themes are woven throughout all levels: communications, reasoning, and connections. New topics include data analysis and discrete mathematics, and the usual content topics are either expanded or modified. The *Standards* makes specific recommendations about the increased and decreased emphasis that should be placed on certain topics, skills, and procedures at all levels.

The evaluation standards focus on assessment of students' performance and curricular programs, with an emphasis on the role of evaluative measures in gathering information on which teachers can base subsequent instruction. A key factor in the general assessment section is alignment, the agreement of the assessment with the curriculum.

For all students to be mathematically literate, the instructional strategies must include collaborative experiences, the use of calculators and computers, exploration activities that enable students to hypothesize and test, applications of mathematics, and experience in problem posing and writing.

Finally, the challenges to teach mathematics as an integrated whole and to link mathematics to the physical world are the relatively new focal points of the standards.

Some teachers—but not most—have been adhering to the principles forwarded by the *Standards* for years. One hopes NCTM's efforts to infect mathematics curricula with those principles (Frye 1989a, 1989b) will increase the number of elementary school classrooms in which the items in Exhibit 2.3 are emphasized and the ones in Exhibit 2.4 are deemphasized (NCTM 1989, 20–21).

Middle School–and Junior High School–Level Outcomes

Traditional Curriculum

In most school systems, middle school includes grades six, seven, and eight; junior high includes grades seven, eight, and nine. Traditional middle or junior high school mathematics curricula impact students in ways very similar to those listed (beginning on page 29) for traditional elementary school curricula. There are, however, these differences:

❏ There is a much more formal treatment of algebra (often labeled prealgebra) and geometry.
❏ More emphasis is placed on percents, ratios, proportions, and formulas (e.g., for rate of speed, interest, area, volume, perimeter, and averages).
❏ There is even more separation among topics and mathematical specialty areas (e.g., between algebra and geometry).
❏ There is even less emphasis on manipulatives and concrete experiences.
❏ Perceptions of students about mathematics deteriorates even further (Dossey et al. 1988, 11).

Students' myopic view and lack of inclination to make sense out of mathematical tasks are illustrated by the beginning ninth graders in the following example.

Exhibit 2.3
Points for increased emphasis in the elementary grades according to the *Standards*.

Emphasize

Conceptual understanding of numbers and relationships between numbers (e.g., between numbers expressed as fractions and numbers expressed as decimals)

Estimation of quantities

Work with approximate figures

Conceptual understanding of fundamental operations

Conceptual understanding of why algorithms work

Mental computations

Application-level understanding of how to select appropriate algorithms

Prediction of computational results

Arithmetic work with numbers resulting from empirical measurements (as opposed to textbook numerals)

Integration of geometry, arithmetic, probability, and data gathering (i.e., measurement),

Exploration of patterns

Use of variables to express relationships

Word problems with a variety of structures

Applications to real-life problems

Problem-solving strategies

Concrete activities with manipulatives

Cooperative work among students

High cognitive-level question/discussion sessions (i.e., thought-provoking as opposed to recitation)

Writing, speaking, and reading about mathematics

Use of calculators and computers to reduce time spent in complex algorithms

Use of calculators and computers as learning tools

Source: NCTM 1989

Exhibit 2.4
Points for decreased emphasis in the elementary grades according to the *Standards*.

Deemphasize

Early attention to reading, writing, and ordering numbers symbolically

Complex paper-and-pencil computations

Treatment of algorithms in isolation from their applications

Use of rounding or other memorized processes for estimating numbers

Addition and subtraction without renaming

Long division without remainders

Paper-and-pencil computations with fractions

Naming geometric figures

Memorization of equivalence between units of measurements

Use of clue words to determine which operations to use in solving word problems

Rote memorization

One-answer-only, one-method-only problems to solve

Teaching by telling

Source: NCTM 1989

❑ **VIGNETTE 2.6**

For the purpose of stimulating discussion and giving her some insights about her students on the first day of algebra I class, Ms. Koa asks one student, Barbara, to multiply 307 and $\frac{4}{5}$ at the board. She computes:

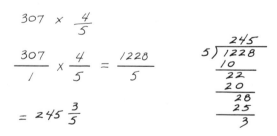

Ms. Koa: "Thank you, Barbara." Barbara starts to erase her work, but Ms. Koa intervenes, "No, please leave it there and work one more next to it. This time find 80% of 307." Barbara writes:

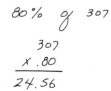

Ms. Koa: So, you found $\frac{4}{5}$ of 307 to be 245$\frac{3}{5}$, but 80% of 307 is 24.56. Does that seem okay to you?

Barbara: I think I did it right. You want me to rework it?

Dudley: The second one's not right because you didn't put the decimal in the right place.

Barbara: But you're supposed to have as many decimal places in the answer as there are in the problem. See two here, so I put two here.

Dudley: But that's because you didn't bring the zero down.

Barbara: I thought you were supposed to . . .

Ms. Koa: Wait a minute. Doesn't anyone care whether or not the answer makes sense? About what would 50% of 300 be?

Lucy: One hundred fifty.

Ms. Koa: Then should 80% of 307 be more or less than 150?

The discussion continues, with most of the students focusing on steps in algorithms and Ms. Koa striving to get them to make sense out of the task.

The failure of Ms. Koa's algebra students to recognize that $\frac{4}{5}$ of 307 is the same as 80% of 307 is not surprising, considering how traditional mathematics curricula isolate topics. Students tend to disassociate fractions from percents, arithmetic from algebra, geometry from numbers, and measurements from numerals that appear in textbooks.

NCTM Standards–Based Curriculum

In middle and junior high school classrooms where the *Standards'* principles are put into practice, the items in Exhibit 2.5 are emphasized, whereas those in Exhibit 2.6 are deemphasized (NCTM 1989, 70–73).

High School–Level Outcomes

Traditional Curriculum

Traditional high school curricula impacts students in much the same ways enumerated for elementary, middle, and junior high grades. But the following also occur at the high school level:

❑ Differences among students' mathematical competence and attitudes are further exaggerated as students are separated into 3- or 4-year course sequences for the "mathematically inclined" college bound; 1- or 2-year course sequences for the "less mathematically inclined" college bound; a 1- or 2-year sequence of business and consumer mathematics courses; or "remedial" mathematics courses.

Exhibit 2.5
Points for increased emphasis in the middle and junior high grades according to the *Standards* (NCTM 1989).

Emphasize

Investigation of open-ended problems

Problem-solving projects that extend for weeks

Representations of a problem and possible solutions verbally, numerically, graphically, geometrically, and symbolically

Speaking, writing, listening, and reading about mathematical ideas

Higher-order cognitive processes (e.g., inductive, deductive, analytical, and divergent thinking)

Interrelating mathematics with other school subjects and to the real world outside of the school

Interrelating topics within mathematics and across mathematical specialties

Real-life problem solving

Conceptual understanding of rational numbers and their relations among themselves and other variables

Inventing algorithms and procedures

Predicting problem solutions and results of algorithms

Discovering concepts and relationships

Distinguishing between *representations of numbers and concepts* and the *numbers and concepts themselves*

Identifying functional relationships and associating mathematical functions to real world situations

Using a variety of methods to solve linear equations and inequalities

Informal investigation of nonlinear relationships

Exploration and application of experimental and theoretical probability models

Application of descriptive statistical methods to real-life decision making

Problem-solving applications of geometric relationships

Acquisition of numbers through measurement and measurement approximations

Using technology (e.g., computers, calculators, and video) for exploration

Using computers and calculators to reduce time spent executing algorithms

Cooperative and group learning activities

Using concrete models and manipulatives

Source: NCTM 1989

❑ The separation among traditional mathematics specialties (e.g., algebra, geometry, trigonometry, statistics, "computer mathematics," "business mathematics," arithmetic, analytical geometry, and calculus) becomes even more distinct in the minds of students.

❑ The treatment of mathematics, except in the consumer and business mathematics courses, becomes even more formalized, abstract, and removed from real-life situations.

❑ Perceptions of the less mathematically inclined students deteriorate even further.

Students' tendencies to adhere faithfully and mindlessly to the execution of algorithms continues

in high school, even in courses that are considered advanced. Here is an illustration.

❑ **VIGNETTE 2.7**

Twelfth grader Rosario diligently follows his calculus teacher's explanation of how to use the derivative of a quadratic function to find maximum and minimum *Y*-values. For homework, Rosario works a number of strictly computational exercises and then gets to the "application word problems" his teacher assigned. The first one reads:

If a rock is tossed upward with an initial velocity of 112 decameters per second from an altitude of 700 decameters above the surface of Mars, its altitude above the surface *s* seconds later is given by $h = -5.6s^2 + 112s + 700$. What is the maximum altitude reached by the rock?

Automatically, Rosario writes "$h = -5.6s^2 + 700$," but then he pauses and thinks to himself, "I wonder what I'm supposed to do with that first part about velocity of 112 decameters and altitude of 700 decameters. She didn't show us what to do with that. Oh, well, all these are maximum and minimum problems, so I know I've got to take the derivative." He writes as he thinks, "the rule is to multiply the coefficient by the exponent and then reduce the exponent by one and just drop constants":

$$h(s) = -5.6s^2 + 112s + 700$$
$$h'(s) = (2)(-5.6)s + 112$$
$$h'(s) = -11.2s + 112$$

He continues, "Now, I've just got to equate this to zero, solve for s and that should give me the answer." He writes:

$$0 = -11.2s + 112$$
$$11.2s = 112$$
$$s = \frac{112}{11.2}$$

Using long division he divides 112 by 11.2 and writes:

$$s = 10$$

Exhibit 2.6
Points for decreased emphasis in the middle and junior high grades according to the *Standards*.

Deemphasize

Practicing routine, one-step tasks

Practicing solving problems categorized by type (e.g., coin, age, and reversed-digit problems)

Recitations and worksheets requiring only rote, one-step memory

Relying on appeal to authority (e.g., the teacher or textbook answer key) for solutions

Learning about topics in isolation from other topics

Developing skills out of context

Memorizing rules, formulas (e.g., in statistics) and algorithms (e.g., cross multiplication or for manipulating algebraic symbols) without understanding why or how they work

Tedious paper-and-pencil computations

Source: NCTM 1989

Rosario: So my answer is 10; better check it in the back of the book. Aw, no! What'd I do wrong? 1260 decameters. I'm not even close! Oh, I wonder if I should have plugged my 10 in for s and solved the function from there. I'll try that.

He writes:

$$h(s) = -5.6s^2 + 112s + 700$$
$$h(10) = -5.6(10^2) + 112(10) + 700$$

After computing both multiplications and the additions by hand he writes 1260 and exclaims to himself, "Oh good, that's right. So, I should work all the rest this way. I wonder why I didn't have to use that 112 and 700 from the beginning of the problem. No matter, this way'll work for all the rest. Okay, next. . . ."

NCTM Standards–Based Curriculum

As you and other teachers develop curriculum and teach in harmony with the *Standards,* high school mathematics courses will tend to emphasize the items in Exhibit 2.7 and deemphasize those in Exhibit 2.8 (NCTM 1989, 126–127).

Exhibit 2.7
Points for increased emphasis in high school according to the *Standards* (NCTM 1989).

Emphasize

The use of real-world problems to motivate the exploration and application of traditional topics from algebra, geometry, trigonometry, and analysis as well as topics recently introduced into the curriculum from probability, statistics, and discrete mathematics

The use of computers to facilitate conceptual understanding of relations (e.g., with computer-based methods of successive approximations and multidimensional geometric representations)

Integration of both geometry and discrete mathematics within other specialty areas and across grade levels

Integration of functions in all specialty areas

Use of calculators and computers to facilitate the execution of algorithms

Deductive arguments expressed in natural rather than artificially rigid forms of communications

Interrelations among topics and specialties

Construction of functions as models for real-world problems

Source: NCTM 1989

Exhibit 2.8
Points for decreased emphasis in high school according to the *Standards*.

Deemphasize

Word problems by type, such as coin, digit, and work

The simplification of radical expressions

The use of factoring to solve equations and to simplify rational expressions

Logarithmic and trigonometric calculations using tables

Solving systems of equations using determinants

Conic sections

Euclidean geometry as a complete axiomatic system

Algorithmic-like approaches to proving theorems (e.g., with two-column format)

Distinction between analytic and Euclidean geometries

Inscribed and circumscribed polygons

Paper-and-pencil calculations

Memorization of formulas and identities

Graphing of functions by hand using table values

Unexplained formulas given as models of real-world problems (e.g., the one given to Rosario in Vignette 2.7)

Source: NCTM 1989

COURSES

The mathematics curriculum in most schools consists primarily of a sequence of courses. Ordinarily, a middle, junior high, or high school mathematics teacher is responsible for four or five class periods a day. In a small school, the five class periods may involve five different courses (e.g., beginning algebra, geometry, intermediate algebra, general mathematics, and precalculus). In a large school, the assignment is more likely to include multiple sections of the same course (e.g., two sections of general mathematics and three sections of geometry). Course titles vary from school district to school district (Hirch and Zweng 1985), but the following listing is representative of many:

❑ In *sixth-grade mathematics,* arithmetic operations with nonnegative rational numbers are the primary concern. Geometric and measurement topics are also emphasized.

❑ In *seventh-grade mathematics,* the emphasis on the arithmetic of rational numbers continues. Applications of arithmetic are extended into areas such as probability and statistics. Negative integers are introduced, as is a more formal treatment of Euclidean geometry.

❑ In *eighth-grade general mathematics* the focus is still on the arithmetic of rational numbers. Some elements of number theory are introduced, as are linear algebraic equations and the Cartesian coordinate systems. The study of geometry emphasizes constructions, areas, and volumes.

❑ *Prealgebra* is ordinarily intended to provide more advanced work for seventh and eighth graders or basic work for ninth and tenth graders. In any case, it is a preparation for elementary algebra, and its content overlaps that of general eighth-grade mathematics and the first half of elementary algebra.

❑ In *elementary algebra,* or *algebra I,* the real-number system is developed. Variable expressions, linear equations, linear inequalities, and operations with polynomials (including those with exponents) are emphasized. Work with quadratic relations may or may not be included, depending on the pace of the course.

❑ *Consumer mathematics* is designed to provide high school students with fundamental mathematical skills needed in everyday life. Such courses are not intended to be a preparation for more advanced work in mathematics. Topics include the applications of arithmetic and algebra to problems in the areas of homemaking, budgeting, banking, marketing, traveling, financing, and purchasing.

❑ *Basic mathematics* is designed to provide junior high and high school students with a review of mathematical work ordinarily included in elementary and middle school courses.

❑ In *geometry,* Euclidean geometry is studied as a system. Applications of trigonometry and coordinate geometry may also be included.

❑ In *intermediate algebra,* or *algebra II,* ideas studied in elementary algebra are extended. Systems of linear equations, quadratic equations, and higher-order relationships are emphasized. Work with statistics, permutations and combinations, probability, complex numbers, sequences and series, and vectors are included. Conceptual understanding of limits, without a formal epsilon-delta definition, is a principal goal.

❑ *Trigonometry* is usually a half-year course for students who have completed intermediate algebra. Content hardly varies among trigonometry courses. Trigonometric functions, trigonometric identities, inverses of trigonometric functions, circular functions, and polar coordinates are standard fare.

❏ *Advanced algebra* is usually a half-year course in which topics from intermediate algebra are reviewed, with applications extended. Topics such as binomial expansion, determinants, and theory of equations are usually added. Considered a preparation for calculus, analytical geometry is emphasized.

❏ *Calculus* is often designed to help students pass the Advanced Placement Examination for college credit (College Board Publications 1990). Topics from algebra and analytical geometry are usually reviewed, followed by treatises on limits of sequences, limits of functions, derivatives and their applications, and integrals and their applications.

❏ In *probability and statistics,* students with a background in algebra study probability models, data-collection techniques, sampling models, and the application of both descriptive and inferential statistical models for interpreting data. A proliferation of courses in probability and statistics may be one way some school district personnel respond to the *Standards'* call for emphasis on discrete mathematics.

Mathematics teachers are sometimes asked to teach courses in computer science. However, such courses are more appropriately conducted by teachers with special preparation in computer science education.

TEACHING UNITS

Each course is organized into *teaching units.* Exhibit 2.9 lists titles for a sample sequence of teaching units that might comprise an algebra II course.

Each teaching unit consists of (1) a learning goal, (2) a set of specific objectives that define the learning goal, (3) a planned sequence of lessons, each consisting of learning activities designed to help students achieve specific objectives, (4) mechanisms for monitoring student progress and utilizing feedback in the design of lessons, and (5) a summative evaluation of student achievement of the learning goal.

The Learning Goal

The *learning goal* is the overall purpose of the teaching unit. The learning goal indicates what students are expected to learn if the teaching unit is successful. In other words, the student-learning outcomes targeted by the unit's teaching functions (i.e., the intended ranges of $T_i(s)$) are defined. For example,

Exhibit 2.9
Sample sequence of teaching units for an algebra II course.

1. Variables, constants, and relations
2. Binary operations with real numbers
3. Variable expressions
4. Open sentences with real-number variables
5. Linear functions
6. Systems of linear equations and inequalities
7. Further applications of linear equations and inequalities
8. Simple operations with polynomials
9. Intermediate operations with polynomials
10. Advanced operations with polynomials
11. Quadratic equations and inequalities
12. Quadratic functions
13. Further applications of quadratic equations and inequalities
14. Complex numbers
15. Exponential and logarithmic functions
16. Systems of higher-order relations
17. Sequences
18. Further applications of sequences
19. Probability functions
20. Further applications of probability functions
21. A look ahead

the learning goal of the sixth unit from Exhibit 2.9, entitled "Systems of Linear Equations and Inequalities," might be as follows:

Students can formulate and efficiently utilize systems of linear equations to solve real-life problems and explain the interrelations within those systems that facilitate problem solving.

The Set of Specific Objectives that Defines the Learning Goal

The learning goal provides direction for designing the teaching unit by identifying the overall student outcome. However, teaching is a complicated art. Taking students from where they are to where they can "formulate and efficiently utilize systems . . . problem solving" involves a complex of different learning stages requiring varying teaching strategies. For students to achieve a learning goal such as the one for the unit on systems of linear equations and inequalities, they must acquire a number of specific skills, abilities, or attitudes. Thus, the learning goal is defined by a *set of specific objectives,* each indicating a particular skill, ability, or attitude that is a necessary but insufficient component of learning-goal achievement. The union of the objectives equals the learning goal. For example, the aforementioned learning goal might be defined by the following objectives. (Keep in mind that the terminology and mathematical notations used in the statement of the objectives are for the teacher's benefit and do not necessarily reflect the terminology or notations to which the students will be exposed.)

A. Given a problem whose solution is facilitated by solving for an equation of the form $f_1(x) + f_2(x) + f_3(x) + \cdots + f_n(x) = 0$, the student explains why the solution is also facilitated by a system of equations of the following form:

$$a_{1,1}x_1 + a_{1,2}x + a_{1,3}x_3 + \cdots + a_{1,n}x_n = 0$$
$$a_{2,1}x_1 + a_{2,2}x + a_{2,3}x_3 + \cdots + a_{2,n}x_n = 0$$
$$a_{3,1}x_1 + a_{3,2}x_3 + a_{3,3}x_3 + \cdots + a_{3,n}x_n = 0$$
$$\vdots$$
$$a_{n,1}x + a_{n,2}x_2 + a_{n,3}x_3 + \cdots + a_{n,n}x_n = 0$$

B. The student describes situations, both real-life and mathematical, that are reflected by each of the following types of pairs of linear equations: (1) simultaneous, (2) inconsistent, and (3) equivalent.

C. Given a system of n n-variable linear equations or inequalities, the student solves for the n variables via the substitution method.

D. Given a system of two two-variable linear equations or inequalities, the student solves for the two variables via the graphing method.

E. Given a system of n n-variable linear equations or inequalities, the student solves for the n variables via the addition method.

F. Given a system of n n-variable linear equations or inequalities, the student solves for the n variables by using matrices.

G. The student explains the difference between problems with solutions that are efficiently facilitated by linear programming and those that are not.

H. The student solves linear programming problems.

I. Given a problem, the student (1) determines whether or not the solution is facilitated by formulating and solving for a system of linear equations or inequalities, and, if so, (2) formulates the system.

The Planned Sequence of Lessons

The paramount components of the teaching units are the *lessons* you design and conduct for the pur-

pose of achieving the stated objectives and, thus, the learning goal. Each lesson consists of *learning activities*. For the sample algebra II unit on systems of linear equations and inequalities, a teacher might engage students in lessons for 3 weeks to help them achieve Objectives A through I. For example,

A. The lesson for Objective A includes the following learning activities:
  1. Students are confronted with three rather complicated problems and for each are directed to formulate a single equation for solving the problem. The students work at the task.
  2. The teacher conducts an inductive questioning/discussion class session, in which students reflect upon their work on the three problems and determine the work could be accomplished more efficiently by formulating a system of simpler equations rather than trying to maintain all the relations between variables in one equation of one unknown.
  3. As homework, students work with additional problems, for each attempting to formulate both a single one-variable equation and a system of equations.
  4. The results of the homework are discussed in class, with the students concluding that the single one-variable equation contains exactly the same information as the corresponding system of equations.

B. The lesson for Objective B includes the following learning activities:
  1. As planned by the teacher, one of the previously assigned homework problems had no solution and another had infinite solutions, so the aforementioned discussion and subsequent inductive questioning session leads students to categorize problems according to whether they lead to pairs of simultaneous, inconsistent, or equivalent equations.
  2. Using direct instruction, the teacher informs the students of the conventional names for the three categories they discovered (i.e., *simultaneous, inconsistent,* and *equivalent*) and provides practice using the names.

C. The lesson for Objective C includes the following learning activities:
  1. The teacher directs one of the students to solve one of the homework problems using the original, single one-variable-equation method. As the student works through the solution, the teacher explains and lists each step of the process. A discussion then ensues, in which an analysis of those steps leads to the formulation of the substitution algorithm

for solving systems of simultaneous equations.

2. Using direct instructional strategies, the teacher explains each step in the substitution method.
3. For homework, ...

.

.

.

I. The lesson for Objective I includes the following learning activities:

1. The teacher engages the students in a deductive questioning/discussion session in which three problems are. . . .

Mechanisms for Monitoring Student Progress and Utilizing Feedback in the Design of Lessons

When you plan a teaching unit, you design its lessons. However, because teaching functions are messy, with a highly complex and unstable domain, you need to monitor students' progress routinely throughout the unit. The feedback from your assessments of their progress should determine the pace of lessons and influence the design of learning activities. For example,

> On the second day of the unit on systems of linear equations and inequalities, the students say, "The new method is the same as the old; it's just working with many small parts rather than one big part." From those comments and other observations, the teacher decides to spend less time discussing the initial homework assignment than originally planned. However, the results of a short diagnostic test on the eighth day indicate a number of unanticipated error patterns in the students' execution of the substitution algorithm. Thus, the teacher takes an extra day to remediate that difficulty.

The assessments about your students' progress that you make for the purpose of guiding the design and conduct of teaching units are referred to as *formative evaluations* (Cangelosi 1990b, 2–6).

A Summative Evaluation of Student Achievement of the Learning Goal

As a teacher, you are expected to make periodic reports to communicate to students, their parents, and your supervisors how well your students are achieving learning goals. Consequently, most teaching units terminate with a test of students' achievement of the learning goal. Your judgments of students' success are referred to as *summative evaluations* (Cangelosi 1990b, 2–6).

The design of teaching units is addressed in Chapter 3, dealing with *determining and defining learning goals,* Chapter 4, dealing with *designing lessons,* Chapters 5 and 6, dealing with *keeping students cooperatively engaged in learning activities,* and Chapter 7, dealing with *evaluating student achievement* for both formative and summative purposes.

APPROACHES TO DESIGNING COURSES
The Follow-a-Textbook Approach

Some teachers "design" courses by religiously following prescribed textbooks page by page; teaching units are equated to textbook chapters. Here, for example, is a glimpse into Ms. McCuller's thoughts as she begins planning a two-semester elementary algebra course.

☐ **VIGNETTE 2.8**

Ms. McCuller thinks to herself: "Let's see, where's the table of contents? Okay, it looks like I've got 16 chapters to cover, from 'The Language of Algebra' to Chapter 16, 'Trigonometry.' I don't remember anything about trigonometry in the district curriculum guide for elementary algebra. I wonder if it's okay to skip that. Probably so, since it's the last chapter, so nothing else would be depending on it. . . . Oh well, I'll cover it unless we run out of time.

"Let's see just how many instructional weeks are available per semester. Where's that district calendar? All right, we've got a total of 36 weeks. But there's 1 week each semester for finals, so that leaves only 34. And then there's standardized test week in the spring, so we've got 17 weeks for the first semester and 16 for the second to cover 16 chapters. So, we should average about 2 weeks per chapter.

"Chapter 1, 'The Language of Algebra' . . . it won't take us but a week to get through this. Same with Chapters 2 and 3; it's all review. So we get through the first three chapters the first 3 weeks. Now, Chapter 4 on inequalities—this'll take us longer. Let's see, pages 114 to 140. That's 26 pages, not too many for 2 weeks. Let's see how involved this gets. . . . This is mostly new for these students. I thought with the NCTM *Standards,* we were supposed to start emphasizing applications! There's not much application in here. How are we supposed to follow the *Standards* if the textbooks don't? Of course, by the time the textbooks catch up, they'll be telling us to do something else! Anyway, two weeks for Chapter 4. . . ."

When Ms. McCuller gets to Chapter 9, "Factoring and Rational Expressions," she exclaims to herself, "This is just the kind of stuff the *Standards* suggests we deemphasize and yet I've got to cover a whole chapter on it. It'll probably take us 4 weeks to get through all these algorithms!"

During the school year, Ms. McCuller manages to cover the book page by page, skipping only the brief "Extending Your Knowledge" and "Computer Excursion" inserts near the end of each chapter. Faithfully, she assigns the even-numbered exercises for every section covered. Student learning is limited mostly to memory-level skills with virtually no conceptual- or application-level achievement. However, most students take comfort in being able to appeal to a single source, the textbook, for all they need to know about mathematics.

The Contrived Problem-Solving Approach

To provide students with heuristic experiences discovering and inventing mathematics, some teachers incorporate concrete mathematical models or problem-solving tasks into every teaching unit (Posamentier and Stepelman 1990, 109–136). The same mathematical topics enumerated in curriculum guides and textbook tables of contents may well be included, but each topic relating to a concept or relation is introduced through a problem-solving or model-analysis experience. For example, consider Vignette 2.9.

❑ VIGNETTE 2.9

Mr. Theron is just beginning a teaching unit intended to help his algebra students extend their abilities to (1) apply arithmetic and geometric sequence formulas they discovered in a previous unit, (2) discover new relations among integers, and (3) invent new algorithms with integers. He introduces the unit by confronting the students with the following problem, which he first read in a book by Posamentier and Stepelman (1990 252–253):

> Form a 3 × 3 matrix with the whole numbers 1, 2, . . . , 9 so that the sum of the elements in each row, column, and diagonal is the same.

He indicates to them that any $n \times n$ matrix of real numbers in which the sum of the numbers in each row, column, and diagonal is the same is called a *magic square* (Sobel and Maletsky 1988, 123–129). For example:

7	2	16	9
12	13	3	6
1	8	10	15
14	11	5	4

Working in small task groups, the students' trial-and-error method succeeds in producing magic squares with the desired attributes; the following is one:

2	7	6
9	5	1
4	3	8

Mr. Theron then leads an inductive questioning/discussion session in which students determine that they can utilize the sum of an arithmetic series formula (i.e., $\sum_{i=1}^{n} a_i = (n/2)(a_1 + a_n)$) that they discovered in a previous unit in formulating a general algorithm, or function, for producing magic squares.

Lessons such as Mr. Theron's, in which students analyze and attempt to solve problems or puzzles that have been contrived because of their mathematical features, provide experiences needed for conceptual-level learning. However, if these are the only types of lessons in which students engage, then they will fail to polish their algorithmic skills and apply what they conceptualized in the contrived situations to real-world situations. Thus, teachers also need to include direct instruction for knowledge-level skills and application lessons in which students work on solutions to real-life problems.

Teachers who adhere to the contrived problem-solving approach to designing courses are hardly able to sequence teaching units in the same order they appear in textbooks. The vast majority of textbooks arrange content so that there is a building of algorithmic skills from easier to more difficult tasks. But teachers (e.g., Mr. Theron) who focus on concept attainment through analysis of contrived problems and models typically design units so that students (1) first attempt the more difficult tasks (e.g., creating a magic square by trial and error), (2) next, discover easier methods from that struggle, and then (3) complete the unit applying the easier method (e.g., creating a magic square via the algorithm).

The Real-World Problem-Solving Approach

Ms. Asgil uses an approach quite similar to Mr. Theron's; however, she uses real-life instead of contrived problems for her students to analyze. Share her thoughts as she begins designing an algebra course.

❑ VIGNETTE 2.10

Ms. Asgil: "In order for these students to appreciate the utility of mathematics they have to discover its power to help them solve their own real-life problems. I ought to have a year-long project that they all work on and to which they'd apply the algebra as they learn it. I once heard about a whole high school curriculum that revolved around a year-long project to build and sell a house. That would be great! Virtually everything I want to teach them about algebra could be applied. There would be functions to formulate and equations to solve to assess costs, work time, construction questions, carpentry decisions, purchasing questions, and on and on. That's a way to really teach math at the application level! But I've got to be realistic. This school won't be ready for that for another 300 years. Then maybe I'll try it!

"Okay, so we can't build a house, but maybe we could try something a little more realistic—like running a school store. That would involve work time, wages, buying, interest, and so on. But, now that I think about it, students would only learn to apply the algebra to store-related problems. What they need is a variety of real-life situations for analysis. . . .

"I've got it! I'll begin the year by conducting a survey to find out what interests them and come up with a list of problems from their real worlds to which we can apply the algebra (e.g., see Exhibit 2.2). Then, I'll introduce each unit with three or four problems built from that list. I could, for example, have those interested in motor vehicles discover functional relations from working on things like effects of tire size on acceleration. Those concerned with body fitness could examine diet and exercise variables against body-fat variables. They might work on those in separate groups and report to the large group; then we could abstract what's common to the solution of all problems. They'd be doing real mathematics that was motivated from their own concerns! Oh, another brilliant idea! If I could get some of their other teachers in on this, we could coordinate some of the problems we're working on with what they're doing in social studies, science, physical education, and so on. Maybe I could. . . ."

The real-life problem-solving approach tends to develop students' appreciation for mathematics and provides experiences necessary for them to learn to apply it creatively in real-life situations. However, the realities of today's schools make it impractical to design courses so that *every* lesson focuses on real-life problems. Although Ms. Asgil's approach is needed and possible, practicality dictates that some learning activities utilize contrived models and problems and others include textbook-type drills. Otherwise, some conceptual and skill-level gaps will go unfilled in most students' mathematical preparation.

Combining Approaches

Students need structured experiences (1) systematically confronting real-life problems, (2) inducting

mathematical principles and processes from analyses of those confrontations, (3) working with mathematical models and on contrived problems to refine and validate those principles and processes, (4) engaging in direct-instruction lessons to develop memory and comprehension skills, (5) engaging in textbook-type drill and practice exercises to polish those skills, and (6) engaging in deductive lessons for application-level achievement of mathematics. How do you go about providing these type of structured experiences for your students? This is the question addressed in subsequent chapters of this textbook.

SELECTION OF LEARNING MATERIALS, RESOURCES, EQUIPMENT, AND FACILITIES

In Vignette 2.8, Ms. McCuller, like many other mathematics teachers, allows textbooks to dictate curricula. Although such blind faith in any textbook is inadvisable, textbook selections as well as other learning materials and resources cannot help but profoundly affect curriculum design and implementation (Usiskin 1985). For his contrived problem-solving lesson with magic squares, Mr. Theron took advantage of an idea he gained from a resource book for teachers. Even how you arrange and equip your classroom influences what and how you teach (Cangelosi 1988a, 165–177; 1990a, 13–20). As Winston Churchill said, "We shape our buildings; thereafter, they shape us."

Your judgment regarding the selection of learning materials, resources, equipment, and facilities should be a function of just what you hope to accomplish with your students (i.e., learning goals) and practical considerations (e.g., cost and convenience). You will, of course, be constrained by budget and administrative considerations. Typically, school mathematics departments are provided with only paltry resources for obtaining anything more than textbooks. As one school superintendent told me, "Textbooks and a classroom with desks, chalk, and chalkboard are all mathematics teachers ever need. Math isn't like science, where they need lab equipment, nor like English, in which they need different books to read." The hope is that one impact of the NCTM *Standards* will be to publicize the need for a variety of learning materials, equipment, and mathematics laboratory facilities for every mathematics teacher.

Textbooks

The degree of control you can exercise regarding the selection of textbooks for your courses varies considerably, depending on your school situation. Typically, panels of teachers and school administrators select textbooks available from state-adopted or district-adopted lists of approved textbooks. In some schools, teachers have virtual control over which textbooks or textbook series are adopted. Of course, options for new texts are hardly open until existing texts are worn or clearly out of date. In other schools, teachers are required to "live with" whatever textbooks have been adopted for them. Subsequent chapters of this book are intended to help you work with whatever text you have.

When selecting a textbook, the following questions should be raised:

❑ *How well do the book's topics match those specified by relevant curriculum guides (e.g., the one you're supposed to follow at your school) and the ones you have listed for your teaching units?* It is not a drawback for the book to include topics you do not plan to include in any of your teaching units as long as the book's treatment of topics you include is not dependent on book topics you delete. However, it is inconvenient to include more than a few topics that are not treated in the book.

❑ *Does the book provide high-quality exercises relevant to the learning objectives you want your students to achieve?* More than anything else, textbooks provide teachers with an abundance of exercises for students to practice. Traditionally, the preponderance of textbook exercises are of the skill-level variety. Even most textbook word problems (e.g., the one Rosario solved in Vignette 2.7) require only algorithmic skills once the wording is deciphered. However, some of the more recently published textbooks also include some concept-building exercises (e.g., the "Explore and Discover" inserts in Elich and Cannon (1989)) and a few word problems that at least border on situations interesting to adolescents (e.g., Keedy et al., *Algebra,* 1986, 371).

❑ *How accurate is the mathematics presented in the textbook?* Virtually all books contain a few misprints and report a few incorrect computational results. Sometimes such mistakes provoke healthy discussions that enhance rather than detract from learning. However, conceptual errors or mathematical treatises that conflict with what you want your students to learn can hinder your lessons. For example, many algebra books define a variable as "a *letter* that stands for a number" (e.g., Brumfiel, Golden, and Heins, 1986, 22; Coxford and Payne 1987, 9; Keedy et al., *Algebra,* 1986, 562). If you take that definition literally, and I assume you want your students to take mathematical definitions literally, then interest rates, age, speed, time, shape, set, location, length, number of, angle, and all the other vari-

ables we deal with in problem solving are not "variables." These books' definitions say a variable is a *letter*—not what the letter stands for, but the letter itself. Such a restrictive definition precludes associations of mathematics with real-life situations. Furthermore, rigorous mathematics defines operations such as addition on numbers, not letters. Operations such as intersection (∩) are defined for sets, not letters. Consequently, you need to consider the conceptual treatment of key topics (e.g., variables, functions, and measurement) in textbooks before adopting one.

❑ *How consistent are the book's organization and presentations with research-based teaching and learning principles?* Few if any mathematics textbooks are written in accordance with research-based teaching and learning principles (principles such as those explained in Chapter 4). Thus, you can expect to have to organize your lessons somewhat differently from your textbook's presentations. However, it would be convenient to use a text that is somewhat in harmony with teaching strategies you employ.

❑ *How readable is the textbook for your students? Will the explanations be intelligible to them?* Typically, students do not read explanations in mathematics textbooks. Generally, they read only examples and exercises (Cangelosi 1985). However, the need for students to read about mathematics is now well publicized (NCTM 1989).

❑ *What practical supplements for the teacher are available?* You may find the annotated teachers' editions, organizational plans for translating the book into teaching units, and test items provided with some books to be helpful. Be particularly cautious regarding validity of tests and test items (as explained in Chapter 7).

❑ *How much does the textbook cost?* Cost factors may or may not be critical, depending on the particular textbook-acquisition arrangement under which your school administrators work.

❑ *How attractively packaged is the book?* The book's aesthetic appeal (e.g., colorful pictures and clever use of white space) may influence the amount of time your students spend with the book.

Sources of Ideas on Teaching

The complexities and dynamics of classrooms dictate that (1) teachers either continue to develop their instructional talents throughout their careers or be incompetent and (2) teachers should not attempt to deal with all their classroom problems without the help of colleagues and instructional supervisors. The traditional model, in which preservice teacher-preparation programs provide their graduates with "teaching tools" and the wish "Good luck in learning how to use these tools on the job!" simply doesn't work for most (Cangelosi 1991, 209). Quality professional support is essential for every teacher (Stallion 1988).

Colleagues

Other teachers, especially mathematics teachers, in your school district and geographical area are probably the most immediate and sympathetic resource for suggestions, information, and thoughts on designing lessons, managing your classroom, dealing with student behavior problems, motivating students, acquiring materials, and evaluating student achievement. Visiting one another's classrooms (Allen et al. 1984), peer coaching (Chase and Wolfe 1989; Chrisco 1989; Raney and Robbins 1989), colleague mentoring (Duke, Cangelosi, and Knight 1988), sharing responsibilities for students (Cangelosi 1988a, 120–124, 198–199), and think sessions are invaluable means for you to learn from other teachers as they learn from you.

Professional Organizations

Besides supporting teachers' causes, professional organizations (such as NCTM, National Education Association (NEA), Mathematical Association of America (MAA), and American Federation of Teachers (AFT)) provide forums for idea-sharing and resource materials in the form of journals, books, pamphlets, and video programs. If you are not already a member, you should join NCTM. Membership benefits include the following:

❑ A subscription to either *Mathematics Teacher* or *Arithmetic Teacher. Mathematics Teacher* contains articles (such as the one in Appendix C) specifically for the purpose of providing middle, junior high, and high school mathematics teachers with practical ideas they can implement in their classrooms. *Arithmetic Teacher* is a similar journal, but it is directed at elementary and middle school teachers.

❑ A subscription to *NCTM News Bulletin,* which reports on current events relevant to the mathematics teaching profession.

❑ A discount on subscriptions to *Journal for Research in Mathematics Education* and to *Arithmetic Teacher* (assuming you selected *Mathematics Teacher* as part of your membership fee). The *Journal for Research in Mathematics Education* includes reports of scholarly studies relevant to questions about teaching and learning of mathematics.

❑ Opportunities to participate in national and regional NCTM conferences consisting of lectures, workshops, seminars, displays, business meetings, and exchanges of ideas among an international group of colleagues.

❑ Ready access to and discounts for acquiring books, monographs, display materials, videotape programs, tests, manipulatives, and computer software relevant to professional improvement and your work with students.

If there isn't a local (district-, county-, or citywide) NCTM affiliate for you to join in your area, then organize one. To do so contact your statewide affiliate or the NCTM headquarters in Reston, Virginia.

Other professional organizations (e.g., NEA and MAA) coordinate many of their activities with NCTM's and can also provide you with invaluable services.

School-District-Sponsored Resource Centers and Workshops

Most school districts maintain a resource center from which their teachers can borrow professional enrichment materials, including publications, computer software, and videotapes. In-service assistance is also provided in the form of periodic workshops and arrangements with universities and colleges for credit courses for enhancing classroom effectiveness.

Colleges, Universities, Foundations, and Research and Development Centers

Besides offering coursework for in-service teachers, colleges and universities, like educational research and development centers (e.g., the National Center for Research on Teacher Education in East Lansing, Michigan, and Far West Laboratory in San Francisco), are a source of professional enrichment materials. Foundations (such as the National Science Foundation in Washington, D.C.) distribute reports on funded projects for both in-service education for teachers (e.g., Math COUNTS at the University of Arizona in Tucson) and professional enhancement materials (e.g., Mathematics Teacher Inservice Project at Utah State University in Logan).

Publishing Houses

As a school faculty member, you can expect to be on the mailing lists of publishing houses, from which you will receive advertisements, catalogues, and sample products of books and other materials. You will find some of these products helpful. The following entries from the reference list for this book have helped many teachers design more effective lessons: Artino, Gaglione, and Shell (1983), Ashlock (1990), Brissenden (1980), Bushaw et al. (1980), Easterday, Henry, and Simpson (1981), Hirsch (1986), Hirsch and Zweng (1985), Hunkins (1989), Johnson (1982,

1986), Krulik and Reys (1980), Nelson and Reys (1976), Posamentier and Stepelman (1990), Salkind and Earl (1973), Saunders (1981), Schoenfeld (1985), Sharron and Reys (1979), Skemp (1973), Sobel and Maletsky (1988), and Souviney (1981).

Sources for Mathematical Topics

Not only are you likely to make use of resources on how to teach mathematics, but you will also use resources on mathematics per se. Besides the usual myriad of mathematics textbooks, there are books about mathematics for both you and your students. From the reference list, for example, are Beskin (1986), Bowers (1988), Collins (1987), Court (1961), Devaney (1990), Dudeney (1958), Gardner (1986), Gnanadesikan et al. (1986), Hoffman (1988), Honsberger (1973, 1976, 1979), Karush (1989), Kasner and Newman (1989), Kogleman and Heller (1986), Nielsen (1962), Niven (1961, 1965, 1981), Packel (1981), Péter (1961), Peterson (1988), Pòlya (1975, 1985), Shapiro (1977), Yaglom (1978), and Zippin (1975).

Given the emphasis in the NCTM *Standards* on students reading about mathematics, engaging students in reading about mathematics from nontextbooks appears particularly important.

Sources for Mathematics History

Cajori (1985, i) quotes J.W. L. Glaisher: "I am sure that no subject loses more than mathematics by any attempt to disassociate it from its history." The need to incorporate topics from the history of mathematics was alluded to in the section "Demystifying Mathematics," beginning on page 13. The following books from the reference list are but a few of the many historical treatises of mathematics: Aaboe (1964), Cajori (1985), Eves (1983a, 1983b), NCTM (1969), and Schiffer and Bowden (1984).

Manipulatives and Concrete Models

Learning activities in which students work with hands-on, concrete objects and models are common in mathematics lessons in the primary grades but are relatively rare at the middle and secondary levels. However, older students (even in high school and college) need experiences working with manipulatives and concrete models (such as those in Exhibit 2.10) to gain conceptual-level understanding of mathematical concepts (e.g., conic sections) and relationships (e.g., the Pythagorean theorem) (Brissenden 1980, 5–32, 131–164). Once secondary school teachers begin involving their students in hands-on activities with concrete objects, they tend to continue doing so because students prefer them to more passive paper-and-pencil exercises and, consequently, are more cooperative, appreciative, and easier to manage. However, manipulatives should not be selected only for the purpose of keeping students busy and entertained, as in the following vignette.

❑ VIGNETTE 2.11

In the faculty lounge at the end of the school day, mathematics teachers Lottie Walker and Fred King have the following exchange:

Exhibit 2.10
Examples of manipulatives and concrete models.

Fred: How'd your day go?

Lottie: Fantastic! We worked with Möbius strips (Sobel and Maletsky 1988, 92–93) in all my classes today. They had a ball, got some great discussions going! They were fascinated.

Fred: What's a Möbius strip?

Lottie: Here, I'll show you. See this strip of paper. I'll mark it A and B, like this. Now, I'll twist it and attach A to B with tape. Now, use your pencil to draw a line from A to B.

Möbius strip.

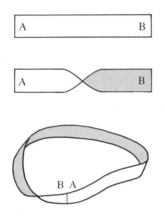

Fred: There, but I never crossed an edge.

Lottie: Use these scissors to cut down the middle on the line.

Fred: Oh, wow! How can that be? It's still only one large band! Why did that happen?

Lottie: That's what the lively discussions in my classes were all about today. I told them if they cooperate during the next unit on polynomial operations, we could do more of these fun sorts of things afterwards.

Ms. Walker seems to think of her Möbius strip activity as an aside from her regular lessons, solely for the purpose of entertaining and fascinating students. Such fascinations can lead some students to appreciate mathematical relationships and motivate them to pursue other mathematical ideas. But more is gained from experiences with concrete objects when those experiences are integrated with other types of activities and are relevant to the learning goal of the unit. In Chapter 8, for example, Mr. Rudd uses the manipulative activity shown in Exhibit 8.23 to help students conceptualize why $a^2 - b^2 = (a + b)(a - b)$.

Materials collected from students' everyday environments usually make manipulatives and mathematical models that are more meaningful to students than prepared instructional materials available from commercial outlets. Such "natural" materials help associate mathematics with real life.

However, the commercial products (such as algebra tiles, create-a-cube puzzles, root blocks, and fraction tiles (Activity Resources Company 1989)) are valuable supplements for contrived problem-solving lessons leading to conceptual-level learning.

Computers, Printers, and Computer Software

Uses

In selecting or organizing materials, equipment, and facilities for a course, you should plan for your own use of computers and how you want your students to use them. You need ready access to your own computer to teach mathematics effectively today as much as you need access to paper, pencil, and textbooks. Teaching responsibilities for which you need a computer include the following.

Producing Documents.   Word-processing capabilities allow you efficiently to produce worksheets, exercises, memos and letters (e.g., to students, parents, and other faculty members), tests, outlines, and lesson plans.

Illustrations.   Combining word processing with art and desktop publishing programs provides a ready means for producing professional-style displays and instructional materials. It took a teacher with a pen 6 minutes to produce the transparency slide illustration depicted in Exhibit 2.11. A teacher generated the one in Exhibit 2.12 in 4 minutes with a computer and printer. The illustration in Exhibit 2.12 is stored in a file the teacher can recall and easily modify for subsequent use.

Simulations, Generating Mathematical Models, and Executing Functions for Classroom Demonstrations.   You can use your computer in conjunction with a classroom display screen for conceptual-level and application-level lessons in which you demonstrate fitting data to curves, manipulating matrices, transforming graphs, rotating solids, plotting graphs, searching for patterns, and other executions of functions. The teacher in Exhibit 2.13, for example, is demonstrating the effects of x approaching 2 on $f(x)$ for $f(x) = (x - 2)/(x^2 - 4)$.

As a Tool for Exploring Mathematics.   You can hardly teach students to discover and invent mathematics unless you remain an active student of mathematics yourself. You need your own computer as a tool for advancing your own mathematical abilities and to gain insights into ideas, which you can share with your students.

Exhibit 2.11
Example of a typical hand-produced transparency.

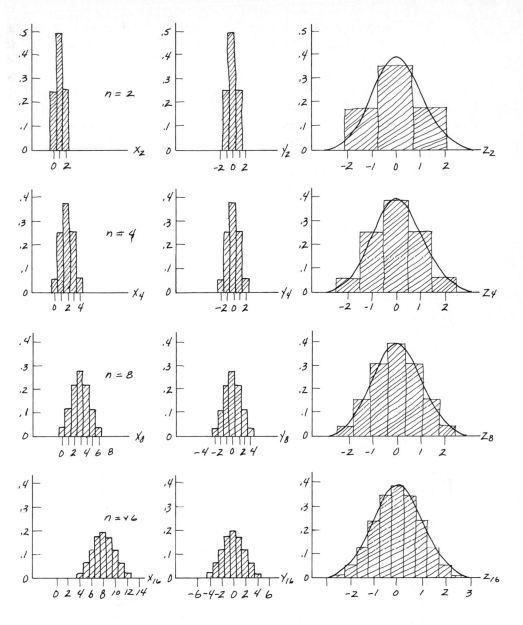

Calculations. By preprogramming your computer to execute multistep, repetitive algorithms, you save time checking students' answers and working out examples for use in class.

Identifying Patterns in Students' Work. Consider the following scenario.

☐ **VIGNETTE 2.12**

Twelve of the 61 students in Mr. Heidingsfelder's two algebra I sections consistently obtain incorrect answers on exercises that involve simplifying rational polynomial expressions such as $(6a^2 - 15ab + 9b^2)/(3b^2 - 4ab + a^2)$. Mr. Heidingsfelder has a computer program that searches out student error patterns from the answers students give on selected exercises. Thus, he administers the selected exercises to the 12 students and has them save their final an-

swers on a computer disk. He feeds the data into this "error-pattern search" program and attempts to diagnose each student's difficulty.

——————

Maintaining Item Pool Files and Generating Tests. As explained in Chapter 7, having computerized item pool files for generating tests is not only a convenience, it also enhances the likelihood that your tests will provide you with valid data on how well students achieve learning goals. Ms. Castillo (Vignette 7.7) demonstrates this use.

Record-Keeping. Maintaining data on 125 students (an average four- or five-section load for mathematics teachers) requires a computer. Exhibit 8.31 illustrates the kind of detailed student test data that can be efficiently managed with a computer.

Exhibit 2.12
Example of a computer-generated transparency.

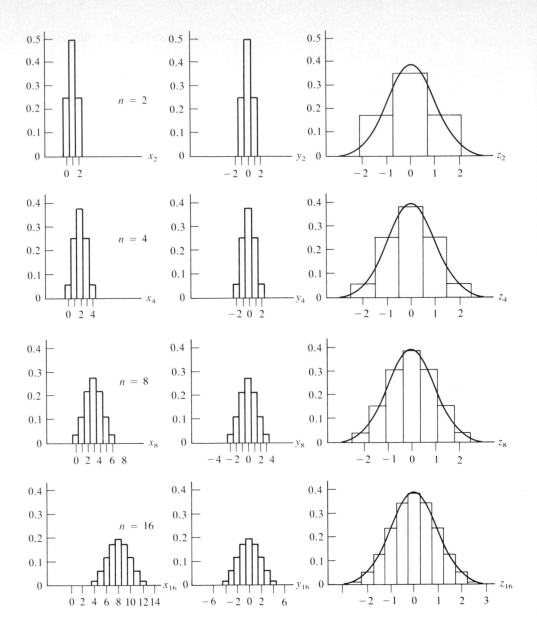

Exhibit 2.13
Teacher using a display computer to demonstrate the influence on $(x - 2)/(x^2 - 4)$ of x-values very near 2.

As recommended by the NCTM *Standards,* your students also need access to computers in school for many activities.

Simulating Mathematical Models and Manipulatives. Mathematics students can engage in contrived problem-solving learning activities with computer-simulated manipulatives and models in much the same way that biology students use computers to simulate animal dissections. For example, in Vignette 1.2, Ms. Lowe used a trash barrel to lead her students to discover a formula for the surface area of a right cylinder. As an alternative to getting her students to imagine the barrel being cut and unrolled in the large-group questioning session, she might have had students work independently with a computer simulation program that allowed them to experiment with a variety of figures emanating from the reshaping of a right cylinder.

Explorations of Mathematical Relationships. Just as language arts students are far more likely to engage in creative writing and editing when they have access to word processing, mathematics students are more likely to experiment with data and test hypotheses creatively when they have a computer to relieve them of mindless work. Consider an example.

❑ **VIGNETTE 2.13**
During an algebra II unit utilizing the Pythagorean theorem, Amanda becomes intrigued by the puzzle of identifying Pythagorean triples (i.e., three integers *a, b,* and *c* such that $a^2 + b^2 = c^2$). She remarks to her teacher, Mr. Johnson, "There should be a way of finding three lengths for sides of right triangles that's easier than trial and error and more trial and error!"

Mr. Johnson: Why don't you see if you can find a pattern by looking at numerous Pythagorean triples and comparing them to one another and also to integer triples that aren't Pythagorean?
Amanda: That would take me all year to come up with enough to pick out a pattern!
Mr. Johnson: Not if we use a computer to do the work for us. We can easily write a program to generate scores of both kinds of triples for you to analyze.

Within 15 minutes Amanda has two lists of triples to analyze. The computer allows Amanda to generate the sample of both Pythagorean and non-Pythagorean triples with very little effort. Thus, she spends her time and energy with the sophisticated analytical task of exploring patterns rather than with the repetitive low-level task of testing triples for whether or not they are Pythagorean.

Over several weeks, with some prodding and guidance from Mr. Johnson, Amanda not only develops and tests

hypotheses about Pythagorean triples, she also involves some of her classmates in the effort. Eventually, she becomes convinced—but doesn't deductively prove—the following:

(*a, b, c*) is Pythagorean if and only if $a = v^2 - u^2$, $b = 2uv$, and $c = u^2 + v^2$ for any positive integer *u* and *v* such that $v > u$, *u* and *v* are relatively prime, and either *u* or *v* is even.

Demonstrating Mathematical Discoveries and Inventions. If students are actually going to engage in the discovery and invention of mathematics, then computers can serve to help them demonstrate and argue their hypotheses and explain their inventions. Consider Vignette 2.14.

❑ **VIGNETTE 2.14**
Mr. Johnson has Amanda report her conjecture about Pythagorean triples to the class, and although she has no formal proof prepared, she challenges anyone to find a Pythagorean triple that doesn't follow her pattern or to find a non-Pythagorean triple that does. Attempts at counterexamples are quickly dispensed with using a computer program that indicates whether or not a given triple is Pythagorean and whether or not it fits Amanda's pattern.

Computer Programming. By programming computers to execute algorithms for them, students enhance their understanding of the algorithms themselves. Posamentier and Stepelman (1990, 148–149), for example, suggest that a lesson for learning an algorithm for solving systems of linear equations might include activities in which students devise a flowchart and write a program for executing that algorithm. To construct the flowchart and BASIC program shown in Exhibit 2.14, students must analyze the algorithm, examining it one step at a time.

Calculations and Executions of Functions. Computers, like calculators, relieve students from the burden of working out algorithms during lessons in which their energies and time should be directed toward more sophisticated cognitive processes (e.g., comprehension, inductive reasoning, deductive reasoning, and creative or divergent thinking). For example, during lessons designed to increase their skill with an algorithm, you may have students execute by hand the algorithm that is programmed in Exhibit 2.14. However, for application-level lessons, you may choose to have them execute it using computers, allowing them to concentrate their time and energy on how to solve problems rather than repeating algorithmic steps.

Exhibit 2.14
Student-generated flowchart and BASIC program for solving $\{ax + by = c, dx + ey = f\}$.

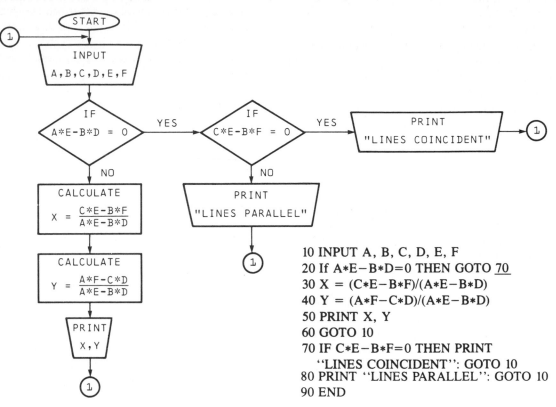

```
10 INPUT A, B, C, D, E, F
20 If A*E−B*D=0 THEN GOTO 70
30 X = (C*E−B*F)/(A*E−B*D)
40 Y = (A*F−C*D)/(A*E−B*D)
50 PRINT X, Y
60 GOTO 10
70 IF C*E−B*F=0 THEN PRINT
      "LINES COINCIDENT": GOTO 10
80 PRINT "LINES PARALLEL": GOTO 10
90 END
```

Source: Excerpted from Posamentier and Stepelman (1990, 149). Reprinted by permission of Merrill, an imprint of Macmillan Publishing Company from *Teaching Secondary School Mathematics*, 3rd ed., by Alfred S. Posamentier and Jay Stepelman. Copyright © 1990 by Merrill Publishing.

Computer-Assisted Instruction (CAI)

Traditionally, the principal use of computers in mathematics classrooms has been in programmed instruction in which students are confronted with exercises (usually computational) and are given feedback on their responses. Programs branch so that a sequence of correct student responses triggers more difficult exercises, whereas incorrect responses trigger easier tasks for students. CAI allows you a degree of flexibility in individualizing lessons according to student achievement levels, especially in accommodating variability in proficiency with algorithms, and affords you more time to conduct conceptual- and application-level learning activities while much of the burden for drill and practice exercises is shouldered by computers. Consider the next vignette.

☐ VIGNETTE 2.15

To help him deal with the multiple stages of mathematical achievement levels among his prealgebra students, Mr. Hornacek uses intraclass grouping, so that different subgroups progress at different rates. He often conducts a lec-

ture, discussion, or questioning session with one group of about 10 while a second group is working independently on textbook exercises and a third group polishes algorithmic skills with the help of CAI programs.

Periodically, the three groups rotate, so Mr. Hornacek spends about the same amount of time with each group while monitoring the other two. He finds this arrangement to be especially important for accommodating the needs of special students (e.g., "learning disabled," "hearing-impaired," and "gifted") who are mainstreamed into his classes. Because he depends on CAI for the major share of activities for algorithmic skills, he's able to devote more personally involved time to the more interesting aspects of teaching, namely, inquiry lessons for higher cognitive learning.

Testing. Some types of tests, especially those using multiple-choice items and error-pattern analyses, are more efficiently administered to students via computers than in the more traditional paper-and-pencil format (Cangelosi 1990b, 131–133). Examples of computer-administered and computer-scored test items are included in Chapter 7.

Students' Maintenance of Records Relative to their Own Progress. Techniques such as precision teaching have proven to be particularly effective in enhancing students' algorithmic skills when students chart their own progress with the aid of computers (Bowden 1991).

Accessibility

Some of the aforementioned uses of computers (such as error-pattern searches) might seem a little futuristic and unrealistic for some school districts. But all these uses are quite practical wherever the teacher has exclusive use of a computer and students have at least shared access to a reasonable number of compatible computers. Slightly over 50% of the nation's middle and secondary school students have some access to computers at school for use in mathematics classes (Dossey et al. 1988, 82–91).

Availability of microcomputers varies considerably among schools. A relatively small portion of schools enjoy the ideal arrangement of having each desk in mathematics classrooms equipped with a personal computer that is interlinked to one of the teacher's and to several printers clustered in one part of the classroom. A few to a dozen computer stations clustered in one part of the mathematics classroom is a more common arrangement. Students take turns completing assignments, engaging in CAI, taking tests, or working on tasks of their choice at these stations. Many schools have one or more computer labs for students to use in doing individual work outside of class time or use by entire classes, depending on scheduling arrangements and demand. School computer labs have traditionally been the domain of business classes (secretarial courses), English classes (for creative writing units), and computer programming classes.

Selection

At some point in your teaching career, you are likely to have the opportunity of selecting computer hardware for your school. Considering today's rate of technological progress, there is not much advice for you today that will not be obsolete tomorrow. Here are two suggestions that seem appropriate for now:

❑ First, identify the software you want (e.g., CAI, mathematical simulations, error-pattern searches, and languages or menus your students can readily use), and then select hardware that can efficiently run that software.

❑ Without compromising your system, try and acquire equipment that is compatible or can be interfaced with existing equipment.

Information about available software can be obtained from computer magazines, software catalogues, computer retail outlets, professional journals for mathematics teachers, libraries, professional conferences for mathematics teachers, college and university departments of educational technology, and school district resource and media centers. Such sources provide information relative to technical compatibility, mathematical content, learning levels, targeted student audiences, user-friendliness, and practical features. However, it is usually necessary for you actually to try programs yourself before deciding which ones are compatible with your needs and goals.

Calculators

Considering the wealth of research supporting the use of calculators as an integral part of lessons and the relatively low cost of powerful hand-held calculators, it seems mad to teach mathematics unless every student has ready access to a calculator (Kansky 1986). Students' use of calculators has risen since the 1986 National Assessment of Educational Progress reported that approximately 95% of secondary students had calculators in their homes but only about 25% had access to calculators in school (Dossey et al. 1988, 79–82).

In selecting calculators, keep in mind their value for other things besides straightforward computational tasks. Like computers, calculators are useful in exploration and discovery activities. Consider the next vignette.

❑   **VIGNETTE 2.16**

Nate works an exercise assigned by his algebra teacher, Ms. Van Dusen, as follows:

Factor $2x^2 - 17x + 21$.

$$(2x - 7)(x - 3)$$

He then engages Ms. Van Dusen in the following conversation.

Nate: Is this right?

Ms. Van Dusen: I don't know. Check it out on your graphics calculator.

Nate: How?

Ms. Van Dusen: Let $Y1 = 2x^2 - 17x + 21$. Good! Now, let $Y2 = (2x - 7)(x - 3)$. Super! Now, graph them both on the same screen.

Nate obtains the results displayed in Exhibit 2.15.

Ms. Van Dusen: If $2x^2 - 17x + 21 = (2x - 7)(x - 3)$, what would you expect about the graphs of $Y1$ and $Y2$?

Exhibit 2.15
Display on Nate's TI-81 graphics calculator with $Y1 = 2x^2 - 17x + 21$ and $Y2 = (2x - 7)(x - 3)$.

Exhibit 2.16
Display on Nate's TI-81 graphics calculator with $Y1 = 2x^2 - 17x + 21$ and $Y2 = (2x - 3)(x - 7)$.

Nate: I don't know.

Ms. Van Dusen: Would $Y1 = Y2$?

Nate: Sure.

Ms. Van Dusen: Then what would be true about their graphs?

Nate: They'd be the same.

Ms. Van Dusen: Look at the two curves on your calculator. Are they the same?

Nate: No. Oh, then $2x^2 - 17x + 21$ isn't the same as $(2x - 7)(x - 3)$ or else there'd be only one curve!

Ms. Van Dusen: You've just invented a test of factoring accuracy.

A minute later, Nate enters $2x^2 - 17x + 21$ for $Y1$ and $(2x - 3)(x - 7)$ for $Y2$ in his graphics calculator and obtains the display shown in Exhibit 2.16.

Measuring Instruments

If you are serious about teaching students real-life applications of mathematics, then your students will need experience working with numbers they obtain

from their real-life environments. *Measurement* is the process by which we make empirical observations (i.e., see, hear, feel, taste, smell, or touch) and record what is observed in the form of numbers. Measuring instruments such as the following provide a conventional means for systematically gathering numbers (or data) during problem solving:

❏ *Clocks, stopwatches, and timers* (for measuring the variable *time*)
❏ *Rulers, tape measures, calipers, trundle wheels, and odometers* (for measuring the variable *distance,* or *length*)
❏ *Thermometers* (for measuring the variable *heat*)
❏ *Barometers* (for measuring the variable *atmospheric pressure*)
❏ *Scales and balances* (for measuring the variable *weight*)
❏ *Protractors* (for measuring the variable *angle size*)
❏ *Unit cubes and containers* (for measuring the variable *volume*)
❏ *Counters* (for measuring the variable *cardinality*)

Such instruments should be standard fare in every mathematics classroom. Measuring instruments that are more specific to certain types of problems should be available at least occasionally (e.g., a *sphygmomanometer* for measuring blood pressure and a *docimeter* for measuring sound levels).

Video and Audio

Compare the learning activities described in the following three vignettes with respect to student attention and involvement in the presentations.

❏ VIGNETTE 2.17

Mr. Barkin's geometry students are poised with pencils and notebooks as he announces, "Let's develop a formula for approximating the area of any circular region." He turns toward the chalkboard and draws a circle. (See Exhibit 2.17.) Looking over his shoulder he says, "Does everyone have a circle in their notes? Okay, let's call the radius of the circle r," as he draws on the board. "And circumscribe the circle in a square like this," he continues. Some students, especially those having difficulty seeing his illustrations until he turns around and moves away, entertain themselves with off-task conversations. Mr. Barkin is slightly annoyed with the noise, but because his back is turned he's not sure who is talking, so for now he ignores it.

Facing the class, he asks, "What is the area of the large rectangle?" Some students don't pay attention to the questions because they are now busy copying the figure that they couldn't see while Mr. Barkin was drawing it. Others are cued to stop talking by Mr. Barkin facing the class.

Leona answers, "Four r-squared." Mr. Barkin: "Why four r-squared?" Leona: "Because. . . ."

The lecture/discussion continues, with Mr. Barkin eventually constructing the octagon whose area approximates that of the circle and concluding that the circle's area is approximately $(3.111. . .)\, r^2$. Exhibit 2.18 illustrates the development of the formula.

Mr. Barkin's presentation was marred by some students' failing to pay attention whenever he turned his back to write on the board. They were restless as he blocked their view of the board, so they entertained themselves in off-task ways. Some of the other students tried to remain on-task but always seemed to be a step behind trying to copy what was on the board as Mr. Barkin went on to the next phase of the explanation.

❏ VIGNETTE 2.18

Like Mr. Barkin, Ms. Ramos conducts a lecture/discussion session in her geometry class to develop an approximation for area of a circular region, as depicted in Exhibit 2.18. However, instead of turning her back to the class to illustrate points on the chalkboard, Ms. Ramos uses an overhead projector and transparencies she prepared before class (Exhibit 2.19). Thus, she is able to monitor the students' behavior throughout and all students are able to see and copy the figures and notes on time.

There is much less off-task behavior than there was in Mr. Barkin's class. Ms. Ramos is able to see when students are finished writing before moving on and whose attention is drifting. Students who appear disengaged are immediately asked a question or hear their name used during the presentation. For example, "How many small squares do we have now, Nancy?" or "Okay, everyone qui-

Exhibit 2.17
Mr. Barkin illustrates area of an approximation to a circular region on the chalkboard with his back to the class.

Exhibit 2.18
Development of a formula for
approximating the area of a circular
region.

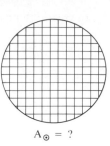

$A_\odot = ?$

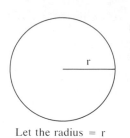

Let the radius $= r$

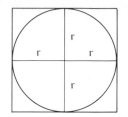

Area of large square $= 4r^2$,
thus $A_\odot < 4r^2$

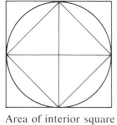

Area of interior square
$= 2r^2$, so
$2r^2 < A_\odot < 4r^2$

each of 9 squares
has an area $= \frac{4}{9} r^2$

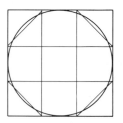

The area of the
octagon $\approx A_\odot$
And the area of the
octagon $= \frac{7}{9}$ of the area of
the large square.

Thus, the area of the octagon $=$
$\frac{7}{9} (4r^2) = \frac{28}{9} r^2 = (3.111\ldots)r^2$.
$\therefore A_\odot \approx (3.111\ldots)r^2$

Exhibit 2.19
Ms. Ramos illustrates area of an
approximation to a circular region
facing the class using an overhead
projector.

etly count the number of squares there are inside the
circle—you too, Scott."

Unlike Mr. Barkin's students, who might be looking at or
copying a figure while he talks about something else, Ms.
Ramos' see only what she wants them to see, since she con-
trols illustrations with a flip of a switch, placement of a transparency, or exposure of only part of a transparency.

❑ **VIGNETTE 2.19**
Mr. Pettis also conducts a lecture/discussion session in his
geometry class to develop an approximation for the area of
a circular region, as depicted in Exhibit 2.18. However,
prior to the session, he videotaped his presentation, along
with computer-generated illustrations. He shows the tape
on a monitor in front of the room as he walks around with

a wireless remote control monitoring students' note-taking. At points he judges appropriate, he pauses the tape, raises questions for discussion, and inserts explanations as needed (Exhibit 2.20).

More than likely your school will equip your classroom with necessities such as an overhead projector and screen. Videotape players, monitors, and cameras probably need to be checked out of the media center. It is up to you to arrange your classroom to take full advantage of such equipment.

The Classroom Arrangements

Consider Mr. Haimowitz's concerns when he first saw the classroom depicted in Exhibit 2.21, to which he is assigned to spend a year conducting five mathematics classes each school day.

❑ **VIGNETTE 2.20**

Surveying the room, Mr. Haimowitz thinks, "This just won't do. First, if I'm at one point in the room, I can't easily get to any one student's desk without negotiating an obstacle course and disturbing other students. If I'm up here explaining something in front of the class and a student in the middle of the fifth row gets off-task, I can't readily walk over to him or her without being a disturbance myself."

Mr. Haimowitz sits down and makes the following "wish list" of classroom features for facilitating his classroom-management style and the type of learning activities he plans to conduct:

1. Quick and easy access between any two points in the room.
2. An area for large-group lecture, discussion, questioning, and desk-work sessions in which students are seated at desks, from which they can view the chalkboard, overhead screen, and video display and listen to whomever has the floor.
3. Areas in which students engage in small-group cooperative learning activities, working on tasks, discussing mathematics, or tutoring one another.
4. Computer stations where students work independently.
5. Work tables for students to work alone, in pairs, or in triples on mathematical laboratory activities.
6. A traffic area for people entering and exiting the room that is easily monitored.
7. A room for Mr. Haimowitz to meet with individuals privately (e.g., to deal with a student's misbehavior away from the rest of the class).
8. A mini-library and quiet reading room for a few students at a time.
9. Cabinets and closets for securely storing equipment and supplies out of sight.
10. A secure teacher's desk at a favorable vantage point.
11. A "for-the-teacher-only" computer station interlinked with a display screen viewed in the large-group areas, students' computers, and printers.

Mr. Haimowitz looks at his room (Exhibit 2.21) and his list and realizes all 11 features are impossible. But he determines to get the most from what he's been handed, so he takes measurements of the room and its equipment and, after making some scale drawings, designs a work-

Exhibit 2.20
Mr. Pettis monitors students as they watch a videotape of him explaining approximating areas of circular regions.

Exhibit 2.21
Mr. Haimowitz's classroom when he initially saw it.

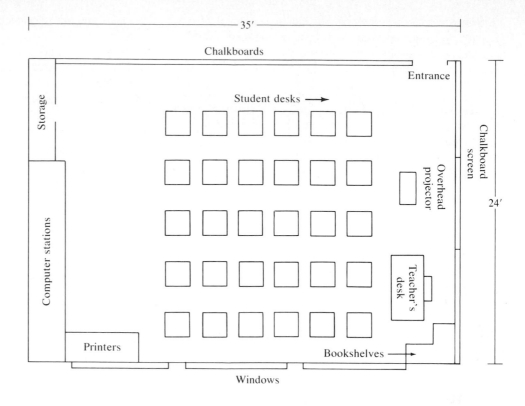

Exhibit 2.22
Mr. Haimowitz's classroom set up for large-group sessions.

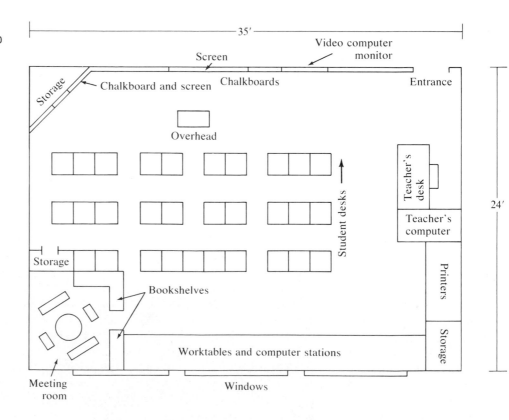

Exhibit 2.23
Mr. Haimowitz's classroom set up
for small-group sessions.

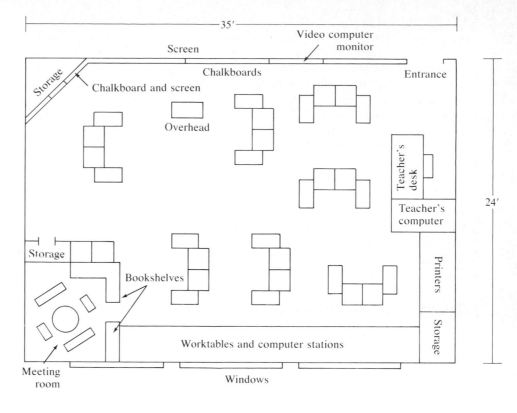

able arrangement. Following a few visits to the school district storehouse, a little trading with a colleague, and some help from a custodian, Mr. Haimowitz begins the school year with the room arranged as indicated by Exhibit 2.22. To accommodate small-group sessions, students rearrange their desks according to Exhibit 2.23.

❏ ❏ ❏ ❏ ❏ ❏ ❏ ❏ ❏ ❏ ❏ ❏ ❏ ❏ ❏ ❏ ❏ ❏ ❏
SELF-ASSESSMENT EXERCISES

1. If you can conveniently do so, examine either a state- or district-level mathematics curriculum guide. Select a list of topics that could conceivably be included in a teaching unit. Describe a unit encompassing those topics as if it were designed solely for the purpose of teaching students mathematics to prepare them to learn more mathematics. Do the same, but this time describe the unit as if it were designed for the purpose of teaching students to apply mathematics to real-life situations. If you are unable to obtain a copy of such a guide conveniently, then complete this exercise using a sample of topics from Appendix B. Compare your work on this exercise with someone else's and discuss similarities and differences with them.

2. Following is a list of suggestions for mathematics curricula. Which of these suggestions are consistent with the NCTM *Standards*? Which are not?

Feel free to refer to Appendix D as you categorize each:
   a. The distinction between geometry and algebra should be maintained throughout coursework in mathematics.
   b. Calculators may be used as a tool for executing an algorithm but only after students have mastered the algorithm using paper and pencil.
   c. Discrete mathematical problems should be integrated throughout the study of mathematics in grades 6 through 12.
   d. Students' abilities to estimate computational results should be afforded at least as much attention as their abilities to find exact numerical answers.
   e. Students should appeal to authoritative sources (e.g., people with more sophisticated understanding of mathematics than themselves) to validate their own hypotheses.
   f. Graphing should be taught along with other forms of expressing relationships (e.g., algebraic sentences and tables) rather than as a distinct topic.
   g. Euclidean geometry should be taught as a complete rational system separate from applied mathematics, which tends to distort its purity.
   h. Students need to read about, write about, and discuss mathematics as an integral part of everyday life.

    i. Students need to appreciate the rare geniuses who handed down the perfect mathematical systems we study today.

    j. Coordinate geometry should be included in the curriculum only after algebra and before calculus.

    k. Topics from probability and statistics should be emphasized in school mathematics more than they have been in the past.

    l. Conceptual-level learning objectives are appropriate for students only after they have reached Piaget's formal-operation stage somewhere between the ages of 11 and 15.

    m. The use of determinants to solve systems of equations should be emphasized less than it has been in traditional curricula.

    n. The use of scientific calculators is favored over calculations using tables.

    o. Mathematical instruction should proceed in small linear increments to avoid student perplexity.

    p. Students' invalid hypotheses should be immediately corrected.

    q. Although it may complicate lessons, connections among related topics should be a paramount concern of instruction.

Compare your responses to this: Parts c, d, f, h, k, m, n, and q are consistent with the *Standards*. The others are not.

3. Examine a mathematics textbook for middle, junior high, or high school students. If the book was to be the primary text for a course you were to teach, to what degree would you follow the sequence of content and presentations in this book? How, if at all, would you deviate from it as you planned your teaching units? Explain the rationale for your decision. How does your response compare with those of others who completed this exercise?

4. Visit a middle or secondary school mathematics classroom. Which one of Mr. Haimowitz's 11 wish-list features are incorporated in the classroom as it is currently arranged? Make a diagram of the room. In a discussion with colleagues, compare the advantages and disadvantages of the arrangement depicted in your diagram to that in Exhibit 2.21 and to that in Exhibit 2.22.

❑ ❑

TAKING WHAT YOU'VE LEARNED TO THE NEXT LEVEL

Now that you've thought about some of the different approaches to developing mathematics curricula and are aware of NCTM's *Standards* for curricula, turn your attention to the task of creating curricula consistent with those standards. The first step is to establish and define learning goals for your students.

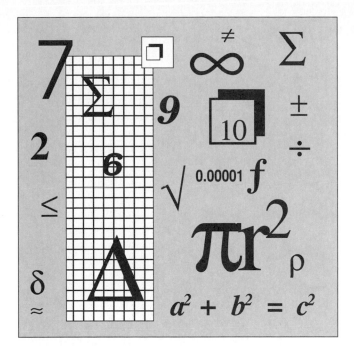

CHAPTER 3
Defining Learning Goals

This chapter provides a model for specifying the mathematical content you plan to include in each teaching unit and the affective and cognitive learning levels you expect your students to achieve with that content. Chapter 3 will help you:

1. Define the learning goal for each unit you teach, using a set of objectives that clarify exactly what students are expected to achieve.
2. Specify the *mathematical content* (i.e., topic) of each objective you set for your students, categorizing it as either (a) a concept, (b) a constant, (c) a relation, (d) an algorithm, or (e) a convention.
3. Specify the *learning level* (i.e., what you will teach students to do with the mathematical content) of each objective as either (a) affective: appreciation, (b) affective: willingness to try, (c) cognitive: simple knowledge, (d) cognitive: knowledge of a process, (e) cognitive: comprehension, (f) cognitive: conceptualization, (g) cognitive: application, or (h) cognitive: creativity.
4. Explain the meanings of the following terms: objective's content, learning level, concept, variable, constant, relation, fact, algorithm, numeral, mathematical convention, shorthand symbol, affective, appreciation, willingness to try, cognitive, knowledge level, simple knowledge, knowledge of a process, intellectual level, comprehension, conceptualization, application, and creativity.

LEARNING GOAL
The Purpose of a Teaching Unit

The first step in designing a teaching unit is to determine and articulate its purpose (i.e., to state its learning goal). *Teaching* is helping students achieve learning goals. Each teaching unit is designed to provide students with experiences that lead them to reach the unit's goal. Here are examples of titles of teaching units, along with their respective learning goals:

1. *Multiplying signed numbers* (seventh-grade mathematics): Understands why (a) $A \cdot B > 0$ if $A > 0$ and $B > 0$, (b) $A \cdot B > 0$ if $A < 0$ and $B < 0$, (c) $A \cdot B < 0$ if $A > 0$ and $B < 0$, (d) $A \cdot B < 0$ if $A < 0$ and $B > 0$, and (e) $A \cdot B = 0$ if $A = 0$ or $B = 0$ and applies these rules for multiplying signed numbers to solve real-life problems.
2. *The number* π (prealgebra): Understands that $\pi = C/d$ for any circle and utilizes that relationship in the solution of real-life problems.
3. *Interest on savings* (consumer mathematics): Understands both simple and compound interest formulas and applies them to solve real-life problems.

4. *Congruence of triangles* (geometry): Understands the rationale underlying certain triangle congruence postulates and theorems, utilizes them to develop and prove additional theorems, and applies triangle congruence relations to solve real-life problems.
5. *Probability of compound events* (intermediate algebra): Establishes appropriate sample spaces for compound events, understands fundamental probability formulas for compound events, and applies the formulas to solve real-life problems.
6. *Analyzing quadratic functions* (algebra II): Understands why the $f(x) = a(x - h)^2 + k$ form of a quadratic function facilitates graphing the function and applies that understanding to the solution of real-life problems.

The Need for Specificity

The learning goal indicates what you intend for your students to gain from a teaching unit. Just how should the unit's lessons be designed so that students will achieve the goal? Before answering that question, the goal needs to be defined in greater detail so that both its *mathematical content* and the *learning levels* that students must display to reach the goal are spelled out. You provide that detail by defining the goal with a set of specific objectives.

A SET OF OBJECTIVES

The teachers who formulated the six preceding learning goals detailed the mathematical content and indicated the specific skills, abilities, or attitudes their students are to display with that content by listing objectives (A, B, C, . . . for each goal), as follows:

   I. *Multiplying signed numbers* (seventh-grade mathematics): Understands why (a) $A \cdot B > 0$ if $A > 0$ and $B > 0$, (b) $A \cdot B > 0$ if $A < 0$ and $B < 0$, (c) $A \cdot B < 0$ if $A > 0$ and $B < 0$, (d) $A \cdot B < 0$ if $A < 0$ and $B > 0$, and (e) $A \cdot B = 0$ if $A = 0$ or $B = 0$ and applies these rules for multiplying signed numbers to solve real-life problems. The student's achievement of this goal depends on how he or she does the following:
   A. When presented with two positive rational numbers, illustrates with a variety of paradigms why the product of those two numbers is positive.
   B. When presented with two rational numbers, one positive and one negative, illustrates with a variety of paradigms why the product of those two numbers is negative.

C. When presented with two negative rational numbers, illustrates with a variety of paradigms why the product of those two numbers is positive.
D. When presented with two rational numbers, one of which is zero, illustrates with a variety of paradigms why the product of those two numbers is zero.
E. Given a rational constant A, explains why $A^2 > 0$ if $A \neq 0$ and $A^2 = 0$ if $A = 0$.
F. Recites the laws for multiplying signed numbers.
G. With the aid of a calculator, simplifies expressions involving nested operations (multiplication and addition) with rational constants, such as

$$12.3 + (30 - 33) \times (-101.1) \times (8.5 - 11.9)$$

H. Given a real-life problem, determines how, if at all, a solution to that problem is facilitated by multiplying signed numbers.
 I. Describes novel paradigms illustrating the rules for multiplying signed numbers that he or she created.
  II. *The number* π (prealgebra): Understands that $\pi = C/d$ for any circle and utilizes that relation in the solution of real-life problems. The student's achievement of this goal depends on how he or she does the following:
  A. Provides an inductive argument for concluding that the ratio of the circumference of any circle to its diameter is π.
  B. Displays a willingness to attempt to develop a method for obtaining a rational approximation of π.
  C. Explains at least three methods for obtaining rational approximations of π: (a) a method for averaging measurements that the students themselves invent, (b) an ancient method (e.g., one listed by von Baravalle (1969)), and (c) a computer-based method.
  D. States the following: (a) π is the ratio of the circumference of any circle to its diameter, (b) π is an irrational number, (c) $\pi \approx 3.1415929$.
  E. Explains why $C = \pi d = 2\pi r$ for a circle with circumference C, diameter d, and radius r.
  F. Solves for the circumference of a circle given either its radius or diameter.
  G. Solves for the diameter and radius of a circle given its circumference.
  H. Given a real-life problem, determines how, if at all, a solution to that problem is facilitated by using the relation $\pi = C/d$.

III. *Interest on savings* (consumer mathematics): Understands both simple and compound interest formulas and applies them to solve real-life problems. The student's achievement of this goal depends on how he or she does the following:

A. Defines the following terms with respect to savings plans: interest, simple interest, and compound interest.

B. Explains the rationale underlying the formula for calculating simple interest, $I = Prt$.

C. For situations involving simple interest on savings, solves for the unknown variables when exactly three of the following four are given: I, P, r, and t.

D. Given a real-life problem, determines how, if at all, a solution to that problem is facilitated by using the relation $I = Prt$.

E. Explains the rationale underlying the following formula for calculating the accumulated amount, A, in a compound interest savings plan:

$$A = P\left(1 + \frac{r}{k}\right)^{kn}$$

where P = the principal, r = the annual rate, k = the number of times per year the interest is compounded, and n = the number of years.

F. For situations involving compound interest on savings, solves for the unknown variables when exactly four of the following five are given: A, P, r, k, and n.

G. Given a real-life problem, determines how, if at all, a solution to that problem is facilitated by using the relation

$$A = P\left(1 + \frac{r}{k}\right)^{kn}$$

IV. *Congruence of triangles* (geometry): Understands the rationale underlying certain triangle congruence postulates and theorems, utilizes them to develop and prove additional theorems, and applies triangle congruence relations to solve real-life problems. The student's achievement of this goal depends on how he or she does the following:

A. Explains the meaning of $\triangle ABC \cong \triangle DEF$, $\overrightarrow{AD}$ bisects $\angle BAC$, and median of a triangle.

B. Provides both an inductive and rational argument (but not necessarily a deductive proof) for why the following relations hold:

1. The theorem that congruence between triangles is an equivalence relation
2. The side-angle-side postulate
3. The theorem that if two sides of a triangle are congruent, then the angles opposite them are congruent
4. The theorem that if $\overline{AB}$ and $\overline{CD}$ bisect each other at F, then $AC = BD$
5. The angle-side-angle theorem
6. The side-side-side theorem
7. The theorem that if two angles of a triangle are congruent, the sides opposite these angles are congruent
8. The angle-bisector theorem

C. Explains deductive proofs for the seven theorems just listed.

D. Recognizes the value of a system of postulates and theorems as a means of verifying relations.

E. Prefers to verify a theorem for himself or herself rather than accepting it on faith in some authority.

F. Originates hypotheses based on the eight relations listed in B.

G. Develops deductive proofs of corollaries to the relations listed in B and to theorems based on student-generated hypotheses.

H. Finds lengths of line segments and measures of angles by executing algorithms based on postulates and theorems formulated in this unit.

I. Given a real-life problem, determines how, if at all, a solution to that problem is facilitated by using relations derived from triangle congruence postulates and theorems.

V. *Probability of compound events* (intermediate algebra): Establishes appropriate sample spaces for compound events, understands fundamental probability formulas for compound events, and applies the formulas to solve real-life problems. The student's achievement of this goal depends on how he or she does the following:

A. Distinguishes between examples and non-examples of each of the following: sample space, compound event, independent events, dependent events, mutually exclusive events, empirical sample space, theoretical sample space, complement of an event, and conditional probability.

B. Defines the terms sample space, compound event, independent event, dependent events, mutually exclusive, empirical sample space, theoretical sample space, complement of an event, and conditional probability.

C. Translates the symbols $P(A)$, $P(A')$, A', $A \cap B$, $A \cup B$, and $A \mid B$.
D. Explains why the following relations hold:
   1. The law of large numbers
   2. $P(A') = 1 - P(A)$
   3. The addition rule for mutually exclusive events
   4. The addition rule for events that are not mutually exclusive
   5. The multiplication rule for independent events
   6. The multiplication rule for dependent events
E. Computes probabilities using algorithms based on relations 2, 3, 4, 5, and 6 of Objective D.
F. Given a real-life problem, determines how, if at all, a solution to that problem is facilitated by using probability principles and methods for compound events.

VI. *Analyzing quadratic functions* (algebra II): Understands why certain methods for facilitating the graphing of quadratic functions work and applies that understanding to the solution of real-life problems. The student's achievement of this goal depends on how he or she does the following:
   A. Given $f(x) = a(x - h)^2 + k$, where x is a real value and a, h, and k are real constants, explains why the following is true regarding the parabolic graph of f:
      1. The line of the axis of symmetry is given by $x = h$.
      2. The vertex is (h, k).
      3. If $a > 0$, then k is the minimum function value and the graph opens upward.
      4. If $a < 0$, then k is the maximum function value and the graph opens downward.
   B. Recites the four relations listed in A.
   C. Given a quadratic function expressed in standard form, uses the algorithm for completing the square to express the function in the form $f(x) = a(x - h)^2 + k$.
   D. Explains why the algorithm for completing the square works in changing the form of a quadratic function as indicated in C.
   E. Explains why
      1. Solving for $f(x) = 0$ yields the x-intercepts of f.
      2. $f(0)$ provides the y-intercept.
      3. The discriminant indicates the number of x-intercepts.
   F. Defines maximum values of a function, minimum values of a function, x-intercept, and y-intercept.
   G. Given a quadratic function, describes its graph using the intercepts and the $f(x) =$

$a(x - h)^2 + k$ form without actually plotting points.
   H. Given a real-life problem, determines how, if at all, a solution to that problem is facilitated by analyzing a quadratic function.
   I. Recognizes the advantages of being able to analyze a function without having to plot very many points of its graph.

THE CONTENT SPECIFIED BY AN OBJECTIVE
The Need to Classify Content

Each objective should specify a *content* so that you clearly know the mathematical topics students are to learn. Reread, for example, the sixth learning goal in the previous section, the one for the unit on analyzing quadratic functions. What "methods for facilitating graphing of quadratic functions" are to be included? Objectives A, C, and F indicate three methods: (1) converting the function to the form $f(x) = a(x - h)^2 + k$ by completing the square and then identifying the graph's axis of symmetry and other features by inspecting a, h, and k, (2) inspecting x where $f(x) = 0$, and (3) inspecting $f(0)$.

Objectives need to be stated so that you know what types of numbers, operations, algorithms, terms, and the like are to be dealt with in the unit's lessons. How those lessons should be designed depends on, among other things, the *type of content* specified in the objectives. As explained in Chapter 4, you design learning activities for teaching about one type of content (e.g., a relation) differently than you would for teaching another type (e.g., a convention). Thus, before designing a learning activity for helping students achieve a particular objective, you need to consider whether the content specified by that objective is a *concept, constant, relation, algorithm, convention,* or other type.

Concept

Look at your present location. Begin listing each individual thing you can see, hear, feel, touch, or taste right now. Like you, the things I'm sensing in my present location are far too numerous to list completely. Before becoming too bored to continue, here's what I managed to list:

1. The computer monitor I'm using at the moment
2. The computer keyboard
3. The black and pink pen and holder my daughter Allison gave me
4. My copy of the book entitled *Cognitive Processes*
5. The calculator lying on my desk

6. My desk
7. The book shelf in front of me
8. My copy of the blue-green book entitled *Modern Mathematics*
9. My copy of the green book entitled *The Mathematical Tourist*
10. My copy of the blue book entitled *Finite Mathematics and Calculus with Applications*
11. My copy of the blue book entitled *Psychology for the Classroom*

.
.
.

99. The tissue box on the shelf
100. My backpack
101. My guitar
102. The pants I'm wearing
103. The shirt I'm wearing
104. The sock on my left foot
105. My left foot

.
.
.

847. My copy of the red book entitled *Teaching Thinking Through Effective Questioning*
848. The photograph of Allison taped on the corner of my maroon disk file box
849. My daughter Amanda's drawing of a cat taped to the wall
850. That shiny, brown, flat, oddly shaped, odorless thing on the floor that appears to be made of hard plastic and is about 6 inches across

.
.
.

1312. The dry taste in my mouth right now
1313. The sound of breeze in the willow outside the window
1314. That itchy feeling on my left hand
1315. The fatigue I'm experiencing as a consequence of making this list
1316. My decision to terminate this list

Our real world is composed of *specifics* we detect with our empirical senses. Specifics are far too numerous for us to deal with efficiently or think about as unique entities. Thus, we categorize and subcategorize specifics according to certain commonalties or attributes. The categories provide a mental filing system for storing, retaining, and thinking about information. The process by which a person groups specifics to form a mental category is referred to as *conceptualizing*. The category itself is a *concept*.

The tedious task of listing 1,316 specifics I detected from my present location was greatly facilitated by the fact that most of the things listed had conventional names associated with categories (i.e.,

concepts) both you and I recognize (e.g., book, desk, and guitar). You've never seen my guitar, but you have a reasonable idea as to what the 101st item on the list is because you've seen other guitars. On the other hand, the 850th item did not fit any concept for which I know a conventional name (other than "thing," and that's not very informative). Thus, more words were used to describe the 850th listing than for others that fit preconceived categories (i.e., book).

Instead of listing each unique item, I could cluster examples of the same concept (e.g., books) and report them as a set. It would require a higher level of thought on my part, but the task would not be nearly as tedious and you would be provided with a more convenient list to read. One-of-a-kind specifics (e.g., I have only one guitar) would still be listed as a singular entity. Compare the following list to the original one:

1. Computer-related equipment
2. Office supplies
3. Three calculators
4. Typical office furnishings
5. Between 50 and 75 teaching methods and learning theory books
6. About 150 mathematics books
7. Many other types of books
8. A dozen bookshelves
9. Me
10. Children's artwork on the walls
11. Children's photographs on the walls
12. Office space confined to a typically structured 12-ft by 13-ft room
13. My guitar
14. Other personal items
15. A few objects I can't identify
16. Natural sounds from outside
17. Some uncomfortable feelings
18. The thoughts in my head

Of the 18 sets in the list, 15 contain more than one element. Thus, those 15 sets are 15 *variables*. The ninth (me), twelfth (a fixed amount of space), and thirteenth (my one guitar) sets contain only one element each. Thus, each of those three is a *constant*. The terms *variable* and *concept* mean the same thing—namely, a set with more than one *element*, or *value*. The following terms or expressions all have the same meaning: *constant, specific, example of a concept, element of a set,* and *value of a variable*.

Six of the nine topics specified by Objective A of the fifth unit are concepts: *sample space, compound event, empirical sample space, theoretical sample space, complement of an event,* and *conditional probability*.

A sample space is the set of all possible outcomes of an experiment. Consider, for example, one particular experiment:

> Joseph and Charog each shoot two foul shots on the basketball court. The number of successful shots for each is recorded.

The following is a sample space for the experiment: {all possible ordered pairs (j, c), where j = the number of successful foul shots Joseph makes and c = the number of successful foul shots Charog makes}, i.e., {(0, 0), (1, 0), (2, 0), (0, 1), (1, 1), (2, 1), (0, 2), (1, 2), (2, 2)}.

Because there are different experiments, sample spaces vary; thus, the idea of a sample space is a concept. Similarly, *compound events, empirical sample spaces, theoretical sample spaces, complements of events,* and *conditional probabilities* all vary from situation to situation, and each is a concept. Some concepts include others, just as sets contain subsets. For example, the idea of *empirical sample space* is *subordinate* to *sample space. Theoretical sample space* is also subordinate to *sample space.*

Examine the following list to (1) determine which entries are concepts and which are constants, (2) identify, for each constant, those concepts on the list for which it is an example, and (3) identify subordinate relations among the concepts:

1. Number
2. Geographic feature
3. 9.013
4. Rational number
5. Irrational number
6. Mountain
7. Miles
8. Former baseball player
9. Mount Olympus
10. Line segment
11. The line segment determined by the following two points: (a) the most extreme point at the left top corner of the textbook page you are now reading and (b) the most extreme point at the right top corner of the same textbook page
12. Limit of a function
13. Baseball Hall of Famer
14. $7(x + 4)/(3x)$, where $x \in \{$ real numbers $\}$
15. Degrees
16. Standard unit of measure
17. Rectangle
18. Jackie Robinson
19. Real number
20. Square (geometric)
21. Derivative of a function
22. Polynomial
23. Meters

Compare how you grouped the 23 items to the following:

1. Number: *a concept*
2. Geographic feature: *a concept*
3. 9.013: a *constant* that is an example of the concepts listed as items 1, 4, and 19 (9.013 could also be considered an example of item 12, limit of a function, and item 14, $7(x + 4)/(3x)$, but such "second-step" examples are not included in the list)
4. Rational number: a *concept* that is subordinate to items 1 and 19
5. Irrational number: a *concept* that is subordinate to items 1 and 19
6. Mountain: a *concept* that is subordinate to item 2
7. Miles: a *concept* that is subordinate to item 16
8. Former baseball player: a *concept*
9. Mount Olympus: a *constant* that is an example of the concepts listed in items 2 and 6
10. Line segment: a *concept*
11. The line segment determined by the following two points: (a) the most extreme point at the left top corner of the textbook page you are now reading and (b) the most extreme point at the right top corner of the same textbook page: a *constant* that is an example of item 10
12. Limit of a function: a *concept*
13. Baseball Hall of Famer: a *concept* that is subordinate to item 8
14. $7(x + 4)/(3x)$ where $x \in \{$ real numbers $\}$: a *concept* that is subordinate to item 22
15. Degrees: a *concept* that is subordinate to item 16
16. Standard unit of measure: a *concept*
17. Rectangle: a *concept*
18. Jackie Robinson: a *constant* that is an example of items 8 and 13
19. Real number: a *concept* that is subordinate to item 1
20. Square (geometric): a *concept* that is subordinate to item 17
21. Derivative of a function: a *concept* that is subordinate to item 12
22. Polynomial: a *concept* that is subordinate to item 1
23. Meters: a *concept* that is subordinate to item 16

Constant

The mathematics content specified by learning objectives usually involves abstract ideas or processes that extend beyond a single constant (e.g., the number 2). Constants are, however, the components of abstractions and provide examples from which students conceptualize and develop process skills. Occasionally, you may want to focus a unit on a particular constant, such as the one entitled "The number π" listed on page 58.

Relation

A *relation* is a particular association either from one concept (i.e., variable) to another, from a concept to a constant, or from one constant to another. Unlike a concept or a constant, a relation denotes a statement. The following are examples of relations:

❏ {Irrational numbers} $\subseteq$ {real numbers}.
❏ $x^2 > -4$ for any real number x.
❏ $\pi \leq 4$.
❏ Cows are not fish.
❏ Jackie Robinson is in baseball's Hall of Fame.
❏ For $\triangle ABC$, if $m\angle B = 90°$, then $AC = \sqrt{(AB)^2 + (BC)^2}$.
❏ $Lim_{x \to a} f(x) = b$ if for every number $\epsilon > 0$ there exist a number $\delta > 0$ such that $|f(x) - b| < \epsilon$ for every x (in the domain of f) satisfying the inequality $0 < |x - a| < \delta$.
❏ $3 + 4 = 22$.

Relations that are always true are referred to as *facts*. Obviously $3 + 4 = 22$ is not a fact. Definitions, theorems, postulates, hypotheses, axioms, functions, binary operations on sets, correspondences, principles, statements, rules, formulas, and identities are types of relations. The study of relations is paramount in mathematics and, consequently, the content specified by most of your objectives is likely to be dominated by relations. How many of the 48 objectives listed on pages 58–60 specify relations? I count 31. Here, for example, are the relations specified by 6 of those 31 objectives:

❏ Objective A of the first unit: *The product of two positive rational numbers is positive.*
❏ Objective A of the second unit: *The ratio of the circumference of any circle to its diameter is π.*
❏ Objective B of the third unit: $I = Prt$.
❏ Objective B of the fourth unit: *Congruence between triangles is an equivalence relation* (as well as seven other relations).
❏ Objective D of the fifth unit: *The law of large numbers* (as well as five other relations).
❏ Objective A of the sixth unit: *Given $f(x) = a(x - h)^2 + k$, the line of the axis of symmetry is given by $x = h$* (as well as three other relations).

Note that each relation makes a complete statement. Concepts simply designate sets, and constants designate specifics.

Algorithm

An *algorithm* is a multistep procedure for obtaining a result. Algorithms are based on relations. The algorithm used to find the distance between the two coordinate points $A(8, 7)$ and $B(3, -5)$ in the following example is based on the Pythagorean theorem, a relation:

$$\begin{aligned} AB &= \sqrt{(8 - 3)^2 + (7 - (-5))^2} \\ &= \sqrt{25 + 144} \\ &= \sqrt{169} \\ &= 13 \end{aligned}$$

Most people with a relatively unsophisticated understanding of the world of mathematics think of mathematics as nothing more than algorithms to be memorized (Cangelosi 1990c). However, an examination of the 48 objectives on pages 58–60 reveals that only 12 (G and H of the first unit; C, F, and G of the second; C and F of the third; H of the fourth, E of the fifth, and C, D, and G of the sixth) specify algorithms for mathematical content. Algorithms include the following.

Arithmetic Computations. Two examples are (1) a long division process using paper and pencil is used to find the quotient of two rational numbers expressed in decimal form and (2) a calculator is used to find the standard deviation of a data sequence.

Reforming Expressions. Two examples are (1) a completing-the-square process is used to change a quadratic function from standard form to the form $f(x) = a(x - h)^2 + k$ and (2) a polynomial is factored.

Translating Statements of Relations. Two examples are (1) a linear equation of one unknown is solved (i.e., the equation is manipulated so that the unknown comprises the left side and a constant comprises the right side) and (2) the formula $\sum_{i=0}^{n-1}(a + id) = \left(\frac{n}{2}\right)(2a + (n - 1)d)$ is used to find the sum of an arithmetic series.

Measuring. Two examples are (1) a protractor is used to obtain the degree measure of an angle and (2) the frequencies of yes and no responses on a survey are tallied.

Convention

The language of mathematics, like any other language, depends on people agreeing to certain *conventions* about what is considered accepted usage for such matters as (1) meanings for symbols and special and technical words, (2) language and communication structures (e.g., for expressing a relation in graphical form) and (3) process or logic structures (e.g., rules for verifying a theorem). Conventions specified as content for learning objectives include the following.

Special Definitions. The meanings of some general-usage words, expressions, and statements vary depending on the mathematical contexts within which they are used. For example,

> The general-usage word *power* ordinarily denotes a *capability of doing something*. In an algebraic context (e.g., x to the nth power), power refers to *the times a number is used as a factor*. In the world of inferential statistics, the power of a statistical test refers to the *probability of rejecting a false null hypothesis*.

Technical Definitions. Some words, expressions, and statements have meaning only within a mathematical structure (e.g., cosine, Cauchy sequence, and $\triangle ABC \cong \triangle DEF$).

Numerals. A *numeral* is a name for a number. Distinguishing between a number and its names (e.g., 2 is a number with an unlimited amount of names, including "2", "$12 \div 6$", and "$\sqrt{4}$") is critical to students' understanding of mathematics.

Shorthand Symbols. Shorthand symbols (such as $\sqrt{}$, $\int_a^b$, $\equiv$, $\leq$, and $\cap$) contribute to the mystery of mathematics for those who have not learned to translate them. On the other hand, such symbols serve two valuable purposes:

❑ Shorthand symbols save time and space in mathematical communications.
❑ By compacting communications, shorthand symbols facilitate the analysis and comprehension of relations. For example, is comprehension of the definition of *standard deviation* easier when it's stated in ordinary English or when using shorthand symbols? Compare the two:

> *Ordinary English:* The standard deviation of a set of data is equal to the principal square root of the number derived by adding the squared differences between each data point and the mean of all the data and then dividing that sum by the number of data points.

Compact form:

$$\sigma = \sqrt{\frac{\sum_{i=1}^{N}(x - \mu)^2}{N}}$$

where σ is the standard deviation of and μ is the mean of the data set $x_1, x_2, x_3, \ldots, x_N$.

As long as a person has been taught the meanings of the symbols, the compact form using shorthand notation makes it easier to recognize critical relationships in the definition (e.g., each difference is squared before the differences are summed).

Communication or Language Structure. Mathematical language includes technical structures (e.g., a Cartesian plane, vector space, group, field, geometry, or matrix) for organizing and expressing ideas and relations. As with other conventions, students need to be taught to comprehend and utilize such structures.

Process or Logic Structures. Standard processes and logic rules for investigation and verification of relations and algorithms are part of mathematical communications. Generally speaking, mathematicians agree on fundamental principles for determining what constitutes valid proofs, whether they be by mathematical induction, counterexamples, indirect methods (i.e., by contradiction), or direct methods.

Other Ways of Classifying Content

Mathematics curricula traditionally include some teaching units focusing not on specific mathematical topics (e.g., congruence of triangles) but on types of problems addressed by mathematical processes (e.g., travel problems). Such a unit might include an objective such as the following:

> Solves problems relative to scheduling plane, train, and automobile travel.

Although you may occasionally find it helpful to include such a unit, a curriculum consistent with the *Standards* (NCTM 1989) is organized around mathematical content topics. Different types of problems (e.g., ones relating to travel) and general problem-solving processes are integrated throughout all units rather than being confined to separate units.

THE LEARNING LEVEL SPECIFIED BY AN OBJECTIVE
The Need to Classify Learning Levels

Compare the following five objectives for similarities and differences:

1. Willingly attempts to develop a general formula for making it easier (than either factoring or completing the square) to solve quadratic equations.
2. Explains why the quadratic formula yields the roots for any one-variable quadratic equation with real coefficients.
3. States the quadratic formula.
4. Given a one-variable quadratic equation with real coefficients, finds the roots of the equations using the quadratic formula.
5. Given a real-life problem, determines how, if at all, a solution to that problem is facilitated by setting up and solving for a quadratic equation.

All five of these objectives specify the same mathematical content, namely, the quadratic formula. However, no two of the five objectives are the same. The objectives differ in the way the student is expected to think about and deal with the quadratic formula. The first is concerned with the student's willingness to develop the formula. The second's concern focuses on the student's understanding of why the formula works. The third strives for the student to remember the formula. The fourth deals with the student's skill in executing an algorithm based on the formula. The fifth targets the student's ability to apply the formula to solve real-life problems.

In summary, each objective differs from the other four in the *learning level* it specifies. Just as an objective's mathematical content influences how you go about teaching to that objective (e.g., you teach about the quadratic formula differently than you teach about conditional probabilities), so should how you teach depend on the objective's learning level.

Learning Domains

You cannot design appropriate lessons until you have identified the learning levels of the targeted objectives. Thus, it is critical that when you formulate an objective, you leave no doubt about the learning level.

Familiarity with one of the published schemes for classifying objectives according to their targeted learning levels will help you clarify your own objectives. The scheme presented in the remainder of this chapter is especially adapted from a variety of sources (Bloom 1984; Cangelosi 1980; 1982, 90–95; 1990b, 7–19; Guilford 1959; Krathwohl, Bloom, and Masia 1964) for teaching mathematics in harmony with the *Standards* (NCTM 1989).

Two *learning domains* are included: *affective* and *cognitive*. If the intent of the objective is for students to develop a particular attitude or feeling (e.g., a desire to prove a theorem or willingness to work toward the solution of problems), the learning level of the objective falls within the *affective domain*.

If the intent of the objective is for students to be able to do something mentally (e.g., remember a formula or deduce a method for solving a problem), the learning level of the objective falls within the *cognitive domain*.

Affective Objectives

Unlike cognitive objectives, *affective* objectives are not concerned with students' abilities with content but rather with their attitudes about content. The affective domain consists of two learning levels: *appreciation* and *willingness to try*.

Appreciation
Students achieve an objective at the appreciation level by *believing that the content specified in the objective has value*. The following are examples of appreciation-level objectives:

❑ Believes that an understanding of systems of linear equations can help solve problems he or she cares about.
❑ Prefers to formulate algebraic open sentences when solving word problems rather than having the sentence set up by someone else.

Achievement of an appreciation-level objective requires students to hold certain beliefs but does not require them to act upon those beliefs.

Willingness to Try
Students achieve an objective at the willingness-to-try level by *choosing to attempt a mathematical task specified by the objective*. By believing that an understanding of systems of linear equations can help solve problems he or she cares about, the student has achieved at the appreciation level. But to learn content at the willingness-to-act level, the student has to act upon that belief (e.g., by trying to learn

about systems of linear equations). The following are examples of willingness-to-try level objectives:

❏ Attempts to formulate algebraic open sentences when solving word problems before turning to someone else to set them up.
❏ When executing a paper-and-pencil algorithm for using trigonometric relations to solve problems, lists sequential results of the process neatly and in an orderly manner so that the work can readily be checked for errors.

Knowledge-Level and Intellectual-Level Cognition

There are two types of objectives that specify learning levels in the cognitive domain: (1) *Knowledge level* and (2) *intellectual level*. An objective requiring students to *remember* some specified content is knowledge level. An objective requiring students to *use reasoning to make judgments* relative to the specified content is intellectual level.

Knowledge-Level Cognitive Objectives

Because of the differences between how achievement of two types of knowledge-level objectives occurs (as explained in Chapter 4) and is assessed (as explained in Chapter 7), a distinction is made between *simple-knowledge* and *knowledge-of-a-process* learning levels.

Simple Knowledge
An objective requiring students to remember *a specified response (but not a multistep sequence of responses) to a specified stimulus* is at the *simple-knowledge* level. The following are examples of simple-knowledge objectives:

❏ States the definitions of the six trigonometric functions.
❏ Associates the notation $A|B$, where A, B ∈ {integers}, with the statement A is a factor of B.

These two objectives, like all simple-knowledge objectives, indicate responses for students to remember when presented with certain stimuli. The stimulus in the first is the name of a trigonometric function (e.g., sine of an angle), and the response is the ratio that defines that function (e.g., opposite over hypotenuse). The stimulus for the second is "$A|B$"; the desired response is "A is a factor of B."

Knowledge of a Process
An objective requiring students to remember a *sequence of steps in a procedure (usually an algorithm)* is at the *knowledge-of-a-process* level. The following are examples of knowledge-of-a-process objectives:

❏ Given the dimensions of a triangle, computes the area of its interior.
❏ Uses the chain rule to compute the derivative of $f(g(x))$, where f and g are algebraic functions such that g has a derivative at x and f has a derivative at $g(x)$.

Knowledge-of-a-process objectives are concerned with students' knowing how to execute the steps in methods for finding answers or accomplishing tasks. Because you know the answer to the question "What is 9 + 3?" without figuring it out, you have achieved a simple-knowledge-level objective dealing with arithmetic facts. However, unless you are quite unusual in this regard, you don't know the answer to the question "What is 168 + 73?" What you do know is how to execute the steps in an algorithm for finding the sum of any two whole numbers such as 168 and 73. This latter skill is indicative of your achievement of a knowledge-of-a-process objective.

Intellectual-Level Cognitive Objectives

Intellectual-level cognitive objectives require mental behaviors that go beyond use of the memory. Four types of intellectual learning levels are considered herein: *comprehension, conceptualization, application,* and *creativity.*

Comprehension
There are two types of *comprehension-level* objectives:

Comprehension of a Message. A comprehension-level objective specifying a particular message as content requires students to *translate or interpret the meaning of the message.* The following are examples:

❏ Explains in her or his own words the ϵ, δ definition of the limit of a sequence.
❏ Explains the rationale for the proof of the Pythagorean theorem as presented by Clemens, O'Daffer, and Cooney (1984, 226–227).

Comprehension of a Communication Mode. A comprehension-level objective specifying a particular mode for communicating messages as content requires students to *demonstrate facility in using that mode.* The following are examples:

❏ Describes in his or her own words the relation between x and $f(x)$ after viewing a graph of the function $f(x)$ in a Cartesian plane.

❑ Explains how to translate summation notation in the form $\sum\limits_{i=a}^{n} f(i)$, where a and n are integers such that $a \le n$.

Comprehension objectives are concerned with students being able to interpret and translate ideas expressed by others.

Conceptualization

A *conceptualization* objective requires students to *use inductive reasoning* either to *distinguish examples of a particular concept from nonexamples of that concept* or to *discover why a particular mathematical relation exists*. Thus, there are two types of conceptualization objectives, those that specify a concept as content and those that specify a relation as content.

Conceptualization of a Concept. The following are examples of conceptualization objectives concerned with students being able to distinguish examples of one concept from those of another:

❑ Partitions a set of relations into functions and nonfunctions and, for each of the given relations, explains why it was so classified.
❑ Given a geometric figure (either concrete or abstract), discriminates between its surface area and its other quantitative characteristics (such as height, volume, and angle sizes).

Conceptualization of a Relation. The following are examples of conceptualization objectives concerned with students discovering why certain mathematical relations exist:

❑ Explains why the area of a rectangle equals the product of its length and width.
❑ Explains why $x^2 < x$ if $0 < x < 1$.

Application

An *application* objective requires students to *use deductive reasoning to decide how to utilize, if at all, a particular mathematical concept, relation, or process to solve problems*. Moreover, when confronted with a problem, students who achieve an application-level objective can determine whether or not the content specified by the objective is appropriate to use in formulating a solution to the problem. The following are examples of application-level objectives:

❑ Given a real-life problem, determines how, if at all, a solution to that problem is facilitated by setting up a system of linear equations.
❑ Given a real-life problem, decides if the solution requires computing the area of a polygonal region and, if so, determines how to find that area.

Sometimes knowledge-of-a-process-level objectives are confused with application-level objectives. Compare the previous objective to the following knowledge-of-a-process objective:

Given the dimensions of a polygonal region, computes the area of the region.

Both objectives deal with computing the area of a polygonal region. But the application objective requires students to *decide when* to compute it, whereas the knowledge-of-a-process objective requires students to *remember how* to compute it. Although the two types of learning levels are closely related, there is quite a difference between designing learning activities for application-level achievement and those for knowledge-of-a-process-level achievement.

Creativity

What is the fifth term in the infinite sequence 0, 5, 10, 15, . . . ? Most people who comprehend the question reason that the fifth number should be 20. They recognize the arithmetic sequence of uniformly increasing multiples of 5 beginning with 0. Such a response requires *convergent thinking* because such thinking produces the expected answer. But suppose a student's thinking *diverges* from the usual pattern, as in the following example.

❑ **VIGNETTE 3.1**

Ms. Strong: What is the fifth term in the infinite sequence 0, 5, 10, 15, and so forth?

Willie: Twenty-six.

Ms. Strong: Why 26?

Willie: Because each number is different from a perfect square by exactly 1, following a pattern.
Willie writes:

$$0 = 1^2 - 1$$
$$5 = 2^2 + 1$$
$$10 = 3^2 + 1$$
$$15 = 4^2 - 1$$

Willie: So, the pattern repeats with $n^2 - 1$ once followed by $n^2 + 1$ twice, then another $n^2 - 1$ and so on.

_____

Willie's divergent reasoning justifies 26 for the fifth term just as well as convergent reasoning justifies 20. *Divergent thinking* is reasoning that is *atypical* and produces an acceptable but unanticipated response. Do not confuse divergent thinking with the thinking of the student in the following example:

❏ **VIGNETTE 3.2**

Ms. Strong: What is the fifth term in the infinite sequence 0, 5, 10, 15, and so forth?
Brenda: Seventeen.
Ms. Strong: Why 17?
Brenda: I don't know. Did I guess it right?

Brenda's unanticipated answer does not appear to be the result of divergent thinking.

An objective that specifies *creativity* as its learning level requires students to *think divergently to originate ideas, hypotheses, or methods.* The condition of originality is met as long as the idea, hypothesis, or method is novel to the student. A student, for example, displays achievement at the creativity learning level by "originating" a proof to a theorem even if that proof has been previously developed. However, the student must design the proof without knowledge of the earlier work.

The following are examples of creativity-level objectives:

❏ Describes novel paradigms he or she originates for illustrating the following relation: If $f(x) = ax^2 + bx + c$, where x is a real variable and a, b, and c are real constants, then $f'(x) = 2ax + b$.
❏ Generates novel hypotheses about angle constructions using a straightedge and compass and either proves or disproves them.

USING THE SCHEME FOR CLASSIFYING LEARNING LEVELS

You cannot design lessons for a teaching unit until you have defined the unit's goal in terms of objectives, each of which clearly specifies the targeted content and learning level. The scheme for classifying objectives according to learning levels (summarized in Exhibit 3.1) provides you with a mechanism for (1) organizing your thoughts about how you want your students to interact with mathematical content and (2) clarifying and communicating the affective or cognitive level targeted by each objective.

The learning level you intend for even a well-written objective may not be communicated clearly until you actually label the objective according to the scheme. For example, does the teacher who formulated the following objective intend for students to (1) recall an existing proof (simple knowledge), (2) explain why an existing proof of the theorem is valid (comprehension level), (3) discover why the relation underlying the theorem holds (conceptualiza-

Exhibit 3.1
Scheme for categorizing learning levels specified by objectives.

> **Affective Domain**
> I. Appreciation level
> II. Willingness to try
>
> **Cognitive Domain**
> I. Knowledge level
>   A. Simple knowledge
>   B. Knowledge of a process
> II. Intellectual level
>   A. Comprehension
>   B. Conceptualization
>   C. Application
>   D. Creativity

tion level), or (4) originate a proof for the theorem (creativity level):

Proves that $\sqrt{2}$ is not rational.

Attaching a learning-level label to the objective would clarify the matter (e.g., proves that $\sqrt{2}$ is not rational (*comprehension*)). You are advised to label objectives you formulate so that there is no question regarding the learning level you plan to target. Objectives listed in subsequent chapters of this book are so labeled.

❏❏❏❏❏❏❏❏❏❏❏❏❏❏❏❏❏❏❏

SELF-ASSESSMENT EXERCISES

1. Reexamine the six sets of objectives listed on pages 58–60. Although the wording of the objectives does not totally communicate exactly what the teachers who formulated those objectives had in mind (e.g., the learning levels are not clearly labeled), infer the teachers' intentions by analyzing each objective to (a) identify its content, (b) categorize the type of content as either concept, constant, relation, algorithm, or convention, and (c) categorize the learning level according to the scheme presented in this chapter. Keeping in mind that differences may be due to ambiguities in the phrasing of objectives, compare your responses to those in Exhibit 3.2.
2. In your response to Exercise 1 of Chapter 2, you described a teaching unit as if it were designed for the purpose of teaching students to apply the unit's mathematical topics to real-life situations.

Exhibit 3.2
Content and learning levels specified by the objectives on pages 58–60.

Unit	Obj.	Content	Type of Content	Learning Level
I	A	The product of two positive rational numbers is positive.	Relation	Conceptualization
I	B	The product of a positive and negative rational number is negative.	Relation	Conceptualization
I	C	The product of two negative rational numbers is positive.	Relation	Conceptualization
I	D	The product of zero and another rational number is zero.	Relation	Conceptualization
I	E	$A^2 > 0$ for any nonzero rational and $0^2 = 0$.	Relation	Conceptualization
I	F	The laws for multiplying signed numbers (as listed in Obj. A–E).	Relation	Simple knowledge
I	G	Calculator-assisted algorithm for simplifying nested operations of multiplication and addition of rational constants.	Algorithm	Knowledge of a process
I	H	The laws for multiplying signed numbers (as listed in Obj. A–E).	Relation	Application
I	I	Paradigms for multiplying signed numbers.	Relation	Creativity
II	A	The ratio of the circumference of any circle to its diameter is π.	Relation	Conceptualization
II	B	Methods for obtaining rational approximations of π.	Algorithm	Willingness to try
II	C	Methods for obtaining rational approximations of π.	Algorithm	Conceptualization
II	D	Facts about π (definition, approximations, type of number).	Relation	Simple knowledge
II	E	$c = \pi d = 2\pi r$	Relation	Conceptualization
II	F	$c = \pi d = 2\pi r$	Algorithm	Knowledge of a process
II	G	$d = c/\pi$ and $r = c/(2\pi)$	Algorithm	Knowledge of a process
II	H	$\pi = C/d$	Relation	Application
III	A	Interest, simple interest, compound interest.	Convention	Simple knowledge
III	B	$I = Prt$	Relation	Conceptualization
III	C	$I = Prt$	Algorithm	Knowledge of a process
III	D	$I = Prt$	Relation	Application
III	E	$A = P(1 + r/k)^{kn}$	Relation	Conceptualization
III	F	$A = P(1 + r/k)^{kn}$	Algorithm	Knowledge of a process
III	G	$A = P(1 + r/k)^{kn}$	Relation	Application
IV	A	$\triangle ABC \cong \triangle DEF$, AD bisects $\angle BAC$, and median of a triangle.	Convention	Simple knowledge
IV	B	The eight relations listed on page 59.	Relation	Conceptualization
IV	C	The seven theorems listed on page 59.	Relation	Comprehension
IV	D	Systems of postulates and theorems.	Convention	Appreciation

Exhibit 3.2 continued

Unit	Obj.	Content	Type of Content	Learning Level
IV	E	Systems of postulates and theorems.	Convention	Willingness to try
IV	F	The eight relations listed on page 59.	Relation	Creativity
IV	G	Corollaries and theorems based on the eight relations listed on page 59.	Relation	Creativity
IV	H	Algorithms based on triangle congruence relations.	Algorithm	Knowledge of a process
IV	I	Triangle congruence relations.	Relation	Application
V	A	Sample space, compound event, independent event, dependent event, mutually exclusive events, empirical sample space, theoretical sample space, complement of an event, and conditional probability.	Concept	Conceptualization
V	B	Names for the concepts listed in Objective A.	Convention	Simple knowledge
V	C	$P(A)$, $P'(A)$, A', $A \cap B$, $A \cup B$, and $A \mid B$.	Convention	Simple knowledge
V	D	The six relations listed on page 60.	Relation	Conceptualization
V	E	Algorithms based on relations 2–6 listed on page 60.	Algorithm	Knowledge of a process
V	F	The six relations listed on page 60.	Relation	Application
VI	A	The four relations listed on page 60.	Relation	Conceptualization
VI	B	The four relations listed on page 60.	Relation	Simple knowledge
VI	C	Completing-the-square algorithm.	Algorithm	Knowledge of a process
VI	D	Completing-the-square algorithm.	Algorithm	Conceptualization
VI	E	The three relations listed for objective E on page 60.	Relation	Conceptualization
VI	F	Maximum and minimum values of a function, x- and y-intercepts.	Convention	Simple knowledge
VI	G	Algorithms based on relations listed for objectives A and E.	Algorithm	Knowledge of a process
VI	H	Relations listed for objectives A and E.	Relation	Application
VI	I	Algorithms based on relations listed for objectives A and E.	Algorithm	Appreciation

Write a goal for that unit and then define the goal by formulating a set of objectives. Label the learning level of each objective using the scheme presented in this chapter. Compare your work on this exercise to someone else's.

3. Select the one response to each of the following multiple-choice items that either completes the statement so that it is true or accurately answers the question:
  a. Which one of the following is a concept?
    i. December 10, 1968
    ii. 10 hours, 14 minutes, 19 seconds
    iii. A point in time
  b. Which one of the following is a constant?
    i. 14 meters
    ii. The distance between two points
    iii. Perimeter
  c. Which one of the following is a relation from a constant to a concept?
    i. Ernest Hemingway wrote books.
    ii. Books are written by people
    iii. George Bush succeeded Ronald Reagan in the White House
  d. Which one of the following is a relation between two constants?
    i. Marcel Barry is 24 years old.

    ii. $x \in$ {integers}
    iii. $-9 \in$ {integers}
    iv. {$1.2, 4, 0.3, -1$} $\subset$ {real numbers $x \mid -5 \le x \le 5$}

e. Which one of the following is a relation between two concepts?
    i. The set of all real numbers x such that $x^2 \ge 2x$
    ii. $x^2 \ge 2x$ for all real values of x
    iii. $m \angle \theta = 33°$
    iv. $8 + 9 > 21$

f. Which one of the following is a fact?
    i. $\dfrac{-b \pm \sqrt{b^2 - 4ac}}{2a}$
    ii. $\cos \theta = 1/\tan \theta$
    iii. {Rational numbers} $\cap$ {irrational numbers} $= \emptyset$
    iv. A relation is a function.

g. A concept is a _____ .
    i. Relation
    ii. Constant
    iii. Variable
    iv. Numeral

h. A numeral is a _____ .
    i. Relation
    ii. Concept
    iii. Number

i. Students' proficiency with an algorithm depends on their achievement of what type of learning objective?
    i. Appreciation
    ii. Conceptualization
    iii. Application
    iv. Knowledge of a process

j. The content of comprehension level objectives is likely to involve a(n) _____ .
    i. Concept
    ii. Communication
    iii. Algorithm

k. Students learn the meaning of shorthand symbols by _____ .
    i. Inductive reasoning
    ii. Deductive reasoning
    iii. Being informed
    iv. Creative invention

l. Which one of the following learning levels requires intellectual-level reasoning?
    i. Application
    ii. Willingness to try
    iii. Knowledge of a process

m. Simple knowledge-level objectives are _____ .
    i. Affective
    ii. Cognitive
    iii. Intellectual
    iv. Knowledge of a process

n. Acceptable form for presenting a proof is a _____ .
    i. constant
    ii. convention
    iii. discovery

Compare your responses to the following: a. (iii); b. (i); c. (i); d. (i); e. (ii); f. (iii); g. (iii); h. (v); i. (iv); j. (ii); k. (iii); l. (i); m. (ii); n. (ii).

❑ ❑ ❑ ❑ ❑ ❑ ❑ ❑ ❑ ❑ ❑ ❑ ❑ ❑ ❑ ❑ ❑ ❑ ❑ ❑

TAKING WHAT YOU'VE LEARNED TO THE NEXT LEVEL

Now that you can proficiently define learning goals by formulating objectives that specify both the targeted content and learning level, turn your attention to questions regarding the following:

1. How to sequence a unit's objectives so that students efficiently achieve them.
2. How to design a unit's lessons so that learning activities are appropriate for both the content and learning level of each objective.

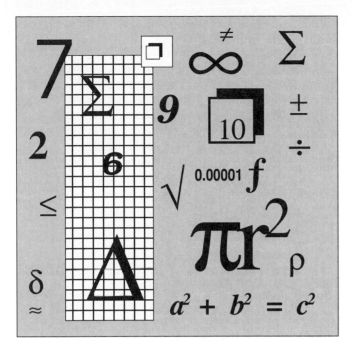

CHAPTER 4
Research-Based Approaches to Designing Lessons

This chapter explains how to design lessons for teaching units that are consistent with a *Standards*-based curriculum (NCTM 1989). Chapter 4 will help you:

1. Explain the nine-stage process by which people apply mathematics in solving real-life problems (*conceptualization*).
2. Explain the types of learning activities students need to experience so that they are able to apply mathematics efficiently and creatively in solving real-life problems (*conceptualization*).
3. Confronted with the task of designing a teaching unit relevant to a learning goal consistent with the NCTM *Standards,* appropriately define that goal with a *sequence* of objectives (*application*).
4. Explain the meanings of the following terms: inductive reasoning, inductive learning activity, psychological noise, direct instruction, mnemonics, overlearning, literal comprehension, interpretive comprehension, error-pattern analysis, deductive reasoning, deductive learning activity, and synectics (*comprehension*).
5. Given a group of middle or secondary school students with whom you are familiar and an objective appropriate for those students that specifies (a) a mathematical content with which you are familiar and (b) an *affective* learning level, design learning activities that will help those students achieve the objective (*application*).
6. Given a group of middle or secondary school students with whom you are familiar and an objective appropriate for those students that specifies (a) a mathematical content with which you are familiar and (b) a *conceptualization* learning level, design learning activities that will help those students achieve the objective (*application*).
7. Given a group of middle or secondary school students with whom you are familiar and an objective appropriate for those students that specifies (a) a mathematical content with which you are familiar and (b) a *simple-knowledge* learning level, design learning activities that will help those students achieve the objective (*application*).
8. Given a group of middle or secondary school students with whom you are familiar and an objective appropriate for those students that specifies (a) a mathematical content with which you are familiar and (b) a *comprehension* learning level, design learning activities that will help those students achieve the objective (*application*).
9. Given a group of middle or secondary school students with whom you are familiar and an objective appropriate for those students that specifies (a) a mathematical content with which you are familiar and (b) a *knowledge-of-a-process* learning level, design learning activities that will help those students achieve the objective (*application*).

10. Given a group of middle or secondary school students with whom you are familiar and an objective appropriate for those students that specifies (a) a mathematical content with which you are familiar and (b) an *application* learning level, design learning activities that will help those students achieve the objective (*application*).

11. Given a group of middle or secondary school students with whom you are familiar and an objective appropriate for those students that specifies (a) a mathematical content with which you are familiar and (b) a *creativity* learning level, design learning activities that will help those students achieve the objective (*application*).

REQUISITES FOR LEARNING TO APPLY MATHEMATICS TO REAL-LIFE PROBLEM-SOLVING
Problem-Solving in the Real World

A major proportion of the teaching units comprising a mathematics course consistent with the *Standards* (NCTM 1989) include learning activities that teach students to apply mathematics to real-life problem-solving. Before addressing questions regarding how to design those learning activities, examine the process by which one student goes about solving a problem from her real world.

❏ **VIGNETTE 4.1**
Fifteen-year-old Brenda and her two brothers have just been told by their dad that because he's tired of them leaving lights on in the house while he has to pay "outrageous" electric bills, he will charge them 25¢ each time he catches one of them leaving lights on unnecessarily. Brenda retires to her room and thinks to herself: "Twenty-five cents just

for leaving a light on isn't fair! It doesn't cost that much to burn a light bulb, or does it? I ought to be able to figure what it cost and show Dad that 25¢ just isn't fair. Let's see, for a problem, Mr. Martinez [her mathematics teacher] has us write out the question we want to answer. Okay, here it is: How much does it cost to leave a light bulb on? Then, from that I should be able to identify the main variable to solve. The variable is *number of dollars the electric company charges us for burning one bulb.* [See Exhibit 4.1.]

"So how should I solve for that variable? I could do an experiment. On the first of next month, I'll put a brand new bulb in my lamp and keep it on for a whole month. The next month, I'll keep the lamp off. Then I can find the difference between the electric bill for the month with the lamp on and the one for when it was off. Oh! What size bulb should I use? That's a variable that'll influence the results. Let's see, it's got a 60-watt one now. I'll stick with that and do the experiment for 60-watt bulbs, so size of the bulb will be constant rather than another variable to deal with.

"Oh! Oh! This experiment will take more than 2 months and I'll have to convince Dad to not charge me for leaving the lamp on all month. He should agree since it's *necessary* for the experiment and he said he'd charge us only for unnecessary lights. But 2 months is too long to make my point. There must be some way to shorten this.

"I've got it! I could use last month's bills for the 'off' month and then I'd only have to wait for the 'on' month. That'd get me the results in half the time! Naw, that's not going to work because I used the lamp for some of the time last month. This is going to have to take two months. . . . But even with the two months, there are still too many variables to worry about, like differences in how much we run the heat and electric fans and stuff. I've got to find a better way to do this. I don't know, but maybe if I looked at some old electric bills I might get some ideas."

Exhibit 4.1
Brenda works on her light-bulb problem.

Exhibit 4.2
Brenda's data source.

CITY OF LOGANA

ᴇᴜ   Electric & Utilities Company
billing date: 12/27/91   account no.: 32-260-01-2
description

Electric Meter Billing
date: 12/20   reading: 75698   kilowatt-hours: 733

charge for electricity:	$53.51
charge for sewer:	$11.00
waste charge:	$4.75
utility tax:	$3.24

TOTAL AMOUNT DUE: $72.52
DATE DUE: 1/16/92

Brenda collects some old electric bills (such as the one in Exhibit 4.2); she examines them at her desk and thinks: "This gives me an idea! Maybe I don't have to do an experiment after all. Last month, they charged us $53.51. And it says we used 733 kilowatt hours. From that I ought to be able to figure how much they charge us by the kilowatt hour. Let's see, the rate must be less than 25¢ or so. I'll divide 733 by 53.51. Here's my calculator, okay, ahh 733 divide by 53.51 is . . . What? $13.70! That can't be! Electricity can't be that expensive. Oh, I know! I should've divided the dollar amount by the kilowatt hours instead of into them. So, it's 53.51 divided by 733 equals 0.073. So the rate is 7.3¢.

Brenda's computation of the electric rate.

$$Kilowatt\text{-}hours = 733$$
$$Cost\ to\ customer = \$53.51$$
$$7\cancel{3}3 \div 5\cancel{3}.51 = 1\cancel{3}.\cancel{7}0$$
$$53.51 \div 733 = 0.073$$
$$Rate = \$0.073\ per\ Kilowatt\text{-}hour$$

"Maybe from this, I can solve for my variable, *cost of burning one 60-watt bulb*, without having to do an experiment. But what's a kilowatt-hour? It's in my science book, better look it up. It's, uhh, 'power consumption of 1,000 watts for 1 hour.' This light bulb is 60 watts, so it burns . . . 60 divided by 1000 watts per hour. So, if the rate is 7.3¢ per kilowatt hour, it cost 0.06 times 0.073 dollars to burn the bulb for an hour. That's about $0.0044 every hour.

"So to leave one light bulb on all day would be 24 times 0.0044, or 0.1056, which isn't much more than a tenth of a cent. Gosh! Is that all it cost? It doesn't seem right for Dad to charge us 25¢. Oh, no! I've been doing this in dollars, so that's 0.1056 of a dollar, not of a cent. So, it's

Brenda's computation of the cost of burning one 60-watt bulb for a day.

$$A\ Kilowatt\text{-}hour =$$
the power consumption of 1000 watts for one hour.
The light bulb is 60 watts.
$$60 \div 1000 = 0.06$$
$$Rate = \$0.073\ per\ Kilowatt\text{-}hour.$$
$$0.06 \times 0.073 = 0.0044.$$
It cost $0.0044 each hour to burn a 60 watt light bulb.
$$24 \times 0.0044 = 0.1056.$$
~~It cost about 1.05 cents to burn a 60 watt bulb for a day.~~
It cost about 10.5 cents to burn a 60 watt bulb for a day.

really about $10\frac{1}{2}$ cents. And that's for only one 60-watt bulb. Let's see, my overhead light has three 60-watt bulbs . . . leaving lights on can get pretty expensive. But 25¢ is still too high for him to charge us. I'll show him these figures and see if we can negotiate this down."

Brenda hurries out of her room but quickly returns to shut off the lights before speaking to her father.

Research studies suggest that most people do *not* confidently address problems, nor do they systematically formulate solutions as Brenda did (Cangelosi 1990c; Schoenfeld 1985). Brenda's confident, systematic pursuit of a solution grew out of her experiences with a mathematics teacher who consciously taught her a process that includes nine stages:

1. *The person is confronted with a puzzling question or questions (e.g., regarding how to do something or explain a phenomenon) that he or she wants to answer.* In Brenda's case, the overall question was, Is it fair for her dad to charge her and her brothers 25¢ each time they leave on a lightbulb?

2. *The person clarifies the question or questions posed by the problem, often in terms of more spe-*

cific questions about quantities. Brenda refined the overall question about fairness of 25¢ per incident to the more mathematical question: How much does it cost to leave a light bulb on?

3. *The principal variable or variables to be solved are identified.* Brenda inferred the variable *number of dollars the electric company charges us for burning one bulb* from the question How much does it cost to leave on a light bulb?

4. *The situation is visualized so that relevant relations involving the principal variable or variables are identified and possible solution designs are considered.* Brenda thought about how a bulb's wattage rating affects the cost of burning the bulb and how burning a bulb impacts the total monthly electric bill. This led her to consider experimenting with one 60-watt bulb for 2 months. After judging that plan impractical, she identified relations involving the rate the company charges for electricity. From there, she decided she could determine the rate from a previous monthly bill and figure the cost of burning the 60-watt bulb.

5. *The solution plan is finalized, including (a) selection of measurements (i.e., how data are to be collected), (b) identification of relations to establish, and (c) selection of algorithms to execute.* For this stage, Brenda decided to use a previous bill as the data source for the dollars charged and the kilowatt hours consumed. Those figures were to be used in calculating the rate and then the cost of burning one 60-watt bulb for a day.

6. *Data are gathered (i.e., measurements taken).* Brenda read the relevant information from the bill.

7. *The processes, formulas, or algorithms are executed with the data.* Brenda completed the computations leading to the figures of $0.073 per kilowatt hour and 10.56¢ per day for burning a 60-watt bulb.

8. *Results of the executions of processes, formulas, or algorithms are interpreted to shed light on the original question or questions.* Brenda compared the 10.5¢ per day figure to the 25¢ per incident her father is charging.

9. *The person makes a value judgment regarding the original question or questions.* Brenda decided she has a reasonable chance of using her findings to negotiate successfully with her father.

Requisite Attitudes, Skills, and Abilities

Students' successes in applying the nine-stage process to solving problems from their own real worlds depends how well they have acquired the following attitudes, skills, and abilities.

Confidence and Willingness to Pursue Solutions to Problems. The dogged pursuit of problem solutions requires (1) confidence in the potential for success, (2) freedom from fear of the consequences of failure, and (3) an appreciation for truth. "Appreciation for truth" may appear corny, but Brenda probably would not have systematically persisted in solving the light-bulb problem had she been more interested in fooling her father into changing his mind than in presenting him with accurate information. Such persistence and appreciation are learned behaviors.

Conceptual-Level Understanding of the Mathematical Concepts, Relations, and Processes from which They Expect to Draw Problem Solutions. Unless students understand how examples and nonexamples of concepts differ and why relations and processes work, they won't recognize how to apply concepts, relations, and processes in novel situations with real-world clutter (i.e., information irrelevant to the problem or its solution). Brenda, for example, had never before tried to solve for an electric rate, but because she had conceptualized the concept of rate and understood why relations such as *rate* × *time* = *distance* and *rate* × *principal* = *interest* work, she was able to associate that understanding with the question about leaving on lights.

Knowledge of Necessary Language and Structural Conventions for Organizing, Maintaining, and Relating Mathematics to Problem-Solving. Language and process conventions provide a means for (1) organizing and storing concepts, relations, and processes and (2) communicating about them. Brenda, for example, retrieved mathematics she had conceptualized and stored under such labels as "rate" and "multiplication of rational numbers" for use in solving her problem. Her knowledge of conventions helped her organize what she understands, utilize common devices such as a calculator, and report her findings to her father.

Ability to Discriminate Between Appropriate and Inappropriate Mathematical Concepts, Relations, and Processes According to Problem Situations. How to decide when to use the mathematics one knows is a learned ability. Brenda, for example, recognized certain features of her problem situation that led her to use one type of mathematics rather than another.

Skills in Recalling or Retrieving Formulas and Executing Algorithms and Other Processes. Accuracy of solutions depends not only on selecting appropriate mathematics but also on correctly executing processes by hand, calculator, or computer. Brenda didn't remember the meaning of kilowatt-hour, but she knew where to look it up. Also, she knew how to compute with her calculator and how to use estimation for monitoring answers.

Requisite Learning Experiences

Relative to the mathematical content of any teaching unit, students acquire requisite attitudes, skills, and abilities for applying that content to real-world problem solving by engaging in learning activities that provide them with the following:

1. Successful experiences working with the content on problems from their own real worlds.
2. Inductive instruction leading to conceptual-level learning (e.g., the learning activity on surface area of right cylinder in which Ms. Lowe engaged her students in Vignette 1.2).
3. Direct and expository instruction accompanied by error-pattern analysis and practice exercises leading to knowledge of conventions, relations, and algorithms (e.g., Ms. Allen's lesson in Vignette 4.17).
4. Deductive instruction leading to application-level learning (e.g., Mr. Wilson's lesson in Vignette 4.20).

Among other things (e.g., engagement in questioning sessions), such learning activities involve students in working on four types of tasks:

❏ *Solving contrived problems.* Contrived problems (e.g., the one Mr. Theron used in Vignette 2.9) are a convenient complement to real-world problems for inductive lessons providing students with experiences discovering and inventing mathematics.
❏ *Skill-level exercises.* Mathematics textbooks are filled with these types of exercises, which are necessary for polishing students' skills with algorithms and other processes. They provide practice in computations, solving open sentences, translating expressions from one form to another (e.g., a function from algebraic to graphic form), reforming expressions (e.g., factoring a polynomial), simplifying expressions, and using mathematical language.
❏ *Solving real-world problems.* Real-life problems are used to motivate students to work on the mathematical content of the unit and to help them bridge school mathematics with real-world mathematics. However, with 15 to 40 students per class, it is impractical to restrict problem-solving activities to real-life situations. Thus, real-world problems used in application-level lessons are complemented with textbook word problems.
❏ *Solving textbook word problems.* Solving textbook word problems involves students in some, but not all, of the aspects of real-world problem solving.

Compare the nine stages of real-world problem solving (as listed on pages 75–76) to the task of solving textbook word problems:

1. With a real-world problem, students are confronted with puzzling questions they want to answer. Textbook word problems (e.g., What is the height of a tree if it casts a 75-foot shadow when the angle of elevation of the sun is 27°?) present puzzling questions but rarely are they questions students feel a need to answer.
2. To solve a real-world problem, students must clarify the questions posed by problems, often in terms of more specific questions about quantities. With textbook word problems, the specific questions involving quantities (e.g., What is the maximum area of the patio?) are typically articulated for students. Thus, instead of taxing students' abilities to formulate questions, students' reading comprehension skills are tested.
3. With both real-world and textbook word problems, principal variables to be solved must be inferred from the questions about quantities.
4. To solve real-world problems, students must visualize situations so that relevant relations involving the principal variables are identified and possible solution designs are considered. Typically, this step is unnecessary for solving textbook word problems because all relevant data are given and open sentences can be formulated simply by following the pattern established by the examples and other word problems in the sections where the problems appear.
5. The solution plan for real-world problems needs to be finalized, but this is unnecessary for textbook word problems, as alluded to in point 4.
6. Numbers used in real-world problem solving result from measurements. Numbers used in textbook word problems are usually given.
7. Both real-world and textbook word problems require students to execute processes, formulas, or algorithms.
8. Results of executions of processes, formulas, or algorithms are interpreted to shed light on the original questions posed by real-world problems. Simply obtaining the results, not interpreting them, is all that is typically required for textbook word problems (e.g., finding the height of the tree that cast the 75-foot shadow is sufficient; it is not necessary to decide if it is practical to move the tree).

9. Unlike real-world problems, solving textbook word problems does not require students to make value judgments.

Exhibit 4.3 summarizes some of the principal similarities and differences between students solving real-world and textbook word problems. Techniques for modifying textbook word problems so they are more representative of real-world problems are illustrated by Mr. Pepper as he begins designing an application-level learning activity in Vignette 1.4.

SEQUENCING THE OBJECTIVES OF A TEACHING UNIT

Reexamine Exhibit 3.2 and note the various learning levels included in each of the six sets of objectives. For each of these units, the objectives are listed in the approximate order in which they should be taught; there are some exceptions, however. Because these units are intended to develop application-level understanding of certain mathematical topics, the lessons for each should roughly be sequenced according to the following pattern:

Learning activities for objectives specifying any particular concept or relation are sequenced so that *conceptualization*-level learning occurs first, followed by *knowledge and comprehension*-level learning; *application*-level learning comes last. Learning activities for other learning levels (e.g., *affective* or *creativity*) are inserted as appropriate.

Here are some general principles to keep in mind:

❑ *Ordinarily, names of concepts or relations should not be introduced before students have been engaged in inductive activities for conceptualizing the concept or relation.* Memorizing the words (e.g., "sample space" or "Pythagorean theorem") to attach to a concept (sample space) or relation (Pythagorean theorem) before that concept or relation is understood is meaningless for students.
❑ *Comprehension objectives relative to certain messages (e.g., the proof of the side-angle-side theorem as presented in a textbook) or to certain communication modes (e.g., use of the summation notation, Σ) should be taught before conducting learning activities that depend on those messages or communications modes.* Students experience consid-

Exhibit 4.3
Solving real-world problems compared to solving textbook word problems.

Characteristic	Real Problems	Textbook Word Problems
Problem is personalized with student having felt a need to solve it.	Yes	No
Questions posed by the problem are clarified and articulated for the student.	No	Yes
Reading comprehension skills are likely to be taxed.	No	Yes
Principal variables must be inferred from questions posed by the problem.	Yes	Yes
Type of problem is categorized for the student according to the type of mathematics needed.	No	Yes
Student is likely to have to select the type of mathematics to be used.	Yes	No
Measurement procedures must be selected and data collected.	Yes	No
Irrelevant data and information (i.e., clutter) are present.	Yes	No
Student needs to execute formulas, processes, or algorithms.	Yes	Yes
Solutions have pat answers.	No	Yes
Student must interpret results and make value judgments.	Yes	No

erable difficulty following lessons in which teachers either assume they understand messages they've yet to comprehend or communicate via modes they've not learned to use.

❏ *Ordinarily, relations should not be memorized before students are engaged in inductive activities for conceptualizing the relation.* Memorizing a relation (e.g., the product of two negative integers is positive) is far more meaningful after students have discovered why the relation exists.

❏ *Students are ready to engage in deductive learning activities for application-level objectives relative to a particular relation only after they have conceptualized the relation and acquired relevant comprehension and knowledge-level skills (e.g., how to execute algorithms based on the relation).*

❏ *If creativity or affective objectives are targeted by a unit, then learning activities for them are ordinarily scattered throughout the unit.* Both creative and affective behaviors are usually acquired by experiences that extend over the entire course of a unit rather than tending to appear near the beginning (as with conceptualization learning), the middle (as with comprehension and knowledge levels), or the end (as with application).

As an example, consider the order in which the nine objectives of the unit on congruence of triangles (page 59 and Exhibit 3.2) might be taught:

1. The content of Objective A involves simple knowledge of the conventional names associated with two relations ($\triangle ABC \cong \triangle DEF$ and $\overrightarrow{AD}$ bisects $\angle BAC$) and one concept (median of a triangle). The teacher who designed this unit indicates that this objective would be taught first because conceptualization of those two relations and one concept was taught in a previous unit. Thus the unit is to begin with the objective of making sure students are familiar with some of the vocabulary that is to be used in subsequent lessons.
2. Next, the teacher plans to help students conceptualize the first of the eight relations listed for Objective B and then to comprehend a proof for that relation (the first part of Objective C). After an inductive lesson to help students conceptualize the side-angle-side postulate (second part of Objective B), the teacher plans to alternate conceptualization lessons (Objective B) and comprehension lessons (Objective C) for each of the remaining six theorems on the list.
3. Affective Objectives D and E are taught throughout the unit with learning activities that are integrated with those for the cognitive objectives.
4. The teacher plans to address the two creativity objectives, Objectives F and G, after formative

feedback suggests that the students have achieved Objectives A, B, and C.
5. Objective H is taught via direct instruction and, finally, Objective I is achieved by deductive methods.

LEARNING ACTIVITIES FOR AFFECTIVE OBJECTIVES
Appreciation

When you teach for an *appreciation* objective, you are attempting to influence students' preferences, opinions, or desires regarding content specified by the objective. Students who learn to *value* mathematical content are intrinsically motivated to increase their skills and abilities with it and, thus, achieve the cognitive objectives you establish for the unit.

Telling students about the importance and value of certain mathematics is generally ineffectual as a learning activity for an appreciation objective. Consider the following vignette.

❏ **VIGNETTE 4.2**
Mr. Shaver realizes that if his algebra students appreciate the value of being able to use permutation and combination formulas efficiently, they will be more receptive to achieving the cognitive objectives of his unit on those topics. Thus, his initial objective for the unit is for each student to:

> Recognize the advantage of being able to use the following formulas in problem-solving situations:
>
> **1.** $_nP_r = (n!)/((n - r)!)$
> **2.** $_nC_r = (n!)/((n - r)!r!)$
> (*appreciation*).

In an attempt to achieve that objective, he tells the class: "Today, people, we're going to begin studying about permutations and combinations. We need to learn about permutations and combinations so that we can extend our abilities to solve probability problems. Now, I know you enjoy working with probabilities because solving probability problems helps us make critical decisions in our lives.

"Well, once you understand how to use permutations and combinations, you'll be able to solve some really neat probability problems that'll actually make a difference in your own lives. You're going to enjoy this first activity. First, think about how many ways you can arrange . . . ."

In general, students do not learn to appreciate something by being told what they enjoy and will find important (Cangelosi 1988a, 89, 130–138).

Rather than wasting time with lip service for his appreciation-level objective, Mr. Shaver should integrate learning activities for the appreciation objective into lessons for his cognitive objectives so that the following occur:

1. *The first few examples used to introduce the content involve situations in which most students have already demonstrated an interest.* Questions such as those listed in Exhibit 2.2 can get students' attention and entice them into the study of the mathematics.
2. *Initial tasks to which the mathematical content is applied are selected so that the value of the new concept, relation, or process is readily demonstrated.* For example, if the content is the formula for computing rectangular areas (i.e., $A = l \cdot w$), then which one of the following tasks would better demonstrate the advantages of having such a formula?

❑ Find the area of the following rectangle:

❑ Find the area of the following rectangle:

If the content is the quadratic formula, then which one of the following tasks would better demonstrate the advantages of having such a formula?

❑ Find the real roots of the following equation:

$$x^2 - 4x = 21$$

❑ Find the real roots of the following equation:

$$15x^2 - 7x = 2$$

It is just as easy to count the unit squares to find the area of the 4-by-2 rectangle as it is to use the area formula. The value of the formula is apparent for the task of finding the area of the 16-by-6 rectangle, since, with the formula, students need to count only the number of units on two edges rather than all 96 squares.

Similarly, the value of the quadratic formula is demonstrated with the second rather than the first equation. The first is more easily solved by factoring.

3. *Whenever the unit's learning goal requires the introduction of a new concept or relation, students discover the concept or relation for themselves.* Achievement of conceptualization objectives normally requires students to be engaged in inductive learning activities in which they work toward such discoveries. These types of activities have the added benefit of developing in students a feeling of ownership in the mathematical content. Ms. Lowe's students (Vignette 1.2) discovered relations that led them to an area formula for a "Norton." Those students are more likely to appreciate the relations than students who are simply told about them.

Note how learning activities for an appreciation-level objective are integrated with lessons for cognitive objectives in the following vignette.

❑ **VIGNETTE 4.3**

The first few lessons of Mr. Polonia's unit on permutations and combinations include learning activities designed to help his algebra students achieve three objectives:

1. Recognize the advantage of being able to use the following formulas in problem-solving situations:
   $_nP_r = (n!)/((n - r)!)$
   $_nC_r = (n!)/((n - r)!r!)$
   (*appreciation*).
2. Discriminate between examples and nonexamples of each of the following two concepts: permutations and combinations (*conceptualization*).
3. Explain why each of the following relations hold:
   $_nP_r = (n!)/((n - r)!)$
   $_nC_r = (n!)/(n - r)!r!)$
   (*conceptualization*).

Mr. Polonia begins the first learning activity by telling the class: "Over the past two weeks, I've kept notes on comments I've overheard students make. Here, I'll show you five of them. I won't tell you who said what, but you may recognize your own words in one."

He reads each as he displays the following on the overhead projector:

Did you notice that at the [school] dances they never play two slow songs in a row? I think they're afraid of too much close dancing.

One of us is bound to win the drawing; they pick five winners!

Almost every time a teacher picks a group to do something, there are more nonblacks than blacks—like

Johnson today, he picked me and two whites to supervise the drawing.

Mrs. Simmons has never chosen one of my poems for the newspaper.

You ought to try the lunch room; there'll always be at least one thing you like.

Mr. Polonia continues: "Tomorrow, we will divide up into small groups with each group assigned to analyze one of these statements for implications and causes. Let's take one to show you what we'll be doing."

He displays the following:

> Almost every time a teacher picks a group to do something, there are more nonblacks than blacks—like Johnson today, he picked me and two whites to supervise the drawing.

Mr. Polonia: This statement hints at the possibility of racial bias influencing teachers' selections of student groups and committees. How might we examine the validity of that suggestion?

Theresa: We could keep a record of groups that teachers select over the next month or so and see how often blacks are in the minority.

Tracy: And if blacks are in the minority most of the time, then that would show bias.

Eva: I don't think so.

Tracy: Why?

Eva: We black students are a minority in the school, so you expect most of the groups would have more nonblacks.

Milton: I think it's because the teachers always want to have one black in a group, so they have to spread us out in all the groups.

Mr. Polonia: How often would black students be in the majority of the groups if the teachers never considered color when they picked groups?

Don: That's impossible. A few teachers are out-and-out prejudiced, but the others bend over backward to show they're not.

Mr. Polonia: Maybe so, but if we figured what the numbers would be if the choices were never biased, then we'd have something to compare with the actual choices Theresa suggests we record.

Tracy: Well, if there were no bias, then the percentage of groups with a majority of black students should equal the percentage of black students.

Mr. Polonia: Okay, in this class we have nine black students and 15 nonblack students. That's . . .

Eva: Nine out of 24 is 37.5 percent.

Tracy: Right. So, 37.5 percent of the groups in this class ought to have a black majority and the other . . .

Eva: 62.5 percent.

Tracy: The other 62.5 percent should have a black minority.

Estelle: I don't think it's that simple because. . . .

After a few more minutes, Mr. Polonia calls a halt to the discussion and directs the students as follows: "I would like for us to continue to work on this problem, but to move us toward developing a model, let's limit the situation for now to selecting groups of 3 people each from this class. Remember 9 of us are black and 15 are nonblack. The question is, If there is no bias in the selection of a group of 3, what are the chances that either 2 of the 3 or 3 of the 3 will be black? What's the first thing we need to do to figure that chance?"

Eva: Make a sample space.

Mr. Polonia: The sample space for this problem might be quite long. So, for homework let's break up the work by having each of you list all the possible groups of three from the class of which you yourself are a member. Tomorrow, we'll eliminate the duplications, combine the rest and, voilà! We'll have our sample space.

After further clarification of the assignment, the students begin the work, returning the next day to learn that there are many more possible groups of three than they had expected—2,024 in all. In class they complete the arduous task of counting the number of groups for each relevant category and to the surprise of many discover the following:

> 4% of the groups are all black.
>
> 27% contain two blacks and one nonblack.
>
> 47% contain two nonblacks and one black.
>
> 22% contain all nonblacks.

Thus, they conclude that under the no-bias supposition, 31% of the time a group of three would have a black majority. After further discussions regarding the implications of their findings (e.g., regarding how much above or below the 31% figure should be tolerated before the figures are indicative of bias), Mr. Polonia directs their attention on the process by which they obtained the 31% figure. All agree that the process was quite tedious and that they should search for easier ways.

From work with other examples, Mr. Polonia leads the students over the next few days to conceptualize permutations and combinations and to discover formulas for computing them.

Because Mr. Polonia was concerned with the appreciation objective as well as his cognitive objectives, he carefully chose initial examples that would get students' attention. Once he had them working on a problem, the mathematical content to be taught (i.e., permutation and combination formulas) came as a welcome tool for making their work easier and more efficient. Because the formulas were inducted from patterns established in their own work, students felt they owned the mathematics. How to design learning activities whereby students discover concepts and relations from their own work with examples is addressed in the section of this chapter entitled "Learning Activities for Conceptualization-Level Objectives."

Willingness to Try

Even though students have learned to appreciate certain mathematical content, they still may not attempt to work vigorously with it because they lack confidence that they will use it successfully in situations they find meaningful. Until they have accumulated experiences successfully using mathematics, they tend to be reluctant to pursue problem solutions in the manner displayed by Mr. Polonia's students in Vignette 4.3 and Brenda in Vignette 4.1.

Willingness to try objectives, such as the following one, require learning activities similar to appreciation objectives:

> Attempts to solve problems involving permutations and combinations and discover models that facilitate efficient solutions to such problems (*willingness to try*).

But to take students that one extra affective level from appreciation to willingness to try, you must select problems or tasks for them that are interesting enough to maintain their attention and yet easy enough for them to experience success. Keep the following in mind:

❏ *Until students gain confidence in their problem-solving abilities and in the benefits of working on perplexing mathematical tasks, most of the mathematical tasks you assigned them should be such that they will feel successful before becoming frustrated.* As their confidence builds, you gradually work in more perplexing and challenging work.
❏ *The more a task relates to what already interests students, the more students tend to tolerate perplexity and frustrations before giving up.* It is quite a challenge for you to have to judge that fine line between interest and frustration.
❏ *Achievement of willingness-to-try objectives requires a learning environment in which students feel free to experiment, question, hypothesize, and make errors without fear of ridicule, embarrassment, or loss of status.* Chapter 5 contains ideas to help you create such an environment in your classroom.
❏ *By presenting students with problems requiring applications of previously acquired mathematical skills and abilities (e.g., from prior units), students not only maintain and improve upon earlier*

achievements, they are also provided additional opportunities to succeed with mathematics. As explained in a subsequent section of this chapter, achievement of application-level objectives requires that students be confronted with problems to which the content of the objective applies as well as problems to which content from previously achieved objectives is applicable. These application-level learning activities provide students with experiences with success, since they include opportunities for them to apply previously learned mathematics.

LEARNING ACTIVITIES FOR CONCEPTUALIZATION-LEVEL OBJECTIVES
Challenging but Critical to Teach

Designing learning activities for conceptualization objectives will tax your understanding of your students, pedagogical principles, and mathematics. Coming up with choice examples, problems, and leading questions necessary to stimulate students to discover concepts and relations is challenging, to say the least. However, once students have conceptualized a concept or relation, it is much easier to teach them related content at other learning levels (e.g., knowledge of a process or application). For example:

❏ Students who have already conceptualized the idea of *limit of a function* will more easily achieve the simple knowledge objective of remembering the ϵ, δ definition of limit of a function than students who don't understand the interplay among ϵ, δ, and other variables in the wording of the definition.
❏ Students who have conceptualized the Pythagorean relation are less likely to make one of the more common computational errors made when executing algorithms based on that relation. One such error is illustrated in the following work:

What is the distance between (0, 6) and (10, 0)?

$$d = \sqrt{(10-0)^2 + (0-6)^2} = \sqrt{100 + 36} = 10 + 6 = 16$$

The failure of most students to learn (1) to use the language of mathematics, (2) how to work multistep problems, (3) to associate mathematics with real-world situations, and (4) to enjoy mathematics is well publicized (Dossey et al. 1988; "U.S. Students again Rank near Bottom in Math and Sciences," 1989; "U.S. Teens Lag Behind in Math, Science,"

1989). Many of the difficulties students experience with language, problem-solving, algorithms, applications, and attitudes can be traced to conceptualization gaps in their learning (Ball 1988a; Bourne et al. 1986, 125–195, 235–311). Such gaps are hardly surprising in light of the fact that many teachers never even consider conducting conceptual-level lessons (NCTM, in press; Jesunathadas 1990).

Inductive Reasoning

In order to conceptualize, students must *reason inductively* (Bourne et al. 1986, p. 17). *Inductive reasoning is generalizing from encounters with specifics.* It is the *cognitive process by which people discover commonalties among specific examples and leads them to formulate abstract categories and generalizations.* Students are using inductive reasoning in the following vignettes.

❑ VIGNETTE 4.4
Over the past month, Rubin has encountered variables in his psychology, chemistry, and mathematics courses. During that time, he has noticed differences and similarities among those variables. Although he never made a conscious effort to do so, he has begun to create a dichotomy between two types:

The first type includes variables such as these: aptitudes people have for learning; temperature fluctuations; $\{x \in \text{real numbers} \mid -2 \leq 5x + 3 \leq 10\}$.

The second type includes variables such as these: different types of emotional disorders; atomic numbers of chemical elements; $\{x \in \text{integers} \mid x^2 - 25 \leq 99\}$.

Rubin thinks of the first type as more difficult to deal with because, as he says, "It's too packed in to list two things that are next to one another." Rubin has apparently begun to form the concept of *continuous data* and the concept of *discrete data.* He does not, however, know the concepts by those names.

❑ VIGNETTE 4.5
After completing a homework assignment in which she used a protractor to measure the angles of six triangles her teacher drew on a work sheet, Robin looks at the resulting six triples: (100°, 45°, 35°), (80°, 61°, 41°), (30°, 60°, 90°), (142°, 15°, 23°), (60°, 60°, 60°), and (30°, 30°, 118°).

She thinks: "Anytime there's a big angle, the other two are small." She then attempts to draw a triangle with two "big" angles and finds it is impossible. Experimenting with triangles that are nearly equiangular, she finds all their angles are near 60°. Curious about the phenomenon, she measures the angles of 16 different triangles determined by concrete objects about her (e.g., two edges of a mirror). She then thinks: "Adding up the degrees of three angles of *any* triangle will give me about 180."

❑ VIGNETTE 4.6
While exploring different functions with the aid of a computer program, Christi notices that $f(i)$ for $i = 0, 1, 2, \ldots,$ 25 is always a prime number when $f(i) = i^2 - i + 41$. Christi concludes she has discovered a function from the set of integers into the set of primes.

In the first case, Rubin organized specific variables into two categories, thus abstracting two concepts. Robin formulated a hypothesis from her experiences with specific triangles, thus abstracting a relation. As illustrated by Christi's example, inductive reasoning can sometimes lead to a generalization that can be disproven with a counterexample (e.g., let $i = 41$). But, disproving the conclusion does not discredit the reasoning.

Inductive Learning Activities

An *inductive learning activity* is one that *stimulates students to reason inductively.* This is accomplished in seven stages:

1. *Task confrontation.* If the objective's content is a concept, then students are presented with a task requiring them to sort and categorize specifics. For a relation, the task is to solve problems.
2. *Task work.* The students work through the task. The teacher orchestrates the activity, managing the environment and providing guidance but allowing students to complete the task themselves.
3. *Reflection on work.* For a concept, students explain their rationales for categorizing the specifics as they did. For a relation, students analyze the process by which problems were addressed or solved. The teacher raises leading questions, stimulates thought, and clarifies students' expressions.
4. *Generalization.* For a concept, concept attributes (i.e., what sets examples of the concept apart from the nonexamples) are pointed out and the concept is identified. For a relation, a common pattern utilized in problem solutions is identified and a relation is hypothesized.
5. *Articulation.* The concept is defined or the statement of the relation is agreed upon.
6. *Verification.* For a concept, the definition is tested with examples (which should fit) and nonexamples (which should not fit). For a relation, attempts are made to produce a counterexample for the statement. Further verification is pursued, depending on the teacher's judgment of the situation. The level of verification can vary from a seems to work—intuitively clear approach to a failure to produce counterexamples approach to a deductive proof approach.

7. *Refinement.* The definition of the concept or the statement of the relation is modified in light of the outcome of the verification stage. Prior stages are reengaged as judged necessary by the teacher.

Conceptualizing Concepts

Concept Attributes and Psychological Noise

One aspect of designing learning activities for conceptualization objectives that teachers find particularly difficult is formulating appropriate examples and nonexamples for students to categorize (Cangelosi 1988b). As you determine sets of examples and nonexamples to present to students, attention to two ideas is critical: Concept attributes and psychological noise.

Concept Attributes. All examples of a particular concept share a common set of attributes. The attributes define the concept. An *even number,* for example, is any integer that is a multiple of 2. Thus, the attributes of the concept *even number* are (a) integer and (b) multiple of 2. Any specific that does not meet both these requirements (e.g., 11, $\sqrt{8}$, or the book you are now reading) is not an even number. Similarly, any specific that has both these defining attributes (e.g., $-\sqrt{16}, 0, 33 + 47, 3.3 + 2.7,$ or 196) is an even number.

Psychological Noise. A characteristic of an example of a concept that is *not* an attribute of the concept is *psychological noise.* For instance, 64 is an example of the concept *even number.* But besides the attributes of even numbers (i.e., integer and multiple of 2), 64 has other characteristics (e.g., less than 70, positive, divisible by 16, a square root of 4096) that distinguish it from other even numbers. Those other features of 64 are *psychological noise* with respect to being an example of an even number.

Attributes of attributes are considered attributes, not psychological noise. For instance, 64 is a real number. Since all integers (a defining attribute of the concept *even number*) are real numbers, then *real number* is not psychological noise for 64. Psychological noise includes only characteristics that are not common to all examples of the concept.

As you select examples and nonexamples for your concept-attainment lessons, you will need to be aware of the role played by psychological noise so that noise facilitates rather than hinders learning. Here is a simple illustration.

☐ VIGNETTE 4.7

Mr. Edwards is using inductive questioning strategies with individual kindergarten students to help them conceptualize *set cardinality,* or "number of."

He displays Exhibit 4.4 to Stacy and asks her, "Which two groups are alike?" Stacy, pointing to sets *A* and *B,* replies, "These."

Mr. Edwards: Why?
Stacy: Because they're not round like the other.
Mr. Edwards: Thank you. Now, can you see a way that this group of round things is like one of the other groups?
Stacy: No, it's different.

Mr. Edwards shows Stacy Exhibit 4.5. "Which of these two groups are alike?" Stacy points to *A* and *C* and says, "Because they have the same amount." Mr. Edwards: "Thank you. Now, let's go back and look at this one again." Mr. Edwards displays Exhibit 4.4 again and the activity continues.

Note how Mr. Edwards manipulated examples to control for psychological noise. Had Stacy immediately categorized by cardinality upon seeing Exhibit 4.4, Mr. Edwards would have moved to a noisier situation (e.g., Exhibit 4.6) where the noise varies more among the examples. But since she experienced difficulty with Exhibit 4.4, he reduced the noise by moving to Exhibit 4.5. In any case, Stacy eventually needs to recognize similarities and differences in cardinality even in high-noise situations, because the real world is quite noisy.

In general, how well students conceptualize a concept is dependent on how well they learn to distinguish between psychological noise and concept attributes when classifying examples. Distinguishing between examples and nonexamples in high-noise situations is indicative of a higher conceptual achievement level than when the distinction is made in low-noise situations.

Incorporating the Seven Stages into a Concept Lesson

In the following scenario, note how the teacher plans and orchestrates each of the seven stages and utilizes both concept attributes and psychological noise.

Exhibit 4.4
Which two sets are alike?

A   B   C

Exhibit 4.5
Examples used by Mr. Edwards that have less variability of psychological noise than Exhibit 4.4.

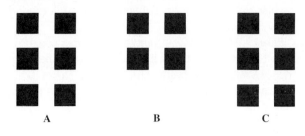

A　　　　　B　　　　　C

Exhibit 4.6
Examples with greater variability in psychological noise than Exhibit 4.4.

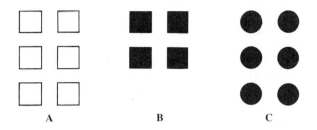

A　　　　　B　　　　　C

❑ VIGNETTE 4.8

Mr. Citerelli thinks as he designs the initial lesson for a unit on arithmetic and geometric sequences he plans to conduct for his intermediate algebra class: "This first objective is the key to the whole unit. All the others depend on it. I'd better concentrate this first lesson on it. Let's see, it says:

> Distinguishes between examples of arithmetic sequences and examples of other types of sequences and explains the defining attributes of an arithmetic sequence (*conceptualization*).

"So the learning level is *conceptualization* and the content is the concept *arithmetic sequence.* That means inductive learning activities beginning with task confrontation sorting through examples and nonexamples. The first thing I've got to do is come up with just the right sequences, arithmetic and nonarithmetic, for them to ponder.

"Better start with a list of arithmetic sequences and then I can match each with a nonarithmetic sequence that is similar regarding psychological noise. I don't want them to abstract the noise as part of the concept. . . ."

With the help of the course textbook and further thought, he develops the following two lists:

Examples
❑ 3, 3.1, 3.2, 3.3, 3.4, 3.5, 3.6
❑ −13, −2, 9, . . . , 130, 141, 152
❑ 15, 10, 5, 0, −5, −10, . . .
❑ 22.6, 22.6, 22.6, 22.6, 22.6, 22.6

Nonexamples
❑ 7, 0.7, 0.07, 0.007, 0.0007, 0.00007
❑ 46, 6.78, 2.60, 1.61, . . . , 1.02, 1.00, 1.00, 1.00
❑ . . . , 16, 9, 4, 1, 0, 1, 4, 16, . . .
❑ 1, 2, 4, 8, 16, . . . , 1,048,576
❑ 1, 1, 2, 3, 5, 8, 13, 21, . . .

He thinks: "Not bad. The psychological noise in the examples varies, so they're unlikely to develop too narrow of a concept. The characteristics of the nonexamples match the noise in the examples, so they should be able to sort out the attributes from the noise. Oh, oh! I really should toss in a few real-life sequences just so they'll maintain the association between the mathematics and the world. That's going to complicate things. I'll just think of a few."

Six minutes later he adds the following to the list:

Examples
❑ Until it's won, the amount of money each hour in a radio giveaway jackpot that begins with $100 and increases by $20 every hour until there is a winner.
❑ The amount of money in Betty's jar each Saturday if she starts with $60 and puts in exactly $7.50 each Friday night. (She never removes money nor puts any in at any other time.)
❑ The number of bricks in the first, second, third, fourth, . . . row that are stacked in a pyramid arrangement with 12 on the bottom and 1 on the top.

Nonexamples
❑ The monthly savings account balance of a person who puts in $750 the first month and leaves it there, allowing it to collect interest at the rate of 4% compounded monthly.
❑ The ages of all the people in our class, listed in alphabetical order.

He thinks: "I'll try starting this off with the whole class of students in a large group. I'll present them with one list on a sheet with the examples and nonexamples mixed up and have them try to pull one group out according to some common attributes. I'm afraid that would really take a long time and might get us into some other concepts I don't want to take time for. At least that's likely with this list; it's pretty complex for them. Of course, they already know what a sequence is; that won't be a problem. But having them all see uniform differences between consecutive elements is problematic unless I use a simpler list. But I hate to simplify it and chance them developing an overly limited concept of arithmetic sequences. . . .

"I know! Instead of making the list easier to distinguish examples from nonexamples, I'll give them a head start on the task by having them already grouped and getting them to explain how the examples are like each other but different from the nonexamples. That way I can keep the same variety of psychological noise and not chance the activity being drawn out and heading out on a tangent. This'll give me more control of the situation."

Mr. Citerelli rearranges the list and adds the workspace at the bottom, as shown in Exhibit 4.7. He makes a copy for each student, one for him to use in class, and one for his file for use with subsequent classes.

He plans the remainder of the learning activities for the objective.

On the first day of the unit, Mr. Citerelli directs the students to take 10 minutes to examine the two lists silently and to make and write out a conjecture as to how the examples are like one another and different from the nonexamples. After each student writes something in the first blank, he engages the class in a questioning/discussion session. From engaging in such sessions before, the students have learned that whenever Mr. Citerelli calls on someone and says "Keep it going," the following procedures are in effect until Mr. Citerelli interrupts:

> One student at a time has the floor. Anyone wanting to speak raises her or his hand to request the floor from the student who is speaking.

Mr. Citerelli: Bill, read your first conjecture.

Bill: The examples are alike because they're all in the same column. The nonexamples are in a different column.

Mr. Citerelli: That surely can't be contradicted. Now, let's hear an idea that might explain what I had in mind when I grouped the examples on the left and the nonexamples on the right? Okay, Mavis, you start; keep it going.

Mavis: The first thing I noticed is that both columns contain sequences. But those on the left have more of a pattern to them. Jeannie.

Jeannie: The ones on the right have patterns also. So, just having a pattern can't be it. Okay, Mark.

Mark: Not all of them. Look at the second one.

Jeannie: Sure it does—.

Mr. Citerelli: Excuse me. Let's let these two hash this out in a two-way discussion while the rest of us listen. Please continue, Jeannie.

Jeannie: The numbers in that second one are getting smaller; that's a pattern.

Mark: Not the last two.

Jeannie: They might, if we saw more decimal places. I think it has something to do with taking square roots. I played around with roots on my calculator and there's something related to roots of 46 with those numbers.

Mr. Citerelli: Excuse me. Mark, do you agree that at least some of the nonexample sequences have predictable patterns?

Mark: Sure.

Mr. Citerelli: Those that also agree raise your hands. It looks like that's one thing we agree on. Bill, would you please come up to the board and help us keep track of the points on which we all agree?

As the discussion continues, Bill takes notes on the board.

Mr. Citerelli: Mavis, do you want to modify your conjecture?

Mavis: No, but I'll withdraw it since we agreed that some nonexamples have patterns also.

Mr. Citerelli: Thank you. Inez, read yours and then keep it going.

Inez: You get the next number by adding something to the one before. Okay, Chico.

Chico: That's not right because look at the last nonexample. You add some to get to the next one. One plus one is two, one plus two is three, three plus five is eight and so on. So, if Inez is right, then that one should be on the left side. Okay, Luis.

Luis: Besides if Inez is right that you just added something, then the numbers should all be going up . . . and two of 'em go down and one stays the same!

Mr. Citerelli: Excuse me, let's hear from Inez, since it's her conjecture we're discussing.

Inez: First of all, Luis, if you add negatives, the numbers go down. And then, I changed my conjecture so that it's this: You get the next number by adding the *same* amount to each one.

Mr. Citerelli: I see Bill has written down Inez' revised conjecture. Bill, would you please write the first example under that?

Bill writes 3, 3.1, 3.2, 3.3, 3.4, 3.5, 3.6.

Mr. Citerelli: Thanks. Now, write the first nonexample over here.

Bill writes 7, 0.7, 0.07, 0.007, 0.0007, 0.00007.

Mr. Citerelli: Now, if Inez' conjecture holds, what should be true about these two sequences Bill just wrote? Okay, Bill.

Bill: You should be able to add the same thing to each of these to get the next one and you shouldn't be able to do that over here.

Mr. Citerelli: I need a volunteer to use Bill's test. Okay, Habebe. Now, if Habebe shows that Inez' conjecture fails Bill's test, what will we know? Mavis.

Mavis: That the conjecture is wrong.

Mr. Citerelli: And what if it passes, James?

James: I don't know. What was the question?

Mr.Citerelli: What was the question, Bill?

Bill: Here, I wrote it down.

James: Then the conjecture is right.

Mr. Citerelli: Do you agree, Anita? Keep it going.

Anita: Well, the conjecture is right. I agree with it. Chico.

Chico: But that's not what Mr. Citerelli asked. He asked *if* passing the test proves it's true and the answer is no. Luis.

Luis: It's got to work for all of them and I see one it doesn't work for. . . .

Mr. Citerelli: Let's let Habebe perform Bill's test. (See Exhibit 4.8.)

Exhibit 4.7
Worksheet Mr. Citerelli uses on the first day of his conceptualization lesson on arithmetic sequences.

EXAMPLES	NON-EXAMPLES
3, 3.1, 3.2, 3.3, 3.4, 3.5, 3.6	7, 0.7, 0.07, 0.007, 0.0007, 0.00007
-13, -2, 9 ... 130, 141, 152	46, 6.78, 2.60, 1.61 ... 1.02, 1.00, 1.00, 1.00
Until it's won, the amount of money each hour in a radio giveaway jackpot that begins with $100 and increases by $20 every hour until there is a winner.	The monthly savings account balance of a person who puts in $750 the first month and leaves it there, allowing it to collect interest at the rate of 4% compounded monthly
15, 10, 5, 0, -5, -10 ...	The ages of all the people in our class, listed in alphabetical order
The amount of money in Betty's jar each Saturday if she starts with $60 and puts in exactly $7.50 each Friday night. (She never removes money nor puts any in at any other time.)	... 16, 9, 4, 1, 0, 1, 4, 16 ...
22.6, 22.6, 22.6, 22.6, 22.6, 22.6	1, 2, 4, 8, 16 ... 1,048,576
The number of bricks in the first, second, third, fourth, etc. row that are arranged as follows:	1, 1, 2, 3, 5, 8, 13, 21 ...

HOW ARE THE EXAMPLES ALIKE? HOW DO THEY DIFFER FROM THE NON-EXAMPLES?

Write your 1st conjecture here: _____

_____

_____

Write your 2nd conjecture here: _____

_____

_____

Write your 3rd conjecture here: _____

_____

_____

Write your 4th conjecture here: _____

_____

_____

Exhibit 4.8
Habebe uses Bill's test on Inez'
conjecture.

Habebe writes down the following:

$$3 + 0.1 = 3.1$$
$$3.1 + 0.1 = 3.2$$
$$3.2 + 0.1 = 3.3$$
$$3.3 + 0.1 = 3.4$$
$$3.4 + 0.1 = 3.5$$
$$3.5 + 0.1 = 3.6$$

Habebe: But it doesn't work for this other sequence because to get from 7 to 0.7 you have to add some negative number that's different than the one you add to get from 0.7 to 0.07.

Mr. Citerelli: While Habebe and Bill do it at the board, I'd like for the rest of you to find the difference for each of these at your places. Bill you may use that calculator on my desk. Habebe, I'll get yours for you.

A few minutes after the following list appears on the board, everyone agrees that Inez' conjecture passes that first test:

$$7 + (-6.3) = 0.7$$
$$0.7 + (-0.63) = 0.07$$
$$0.07 + (-0.063) = 0.007$$
$$0.007 + (-0.0063) = 0.0007$$
$$0.0007 + (-0.00063) = 0.00007$$

Mr. Citerelli then directs the students to quietly perform the test on the remainder of the examples and nonexamples. During the activity, he circulates among them, looking at their work and occasionally whispering a probing question to individuals.

Twelve minutes later, the class returns to a questioning/discussion activity and the group agrees to Inez' conjecture. Then Mr. Citerelli directs each of them quickly to formulate two more example sequences.

Mr. Citerelli: Mavis, Luis, and J. J., please write yours on the board.

Mavis: 5, 10, 15, 20, . . .
Luis: 0, 0, 0, 0, 0, 0, 0, 0
J.J.: $\frac{1}{2}$, 0, $-\frac{1}{2}$, -1, $-\frac{3}{2}$, -2

Mr. Citerelli: (Gesturing toward the three examples to illustrate his question) Think about what just went through your mind when you determined the third number of your sequence. What told you what it should be, when you went from here to here? J.J.

J.J.: I knew I had to add the same thing to the second I had added to the first.

Mr. Citerelli: How'd you decide what to add to the first, J.J.?

J.J.: Just made up a number; it doesn't make any difference what you add until after the second.

Mr. Citerelli: How'd you pick the first number, Alysia?

Alysia: I don't know.

Mr. Citerelli: Read your sequence.

Alysia: Nine, 10, 11, 12, 13.

Mr. Citerelli: Why 9?

Alysia: I just like 9. My birthday is on the ninth.

Mr. Citerelli: And why 1?

Alysia: What do you mean?

Mr. Citerelli: Mavis chose a difference of 5, Luis chose 0, and J.J. picked $-\frac{1}{2}$. Why did you choose to create differences of 1?

Alysia: I don't know; it just seemed simple.

Mr. Citerelli: So Alysia is telling us that you get to pick anything you want for your first number and anything you want for the difference, but then after that everything else is determined for you. Is that right, Mark?

Mark: Yes.

Mr. Citerelli: Is that right, Jeannie?

Jeannie: Yes.

Mr. Citerelli: Is that right, Gomer?

Gomer: No.

Mr. Citerelli: And why not?

Gomer: Because you wouldn't keep asking the question over and over if you agreed with their answers.

Mr. Citerelli: What have you got to say about all this, Inez? Keep it going.

Inez: Once you've got the first number and the difference between them, the pattern is set. Jacelyn.

Jacelyn: But how do you determine when to cut off the sequence?

Mr. Citerelli: Eureka! Thank you! That's what I was waiting to hear. Write down the three variables that determine any example sequence. Quickly, right now, on the paper in front of you! Okay, what have you got, Gomer? Keep it going.

Gomer: The first number, the second number, and how many numbers. Inez.

Inez: Instead of the second number, it should be the difference between the numbers. Mavis.

Mavis: But if you know the first and second, you know the difference. So, it's the same thing.

Inez: Oh, okay.

Mr. Citerelli: But you don't have the floor. Summarize what Gomer, Inez, and Mavis concluded about sequences that fit our example, Linda.

Linda: All you need for these is the first number, the difference that's the same between numbers, and how many numbers.

Mr. Citerelli: And what was Mavis' point, Linda?

Linda: Oh, yea! You can figure the difference from the first two numbers. Yes, Jeannie.

Jeannie: Shouldn't we give these sequences a name?

Mr. Citerelli: Pick somebody to make up one for us.

Jeannie: I think Bill should. He did all the writing on the board.

Mr. Citerelli: Bill?

Bill: How about "addition sequences," since you add the same thing to go from one to the other.

Mr. Citerelli: I like that. So for now, let's call them addition sequences. Yes, what is it, Gomer?

Gomer: You said for now. That usually means there's already a name. What's the real name?

Mr. Citerelli: The real name is whatever we decide. But you'll find out there's a conventional name when you do your homework assignment from the text. Not now, don't get your books out yet! Let's get back to defining an addition sequence. As Linda said, we've got three determining variables: The first number, the difference between numbers, and the number of numbers.

Mr. Citerelli turns on the overhead projector; the students take the cue that they should be ready to take notes carefully. Mr. Citerelli uses the overhead projector to highlight what is said.

Mr. Citerelli: If we let a be the first member of an addition sequence, what will the second one be? Okay, J.J.

J.J.: a plus whatever the difference is.

Mr. Citerelli: Name that difference for us, Helen.

Helen: d.

Mr. Citerelli: So the second number is what, Mavis?

Mavis: a plus d.

Mr. Citerelli: And the third, Habebe?

Habebe: a plus d plus d.

Mr. Citerelli: Simplify Habebe's expression for us, Helen.

Helen: a plus $2d$.

Mr. Citerelli: And the fourth number, Inez?

Inez: a plus $3d$.

Mr. Citerelli: And the fifth number, Allan?

Allan: a plus $4d$.

Mr. Citerelli: And the nth number, Jacelyn?

Jacelyn: a plus $5d$.

Mr. Citerelli: And the n + first number, Linda?

Linda: Wait a minute! Jacelyn said a plus $5d$, but you didn't ask her for the sixth number, you asked her for the nth. So it's not necessarily a plus $5d$, because n could be anything.

Mr. Citerelli: Oh, that's my fault. I didn't define n, did I? Now, I can't even remember what I wanted it to be.

Quite a few students anxiously raise their hands to be recognized, but Mr. Citerelli just waves his hand and says, "Just a moment, let me reconstruct my thoughts before I forgot what I was doing. Let's see. . . ." The following is now displayed on the overhead projector screen:

1st	a
2nd	$a + d$
3rd	$a + 2d$
4th	$a + 3d$
5th	$a + 4d$
.	.
.	.
.	.
nth	$a + ??$

Mr. Citerelli: Oh, I remember now. I was getting tired of listing each one of these at a time, so I thought maybe we could just come up with a general nth term. So what is n now? Okay, Gomer.

Gomer: *n* is the one you want.

Mr. Citerelli: Okay. Do you want to put that another way, Linda?

Linda: *n* is the position of any number in the sequence. So the *n*th term is *a* plus *n* times *d*.

As Mr. Citerelli writes down *a* + *nd* in place of *a* + ??, at least 15 hands are raised as students are eager to correct the error.

Mr. Citerelli: Okay, what's wrong now? Jacelyn.

Jacelyn: It's not *nd*. It should be *n* minus 1 times *d*.

Mr. Citerelli: Is this what you mean?

The line on the screen now reads:

$$n\text{th} \qquad a + (n - 1)d$$

Jacelyn: Right.

Mr. Citerelli: But why?

Jacelyn: Look at the others. What you multiply *d* by is always one less than the position of the number.

Mr. Citerelli: Who agrees with Jacelyn? Everybody! Okay, we're about out of time. Here's the assignment that's due at the start of class tomorrow. Please use the rest of today's period to get started.

He distributes the sheet that appears in Exhibit 4.9.

The next day, Mr. Citerelli has Leon, Jeannie, James, Luis, and Candice write their definitions from Item I of the homework on the chalkboard:

Leon: An arithmetic sequence is one that has the same difference between any two numbers. The first number is *a*, the difference is *d*, and the last one is *n*.

Jeannie: A sequence is an addition sequence if and only if the first number is *a*, the next is *a* + *d*, the next *a* + 2*d*, the next *a* + 3*d*, and so on so; the *n*th number is *a* + (*n* − 1)*d*. (*d* can be positive or negative or zero.)

James: An arithmetic sequence, or arithmetic progression, is a sequence in which each term after the first is obtained by adding a constant *d* to the preceding term. In the sequence above, the common difference *d* is 5.

Luis: An addition sequence is one that has the same difference, *d*, between any two terms, like *a*, all the way to *n*.

Candice: Addition, or arithmetic, sequences, or progressions, are ones in which its *n*th term is *a* + (*n* − 1)*d*.

Exhibit 4.9

Mr. Citerelli's homework assignment after the first day of his conceptual lesson.

I. Using *a* to represent the first term, *d* for the common difference between consecutive members, and *n* for the number of terms, define what we called in class today an addition sequence (i.e., what your textbook calls an arithmetic sequence.)

II. Carefully read Section 13-2 beginning on pages 474−475 of your textbook. Be sure to familiarize yourself with the meanings of the following terms: arithmetic sequence, progression, common difference, and arithmetic means of two numbers. Add those terms and their definitions to the glossary in your note book.

III. For each of the following sequences, determine whether it is arithmetic or not. If it is, then solve for *a*, *d*, and *n* as according to your definition in I. If the sequence is not arithmetic, then prove that by illustrating that the difference between one pair of consecutive members does not equal the difference between some other pair of consecutive members.

A. $\sqrt{3}, -\sqrt{3}, -3\sqrt{3}, -5\sqrt{3}, -7\sqrt{3}$

B. −1, 0, −1, 0, −1, 0, −1, 0, −1, 0, −1, 0

C. 7.1 + π, 7.1 + 2π, 7.1 + 3π, . . . , 7.1 + 1000π

D. All whole numbers arranged in ascending order

E. All integers arranged in ascending order

F. The sequence of digits in the numeral π (i.e., 3, 1, 4, 1, 5, 9, 2, 6, 5, . . .)

G. The amount of money you spend each month beginning with January of last year

H. $f(1), f(2), f(3), f(4), \ldots$, where $f(x) = x^2 - 5$

I. $f(1), f(2), f(3), f(4), \ldots$, where $f(x) = x - 5$

J. The accumulated total, by inning, of outs the visiting team makes in one regular nine-inning baseball game

K. The accumulated total, by inning, of outs both teams make in a regular nine-inning baseball game

IV. Work the following exercises from page 476 of your text: 1, 7, 8, 9, 15, 19, 22.

Mr. Citerelli: Please spend the next 9 minutes comparing your definition to the ones on the board. Decide which ones, if any, are equivalent to yours. Which ones of these define an addition or arithmetic sequence as we described it yesterday? How about your own definition? Okay, you've got 8.5 minutes. . . .

Okay, time's up. Let's look at Leon's first. Read it for us, Eldon.

Eldon: An arithmetic sequence is one that has the same difference between any two numbers. The first number is *a*, the difference is *d*, and the last one is *n*.

Mr. Citerelli: What do you think about that one, Eldon? Keep it going.

Eldon: Well, it's not the same as mine, but it's the same idea. I think it's right. Okay, Jeannie.

Jeannie: But he's got *n* as a member of the sequence. *n* isn't in the sequence. It's . . .

Mark: Sure it is, it's the . . .

Jeannie: Hey, you don't have the floor; I didn't call on you! As I was saying, *n* is the place of any one member of the sequence, not the member itself. Okay, Mark.

Mark: What's the difference? The place is part of the sequence. Jeannie.

Jeannie: I'm going to ask you a question, Mark, but you've got to give me the floor right back. Okay? Which seat are you in right now in this row, Mark?

Mark: You can see I'm in the fourth. Jeannie.

Jeannie: Okay. Fourth is your place, but it's not *you*! Mark.

Mark: Okay, I see what you're saying. Uhh, Habebe.

Habebe: There's something else wrong with Leon's definition. It says *d* is the difference between *any* two numbers. Leon.

Leon: That's the whole idea of an arithmetic sequence; they've got the same difference between the members. Habebe.

Habebe: Here, let me show you.

Habebe writes the following on the board: 5, 10, 15, 20, 25, 30.

Habebe: Is this an arithmetic sequence? ... You agree, but the difference between 25 and 10 is 15 and the difference between 25 and 20 is 5. See, it's not the same between every two members. Leon.

Leon: You know what I mean. By the difference between two numbers, I mean numbers next to each other.

Mr. Citerelli: Excuse me. What adjective might Leon add to clear up this matter. Mavis. Keep it going.

Mavis: Next to? Linda.

Linda: Neighboring. J.J.

J.J.: That's what I was going to say. Okay, Habebe.

Habebe: I like consecutive. Leon.

Leon: So, if I said, 'An arithmetic sequence is one that has the same difference between *consecutive* numbers,' it would be all right?

Mr. Citerelli: Excuse me. Everybody locate their work for sequence B in item III on the homework. Take 45 seconds to examine that and then think about Leon's question. Is 'same difference between consecutive numbers' adequate for the definition? Okay, Inez, keep it going.

Inez: I said B wasn't arithmetic because to get from the first to the second, *d* must be 1, but from the second to the third, *d* must be − 1. It makes a difference which way you're going. I think it's easier to write the definition kind of like Jeannie's. Leon.

Leon: I'm going to change mine. Let's talk about somebody else's definition.

Mr. Citerelli: Okay, what about Jeannie's? Read it, Bill, and keep it going.

Bill: A sequence is an addition sequence if and only if the first number is *a*, the next is *a* + *d*, the next is *a* + 2*d*, the next *a* + 3*d*, and so on so; the *n*th number is *a* + (*n* − 1)*d*. *d* can be positive or negative or zero. Gomer.

Gomer: Do you have to say that last part? Isn't that understood as long as we know *d* is a number? Jeannie.

Jeannie: You're right. Just scratch that. Anybody else?

Mr. Citerelli: Nobody wants the floor to argue with Jeannie's definition? Okay, let's look at James'. Gomer, keep it going.

Gomer: He didn't use the *a*, *d*, and *n* like we were supposed to. Mark.

Mark: And what's that part about the common difference being 5? James.

James: I don't know. That's just what the book said.

Mr. Citerelli: If you're going to copy straight from the book, it would be a good idea to credit the authors. Jeannie?

Jeannie (looking in the book): I see where the difference-of-five business comes from; it's referring to an example that's not part of the definition.

Mr. Citerelli: I suggest we accept Jeannie's revised definition for an arithmetic sequence and move on. Yes, Mavis.

Mavis: Why 'revised'?

Mr. Citerelli: Oh! She deleted this part about *d* being positive, negative, or zero. Okay? Fine. Let's take a look at item III on the homework. Yes, Inez.

Inez: I was really confused by E.

Mr. Citerelli: Read it please.

Inez: All integers arranged in ascending order.

Mr. Citerelli: Write those on the board for us, Candice.

Candice writes: . . . , − 2, − 1, 0, 1, 2, ...

Mr. Citerelli: How many of you said that's arithmetic? And raise your hand if you said it wasn't. Interesting! Why did you call it arithmetic, Chico?

Chico: Because there's the same difference, *d*, between any two *consecutive* numbers.

Mr. Citerelli: Why did you say it isn't arithmetic, Sydna?

Sydna: Because it has no *a*. I couldn't solve for *a*. If it's an addition sequence, it's got to have an *a*.

Mr. Citerelli: Inez, you didn't raise your hand either way. Why not?

Inez: I agree with Sydna. Our definition says you've got to have a first member. The book's definition says 'first term.' But I also agree with Chico. You can't disprove its arithmetic by the way you told us. Any two consecutive numbers have the same difference. So what are we supposed to do?

Mr. Citerelli: Helen?

Helen: Let's just throw out that one. It's a bad item.

Mr. Citerelli: It may be a bad item, but I don't want to throw out that sequence. We have a decision to make. We must decide if we want to keep our current definition and restrict arithmetic sequences to those with a first member. Or we can modify the definition to include sequences that are *open* on the left side. Gomer?

Gomer: Which one is right?

Mr. Citerelli: According to our textbook, what's right? Jacelyn.

Jacelyn: You got to have a first member. And if that's the case, we've got to include that when we show a sequence isn't arithmetic.

Mr. Citerelli: Okay, keep that in mind. But before we decide, let me read you a definition from this book, the *CRC Standard Mathematical Tables* (Beyer 1987, 8): "An arithmetic progression is a sequence of numbers such that each number differs from the previous number by a constant amount, called the common difference". Now, it goes on to mention a first term, but it's not part of the definition. What do you think? Alysia.

Alysia: Let's stick with our textbook and Jeannie's definition and have a first member.

Mr. Citerelli: Raise your hand if you agree with Alysia. So be it. But remember that in another place, time, and textbook, it may be defined to include those without a first member.

Discussion of the homework continues.

Conceptualizing Relations

Necessary Conditions and Psychological Noise for Relations

As with conceptualizing concepts, lessons for conceptualizing relations require inductive activities involving the seven stages listed on pages 83–84. In the first stage, students confront problems to which the relation is relevant. As you select problems for stimulating inductive thinking, keep two ideas in mind.

Necessary Conditions for the Relation. A necessary condition for a relation is analogous to an attribute of a concept. For a relation to be relevant to the solution of a particular problem, certain conditions must exist within the context of that problem. Consider, for instance, the Pythagorean relation:

> The square of the length of the hypotenuse of a right triangle equals the sum of the squares of the lengths of its legs.

For the Pythagorean relation to be relevant to a problem, the solution must somehow be facilitated by finding the length of a side of a right triangle. Thus, one *necessary condition* for the Pythagorean relation is for the problem to involve a right triangle.

Psychological Noise in the Examples. Characteristics and circumstances of a problem to which a relation is relevant that are not necessary conditions comprise the psychological noise for that problem relative to that relation. Consider, for instance, the following problem:

> A store advertises that a television selling for $387.99 has a 25-inch screen. Actually, the height of the screen is approximately 15.5 inches and its width 19.5 inches. Is the advertisement truthful regarding the size of the screen?

Since finding the length of the side of a right triangle will help solve the problem, the Pythagorean relation is relevant to this problem. But features of the problem, such as the following, are *psychological noise* because they are not features of all problems to which the Pythagorean relation applies:

❑ A television is advertised for sale.
❑ The television sells for $387.99.
❑ Measurements of lengths are reported in inches.
❑ The lengths of the triangle's legs are 15.5 inches and 19.5 inches.
❑ The variable that needs to be found is a right triangle's hypotenuse, not one of its legs.

A Seven-Stage Lesson for Conceptualizing a Relation

In the following vignette, students discover a relation from their analysis of how they solved problems with a variety of psychological noise.

❑ VIGNETTE 4.9

In the 9 years Ms. Smith has been teaching mathematics, she's noticed that most students who learn about rate relations in one context (e.g., simple interest on savings = $p \cdot r \cdot t$) do not recognize rate relations in other contexts (e.g., distance = $r \cdot t$). Thus, when she planned the seventh-grade mathematics course she's currently teaching, she decided to attempt a unit on general rate relations rather than treating interest rates on savings, rates of travel, interest on loan rates, discount rates, and other types of rate problems separately.

Now, she's in the process of designing the learning activities for the first objective of that unit; the objective is:

> Explains why the accumulative effect of the application of a rate per unit over an observed frequency of that unit is given by the product of the rate and the frequency (conceptualization).

She thinks: "It was really tough for me to put the relation that's the content of this objective into words. But I know what I mean. It's the general relation that includes distance formulas, interest rate formulas, rate pricing formulas, and anything else that's so much per unit. The learning level is conceptualization, so I need inductive learning activities, beginning with one where they have to work through sample problems without benefit of knowing the relation ahead of time.

"I think I'll begin with them in small task groups, each working on a different problem with different psychological noise. Maybe I can assign the problems according to their own personal interests. After 7 weeks with these people, I know most of them pretty well. Okay, I'll begin with a list of different types of problems to which rate relations are applicable. Let's see, there's distance when traveling, and bank interest . . . savings and loans. Then there are mark-ups and discounts at stores. Oh, yeah! Sales commission is another. But except for the distance ones, these all have something to do with money. I need more variety or else they'll always think of rates as either on money or for distance. I also need to make these germane to their own lives. The savings interest is more relevant to them today than bank loans. What kinds of problems does the text have? . . . They're scattered throughout, but not many will tease my students' interests. . . . Some of these I can modify for them.

"I should do this systematically and start with a list of areas from which to draw the problems. Distance is one for sure and one on interest on savings. How about one for the sports fans in the class—commissions for sports agents would be good. Oh, that reminds me! Rachael was discussing selling greeting cards for one of those mail-order firms. How does that work? They get so many prizes for selling so many dollars worth of cards. That's like a commission. Maybe that could produce a problem for Rachael and a couple of others to work on."

With further thought, Ms. Smith develops the following list of problem areas:

1. Distance in traveling
2. Interest on savings
3. Interest on borrowing
4. Commissions for celebrities' agents
5. Prizes for selling (e.g., mail-order greeting cards)
6. Discounts at stores
7. Cooking/diet-related rates
8. Prize-winning rates on radio giveaway shows
9. Bonus gifts for purchases (e.g., a number of free music tapes based on number purchased)
10. Physical fitness or growth (e.g., percent body fat, rate of improvement in weight lifting, growth rate, etc.)
11. Sports performance rates (e.g., percent of foul shots, batting averages, etc.)

Looking over the list she thinks: "How many problems do I actually need? Each task group should have at least three people and no more than five. With 31 in the class, that means eight groups, so eight problems.... Well, a traveling distance problem is practically mandatory, since I'm expected to cover that and they'll be tested on rate times time equal distance on the standardized tests. So,..." After formulating the travel problem, she thinks: "Interest problems are also mandatory."

After developing two interest problems, she continues: "Five more to go. Some of the students might have had and even remember distance and bank interest formulas from fifth or sixth grade. It'd be too bad if they just recall the formulas rather than discover them for themselves. But none of them will have pat formulas for any of these other areas. So, I'll make sure to assign kids who are likely to recall the formulas to the other areas. Oh! Now that I think about it, it wouldn't be so bad if one or two of the groups recalled a formula and then we could compare it to how the other problems are solved. That way we could illustrate that all the solutions are based on the same relations.... Oh, another idea! When I assign the task, I'll require each group to diagram just what's happening. That way, it'll be easier for them to pick up a common pattern when we get into third- and fourth-stage activities. I'd better try that out for one of these I've already developed. The distance problem says:

> Ron misses his bus one morning and has 25 minutes to walk the 4 miles to school. Will he make it on time if he covers 0.15 miles each minute?

"How would they probably diagram that? Let's see . . . ." She illustrates a solution with the diagram in Exhibit 4.10.

She then develops a problem for the "prizes for greeting cards" category and draws a diagram (see Exhibit

Exhibit 4.10
Diagram illustrating Ms. Smith's students' solution to Ron's walking-to-school problem.

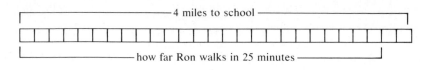

$$0.15 + 0.15 + 0.15 + 0.15 + 0.15 + 0.15 + 0.15 + 0.15 + 0.15 + 0.15 + 0.15$$
$$+ 0.15 + 0.15 + 0.15 + 0.15 + 0.15 + 0.15 + 0.15 + 0.15 + 0.15 + 0.15 +$$
$$0.15 + 0.15 + 0.15 + 0.15 = 3.75, \text{ just short of 4 miles}$$

Exhibit 4.11
Diagram illustrating Ms. Smith's students' solution to Mary's selling-greeting-cards problem.

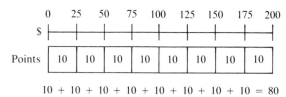

$$10 + 10 + 10 + 10 + 10 + 10 + 10 + 10 = 80$$

4.11) she expects is similar to the one Rachael and others would use to illustrate their solution:

> For every $25 worth of greeting cards Mary sells for a mail-order company, she receives 10 points toward prizes from their catalog. For example, it takes 30 points to get a pen-and-pencil set and 150 points to get an audiocassette player/recorder. How many points would Mary get for selling $200 worth of greeting cards?

Convinced that the solutions to the problem will all produce comparable diagrams, Ms. Smith continues working until her list of problems for the initial learning activities is as follows:

1. Ron misses his bus one morning and has 25 minutes to walk the 4 miles to school. Will he make it on time if he covers 0.15 miles each minute?
2. City Bank is now paying 4¢ for each dollar that remains in a savings account for a whole year. How much interest will Lois make by leaving $60 in a City Bank savings account for a year?
3. Ernie asks Sally, "Would you lend me $15?" Sally: "Why should I?" Ernie: "Because I need to pick up my bike that's being fixed." Sally: "No, I mean what's in it for me?" Ernie: "I'll pay you back in a month when I get paid for my paper route. But until I get my bike I can't work." Sally: "You still haven't given me a good reason for lending it to you." Ernie: "Okay! I'll give you a nickel more on the dollar." Sally: "Make it a dime on the dollar for each week until you pay, and you've got a deal." If Ernie accepts the deal, how much more than $15 will he owe Sally if he waits 4 weeks to pay her back?

4. For every $25 worth of greeting cards Mary sells for a mail-order company, she receives 10 points toward prizes from their catalog. For example, it takes 30 points to get a pen-and-pencil set and 150 points to get an audiocassette player/recorder. How many points would Mary get for selling $200 worth of greeting cards?
5. Mau-Lin wants to buy clothes at a store that will cost her $45 today. However, she knows that in a week the store will have a sale marking everything down by 20%. How much will she save by waiting a week to purchase the clothes?
6. Lucy Davis is an agent for professional athletes. For her services negotiating their contracts, she is paid 5¢ for every dollar her clients earn from those contracts. How much will Lucy earn from a $125,000 contract?
7. A mail-order company that sells compact discs advertises that for every 12 discs purchased, a customer may select a free disc. How many discs would a customer need to purchase to receive 7 free discs?
8. Every school day, Woody eats a Whiz-O candy bar at lunch. Each Whiz-O contains 312 calories. How many calories does this habit add to Woody's diet during nine weeks of school?

Pleased with the eight problems, Ms. Smith thinks: "That takes care of the most difficult part of designing this lesson. Now, to match students to the problems—I'd better see that the less motivated ones are assigned something with which they can identify. Also, there should be at least one energetic thinker in each group. Okay, Rachael goes to group and problem 4. She's bound to be interested in the greeting cards. Bart and Pete should be in separate groups, they get goofy together. Bart to group 1 and Pete to 2. Let's see, Patrice should. . . ."

With the groups of three or four each assigned, Ms. Smith prepares to organize and manage the small-group activity efficiently by preparing a direction sheet for each of the 31 students that contains the following:

1. Instructions on how to locate the other members of the task group using a mathematical expression on the card.
2. The mathematical expression (e.g., the sum of the multiplicative inverses 1, 2, 3, and 4)
3. The number of people in the task group to which the student is to join (three or four)

Exhibit 4.12
Direction sheet for one of Ms. Smith's students.

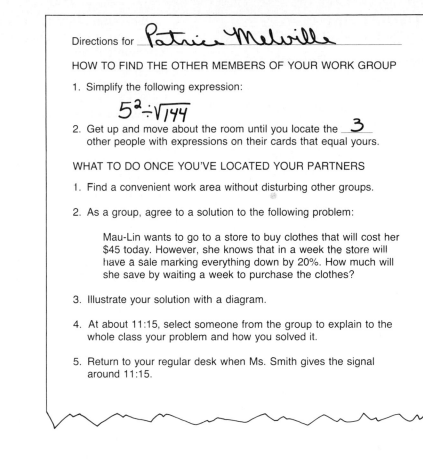

Directions for *Patrice Melville*

HOW TO FIND THE OTHER MEMBERS OF YOUR WORK GROUP

1. Simplify the following expression:

$$5^2 \div \sqrt{144}$$

2. Get up and move about the room until you locate the __3__ other people with expressions on their cards that equal yours.

WHAT TO DO ONCE YOU'VE LOCATED YOUR PARTNERS

1. Find a convenient work area without disturbing other groups.

2. As a group, agree to a solution to the following problem:

   Mau-Lin wants to go to a store to buy clothes that will cost her $45 today. However, she knows that in a week the store will have a sale marking everything down by 20%. How much will she save by waiting a week to purchase the clothes?

3. Illustrate your solution with a diagram.

4. At about 11:15, select someone from the group to explain to the whole class your problem and how you solved it.

5. Return to your regular desk when Ms. Smith gives the signal around 11:15.

4. Instructions on what the task group is to do (one of the eight problems is stated, along with what the group is to accomplish relative to the problem)

Exhibit 4.12 displays one of the 31 direction sheets.

Just before the students enter her classroom for the hour in which she plans to begin the unit and teach to the conceptual objective on rate relations, Ms. Smith tapes each student's sheet under his or her desktop. Initially, the students are not aware the sheets are there.

The students are seated at their regular places when Ms. Smith begins the activity with these directions: "For the next 15 or so minutes we will be working in three- or four-member task groups. Directions for locating your partners and the task your group is to complete are attached to the underside of your desktop. Please find the sheets now and begin following the directions."

As Ms. Smith walks about the room monitoring behavior, the students quickly locate their partners and within minutes are on-task working out solutions to the problems. At 11:13, Ms. Smith calls for the first of the eight reports to the class.

Explanations of solutions for the first four problems (those involving Ron's rate of walking, City Bank's interest rate, Sally's interest rate, and point rate for selling greeting cards) produce diagrams and repeated addition procedures similar to Exhibits 4.10 and 4.11. Group 5 (the ones solving Mau-Lin's discount rate problem) simply multiplies 45 by 0.20 for their answer, but Ms. Smith directs them to illustrate the multiplication with a diagram.

Group 6 fails to solve the sports agent rate problem. They complain that they "couldn't add something 125,000 times." Other students ask, "Why didn't you just multiply?" Group 7 simply multiplies 12 by 7 but also illustrates their logic with a diagram similar to Exhibit 4.11. Much as the first four groups, Group 8 uses repeated addition and a diagram in its solution.

In the ensuing discussion, similarities among the solutions to the eight problems are pointed out by different students responding to Ms. Smith's probing questions (e.g., "Why did Group 6 want to add five 125,000 times instead of 125,000 five times?"). However, before a generalization is formalized by the class, Ms. Smith halts the activity and directs everyone to make a copy of each group's illustration and computations. As part of the homework assignment, each student is to develop a formula for solving these types of rate problems.

The following day, students' formulas are reported and discussed and the class agrees to a "multiplication rule" for computing the accumulative effects of a rate applied to a frequency. Ms. Smith engages the class in a verification activity in which students apply their formula to additional problems and then develop a proof based on multiplication being repeated addition.

_____

LEARNING ACTIVITIES FOR SIMPLE-KNOWLEDGE-LEVEL OBJECTIVES
Facilitating Reception and Retention through Direct Instruction

Students achieve conceptualization objectives by making decisions about information (e.g., classifying it or identifying patterns in procedures for acquiring information). On the other hand, students achieve simple knowledge objectives by accurately *receiving* and *retaining* information. Reception and retention is accomplished through a five-stage *direct instruction* process that includes:

1. Exposition
2. Explication
3. Mnemonics
4. Monitoring and Feedback
5. Overlearning

Exposition
Students are exposed to the content they are to remember. Consider the following example.

❑ VIGNETTE 4.10
Ms. Corbridge's students have already conceptualized Fibonacci sequences. Now she wants them to achieve the following objective:

Defines "Fibonacci number" (*simple knowledge).*

As part of a homework assignment, she directs the students to copy the definition of Fibonacci numbers from page 301 of their texts and into the glossary they maintain in their notebooks. The next day, she displays the definition on the overhead screen, reads it, and asks them to check the accuracy of the copies in their glossaries.

Explication
The students are provided with an explanation as to just how they are to respond to the content's stimulus. For example, Ms. Corbridge tells her students, "Anytime you see or hear the words 'Fibonacci number,' you are to think, 'a member of the infinite sequence whose first two terms are both 1 and whose subsequent terms are the sum of the previous two: 1, 1, 2, 3, 5, 8, and so forth.' Also, anytime you see that sequence, think 'Fibonacci.' "

Mnemonics
Mnemonic is a word derived from *Mnemosyne,* the name of the ancient Greek goddess of memory. The word means *aiding the memory* (Bourne et al. 1986, 98).

For some, but not all, simple-knowledge objectives, you might consider providing students with mnemonic devices to enhance retention. Mnemonic devices have proven to be effective in helping students remember *new* information (Joyce and Weil 1986, 89–96). I, for example, informed you about the derivation of mnemonic as an aid to helping you remember the definition. Thus, I gave you a mnemonic aid. However, unless you are already familiar with the goddess Mnemosyne, my mnemonic device is not likely to be very effective. The most effective mnemonic devices link the new information to be remembered to something already familiar to the student. For example,

❑ To help students remember that whole numbers refer to {0, 1, 2, . . .}, whereas counting numbers refer to {1, 2, 3, . . .}, a teacher says, "The set of whole numbers is the one with the *hole* in it. The hole is the zero."

❑ If Ms. Corbridge related the history of Fibonacci numbers with her conceptual-level lesson on Fibonacci sequences, she probably needs no mnemonic devices to help her students to remember the meaning of Fibonacci numbers. However, if the students have yet to associate the sequence with Leonardo Fibonacci, then she might consider a mnemonic gimmick to help them remember. For example, she could tell her students, "The word Fibonacci reminds me of 'fibbed on arithmetic' because Fibonacci sequences are sort of like arithmetic sequences, since you have to add to find the next member. But they're not arithmetic because you don't keep adding the same number."

Usually, it isn't necessary to use mnemonics for remembering formulas based on relations that students already conceptualize. Mnemonic devices are more helpful for recalling conventions that are not the logical result of a familiar relation.

Monitoring and Feedback
The accuracy with which students recall what they are supposed to have memorized is tested and monitored. Correct responses are positively reinforced and errors corrected. Consider the next vignette.

❑ VIGNETTE 4.11
Matt asks Ms. Corbridge, "Is 300 one of those kinds of numbers?" Ms. Corbridge: "What kind of numbers?" Matt: "You know, the kind you were talking about." Ms. Corbridge: "What's the name?" Matt: "You know, Fibba-something." Ms. Corbridge: "What's Matt talking about, Riley?" Riley: "Fibonacci numbers." Ms. Corbridge: "Oh!

Thank you, Riley. Fibonacci numbers! Repeat your question using the words Fibonacci numbers.''

Overlearning

Students *overlearn* by continuing to practice recalling content even after they have memorized it. Overlearning increases resistance to forgetting and facilitates long-term retention of information (Chance 1988, 221–222). For example, even after the completion of the unit in which she introduced the Fibonacci sequence, Ms. Corbridge continues to confront students with tasks requiring them to use their knowledge of the meaning of Fibonacci numbers.

A Five-Stage Lesson for a Simple-Knowledge Objective

In the following vignette, a teacher plans learning activities to include the five stages leading to simple-knowledge-level learning.

❏ **VIGNETTE 4.12**

Ms. O'Connell designs the learning activities for the following objective:

States the definitions of the six trigonometric functions (*simple knowledge*).

She thinks: ''This lesson follows the conceptual-level one on the relation between the size of one of the acute angles of a right triangle and the relative lengths of the triangle's legs. So, I hope they'll already understand how the value of angle θ affects the ratio of one side to another.'' She draws and muses over the following:

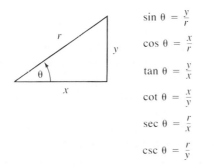

$$\sin \theta = \frac{y}{r}$$
$$\cos \theta = \frac{x}{r}$$
$$\tan \theta = \frac{y}{x}$$
$$\cot \theta = \frac{x}{y}$$
$$\sec \theta = \frac{r}{x}$$
$$\csc \theta = \frac{r}{y}$$

She thinks: ''So all we really need to do here is to get them to associate these six names with the right ratios. How can I help them keep the names straight? They're familiar with tangents and secants relative to circles. So, maybe I could show them these ratios and show how y/x is associated with tangent and r/x with secant. . . . Hmmm, then I'd have to get into circular functions and they're not ready for that yet. Besides it would take more time than I

care to spend just so they'll see some logic behind the names. On the other hand, if we took the trouble to do that, I bet they'd never forget the names that go with the ratios. No, I need to remember this is to be a simple-knowledge lesson and just give them straightforward, direct instruction. I'll just tell them the names, sine θ is *y* over *r*, cosine θ is *x* over *r*, and so forth. . . . Oh, no! That's not the terminology they need to know at this point. We've worked only with right triangles independent of coordinate planes and circles to this point. So I'd better use these.''

She modifies her notes to read:

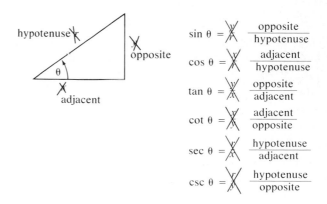

She continues: ''That's better, and I think that's the way the book starts off too. Better check that. . . . Yep, that's good; I'm in line with the book.

''Okay, so the first thing I'll do is write each function on the overhead and—No, here's a better idea! I start by having them list all six possible ratios. That way they'll automatically know the right side of all these equations as permutations of three sides taken two at a time. It'll serve as a mnemonic. Then after they've listed them, I'll start naming them—getting them to write each out and saying it aloud. Might as well expose this stuff to as many of their senses as we can. I'd get them to smell these relations if I could. Hmm, actually I could appeal to their sense of touch with some concrete models of each function. . . . Not a bad idea! I'm not taking that trouble this time, but maybe with another class.

''Oh! Also, I've got to make sure they get the abbreviations down. Better include those right from the start. Okay, so I get all the functions listed and names and abbreviations for them. Then to explain just what they're to remember—they've got to respond with the right name to a ratio and also respond with the ratio for a name. I'll explain that to them and test them both ways. . . .

''I wish I could think of some good mnemonics for these. I ought to check with Frank; he's taught this for years. I'll bet he's come up with some effective gimmicks. . . . Hmm, how did I ever remember these? My teachers never used mnemonics, but I never forgot. Let's see . . . I remember! The sine and cosine have the hypotenuse in the denominator, and the sine has opposite for the numerator, so there's nothing left but adjacent for cosine's numerator. Tangent and cotangent are the ones without the hypotenuse and the numerators follow the same order as sine and cosine, opposite for the function and adjacent for the cofunction. I used to remember that cosecant is the reciprocal of sine and secant is the reciprocal of cosine. I wonder if sharing that with them would work as a mnemonic? Maybe it would be better to leave them to their own devices. . . . I don't know. . . . Think I won't tell this class and see what they come up with. In fourth period, I'll tell them and see if they have an easier time remembering.

"Memorization and practice for homework, along with some computational practice, and then a quick quiz first thing the next day. We'll go over the quiz right away and correct errors. Overlearning shouldn't be difficult; they'll be using the names with these ratios for the rest of the unit as well as for the next three units. If they get these correct now, there's no way I'll let them forget them before the summer."

LEARNING ACTIVITIES FOR COMPREHENSION-LEVEL OBJECTIVES

By engaging students in learning activities that lead them to comprehend mathematical communications, you obviate one of the more mystifying aspects of mathematics, namely, negotiating its language. Comprehension-level lessons provide students with systematic strategies for understanding mathematical *messages* and acquiring meaning from *communication modes* that are conventional in mathematics.

Comprehension of a Particular Message

Literal and Interpretive Understanding
Lessons for comprehension of particular messages should be concerned with two stages of understanding.

Literal Understanding. Students literally understand a message if they can accurately translate its explicit meaning. For example, Cathy examines the following definition of the absolute value of a real number:

$$|x| = x \text{ iff } x \geq 0 \quad \text{and} \quad |x| = -x \text{ iff } x \leq 0$$

She then displays *literal understanding* of the definition by formulating the following explanation: "The absolute value of a number is the number itself if and only if the number is positive or zero. The absolute value of a number is its opposite if and only if the number is negative or zero."

Interpretive Understanding. Students understand a message at an interpretive level if they can infer implicit meaning and explain how aspects of the communication are used to convey the message. For example, Cathy examines the following definition of absolute value of a real number:

$$|x| = x \text{ iff } x \geq 0 \quad \text{and} \quad |x| = -x \text{ iff } x \leq 0$$

She then displays *interpretive understanding* of the definition by extending her previous explanation with the following: "This means that the absolute value of any number is nonnegative. The absolute value of 10, for instance, is just 10 because, as the definition says, the absolute value of a positive number is the number itself. But for -10, the absolute value is its negative and the negative of a negative is positive, so the absolute value of -10 is 10. Zero doesn't have an opposite, so, when they wrote the definition, they included it in both cases."

Designing Learning Activities for Literal Understanding
Interpretive understanding depends on literal understanding. Thus, the initial phase of your lesson should promote literal understanding. To design the learning activities, you will need to analyze the message to be comprehended, identifying the requirements of students regarding the following.

Vocabulary. What general, special, and technical terms will they need to understand in order to translate the message? Meanings of words and expressions are learned through simple-knowledge-level lessons. Are there any prerequisite simple-knowledge-level objectives that should be achieved before students are ready for the comprehension-level activities?

Symbol Meanings. What shorthand symbols used in communicating the message will students need to be able to translate? In the previous example, Cathy translated the symbols $|x|$, iff, $\geq$, and $\leq$.

Concepts. What concepts does the author of the message assume the students have conceptualized prior to receiving the communications? In the previous example, Cathy's understanding of the definition depended on her prior conceptualization of nonnegative numbers.

Relations. What relations does the author of the message assume the students have conceptualized prior to receiving the communications? In the previous example, Cathy's understanding of the definition depended on her prior conceptualization of the following relation: A real number and its opposite are equidistant from zero.

Communication Modes. What conventional mathematical modes of communication are used to convey the message that students need to be able to comprehend? Cathy's explanation in the previous example suggests that she understands how to read mathematical definitions. She seems to understand that "if and only if" serves as a two-way implication. Comprehending a definition requires specialized skills, as does comprehending proofs, word problems, graphs, and other types of communications modes.

Once these five prerequisites are achieved, *literal* understanding of a message is effected through *direct instruction* in which the following occur:

1. *The message is sent to the students* (e.g., the definition of absolute value is stated orally and in writing).
2. *The message is rephrased and explained* (e.g., "the absolute value of a number is the difference between the number and zero, but without concern for whether the number itself is greater than or less than zero").
3. *Students are questioned about specifics in the message* (e.g., "Is negative *x* in this second case a positive or negative number?").
4. *Students are provided with feedback on their responses to the aforementioned questions.* (e.g., "I agree that the absolute value of a number can never be negative, but for this case negative *x* is a positive number").

Designing Activities for Interpretive Understanding

Interpretive understanding of a message is achieved with learning activities that utilize more inquiry and open-ended questions and discussions than the direct instruction for literal understanding. Students are stimulated to examine the message, extracting its main idea, data base or facts, assumptions, and conclusions.

A Lesson for Comprehension of a Particular Message

In the following example, note how Mr. Matsumoto shifts from direct instructional activities during the literal understanding phase to activities in which students generate ideas during the phase for interpretive understanding.

❑ **VIGNETTE 4.13**

As part of a unit on aspects of number theory, Mr. Matsumoto would like for his students to *conceptualize* the following relation:

$$\sqrt{2} \notin \{\text{rationals}\}$$

However, he realizes that such an objective is a bit ambitious for this class, so he settles for helping them to comprehend a classic proof for why $\sqrt{2}$ is not rational. Thus, his unit includes this objective:

Explains the classic proof by contradiction (using the supposition of $\sqrt{2} = p/q$, where $(p, q) = 1$) of the theorem:

$$\sqrt{2} \notin \{\text{rationals}\}$$

(*comprehension*).

He thinks, as he designs the lesson for the objective: "I'd better recreate this proof for myself to make sure I thoroughly understand it."

He writes out the proof as shown in Exhibit 4.13.

Looking over his work, he thinks: "That's a nice proof; there's a lot going on for them to understand. It's really too gimmicky for them to conceptualize the theorem from it, but they'll gain a lot just from comprehending the argument.

"I've got to present this to them. I'll write it on the overhead as I explain the logic behind each step. But first, I'd better decide on the form for the presentation. This version [Exhibit 4.13] is too full of symbols for them. I'll go through my checklist of prerequisites for literal comprehension first. . . . Okay, *vocabulary:* They already know rationals, integers, irrationals, relatively prime—but not that symbol [$(p, q) = 1$]; I'll write it out for them. Okay, they also know the definitions for even and odd; there's no new vocabulary here.

"Now, for *symbols:* I already said I should write out *p* and *q* are relatively prime for $(p, q) = 1$. Let's see . . . all the set symbols are familiar to them and so is the implies symbol [$\Rightarrow$]; I can leave those. Such that [∍] and there exist [∃] have to go. And I'd better write out the names of the sets or else Jim and Blaine will be distracted.

"*Concepts:* Let's see . . . the only concept here they lack is the big one, *irrational numbers.* They know the definition, but most haven't conceptualized the set. This lesson won't lead to conceptualization, but it's a step in that direction. . . . There's no lesson for prerequisite concepts needed.

"*Relations:* Oh, oh! They comprehend the definition of rational numbers, but the fact that a rational can be ex-

Exhibit 4.13
Mr. Matsumoto's proof as he
originally wrote it.

To prove $\sqrt{2} \notin \{\text{rationals}\}$:

Suppose $\sqrt{2} \in \{\text{rational}\}$

$\sqrt{2} \in \{\text{rationals}\} \Rightarrow \exists \, p, q \in \{\text{integers}\} \ni (p, q) = 1$ and $\sqrt{2} = \frac{p}{q}$.

$\sqrt{2} = \frac{p}{q} \Rightarrow 2 = \frac{p^2}{q^2} \Rightarrow 2q^2 = p^2$. Thus, $p^2 \in \{\text{evens}\}$.

Lemma:
  To prove $a^2 \in \{\text{evens}\} \Rightarrow a \in \{\text{evens}\}$.
  Proof: Suppose $a \notin \{\text{evens}\}$
    $a \notin \{\text{evens}\} \Rightarrow a \in \{\text{odds}\} \Rightarrow \exists \, i \in \{\text{integers}\} \ni a = 2i+1$.
    $a = 2i+1 \Rightarrow a^2 = 4i^2 + 4i + 1 \Rightarrow a^2 = 2(2i^2 + 2i) + 1 \Rightarrow a^2 \in \{\text{odds}\}$
    But $a^2 \in \{\text{evens}\}$ $\otimes$
    $\therefore a \notin \{\text{odds}\} \Rightarrow a \in \{\text{evens}\}$.

Thus, $p^2 \in \{\text{evens}\} \Rightarrow p \in \{\text{evens}\}$.

$p \in \{\text{evens}\} \Rightarrow \exists \, j \in \{\text{integers}\} \ni p = 2j$.

$\therefore 2q^2 = p^2 \Rightarrow 2q^2 = (2j)^2 \Rightarrow 2q^2 = 4j^2 \Rightarrow q^2 = 2j^2 \Rightarrow q^2 \in \{\text{evens}\}$.

$q^2 \in \{\text{evens}\} \Rightarrow q \in \{\text{evens}\}$

$\therefore q, p \in \{\text{evens}\}$

But $(p, q) = 1$ $\otimes$

$\therefore \sqrt{2} \notin \{\text{rationals}\}$.

pressed as the ratio of *relatively prime* integers is something that most of them haven't really internalized. So, I need to precede this lesson with a conceptual one on the relation $[x \in \{\text{rationals}\} \Rightarrow \exists \, p, q \in \{\text{integers}\} \ni (p, q) = 1$ and $x = \frac{p}{q}]$. That shouldn't be very difficult because, it's just a matter of combining two relations they've already conceptualized. . . . Okay, the other relation is the one proved by the lemma. I'd better do a conceptual lesson on that also. In fact, I ought to prove the lemma ahead of time, so we don't have to confuse this proof with that one. That'll make this proof easier for them to follow. So, I've got two conceptual lessons and one comprehension-of-a-proof lesson to conduct before this one!

"*Communication modes:* We're okay here. They're familiar with these paragraph-type proofs, as well as proofs by contradiction. Getting the lemma out of there will simplify things also."

After planning and conducting lessons for the following three prerequisite objectives, Mr. Matsumoto is ready for the comprehension lesson:

1. Explains why any rational number can be expressed as the ratio of two relatively prime integers (*conceptualization*).
2. Explains why if the square of an integer is even, then so is the integer (*conceptualization*).
3. Explains a proof of the following theorem:
   $k^2 \in \{\text{evens}\} \Rightarrow k \in \{\text{evens}\}$ (*comprehension*).

He begins the literal-understanding phase of the lesson by telling the students that they will be examining a classic proof and their job is to understand it well enough to explain why it's a valid proof. Having informed them of that objective, he directs them to copy the proof as he presents it step by step and to raise any questions to clarify the meaning of any step.

After presenting the proof and responding to students' questions, Mr. Matsumoto summarizes the argument and then queries students with exchanges such as the following:

Mr. Matsumoto: How could the author of this proof make this statement, right here, that radical-2 equals *p* over *q*, Wendy?

Wendy: There's a *p* and *q* like that for any rational number. We showed that yesterday.

Mr. Matsumoto: Thank you. How did we get from $a = 2i + 1$ to $a^2 = 4i^2 + 4i + 1$, right here, Nadine?

Nadine: You just square both sides of the equation, and that's what you get.

Mr. Matsumoto: What does this encircled *X* mean right here, Jake?

Jake: That means you did something wrong?

Mr. Matsumoto: What do you mean, wrong, Jake?

Jake: There's a mistake that you've got to do over.

Mr. Matsumoto: Actually, this indicates a point where we made a statement that contradicts an earlier statement. That's different from being wrong; it's . . . .

After completing this activity in which students are given feedback on their responses to Mr. Matsumoto's questions about the meaning of different aspects of the proof, Mr. Matsumoto begins raising more open-ended questions to elicit more in-depth ideas students might have about the proof. He begins this interpretive phase of the lesson with the following:

Mr. Matsumoto: I'd like for everyone to take 6 silent minutes to outline on a sheet of paper the main ideas of this proof. Use brief phrases for headings and sub-headings that illustrate the logic of the argument. Okay, go.

He walks around the room, monitoring the work and selecting papers for the class to discuss. At the end of the 6 minutes he asks several students to put their outlines on the board. Included is Adam's, which appears in Exhibit 4.14.

Mr. Matsumoto: I really like the way Adam listed each climactic point in the proof, I through VII. Yes, Chen?

Chen: What does that word cli-whatever mean?

Mr. Matsumoto: Climactic. Look at what Adam has pulled from the proof. He didn't list, for example, this step here where we go from radical-2 equals p over q to 2 equals p-squared over q-squared. But he did list p is even. Why, Chen, do you think he listed one but not the other?

Chen: Because just squaring both sides of that equation is just a step leading to something. But p is even is something we are trying to show.

Mr. Matsumoto: I agree. What do we call a part of a story when something comes together at the end? It sounds sort of like climactic. Grace?

Grace: Climax.

Mr. Matsumoto: The things Adam listed are climax points of the proof leading to the big conclusion in what he calls VII. Okay, Julio.

Julio: Proofs aren't stories.

Mr. Matsumoto: Anybody want to debate Julio's point? Okay, Grace.

Grace: Sure proofs are stories. They tell the story of why something is true. Like showing that the square of 2 is irrational.

Julio: You mean the square *root* of 2 is irrational!

Grace: Right, what did I say?

Mr. Matsumoto: You said square, even though you meant square root. But there's something else I want to pick on that Grace said. She said we proved the square root of 2 is *irrational*. Is that what we proved, Johnny?

Johnny: Yep, that's right.

Mr. Matsumoto: Irrational, or just not rational? Nettie.

Nettie: It's the same thing. If a number is not rational, then it's irrational.

Mr. Matsumoto: Adam?

Adam: That's true *if* we know the number is real. We never proved that radical-2 is real, so we didn't prove it's irrational, just not rational.

The discussion about the proof continues for another 12 minutes and then Mr. Matsumoto moves on to another objective.

Comprehension of a Communications Mode

Mathematical language contains specialized communications with conventions that students need to understand before comprehending messages via those modes. For example,

Exhibit 4.14
Adam's outline of the proof that $\sqrt{2} \notin$ {rationals}.

Want: To show that $\sqrt{2}$ is not rational

I. Assume $\sqrt{2}$ is rational

II. So $\sqrt{2} = \frac{p}{q}$ so that p and q are relatively prime

III. p is even

IV. q is even

V. III and IV contradict II

VI. So I is false

VII. Conclusion: $\sqrt{2}$ is not rational

❑ Ruth understands the common logic structure of mathematical definitions. Thus, when she confronts the definition of convex set for the first time, she knows to look for features common to all convex sets that other sets do not have. Her understanding of definitions in general serves as an advanced organizer for comprehending unfamiliar definitions.

❑ Exhibit 4.15 contains the graphs of scores of two classes of students who took the same history test. From just glancing at it, Edwin reads graphs of real functions in Cartesian planes well enough to note that

1. As a group, the second-period class scored higher on the test than the first-period class because points on the second-period's graph tend to be farther to the right.
2. The two classes contain approximately the same number of students because the areas under the curves are about the same.
3. The first-period scores are more homogenous than the second-period scores because the scores for the first period are "piled up" and clustered together, whereas the second period scores are spread farther out.

A lesson for a comprehension of a communications mode should include learning activities that (1) use direct teaching methods to inform students about the special conventions of the mode and (2) use inquiry methods for helping students develop

Exhibit 4.15
Graphs of history test scores from two classes.

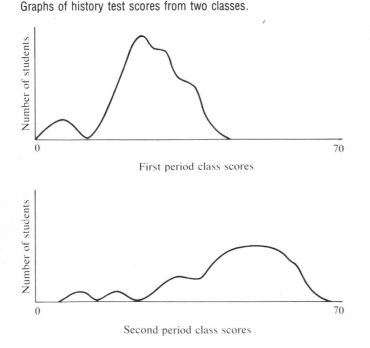

strategies for using that mode. Consider the next vignette.

❑ **VIGNETTE 4.14**

Ms. McGiver has planned her prealgebra course so that students confront textbook word problems in every unit. However, after the first two units, she realizes that students are experiencing difficulty solving word problems, not necessarily because they don't understand the particular mathematics applicable to the problem but because they have never developed strategies for solving word problems in general. Thus, she decides to insert a special unit designed to teach general strategies for solving any kind of word problem. Her first objective is to get them to *comprehend* problems as typically presented in textbooks. She states the objective as follows:

> From reading a textbook word problem, (a) identifies the question posed by the problem, (b) clarifies the question in his or her own words, (c) specifies the variable to be solved, and (d) lists facts or data provided in the statement of the problem (*comprehension*).

Ms. McGiver begins her lesson by displaying the following word problem with the instructions, "Just read this carefully without trying to solve it."

> Tom is on a television quiz show. He scores 5 points by correctly answering his first quiz show question. He then misses the second question and loses 10 points. What is his score after the two questions?

Ms. McGiver knows that everyone in the class can readily solve that problem. So, she's not surprised to hear some students blurt, "Aw, that's easy! It's −5." But rather than accept their solutions she insists they follow her directions:

Ms. McGiver: Now, that you've read the problem, I want you to copy down and answer these questions:

She displays the following:

1. Solving this problem answers what question?
2. What *variable* does answering the question require you to find?
3. What information are you given with which to work?

After several minutes, she begins a discussion.

Ms. McGiver: How did you answer the first question, Stephanie?
Stephanie: What is his score after the two questions?

Ms. McGiver: Did anyone answer that question in a way that's essentially different from Stephanie's? Okay, Michelle?

Michelle: I put −5. Isn't that right?

A number of students interrupt, saying, "That's what I got; −5!" But Ms. McGiver gives them an icy stare, then turns back to Michelle.

Ms. McGiver: What is the question you were to answer?

Michelle: What was the score after the two questions?

Ms. McGiver: No, read the first question from your paper.

Michelle: Solving this problem answers what question?

Ms. McGiver: Now, answer *that* question, Warren.

Warren: What is the score after two questions?

Ms. McGiver: If your answer to the first question doesn't essentially agree with what Stephanie and Warren read, then change it right now so it does. . . . Okay, how did you answer the second question, Bonita?

Bonita: How many points Bill is behind.

Ms. McGiver: Behind! Why behind, Bonita?

Bonita: Because he lost more points than he gained.

Ms. McGiver: Angelo?

Angelo: The variable is how many points he has left. You don't know if he's behind or not until you solve the problem.

Rita: But 10 is bigger than 5.

Ms. McGiver: You didn't listen to what Angelo said. Repeat what you said, Angelo.

Angelo: Just that you've got to know the variable before you solve for it. They're naming the variable after they solve it, so it's no longer a variable.

Ms. McGiver: Angelo, you're getting into some pretty sophisticated ideas there. Thank you. I think Angelo has hit on the reason we're confused. We need to try this on a problem that you won't solve so easily and then answer these questions before you—quote—know the solution. Here's the problem. Answer the same questions for it.

She displays the following:

An airplane travels at 250 miles per hour for 2 hours in a direction of 138° from Albion, N.Y. At the end of this time, how far west of Albion is the plane?

Some of the students grumble that the problem is too hard, but Ms. McGiver simply uses a stern look and a gesture to tell them to just answer the three questions. After 4 minutes, she begins.

Ms. McGiver: Read your answer to the first question, Hartense.

Hartense: How far west of Albion is the plane?

Ms. McGiver: Anybody disagree? Okay, what do you have for the second question, Wil?

Wil: How far west the plane is.

Ms. McGiver: Far west from where, Joan?

Joan: From that place in New York.

Ms. McGiver: What kind of variable is it? . . . Anybody? . . . Okay, Stephanie.

Stephanie: What do you mean?

Ms. McGiver: I mean is it an angle size, distance, weight, or what?

Stephanie: It's a distance.

Ms. McGiver: So what's the variable, Mike?

Mike: The distance from the town.

Ms. McGiver: Okay, what did you put for the third question, Zeke?

Zeke: I made a list: airplane going 250 miles an hour, 2 hours, at 138°.

Ms. McGiver: Does anyone have any more to add? Okay, Joe.

Joe: It's by Albion, New York.

Ms. McGiver: Now, let's go back and answer the questions again for the first problem.

After they go through the first problem again, Ms. McGiver explains that they are to answer those three questions for every work problem they work for this class until she notifies them differently. She plans to continue going over this process for comprehending word problems until they appear to do it automatically.

LEARNING ACTIVITIES FOR KNOWLEDGE-OF-A-PROCESS OBJECTIVES
Processes, the Most Common Type of Content

Virtually all school mathematics textbooks are dominated by *processes* for students to learn. There are processes (step-by-step procedures) for constructing angles with a straightedge and compass, measuring distances, finding the quotient of two rational numbers expressed in decimal form, solving systems of linear equations, graphing algebraic functions, factoring polynomials, interpolating from logarithmic tables, integrating a function, converting rational numbers expressed as percentages to fractions, using the quadratic formulas to identify roots, determining if a set is closed under a given operation, determining if a relation is a function, and so on. The reason most people view mathematics as tedious, boring, and difficult may well stem from the typical perception that mathematics consists of a massive set of processes to be memorized (Cangelosi 1990c).

An algorithm is a procedure that includes a sequence of binary operations. Most processes specified as content for objectives do involve binary operations and are, thus, algorithms.

Facilitating Process Skills through Direct Instruction

Gaining proficiency with an algorithm usually means students must be engaged in learning activities that are more tedious and less interesting than learning activities for other types of objectives (e.g., conceptualization). Sometimes games (e.g., the one integrated into Ms. Saucony's lesson in Vignette 6.13) can be used to relieve tedium and boredom during the practice stages of lessons for knowledge-of-a-process objectives. In any case, knowledge of a process is effected through *direct instruction* in a *nine-stage* lesson.

Before you can design learning activities that will take students through the nine stages of the lesson, you must:

1. analyze the process, delineating the steps for students to execute
2. from an examination of the steps in the process, identify any prerequisite skills or abilities students might need to acquire before being ready to learn the process

Analyze the Process

The first few times you analyze the process, you may be quite surprised to discover that algorithms involve more steps than you, who are already proficient with the algorithm, had imagined. Shoenfeld (1985, 61) points out, "It is easy to underestimate the complexity of ostensibly simple procedures, especially after one has long since mastered them." Consider the next vignette.

❑ VIGNETTE 4.15

Mr. Champagne proficiently factors quadratic trinomials with one variable and integer coefficients without much conscious effort. Thus, he doesn't consider the algorithm to be very complex until he thinks about each step his students will need to remember when they learn it for the first time. To factor $x^2 + 10x + 21$, they will need to

1. Recognize that this is a quadratic trinomial in standard form.
2. Look for the greatest integer factor that is common to all three terms.
3. Since, in this case, there is nothing to "take out" (i.e., no F in which $FAx^2 + FBx + FC$ becomes $F(Ax^2 + Bx + C)$), attempt to factor the trinomial into two first-degree binomials.
4. Write down $(x \quad) (x \quad)$.
5. Note that all coefficients are positive, so insert $+$'s as follows: $(x + \quad) (x + \quad)$.
6. Note that the constant term is 21.
7. List each whole-number pair whose product is 21: (21, 1), and (7, 3).
8. Note that the coefficient for the middle term is 10.
9. Determine which, if either, of the pairs listed in step 7 has a sum of 10.
10. Note that $7 + 3 = 10$.
11. Note 7 and 3 should be inserted in the blanks from step 5 (in either order).
12. Insert 7 and 3 as follows: $(x + 7) (x + 3)$.

You may think that enumerating 12 steps for the algorithm Mr. Champagne plans to teach is "complicating the simple." However, please keep in mind that Mr. Champagne's students are just being introduced to this algorithm, and each step represents a potential hurdle that he may have to help them negotiate.

Identify Any Prerequisite Skills or Abilities Students Might Need

Mr. Champagne, after examining the process, should feel confident that his students are skilled at factoring integers before attempting to teach the algorithm in the example.

Once you have the steps in the process clearly delineated in your mind and students have achieved prerequisite objectives, conduct the following nine stages of the lesson:

1. *Explanation of the purpose of the process.* Algorithms are based on relations. If your students have experienced conceptualization-level lessons on relations relevant to a process before you attempt to teach them knowledge of the process, then explaining the purpose of the process is a trivial task. The first stage generally involves nothing more than making an announcement such as, "This algorithm provides us with an efficient way of using our calculators to determine whether a quadratic equation has two, one, or no real roots."

2. *Explanation and practice on estimating or anticipating outcomes from the process.* Although process skills are acquired through knowledge-level learning, students need to get into the habit of estimating or anticipating outcomes before executing the process. This (a) tends to add a little interest to the task as students may become interested in checking their prediction skills, (b) provides an informal check on the accuracy of the process, and (c) maintains some connection between the process and problem solving. Consider this example.

❏ **VIGNETTE 4.16**

Jenny works the following two exercises from her textbook:

Find the volume of the right cylinder:

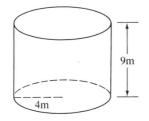

Find the volume of the cone:

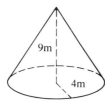

She thinks for the first, "Okay, that's just 9 times 4, which is 36 square centimeters. No, this is volume, so the answer should come out in cubic, not square, centimeters. What'd I do wrong. What's the formula again? . . . Oh, yeah, here it is; it's $\pi r^2 h$. Glad I caught that! So the answer is . . . punch up π on my calculator times 16 times 9 equals . . . 452.389 and so on. Okay, 452.39.

Now, for the next one. . . . This is a cone, but the figures are the same as for the last one. Let's see, this answer should be less than my last one because the top is squeezed down. I bet about 200 cm². Okay, what's the formula? . . . 0.333 times π times 16 times 9 is . . . 150.645 and so on. So, 150.65. Why so much smaller? Oh, yeah, this formula is one-third of that one, not one-half."

---

3. *Explanation of a general overview of the process.* In this stage, students are provided with an outline of the process they'll be executing. This is particularly important for algorithms with many steps, in which students are likely to get so involved in detail that they lose sight of the overall process. For example, Mr. Anselmo tells his students, "To use this formula to solve quadratic equations, you will first put the equation in standard form so you can identify *A, B,* and *C*. Then plug in the values for *A, B,* and *C* and work through the computations with your calculators, making sure you follow the order of operations. The computation will eventually get down to two cases, one for this plus and one for this minus. From there, you'll be working them out as two

separate computations. Each results in a potential root."

4. *Step-by-step explanation of the process.* This is the paramount stage of the lesson, in which the process is delivered to the student. You begin by explaining the first step of the process to the students and then having them try it. You then explain how the result of the first step triggers the second, and the second step is explained and tried. Movement to subsequent steps and the steps themselves are each explained and tried in turn.

Consider teaching students three additional steps to be executed after the results from the process are obtained: (a) compare results to previous estimate or anticipated outcome, (b) check the results, and (c) redo previous steps to rectify any error detected.

5. *Trial test execution of the process.* Students are assigned exercises selected to demonstrate any error patterns they may have learned by mistake. The purpose of this stage is to obtain formative feedback on just which aspects of the process students execute correctly and which ones they do not. This includes how they go about (a) estimating or anticipating outcomes, (b) executing each step in the process itself, and (c) checking for and correcting errors.

Exhibit 4.16 illustrates sample exercises, including the teacher's annotations to a student's responses.

6. *Error-pattern analysis.* Students' responses to the trial exercises are analyzed to diagnose how students are executing the process (e.g., as indicated by the teacher's annotations in Exhibit 4.16). Chapter 7, "Assessing Student Achievement," provides explicit suggestions for analyzing students' error patterns.

7. *Correction.* Students are provided with additional explanations as warranted by the error-pattern analysis.

8. *Practice.* Students polish their skills and overlearn the process through practice exercises.

9. *Recycle prior phases as warranted by formative feedback.* Students' work continues to be monitored as they use the process in subsequent learning activities for other unit objectives.

A Nine-Stage Lesson for a Knowledge-of-a-Process Objective

Here is an example of a teacher engaging students in learning activities relevant to a knowledge-of-a-process objective.

Exhibit 4.16
Sample exercise completed by a student with teacher's error-pattern analysis.

Name *Neil* _____ Exercise on Multiplying Binomials

Simplify:

what does this equal if x = 3?

1. $(x + 7)(x + 4)$

$x^2 + 7x + 4x + 28$

$x^2 + 11x + 28$ } *what does this equal if x = 3?*

FOIL — LAST
1st outside inside

what does this equal if x = 3?

2. $(4x - 2)(x - 1)$

$\cancel{4}x^2 - \cancel{2}x - \cancel{2}x + \cancel{2}$

~~4x²-2x-2x+1~~

$2x^2 - x - 2x + 1$

$2x^2 - 3x + 1$ } *what does this equal if x = 3?*

3. $(x - 7)(2x + 3)$

$2x^2 - 14x + 3x - 21$

$2x^2 - 11x - 21$

4. $(3x - 1)(3x + 1)$

5. $(x - 1/4)(x + 1/4)$

6. $(2x - 1/3)(x + 5/6)$

x + 2/5 = 0 ⟹ But 3x + 2 = 0 x + 2/3 is not always equal to 3x + 2!

$9x^2 - 3x + 3x - 1$

$9x^2 + 0 - 1$

$9x^2 - 1$

④ $(4x - 1)(4x + 1)$

$16x^2 - 4x + 4x - 1$

$16x^2 - 1$

⑥ $(12x - 2)(6x + 5)$

$\cancel{7}2x^2 - \cancel{1}2x + \cancel{6}0x - \cancel{1}0$

$36x^2 - 6x + 30 - 5$

Neil:

3 of these are correct and 3 are incorrect. Find out which ones are incorrect by trying some values for x in the original binomials and then again in your final product.

I think you'll find that on the three you missed that you made only one mistake in the process:

3x² + 6x + 3 = 0   x² + 2x + 1 = 0   But   3x² + 6x + 3   Does not necessarily   Equal   x² + 2x + 1

you confused ~~multiplying~~ an expression like $3x^2 + 6x + 3$ or x + 2/3 x + 1/3 with equations like $3x^2 + 6x + 3 = 0$ and $x + \frac{2}{3} + \frac{1}{3} = 0$

❑ **VIGNETTE 4.17**

Ms. Allen is about two-thirds through a unit on derivatives of algebraic functions with her calculus class. The previous unit was on limits of functions, and, in this unit, she has already completed lessons for (1) conceptualization of the derivative of an algebraic function, (2) conceptualization of some relevant relations involving continuity and tangent lines, (3) knowledge of some relevant vocabulary and shorthand notations, and (4) comprehension of the proofs for a few related theorems.

Having already delineated the steps in the algorithm and feeling confident that the students have achieved the prerequisites, Ms. Allen begins a lesson for the following objective:

Given a continuous function $f : A \rightarrow B$, where $A, B \subseteq$ {reals} and $f(x) = a_0x^n + a_1x^{n-1} + a_2x^{n-2} + \cdots + a_{n-2}x^2 + a_{n-1}x + a_n$, computes $f'(x)$ using the algorithm based on the following relation:

$$f'(x) = na_0x^{n-1} + (n-1)a_1x^{n-2} + (n-2)a_2x^{n-3} + \cdots + 3a_{n-3}x^2 + 2a_{n-2}x + a_{n-1} + 0$$

(*knowledge of a process*).

Tying into the previous lesson, she tells the class: "Recall our definition of the derivative of f at x." She displays on the overhead:

$$f'(x) = \lim_{h \to 0} \frac{f(x+h) - f(x)}{h}$$

Ms. Allen: From theorems 5-1 and 5-3, we know two things.

She displays and reads the following:

$$f(x) = a_0x^n + a_1x^{n-1} + a_2x^{n-2} + \cdots + a_{n-2}x^2 + a_{n-1}x + a_n$$

Ms. Allen: If f has a derivative at x, then . . .

She displays and reads the following:

$$f'(x) = D_x(a_0x^n) + D_x(a_1x^{n-1}) + D_x(a_2x^{n-2}) + \cdots + D_x(a_{n-2}x^2) + D_x(a_{n-1}x) + D_x(a_n)$$

and

$$D_x(bx^m) = mbx^{m-1}$$

Ms. Allen: Those two relations provide the basis for the algorithm you're about to learn. We'll use this algorithm to find the derivative of *f* at *x*. From this first relation we get from theorem 5-1, we'll be finding the derivative of each term of *f* one at a time. This second relation from theorem 5-3 will be used to find each term's derivative. After the algorithm has been executed completely, what do you think we'll be left with? . . . Jena?

Jena: *f* prime of *x*.

Ms. Allen: I agree, but what will *f* prime of *x* look like, Michael?

Michael: It'll be the derivative of *f* at *x*.

Ms. Allen: True, but—I'm sorry, I didn't word my question very clearly. Let me try again. Since *f(x)* is a polynomial, will *f'(x)* also be a polynomial, and, if so, how will the two differ? Let me give everyone a chance to formulate his or her own answer. . . . Okay, Dean.

Dean: *f'* will be a polynomial of one less degree than *f*.

Ms. Allen: Okay, let me write that down as you get it in your notes . . . . Anything else we can predict about *f'*, Kayleen?

Kayleen: The constant of *f* will go to zero, so you'll have one less term.

Ms. Allen: Okay, here I'll get that down. . . .

Ms. Allen is now ready to shift into the fourth phase of the lesson, in which she'll enumerate, display, explain, and use an example to illustrate each step of the algorithm. (See Exhibit 4.17.)

She has Randy serve as chalkboard scribe. He is to follow her directions, working through an example at the board as she uses the overhead to list each step. The students know from previous activities that she expects them to record the steps and work the example in their notebooks.

Ms. Allen: Akeem, when we're done today, would you mind if I duplicate your notes for Randy—at least the ones he'll miss while he's at the board?

Akeem: No problem.

Ms. Allen: Thank you. Okay, get this function down as Randy writes it on the board.

$$g(x) = 2x + 9x^4 - 17.4 - x^2 + 3/x + 5/x^2 - 2x^4 - 1/x$$

Our first step is to write the function in standard form, with all variables expressed in numerators with integer coefficients.

She displays the following general form under the rule on the overhead:

$$f(x) = a_0x^n + a_1x^{n-1} + a_2x^{n-2} + \cdots + a_{n-2}x^2 + a_{n-1}x + a_n$$

Ms. Allen: Let's do that for Randy's example.

Randy writes the following on the board as the students try the task at their places:

$$g(x) = 7x^4 - x^2 + 2x - 17.4 + 2/x + 5/x^2$$
$$g(x) = 7x^4 - x^2 + 2x - 17.4 + 2x^{-1} + 5x^{-2}$$

Exhibit 4.17
Ms. Allen lists rules for differentiation algorithm on the overhead projector as Randy differentiates *g(x)* at the chalkboard.

Ms. Allen: If your *g* in standard form doesn't look like Randy's, then change it if you see what you did wrong. If yours doesn't agree and you don't know why, then ask me about it now. . . . Okay, great! . . . Next we think about what the derivative of the function should look like. In Randy's example, *g* is what degree, Ruth?

Ruth: Fourth.

Ms. Allen: So, *g'* will have what degree, Ross?

Ross: Third.

Ms. Allen: And how many terms does *g* have, Jena?

Jena: I don't know.

Ms. Allen: Count them.

Jena: Oh, okay! . . . Six.

Ms. Allen: So, how many terms should we expect for *g'*, Humula?

Humula: Six.

Ms. Allen: What's the derivative of a constant, Humula?

Humula: Zero.

Ms. Allen: Is one of the six terms of *g* a constant, Humula?

Humula: Yes, so *g'* will have five terms.

Ms. Allen: So, now that we have the function in standard form with no variables in denominators, the next step is to apply theorems 5-1 and 5-3 and find the derivative of each term individually. Let's do it for the first term of *g*. The rule is multiply the coefficient by the exponent and reduce the exponent by one and then simplify. In general, *bx* to the *m*th becomes *mbx* to the *m* minus first. Work it for the first term for Randy's example. . . . Does anyone disagree with $28x^3$? . . . Okay, repeat the process for each of the other terms one at a time. . . .

Several minutes later the explanation of the steps is completed and Ms. Allen has them differentiate a variety of algebraic functions on a worksheet. She circulates about the room monitoring work and providing help as needed (Exhibit 4.18). Rather than reexplaining the algorithm to individual students, she provides very specific directions. Here's one case in point:

Estes: How do you do this one?

Ms. Allen: What's this rule say right here in your notebook?

Estes: Find the derivative of each term one at a time.

Ms. Allen: Then do it.

Estes: But this one's funny. What do I do with these negatives?

Ms. Allen: Follow this rule from your notebook.

Estes: You mean you can do that even for the negative of a negative?

Ms. Allen: Yes. Try it and I'll check with you after you've had a chance to complete this one and the next three.

From such exchanges and monitoring the work, Ms. Allen is convinced that students generally know the algorithm, but about 10 tend to get careless in manipulating expressions with negative exponents and negative coefficients, especially when the coefficient is − 1. Thus, she decides to include a larger share than she originally planned of functions with such expressions in the practice exercises for homework.

She plans to continue to check on their skill with this algorithm as students use it during the next lesson, which begins the next day and focuses on the following objective:

Given a real-life problem, determines how, if at all, a solution to that problem is facilitated by finding the derivative of an algebraic function (*application*).

Exhibit 4.18
Ms. Allen providing individual help.

LEARNING ACTIVITIES FOR APPLICATION-LEVEL OBJECTIVES
Problem-Solving

When confronted with a problem, a student who has achieved an application-level objective can determine how, if at all, the mathematical content of that objective can be utilized in a solution to the problem. During application-level lessons, students learn to put into practice previously conceptualized concepts and relations and previously memorized conventions and processes.

Because of the inextricable alliance between application-level learning and problem solving, it might be helpful at this point for you to reread the sections entitled "Real-Life Problems" beginning on page 25 and "Requisites for Learning to Apply Mathematics to Real-Life Problem-Solving" beginning on page 74.

Deductive Reasoning

Application-level learning depends on students using *deductive reasoning* (Beyer 1987, 30–32). *Deductive reasoning is inferring that a specific* (e.g., a constant or problem) *is subsumed by a more general idea* (i.e., concept) *or rule* (i.e., abstract relation). *It is the cognitive process by which people determine whether or not what they know about a concept or abstract relation is applicable to some unique situation.*

The use of *syllogisms* is inherent in deductive reasoning. A syllogism is a scheme for inferring problem solutions in which a conclusion is drawn from a *major premise* and a *minor premise*. The major premise is a general rule or abstraction. The minor premise is a relation of a specific to the general rule or abstraction. The conclusion is a logical consequence of the combined premises. Consider the following example:

Major premise: If the discriminant ($b^2 - 4ac$) of a quadratic equation is positive and not a perfect square, the equation has two irrational roots.

Minor premise: The discriminant of $x^2 - x - 18 = 0$ (i.e., 73) is positive but not a perfect square.

Conclusion: $x^2 - x - 18 = 0$ has two irrational roots.

Deductive reasoning is the foundation of formal proofs of theorems. Although they do not normally express the ideas formally, people use that same syllogistic, deductive reasoning in real-life problem solving. Consider this vignette.

❑ **VIGNETTE 4.18**

Anna is building a playhouse with her children. She has the problem of figuring how to precut the rafter ends so that they will be vertical to the ground when in place. She sketches the following diagram with her planned dimensions for the rafters:

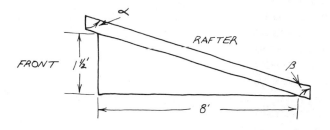

Looking at her diagram, she thinks, "What should α and β be? α = β because they're opposite angles of a parallelogram. Okay, so how do I solve for one of them? β has got to be the same as this angle right here; I'll call it Θ." She inserts Θ:

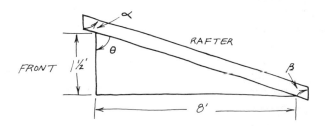

Anna begins to doubt that β = Θ, thinking, "Or does it? Let's see, these two lines are parallel, so we have . . . Okay, that's right, β = Θ! Alright, I should be able to find Θ, since it's part of this triangle—in fact, a right triangle! A right triangle with two known sides, that means I can use a little trig here. Okay, I know Θ's opposite side and its adjacent side. So, tangent is the operable word here. Tangent Θ is 8 over $1\frac{1}{2}$ so—get this calculator working, arctan, open parenthesis, 8, divide by 1.5, close parenthesis, equals . . . 1.38544. . . . That's not right! Oh, no wonder, the calculator is set for radians. Okay, switch to degrees and try it again. Ahh! 79.38. . . . That's more like it. . . . Okay, so I cut these two angles at almost 80°."

Anna used several syllogisms in formulating a solution to her problem:

Major premise: Opposite angles of a parallelogram are congruent.

Minor premise: The angle with α degrees and the one with β degrees are opposite angles of a parallelogram.

Conclusion: α = β.

Major premise: The tangent of an acute angle of a right triangle is the ratio of the side opposite to the angle to the side adjacent to the angle.

Minor premise: The angle with Θ degrees belongs to a right triangle whose opposite side measures 8 feet and adjacent side measures 1.5 feet.

Conclusion: $\Theta = \tan^{-1}(8/1.5)$.

Facilitating Application-Level Learning

A *deductive learning activity* is one that *stimulates students to reason deductively.* An application-level objective is achieved through a four-stage lesson; the first two stages utilize deductive learning activities. The four stages are:

1. Initial problem confrontation and analysis
2. Subsequent problem confrontation and analysis
3. Rule articulation
4. Extension into subsequent lessons

Initial Problem Confrontation and Analysis. In the initial activity of this phase of the lesson, you confront students with a pair of problems. The pair is chosen so that the problems are very similar except that the content of the application-level objective applies to the solution of one of the problems but not the other. Suppose, for example, that the following objective is to be achieved:

> Given a real-life problem, decides if the solution requires computing the area of a polygonal region, and, if so, determines how to find that area (*application*).

The content of the objective applies to the solution of the first of the following pair of problems, but not the second:

A. The front wall surrounding the chalkboard is quite drab. Students suggest that they make decorative posters on standard sheets of cardboard and use them to cover the wall completely, as begun in Exhibit 4.19. How many posters will be needed to complete the task?

B. There is a nasty-looking crack just above the chalkboard on one side wall of the classroom. Students suggest that they make decorative posters and use

Exhibit 4.19
Classroom wall partially covered with decorative posters.

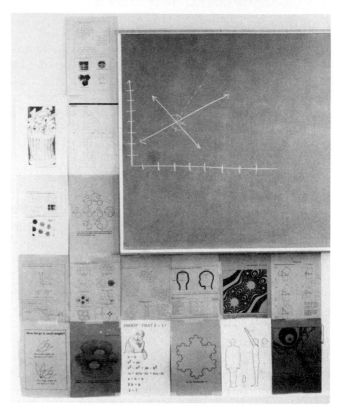

them to hide the crack, as begun in Exhibit 4.20. How many sheets will be needed to complete the task?

You then engage students in a *deductive questioning/discussion* session in which students describe how they would go about solving each problem and then explain why the objective's content was used in one case, but not the other, as in the following vignette.

❏ VIGNETTE 4.19

Mr. Cummings uses the two sample problems (listed as A and B) for the aforementioned objective on polygonal area. He engages one student in the following exchange:

Mr. Cummings: How would you go about solving problem A?

Patsy: I'd divide the wall around the board into rectangles and then find out how many sheets would fit into each rectangle.

Mr. Cummings: But how would you go about finding out the number of sheets to use?

Patsy: I'd have to just puzzle the sheets in.

Mr. Cummings: But how would you know how many puzzle pieces to use?

Exhibit 4.20
Side wall of classroom with crack partially covered by decorative sheets.

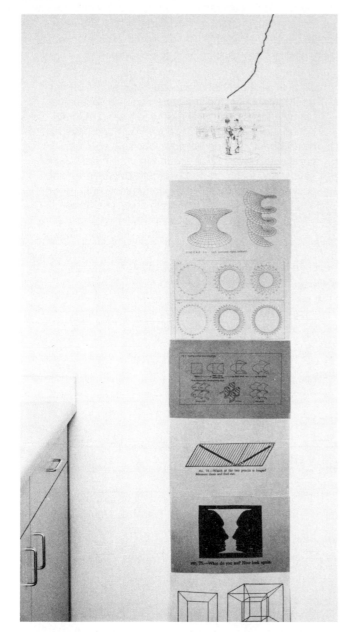

Patsy: By trying it.
Mr. Cummings: But suppose you wanted to find out how many sheets you needed without wasting a bunch of sheets. Is there an easier way?
Patsy: Oh, you mean by computing the area of the wall. Yeah! I could add up the rectangle's areas and divide that by the area of one sheet. Then I'd have it.
Mr. Cummings: Now, what about problem B. How would you solve that one?
Patsy: Just measure the length of the crack and divide that by the width of a sheet and that would give you the number of posters.

Mr. Cummings: Why didn't you compute areas for problem B like you did for problem A?
Patsy: B isn't an area problem.
Mr. Cummings: Why not? How is it different from A? They seem pretty similar to me.
Patsy: With A we had to spread the posters all out. In B the sheets are lined up in just one row.

Subsequent Problem Confrontation and Analysis. Learning activities for the second stage are similar to those of the first, except students analyze solutions to additional pairs of problems. The pairs are selected so that students are exposed to a wide variety of circumstances and varying psychological noise in which to determine if the content is applicable. For the objective on areas of polygonal regions, subsequent problems would include circumstances other than covering a wall with posters.

How many pairs of problems to include and how difficult each is should depend on how easily students are distinguishing between problems to which the content applies and those to which it doesn't. If they readily explain why the content works in one case but not another, then you should engage them in more difficult problems. On the other hand, select easier problems and delay the start of the third phase if they are experiencing serious difficulties.

Rule Articulation. In this stage, students formulate rules for when the content of the objective applies to the solution of a problem. If conceptualization of the content preceded the lesson, then this often involves no more than rephrasing rules discovered during conceptualization lessons. In cases in which students began the application lesson with some conceptual learning gaps relative to the content, this phase may require some inductive learning activities to help them rediscover rules.

Extension into Subsequent Lessons. As suggested in Chapter 1, teaching functions are messy; one lesson does not always end before another begins. Achievement of one application-level objective is enhanced during the first two phases of lessons for subsequent application-level objectives. In the previous example, Mr. Cummings' questions stimulated Patsy to reason deductively about lengths (a topic from a previous unit) for the problem to which area computations did not apply. In a subsequent unit on volume, Mr. Cummings will probably pair a problem that can be solved via a volume relation with one that can be solved via an area relation. Thus, application lessons on one content extend into those for subsequent content.

A Four-Stage Lesson for an Application Objective

Here is an example of an application-level lesson.

❏ VIGNETTE 4.20

Exhibit 4.21 depicts what Mr. Wilson call his "solution blueprint form." He got the idea for the form while attending an NCTM convention (Cangelosi 1989b), and it has proven so successful that he now incorporates it into every application-level lesson he teaches.

Mr. Wilson is beginning a lesson for the following objective:

Given a real-life problem, decides if use of either the multiplication principle for independent events, permutation formula, or combination formula will help solve the problem (*application*).

He directs his students: "Please take out one copy of our solution blueprint form. Now, label it "Jill and Jack's Locker Security Problem." Read Jill and Jack's locker security problem as I display it on the overhead":

Jill and Jack are debating whether it would be better if their school lockers were secured with combination locks or with key locks. Jill says, "Combination locks are better because you don't have to worry about keeping up with your key; you just carry your combination around in your head." Jack says, "Key locks are more secure because a thief could just keep trying your combination until he or she got the right one." Jill counters, "The thief

Exhibit 4.21
Solution blueprint form Mr. Wilson uses with his students.

Solution Blueprint

Question(s) posed by the problem:

_____

Principal variable(s):

_____

Other variables affecting results:

_____

Possible approaches to consider:

_____

Delimited principal variable(s):

_____

Solution plan:

   Overall design

_____

   Measurements to make

_____

   Relations to establish

_____

   Algorithms

_____

Results:

_____

Conclusions:

_____

How you would solve this type of problem in the future?

_____

would have to try over a hundred combinations before finding yours and, besides, out of hundreds of locks, one key will be able to open more than one locker."

Mr. Wilson: Let's help settle the debate by finding out whether combination locks or key locks are more vulnerable to being opened by a thief. Everyone write the question posed by the problem on the form. . . . Read yours, Gene.

Gene: Which type of lock is more secure from a thief, combination or key?

Mr. Wilson: Does anyone disagree with Gene's answer? Okay, great! Now, what variables do we have to address, Larry?

Larry: Uhh, wait a minute. . . . Just how secure the combination lock is and how secure the key lock is.

Mr. Wilson: Everybody write that down. . . . What other variables are going to affect our results besides the two principal variables, Rembert?

Rembert: Oh, stuff like—ahh—how many thieves there are and a bunch of others.

Mr. Wilson: Good! Let's have Devon, Marilyn, Lynae, and Wanda each list one. Start, Devon.

Devon: How many keys the thief has.

Marilyn: How many numbers on the combination locks.

Lynae: How many locks out of so many one key will fit.

Wanda: I was going to say the same thing as Marilyn.

Mr. Wilson: Any other *other* variables anybody wants to list? Brent?

Brent: How about the number of numbers in each combination?

Mr. Wilson: Yes, Winnie.

Winnie: All our locks use three-number combinations. Can't we just stick with that?

Mr. Wilson: If it's okay with you, Brent, let's make three the constant number of numbers in any one combination. Okay, considering this list of other variables, I'm going to move us along a little faster on this by telling you that I did a little research before class. I got Coach Bailey to loan me 100 locks and one randomly selected key. The key opened 5 of the 100 locks. Also, I noted that most locks used in school have 50 numbers on them. So, I suggest that for purposes of Jill and Jack's locker security problem, we control for some of these other variables by delimiting our two principal variables so that we solve the problem for one thief operating with one key that'll open 5 percent of the locks. And also that each combination lock has 50 numbers. Assuming you agree to that, what are our two principal variables after they've been delimited, Hank?

Hank: What's delimited mean again?

Mr. Wilson: Read the two general principal variables from the second line on your blueprint form, Hank.

Hank: How secure the combination lock is one. The other is how secure the key lock is.

Mr. Wilson: Those are two great variables, but there's one difficulty with them if we're going to solve this problem. . . . What is it, Rembert?

Rembert: They're so general that we can't measure them. We need some mathematical variables.

Mr. Wilson: The delimited variables should be narrower, and—we hope—quantifiable. . . . So, what are the delimited variables, Hank?

Hank: I want to pass. Would you ask somebody else?

Mr. Wilson: Sure. Reed?

Reed: One is the chance that the thief with the one key that opens 5 percent of the locks will open your key lock. The other one is the chance that a thief who's willing to try a lot of combinations will open your combination lock.

Mr. Wilson: I'll buy that. Everybody get those down. . . . Could we use a shorthand symbol for those so we can refer to them easily while we work on solutions for each? What do you want to call them, Hank?

Hank: K and C.

Mr. Wilson: Let's take Hank's suggestion and call the event that the thief opens your key lock K and opens your combination lock C. And since it's the probability of those events we're interested in, let's use our conventional notation and call our delimited variables $P(K)$ and $P(C)$, respectively.

At this point, the solution blueprint form has been filled in down to the Solution Plan.

Mr. Wilson: After we solve for $P(K)$ and $P(C)$, what should we do next, Winnie?

Winnie: We compare them to see which is greater. If K is a more likely event, then Jack is right and key locks should be used. If C is more likely, then Jill is right and combinations are better.

Mr. Wilson: Okay, then let's split Jill and Jack's locker security problem into two subproblems. One is to figure $P(K)$ and the other to figure $P(C)$. Let's do $P(C)$ first. How do we go about solving for $P(C)$? . . . Ilone.

Ilone: You've got to figure how many possible combinations there are on the lock.

Mr. Wilson: How many numbers on the lock, Hank?

Hank: 50.

Mr. Wilson: How many numbers in one combination, Tracy?

Tracy: Three.

Mr. Wilson: So, each of you silently figure how many possible lock combinations there are. You have 3 minutes. . . . What did you get, Rembert?

Rembert: 19,600.

Mr. Wilson: What did you do to get that, and why did you decide to do it that way?

Rembert: It's a combination of 50 things taken 3 at a time, so I just used the combination function on my calculator.

Mr. Wilson: By the number of hands raised, it looks like a few people want to debate your method. . . . Okay, Kabul, you and Rembert stand up and debate the differences in your approaches.

Kabul: It's not a combination; it's a permutation.

Rembert: Why do you think they call them combination locks? Sure it's a combination.

Kabul: I don't know why they call them combinations, but I do know the order of the three numbers makes a difference. If the lock's combination is 20, 30, 40, then 40, 30, 20 won't open it. So it's a permutation, not a combination.

Rembert: So, what's the answer?

Kabul: 117,600.

Mr. Wilson: I see some other folks are anxious to speak. . . . Yes, Marilyn.

Marilyn: But it's not a permutation either. A number can be repeated in a lock combination. What about 20, 20, 30?

Mr. Wilson: What's the rule for when permutations apply to a situation, Cassandra?

Cassandra: When you want to know how many ways so many things can happen out of so many. But there can't be any repeats in any one way. That's what we said the other day.

Mr. Wilson: And can a lock combination have repeats such as 23, 14, 23, Nancy?

Nancy: Sure, and that's why Marilyn is right.

Mr. Wilson: So if permutations don't apply, what does? . . . Okay, Devon.

Devon: It'd be however many numbers times itself times itself.

Mr. Wilson: Therefore, what? Finish the syllogism for the combination lock problem, Rembert.

Rembert: Therefore, the possible number of lock combinations is 50 times 50 times 50.

Mr. Wilson: So, what's $P(C)$, Kabul?

Kabul: Almost zero; it's 1 divided by 50^3. That's . . . 0.000008 on my calculator.

Mr. Wilson: Now, let's move to the other subproblem in Jill and Jack's overall problem. . . . What's the other variable we need to solve for, Anson?

Anson: $P(K)$.

Mr. Wilson: How do we solve for $P(K)$, Nancy?

Nancy: You said it's 5 percent. A thief with a key can open 5 out of every 100 key locks. That means key locks are not nearly as secure as combination locks.

Mr. Wilson: Before you compare $P(K)$ to $P(C)$, explain how you got $P(K) = 0.05$, Nancy.

Nancy: You did it by experimenting.

Mr. Wilson: You mean we don't have to use any permutation or combination formulas or even the multiplication principle for $P(K)$ like we did for $P(C)$? . . . Marie.

Marie: No, it's just one key that fits 5 out of 100 locks. If the thief tries your lock, there's a 5 percent chance he

or she'll get in. There's not so many things to group out of so many—repeating or not repeating.

Mr. Wilson: Oh, grouping! Are you saying if there's no *grouping,* or *arrangements,* then we don't have a case for permutations, combinations, or the multiplication rule? I understand. Let's go ahead and complete the solution blueprint form for Jill and Jack's overall problem.

Without further discussion, the students complete their forms.

Mr. Wilson continues the lesson by presenting another pair of problems that he considers more difficult than the ones involving $P(C)$ and $P(K)$. However, the students solve them efficiently and appear to distinguish clearly among problems to which combinations apply, permutations apply, the multiplication principle applies, and none of those apply. He thus decides to end the lesson without confronting them with additional problems in class. For homework he assigns eight more problems. Permutations are applicable to two of them, combinations to two, and the multiplication principle to one other. The other three can be solved by applying prior content. He checks the homework to assess if additional learning activities are needed.

Also, in the next application lesson on binomial distributions, combinations are again applied and permutations are used as nonexample problems.

LEARNING ACTIVITIES FOR DEVELOPING MATHEMATICAL CREATIVITY
Some Thoughts on Creativity

An objective that specifies *creativity* as its learning level requires students to *think divergently to originate ideas, hypotheses, or methods.* Creativity is the development of new mental patterns. People tend to produce creative ideas in response to dissatisfaction with available methods, ideas, beliefs, and principles for dealing with perplexing situations.

Contrary to the popular belief that aptitude for creative production is found only in rare, exceptional individuals, virtually everyone possesses creative talents (Torrance 1966). What is rare is for that talent to be recognized and rewarded. Historically, society and its institutions (e.g., schools and churches) have frowned upon and generally discouraged creative thinking (Strom 1969, 222–236). Divergent reasoning threatens common beliefs and established "truths." Irrational thought and emotionally controlled behaviors are often associated with mental instability. However, Gordon (1961, 6) suggests that irrational, emotionally charged thought tends to produce an environment more conducive to creative production than rational, controlled thought. Joyce and Weil (1986, 165) state, "Nonrational interplay leaves room for open-ended thoughts that can lead to a mental state in which new ideas are possible. The basis for decisions, however, is always rational; the irrational state is the best mental state for exploring and expanding ideas, but it is not a decision-making state."

Creativity thrives in an environment in which ideas are valued on their own merit, not on the basis of how they were produced nor who produced them (Strom 1969, 258–267). In such an environment, irrationally produced ideas are evaluated with the same regard as those resulting from a rational process. The attention afforded an idea should not depend on the eminence of its originator.

Gordon's (1961) studies challenge typical views about creativity with four ideas:

1. Creativity is important in everyday circumstances; it should not only be associated with the development of great works.
2. Creativity is utilized in all fields, not just the arts.
3. Creative thoughts can be generated by groups as well as solitary individuals via similar processes. This is contrary to the common view that creativity must be an intensely personal experience.
4. The creative process is not mysterious; it can be described and people can be taught to use it.

Gordon's fourth point is critical to justifying the inclusion of creativity-level lessons in curricula. However, how best to teach for creativity is still not well understood. One difficulty is resolving the phenomenon that creative thoughts seem to rise unpredictably (Bourne et al. 1986, 9–10).

Preserving Creativity

Studies indicate a steady decline in most students' curiosity and creative activities during their school years (Strom 1969, 259–260):

> Given the great number of children with creative prospect and the fact that it represents a natural evolving process, the first concern among educators ought to be one of preservation. Creativity will develop if allowed to grow, if teachers permit and encourage a course already begun (see Gowan, et al. 1967). A primary clue comes from the process itself—allowing inquiry, manipulation, questioning, guessing, and the combination of remote thought elements. Generally, however, the preferred cognitive style of learning creatively is discouraged [in typical classrooms]. Studies indicate that discontinuities in creative development occur at several grade levels and that the losses are accompanied by a decline in pupil curiosity and interest in learning. At the same grade levels at which creative loss occurs, increases are

noted in the incidence of emotional disturbance and egregious behavior. Among Anglo-American cultures, the greatest slump in creative development seems to coincide with the fourth grade; smaller drops take place at kindergarten and seventh grade. Children at each of these grades perform less well than they did one year earlier and less well than children in the grade below them on measures of divergent thinking, imagination, and originality. This problem was ignored, since it was judged to be a developmental phenomena instead of man-made or culture-related (Torrance 1962). Not long ago it was first recognized that in certain cultures the development of creative thinking abilities are continuous. And, even in our own country, under selective teachers who encourage creative boys and girls and reward creative behavior, no slump occurs at grade four.

As a teacher, you can choose not to include creativity-level objectives in your curricula. However, simply managing to preserve students' creativity and allowing it to grow requires some conscious effort on your part.

Fostering Creativity

Consistent with the NCTM (1989) *Standards,* you may choose not only to preserve your students' creativity but also to conduct learning activities that help them achieve creativity-level objectives. Just as activities for affective objectives can be efficiently integrated into lessons for cognitive objectives (e.g., in Vignette 4.3), so too can activities fostering creativity be interwoven with those for other types of objectives (especially conceptualization). The strategy is to conduct these other lessons so that students feel free to question, make mistakes, and disagree with ideas, even yours. Particularly important is for them to be positively reinforced (Cangelosi 1988a, 35–37) for depending on themselves and on their own devices for decision making and problem solving.

Although the creative process is not well understood, some promising methods for teaching for creativity have been tried and studied with promising results (Bourne et al. 1986, 9). Strom (1969, 261) recommends students be exposed to examples of creative production (e.g., through historical accounts of mathematical inventions and discoveries and through teachers' modeling divergent thinking in "think-aloud" sessions). Beyer (1987, 35–37) points out the importance of heuristic activities such as brainstorming, open-ended questioning sessions, and discussions in which ideas for consideration are critiqued regarding purpose, structure, advantages, and disadvantages.

One of the more systematic and researched methods for fostering creativity is referred to by its designer, William J. J. Gordon (1961), as *synectics* (Joyce and Weil, 1986, 159–183).

Synectics

Synectics is a means by which *metaphors* and *analogies* are used to lead students into an illogic state for situations where rational logic fails. The intent is for students to free themselves of convergent thinking and to develop empathy with ideas that conflict with their own. Three types of analogies are used in learning activities based on synectics:

1. *Direct analogies.* Students raise and analyze comparisons between the mathematical content and some familiar object or concept. For example,

   ❏ How is a function like a tossed salad?
   ❏ What's the difference between a continuous sequence and frozen yogurt?
   ❏ Which is rounder, a hexagon or a television show?

2. *Personal analogies.* Students empathize with the content, losing themselves in some imaginary world. For example,

   ❏ Be the function f: $(-1, 6)$→{reals} such that $f(x) = 3/(6 - x)$. Describe how you feel as x moves from -1 to about 5.75. Describe how you feel as x moves from 5.75 nearer and nearer to 6.
   ❏ You're the set of rational numbers, and you must give up one of your infinite subsets to the set of irrational numbers. You get to choose which one to give away. Which one is it and why?
   ❏ You have just invented a way of constructing an equilateral right triangle. How do you feel about your invention? How will this accomplishment change your life?

3. *Compressed conflicts.* Compressed conflicts usually involve metaphors containing conflicting ideas.

   ❏ Draw a continuously discrete graph.
   ❏ How would mathematics be different if only parallel lines could be perpendicular?
   ❏ Show how an infinite set is small.

The metaphors and analogies are intended to stimulate students to reconceptualize old ideas, thus promoting divergent thinking.

A Lesson Designed to Foster Creativity

Synectics are used in the following example.

❏ VIGNETTE 4.21

Ms. Ferney routinely mixes learning activities for creativity with lessons for other types of objectives. Her algebra class already possesses conceptual-level understanding of functions, density, and continuity, along with a comprehension-level understanding of the language associated with those concepts. They have not, however, been introduced to the idea of limits of a function. At this point, she intends to help them achieve the following objective:

> Generates a variety of novel functions and describes their features, including some suggesting the idea of limits *(creativity)*.

She directs the students to begin writing down functions of their own design. She insists that at least one of the functions have a domain that is not a set of numbers. After 6 minutes she calls a halt to the activity and asks Brook to write one of his on the board; he writes the following and then returns to his place:

$$q(a) = -\sqrt{|9 - a|}$$

Ms. Ferney: Please take a blank sheet of paper and number it from -3 to 2. Leave about three lines between numerals to write answers to respond to items I'm about to give. . . . Number -3: How is Brook's function like a night light? . . . Number -2: If you were Brook's function, why do you suppose you'd be accused of being fickle? How would you answer your critics? . . . Number -1: Why would anyone call Brook's function a variable constant? . . . Number 0: Write out a question about Brook's function for the class to discuss. . . . Number 1: Write out another question about Brook's function for the class to discuss. . . . Number 2: Write out yet another question about Brook's function for the class to discuss. . . . How did you answer item -3, Katrina?

Katrina: A night light is for security and the function is very secure because you can't take the square root of a negative number, and by putting in the absolute value, that protects you from having negative inside the radical.

Additional responses to each of the six items are reported and discussed in detail. Other functions are put on the board; similar questions are raised, and the responses are discussed.

❑❑❑❑❑❑❑❑❑❑❑❑❑❑❑❑❑❑❑❑

SELF-ASSESSMENT EXERCISES

1. Select the one response to each of the following multiple-choice items that either completes the statement so that it is true or accurately answers the question:

 a. With which one of the following do students usually have to deal when solving real-life problems but not when solving most textbook word problems?
   i. Variables
   ii. Relations
   iii. Need to execute algorithms
   iv. Irrelevant data

 b. Which one of the following do students usually have to determine in order to solve most textbook word problems?
   i. The variable to be solved as indicated by the question given in the problem
   ii. The implications of the solution outcome
   iii. What measurements to make
   iv. Whether or not mathematics should be used to solve the problem

 c. Ordinarily, the lesson for a conceptualization-of-a-relation objective should be sequenced in a unit so that _____ .
   i. Students memorize the relation before it is conceptualized.
   ii. Students memorize the relation after it is conceptualized.
   iii. Achievement of the objective culminates the unit.
   iv. Students learn to apply the relation before it is conceptualized.

 d. Learning activities for which one of the following types of objectives are *least* likely to be effectively integrated into lessons for other types of objectives?
   i. Willingness to try
   ii. Creativity
   iii. Knowledge of a process
   iv. Appreciation

 e. Which one of the following strategies is *least* likely to enhance students' achievement of an appreciation objective?
   i. Students use the objective's content to solve problems that concern them.
   ii. The teacher tells students how important understanding the content will be to them.
   iii. The teacher demonstrates that use of the content can save time.
   iv. Students discover and invent mathematics for themselves.

 f. Student perplexity is a critical ingredient in learning activities for all *but* which one of the following types of objectives?
   i. Creativity
   ii. Simple knowledge
   iii. Conceptualization
   iv. Application

 g. According to this textbook, for which type of objective is it the most difficult to design lessons and also the type upon which virtually all other types of objectives depend?
   i. Creativity
   ii. Application
   iii. Knowledge of a process
   iv. Conceptualization

 h. Lessons for application objectives require _____ .
   i. Direct instruction
   ii. Inductive learning activities
   iii. Deductive learning activities
   iv. Use of mnemonics

 i. Lessons for conceptualization objectives require _____ .
   i. Direct instruction
   ii. Inductive learning activities
   iii. Deductive learning activities
   iv. Error-pattern analysis

 j. Lessons for simple-knowledge objectives require _____ .
   i. Direct instruction
   ii. Inductive learning activities
   iii. Deductive learning activities
   iv. Error-pattern analysis

 k. Lessons for knowledge-of-a-process objectives require _____ .
   i. Direct instruction
   ii. Inductive learning activities
   iii. Deductive learning activities
   iv. Use of mnemonics

 l. Literal and interpretive understanding are associated with what level of learning?
   i. Conceptualization
   ii. Application
   iii. Comprehension
   iv. Creativity

 m. Synectics is used in learning activities for what type of objective?
   i. Willingness to try
   ii. Comprehension
   iii. Application
   iv. Creativity

 n. Error-pattern analysis is used in learning activities for what type of objective?
   i. Simple knowledge
   ii. Comprehension

    iii. Willingness to try
    iv. Knowledge of a process
  o. Students are stimulated to formulate generalizations from work with specifics during

    _____ .

    i. Inductive learning activities
    ii. Direct instruction
    iii. Deductive learning activities
    iv. Lessons for interpretive understanding
  p. Students utilize syllogisms during

    _____ .

    i. Inductive learning activities
    ii. Direct instruction
    iii. Deductive learning activities
    iv. Lessons for interpretive understanding
  Compare your responses to the following: a. (iv);
b. (i); c. (ii); d. (iii); e. (ii); f. (ii); g. (iv); h. (iii); i.
(ii); j. (i); k. (i); l. (iii); m. (iv); n. (iv); o (i); p. (iii).

2. Recall a real-life problem you once solved. Analyze the process by which you solved it by describing just what you did with each of the nine stages
listed on pages 75–76.

3. Solve one of the word problems in a mathematics
textbook. Analyze the process by which you
solved it. Now compare that process to the one
you described for Exercise 2. List the similarities
and differences between the processes. Exchange
your list with that of someone else who worked
this exercise. Discuss them.

4. In your response to Exercise 2 in Chapter 3, you
formulated a set of objectives. In light of your
work with Chapter 4, sequence the objectives according to when you would address them in a
unit. Also, you may want to modify some and delete or add others. For each of the objectives, design and describe a lesson for helping a group of
students achieve that objective. For each objective, make sure that your design is guided by
principles for learning activities pertaining to the
objective's learning level. Compare your work on
this exercise with someone else's.

❑❑❑❑❑❑❑❑❑❑❑❑❑❑❑❑❑❑❑❑

TAKING WHAT YOU'VE LEARNED TO THE NEXT LEVEL

No matter how well you design lessons with (1)
attention-grabbing problems and examples for affective objectives, (2) inductive learning activities for
conceptualization objectives, (3) direct instructional
activities for simple knowledge objectives, (4) direct
and inquiry activities for comprehension objectives,
(5) direct instructional and error-pattern-analysis
activities for knowledge-of-a-process objectives, (6)
deductive learning activities for application objectives, and (7) various heuristic activities, including
synectics, for creativity objectives, your efforts may
still fail if you do not solve the most worrisome task
faced by teachers, especially beginning teachers
(Cangelosi et al. 1988; Doyle 1986; Steere 1988, 5–9;
Weber 1986). That task is to obtain and maintain
your students' cooperation so that they willingly engage in your well-designed learning activities. It
does little good for you to present a perfectly clear
explanation of a process unless your students are
following along with you as you intend. Masterfully
selected examples and problems raised during ques-
tioning/discussion sessions go for naught unless students courteously engage in exchanges and seriously address the issues at hand. Error-pattern
analysis is useless unless students are motivated to
improve their skills. The success of homework and
seatwork assignments depends on the effort students are willing to put forth. Formative feedback
hardly serves as a guide to you if students either fail
to try or cheat on measures of their achievements.

    How to elicit students' cooperation and engage
them in your direct instructional, inductive, deductive, individualized work, homework, and other
types of learning activities are the topics of Chapters
5 and 6.

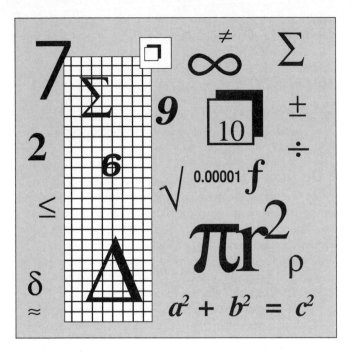

CHAPTER 5
Managing Student Behavior

This chapter suggests ways for you to gain and maintain your students' cooperation. Chapter 5 will help you:

1. Differentiate between examples and nonexamples of each of the following: (a) allocated time, (b) transition time, (c) on-task behavior, (d) engaged behavior, (e) off-task behavior, (f) disruptive behavior, (g) isolated behavior, (h) behavior pattern, (i) businesslike classroom environment, (j) descriptive communication, (k) judgmental communication, (l) supportive reply, (m) assertive communication, (n) hostile communication, and (o) passive communication (*conceptualization*).
2. Explain why the success of teachers' lessons is dependent on how well they plan and implement ways of teaching students to be on-task (*conceptualization*).
3. Given a teaching assignment for a specific mathematics course, describe how to incorporate a plan for managing student behavior within the overall plan for that course (*application*).
4. Explain fundamental principles for (a) communicating with students in a way that increases the likelihood that they will choose on-task instead of off-task behaviors, (b) establishing a favorable climate for learning mathematics, (c) establishing rules of student conduct, (d) establishing classroom procedures, and (e) dealing with off-task behaviors (*conceptualization*).

A WELL-DESIGNED LESSON GONE AWRY

Chapter 4 provided suggestions for designing lessons consistent with research-based principles. However, even when you design a lesson that is appropriate for your objective, learning activities are unlikely to go as planned unless you include measures for gaining and maintaining students' cooperation. Consider the following vignette.

❏ VIGNETTE 5.1
As part of an algebra I unit on graphs and linear equations, Ms. Lewis planned a lesson intended to help students achieve the following objective:

Explains why the graph of $y = ax + b$ (where x and y are real variables and a and b are real constants) is a line (*conceptualization*).

At the end of Monday's class she makes the following homework assignment: Solve each of the following for x and plot the solution on a number line:

$$-4 = 3x - 1 \qquad -2 = 3x - 1$$
$$0 = 3x - 1 \qquad 3 = 3x - 1$$
$$4 = 3x - 1 \qquad 10 = 3x - 1$$

For Tuesday, she plans to have the students transfer the six number lines from their homework onto a Cartesian plane, as indicated in Exhibit 5.1. Then she wants to ask them leading questions to get them to discover that when the number lines are located where $y = -4$, $y = -2$, $y = 0$, $y = 3$, $y = 4$, and $y = 10$, respectively, the solution points for x are contained by a single line.

She plans a few more examples along with a few non-examples (e.g., a set of equations that include $3 = x - 7$ and $-4 = x + 5$ and another set of the form $y = 3x^2 - 1$) on which the students are to repeat the homework task and then discuss the outcomes to discover the relation specified by the objective.

It's now Tuesday, and the bell to begin the class has just rung. Ms. Lewis moves to the front of the room as some students stream into the room while others sit at their desks passing time in various ways. Joyce and Junie are talking about their plans for that night while Randall feverishly works on his history assignment. Ms. Lewis attempts to speak above the rising noise level in the room as she yells, "Okay, people, settle down. . . . Hey! Patrick, did you hear me?" Patrick: "No, ma'am. What'd you say?" Ms. Lewis: "If you weren't so involved with Cindy over there, maybe you'd hear something!" Laughter erupts from the class, as comments are made like, "Wooo, Patrick is involved with Cindy!" Feeling embarrassed that once again she's having trouble getting the class' attention, Ms. Lewis gives a half-hearted laugh at the joke on Patrick, but she realizes that her comment was counterproductive with respect to getting the lesson started.

Raising her voice above the din, Ms. Lewis calls roll:

Ms. Lewis: Genan?
Genan: Here.
Ms. Lewis: Paulette?

Exhibit 5.1
How Ms. Lewis plans for students to transfer the points they plot for homework onto a Cartesian plane.

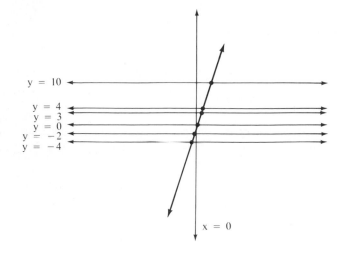

Paulette: Here.
Ms. Lewis: James? . . . James, aren't you here? James, answer the roll!
James: —Oh! Yes, I'm here.
Ms. Lewis: Answer me right away next time. Jeannie? Has anyone seen Jeannie?
Davilon: Oh, yeah, she's still in orchestra.
Ms. Lewis: Why doesn't anyone ever tell me these things? . . . Okay, Winston?

Eighteen minutes after the bell, the roll has been taken, the absentee list is posted on the door to be picked up by the office staff, and the students are finally settled well enough for Ms. Lewis to begin putting her lesson plan into effect. She announces, "Take out your homework." This leads to another eruption of student comments and quips (e.g., "What homework? I didn't know you were going to pick this up!"). Ms. Lewis responds, "If you had listened, yesterday, you'd know about the homework. Melissa, do you have yours? . . . Great, you're so dependable! Write it up on the board for me."

Some students pay attention while others entertain themselves in other ways, as Melissa writes the following on the board:

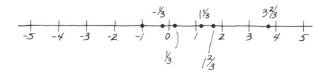

Ms. Lewis says to Melissa: "That's not how you were supposed to do it. Did anybody do this the way I told you to?" Remembering that Ms. Lewis had just praised her for being dependable, Melissa feels embarrassed. Another round of remarks and quips are heard from the class, and Ms. Lewis is clearly annoyed. She says, "Okay, settle down. Let me show you how you were supposed to do this assignment." As Melissa sheepishly returns to her place, Ms. Lewis begins writing on the board, using a *separate* number line to plot each of the six points (Exhibit 5.2). As Ms. Lewis writes on the board with her back to the class, a number of students pass the time by talking and doing things unrelated to mathematics. As she writes, Ms. Lewis worries that the noise in her room is distracting neighboring classes, so she yells out "over-the-shoulder" comments such as, "Pipe down!" "That's enough noise already!" and "If you don't get this now, you won't know it for the test!"

With each of the six points plotted on separate number lines on the board, Ms. Lewis directs the class, "Now, take out a sheet of graph paper and draw this first number line on the line where $y = -4$. Then do the second one on the horizontal line where $y = 0$, and . . . ." As she continues with the directions, some students are searching for graph paper while others are trying to borrow some. Only a few are actually listening to the directions.

Exhibit 5.2
Ms. Lewis steps in for Melissa.

Exhibit 5.3
Ms. Lewis does not get to all the
students requesting her help.

Six minutes later, everyone has graph paper and is ready to follow Ms. Lewis' fourth repeat of the directions. She starts again, "Now, this time *listen*! Here, I'll show you on the chalkboard graph." Midway through the explanation, Andrew enters the room and walks up to Ms. Lewis with an admit slip for being late. "Would you sign this for me, Mrs. Lewis?" Ms. Lewis: "Why are you late?"

Eight minutes later, some of the students are quietly working on the task, others are waiting for Ms. Lewis to provide them individual help, and others have completed the task and have begun to think about other things. Ms. Lewis tries to get to each student requesting help, but time doesn't permit (Exhibit 5.3).

Finally, she calls for their attention and tells the class, "This is what you should have done on your graph paper." She then produces the drawing in Exhibit 5.4 on the chalkboard graph.

To lead the students to discover the relationship specified by the objective, she asks, "What can you say about these six points?" A number of students shout out replies.

Exhibit 5.4

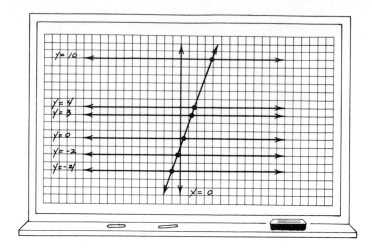

Ms. Lewis: Pipe down! We talk one at a time in here. . . . That's better. Okay, Eileen.

Eileen: They're all lined up in a row.

Ms. Lewis: That's right! Now, what does that tell us?

The discussion continues, but the students don't appear to be relating the six equations to $y = 3x - 1$ and the bell to end the period is about to ring. Frustrated, Ms. Lewis aborts her plan to use inductive questions leading students to discover the relation for themselves. She says, "Okay, this is what you're supposed to understand. We could express these six equations as one by writing $y = 3x - 1$ and then plot the coordinate points (x, y) like . . . ."

The bell rings and the students rush for the door before Ms. Lewis finishes the explanation and before she assigns homework.

A TEACHER'S MOST PERPLEXING PROBLEM

Why do some teachers orchestrate smoothly operating classrooms, where students cooperatively and efficiently go about the business of learning with minimal disruptions (e.g., Mr. Citerelli in Vignette 4.8), whereas others (e.g., Ms. Lewis) ineffectively struggle with student misbehaviors, trying to involve them in planned learning activities? Whether your teaching experiences are satisfying or marked by constant, frustrating struggles trying to get students to cooperate with you depends largely on how well you apply fundamental, research-based classroom-management principles. Overwhelmingly, teachers indicate classroom-management and discipline problems cause their greatest difficulties and lead to feelings of inadequacy during their first 2 years of teaching (Cangelosi et al. 1988; Evertson 1989). According to studies conducted over the past 75 years, improper management of student behavior is the leading cause of teacher failure (Bridges 1986, 5).

ALLOCATED AND TRANSITION TIMES

Examine the 1-day's lesson plan given in Exhibit 5.5. Note that five learning activities are planned:

1. Item 1 of the agenda indicates that the students are to work on exercises from page 124 of their text at the very beginning of the period.
2. Items 4–6 indicate that the students are to transfer results from their previous homework onto a single Cartesian plane and then engage in a questioning/discussion session intended to culminate with two discoveries.
3. Item 7 indicates that the students are to work individually at their places as the teacher provides one-to-one help.
4. Items 8–9 indicate that the students are to engage in a questioning/discussion session intended to culminate in a discovery.
5. Items 10–11 indicate that the students are to engage in a homework assignment.

The time periods in which you plan for your students to be involved in learning activities are referred to as *allocated time*. Thus, the lesson plan in Exhibit 5.5 provides for five different *allocated time* periods. The time students spend *between learning activities* is referred to as *transition time*. If the lesson plan of Exhibit 5.5 is followed, transition time should occur during the following periods:

1. While students are entering the room, obtaining the directions for the initial assignment, taking out their homework, and locating the materials to begin the exercises from page 124.
2. As indicated by item 3, when they have just stopped the first learning activity and are receiving directions for the second.
3. Just after the learning activity in item 6, as they receive directions for and prepare to work on the exercises indicated by item 7.

Exhibit 5.5
Example of a day's lesson plan.

Unit: #6, Graphs and Linear Equations / *Day:* 2nd / *Date:* Tues., 10/18

Objectives: #3. Explains why the graph of $y = ax + b$ (where x and y are real variables and a and b are real constants) is a line (*conceptualization*)

#4. States that the graph of $y = ax + b$ (where x and y are real variables and a and b are real constants) is a line (*simple knowledge*)

Agenda for the class session:

1. As students enter the room, direct them to begin immediately the following assignment appearing on the board:

    A. Take out your homework and place it on your desk.

    B. Work exercise items 13, 14, 18, 21, and 23 from page 124 of the text.

2. As they work on the assignment, move from student to student silently taking roll and checking homework. Note whose homework you want to use as examples for explanations to the class.

3. Call a halt to the individual work. Have someone put her or his homework on the board as everyone else takes out a sheet of graph paper.

4. Direct the person at the board to transfer the six number lines, each with a plotted solution for x, onto the board graph where $y = -4, -2, 0, 3, 4,$ and $10,$ respectively. Direct those at their places to do the same on their graph papers.

5. Use leading questions to lead them to discover that the six points are collinear as follows:

6. Use leading questions to get them to associate the six equations with $y = 3x - 1$.

7. Have the person at the board return to his or her place and assign everyone to repeat the procedure completed for homework and in item 4 above on each of the following sets of equations:

$-9 = 5x + 4$	$4 = -2x$	$3 = x - 7$	$-1 = 3x^2 - 1$
$-5 = 5x + 4$	$1 = -2x$	$-4 = x - 5$	$1 = 3x^2 - 1$
$0.9 = 5x + 4$	$0 = -2x$	$0 = 7x - 1$	$8 = 3x^2 - 1$
$3 = 5x + 4$	$-12 = -2x$	$13 = x - 7$	$9 = 3x^2 - 1$

Keep the previous work on the board, so as they are working you can provide efficient help as you circulate about the room working with individuals.

8. When at least 75% of the class have completed the first three sets and five have completed all four sets, call a halt to the work and engage them in an inductive questioning session to get them to discover the relation specified by Objective #3.

9. After they've articulated the relation, have them enter it into their notes and have at least five people repeat it aloud.

10. Assign: (a) Complete the exercise begun at the beginning of class, (b) study pp. 126-127, working through the examples, and (c) work each exercise items 1, 5, 7, 9, 15, 17, 21, and 22 from pp. 127-128.

11. As time permits, have them begin the r homework.

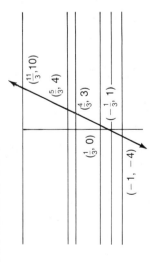

Points: $\left(\frac{11}{3}, 10\right)$, $\left(\frac{5}{3}, 4\right)$, $\left(\frac{4}{3}, 3\right)$, $\left(\frac{1}{3}, 0\right)$, $\left(-\frac{1}{3}, 1\right)$, $(-1, -4)$

4. When the teacher calls a halt to the individual work exercises and directs the students into the questioning/discussion session indicated by items 7–8.
5. While the teacher assigns the homework.
6. As the class session ends and the students exit the classroom or wait for their next class.

STUDENT BEHAVIORS
On-Task Behavior

A student's behavior is *on-task* whenever the student is attempting to follow the teacher's directions during either transition or allocated time. The students in the following examples are *on-task*:

❑ As Joe enters the classroom for his algebra I class, he sees his teacher point to the assignment on the board. He immediately goes to his desk and begins the assignment.
❑ During a questioning/discussion session, Jolene listens to what her teacher and peers are saying, occasionally volunteering her own questions, comments, and responses to others' questions.

Engaged Behavior

A student exhibits *engaged* behavior by being on-task during allocated time. In other words, whenever students are attempting to participate in a learning activity as planned by the teacher, the students are *engaged in the learning activity*. The students in the following examples display engaged behaviors:

❑ During a questioning/discussion session, Jolene listens to what her teacher and peers are saying, occasionally volunteering her own questions, comments, and responses to others' questions.
❑ Carol works on the textbook exercises assigned by her teacher.

Off-Task Behavior

A student's behavior is *off-task* whenever the student fails to be on-task during either transition or allocated time. The students in the following examples are *off-task*:

❑ As Marlene enters the classroom for algebra I class, she ignores her teacher's directions to begin the assigned exercises; instead, she grabs Justin and begins arguing with him over a disagreement they had earlier.

❑ During a questioning/discussion session about graphs of linear equations, Steven quietly daydreams about the car he plans to buy.

Disruptive Behavior

A student's behavior is *disruptive* if it is off-task in such a way that it interferes with other students being on-task. Thus, a student who is being disruptive not only fails to cooperate during transition or allocated time but also prevents or discourages others from behaving in accordance with the teacher's plans. The students in the following examples are being *disruptive*:

❑ As Marlene enters the classroom for algebra I class, she ignores her teacher's directions to begin the assigned exercises; instead, she grabs Justin and begins arguing with him.
❑ During a questioning/discussion session about graphs of linear equations, Rudolph interrupts others while they are talking and makes jokes that distract others from concentrating on the planned mathematical topic.

Exhibit 5.6 provides examples of student behaviors classified as *on-task, engaged, off-task,* and *disruptive*.

Isolated Behavior

An incident in which a student exhibits a particular behavior is considered *isolated* if that behavior is not habitual for that student. In the following examples, Debbie's *off-task* behavior during a particular lecture and Frank's *on-task* behavior during a particular exercise are *isolated*:

❑ Ordinarily, Debbie diligently listens to and takes notes during her teacher's lectures. However, today she is excited about being offered a job and she thinks about the job rather than concentrating on her teacher's explanations about the graphs of linear equations.
❑ Ordinarily, Frank puts very little effort into his mathematics assignments, completing only mindless one-step exercises and skipping others. However, because an unusual aspect of today's assignment interests him, he assiduously works through every exercise.

Behavior Pattern

A student displays a *behavior pattern* by habitually repeating a particular type of behavior. For example,

Exhibit 5.6
Examples of student behaviors

On-Task

Engaged in Learning Activities

❑ Responding to questions during a questioning/discussion session in a manner consistent with the procedures established by the teacher.
❑ Attempting to solve a problem posed in class.
❑ Making suggestions, raising questions, and posing problems as directed by the teacher for group discussion session.

On-Task During Transition Time

❑ Listening to the teacher's directions for the next learning activity.
❑ Moving from a small-group to a large-group class arrangement as directed by the teacher.
❑ After completing a test, patiently and quietly waiting for other students to finish theirs.

Off-Task

Disruptive

❑ Throwing paper across the room while the teacher is explaining an algorithm at the chalkboard.
❑ Fighting with another student as the two are about to leave the classroom.
❑ Making a rude remark in response to the teacher's question.

Nondisruptive

❑ Daydreaming during an explanation of an algorithm.
❑ Working on a writing assignment for English class during time allocated for individualized work on a mathematics exercise.
❑ Discreetly using unauthorized notes to cheat on a test.

❑ Debbie almost always listens diligently to her teacher's lectures and carefully takes notes.
❑ Christine and Walt frequently talk to one another in mathematics class, but the conversations are rarely about mathematics.

TEACHING STUDENTS TO BE ON-TASK
Learned Behavior

Socializing with friends, eating, sleeping, partying, watching television, and playing games are the kinds of behaviors that people (e.g., your students) are ordinarily inclined to exhibit. Entering a classroom in an orderly fashion, working on mathematics exercises, listening to a lecture, engaging in an inductive questioning session, taking tests, raising a hand before speaking, and doing homework are the kinds of behaviors we expect from our students. Since such on-task behaviors tend to conflict with those that people are naturally inclined to exhibit, on-task behaviors need to be *taught* to students. On-

task behaviors (e.g., the six listed in Exhibit 5.6) are *learned* by students. If you expect your students to choose to cooperate with you and be on-task, then you need to *teach* them just how to do that and make sure their efforts are reinforced.

Communicating Expectations

You are responsible for helping your students achieve learning objectives and, thus, engaging them in learning activities. This requires motivating them to be on-task themselves and preventing them from disrupting the learning opportunities of their classmates. But because of experiences they may have had with other teachers who were either less conscientious or less able than you in obtaining and maintaining their cooperation, they may initially come to your class not knowing just how serious you are regarding these responsibilities. So, one of your first tasks will be to begin communicating exactly how you expect them to conduct themselves in your classroom. Consider how the teacher in the following vignette fails to heed that advice.

❑ **VIGNETTE 5.2**

Mr. Boone is conducting the third day's lesson of an algebra I class. He asks, "Who can tell me what a *variable* is?" Four students raise their hands, but before Mr. Boone calls on one of them, Mike yells out, "A variable is a letter that stands for a number."

Mr. Boone: Where did you learn that?
Robin: That's what we had in prealg—.
Mr. Boone: We are supposed to wait our turn to talk.
Robin: Mike didn't!
Mr. Boone: Then, Mike was rude. Anyway, this is really important, get it down.

Mr. Boone writes down the statement shown in Exhibit 5.7 on the overhead projector. Most of the students are unable to read what's on the overhead screen; some don't bother trying. Carney whispers to Mai-Lin, "What's that say?" Mr. Boone sees them and snaps, "Apparently you two don't need to understand this or else you wouldn't be wasting your time talking!"

Near the end of the period, Mr. Boone makes a homework assignment and warns, "I'll be checking to see that it's done first thing tomorrow. If you don't have it, you'll lose points on your grade."

The next day, he has the students place their homework papers on their desks and he quickly walks by each desk, checking the names of those who don't have anything written down for the assignment. No further reference is made to the homework.

Although Mr. Boone said, "We're supposed to wait our turn to talk," he tolerated Mike speaking ahead of those who raised their hands and tried to speak in turn. Thus, he unwittingly communicated to the class that he does not take his own dictates very seriously and does not expect them to either. By presenting the important definition on the overhead so that it was difficult for most of the class to read, he unwittingly hinted that the mathematical content isn't important enough for him to take the trouble to express it clearly. Mr. Boone also played down the importance of the mathematical topic at hand by raising the irrelevant question, "Where did you learn that?" Calling Mike "rude" and being sarcastic with Carney and Mai-Lin encourages antagonistic relationships. Students learn that they are expected to compete with Mr. Boone in a game of "put-downs." The way in which homework was assigned and checked suggested that the experience of doing the homework is not as important as having something down on paper to avoid a loss of points.

By contrast, the messages students receive in the following vignette are the messages their teacher intends for them to receive:

❑ **VIGNETTE 5.3**

Ms. Strong is conducting the third day's lesson of an algebra I class. She says, "I'm going to ask you a question. You are to take 30 seconds to formulate an answer silently in your mind. Then, if you want to share it with the class, please raise your hand to be recognized. The question is, What is a variable?" Sybil yells, "It's a—." Ms. Strong immediately faces Sybil, interrupting her with a stern look and a gesture silently indicating silence. Thirty seconds later, Ms. Strong calls on John, who says, "A variable is a letter that stands for a number." "That's a definition that appears in some books. I'm glad you remembered it. However, you need to understand a different definition for variable for the work we'll be doing in here. Here's our definition," she replies as she displays the overhead transparency slide shown in Exhibit 5.8.

Near the end of the period, Ms. Strong makes a homework assignment that's clearly related to the day's lesson about variables. The next day, she begins the period with a short test. Students who worked diligently on the homework assignment have no trouble with the test, but other students find it too difficult.

Exhibit 5.7

A variable is a quantity, quality, or characteristic that can assume more than one value.

Exhibit 5.8

A <u>VARIABLE</u> is a quantity, quality, or characteristic that can assume more than one value.

Reinforcing On-Task Behaviors

Once students learn how you expect them to behave, you need to make sure that their cooperative, on-task behaviors are *positively reinforced*. A *positive reinforcer* is a stimulus occurring after a behavior that increases the probability of that behavior being repeated in the future. In the previous example, Ms. Strong positively reinforced students doing homework by following up the assignment with a short test that was rewarding only for those who had done the homework. She also avoided positively reinforcing Sybil's speaking-out-of-turn behavior by not allowing her to have the floor.

Consistent, positive reinforcement of isolated behaviors results in the formation of behavior patterns; furthermore, students will extinguish a behavior that proves unrewarding (Cangelosi 1988a, 33–37, 218–220). Thus, it is critical for you to make sure that your students' on-task behaviors are positively reinforced and their off-task behaviors are not.

Planning for Students to Be On-Task

Students' understanding of your expectations, positive reinforcement of on-task behaviors, and discouragement of off-task behaviors are such critical factors to your teaching success that you cannot afford to allow them to be functions of chance. You need deliberately to design strategies for teaching students to be on-task as an integral part of your plans for teaching them mathematics. Such plans should include methods for (1) establishing a favorable climate for learning mathematics, (2) communicating effectively, (3) establishing rules of conduct, (4) establishing classroom procedures, (5) conducting engaging learning activities, and (6) dealing with off-task behaviors. These topics are addressed in the remainder of this chapter and in Chapter 6.

ESTABLISHING A FAVORABLE CLIMATE FOR LEARNING MATHEMATICS
Priority on the Business of Learning

Your students are in the *business of learning*; you are in the *business of teaching* (i.e., helping them learn). Vignette 5.1 illustrates a case in which a teacher, Ms. Lewis, struggles unsuccessfully to get her students engaged in learning activities. Her students did not appear to consider learning mathematics very serious business. As is true in many classrooms (Jones 1979), a major portion of the time students spent in Ms. Lewis' class was wasted with matters unrelated to the business of learning (e.g., taking roll, inefficient transitions, and off-task verbal exchanges). Whether your teaching experiences are dominated by exhausting, frustrating struggles with off-task student behaviors or by satisfying efforts engaging students in smoothly run learning activities depends largely on whether your students consider your classroom a place for wasting time or a place for conducting the business of learning mathematics.

Students determine that learning mathematics is serious business in your classroom not because you tell them so but because of the attitude you display from the first day you walk in the room. First of all, *you* must sincerely believe that the lessons you plan for your students are vital to their achievement of worthwhile learning goals. Then you demonstrate that belief by getting the class off to a businesslike start, being prepared and organized, modeling professional, purposeful behavior, orchestrating efficient transitions, and maintaining a comfortable, nonthreatening environment.

A Businesslike Beginning

Students arrive in your class on the first school day with some preconceived notions about your expectations for them. The vast majority anticipate being required to follow teachers' directions and know that antisocial behaviors (e.g., fighting), blatant rudeness, and highly disruptive behaviors (e.g., screaming in class) are not generally tolerated. But experience has taught them that teachers vary considerably when it comes to dedication to their work, what they tolerate, expectations, awareness of what students are doing, assertiveness, decisiveness, predictability, respect for students, and respect for themselves. In their initial encounters with you, they will not yet know the following:

❑ How seriously you take your responsibility for helping them learn.
❑ Which specific student behaviors you expect, which you demand, which you tolerate, which you appreciate, which you detect, which you ignore, which you reward, and which you punish.
❑ How predictably you react to their behaviors.

Thus, your students are initially filled with uncertainties about you. During this period of uncertainty, they will be observing your reactions, assessing your attitudes, assessing their place in the social order of the class, assessing their relationship with you, and determining how they will behave in your classroom. Because students tend to be more attentive to your words, actions, and reactions, during this "feeling-out" period of uncertainty, it is an opportune time for you to communicate some definitive messages that establish the classroom climate and set the standards of behavior for the rest of the course. Thus, it is critical that you begin each course in a very businesslike fashion, tending to the work at hand: learning and teaching mathematics.

Being businesslike does not imply being somber, stiff, or formal. The business of learning and teaching mathematics is best conducted in a friendly, relaxed atmosphere where hearty laughter is appreciated. Being businesslike does imply that learning activities, whether enjoyable or tedious, are considered important and that matters unrelated to the learning of mathematics are dispatched efficiently.

To effect a businesslike beginning to your course, immediately involve students in a learning activity with the following features:

❑ *Directions for the activity are simple and unlikely to confuse anyone.* This allows your students to get to the business of learning mathematics without experiencing bewilderment over what they are supposed to be doing. This initial experience teaches students to expect to understand your directions and enhances the probability that they will attend to them in the future. If students are confused by your initial directions, they may not be as willing to try to understand subsequent ones. Later, after they have developed a pattern of

attending to your directions, you can begin introducing more complicated procedures to be followed.
❑ *The activity involves them in a task that is novel for them but one in which they are likely to succeed and experience satisfaction.* Leaving them with the impression that they successfully learned something should serve to provide positive reinforcement for engaged behaviors.
❑ *All students are concurrently engaged in the same activity.* Later in the course, it will be advantageous to have students working on differentiated learning activities. But in the early stages of the course, having all students working on the same task allows you to keep directions simple, monitor the class as a whole, and compare how different students approach the common task. Besides, until you become better acquainted with students, you hardly have a basis for deciding how to individualize.
❑ *The activity is structured so that you are free to monitor student conduct and immediately stem any displays of off-task behaviors.* Jacob Kounin (1977) demonstrated that students are more likely to cooperate with a teacher they believe is "on top of things" and in control of classroom activities. He coined the term "withitness" to refer to a teacher's awareness of what students are doing. You are in a better position to be *with it* during activities in which you are free to move about the classroom and position yourself near students than at times when your movements are restricted (e.g., when stationed at a chalkboard, standing behind a lectern, or sitting at your desk). Surely you want to be especially with it during the early stages of a course.

The following vignette illustrates an ideally designed beginning to a course.

❑ **VIGNETTE 5.4**

It is the opening day of a new term at Faultline High School. The bell ending the third period rings; there are 5 minutes before the bell for the fourth period. Mr. Krebs, in preparation for the arrival of his fourth-period geometry class, turns on a video player showing a tape on a prominently displayed monitor with the volume control set rather loud. As required by school policy, Mr. Krebs stations himself just outside his classroom during the change of periods. As students enter the room, they hear Mr. Krebs' voice emanating from the video monitor repeating the following message, which also appears in print on the screen (see Exhibit 5.9): "Please sit in the desk displaying a card with your name. If no desk has your name card on it, please sit at one of the desks with a blank card. There you will find a marking pen for you to print and display your first

Exhibit 5.9
Opening day in Mr. Kreb's
fourth-period geometry class.

name. Once seated at your desk, please remove the questionnaire from inside your desk. Clear the top of your desk except for the questionnaire, a pen or pencil, and your name card. Write answers to items one through four on the questionnaire and wait at your desk for further instructions. Thank you. This message will be repeated until the beginning of the fourth period. After the bell, the directions for today's first lesson will appear on the screen." Exhibit 5.10 depicts the questionnaire.

Five seconds after the bell, the message stops repeating and Mr. Krebs is circulating among the students. He gently taps one inattentive student on the shoulder and points toward the monitor. The students takes the cue. Several times students attempt to speak to him, but he responds with a gesture indicating for them to watch the screen. Mr. Krebs' image appears on the video screen with the following message as Mr. Krebs himself continues to move about the room monitoring the students: "I am about to show you two objects. One, we'll call object A, the other object B. Here they are":

"Both objects are trees. *Describe* how they look different in the blanks for item 5 on your questionnaire. . . . If you wrote that object B is larger, then I can't argue with you. But if so, take about 25 seconds more to describe in what way object B is bigger than object A. . . . Thank you. Now, I'll show you objects C and D:"

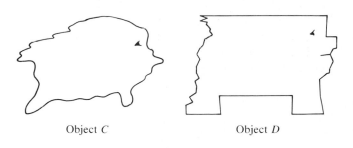

Object *C*   Object *D*

The video presentation continues in a similar vein with students describing differences between each of the pairs for items 6, 7, 8, 9, and 10.

Object *A*

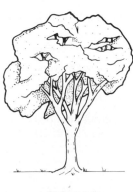

Object *B*

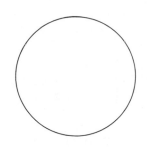

Object *E*

Object *F*

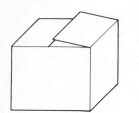

Object *G*

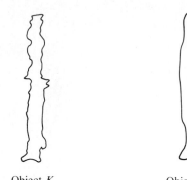

Object *K*   Object *L*

Object *H*

Object *I*

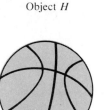

Object *J*

As this continues, Mr. Krebs is circulating about the room reading over students' shoulders as they write. After item 10, the video program signs off and Mr. Krebs engages the students in a questioning/discussion session in which they share responses to items 5 through 10. Mr. Krebs highlights descriptors such as taller, wider, pointier,

Exhibit 5.10
Questionnaire Mr. Krebs used on the first day of class.

1. What is your name? _____

2. Name two things that are more fun for you than filling out this questionnaire.
   _____
   _____

3. Name two things that are less fun for you than filling out this questionnaire.
   _____
   _____

4. What do you think geometry is? _____
   _____
   _____

   WAIT FOR FURTHER DIRECTIONS FROM
   THE VIDEO SCREEN
   BEFORE FILLING OUT THE REST OF
   THIS QUESTIONNAIRE.

5. How does object A look different from object B?
   _____
   _____

6. How does object C look different from object D?
   _____
   _____

7. How does object E look different from object F?
   _____
   _____

8. How does object G look different from object H?
   _____
   _____

9. How does object I look different from object J?
   _____
   _____

10. How does object K look different from object L?
    _____
    _____

rounder, boxier, smoother, and rougher. He plays upon these descriptors to explain what geometry is all about.

Mr. Krebs collects the completed questionnaires; he will use their responses to the first four items in assessing their attitudes and perceptions about geometry. He then distributes copies of the course syllabus and uses it to preview the course for the students. Textbooks are distributed and some administrative matters are taken care of just before the bell sounds.

Mr. Krebs had checked roll and posted the attendance report outside the classroom door for the office personnel while the students were in the midst of the video presentation.

Preparation and Organization

Mr. Krebs left his students with the impression that he expects directions to be followed and that the business of learning is to be afforded the highest priority in his classroom. Reread the scenario and list some of the specific steps he took to convey that message. For example, he did the following:

❑ *Prepared the videotaped presentation.* This use of technology managed to grab students' attention, freed Mr. Krebs to remain near the students monitoring their behaviors, and gave the students the impression that he has his classroom organized and under control.
❑ *Prepared name cards and placed them on desks.* Mr. Krebs used the class list to make the name cards and assign seats. The fact that these arrangements were made ahead of time gives students still another hint that *this* classroom is an orderly place. Even though he has approximately 150 students per term in his five sections of mathematics, because of the name cards Mr. Krebs can call each student by her or his name on the very first day of class. This allows Mr. Krebs, for example, to use the name of a student whose attention appears to be drifting in the midst of the questioning/discussion session. A student is more likely to be efficiently cued back on-task when hearing his or her name being used than when hearing "the person in the pink shirt." The name cards also facilitated roll taking.
❑ *Prepared a questionnaire and specific directions.* Students were kept busy from the moment they entered the room. The specificity of the directions and the structure of the questionnaire reduced transition time, leaving more time for the business of learning.
❑ *Prepared a learning activity that rapidly moved students' attention from the familiar (trees, balls, boxes, and sticks) to an overview of geometry.* Students experienced success in an activity that for them was novel.
❑ *Prepared a course syllabus.* A course syllabus, especially if it is well-organized and professional looking, provides a businesslike touch to the beginning of a course and serves as an advanced organizer as the course progresses. Appendix E provides an example of a course syllabus.
❑ *Organized supplies and materials ahead of time so that administrative matters (e.g., distributing textbooks) could be efficiently completed.* Transition time was reduced, thus allowing more allocated time for students to get to the business of learning mathematics.

Your preparation and organization for the first day's lesson sends students a message that helps set the tone for the rest of the course. Being prepared and organized—not only for the first day but for the entire school year in all your courses—requires planning that begins weeks prior to the opening day of school.

Before the start of a school year, spend some time alone in your classroom visualizing exactly what you want to be going on there throughout the upcoming school session. Picture yourself conducting different learning activities and managing transition times. What traffic patterns for student movement do you want followed? How will you control the sounds in your classroom? For example, do you want only one person speaking at a time during large-group sessions and several speaking in hushed tones during small-group activities? What procedures do you want students to follow for such matters as sharpening pencils, using computers, going to the rest room, and obtaining and returning supplies? How do you plan to make time for completing the work that does not involve interacting with students? Anticipate problems that might arise (e.g., students refusing to follow directions or supplies that don't arrive on time) and simulate alternative ways of responding to those problems.

Here is a list of questions one teacher made for himself in preparation for the opening of school (Cangelosi 1988a, 55–57):

I. Classroom organization and ongoing routines
   A. What different types of learning activities (e.g., video presentations, large-group demonstrations, small-group buzz sessions, and independent project work) do I expect to conduct this term?
   B. How should the room be organized (e.g., placement of furniture, screens, and displays) to accommodate the different types of

learning activities and the corresponding transition times?

C. What rules of conduct will be needed to maximize engagement during the different types of learning activities and to maximize on-task behaviors during transition times?

D. What rules of conduct will be needed to discourage disruptions to other classes or persons located in or near the school?

E. What rules of conduct are needed to provide a safe, secure environment in which students and other persons need not fear embarrassment or harassment?

F. How will rules be determined (e.g., strictly by me, by me with input from the students, democratically, or some combination of these)?

G. When will rules be determined (e.g., from the very beginning, as needs arise, or both)?

H. How will rules be taught to students?

I. How will rules be enforced?

J. What other parts of the building (e.g., detention room or other classrooms) can be utilized for separating students from the rest of the class?

K. Whom, among building personnel, can I depend on to help handle short-range discipline problems and whom can I count on for long-range problems?

L. How do I want to utilize the help of parents?

M. What ongoing routine tasks (e.g., reporting daily attendance) will I be expected to carry out for the school administration?

N. What events on the school calendar will need to be considered as I schedule the class' learning activities?

O. What possible emergencies (e.g., fire or student suffering physical trauma) might be anticipated and, considering school policies, how should I handle them?

II. One-time-only tasks

A. How will I communicate the general school policies to my students?

B. What special administrative tasks will I be required to complete (e.g., identifying number of students on the reduced-payment lunch program and checking health records)?

C. What supplies (e.g., textbooks) will have to be distributed?

D. Are supplies available and ready for distribution in adequate quantities?

E. How will I distribute and account for supplies?

F. Are display cards with students' names ready?

G. How should I handle students who appear on the first day but are not on my roll?

H. What procedures will be used initially to direct students into the classroom and to assigned places?

I. For whom on the student roster might special provisions or assistance be needed for certain types of activities (e.g., students with hearing losses and students confined to wheelchairs)?

III. Reminders for the first week's learning activities

A. Do lesson plans for the first week call primarily for learning activities that (1) have uncomplicated, simple-to-follow directions, (2) are challenging but with which all students will experience success, (3) have built-in positive reinforcers for engagement, and (4) simultaneously involve all students?

B. Do the first week's lesson plans allow me to spend adequate time observing students, getting to know them, identifying needs, and collecting information that will help me make curricula decisions and design future learning activities?

C. Do plans allow me to be free during the first week to monitor student activities closely and be in a particularly advantageous position to discourage off-task behaviors before off-task patterns emerge and positively reinforce on-task behaviors so that on-task patterns do emerge?

Modeling Businesslike, Purposeful Behavior

You teach your students the importance of learning mathematics and being on-task in your classroom more by the attitudes you consistently demonstrate than by telling them, "It's important to learn mathematics," and "You should pay attention." Your classroom behavior serves as a model for students to imitate. Which of the teachers in the next two vignettes demonstrates to her class that she affords the business of learning and teaching mathematics highest priority? Which one allows herself to be easily distracted from that business?

❏ **VIGNETTE 5.5**

Just as the third-period bell rings signaling the beginning of prealgebra class, one of Ms. Simmons' students, Cole, begins telling her about a movie he saw last night. Not wanting to seem uninterested, Ms. Simmons continues to talk with Cole, delaying the start of the lesson by 6 minutes.

Later during the period, while explaining to the class the differences between prime and composite numbers,

Ms. Simmons notices Doris staring off into space, seemingly oblivious to the explanation. Without moving from her position in the front of the room, Ms. Simmons stops her presentation to the class and says to Doris, "Earth to Doris, earth to Doris—come in Doris, return to this planet for your math lesson!" Doris glares back at Ms. Simmons who retorts, "Don't glare at me, young lady! You're the one in outer space instead of where you should be!" Embarrassed in front of her friends, Doris half-smiles and appears to pay attention. Ms. Simmons says, "That's better; now, keep paying attention." But Doris isn't thinking about the prime and composite numbers about which Ms. Simmons is talking. As she pretends to attend to mathematics, Doris' mind is focused on her embarrassment. She feels Ms. Simmons insulted her. Furthermore, some of the other students who were engaged in the learning activity prior to the incident are no longer concentrating on mathematics.

A few more minutes into the explanation, Ms. Simmons notices Mr. Thibodeaux, the principal, beckoning her to the door. She abruptly stops the lesson with, "Just a minute, class. I have some business to take care of with Mr. Thibodeaux." In a few minutes, the class gets noisy and Ms. Simmons turns from her conversation in the doorway to yell, "Knock it off in here! I can't hear what Mr. Thibodeaux is saying; it's important!" Eight minutes later, Ms. Simmons is ready to reengage the students in the lesson, but it takes a while for most of them to shift their thoughts back to mathematics.

❑ VIGNETTE 5.6

Just as the third-period bell rings signaling the beginning of prealgebra class, one of Ms. Von Brock's students, Emerald, begins telling her about a movie she saw last night. Not wanting to seem uninterested but recognizing that the lesson should begin, Ms. Von Brock says, "I really want to hear about that movie, but I'm afraid it's time to start class. Please tell me about it when we have the time."

Later during the period while explaining to the class the differences between prime and composite numbers, Ms. Von Brock notices Jefferson staring off into space, seemingly oblivious to the explanation. Without missing a word in her presentation to the class, Ms. Von Brock moves by Jefferson and gently pats him on the shoulder. Jefferson "wakes up" from his daydream and appears to be attending to the explanation, which continues without interruption as she moves about the room.

A few minutes later, Ms. Von Brock notices Ms. Henderson-Clark, the principal, beckoning her to the door. Rather than stop in midexplanation, she acknowledges Ms. Henderson-Clark with a hand signal indicating "just a moment, I can't stop now." In 2 minutes, with Ms. Henderson-Clark still waiting in the doorway, Ms. Von Brock reaches a stopping point and tells the class, "Keep that last thought in mind—all composite numbers can be expressed as the product of factors, each of which is prime—while I quickly find out what Ms. Henderson-Clark needs." At the door,

Ms. Henderson-Clark attempts to engage Ms. Von Brock in a conversation about a meeting to be held that night. However, Ms. Von Brock responds with, "I can't stop my lesson right now. Please come back in 25 minutes, I'll have them doing independent work then." After that 22-second interruption, she returns to the explanation, by asking, "Now, what was the last thought I asked you to keep in mind? . . . Okay, Maxine." Maxine: "You said that all . . . ."

Efficient Transitions

Unlike Ms. Simmons, Ms. Von Brock indicated to her students that time allocated for learning is too precious to be wasted. By efficiently using the transition times between learning activities, you not only save allocated time, you also communicate to your students the importance of getting down to business. The efficiency of your transitions is at least partially dependent on how you manage to take care of administrative chores, direct students into learning activities, distribute learning materials, and prepare illustrations and audiovisual aids.

Taking Care of Administrative Chores

Administrative chores (e.g., checking the roll and completing accident reports) are a necessary aspect of your responsibilities as a teacher. However, it is not necessary to spend over a third of your class time, as many teachers do, with such noninstructional matters (Cangelosi 1988a, 19; Jones 1979). As Mr. Krebs demonstrated in Vignette 5.4, you can check attendance, homework, and other things while students are busy working on an assignment or test. A seating chart and prepared forms with students' names and grids for checking off such things as whether or not an assignment has been completed facilitate record-keeping and other routine matters with minimal infringement on class time.

Directing Students into Learning Activities

The directions for a learning activity can be delivered during the preceding transition period. That transition period is efficient only if those directions are delivered concisely and clearly enough for students to be properly engaged in the learning activity with only minimal delays. Suggestions for giving directions are provided in Chapter 6. For now, keep in mind how Mr. Krebs (Vignette 5.4), managed to communicate very specific directions to students while remaining free to monitor student behavior closely during the transition period.

Distributing Learning Materials

Having materials laid out for students ahead of time helps streamline transition periods. Mr. Krebs, for example (Vignette 5.4), had the questionnaires tucked away in students' desks before they arrived. However, materials in students' hands before they are needed can be a distraction. The teacher in Vignette 5.7 manages to distribute materials ahead of time in a way that heightens students' curiosity without being a distraction.

❑ **VIGNETTE 5.7**

With the help of his student aide, Mr. Deer seals enough seven-piece tangram sets in envelopes for each student in his fifth-period geometry class (see Exhibit 5.11). Written on each envelope is "Do not open until Mr. Deer tells you to." Prior to fifth period, Mr. Deer and the aide tape the envelopes to the bottom of the students' desks.

Mr. Deer spends the first 30 minutes of fifth period reviewing homework and conducting a lecture/discussion session. After that, he places his hands on his head and directs the students into small-task-group sessions as follows: "Everyone put their hands on their heads like this. . . . Thank you. Please keep them there until you see me take mine down. Beneath the seat of your desk is an envelope containing some tangrams we're about to use. Tangrams are . . . ." (He explains what they are to do with the tangrams.) "Now" (he removes his hands), "locate the envelopes, open them, and go to work."

Preparing Illustrations and Audiovisual Aids

Contrast the efficiency of the transition in Vignette 5.8 to that of the transition in Vignette 5.9.

❑ **VIGNETTE 5.8**

Mr. Burson's class just completed a learning activity in which several students illustrated problem solutions on the chalkboard. The class is now in transition as Mr. Burson prepares to present a proof he wants the class to comprehend. As the students sit and wait, Mr. Burson erases the students' work from the board and then takes 6 more minutes to copy the proof onto the board. In the meantime, students find ways to kill the time.

❑ **VIGNETTE 5.9**

Mr. Bretan's class just completed a learning activity in which several students illustrated problem solutions on the chalkboard. Now, Mr. Bretan shifts to the next learning activity by turning on the overhead projector to display a proof he had previously copied onto a transparency slide. He begins explaining the proof.

Whenever feasible, consider preparing visual and even audio presentations before they are needed in class. This initially infringes on your out-of-class time, but remember that these materials will still be available for use in subsequent classes. Thus, the net savings in time works in your favor. Because he did not take students' time writing on the chalkboard with his back to the class, Mr. Bretan minimized transition time and facilitated keeping students on-task. Overhead projectors, videocassette recorders, and microcomputers (especially with word processing, desktop publishing, and graphic capabilities) are only three of the widely available

Exhibit 5.11
Tangrams Mr. Deer attached under the desks.

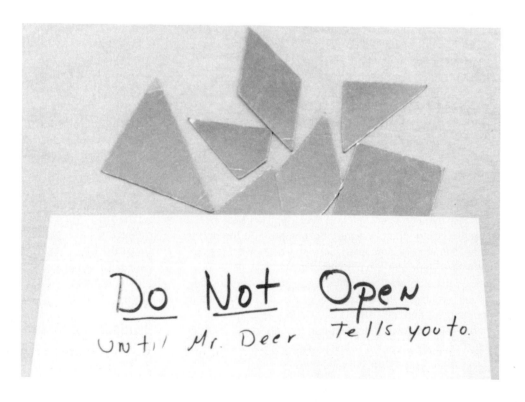

cost-effective devices that make it easier for you to conduct high-quality professional demonstrations to streamline transitions and enhance the businesslike atmosphere of your classroom.

A Comfortable, Nonthreatening Environment

Middle, junior high, and high schools are frightening places for many students (McLaren 1989). Many school environments are contaminated by an atmosphere in which students fear that the immediate risks of becoming enthusiastic about learning outweigh the long-range benefits. Why does such an atmosphere exist? The following contributing factors have been suggested (Cangelosi 1988a, 76):

❑ The threat of physical violence in schools may be so great in the minds of some students that they are more concerned about surviving each school day without being seriously injured than they are about academic concerns.

❑ Some students may fear that their efforts to achieve learning goals will be ridiculed by peers who do not value academic achievement.

❑ Some students believe that if they put an effort into learning activities and still fail to achieve learning goals, they will either be labeled "stupid" or will fail to live up to a previously acquired label of "smart."

❑ Because they feel that a teacher has challenged or embarrassed them in front of their peers, some students consider engaging in learning activities to be tantamount to collaborating with a resented authority figure.

The existence of any or all of the aforementioned factors does not excuse misbehavior or disengagement in learning activities. However, to establish a climate in your classroom that is favorable to learning mathematics, you must see to it that fear and discomfort are overcome by students learning that your classroom is a safe haven for intellectual pursuits. You teach your students that attitude by the manner in which you communicate with them and establishing and consistently enforcing sensible rules of conduct.

COMMUNICATING EFFECTIVELY
Proximity and Body Language

Put yourself in the place of a student sitting in Ms. Spencer's class. As pictured in Exhibit 5.12, she's telling you and your classmates something.

Now, visualize yourself in Ms. Castillo's class. As pictured in Exhibit 5.13, she's telling you and your classmates something.

Exhibit 5.12
Ms. Spencer speaking to you.

To which of the two teachers do you think you might listen more carefully? Research suggests that students are more likely to listen to a teacher who is facing them, making eye contact, and nearby than one in the posture illustrated by Ms. Spencer in Exhibit 5.12 (Cangelosi 1988a, 89–91; Jones 1979). Ms. Spencer's body language suggests that she doesn't take what she's saying seriously enough to face her listeners. Ms. Castillo's body language clearly tells students, "I'm talking to you and I expect you to be listening to this important message!" Your posture, body position, location in the room, use of eye contact, gestures, and facial expressions provide students with an indication of the degree to which you are in control, care for them, and expect to be taken seriously.

Exhibit 5.13
Ms. Castillo speaking to you.

Get in the habit of facing and making eye contact with students to whom you are speaking. When addressing the entire class, move your eyes about the room, making eye contact with one student after another. Managing to focus your eyes on each individual student regularly during the course of classroom activities, occasionally making positive expressions and gestures (e.g., smile, wink, or thumb up) when you've caught his or her eye, helps establish an atmosphere of mutual respect.

When addressing only one or two students at a time, body positioning can be used to indicate clearly to whom your message is intended. Which teacher in the following two vignettes displays the more effective use of body language?

❑ **VIGNETTE 5.10**

Mr. Adams' students are at their desks individually working on an assignment as he moves about the room answering questions and providing one-to-one help. While reviewing an algorithm with Bernice, he hears Charlie and Leona talking from their desks across the room. Without turning from Bernice, he yells, "No more talking, you two!" Others in the class stop their work to find out to whom he's speaking.

❑ **VIGNETTE 5.11**

Ms. Petrovich's students are at their desks individually working on an assignment as she moves about the room answering questions and providing one-to-one help. While reviewing an algorithm with Terry, she hears Moe and Bernie talking from their desks across the room. She softly tells Terry, "Excuse me, I'll be back within 35 seconds." Ms. Petrovich pivots and faces Moe and Bernie, calmly walks directly toward them, and squats down so they are on the same eye level. With her shoulders parallel to Moe's, she looks Moe in the eyes and softly says, "I would like for you two to work on these exercises without further talk." She immediately turns directly to Bernie, achieves eye contact, and repeats the message. Standing up, she pivots and returns to Terry.

Ms. Petrovich's mannerisms made it clear that what she had to say was meant only for Moe and Bernie. Other students didn't need to stop their work to find out that her message didn't apply to them. It is to your advantage to speak so the entire class can hear you *only* when you expect all students to focus their attention on your words. Having experiences stopping their work to listen to you only to find out you are speaking to someone else conditions students to "turn you off."

Descriptive Versus Judgmental Communications

Students feel less threatened, less defensive, and more willing to engage in learning activities when working with teachers who consistently use *descriptive* language than when working with teachers who use *judgmental* language (Van Horn 1982). *Descriptive language verbally portrays a situation, behavior, achievement, or feeling. Judgmental language verbally summarizes an evaluation of a person, achievement, or behavior with a characterization or label* (Cangelosi 1988a, 83). Judgmental language that focuses on personalities is especially detrimental to a climate of cooperation in the classroom (Ginott 1972).

Mr. Farr uses *descriptive* language in the following examples:

❑ Ken and Oral begin talking to one another as Belinda is addressing the class explaining how she solved a problem. Mr. Farr says, "Excuse me, Belinda." Turning to Ken and Oral, he says, "Your talking is preventing me from concentrating on what Belinda is explaining to us."

❑ After Belinda's explanation of how she solved the problem, Mr. Farr exclaims, "By multiplying the expression by x minus three over x minus three, you made it obvious that the limit had to be 14. I'm glad you thought of doing that!"

❑ Mr. Farr returns Robin's test paper with the following comment written by one of the items: "You completed the steps of the algorithm without a single error. However, your answer doesn't take into account that the denominator cannot be zero."

Judgmental language is used by Ms. Camparell in these next three examples:

❑ Kay and Malcom begin talking to one another as Gail is addressing the class explaining how she solved a problem. Ms. Camparell says, "Excuse me, Gail, but there are a couple of rude people in here!"

❑ After Gail's explanation of how she solved the problem, Ms. Camparell exclaims, "Gail, you are quite a mathematician; that was ingenious!"

❑ Ms. Camparell returns Ricardo's test paper with the following comment written by one of the items: "You're too mechanical. You've got to be more of a thinker."

The extra thought required in using descriptive instead of judgmental language will be well worth the benefits in terms of student attitudes and classroom climate. You should consistently make descriptive instead of judgmental comments to your students for the following reasons:

❑ *Descriptive language is far richer in information than is judgmental language.* Students gain specific information about their work, behavior, or situation from your descriptive comments. Judgmental comments provide only broad labels (e.g., "good" and "bad") that students would be better off determining for themselves in light of specific information. Once your students learn that your comments tend to be filled with helpful information, they are likely to be more attentive to your words.

❑ *Descriptive language focuses on the business at hand, not on personalities.* Communicating about work to be performed rather than judgments about those performing the work enhances the businesslike atmosphere of the classroom. Com-

ments such as "You're rude!" or "You're smart!" detract from the business of engaging in mathematical learning activities.

❑ *Unlike judgmental language, descriptive language avoids the labeling of students and the dangerous practice of confounding academic achievement with self-worth.* The delicate and complex relationship among students' self-concepts, desires to be loved and accepted, and experiences with successes and failures is a topic for extensive study reported elsewhere (e.g., Cangelosi 1988a, 23–41, 83–110; Dreikurs 1968; Ginott 1965, 1972; Harris 1969). It is a common mistake to think that students will be motivated to cooperate and study diligently because their teachers praise them for appropriate behaviors and academic achievements and withhold praise or criticize them for misbehaving and failing to achieve. To the contrary, such tactics are more likely to backfire than to motivate desirable behaviors and efforts. For example, Ms. Camparell's reference to Kay and Malcom as "rude people" may lead them to believe she no longer respects them and their only course is to try and live down to their reputations as rude people. Also, overhearing Ms. Camparell label Gail "quite a mathematician" triggered this thought in the mind of another student: "I didn't solve the problem, so I must not be much of a mathematician!" The praise may also have a negative effect on Gail's attitude as she may feel pressure to live up to Ms. Camparell's label. In time, she might protect her reputation as "quite a mathematician" simply by avoiding attempts at mathematical tasks at which she could fail.

Supportive Versus Nonsupportive Replies

Here is a teacher attempting to encourage a student to pursue a mathematical task confidently, only to reap the opposite effect.

❑ **VIGNETTE 5.12**

Mr. DeCarlo is moving about his classroom as his students work individually on factoring polynomials. As he passes Rosalie, she says, "I can't figure these out; they're too hard for me!" Mr. DeCarlo responds, "Rosalie, these should be easy for a smart girl like you! Here, I'll show you how simple they are."

What impact do you think Mr. DeCarlo's well-intentioned response had on Rosalie's thinking about doing mathematics and working with him? She said the exercises are hard. He said they should be easy for a smart girl. Besides denying her feelings, Mr. DeCarlo has indicated that if she thinks the exercises are hard, she's not smart. Rosalie is less inclined to work with Mr. DeCarlo because in her mind, he doesn't listen to what she says (he contradicted her statement) and he thinks she's stupid.

Because his response to Rosalie's expression of frustration failed to demonstrate that he understood that she was experiencing difficulty, Mr. DeCarlo's reply was *nonsupportive.* A reply to an expression of feelings (usually frustration) is considered *supportive* if the response clearly indicates that the feelings have been recognized and not judged to be right or wrong. Here is an example of a teacher making a supportive reply.

❏ VIGNETTE 5.13

Mr. Marciano is moving about his classroom as his students work individually on factoring polynomials. As he passes Seritta, she says, "I can't figure these out; they're too hard for me!" Mr. Marciano responds, "You're having difficulty identifying the common terms. That can be a real struggle. Let's look at this one."

Mr. Marciano demonstrated that he heard and understood what Seritta said. Once he let her know that he recognizes her frustration and she doesn't have to feel uncomfortable about it, Seritta is ready to work with him on the mathematics. He listened to her and now she is prepared to listen to him.

Assertive Versus Hostile or Passive Communications

Studies examining traits of teachers whose students display high levels of on-task behaviors suggest that your students are more likely to cooperate with you and be on-task if you consistently communicate with them in an *assertive* manner rather than in either a *hostile* or *passive* manner (Canter and Canter 1976).

Your communications are *assertive* when you send exactly the message that you want to send being neither intimidating nor intimidated. Consider the following vignette.

❏ VIGNETTE 5.14

"Mrs. Fisher, you know those problem solutions you wanted us to give you Friday?" says Paulette, a student in Ms. Fisher's statistics class. Ms. Fisher: "Yes, Paulette. What about them?" Paulette: "Could we wait 'til Monday to finish to turn them in?" Others in the class chime in with comments such as, "Oh, please Mrs. Fisher, be nice just this once!" Paulette: "We've got a game Thursday night and I know you want to support the team!" Chen: "You wouldn't want us to miss the game, would you?"

Ms. Fisher is tempted to "be nice," "show support for the team," and enjoy the students' cheers if she gives in to their wishes. However, she also realizes the consequences of delaying the assignment. Some students will fall behind in their work. If she doesn't get their work until Monday, she won't be able to examine and annotate them over the weekend, disrupting her schedule. Furthermore, she knows that by adjusting their own schedules, the students could complete the work on time without missing the game.

Ms. Fisher announces to the class, "I understand that you are worried about making it to this important game and still finishing your work on time. You have cause for concern. Because changing the due date will mess up our schedule and because I need the weekend to go over your work and provide you with feedback, the work is still due on Friday." "That's not fair!" cries Porter. Ms. Fisher: "Yes, I know it seems unfair to you. Now, let's turn our books to page 101. . . ."

A less-assertive teacher in Ms. Fisher's situation might have feared jeopardizing a friendly relationship with the students by not agreeing to their request. Actually, her assertive communications enhance her relationship with students because students learn that she takes their work very seriously and her plans for them are well thought out and not changed whimsically. Furthermore, had she altered her plans, thus inconveniencing herself and causing the class to fall behind, she might have disappointed herself for failing to do what she thought best. Such disappointments often lead to feelings of resentment directed toward the students (Wolpe and Lazarus 1966).

Rather than being assertive, your communications are *hostile* when they are intimidating or include personal innuendoes and insults. Ms. Fisher would have displayed *hostile* communications if she had responded to the students' request as follows:

"You people are always trying to get out of work! Do you think your game is more important than mathematics? Mathematics will take you a lot farther in life than games. Besides, if you weren't so lazy, you'd have these problems solved in plenty of time for your game!"

Hostile communications encourage antagonistic feelings that detract from an atmosphere conducive to cooperation and learning.

Passive communications erode the teacher's ability to control classroom activities. Your communications are *passive* when you fail to convey the message you want because you are intimidated or fearful of the reactions of the recipients of your message. Ms. Fisher's communications would have been *passive* if she had responded to the students' request as follows:

> "Well, we really need to have the problems solved by Friday. I really should be going over them this weekend. I wish you wouldn't ask me to do this because I . . . but, okay, just this once—since this is an important game."

Being Responsible for One's Own Conduct

People who frequently communicate passively tend to feel that others control their lives for them. However, except for the relatively unusual cases where one person physically accosts another, one person cannot *make* another do something. Once students realize this and realize that you hold each of them responsible for her or his own conduct, they no longer have excuses for misbehavior. Eavesdrop on the otherwise private conversation between two teachers in Vignette 5.15.

❏ **VIGNETTE 5.15**

Mr. Suarez: Didn't you have Carolyn Smith in prealgebra last year?

Ms. Michelli: Yes. How's she getting along in algebra I?

Mr. Suarez: Awful! Today, I asked her why she didn't have her homework and she told me she had better blinking things to do then my blinking homework.

Ms. Michelli: Except I bet she didn't say 'blinking.' Her vocabulary is more to the point.

Mr. Suarez: Exactly, she used a very vulgar word out loud in front of the whole class.

Ms. Michelli: What did you do?

Mr. Suarez: I was really dumfounded; I didn't know what to do. So, I bought myself some time by telling her to meet me after school today.

Ms. Michelli: If she shows up, what do you plan to do?

Mr. Suarez: I had planned to take firm measures to prevent her from pulling this kind of thing again. But then, Bill, who has her for biology, told me she's an abused child and we need to give her every break. After he told me the kinds of things she's suffered, I understand why she's so uncooperative. How do you think I should handle it?

Ms. Michelli: First of all, knowing about her unfortunate situation helps us understand why she misbehaves. But you don't do her a favor by ever excusing misbehavior. Sure, she has it rougher than the rest of us, but she's still capable of conducting herself in a civil, cooperative way in your classroom. Our job is to hold her to the same standards of classroom conduct we expect of everybody else. Because we're aware of her background, it's easier for us to respond to her misbehaviors constructively rather than angrily.

Mr. Suarez: So, I should stick with my plan for being firm with her.

Ms. Michelli: Let's hear it, and you also need to come up with a strategy if she fails to show up this afternoon.

Mr. Suarez: Well, first, in no uncertain terms I plan to tell her that . . . .

To lead students to understand that only they are in control of their own conduct, consistently use language that is free of suggestions that one person can determine how another chooses to behave. Purge utterances such as the following from your communications with students:

❏ You made me lose control.
❏ You hurt his feelings!
❏ Watch out or you'll get her into trouble.
❏ Does he make you mad?
❏ If she can prove the theorem, so can you.

Replace such phrases with remarks like these:

❏ It's difficult for me to control myself when you do that.
❏ He felt bad after you said that!
❏ Be careful not to influence her to do something she'll regret.
❏ Do you get mad when he does that?
❏ We know the theorem can be proved; she did it.

Remind students that they are in control of and responsible for their own conduct whenever they say things such as, "Well, Sue made me do it!" or "Why blame me, I wasn't the only one!"

Communicating with Parents

A Cooperative Partnership

Ideally, you, each student, and the student's parents form a cooperative team working together for the benefit of the student. Unfortunately, all parents are not able and willing to contribute to such a team. But whenever you do elicit parents' cooperation in support of your work with their children, you reap a significant advantage in managing student behavior and, thus, helping students achieve learning goals. Most, though not all, parents are in a position to do the following:

❏ Encourage their children to cooperate with you and work at mathematics.
❏ Provide time and space for their children to do homework and monitor their attention to homework assignments.

❑ Motivate their children to attend school regularly.

❑ Work with you in addressing discipline problems their children might present in your classroom.

The key to gaining parents' cooperation is establishing and maintaining an active, two-way channel of communications. Such a channel for each student needs to be opened well before either problems arise that call for immediate parental help (e.g., serious disruptive behavior patterns) or summative evaluations of student achievement (especially one involving low or failing grades) must be reported. You open communication channels before crises arise by keeping parents apprised of the learning goals their children should be striving to achieve and how you are attempting to help them reach those goals. Parents need to be informed about how they can help in the process. Basically, you have two vehicles for keeping parents informed, *conferences* and *written communiques.*

Teacher/Parent Conferences

Except for formal "back-to-school nights" held several times a year in most middle, junior, and senior high schools, parents typically expect to have conferences with teachers only to receive news about *summative* evaluations of their children's achievement (i.e., grades) or when a serious discipline problem arises. To establish open channels of communications, however, you need to hold conferences with parents that focus on *formative* evaluations. Note in the following vignette how the teacher keeps steering the conversation away from the parent's obsession with "Is he causing you trouble?" and "Is he going to pass?" and toward "Let's talk about what we're trying to accomplish and how we can get it accomplished":

❑ **VIGNETTE 5.16**

Ms. Sloan teaches 148 students in five sections of mathematics. She does not have time to confer with her students' parents as frequently as she would like. However, by routinely calling three parents every school day and limiting each phone conference to a maximum of 10 minutes, she's able to speak with a parent of each student at least once every 10 weeks. Here's her initial conference with Redfield's mother:

Ms. Breaux: Hello.

Ms. Sloan: Ms. Breaux?

Ms. Breaux: Yes, this is Ms. Breaux.

Ms. Sloan: Ms. Breaux, this is Nancy Sloan, Redfield's prealgebra teacher. If you can manage the time right now, I'd like to spend about 5 minutes talking with you about Redfield's work in mathematics. Can you do that

right now, or should I call you back at a more convenient time?

Ms. Breaux: Oh, this is fine. Is Redfield giving you some kind of trouble? Isn't he doing his work?

Ms. Sloan: He's been very cooperative with me and seems to be working very hard. I just wanted to get acquainted with you and let you know some of the things we're trying to accomplish in mathematics class.

Ms. Breaux: Do you think he'll pass? I never could do math myself, so I can't help him with his homework.

Ms. Sloan: We're just beginning a lesson on rates and percents, and right now we're looking at ways to determine the best prices when shopping.

Ms. Breaux: That sounds more interesting than the math I had in school. Will he be able to learn it?

Ms. Sloan: Yes, he should improve both his skill with percentages and, more importantly, his ability to apply mathematics to his everyday real life. Tomorrow, I'm going to ask them to find newspaper ads that include things like interest rates at banks and discount sales at stores.

Ms. Breaux: It'd be good for him to look at a newspaper instead of watching TV all the time.

Ms. Sloan: Oh, you've given me an idea! Let's use his taste for television to build his interest in using mathematics to solve shopping problems. I'll ask him to make a record of rate-related and percentage-related information from television commercials. Anytime he happens to be watching TV, he should take notes that we'll use in mathematics class.

Ms. Breaux: I can make sure he has a pad and pencil anytime he's in front of that television.

Ms. Sloan: That would really help. Thank you very much.

Ms. Breaux: Anything else?

Ms. Sloan: Does Redfield have a regular time set aside for homework?

Ms. Breaux: No, but I sure could make him do that. How much time does he need?

Ms. Sloan: He takes five subjects. The assignments vary a lot from subject to subject. For mathematics, he needs around 45 minutes a night. Would you please help him schedule a homework routine?

Ms. Breaux: That's a good idea. I'm working tonight, so I won't see him until late. If he's not up, I'll catch him in the morning.

Ms. Sloan: I really appreciate you working with me. My time is up; I've got to phone some other parents—but please feel free to call me. I'll check back with you midway through the term, or sooner if necessary.

Ms. Breaux: Thank you so much for calling. Good-bye.

Ms. Sloan: Good-bye, Ms. Breaux.

Regularly scheduled face-to-face teacher/parent conferences are common in most elementary schools. Although not as common and more difficult to schedule, more and more secondary schools are also setting aside days for such conferences, especially for reporting summative evaluations. School-sponsored teacher/parent conferences and, especially, individual teacher initiatives such as Ms. Sloan's make it easier to solicit parents' help in crisis situations. Consider the next vignette.

❑ VIGNETTE 5.17

For two weeks, Theresa has displayed a pattern of disruptive talking in Mr. Boher's general mathematics class. The second time he stops today's lesson to deal with the problem, he asks her to meet with him after school for yet another discussion on how they can solve the problem. Today, after school, he informs her that he will arrange a conference with her parents for the purpose of devising a way to motivate her to terminate the disruptive talking pattern.

The next day, Mr. Boher, Theresa, and her father meet and at Mr. Boher's insistence agree to the following plan:

Beginning the next day, and continuing for the next two weeks, the first time Mr. Boher detects Theresa talking disruptively in mathematics class, he will issue her a warning. If she continues or disrupts the class a second time that day, he'll direct her to leave class and wait for the next period in the office. Each day she doesn't stay until the end of class, she reports to Mr. Boher to make up missed work. On those days, she'll miss her bus and her father will pick her up at 4:30 when Mr. Boher leaves the building. At the end of the 2 weeks, if Theresa has stayed to the end of at least 7 of the 10 class sessions, she'll be declared "cured," and the "treatment" will be terminated. If she has to meet after school more than 3 of the 10 days, then another three-way conference will be held to map out an alternative strategy.

Consider the following six suggestions for face-to-face teacher/parent conferences (Cangelosi 1988a, 104):

1. Prepare an agenda for the conference that specifies (a) the purpose of the meeting (e.g., to increase the rate at which the student completes homework assignments); (b) a sequence of topics to be discussed; and (c) a beginning and ending time for the conference.
2. Except for special situations, invite the student to attend and participate in the conference. (Healthier, more-open attitudes are more likely to emerge when the student, the guardian, and you are *all* involved.)
3. Schedule the meeting in a small conference room or other setting where distractions (e.g., a telephone) are minimal and there is little chance for outsiders to overhear the conversation.
4. Provide a copy of the agenda to each person in attendance. During the meeting, direct attention to the topic at hand by referring to the appropriate agenda item and by using other visuals (e.g., report card or test).
5. Throughout the conference, concentrate remarks on descriptions of events, behaviors, and circumstances. Focus on needs, goals, and plans for accomplishing goals. Completely avoid characterizations and personality judgments.
6. During the conference be an active listener so that you facilitate two-way communications between you and those at the meeting and thus increase the likelihood that you get your planned message across and learn from the others at the meeting and pick up ideas for working more effectively with the student.

Written Communiques

Out of necessity, teacher/parent conferences are infrequent. Some teachers supplement conferences with weekly or monthly newsletters designed to apprise parents of what is going on in the courses their children are taking. Exhibit 5.14 shows an example of weekly newsletters one teacher sent parents.

By taking the time to write such form letters, you foster the goodwill and understanding of parents. Their understanding of what you are trying to accomplish with their children will serve you when you want to call on them for help.

Professional Confidences

Violations of Trust

Does anything bother you about the teacher's conduct in the following situation?

❑ VIGNETTE 5.18

In a teacher/parent conference with Lamar Monson's father, Ms. Bangater says, "Lamar is one of my better mathematicians. If only all my students caught on so fast! Do you know Ward Anderson?" Mr. Monson: "It seems as if Lamar has mentioned him before." Ms. Bangater: "You can't imagine the trouble I have getting that kid to understand anything!"

Trust between a professional teacher and a student is a critical ingredient in establishing a classroom climate conducive to cooperation and on-task behaviors. Teachers violate that trust by gossiping about students or sharing information gained through teaching with unauthorized persons. Ms. Bangater's comments to Lamar's father should have

Exhibit 5.14
Sample of a weekly newsletter one
teacher sends to parents.

**PARENTS' NEWSLETTER FOR GEOMETRY
2ND PERIOD**

From Charog Berg, Teacher
Vol. 1, No. 13, Week of November 25

Looking Back
Our last letter mentioned that we had begun a unit on quadrilaterals and polygons. I think most of the students were somewhat bored with the 1.5 days we spent reviewing and using definitions of the terms trapezoid, parallelogram, rectangle, rhombus, square, perimeter, base, and height. I was pleasantly surprised that most already possessed a working vocabulary of these terms from their work from previous mathematics courses.

Enthusiasm picked up when we delved into some hands-on problems that led to some useful discoveries about quadrilaterals. Ultimately the students developed some shortcut algorithms based on relations and theorems they discovered. Toward the end of the unit, we worked on applying our discoveries to real-life problem situations. This might explain why your daughter or son spent time gathering measurements from around your living space.

The results of the unit test given on November 22 proved interesting—to me anyway. The scores were somewhat higher than I had anticipated; I felt pleased about that. But what really surprised me was that according to my statistical analysis of the results, the class did far better on the parts of the test that taxed their thinking abilities than on the parts where they only had to remember something.

This Week
This week we will be working on more-sophisticated problems involving parallelograms and their relations in three-dimensional space. I hope that words such as plane and half-plane will creep into your son's or daughter's vocabulary as we begin examining the space about us in terms of sheets of points. One of the purposes is to get the students to analyze spatial problems systematically, but in a way that does not occur to most people.

Homework assignments will include: (a) Study and work selected exercises from pages 264–269 for Tuesday's class; (b) watch the television program entitled "Spatial Fractions" from 7:00 to 8:30 on Channel 7 Tuesday night and be prepared to discuss its contents on Wednesday; (c) begin working on the worksheet to be distributed on Wednesday and have it completed for Friday's class; (d) study for a test on Monday, December 2.

Looking Forward
After we review the test results on Tuesday, December 3, we'll tie together what we learned from these last two units with some work with mosaics and mapping three-dimensional space. This will lead us into the study of geometric similarities and proportions.

---

been confined to Lamar's achievements, behaviors, and work; there is no need to share information or judgments about other students. Once students acquire the idea that a teacher gossips about them, they tend to be very guarded around that teacher, failing either to share ideas or to attempt difficult tasks.

Privileged Information

When and to whom should you communicate information and express your judgments about students' achievements and behaviors? The following guidelines have been published (Cangelosi 1988a, 107):

1. In most cases, the *student* needs to be kept apprised of his or her own status regarding achievement of learning goals and evaluations of personal behaviors.
2. The student's *guardians* often need to be aware of their child's level of achievement and behaviors for two reasons:

❏ Guardians who understand just what their children are and are not accomplishing in school are in an advantageous position to serve as partners with teachers in helping their children cooperate and achieve.

❑ Guardians are legally responsible for their children's welfare. They do, after all, delegate and entrust some of their responsibilities to teachers. They should know how the school is impacting their children.

3. *Professional personnel (e.g., a guidance counselor or another of the student's teachers) who have instructional responsibilities for that student* sometimes need to know about the student's achievement and behaviors so that they are in a better position to help that student.

4. *Professional personnel (e.g., the principal, subject-area supervisor, or curriculum director) whose judgments impact the curricula and conduct of the school* sometimes need to be aware of an individual student's achievements or behaviors so that they will be in an advantageous position to make school-level decisions.

5. Because a school often acts as an agency that qualifies students for occupations, other institutions, or for privileges (e.g., scholarships), it may sometimes be necessary for a *representative of an institution to which a student has applied* to have knowledge of evaluations of that student's achievements and behaviors. However, school personnel should seriously consider following a policy that they release information on an individual student's achievements and behaviors to such representatives only with that student's and his or her guardians' authorization.

ESTABLISHING RULES OF CONDUCT AND CLASSROOM PROCEDURES
Necessary Rules of Conduct

In virtually all schools, there is a published set of *school rules* for student conduct (e.g., fighting is prohibited on school property). Furthermore, each teacher typically has his or her own set of rules for how students are to conduct themselves in the classroom. The *classroom rules of conduct* you establish should provide students with general guidelines for their behavior while under your supervision. The purposes of those rules are to:

1. Secure the safety and comfort of the learning environment.
2. Maximize on-task behaviors and minimize off-task behaviors.
3. Prevent the activities of the class from disturbing other classes and others outside of the class.
4. Maintain acceptable standards of decorum among students, school personnel, and visitors to the school campus (Cangelosi 1990a, 29).

A few well-understood, broadly stated rules that clearly serve the four aforementioned purposes are preferable to a great number of specific, difficult-to-remember rules (Emmer et al. 1989, 21–23). For example, rules similar to those listed in Exhibit 5.15 may be all you need, providing you make sure your students clearly understand them and that they are consistently enforced.

Having such rules prominently displayed in the classroom reminds students of how you expect them to behave and helps you efficiently respond to students' disruptive behaviors. Consider the following vignette.

❑ VIGNETTE 5.19

Mr. Martinez has the rules listed in Exhibit 5.15 displayed on the front wall of his classroom. While explaining the algorithm for bisecting an angle with a straightedge and compass, he notices Don lightly pricking Justin's arm with the point of his compass. Justin jerks away, turns to Don, and whispers between gritted teeth, "Cut it out!" With the class' attention to the explanation already disrupted, Mr. Martinez stops speaking to the class, walks directly to Don, looks him in the eye, and says, "Please meet with me right after class today, so we can schedule a time to discuss

Exhibit 5.15
The rules of conduct Mr. Martinez displays in his classroom.

Classroom Rules of Conduct

Rule 1:
Respect your own rights and those of others. (*Note:* All students in this class have the right to go about the business of learning mathematics free from fear of being harmed, intimidated, or embarrassed. Mr. Martinez has the right to go about the business of helping students learn mathematics in the manner in which he is professionally prepared without interference from others.)

Rule 2:
Follow directions and procedures as indicated by Mr. Martinez.

Rule 3:
Adhere to school rules.

ways to prevent you from violating rule 1 again." Mr. Martinez continues the explanation.

Although rules (such as Mr. Martinez') are necessary because they serve the aforementioned four purposes, having *unnecessary* rules can be disruptive and detract from a businesslike atmosphere, as in the next vignette.

❏ **VIGNETTE 5.20**

Mr. Leggio grew up with the idea that it is rude for men to wear hats indoors. Without much thought, he instituted a "no-hat-wearing" rule for the male students in his classroom. His efforts to enforce the rule have caused a number of disruptions to learning activities. On most days, Mr. Leggio stands by the doorway at the beginning of each period to check on students for such things as chewing gum and boys wearing hats. Often, this delays the start of learning activities.

Today, while Mr. Leggio is writing on the chalkboard, Mark slips on a baseball hat. Ten minutes later, Mr. Leggio notices it, stops the lesson and snaps, "I'll take that hat, young man!"

Mark: Why?
Mr. Leggio: You know you're not supposed to wear a hat in here!
Mark: Why?
Mr. Leggio: Because it's not polite.
Mark: Who does it hurt?
Mr. Leggio: Me. I can't teach you when you're wearing a hat!

The class laughs and Mr. Leggio begins to feel uncomfortable. Feeling a need to assert his authority, he yells, "Either you give me the hat right now, or you're out of this class for good!" Mark grins and slowly swaggers up to the front of the room and gives up his hat. Mark turns away from Mr. Leggio making a face mocking Mr. Leggio as he slowly returns to his desk. The class laughs, but Mr. Leggio is not sure why as he continues the lesson.

Mr. Leggio cannot justify his no-hat-wearing rule on the basis of the first three of the four purposes for having classroom rules of conduct (i.e., (1) securing the safety and comfort of the learning environment, (2) maximizing on-task behaviors and minimizing off-task behaviors, or (3) preventing the activities of the class from disturbing other classes and others outside of the class). He may argue that the rule helps maintain acceptable standards of decorum among students, school personnel, and visitors to the school campus. However, he should be careful that any rule based on that fourth purpose clearly helps maintain an atmosphere of politeness

and cooperation, not just imposes his personal tastes upon students.

The unpleasant consequences of having *unnecessary* rules of conduct include these:

❏ Teachers become responsible for enforcing rules that are difficult to defend.
❏ When students find some rules to be unimportant, they generalize that others may be unimportant also.
❏ Students who are penalized for resisting unnecessary rules are likely to become disenchanted with school and distracted from the business of learning.

Procedures for Smoothly Operating Classrooms

Whereas rules of conduct define general standards for behavior, *classroom procedures* are the specific operational routines for students to follow. How smoothly classroom operations proceed typically depends on how well procedures have been established for movement about the room, use of supplies, transitions between learning activities, large-group sessions, small-group sessions, individualized work, and administrative duties. As indicated on pages 131–132, you need to determine such procedures when you organize your classroom and courses for an upcoming school term. During the course of a term, however, situations may arise that lead you either to modify previous procedures or to develop new ones. For example, consider the next vignette.

❏ **VIGNETTE 5.21**

Mr. Hood has organized his third-period general mathematics course so that group-learning activities (e.g., lecture, discussion, and questioning sessions) are confined to Mondays, Tuesdays, Thursdays, and Fridays. Wednesdays are saved for individual, make-up, catch-up, and enrichment work. Every Wednesday, students are free to determine how they spend their time as long as they are in the classroom independently working on mathematics in a way that does not disturb their classmates.

Mr. Hood's classroom is arranged similarly to the one diagrammed in Exhibit 2.19. There are 12 microcomputers in the room to accommodate the 29 third-period students.

A month into the general mathematics course, Mr. Hood discovers that on Wednesdays the student demand for use of the computers exceeds the availability of computer time. Students regularly complain that they don't get to the machines because they are dominated by some of their classmates. Another complaint involves diskette abuse. The following procedure that Mr. Hood had been using for maintaining and using diskettes is apparently not working:

Each student is provided storage space in the file boxes kept on the computer tables. To use a computer, a student retrieves one of her or his own diskettes from the file, inserts it in an available machine, completes the work, and returns the diskette to the file.

Students indicate that others are tampering with their diskettes and misfiling them so they cannot easily locate theirs. On some Wednesdays, arguments have erupted over allegations of diskette-stealing as well as "computer-hogging" (see Exhibit 5.16).

Mr. Hood discusses ways of working out more efficient procedures for use of the computers on Wednesdays and of diskette use and maintenance. Based on input from the students, Mr. Hood establishes the following procedures for use of the computers on Wednesdays:

The 12 computer stations are numbered 1 through 12. During the last 10 minutes of class each Tuesday, Mr. Hood will circulate among the students a clipboard containing the sign-up sheet for scheduling computer time on Wednesday. The sheet indicates five 10-minute blocks of time for each station. Each student schedules up to 20 minutes of computer time the first time the sheet is passed around the room. The clipboard is recirculated, in reverse order, until either all students' computer-time needs have been filled or all the 10-minute blocks are exhausted.

Regarding diskette use, the procedures are revised as follows:

The file boxes will be discarded. Each student is responsible for the security of his or her own

diskettes kept in a portable storage box. Students carry their boxes to and from the computer stations.

Teaching Rules and Procedures to Students

Formulating necessary rules and routine procedures will lead to a smoothly operating classroom only if students (1) comprehend the rules and procedures, (2) understand just how to follow them, and (3) are positively reinforced for following them and suffer consequences for violating them. Thus, you need to apply sound pedagogical principles to teach students deliberately about rules and procedures just as you do to teach them about mathematics. The time you spend explaining and demonstrating rules and routine procedures will result in time saved because students will spend more time on-task and transitions will be more efficient.

DEALING WITH OFF-TASK BEHAVIORS
A Systematic Approach

By establishing a favorable classroom climate, communicating effectively, establishing necessary rules and procedures, and conducting engaging learning activities (the topic of Chapter 6), you will avoid many of the off-task behaviors that are so pervasive in most of today's classrooms. However, with a group of 30 or so adolescents, you will still have to deal with some isolated off-task behaviors and off-task behavior patterns. The key to dealing effectively with off-task behaviors—including those that are

Exhibit 5.16
Mr. Hood needs to change procedures for students accessing classroom computers.

disruptive, rude, or even antisocial—is to calmly utilize systematic teaching strategies for getting students to supplant the off-task behaviors with on-task ones. It is quite natural for teachers to *feel* like retaliating against and displaying their power over students who are infringing on the rights of those about them. But such responses are virtually always counterproductive (Cangelosi 1988a, 183–214). Rather than allowing emotions to cloud her thinking, the teacher in the following vignette systematically and thoughtfully deals with a serious disruptive behavior pattern.

❏ VIGNETTE 5.22

Matthew, one of Ms. Asgill's algebra I students, is working in a small-group activity with five others playing a game called Complete the Equation. The student conducting the game draws the next "rule" card and reads aloud, "the square root of an odd integer." The players hurriedly try some ideas out on their calculators, attempting to come up with the number that will complete the equation they've built to this point. . . . Suddenly, Oliver exclaims, "I got it—equation!" Matthew stands up and yells, "Oliver, you cheat, I was about to get mine!" With that, Matthew shoves Oliver, toppling him backward and upsetting the game board and other materials. Having observed the incident from her position across the room working with another group, Ms. Asgill walks unhesitatingly between Matthew and Oliver, looks Matthew in the eye, and in a calm voice says, "Step into the hallway with me." Indicating with a gesture that he is to go first, she follows him to a point just outside the classroom. She faces him directly as his back is to a wall. Looking directly into Matthew's eyes, she firmly but calmly says, "You stay right here until I get back. I'm going to see if I can help Oliver; he may be hurt." She turns away before Matthew has a chance to reply. Actually, she already noted that Oliver didn't appear hurt, but she immediately returns to the scene of the game, where an audience has gathered around Oliver, who is announcing his plans for retaliation. Ms. Asgill interrupts him with, "I'm sorry this happened, but I'm pleased that you are not hurt." Cutting off a student starting to criticize Matthew, Ms. Asgill continues, "Eric and Beatrice, please pick up this mess and set up the game again. We'll start over with Oliver conducting for three players." Raising her voice, she announces, "Everyone return to your work. Thank you."

Quickly returning to Matthew standing against the hallway wall, she says, "I do not have time to deal with the way you behaved during Complete the Equation. Right now, I have a class to teach and you need to continue practicing with equations. We'll have time to discuss how we can stop these disruptions before the first bell tomorrow morning. As soon as your bus arrives tomorrow, meet me at my desk. Will you remember or should I call your house tonight to remind you?" Matthew replies, "I'll remember." Ms. Asgill responds, "Very well, it's up to you. We have only 13 more class minutes to work with equations. Go get

your textbook and notebook and bring them with you to my desk." There, Ms. Asgill directs him to complete an exercise at a desk away from the other students. The exercise works on the same skills that Complete the Equation is designed to develop.

Later in the day, when she finally has a chance to be alone, Ms. Asgill thinks: "I bought myself some time to decide what to do about Matthew's hostile outbursts. . . . I took a chance stepping in front of him while he was still angry. Suppose he had turned on me? Then I wouldn't have him in my class anymore, and I wouldn't have to be here trying to figure out a solution.

"This is the third time he's had a disruptive outburst—but it's the first time he's gotten physically violent. Every time it's been during some type of group activity where there's a lot of student interaction. I don't know if he's been the instigator each time, but he's been right in the middle. But I'm not going to worry with who caused what, just with preventing this from happening again before somebody really gets hurt.

"Until he's learned that antisocial behavior isn't tolerated in my classroom, he'll have to be excluded from student-centered activities—nothing where he interacts with others unless I'm right on top of things orchestrating every move.

"That takes care of the immediate goal of preventing recurrences. But if he doesn't learn to control that temper at least in my class, another outburst will eventually occur, and besides—I don't want to have to keep him separated for the rest of the year. . . . Tomorrow, maybe I should explain my dilemma to him and ask what he would do to solve the problem if he were in my place. That tactic worked well before with Janice. . . . But no, Matthew isn't ready for that; he's far too defensive. He'd start trying to tell me how it's so unfair, that he's always being picked on. Here's what I'll try:

1. Tomorrow, I will not even attempt to explain my reasons for what I'm doing (otherwise he'd try to argue with those reasons and I don't need that). I will simply tell him what we're going to do and not try to defend the plan.
2. Whenever he would normally be in a group activity that I'm not personally directing, I will assign work for him to do by himself at a desk away from the others. As far as possible, his assignment will target the same objective as the group activity.
3. I'll watch for indicators that he is progressing toward willingness to cooperate in activities with other students.
4. As I see encouraging indications, I will gradually work him back in with the other students. But I will begin very slowly and only with brief, noncompetitive-type activities.

"Now, to prepare for this. . . . I'd better come up with a contingency plan if he doesn't show up for our meeting tomorrow morning. . . ."

_____

Note how Ms. Asgill viewed the problem of eliminating the undesirable behavior pattern as she would view a problem of how to help a student achieve a learning objective. By applying teaching techniques to the job of teaching students to choose cooperative on-task behaviors instead of uncooperative off-task behaviors, she is able to focus her time, energy, and thought on the real issues at hand. In the vignette, she did not try to moralize to Matthew about the evils of fighting. She realized that such preaching would fall on deaf ears.

Teachers who do not systematically focus on the behavior to be altered tend to compound difficulties by dwelling on irrelevant issues. For example,

❑ In Vignette 5.1, Ms. Lewis called attention to Patrick's "involvement with Cindy" instead of focusing attention on the business at hand. Later, she asked Andrew, "Why are you late?" instead of quickly directing him to his seat and continuing with the lesson.

❑ In Vignette 5.5, Ms. Simmons dwelt on Doris' daydreaming to make a joke at Doris' expense.

Do not interpret your students' off-task behaviors as a personal attack on you. It's annoying to have your plans disrupted, your efforts ignored, and your authority questioned by adolescents. But they do it out of ignorance, boredom, or frustration or for other reasons that do not threaten your personal worth. Keeping this in mind helps you maintain your wits well enough to take decisive, effective action that terminates the misbehavior and reduces the probability of it recurring in the future.

Thirteen Suggestions

Here are 13 suggestions for confronting off-task student behaviors:

1. Confront Off-Task Behaviors as You Would Confront Situations in which Students Lack Necessary Prerequisites to Learning the Mathematics You Plan to Teach Them. How would you react in the following situation?

❑ **VIGNETTE 5.23**

You have just begun a unit with your intermediate algebra class on logarithmic functions. With the help of an overhead projector, you explain the following definition:

$\log_b x = y$ if and only if $b^y = x$.

Feeling confident that your presentation went well, you move to the next stage of the learning activity and distribute a worksheet with the following exercises:
Fill in the blanks so the statements are true:

If $\log_3 9 = y$, then $y =$ _____ .

$\log_{10} 1000 = 3$ because $10^{\underline{\quad}} =$ _____ .

If $\log_a 8 = 3$, then $a =$ _____ .

Since $3^{-1} = \frac{1}{3}$, $\log_{\underline{\quad}} \frac{1}{3} =$ _____ .

If $\log_5 x = 1$, then $x =$ _____ .

Directing the students to complete the sheet quickly, you walk around the room checking on how they are doing. You note Chuck staring intently at the first one, with the blank left unfilled. "What are you thinking about for this first one?" you softly ask him. Chuck replies, "I don't know how to do it." You respond, "What's the definition of a logarithmic function?" Chuck immediately writes:

$$\log_b x = y \quad \text{if and only if} \quad b^y = x$$

You: In this first one, what's b in the definition?
Chuck: 3.
You: What's x?
Chuck: 9.
You: Then what's y?
Chuck: That's what I can't figure.
You: What does the definition say y should be?
Chuck: It's that little number at the top right here. (He points to the exponent y in the definition.)
You: What's that little number called in that equation?
Chuck: I don't know.
You: Have you heard of the word exponent?
Chuck: I guess so.
You: What's 3^2?
Chuck: I don't know.
You: What's 3 times 3?
Chuck: Nine.
You: What's 3^2?
Chuck: I don't know.
You: What's 5 times 5 times 5?
Chuck: Uhh, 5 times 5 is 25 times 5 is, ahh . . . 125.
You: What's 5^3?
Chuck: I don't know.
You: You know, like this: 5^3.
Chuck: I don't know.

Although you know that Chuck has completed courses in beginning algebra and geometry and that you've "covered" exponents with this class earlier in the course, it appears that Chuck does not know enough about exponents to be ready for this current unit on logarithmic functions.

It's a frustrating situation for you; Chuck is unable to participate in the learning activities for the unit that you've planned. But are you angry with or threatened by Chuck not understanding what he should understand? My guess is that rather than reacting in anger to his lack of mathematical proficiency, you are thinking about the steps you should take to help Chuck heal this learning gap. Either you need to do the remedial work yourself or refer Chuck to some other source of help (e.g., a tutor or placement in a lower-level mathematics class).

Now imagine yourself in the next situation.

❑ VIGNETTE 5.24

You have just begun a unit with your intermediate algebra class on logarithmic functions. With the help of an overhead projector, you explain the definition of a logarithmic function.

Feeling confident that your presentation went well, you move to the next stage of the learning activity and distribute a worksheet for the students to complete quietly at their desks. As you walk around the room checking on how students are doing, you notice Aretha and Armond engrossed in a conversation having nothing to do with your lesson. Neither has even attempted the first item on the worksheet.

Unless the students quickly complete the worksheet as you directed them to do, the next phase of your lesson will be meaningless. Quickly you go over to Aretha and Armond and say, "Let's get to work, you only have 4 more minutes to finish these." They look at you, smile, and say, "Okay, we will." You walk away, only to look back to see that they are once again talking and have not begun the exercises.

Most of us are more likely to react in anger to students' lack of cooperative, on-task behaviors than to their lack of some prerequisite academic learning. But being on-task is also prerequisite to successful participation in learning activities and also needs to be *taught* to students. Students learn to supplant off-task behaviors with requisite on-task behaviors when we respond to their displays of off-task behaviors with sound, systematic pedagogical techniques, not when we react emotionally.

2. Deal Decisively with an Off-Task Behavior or Don't Deal with It at All. What are students learning about the need to follow Ms. Rockwell's directives from their experiences in this example?

❑ VIGNETTE 5.25

Some of Ms. Rockwell's students are busy taking a test while others are supposedly working with computers in the back of the room. As Ms. Rockwell is doing paper work at her desk, she becomes concerned that conversations among those at the computer stations are interfering with the thoughts of the test-takers. She yells from her desk, "No talking in the back!" The students stop talking momentarily, but within a minute the conversations are again loud. "Didn't I say no talking?" Ms. Rockwell yells. This time, the noise level hardly drops at all. Five minutes later, Ms.

Rockwell tries, "Hey, you back there, I've already told you to stop talking! This is your last warning." In another 4 minutes, she tries again, "How many times do I have to say—no talking?" The talking continues.

Ms. Rockwell's test-takers should have been afforded the opportunity to work in undisturbed silence. Thus, the disruptive talking should have been dealt with—not ignored. However, *ignoring* the talking would have been preferable to Ms. Rockwell's indecisive approach. She actually reminded her students that she told them "no talking" while allowing the talking to continue. She might as well have said, "See, you don't have to worry about what I tell you. There are no consequences." She should not give commands she doesn't plan to enforce (e.g., by walking to the back of the room, turning off the computers, having the students wait in another location (e.g., office, gym, outside, or a colleague's classroom) until after the test, and having them make up the computer work after school).

3. Control the Time and Place for Dealing with Disruptions. In Vignette 5.22, Ms. Asgill focuses her immediate efforts on getting the class reengaged in the learning activities after Matthew's outburst. She waited to develop a plan for dealing with Matthew in a setting that she could readily control until she had adequate time to do so. Had she attempted to teach Matthew to change his disruptive behavior pattern at the scene of the incident right after it occurred, she would have had to contend with the following:

❑ She would be burdened with supervising the rest of the students and thus could not focus her full attention on working out a solution to the problem with Matthew.
❑ Matthew would have an audience of peers whose perceptions are more important to him than anything Ms. Asgill might be trying to tell him at the moment.
❑ She would have little time to think through a plan.
❑ Neither she nor Matthew would have time to cool down from the incident.

Don't feel obliged to demonstrate your authority by dealing with a student who has been disruptive in front of the class. It is usually more efficient to get everyone back on-task first and then work on preventing future occurrences at a time and place away from other students. It is easier to work with a disrupter when he or she is not on stage in front of peers. There's no need to be concerned that other students will think that the disruption went unpunished; word will get back that you handled the situation decisively (Cangelosi 1990a, 53).

4. Leave Students Face-Saving Ways to Terminate Misbehaviors.

You are asking for trouble by ever doing anything that leads students to feel embarrassed in front of their peers. If you expect dignified behaviors from your students, you need to avoid situations where a student feels her or his dignity is compromised. Thus, your strategies for dealing with off-task behaviors—even annoying, rude ones—should allow students face-saving ways of choosing on-task behaviors. This is often difficult to do. When students behave rudely, it is tempting to respond with clever comebacks or put-downs. Not only does this practice destroy a healthy climate, it can also backfire, as it did in the following vignette (Cangelosi 1988a, 196–197).

❏ VIGNETTE 5.26

Mr. Sceroler is urging his eighth-grade class to get their homework in on time as he says, "There's nothing I can do if you don't have the work for me to see." Ronald from the back of the room, in a barely audible tone, quips to the student next to him, "He could always go _____ off!" Having overheard the comment, Mr. Sceroler yells at Ronald, "What was that you said?" Ronald begins to grin and look around at his classmates. "You were trying to show off for us and now you can't say anything! What did you say?" Ronald whispers with his head down, "Nothing." Mr. Sceroler sees Ronald back down and begins to feel confident as he continues, "What was that? Speak up. What did you say?" Now facing Mr. Sceroler, Ronald says in a loud voice, "I said I didn't say nothin'!" Mr. Sceroler retorts, "You can't even use decent English. Of course you didn't say anything. You aren't capable of saying anything, are you?" Some class members laugh. Enjoying the audience, Mr. Sceroler smiles. Ronald, very concerned with what his classmates are thinking, suddenly stands up and shouts at Mr. Sceroler, "I said you could always go _____ off, but then I forgot, you don't have a _____ !"

By trying to outwit Ronald instead of providing him with a face-saving way of getting back on-task, Mr. Sceroler extended what would have been a self-terminating incident into a most-unfortunate confrontation with unhappy consequences for all concerned. After hearing Ronald's initial remark, what was Mr. Sceroler's purpose in asking, "What was that you said?" Ronald tried to end the incident by not replying, but Mr. Sceroler's persistence left Ronald with only two options—either lying or repeating what would surely be interpreted as an obscenity. Had the teacher in this example behaved professionally as a secure adult instead of trying to demonstrate his superiority over an adolescent, he would have either ignored the remark or politely directed Ronald to meet with him at a more convenient time.

5. Terminate Disruptions without Playing the "Detective Game."

In the previous anecdote, Mr. Sceroler knew that Ronald was the one who made the rude comment. However, many times, teachers are unable to detect the source of disruptions. Vignette 5.27 illustrates such an example.

❏ VIGNETTE 5.27

Mr. Cambell's lectures, class discussions, and individual help sessions are habitually interrupted by a few students who covertly hoot, "Ooohh-ooooh-ooooh." Initially, he reacts to the disruptive noise by asking, "Okay, who's the owl in here?" His frequent attempts to identify the culprits are fruitless. Students are getting bolder with the hooting and more clever at concealing the sources. Apparently, more students are joining in on the game.

Frustrated, Mr. Cambell seeks the advice of another mathematics teacher, Ms. Les. She suggests that the students don't really intend to make his life so miserable, which is what he's allowing to happen, but that they are simply enjoying a game of cat and mouse that he's unwittingly playing with them. She says he can terminate the game by no longer trying to catch the culprits. She advises him to devise a plan for getting the culprits to stop their discourteous disruptions without having to identify them. She tells him: "Stop worrying about identifying the hooters. Confront the class with the fact that you do not appreciate the rudeness. Explain that you are responsible for teaching them mathematics, but that you cannot do so effectively when they are making that noise. Ask them to respect your rights and one another's rights to go about the business of teaching and learning.

"Follow up that little speech with some action. Anytime you've got a lesson going in which you're lecturing, conducting a discussion, or explaining something and you hear that noise, immediately initiate an alternative activity that doesn't require you to speak to students—one that is less pleasant and allows you to monitor their every move closely."

Taking Ms. Les' advice, Mr. Cambell explains his feelings to the class and there is no hooting for several days. Then while explaining how to find the standard deviation of a distribution, Mr. Cambell hears the dreaded "Ooohh-ooooh-ooooh." Abruptly, he stops the explanation and silently and calmly displays a transparency on the overhead with the following message: "Open your book to page 157. Study the material on standard deviation and work the examples and exercises on pages 157–171. Most of what we planned to talk about in class today is covered on those pages. Do not forget we have a test on Thursday. It covers the unit objectives on means, variances, and standard deviations. Good luck."

Mr. Cambell watches them reluctantly work through the text material without his help. Some students start to ask him questions, but a stern look and signal for silence puts an end to that.

———————————

6. Utilize the Help of Colleagues, Parents, and Supervisors; Don't Be Fooled by the "Myth of the Good Teacher."

In the previous example, Mr. Cambell sought the counsel of a trusted colleague. But, unfortunately, some teachers are deluded by what Canter and Canter (1976, 6–7) refer to as the "myth of the good teacher." According to the myth, really "good" teachers handle all their own discipline problems without outside help; seeking help is considered a sign of weakness. In reality, consulting with colleagues is a mark of professional behavior (Bang-Jensen 1988; Cangelosi 1990a, 56; Raney and Robbins 1989). Furthermore, your supervisors are legally and ethically responsible for supporting your instructional efforts (Cangelosi 1991; Stanley and Popham 1988a; Stiggins and Duke 1988) and parents typically have greater influence over their children than do teachers (Canter and Canter 1976).

7. Have Alternative Lesson Plans Available for Times when Students Do Not Cooperate as You Planned.

Expect your students to cooperate with you and choose to engage in learning activities. Your confident expectations increase the chances that they will. Do not abort a well-designed learning activity as soon as it does not go as smoothly as you planned. However, by being prepared in the event that some students refuse to cooperate, you protect yourself from operating under the stress of having no alternative if the activity should be aborted. Ms. Asgill (Vignette 5.22) and Mr. Cambell (Vignette 5.27) demonstrated the advantage of having alternative and less-enjoyable activities ready for times when students' off-task behaviors rendered their original plans unworkable. Ideally, the alternative activities target the same objectives as the original ones.

8. Concern Yourself with Decreasing Incidences of Nondisruptive Off-Task Behavior as Much as with Decreasing Disruptive Off-Task Behaviors.

Nondisruptive off-task behaviors (e.g., mind-wandering, daydreaming, failing to attempt assignments, being under the influence of drugs during lessons, and sleeping in class) are easier to disregard than disruptive behaviors, which infringe on the rights of the class as a whole. However, you should be concerned with all forms of student off-task behaviors for the following reasons (Cangelosi 1990a, 57–58):

❑ When students are off-task, they fail to benefit from your planned lessons and thus diminish their chances of achieving learning goals. Your responsibility for helping them achieve learning goals includes helping them supplant off-task with on-task behaviors.

❑ Nondisruptive students who are off-task tend to fall behind in a lesson. Once students miss one part of a lesson, they are likely to not learn from a subsequent part, even though they may reengage in the learning activities. Those unable to follow a lesson are likely candidates for boredom and disruptive behaviors.

9. Allow Students to Recognize for Themselves the Natural Consequences of Failing to Attempt Assignments.

When students fail to attempt assignments, some teachers punish them or artificially manipulate their grades. But if your assignments are really necessary for students to succeed, then punishment or grade manipulation may be unnecessary. The teacher in Vignette 5.28 (Cangelosi 1990a, 59–60) comes to realize just that.

❑ VIGNETTE 5.28

Ms. Goldberg, a mathematics teacher, uses a procedure in which each student's grade is determined by the number of points accumulated during a semester. Her students have two means of accumulating points: (1) Half of the total possible points are based on their test scores; (2) the other half are awarded for homework that when turned in on time is scored according to the number of correct responses.

Ms. Goldberg discovers that a number of students receive high marks on their homework but low marks on their test papers. Under her system, such students are able to pass the course. After analyzing the matter she realizes that these students are either copying their homework from others or having others do it for them. Thus, she decides to change her grading procedures. She will annotate students' homework to provide them with feedback, but she will not grade their homework so that it influences their semester reports. Ms. Goldberg begins to make a concerted effort to assign homework and design tests so that completing homework will clearly be an effective way to prepare for tests.

To begin conditioning her students to the new system, she assigns homework one day and then administers a test the next that covers the same objectives as the homework.

———————————

10. Never Use Corporal Punishment.

There may be times when you need to restrain students physically for the purpose of preventing them from injuring themselves or others (including you). But do not confuse necessary physical constraint with the administration of corporal punishment. Corporal punishment is physical pain intentionally inflicted on a student for the purpose of making that student sorry for something she or he did. For you or any other teacher to inflict such a form of punishment is far more harmful than helpful (Curwin and Mendler 1980; Rose 1984; Welsh 1985). Although numerous prominent professional organizations (e.g., the National Education Association, American Federation of Teachers, and American Psychological Association) have issued statements adamantly opposing its use in school and its use has been banned in some states (e.g., New Jersey), corporal punishment continues to be widely, but inconsistently, practiced in schools (National Education Association 1972; Reardon and Reynolds 1979; Van Dyke 1984; Wood 1982). The arguments against the use of corporal punishment and in favor of more effective and less-destructive discipline practices are compelling (see, for example, Azrin, Hake, and Hutchinson 1965; Azrin, Hutchinson, and Sallery 1964; Bandura 1965; Bongiovanni 1979; Cangelosi 1988a, 207–208; Delgado 1963; Hyman and Wise 1979; Kohut and Range 1979; Rust and Kinnard 1983; Strike and Soltis 1986; Sulzer-Azaroff and Mayer 1977; Ulrich and Azrin 1962; Welsh 1985).

11. Don't Try to Build a Student's Character when You Should Be Trying to Keep Him or Her On-Task. In Vignette 5.22, Ms. Asgill didn't preach to Matthew about the evils of fighting; she concentrated on teaching him to refrain from fighting in her classroom. She recognized her responsibility for keeping students engaged for the purpose of achieving learning goals. She believes that the development of students' characters and moral upstanding citizens falls outside of the purview of her responsibilities as a mathematics teacher. Her tactics for stopping the clash between Matthew and Oliver and efficiently reengaging the class were successful, at least in part, because she focused on her role as a teacher and didn't get sidetracked with character-building and moral development.

12. Maintain Your Options; Avoid "Playing Your Last Card." Understand the extent and limits of your authority. Never threaten a student with anything unless you know you can follow through. For example, if you tell a student, "Either start working now or you're out of this class for good!" what are you going to do if the student refuses? You have extended your authority as far as it reaches, exhausting your options. Obtain the help of supervisors well *before* you run out of ways of dealing with problems.

13. Know Yourself and Know Your Students. Continually examine your motives for your work with students. Be receptive to differences among your students. What works with one may be a disaster with another. New ideas should be tried out cautiously—

first with individuals you know best and then extended to others as they prove promising. The better you understand yourself and your students, the more likely you will be able to gain students' cooperation and respond sensitively, flexibly, decisively, and effectively to discipline problems whenever they do occur.

CONDUCTING ENGAGING LEARNING ACTIVITIES

"Math is so dumb!" "Class is boring!" "This stuff is so dry!" "Why should I care about this stuff? I'm never going to use it!" "I don't have time to do this homework!" "It's so boring just sitting here listening to him jabber away about x's and y's!" "None of this has anything to do with me!"

Embedded in those familiar cries are the more common reasons why students get off-task during learning activities. To keep students on-task, not only must you establish a favorable classroom climate, communicate effectively, establish necessary rules and procedures, and effectively deal with off-task behaviors, you must also plan and conduct learning activities that hold students' attention. Chapter 6 provides you with suggestions for doing just that.

☐ ☐ ☐ ☐ ☐ ☐ ☐ ☐ ☐ ☐ ☐ ☐ ☐ ☐ ☐ ☐ ☐ ☐ ☐ ☐

SELF-ASSESSMENT EXERCISES

1. Select the one response to each of the following multiple-choice items that either completes the statement so that it is true or accurately answers the question:
   a. Time for students to achieve learning objectives increases as _____.
      i. More time is spent on knowledge-level activities instead of intellectual-level activities.
      ii. More time is spent on intellectual-level activities instead of knowledge-level activities.
      iii. Allocated time decreases.
      iv. Transition time decreases.
   b. Which one of the following statements is true?
      i. Students who are on-task are engaged in learning activities.
      ii. Students who are off-task are being disruptive.
      iii. Engaged behaviors are never off-task.
   c. Students develop on-task behavior patterns because _____.
      i. Isolated on-task behaviors were positively reinforced.

    ii. Isolated off-task behaviors were positively reinforced.

    iii. Of inherent instincts about right and wrong.

d. Students develop off-task behavior patterns because _____.

    i. Isolated on-task behaviors were positively reinforced.

    ii. Isolated off-task behaviors were positively reinforced.

    iii. Of inherent instincts about right and wrong.

e. A classroom with a businesslike atmosphere is characterized by _____.

    i. Democratic decision-making

    ii. Authoritarian decision-making

    iii. A highly formalized structure

    iv. Purposeful activity

f. Which one of the following contributes to a businesslike classroom atmosphere?

    i. Use of descriptive language

    ii. Use of judgmental language

    iii. Maximizing transition time

    iv. Consistent use of corporal punishment for unbusinesslike student behaviors

g. Students tend to be most receptive to signals about your expectations of them _____.

    i. Right after examinations

    ii. During the first few days of a course

    iii. During the last few days of a course

h. A supportive reply to a student tends to communicate _____.

    i. Assertiveness

    ii. Passiveness

    iii. Acceptance of feelings

    iv. Value judgments

i. By "withitness," Kounin refers to how _____.

    i. Well a teacher maintains students on-task and engaged in learning activities

    ii. Aware a teacher is of what's going on in the classroom

    iii. Well a teacher displays enthusiasm for learning

    iv. Assertively a teacher conducts her/himself with students

Compare your responses to the following: a. (iv); b. (iii); c. (i); d (ii); e. (iv); f. (i); g. (ii); h. (iii); i. (ii).

2. This chapter provided suggestions for managing student behavior (e.g., positively reinforce on-task behaviors, organize and prepare for efficient transitions, focus on the business of learning, and use descriptive instead of judgmental language). In Vignette 5.1, Ms. Lewis failed to heed a number of those suggestions. Reread that vignette and identify behaviors Ms. Lewis exhibited that were inconsistent with the suggestions. Indicate what she might have done differently to improve her classroom climate and to encourage her students to be on-task. Compare your work on this exercise to someone else's.

3. Apparently Mr. Krebs spent an extraordinary amount of time preparing for the class session described by Vignette 5.4. In what ways were his preparations for this class more elaborate than what you expect from most mathematics teachers? How do you think those efforts will pay practical dividends for him throughout the remainder of that geometry course? Compare your response on this exercise to that of someone else.

4. You have just been assigned a classroom and received your teaching schedule for the upcoming school year (e.g., two algebra I sections, one geometry, one consumer mathematics, and one precalculus) at a school familiar to you. Consider how you might answer the questions appearing on pages 131–132 for (a) classroom organization and ongoing routine, (b) one-time-only tasks, and (c) reminders for the first week's learning activities.

5. You have just directed your students to devise proofs independently to a theorem you've just stated. Although you were quite clear that they were to work silently on the proof by themselves, you notice Haywood and Howard talking together. You walk over to them and realize that they are discussing how to prove the theorem. State an example of a *descriptive* comment you could make to them. State an example of a *judgmental* comment you could make to them. What are the relative advantages and disadvantages of making the first instead of the second comment? Compare your work on this exercise with someone else's.

6. After you've assigned students to devise a proof for a theorem, Delcima exclaims to you, "I could never make up my own proof!" State an example of a *supportive* comment you could make to Delcima. State an example of a *nonsupportive* comment you could make. What are the relative advantages and disadvantages of making the first instead of the second comment? Compare your work on this exercise with someone else's.

7. After you've assigned students to devise a proof for a theorem, Billy exclaims to you, "We've already got too much work to do! Do we really have to prove this?" State an example of an *assertive* comment you could make to Billy. State an example of a *passive* comment you could make. State an example of a *hostile* comment you could make. What are the relative advantages and disadvantages of making the first instead of either the second or third comment? Compare your work on this exercise with someone else's.

8. By their comments in the following vignettes, teachers violate principles suggested in this chapter. What principles are they violating? Answer that question before comparing your answer to that given at the end of the second anecdote.

❏ VIGNETTE 5.29

Mr. Zebart confronts Jackie, Fred, and Lamont with evidence that they cheated on a test. "What have you got to say for yourselves?" he asks. Lamont: "I didn't steal the test; Jackie already had it before I even knew about it." Mr. Zebart: "So, Jackie, you not only cheated, but you got these other two to cheat also."

❏ VIGNETTE 5.30

Mr. Meyers, a school custodian, notices one of the teachers, Ms. Orlando, appearing a bit haggard. He says, "You seem a bit out of sorts. Are you okay?" Ms. Orlando: "Oh, thanks for asking. I'm okay—it's just Justin Thomas. He's so frustrating to work with! The next time he gives me trouble, I'm going to have to talk to one of the counselors about him."

Mr. Zebart failed to convey that the students are responsible for and in control of their own behaviors. Ms. Orlando violated a professional trust by sharing privileged information about a student.

9. Observe a mathematics class in a middle, junior high, or high school. Distinguish the transition times from the allocated times in the class period. For each transition period and each allocated period, note one student who is on-task and another who is off-task. Describe the behaviors that led you to believe they were on-task and off-task, respectively. If you were in the teacher's place, what might you do to positively reinforce the on-task behavior? What might you have done to discourage recurrences of the off-task behavior?

10. In your response to Exercise 4 of the Chapter 4 exercises, you described lessons for a sequence of objectives for a teaching unit. Now, formulate and describe a plan for obtaining and maintaining students on-task during that unit. Include your plans for efficient transitions, alternative learning activities, if needed, notes to yourself on communicating with students, and contingency plans for dealing with potential situations in which students are off-task. Compare your work on this exercise to someone else's.

❏ ❏ ❏ ❏ ❏ ❏ ❏ ❏ ❏ ❏ ❏ ❏ ❏ ❏ ❏ ❏ ❏ ❏ ❏ ❏

TAKING WHAT YOU'VE LEARNED TO THE NEXT LEVEL

Keeping in mind the research-based principles for designing lessons suggested in Chapter 4 and those for gaining and maintaining students' cooperation, turn your attention to the concern of Chapter 6: how to conduct learning activities in ways that grab and hold students' attention.

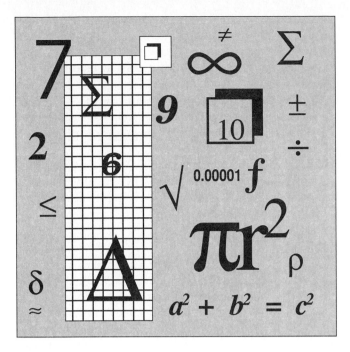

CHAPTER 6
Engaging Students in Learning Activities

This chapter explains how to conduct learning activities in ways that encourage student engagement. Chapter 6 will help you:

1. Select and integrate types of learning activities (e.g., questioning/discussion or independent work) for each teaching unit that are appropriate for your students, you, the learning objectives, and the available resources (*application*).
2. For each of the following types of learning activities, explain effective ways of (a) providing directions, (b) initiating student engagement, (c) maintaining engagement, (d) utilizing formative feedback to regulate pace and determine modifications, and (e) achieving closure:

   ❑ Large-group interactive lecture sessions
   ❑ Large-group intellectual-level questioning/discussion sessions
   ❑ Large-group recitation sessions
   ❑ Small-task-group sessions
   ❑ Independent work sessions (*conceptualization*).

3. Explain how to incorporate meaningful homework assignments into lessons and to teach students to engage in those assignments (*conceptualization*).

INTEGRATING DIFFERENT TYPES OF LEARNING ACTIVITIES INTO LESSONS
The Traditional Approach

As indicated in Chapter 2, most mathematics teachers hardly vary from a four-stage lesson pattern in which the following occur (Jesunathadas 1990):

1. A relation (e.g., fact, definition, or theorem) or algorithm is introduced and explained by the teacher with the aid of a chalkboard or overhead projector to the class as a whole.
2. The teacher illustrates the relation or algorithm to the class with one or two examples from the textbook.
3. Students work individually on textbook exercises similar to the examples illustrated by the teacher as the teacher provides help on a one-to-one basis.
4. Students complete similar exercises for homework that are checked and reviewed at the beginning of the following class period.

This pattern, in which the teacher presents an explanation in a large-group lecture session, presents illustrations in a large-group lecture session, monitors and provides help during an independent work session, and assigns and reviews homework, is repeated monotonously lesson after lesson after lesson.

The Resurrection of an Eighteenth-Century Approach

Until the mid-nineteenth century, the dominant method of teaching mathematics in American schools involved virtually no group instruction or interaction among students. Individually, students found out what to remember or how to execute an algorithm from either teachers' one-to-one oral presentations or from reading text materials. Then students worked individually on exercises that were, in turn, checked by the teacher (Cubberley 1962, 327–329).

With the advent of programmed instruction facilitated by microcomputers, use of this eighteenth-century approach, in which students work independently with virtually no group interaction, is increasing. Precision teaching, an approach successfully used in arithmetic skill development in special-education programs, is gaining in popularity in middle and secondary schools as a consequence of commercially packaged mathematics curricula being sold to school districts (Bowden 1991).

The Suggested Research-Based Approach

When competently executed, the aforementioned direct instructional approach is quite effective in helping students achieve knowledge-level objectives (as indicated in Chapter 4, pages 96–98, 103–108). However, for students to achieve affective and intellectual-level cognitive objectives, they must engage in a wider variety of learning activities (e.g., ones that stimulate inductive reasoning) (as indicated in Chapter 4, pages 79–95, 109–116). This requires lessons that integrate different types of learning activities, including (1) large-group interactive lecture sessions, (2) large-group intellectual-level questioning/discussion sessions, (3) large-group recitation sessions, (4) small-task-group sessions, (5) independent work sessions, and (6) homework assignments. Determining when to use combinations of these types of learning activities and how to keep students engaged in them are the concerns of this chapter.

ENGAGING STUDENTS IN LARGE-GROUP INTERACTIVE LECTURE SESSIONS
Appropriate Uses of Large-Group Interactive Lecture Sessions

Large-Group Sessions
You should plan to use large-group sessions whenever you want all students in the class to be concentrating on a common center of activity (e.g., a speaker, demonstration, or illustration). Such sessions provide an efficient means for class members to share a common experience that they draw upon in subsequent learning activities. For example,

❑ Students individually pattern their own proofs of several theorems on how the proof of another theorem was developed in a large-group discussion session.
❑ While responding to a student's request for individual help on how to execute an algorithm, a teacher refers to notes the student took during a large-group lecture session.

Lectures
A lecture is a monologue. To be engaged in a lecture-type learning activity, students must attentively listen to the lecturer. Taking notes and attempting to follow a prescribed thought pattern may also be a required aspect of engagement. This type of engagement, requiring students to be cognitively active while physically inactive, is not easily maintained for extended time periods. Lectures that continue uninterrupted for more than 10 minutes without being integrated with other types of learning activities are ill advised (Cangelosi 1988a, 144). Quina (1989, 140–141) states:

> In recent years the lecture has been disregarded and maligned by some educators. Much empirical research has been amassed to show shortcomings of the lecture as an instructional vehicle. Some common arguments are that students have too short an attention span to focus on a lecture for more than 10–15 minutes at a time. Without correct feedback it is easy to misunderstand what has been said. NLP (Neurolinguistic Programming) operators say that only 7 percent of what we receive as a message is carried by the words one uses in a speech. The speaker's tonality carries 38 percent of the message and his body posture carries 55 percent of the message (Robbins 1987). Most teachers are not specifically trained in oratorical skills. There is the conjoint problem of teachers tending to focus on subject matter, forgetting *how* they are communicating, and lapsing into a monotone delivery—the deadliest form of a lecture. There is, moreover, the tendency of the lecturing high school teacher to imitate the lecture format, the style of delivery, and the technical vocabulary of the college professor.

This is *not* to say that you should exclude lectures from your teaching. Lectures provide a valuable means by which you can present information, provide explanations, demonstrate processes, and stimulate inductive and deductive reasoning. However, to maintain student interest in lectures, you need to do more than just talk. You must organize and design lectures so that you employ attention-focusing techniques (e.g., illustrations, advanced organizers, and body language) and continuously integrate activities into lectures that stimulate interactions between you and the students.

Interactions

Unless you continue to evoke student responses during a lecture, you will be unable to detect just what message they are receiving, and consequently may dwell on points they already understand, fail to elaborate where needed, and fail to correct misunderstandings. Furthermore, students need feedback on whether or not what they are understanding is what they are supposed to be understanding. Left as passive receptors of your words, they will not remain engaged for very long, even though they may be quite adept at appearing to listen—following you with their eyes, nodding on occasion, and even smiling at humorous sidetracks. Mind-wandering will be rampant unless you frequently solicit student reactions and input.

Interactive Lecture Sessions

To take advantage of lectures as a mode of instruction without losing students in the process, plan for nontraditional *interactive lecture sessions* in which your oral discourses are inextricably meshed with activities that evoke interactions between you and your students. How to utilize and engage students in that type of learning activity is the question addressed in the remainder of this section.

Direct Instructional Methods in Interactive Lecture Sessions

Direct instructional methods appropriate for knowledge-level objectives and literal understanding relative to comprehension-level objectives can readily be incorporated into interactive lecture sessions. Use monologues to present and explicate information, but mix them with interactive techniques that will (1) focus attention, (2) keep students alert, (3) provide you with formative feedback, (4) add variety to the presentation when points need to be repeated, (5) provide students with feedback on their understanding, and (6) positively reinforce their efforts. Consider Vignette 6.1.

☐ VIGNETTE 6.1

Mr. Delaney is in the midst of a large-group interactive lecture session designed to help his students achieve the following objective:

States that for any positive integer n, where n is odd and a is any real number, or for any positive integer n, where n is even and $a \geq 0$, $a^{1/n} = \sqrt[n]{a}$ (*simple knowledge*).

He states the relation specified by the objective, displays it on the overhead projector, and says, "Read this aloud for us, Rudy." Rudy does so, and Mr. Delaney continues, "Now, as Rudy just pointed out to us, a to the one-nth power is defined for two cases." As he speaks, Mr. Delaney illustrates his words with the aid of the overhead projector. "Let's look at the two cases separately. . . . What's the first case, Geraldine?" he asks.

Geraldine: It says n is odd.
Mr. Delaney: And the second case, Lynette?
Lynette: n is even.
Mr. Delaney: The reason it is defined for the two cases separately is because of the way principal roots are defined.

He displays the definition with the overhead and continues, "Remember this definition of a principal root we've been using for the past six weeks. Notice that it represents only the . . . ."

Note that the questions Mr. Delaney used in this direct instructional lesson are not the open-ended, "develop-a-hypothesis" type of questions used in lessons for intellectual cognitive objectives (e.g., those raised by Mr. Citarelli in the inductive lesson in Vignette 4.8). Students' responses during an interactive lecture session using direct instruction are elicited with questions or directives such as "Repeat what I just said," "Read this for me," and "What did we do first?"

Inquiry Instructional Methods in Interactive Lecture Sessions

For intellectual-level objectives, you can use the large-group interactive lecture mode to stimulate students to reason in various ways. If, for instance, your target is a conceptualization objective, examples and nonexamples of the concept or principle can be explained and illustrated in a monologue; then questions and discussions can be used to lead students through an inductive process.

Common Misuses of Large-Group Interactive Lecture Sessions

A high school student once replied to my query about what he had learned from a geometry course with, "I learned all kinds of stuff about logical thinking—how to develop ideas of what might be true and then how to prove whether they are or not. Space—I think of the space around us differently now, as all these points and planes and whatever! I like how I can—." "Your teacher must have done a great job with your class," I commented. "Not really, she made us figure all this stuff out on our own. We learned a lot, but she didn't do much teaching—mostly gave us things to do, asked us a lot of questions, and let us know how we were doing."

This student seems to have a view that most people don't develop until they've been in college for a few years, the view being that to teach, one must lecture. Therein lies the basis for the most common misuse of interactive lecture sessions: *There is too much lecture and not enough interaction.* Unlike the high school student's geometry teacher, some teachers bring from their college experiences the mistaken idea that teaching is spewing forth words of wisdom. The consequence of the overuse of lectures is students being told things they need to figure out for themselves in order to learn at an intellectual level. This results in an overemphasis on knowledge-level learning.

By contrast, interactive lecture sessions are also misused when the interactive aspects degenerate into unstructured "bull sessions." Some teachers, especially those who do not consistently use assertive communications, have difficulty controlling class discussions so that exchanges focus on intended topics. How to manage meaningful discussion sessions is addressed in subsequent sections of this chapter.

Two Contrasting Examples

The teacher in the first of the following two vignettes needs to learn how to conduct a large-group interactive lecture session from the teacher in the second.

❑ VIGNETTE 6.2

Mr. Johnson's 26 students are sitting at their desks. Nine have paper and pencil poised to take notes, but others are involved with their own thoughts as he begins, "Today, class, we're going to study about a measure of central tendency called the arithmetic mean. Some of you may have already heard of it." He turns to the chalkboard and writes, continuing to speak, "The arithmetic mean of N numbers equals the sum of the numbers divided by N." Keeping his side to the class so he can write on the board and glance at the class, he says, "For example, to compute the mean of these numbers, 15, 15, 20, 0, 13, 12, 25, 40, 10, and 20, we would first add the numbers to find the sum. Right?" He looks at the class but doesn't notice whether students appear to respond to his question, turns back and adds the numbers on the board. "So the sum is 170. Now, since we have 10 numbers, N in the formula is 10 and we divide 170 by N or 10. And what does that give us? It

gives us 17.0. So, the arithmetic mean of these numbers is 17.0. Is that clear?"

Mr. Johnson stares at the class momentarily, notices Armond nodding and softly saying, "Yes." With a smile, Mr. Johnson quickly says "Good! Okay, everybody, the arithmetic mean is a very important and useful statistic. Suppose, for example, I wanted to compare this group of numbers—." From his notes he copies the following numbers on the board: 18, 35, 30, 7, 20, and then continues, "to these over here." He points to the previous set of data.

Mr. Johnson: What could we do? . . . Ramon?

Ramon: Compute that arithmetic thing you told us about.

Mr. Johnson: That's right! We could compute the arithmetic mean. . . . 18 plus 35 plus 30 plus 7 plus 20 is 110, and 110 divided by N—which in this case is 5, okay?—is 22.0. Okay? Now, that means this second data set has a higher average than the first—even though the first had more numbers. Any questions? . . . Good! . . . Oh, okay, Angela?

Angela: Why do you write 17.0 instead of just 17? Isn't it the same thing?

Mr. Johnson: Good question. Hmmm, can anybody help Angela out? . . . Well, you see in statistics the number of decimal places indicates something about the accuracy of the computations, and, for that matter, the data-gathering device. So that one decimal point indicates that the statistics are more accurate than if we had just put 17 and 22 and not as accurate if we had put, say 17.00000 or 22.00000. . . . Got it? That was a good question. Do you understand now?

Angela: I guess so.

Mr. Johnson: Good! Now, if there're no more questions, there's some time left to get a head start on your homework.

❑ VIGNETTE 6.3

Ms. Erickson's 27 students are quietly sitting at their desks, each ready with paper and pen or pencil. She has previously taught them how to take notes during large-group interactive lecture sessions so that they record information during the session on a paper and then, after the session, organize the notes and transfer them into their required notebooks.

After distributing the form appearing in Exhibit 6.1, she faces the class from a position near the overhead projector and says, "I'm standing here looking at you people and I just can't get one question out of mind." Very deliberately she walks in front of the fourth row of students and quickly, but obviously, looks at their feet (Exhibit 6.2). Then she moves in front of the first row and repeats the odd behavior with those students. "I just don't know!" she says shaking her head as she returns to her position by the overhead.

She switches on the overhead displaying the first line of Exhibit 6.1 and says, "In the first blank on your form, please write: Do the people sitting in the fourth row have

Exhibit 6.1
Form Ms. Erickson uses during a large-group interactive lecture session.

An Experiment

Question to be answered: _____

_____

Data for Row 4: _____

Data for Row 1: _____

Treatment of data for row 4:

Treatment of data for row 1:

Treatment to compare the two sets of data:

Results: _____

_____

Conclusions: _____

_____

Exhibit 6.2
Why is Ms. Erickson looking at
students' feet?

bigger feet than those in the first row?" She moves closer to the students, obviously monitoring how well her directions are followed. Back by the overhead as they complete the chore, she says, "Now, I've got to figure a way to gather data that will help me answer that question." Grabbing her head with a hand and closing her eyes, she appears to be in deep thought for a few seconds and then suddenly exclaims, "I've got it! We'll use shoe sizes as a measure. That'll be a lot easier than using a ruler on smelly feet!" Some students laugh, and one begins to speak while two others raise their hands. But Ms. Erickson quickly says, "Not now, please, we need to collect some data." She flips an overlay off of the second line of the transparency, exposing "Data for Row 4."

Ms. Erickson: "Those of you in the fourth and first rows, quickly jot down your shoe size on your paper. If you don't know it, either guess or read it off your shoe if you can do it quickly. . . . Starting with Jasmine in the back and moving up to Lester in the front, those of you in the fourth row call out your shoe sizes one at a time so we can write them down in this blank at our places." As the students volunteer the sizes, she fills in the blank on the transparency as follows: 6, 10.5, 8, 5.5, 6, 9. Exposing the next line, "Data for Row 1," on the transparency, she asks, "What do you suppose we're going to do now, Pauline?" Pauline: "Do the same for row 1." Ms. Erickson says, "Okay, you heard her; row 1, give it to us from the back so we can fill in this blank." The numbers 8.5, 8, 7, 5.5, 6.5, 6.5, 9, and 8 are recorded and displayed on the overhead.

Ms. Erickson: "Now, I've got to figure out what to do with these numbers to help me answer the question." Several students raise their hands, but she responds, "Thank you for offering to help, but I want to see what I come up

with." Pointing to the appropriate numbers on the transparency, she seems to think aloud saying, "It's easy enough to compare one number to another. Jasmine's 6 from row 4 is less than Rolando's 8.5 from row 1. But I don't want to just compare one individual's number to another. I want to compare this whole bunch of numbers [circling the set of numbers from row 4 with an overhead pen] to this bunch [circling the numbers from row 1]. . . . I guess we could add all row 4's numbers together and all row 1's together and compare the two sums—the one with the greater sum would have the larger group of feet."

A couple of students try to interrupt with, "But that won't wor—" but Ms. Erickson motions them to stop speaking and asks, "What's the sum from row 4, Lau-chou?"

Lau-chou: . . . 45.
Ms. Erickson: Thank you. And what's the sum for row 1, Stace?
Stace: 59.

"Thank you. So row 1 has the bigger feet, since 59 is greater than 45," Ms. Erickson says as she writes, "59 > 45."

Ms. Erickson: I'll pause to hear what some of you with your hands up have to say. Evangeline?
Evangeline: That's not right; it doesn't work.
Ms. Erickson: You mean 59 isn't greater than 45, Evangeline?
Evangeline: 59 is greater than 45, but there are more feet in row 1.
Ms. Erickson: All the people in row 1 have only two feet, just like the ones in row 4. I carefully counted. [Stu-

dents laugh.] Now that we've taken care of that concern, how about other comments or questions—Brook?

Brook: You know what Evangeline meant! She meant there're more people in row 1. So what you did isn't right.

Ms. Erickson: Alright, let me see if I now understand Evangeline's point. She said we don't want our indicator of how big the feet are to be affected by how many feet, just the size of the feet. . . . So, I've got to figure out a way to compare the sizes of these two groups of numbers when one has more numbers. I'm open for suggestions. Kip?

Kip: You could drop the two extra numbers from row 1; then they'd both have 6.

Ms. Erickson: That seems like a reasonable approach. I like that, but first let's hear another idea—maybe one where we can use all the data. Myra?

Myra: Why not do an average?

Ms. Erickson: What do you mean?

Myra: You know, divide row 4's total by 6 and row 1's by 8.

Ms. Erickson: How will that dividing help? Seems like just an unnecessary step. Tom?

Tom: It evens up the two groups.

Ms. Erickson: Oh, I see what you people have been trying to tell me! Dividing row 4's sum of 45 by 6 counts each number 1/6. And dividing row 1's sum of 59 by 8 counts each number 1/8. And that's fair, since 6 one-sixths is a whole, just as 8 one-eighths is a whole. How am I doing, Jasmine?

Jasmine: A lot better than you were.

Flipping over another overlay, she displays the next two lines of Exhibit 6.1 and says, "Let's write, 'The sum of row four's numbers is 45.' 45 divided by 6 is what, Lester?"

Lester: 7.5.

Ms. Erickson: Thanks. And on the next line we write, 59 divided by 8 is what, Sandy?

Sandy: 7.375.

Ms. Erickson: Since 7.5 is greater than 7.375, I guess we should say that the feet in row 4 are larger than the feet in row 1. That is, of course, if you're willing to trust this particular statistic—which is known as the MEB. Any questions? . . . Yes, Evangeline.

Evangeline: Why the MEB?

Ms. Erickson: Because I just named it that after its three inventors, Myra, Evangeline, and Brook. They're the ones who came up with the idea of dividing the sum. [The class breaks into laughter.]

Ms. Erickson shifts to direct instruction to help students remember the formula, practice using it, and remember its more conventional name, *arithmetic mean,* during the remainder of the session.

Providing Directions

There are some behaviors you expect your students to exhibit during *every* large-group interactive lecture section. As soon as Ms. Erickson's students recognized they were about to begin such a session, they immediately got ready to take notes and focused on her. This is a routine *procedure* she taught them to follow in the very beginning of the course. However, there are also expected behaviors that vary from one large-group interactive lecture session to another. These may involve how to take notes on a form you developed just for one session or how to follow a particular thought pattern (e.g., inductive reasoning for one session and absorbing information for another). For such behaviors not covered by routine procedures, you need to provide students with specific, explicit *directions*.

Providing students with directions is quite unlike conducting inquiry lessons; with directions, there should be no guesswork for students. Very direct, exacting messages are sent. In Vignette 5.4, Mr. Krebs exemplified the art of giving precise directions that get learning activities off to a smooth start.

Initiating Student Engagement

Readiness to Listen

In Vignette 6.2, Mr. Johnson began talking to his class of 26 students, although only 9 were ready to listen and take notes. He should take a lesson from Ms. Erickson and develop the attitude "I don't speak until you're ready to listen!" Remember, if your students aren't ready to listen on cue, you can always shift to an alternate learning activity (as Mr. Cambell did in Vignette 5.25). The rule is not to begin the interactive lecture session until all students appear attentive with necessary materials (e.g., paper and pencil) ready and potential sources of distractions (e.g., a book that won't be used during the session) put away.

Establishing Set

The second rule for initiating engagement is to *establish set*. Establishing set is focusing attention on and setting up the students for the task at hand. Ms. Erickson established set in three ways:

❑ She distributed the form appearing in Exhibit 6.1. This helped structure the situation and provided a focal point to which she could direct students' attention throughout the session. The form gave students an idea of what they would be doing.

❏ Her curious behavior, deliberately staring at feet, encouraged students to take notice and wonder, "What's she going to do next?"

❏ Her deliberate movements established *cues* she would take advantage of for the remainder of the session. For example:

> After distributing the form, she walked directly to a point near the overhead projector and faced the class. From that position she spoke to the students. Silently, she walked directly to a point in front of the fourth row, then to a point in front of the first row, and then back to the position near the overhead where she once again spoke to the class. When she wanted students to look at an illustration, she switched on the overhead projector. When she wanted them to stop looking at it, she turned the overhead off or controlled what they could see with transparency overlays.

These movements conveyed cues to students associating her location and movements with what they should be doing throughout the session (e.g., listen attentively when she's by the overhead).

Communicating to students the purpose of the session also helps establish set. Because Ms. Erickson's session was part of a conceptualization-level lesson and she was stimulating inductive reasoning, she did not explicitly state the purpose in the first stage of the activity. She did, however, indicate that she had a question (Do the people sitting in the fourth row have bigger feet than those in the first row?) they would be addressing. For a session in which direct instructional methods are appropriate (e.g., for a knowledge-of-a-process objective), establishing sets should include an explicit statement of what the session is intended to accomplish.

Maintaining Engagement in Large-Group Interactive Lecture Sessions

Once you have initiated student engagement in a large-group interactive lecture session, that engagement needs to be sustained. Here are suggestions for doing so:

Refer students to an outline of the presentation, session agenda, note-taking form, or other form at climactic or transitional points during the session. Ms. Erickson used the form in Exhibit 6.1 to focus students' attention and structure the activity. Consider taking that idea a step farther by having an outline of the presentation (e.g., Exhibit 6.3), a session agenda (e.g., Exhibit 6.4), or a note-taking form (e.g., Exhibit 6.5) in the hands of students or displayed on an overhead transparency that you can use to direct attention and provide a context for ideas, topics, and subtopics. Having such advanced organizers in students' hands facilitates their note-taking and helps you monitor their engagement (e.g., by sampling what they write on the form in Exhibit 6.5). By using transitional remarks (e.g., "Moving on to item 4. . . .") in conjunction with an outline or agenda, you help students maintain their bearings during sessions.

Make use of illustrations. Not only do pictures, graphs, diagrams, flowcharts, tables, and printed words highlight and supplement oral speech, students are more likely to attend to and comprehend what they see than to what they hear. Of course, illustrations need to be intelligible (such as Ms. Strong's in Vignette 5.3 and unlike Mr. Boone's in Vignette 5.2) and clearly visible to all students. Plan to exhibit illustrations so you need not be confined to one location and unable to monitor the class.

Speak directly to students, moving your eyes about the room and making eye contact with one student after another. Reread the section beginning on page 135 entitled "Proximity and Body Language."

Develop a pattern of nonverbal cues for indicating expected student behaviors without interrupting the session. Ms. Erickson grabbed her head and closed her eyes to indicate that she should be allowed to think without interruption. Later she used a hand motion to let students know it was not yet time for them to raise questions. Note that when she was ready for students to speak, she made it clear by saying, "I'll pause to hear what some of you with your hands up have to say." The likelihood of your students responding to your cues increases after they learn the routine your sessions follow. Ms. Erickson's students, for example, were willing to hold their questions and comments because they knew from previous sessions that she would provide a time for them.

Move about the room purposefully, neither pacing aimlessly nor confining yourself to one location. Ms. Erickson cued student behaviors by her position in the classroom. Quina (1989, 141–142) suggests dividing the room into quadrants:

> Beginning teachers sometimes unconsciously pace the floor, moving from one side of the room to another. The observing students' heads move as though they are watching a tennis match. To avoid this, think where you want to be standing as you develop parts of your lecture. You can divide the room into quadrants and intentionally move into each quadrant at differ-

Exhibit 6.3
Example of presentation outline
distributed to students for an
interactive lecture session.

Topic: Proof by Induction
Date: 3/7

Presentation Outline

I. Review of familiar methods of proving theorem
  A. Direct
  B. By contradiction
II. The types of theorems to which proof by induction applies
III. The logic of a proof by induction
  A. Sequential cases
  B. Is it true for one case?
  C. If it's true for one case, will it be true for the next case?
IV. Some everyday examples of the induction principle
  A. Playing music
  B. On soccer field
  C. In the kitchen
  D. Eating food
  E. Computer programming
V. An example with an arithmetic series, $\sum\limits_{i=1}^{n} i = n(n+1)/2$
VI. Formalizing the process
  A. Show the statement is true for $i = a$.
  B. Show that if the statement is true for some value of i, then it must also be true for $i + 1$.
  C. Draw a conclusion.
VII. Proof of the following theorem:

$$\sum\limits_{i=1}^{n} i^2 = (n/6)(n+1)(2n+1)$$

VIII. Summary

Exhibit 6.4
Example of a class meeting agenda
distributed to students.

Meeting Agenda for 10/18
Algebra II, 4th Period

1. Hello (0.50–0.75 minutes)
2. Formative quiz and roll (15–16 minutes)
3. Review quiz items and discuss some subset of the following questions, as needed according to the quiz review:
  a. What is a proportion?
  b. What types of problems does setting up proportions help solve?
  c. What is the so-called proportion rule?
  d. What are some efficient strategies for estimating solutions to problems involving proportions?
  (10–20 minutes)
4. Lecture presentation on further applying our understanding proportions to problems involving direct and indirect variations (10–15 minutes)
5. Homework assignment (2–4 minutes)
6. Head start on homework (7–21 minutes)
7. Prepare for dismissal (1–1.75 minutes)
8. Be kind to yourself (1310 minutes)

Exhibit 6.5
Example of a note-taking form a teacher distributed to students for use during a lecture presentation.

Topic: Developing the Quadratic Formula	
Date: 1/23	

Main Ideas	Margin Notes
The need for a general method:	
Completing-the-square method:	
The need for an easier method:	
Completion-of-the-square example:	
Generalizing completing-the-square method:	

Exhibit 6.5
continued

Main Ideas	Margin Notes
Reforming expressions to obtain the formula:	
Examples of equations solved with the formula: 1.	
2.	
3.	
Summary:	
What to do next:	

ent stages of your lecture. For example, after introducing the question "Why do we need to communicate?" the teacher may move to the left side of the room, give some information on communicating in pantomime, provide a quick pantomime, then move to the right side of the room to discuss ways we designate things, illustrate by pointing to objects, and then ask a related question, "How is pointing and acting things out like using words?" The teacher may then walk to the back of the room and ask even more pointed questions: "What would happen if we did not have words? What would it be like if words were not available right now?"

The shift in position in the room corresponds to the development of the lecture, providing a spatial metaphor for organization. As the teacher walks back to the front of the room to sum up, the very return to the front of the room, to the beginning point, suggests a completion, a completed square, circle, or other shape. These movements are intentional. They can be planned in advance or they can be used spontaneously. Either way, they are intentional—not random pacing.

Consider the following advantages of videotaping lecture presentations ahead of time and playing them for students in class:

❑ Videotaped lectures can be previewed, edited, and corrected before being presented.
❑ Lecturers on videotape do not lose their trends of thought or get sidetracked in response to other classroom activities (e.g., comments, questions, or distractions). Videotape can be interrupted, restarted, or replayed on demand without loss of words.
❑ During a videotaped lecture presentation, you are free to monitor student behaviors, stopping, starting, and replaying the tape as formative feedback warrants.
❑ Videotaped lectures can be saved and presented in subsequent sessions and with other classes.

Use humor and other attention-grabbing devices without allowing them to distract from the business at hand. You are a teacher, not an entertainer. Don't feel obliged to entertain students. However, by *strategically* injecting humor or dramatics into the sessions, you relieve boredom and increase engagement. "Strategic" is the operative word here. Do not allow student laughter to flatter you into the trap of valuing the entertainment aspects of your sessions more than the educational outcomes. Also be cautious of anyone being offended by your humor or dramatics and of students being the butt of jokes.

Interject students' names into lectures and relate content to areas that interest them. The most impor-

tant concern to virtually any student is herself or himself. Hearing their names stimulates students' attention. For example, ". . . I'll bet Carmen would agree that most of the numbers we gather from the world about us are not perfectly accurate. Larry watches his calories, since he's on the wrestling team. But just how accurately can someone measure caloric intake? And yet we use numbers of calories to compute the . . . ."

When students need to be following a thought pattern, let them hear you think aloud. To be engaged in lectures, students need to listen *actively,* trying to follow prescribed thought patterns. You facilitate this level of engagement by verbally walking students through cognitive processes leading to conclusions.

Except for relatively brief quotes, avoid reading to the class. Rather than read a lecture to students, have them read it for themselves. For a brief quote you want read during a lecture presentation, consider calling on a student to read it aloud. This increases student involvement, adds variety, and distinguishes between messages that originate with you and those from other sources.

Speak on the students' level (both structurally and relative to vocabulary); make sure vocabulary and notations that are requisite for comprehension of the lecture have been previously taught. Students often become disengaged during a lecture because the teacher uses an unfamiliar word, expression, formula, or symbol. The teacher continues, assuming the students understand. But rather than listening, students are trying to figure out what they didn't previously comprehend. Remember, they can't return to a previous passage in a lecture to look up what is missed, as they can with printed material. Once students have missed one point, they are likely to miss subsequent ones.

Strategically vary your voice volume, inflection, pitch, and rhythm according to the message you want to send; avoid a monotone. Even when the message itself is important and exciting, a monotonic speech is a recipe for boredom. Punctuate your sentences with voice variations.

Follow key statements and questions with strategic pauses. If you raise a question, students should be expected at least to formulate an answer in their minds before it is answered for them. Pauses indicate points to be pondered.

Routinely take time to breathe deeply. This helps you to stay alert and control your voice. It also has a calming effect if you happen to be nervous.

Pace your speech so that the sessions move briskly but so that students still have time to absorb your messages and take notes. This point, of course, varies considerably according to the type of lesson you're teaching. A lecture for an inquiry lesson would ordinarily proceed at a slower pace than one using direct instruction. Quina (1989, 143) suggests that between 110 and 130 words per minute is optimal.

Using Formative Feedback

Determining (1) when to move from one phase of a session to the next, (2) how to regulate the pace of the activities, (3) whether to repeat, skip over, or change messages, (4) whether to extend or abbreviate an activity, and (5) how, if at all, the plan for the session should be modified are among the difficult decisions you make as you orchestrate learning activities. These decisions should be based on formative feedback relative to how well students are cooperating and learning.

Unless you obliviously talk to the back wall the whole session, you can't help but acquire formative feedback while conducting large-group interactive lecture sessions. Are students staying on task? If they aren't understanding what is being said, they're not likely to remain attentive. If they already know what is being said, they're not likely to remain attentive. Thus, level of attentiveness, unless it's coerced, is an indicator of how the session is proceeding. There are also the overt displays of understanding or misunderstanding associated with facial expressions, comments, and body language.

But acquisition of accurate formative feedback is too critical to the success of the lesson to be left to chance indications you may be fortunate enough to detect. Formative feedback should be systematically sought by integrating specific tasks for students to perform and pointed questions for them to answer throughout the session. Questions such as, "Are there any questions?" "Does everybody understand?" and "Okay?" do little to inform you about how well students are following the session or understanding the lesson. To provide formative feedback, questions and directives must be more to the point. For example:

❑ We don't know the size of angle β, but we do know something about what other angle? . . . What is it, Leona?
❑ Repeat Leona's answer for us, Amos.
❑ Quickly work this example on your note outlines while I zip around peeking over shoulders.

Not only does the success of a learning activity depend on how well you utilize formative feedback while you're conducting it, but it also depends upon your abilities to conduct activities, such as large-group interactive lecture sessions, improve with experience *if* you use formative feedback to learn what

does and what doesn't work. Chapter 7 deals with evaluating student achievement; it includes ideas for collecting accurate formative data.

Achieving Closure

Students' engagement in interactive lecture sessions is positively reinforced by climactic moments in which it is clear that they have learned something of value. Thus, it is important that they are not left "hanging" for too long. Plan for moments throughout the session in which ideas come together and students recognize progress toward an objective. Timing is critical. Save enough time for summarizing the main points and for students to practice with or apply the mathematical concepts, constants, relations, algorithms, or conventions dealt with during the session.

Once they realize that your interactive lectures are structured so that ideas raised during a session are brought together as a coherent whole at the end of the session, they will tend to stay with you and tolerate perplexity during subsequent sessions.

ENGAGING STUDENTS IN LARGE-GROUP INTELLECTUAL-LEVEL QUESTIONING/DISCUSSION SESSIONS
Intellectual-Level Questions

Compare the type of questions Ms. Ortiz asks to those of Mr. Windley in the following two vignettes.

❑ **VIGNETTE 6.4**

Ms. Ortiz: Yesterday we introduced a family of statistics called what, Amy?

Amy: Measures of variability.

Ms. Ortiz: That's right. Who remembers what it means to say that the *variability* in one group of numbers is greater than that of another? . . . Okay, Eric.

Eric: You told us that the numbers in the group with greater variability have a bigger range.

Ms. Ortiz: What does range mean, Vernon?

Vernon: I don't know.

Ms. Ortiz: It's defined at the top of page 93. Look it up, and I'll come back to you within a minute. . . . Did I say that when comparing two groups of numbers, the one with the greater variability will *always* have a larger range? . . . Okay, Shawn.

Shawn: You said it *probably* would have a greater range, but you also said that wasn't the *only* part of variability. It's also the differences between other numbers in the group besides the biggest and smallest.

Ms. Ortiz: That's correct. Everyone please remember what Shawn just said. Repeat what he said, Encincio.

Encincio: It probably would have a greater range, but range isn't the only part of variability.

Ms. Ortiz: Thank you. . . . I see Vernon has the definition of range ready for us. Read it aloud.

Vernon: The range of a set of numbers is the difference between the greatest and least number in the set.

Ms. Ortiz: What's the formula for computing the range of a data set, Vanessa?

Vanessa: The range equals the greatest number minus the least number.

Ms. Ortiz: Everyone, compute the range of these data on the overhead screen. . . .

❑ **VIGNETTE 6.5**

Mr. Windley: Class, I have the scores from two groups of students who took the same test. Look at the graphs of the two scores. He displays the following:

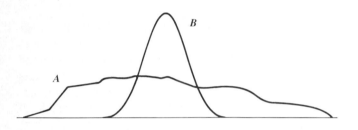

Mr. Windley: In what ways are the two sets of data alike? How are they different from one another? . . . Jack.

Jack: Group A is flatter; B is taller.

Mr. Windley: What makes A flatter than B, Dallas?

Dallas: I don't know; you just drew it that way.

Mr. Windley: What does being drawn flatter versus taller indicate about the data, Dallas?

Dallas: B has higher scores.

Mr. Windley: Which group appears to have the higher average score, Dallas?

Dallas: I don't know.

Mr. Windley: Here, as I move my pen from left to right along the x-axis, you people say 'stop' when I get to the average score for A. (See Exhibit 6.6.)

Various students (when the pen reaches the middle of the segment): Stop!

Mr. Windley: Now let's do the same for B:

Various students (when the pen reaches the same point as before): Stop!

Mr. Windley: So, you're saying the two averages are about what, Dallas?

Dallas: Equal—so I take back what I said before. B's scores aren't any higher than A's.

Mr. Windley: So what does it mean that—Okay, Mailen has something she wants to say.

Mailen: B's scores are more bunched up together in the middle; A's are more spread out.

Mr. Windley: Please keep Mailen's words in your mind as we shift to two other sets of data, C and D. We'll return to A and B shortly.

Exhibit 6.6

He displays the following:

Group C	Group D
18	12
14	9
9	9
5	9
1	8

Mr. Windley: How do C and D differ from one another, Arlo?

Arlo: C is more like A before, the numbers are spread out.

Mr. Windley: What do you think Arlo means by spread out, Turquoise?

Turquoise: It's got higher numbers.

Mr. Windley: Higher, Turquoise?

Turquoise: Yeah, 18's higher than 12.

Mr. Windley: Any reactions to Turquoise's observation, Samone?

Samone: C also has lower numbers than D. 1 is less than 8.

Mr. Windley: Mailen?

Mailen: That's the point. The difference between the highest and lowest in C is greater than the difference between the highest and lowest in D. That's what spread out means.

Mr. Windley: Here's what I hear Mailen saying:

He draws the following on the overhead display:

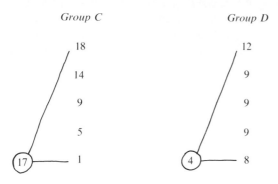

Group C   Group D

Mr. Windley: Jack?

Jack: Also, the difference between the other numbers in C are mostly greater than those for D.

Mr. Windley: Come up here and show us what you mean.

Jack adds to the illustrations so that they look like this:

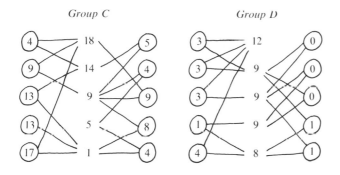

Group C   Group D

Mr. Windley: What did Jack just do, Rosalie?

Rosalie: He added those circled numbers.

Mr. Windley: He *added* them together? Where did he put the sum?

Rosalie: No, that's not what I meant. He wrote them on the overhead.

Mr. Windley: Oh! But how did he come up with those particular numbers? What did he do to find them, Seritta?

Seritta: He subtracted the numbers from each other.

Mr. Windley: What does Seritta mean, Vincent?

Vincent: She means, ahh—can I just come up and show you?

Mr. Windley: Please.

Vincent: . . . He subtracted this number from this one, then this one from this one, and this one from this one, and so on. . . . Just follow his lines here.

Mr. Windley: Now you tell us what Jack just showed us, Samone.

Samone starts to walk toward the front.

Mr. Windley: No, describe what he was showing us from your place—no illustrations, just words.

Samone: Jack took the numbers in pairs and found all possible differences.

Mr. Windley: How many differences among group C, Alvin?

Alvin: . . . 4, 5, 8, 10—10 in C—and also another 10 for D.

Mr. Windley: Jack, you want to tell us something.

Jack: Just that it's the size of the 10 circled numbers for the C group that explains why its graph would be flatter like A was and D's would be taller and skinnier like B was before.

The session continues with the group describing the concept of variability and developing two measures of variability: (1) what is conventionally known as the range and (2) one of their own design they called "the average of all the pairs of differences."

In the first of the two examples, Ms. Ortiz' questions taxed her students' memories. Her questions helped them to remember the definitions of variability and range and how to compute the range. Such questions provide Ms. Ortiz with formative feedback on what students remember and provide students with both corrective feedback and a repetitive drill to help them remember. Such questions are *knowledge-level*.

Mr. Windley's questions, on the other hand, were more open-ended and designed to guide students' thought patterns leading to discovery. Unlike, Ms. Ortiz' questions, Mr. Windley's questions could have more than one correct answer. Mr. Windley's questions taxed students' intellectual cognitive abilities (i.e., conceptualization, comprehension, application, or creativity). Such questions are *intellectual-level*.

Appropriate Uses of Intellectual-Level Questioning/Discussion Sessions

Intellectual-level questioning/discussion sessions in which a teacher raises intellectual-level questions for students to answer, analyze, and discuss are necessary components of lessons for intellectual-level objectives. Such sessions were illustrated in Chapter 4:

❏ In Vignette 4.7, Mr. Citerelli's lesson for a *conceptualization* objective on *arithmetic sequences* included a large-group intellectual-level questioning/discussion session to stimulate inductive reasoning. Questions were raised about the examples and nonexamples listed in Exhibit 4.7; differences and similarities were discussed.

❏ In Vignette 4.13, Mr. Matsumoto's lesson for a *comprehension* objective relative to the *proof of a theorem* (stated in Exhibit 4.13) included a large-group intellectual-level questioning/discussion session to involve the students in interpreting aspects of the proof and analyzing its logical underpinnings. Questions such as the following were raised and discussed: "How did we get from $a = 2i + 1$ to $a^2 = 4i^2 + 4i + 1$?"

❏ In Vignette 4.20, Mr. Wilson's lesson for an *application* objective on *the multiplication principle, permutations, and combinations* included a large-group intellectual-level questioning/discussion session to stimulate deductive reasoning. Questions were addressed leading to a solution of a problem about the relative security of combination and key locks. The form in Exhibit 4.21 was used as an advanced organizer for that session.

❏ In Vignette 4.21, Ms. Ferney's lesson for a *creativity* objective on *functions* included a large-group intellectual-level questioning/discussion session to stimulate divergent thinking. Raising open-ended questions and sharing analyses of responses are inherent in the synectics Ms. Ferney applied.

Common Misuses of Intellectual-Level Questioning/Discussion Sessions

In response to the overemphasis on knowledge-level skills and underemphasis on intellectual-level learning in most mathematics courses today (Carpenter et al. 1988; Dossey et al. 1988, 11; Jesunathadas 1990), arguments favoring an emphasis on inquiry and discovery instruction leading to intellectual-level learning are widely circulated (e.g., by this book and by NCTM (1989)). This push has, unfortunately, nurtured the mistaken belief among some teachers that discovery or inquiry lessons are always superior to direct instruction. Of course, some knowledge-level objectives should be included among the objectives for most teaching units. Direct instruction, not inquiry instruction, is appropriate for knowledge-level objectives. But those well-intentioned teachers who have been "oversold" on the virtues of inquiry instruction inappropriately attempt to get their students to discover content that's not discoverable. They then inappropriately conduct intellectual-level questioning/discussion sessions for what should be knowledge-level objectives. Consider Vignette 6.6.

❏ VIGNETTE 6.6

Ms. Thorpe wants her students to discover why the $\sqrt{}$ symbol is used to denote principal square roots of numbers.

Ms. Thorpe: Why do you think we use this radical symbol [she displays the symbol with the overhead] to show square roots, Olivia?

Olivia: I don't know. . . . Maybe because it looks kind of like a division thing and taking a root is sort of like division.

Ms. Thorpe: Oh, that's a good idea! How about some others? Ellen, what about you?

Ellen: I agree with Olivia.

Ms. Thorpe: Can't you think of something else?

Ellen: . . . Well, it looks kind of like a lightning bolt—maybe, you know, how—but I don't know why you'd use a lightning bolt.

Ms. Thorpe: Any other ideas, class? . . . Okay, well why do you suppose we call it a radical sign?

There is no logically discoverable reason why the radical symbol looks as it does. The symbol is simply a convention whose usage evolved from pre–fifteenth century Arabic use of the word *radix* because of Arab writers thinking of a square number growing out of a root. Late Medieval Latin writers compressed *radix* into a single symbol, R_x. A historical account of how today's conventional radical symbol evolved from R_x is presented by Miller (1969). Sharing such accounts with students serves as a mnemonic for remembering the symbol and its meaning and leads to an appreciation of the human side of mathematics. However, trying to get students to discover the evolution of a convention via intellectual-level questioning/discussion sessions is not only an inefficient use of class time, it's impossible.

For knowledge-level objectives, knowledge-level questioning sessions are appropriate—but not intellectual-level questioning/discussion sessions. There are times when you should raise open-ended questions during direct instructional lessons for knowledge-level objectives. But ordinarily such questions are rhetorical. For example, Ms. Thorpe might have initiated her lesson on knowledge of the radical symbol with a question: "Why do we use this radical symbol for square roots?" But instead of having students try to discover the answer, she should have just paused a moment and then used direct instructional methods to relate the historical account (either in a brief lecture or reading assignment).

Avoiding Ms. Thorpe's type of misuse is a matter of attending to the learning level of your objective. Another type of misuse is more difficult to overcome because it stems from the fact that conducting effective large-group intellectual-level questioning/discussion sessions is a sophisticated art, requiring in-depth understanding of pedagogical principles, students, and mathematics. It is quite a challenge to determine (1) when to raise what questions and with whom, (2) how to respond to students' answers, comments, and questions, and (3) whether a discussion should be abbreviated, extended, or redirected. Besides your academic preparation, experience will help you avoid the following causes of unsuccessful intellectual-level questioning/discussion sessions:

The teacher fails to comprehend students' answers, comments, and questions unless the students use the words the teacher has in mind. For example, consider Vignette 6.7.

❏ VIGNETTE 6.7

Ms. Warrick's class has just completed the first four stages of a conceptualization lesson designed to achieve the following objective:

> Discriminates between examples and nonexamples of relations that are functions and relations that are not functions *(conceptualization)*.

She is now conducting an intellectual-level questioning/discussion session as part of the *articulation* stage. She has in mind the following definition for the students to develop:

f is a function from set A to set B if and only if

1. f is a relation from A to B;
2. For each $a_i \in A$, there exist $b_i \in B$ such that $f(a_i) = b_i$; and
3. $a_1, a_2 \in A$ and $a_1 = a_2$ implies that $f(a_1) = f(a_2)$.

Without yet showing them her definition she says, "Now that we agree on what a function is, let's develop a definition." She uses the overhead to write the following:

f is a function from set A to set B if and only if

1. f is a relation from A to B;
2.
3.

Ms. Warrick: You told me in the discussion that a function from one set to another not only had to be a relation from the one set to the other, but two other things also have to be true. . . . What are those two things? Take 3 minutes at your place to list those for two and three to complete this definition. . . . Okay, what do you have for number two, Puffy?
Puffy: If one of the elements in A is mapped to two b's then the two from B are equal.

Because Ms. Warrick has "For each $a_i \in A$, there exist $b_i \in B$ such that $f(a_i) = b_i$" on her mind and listened only to the first part of Puffy's statement ("If one of the elements in A is mapped to two b's. . . ."), she does not recognize that what Puffy means is tantamount to the third part of the target definition ($a_1, a_2 \in A$ and $a_1 = a_2$ implies that $f(a_1) = f(a_2)$). Thus, Ms. Warrick makes the mistake of responding to Puffy with, "That's a good try, but don't you remember we decided that any one element in A can only be mapped onto one element from B?"

As Ms. Warrick continues to pursue the definition, Puffy is no longer listening; she's trying to figure why her correct response is "wrong."

The teacher fails to play upon students' responses to further probing questions. Even though Ms. Warrick thought Puffy's statement should not have been incorporated into the definition, she could have followed through with analytical questions about Puffy's statement that would have stimulated further thinking. For example, "What do you think Puffy means by an element from A being mapped to two b's?" After calling on another student for that answer, she could turn to Puffy and ask, "Is that what you meant?"

Some teachers, not wanting to appear unaccepting of students' answers, routinely respond with vague praise to virtually anything students say and then proceed with the session as if the students said nothing. For example, consider Vignette 6.8.

❏ VIGNETTE 6.8

Mr. Saunders: What are some of the things we know about rational numbers, Tina?
Tina: Fractions are always rational numbers.
Mr. Saunders: Good! What else, Paul?
Paul: Rational numbers can be expressed as the ratio of two integers p and q, but, ahhh, p's not zero—or one of 'em's not zero.
Mr. Saunders: Super! Katie?
Katie: The decimal form of all rational numbers terminates.
Mr. Saunders: That's a good try. Now, for this lesson what you need to know about rational numbers is that for any two rational numbers you can name, you can always find another that's greater than the one but less than the other. This is because . . . .

Out of frustration with students' answers, the teacher aborts the session in favor of direct instruction, "telling" them what they should have discovered for themselves. When students' responses to questions don't progress the class' thinking along planned lines and students appear restless, it is tempting to change strategies in midsession. However, the difficulty may not stem from students' inability to "get it" as much as from the teacher's failure to:

❑ Structure the session adequately with the aid of outlines, forms, and other advanced organizers for focusing attention (e.g., Exhibits 4.7 and 4.21).
❑ Use appropriate probes that stimulate students to examine their own responses in ways that lead them back on track.
❑ Utilize formative feedback for pacing and modifying activities (e.g., deciding whether to reduce or increase psychological noise of examples).

When students' responses and comments deviate from the planned thought pattern, you need to refocus them with less-open-ended questions. In Vignette 6.5, Mr. Windley applied this strategy when he changed from "Which group appears to have the higher average?" to "Here as I move my pen from left to right along the x-axis, say 'stop' when I get to the average of A."

Another strategy is to "jump" on a student's comment or answer if it has any semblance of directing thinking in the desired direction and reword it just enough to assure that what needs to be said is said. Mr. Windley applied that strategy when he followed one of Mailen's comments with, "Here's what I hear Mailen saying . . . ."

The teacher fails to structure the session sufficiently or be assertive enough to maintain the focus on the business at hand; thus the activity degenerates into random conversation. Critics of inquiry-type instructional activities point out how often open-ended questions and class discussions drift from the intended topic, wasting time that teachers should be using to cover the material with direct approaches. The solution is not to abandon necessary intellectual-level questioning/discussion sessions but to structure activities with advanced organizers and to utilize assertive communications.

Classroom-management strategies for engaging all—not just a few—students in formulating answers to questions are not applied. Affording every student opportunities to respond to questions and participate in discussions seems possible to some only in small group sessions. Examples in the next section

illustrate how you can achieve full student participation in large, whole-class sessions.

Initiating and Maintaining Student Engagement in Large-Group Intellectual-Level Questioning/Discussion Sessions

Teachers typically conduct large-group intellectual-level questioning/discussion sessions so that students answer questions aloud almost as soon as the first one volunteers (Cangelosi 1984b). For example, consider Vignette 6.9.

❑ **VIGNETTE 6.9**

Mr. Grimes is conducting an inductive learning activity designed to help his 28 algebra students achieve the following objective:

> Distinguishes between examples of *variables* and examples of *constants (conceptualization)*.

With the overhead projector he displays the list in Exhibit 6.7.

Mr. Grimes: Notice that some of the elements in this set are marked with blocks and others with balls. Can anyone tell why the ones with blocks belong together and the ones with balls belong together?

Akeem, Jardine, and Sharon eagerly raise their hands. Immediately, Mr. Grimes calls on Jardine.

Jardine: The ones with blocks are all in this room. Gary is here, the screen is there, and most of us are 15 years old.

Akeem and Sharon are waving their hands trying to get Mr. Grimes' attention. Akeem cries, "No, no!" as three other students also raise their hands.

Mr. Grimes: Easy, Akeem. What's the matter?
Akeem: That can't be right because I don't see any 13's in here. And besides one of the ones with a ball is

Exhibit 6.7
Mr. Grimes' overhead transparency for his inductive lesson on variables.

■ GARY ABOUD
● RECTANGLE
● RATIONAL NUMBER
■ 13
■ THE OVERHEAD PROJECTOR SCREEN YOU SEE RIGHT NOW
● PEOPLE IN THIS ROOM
● AGE
■ 15 YEARS OLD

'people in this room.' I think the ones with balls have something to do with numbers.

Mr. Grimes: Okay, Sharon, before you fall out of your desk.

Sharon: The ones with blocks are exact and the—

Mr. Grimes: Excuse me, Sharon, but the rule is that you must counter the previous hypothesis before you give your own.

Sharon: Oh, I'm sorry, what was it again?

Akeem: I said the ones with balls have something to do with numbers, but I see that's not right because 13 is a ball. I thought it was a block at first.

Mr. Grimes: Okay, go on Sharon.

Sharon: Like I was saying, the ones with blocks are exact things—like Gary, not just people in the room, or 13, not just *any* rational number. Do you see what I'm saying?

Mr. Grimes: Do you understand what Sharon said, Vesna?

Vesna: Oh! Ahh, sure.

Mr. Grimes: Good! Yes, Jardine what is it?

Jardine: I don't. Can you explain it more?

Sharon: Look at the ones with the balls. There can be all different kinds of rectangles. A rational number can be 13, 15, or 100.75. People in this room can be any of us. And there's more than one age.

Jardine: Yeah, but Gary is a person in this class and 13's a rational number. So, why do they have blocks instead of balls?

Mr. Grimes: That's a good question! Who wants to answer? Okay, Akeem.

Akeem: It's like Sharon said. They're just one of a kind. Gary is only *one* person in this . . . .

The session continues toward closure, with Mr. Grimes defining a *constant* and then a *variable* with input from Akeem, Jardine, and Sharon.

Mr. Grimes' questioning/discussion session probably helped Akeem, Jardine, and Sharon achieve the objective. But what about the other 25 students in the class? For students to be engaged in activities in which intellectual-level questions are raised, they must do more than passively listen to their classmates' responses. They don't necessarily have to be recognized and state their answers for the group, but they do need to formulate and articulate their own answers.

Because Mr. Grimes allowed Jardine to answer aloud immediately after the initial question was raised, most students did not have time to formulate their own answers. They quit thinking about their own answers to listen to Jardine's. Only the outspoken, quick-to-respond students engaged in the learning activity as they should. Mr. Grimes did not allow enough time to elapse between when ques-

tions were asked and when they were answered aloud for the class. The overall average time teachers wait for students to respond to in-class questions is less than 2 seconds (Arnold, Atwood, and Rogers 1974). After experiencing a few sessions such as Mr. Grimes', in which they are asked questions that they don't have the opportunity to answer, most students learn not even to attempt to formulate their own responses. Some will politely listen to the responses of the few, others entertain themselves with off-task thoughts, and others, if allowed, entertain themselves with disruptive behaviors (Cangelosi 1988a, 155).

How, then, can you conduct intellectual-level questioning/discussion sessions so that all students formulate answers to each question? Here are two possibilities:

You might preface questions with directions for all students to answer each question in their minds without answering aloud or volunteering answers until you ask them to do so. Here's an example of a teacher applying that option to Mr. Grimes' situation.

❑ VIGNETTE 6.10

Mr. Smart is conducting an inductive learning activity designed to help his 28 algebra students achieve the following objective:

> Distinguishes between examples of *variables* and examples of *constants (conceptualization)*.

With the overhead projector he displays the list in Exhibit 6.7.

Mr. Smart: I am going to ask you some questions, but I don't want anyone to answer aloud until I call on her or him. Just answer the questions in your mind.

He then asks them to consider the differences and similarities between those on the list marked with balls and those with blocks. Two students eagerly raise their hands and say, "Oh, Mr. Smart!" He is tempted to call on them to positively reinforce their enthusiasm, but he resists, instead cuing them to follow directions with a gesture and stern look. He waits, watching students' faces. Convinced after 3 minutes that all have thought about the question and most have an answer ready, he asks, "Joyce do you have an answer?" Joyce nods.

Mr. Smart: Good! How about you, Curtis?
Curtis: Yes.
Mr. Smart: Fine! Are you ready, Melissa?
Melissa: Not yet.
Mr. Smart: Just think aloud for us. Let's hear your thoughts about the two kinds of elements on the list.

Melissa: I don't see how they're different. Some of the ones with balls are about mathematics, but then so are some of those with blocks.

Mr. Smart: I think that's an important observation. Now, I'd like some volunteers to share their answers with us. Okay, Ruth?

Ruth: I was thinking like Melissa, and then I . . . .

———————————

You might direct students to write answers to questions on forms you supply or on their own paper as you circulate about the room, quietly reading samples of their responses. Here's an example of a teacher applying this option to Mr. Grimes' situation.

❏ VIGNETTE 6.11

Ms. Cramer is conducting an inductive learning activity designed to help her 28 algebra students achieve the following objective:

> Distinguishes between examples of *variables* and examples of *constants (conceptualization)*.

She distributes the form appearing in Exhibit 6.8 and says, "At the bottom of this handout, please write one paragraph describing why you think the elements with blocks in front go together and why the ones with balls go together. In what ways are all the ones with balls alike but different from the ones with blocks? In what ways are all the ones with blocks alike but different from the ones with balls? . . . You have 9 minutes for this task. I'll be around to read answers, but just keep working. Please don't talk to me during this time. Now, begin." She demonstratively sets the timer on the chronograph she has on her wrist.

As students think and write, Ms. Cramer moves about the room, reading over students' shoulders. Some students are slow to start until she passes their desks and gently taps on their forms. As she samples their writing, she notes to herself students' answers she wants to use in the upcoming large-group discussion and answers she wants to avoid.

At the 9-minute mark, she moves to the front of the room and displays Exhibit 6.9 on the overhead.

Ms. Cramer: Please read yours, Simon.

Simon: Well, I didn't know exact—

Ms. Cramer: Just *read* it from your paper.

Simon: The blocks are alike because they have the blocks, first of all. And then they are all things that you can see or that are numbers. The ball ones have balls in front. They have one geometry thing and two that

Exhibit 6.8
The form Ms. Cramer distributed during her inductive lesson on variables.

> ▪ WILSON McCARDLE
> ● RECTANGLE
> ● RATIONAL NUMBER
> ▪ 13
> ▪ THE OVERHEAD PROJECTOR SCREEN YOU SEE RIGHT NOW
> ● PEOPLE IN THIS ROOM
> ● AGE
> ▪ 15 YEARS OLD
>
> How are the ▪'s alike but different from the ●'s?
> How are the ●'s alike but different from the ▪'s?
>
> _____
> _____
> _____
> _____
> _____
> _____
> _____
> _____
>
> COMPARISON
>
> _____
> _____
> _____

Exhibit 6.9

Person	■	●

are types of numbers and another that's a group of people. They both seem pretty mixed up, alike in some ways and different in others.

Ms. Cramer writes "Simon:" and then "can see or is a number" under the ■ on the transparency and "types of things" under the ● heading.

Ms. Cramer: Read yours, Megan.
Megan: Those with balls are kinds of things, not exact things. The ball ones are things you study about. The blocks are actual things, not just kinds. The blocks are more exact. The blocks also have a weird thing, but I like him anyway.

The class laughs as Ms. Cramer adds to the transparency. She writes "Megan:" under "Person," "actual and exact" under the ■, and "kinds of things" under the ● heading.

Ms. Cramer: On two lines of your form labeled 'Comparison,' quickly write one or two sentences describing how Simon's and Megan's answers are similar. You've got 1 minute.

She quickly moves about the room glancing at their responses as the session continues toward closure.

———————

You might also consider having students formulate and discuss answers in small task groups and then making group reports of their findings and conclusions to the large group. Engaging students in these types of cooperative group sessions is addressed in a subsequent section of this chapter.

Here are some additional ideas to keep in mind as you go about designing and conducting large-group intellectual-level questioning/discussion sessions:

❏ Apply the same principles for providing directions (e.g., be direct and exacting) and initiating student engagement (e.g., establish set) as you

would for large-group interactive lecture sessions (see pp. 161–166).
❏ Formative feedback is inherent in questioning sessions; use it to regulate activities.
❏ As with interactive lecture sessions, climatic moments in which students recognize that they've learned something and final closure are critical to the success of intellectual-level questioning/discussion sessions.

Responding to Students' Questions

If students feel they've been asked a lot of questions during these sessions but haven't had their own questions answered, they feel unfulfilled; thus, closure is not achieved. Keep in mind that you not only should raise questions for students' responses, but you also need to respond to students' questions. Your strategies for addressing their intellectual-level questions should differ from those for their knowledge-level questions.

Student-Initiated Intellectual-Level Questions
Imagine yourself conducting a large-group session as part of an application-level lesson on compound probability. A student, Jennifer, asks you:

"In biology class, we learned about this genetic thing—a defect in which if parents had it, there's a 25 percent chance that a kid they have will also. What if they have two kids, what are the chances that one or both will have the defect? Is it 50 percent or does it stay 25 percent?"

Such a question is answerable via a cognitive process—namely, deductive reasoning that involves more than just recalling a response. Being in the midst of an application-level lesson dealing with the content of the question, compound probability, you want to respond in a way that will advance the cause of the lesson. You have at least four options:

1. Answer the questions directly
2. Use think-aloud strategy
3. Probe back to the student
4. Probe and redirect the question to other students

Answer the Question Directly.   This would be the easiest and quickest thing to do. Give the answer, and since it's an intellectual-level question, explain the rationale for it. For example,

You: Actually, Jennifer, I think the probability would be somewhere between 25 percent and 50 percent. Think of the probability of neither of the two children inheriting the defect. The chances of the first not having it is 75 percent; the chances of the second not having is also 75 percent. It's a compound probability of two independent events, so you multiply 0.75 by 0.75. And that would be . . . about 0.56 according to my calculator. So, if there's a 56 percent chance of neither having it, there must be a 44 percent chance that one or both will get it. . . . Okay?

Use a Think-Aloud Strategy.   Rather than explaining the answer directly, you may spend more time demonstrating what goes through one's mind when formulating a solution. For Jennifer's question, you would be modeling the application-level behavior you want the students to learn:

You: Gracious, Jennifer, that's a challenging question. Let's see, how would I go about solving that one? . . . You've got two kids, the first or older one, and then the second. The probability of the first having the defect is 25 percent, did you say? . . . Okay. And is the probability of the second one having it affected by whether or not the first one has it? . . . No. So, no matter what, the probability for the second is also 25 percent. So, the first thing that comes to mind is to add the two and I get the 50 percent that you got, Jennifer. . . . Let me see, is that right? It couldn't be because if the parents had five children, for example, that would be 0.25 five times, and that would be a probability of 1.25 or 125 percent—that's impossible. The probability has got to be less than 1. . . . Oh, let's try it case by case. What's the probability of the first having it and the second not? . . . Chances are 0.25 for the first and then 0.75 for the second not to have it. That's what? The multiplication rule applies, so 0.25 times 0.75 is . . . about 0.19. That takes care of one case. Now, what about the first not having it, but the second one does—

that's another 0.19. What's left? . . . Both of them having it. That's 0.25 times 0.25 which is . . . about 0.06. . . . That's all the possibilities, so add them up, since they're mutually exclusive events and we get . . . 44 percent. Does that seem right? Oh! I shouldn't have spent all that time; I just thought of an easier way. Couldn't we have just looked at the complement? Then we'd only have one case to figure! The probability of neither child having the defect would be simply 0.75 squared and that's . . . about 0.56. . . . So, our answer should be 100 percent minus 56 percent, or 44 percent—same thing as before, but we found it with less work.

Probe Back to the Student.   Even more time-consuming but probably more beneficial for the student is to respond with a sequence of your own questions that stimulate the students to engage in the type of reasoning demonstrated by the think-aloud example:

You: What makes you think it might be 50 percent?
Jennifer: There's 25 percent chance the first one has it, right?
You: Right.
Jennifer: And 25 percent for the second one. So, that's another 25 percent chance—giving you a total of 50 percent.
You: Then what would the probability be of having at least one child with the defect if the family had five children?
Jennifer: Five times 0.25.
You: Which is?
Jennifer: . . . ahh, 1.25. . . . That's not possible!
You: Why don't you try a case-by-case strategy?
Jennifer: Like what?
You: Here, come up to the board and . . . .

You would continue along these lines, leading Jennifer through the thought process.

Probe and Redirect the Question to Other Students.   To involve more students in the activity, respond with leading questions, but direct them to other students as well as Jennifer:

You: Which do you think is right, 50 or 25 percent, Wade?
Wade: It's got to be more than 25 percent because that's the probability if they had only one child.
You: So does that make it 50 percent, Agnes?
Agnes: That's all that's left.

You: Okay, class, assuming Agnes is correct, compute the probability of at least one child having the defect if the family has five instead of only two children. Quickly, now, every-one. . . . Okay, what did you get, Jennifer?

Jennifer: 1.25, but that can't be because . . . .

Student-Initiated Knowledge-Level Questions

Imagine yourself conducting a large group session as part of a lesson on compound probability when a student, Janet, asks you, "What does mutually exclusive mean?" Such a question is answerable by recalling a response, in this case, a definition. Your options, of which there are at least five, are simpler to implement than those for intellectual-level questions:

1. Answer the question directly
2. Use a "how-might-we-find-that-out" strategy
3. Refer the student to a source to be used right away
4. Refer the student to a source to be used at a later time
5. Redirect the question to another student

Answer the Question Directly. For example:

You: Two events are mutually exclusive if they are so related that one cannot happen if the other does. For example, you cannot get *both* an A and a D on Thursday's test. If you get an A, you can't get a D. If you get a D, you can't get an A. The two events are mutually exclusive.

Use a "How-Might-We-Find-That-Out" Strategy. For example:

You: We really need to know what that means. Where should we go to look that up?

Janet: It's probably in the book, but I don't know where.

You: Why don't you try the index? That should give us some page numbers.

Refer the Student to a Source to Be Used Right Away. For example:

You: Quickly, get the mathematics dictionary off the shelf. Look up the definition and read it to the class.

Refer the Student to a Source to Be Used at a Later Time. For example:

You: You can find the definition in your textbook or you may use my mathematics dictionary.

Please look it up in one or the other and share it first thing in class tomorrow.

Redirect the Question to Another Student. For example:

You: Who remembers the definition of mutually exclusive? . . . Okay, Salvador.

Salvador: You said it's when two things can't happen at the same time.

ENGAGING STUDENTS IN LARGE-GROUP RECITATION SESSIONS
Knowledge-Level Questions

To the eyes of an untrained classroom observer, large-group recitation sessions may hardly be distinguishable from large-group intellectual-level questioning/discussion sessions. In both types of sessions, the teacher raises questions for students to answer. However, the level of questions and the level of student learning differ dramatically. Recitation sessions are dominated by knowledge-level questions requiring students to *remember* answers or how to find answers, *not* to use reasoning to formulate answers. Ms. Ortiz (Vignette 6.4) conducted an exemplary large-group recitation session. Her questions (such as, "What's the formula for computing the range of a data set?") were *knowledge-level* questions.

Appropriate Uses of Large-Group Recitation Sessions

Recitation sessions in which a teacher raises knowledge-level questions provide students with reviews of what they need to remember, experiences hearing correct answers they need to retain in memory, and feedback on the accuracy of what they remember. Furthermore, the teacher gains formative feedback on what students do and don't know. Such sessions play an important role in knowledge-level lessons.

Common Misuses of Large-Group Recitation Sessions

As with other types of learning activities, recitations are not always used as they should; the more common misuses include the following:

A teacher attempts to help students achieve an intellectual-level objective via a recitation instead of an intellectual-level questioning/discussion session. Ordinarily, this is a consequence of a teacher either not knowing how to ask intellectual-level questions or becoming so frustrated with students' responses to intellectual-level questions that he or she shifts to knowledge-level questions.

A teacher uses a large-group recitation session to test what students know, using the results to make summative evaluations affecting students' grades. As indicated in Chapter 7, there are far more accurate and efficient ways of collecting data on student achievement for grading purposes than holding a large-group recitation. Some teachers and many students think of in-class questioning sessions as times for "putting students on the spot" and "proving how smart" (and, thus, dumb) they are. Such an attitude detracts from the value of any large-group questioning session, either intellectual-level or knowledge-level, as a learning activity. Testing for summative evaluation purposes needs to be clearly distinguished from learning activities.

A teacher attempts to use students' anticipation of such a session to motivate them to memorize what they need to know or else be embarrassed in front of their peers. As indicated in Chapter 5 and by numerous classroom-management research studies (Cangelosi 1988a, 76–79), the threat of being embarrassed in the classroom tends to discourage rather than encourage student engagement and effort.

A large-group recitation session is used to provide students with practice on a particular skill that could be more efficiently practiced in another type of learning activity arrangement (e.g., an independent work session). Consider Vignette 6.12.

❑ VIGNETTE 6.12

To help his students remember rules they've studied for graphing different types of functions, Mr. Winn conducts a large-group recitation session, part of which proceeds as follows:

Mr. Winn: What will the graph of $3x - 7 = 10y + 1$ look like, Deanna?
Deanna: It would be a line.
Mr. Winn: How do you know that?
Deanna: Because the highest power of the variable is 1.
Mr. Winn: That's right. Now, what does the graph of $y = x^2 - 16x + 5$ look like, Gail?
Gail: A parabola.
Mr. Winn: What rule did you use?
Gail: The exponent of the . . . .

Although there's nothing particularly wrong with Mr. Winn's recitation session, there may well be times when this type of activity would more efficiently provide practice for students if it were designed as an independent work session. With the independent work session, each student could respond to all Mr. Winn's questions on an exercise sheet. He could provide some individual help during the session and then check answers in a large-group setting afterwards.

Initiating and Maintaining Student Engagement in Recitation Sessions

Here are some ideas to keep in mind when designing and conducting large-group recitation sessions:

Games can be used to excite student interest. The term *recitation* is associated with boredom in the minds of most people. Yet, television quiz shows and board games such as Trivial Pursuit enjoy immense popularity although they are forms of recitations (i.e., knowledge-level questions are addressed). Thus, you might consider tailoring some of your recitation sessions along the lines of some of the popular quiz games. Consider Vignette 6.13.

❑ VIGNETTE 6.13

Ms. Saucony periodically has her algebra II students play a game with the following rules:

1. One student is selected as the *game conductor,* another, as *game scorekeeper.*
2. The rest of the class is divided into two teams, A and B.
3. Six members of each team are selected to serve as that team's *panel.*
4. Panels A and B sit at separate tables in front of the room, as depicted in Exhibit 6.10.
5. The game conductor randomly draws the name of a nonpanelist member of one of the teams. That student then selects one of the following categories for the first question to the opposing team:

   ❑ Geometric terms, symbols, and expressions
   ❑ Algebraic terms, symbols, and expressions
   ❑ Statistical terms, symbols, and expressions
   ❑ Trigonometric terms, symbols, and expressions
   ❑ Geometric relations
   ❑ Algebraic relations
   ❑ Statistical relations
   ❑ Trigonometric relations
   ❑ Mathematical history
   ❑ Potpourri

6. The game conductor randomly draws a question card from the selected category and asks the question to the panel (panel A if the student selecting the category is from B and vice versa).
7. The panel members have 15 seconds to confer and answer the question. If they answer, their team is awarded

Exhibit 6.10
The recitation session in Ms. Saucony's algebra II class is patterned after a television game show.

two points. If they fail, then the panel members call on a nonpanelist from their team for the answer. If the team member correctly answers the question, the team gets one point. If that member doesn't, then the conductor asks the same question to the other panel, and that team goes through the same process. If no correct answer is forthcoming, then the conductor announces the correct answer and no points are awarded.

8. A second nonpanelist is randomly chosen to select a category and steps 6 and 7 are repeated with the following exceptions:

❏ A new category has to be selected; no previously selected category can be chosen until all categories have been used once.
❏ Each time a panel calls on one of its nonpanelist team members to answer a question, they must select a student who has not been called on earlier in the game.

9. The game continues along these lines (repeating the cycle established in steps 6–8) until a prespecified number of questions has been asked.

Most recitation sessions should probably be integrated with other types of learning activities. This idea is in contrast to the previous one, in which an elaborate game is set up for a recitation. Such games, though usually quite engaging for most students, are time-consuming and can hardly be used every day. As you conduct various types of learning activities, even ones targeting intellectual-level objectives, it's wise to insert knowledge-level questions

relative to content that is relevant at the time. For example, consider the next vignette.

❏ **VIGNETTE 6.14**
As Mr. Willoughby is conducting an inductive lesson on compound probability relations, a student remarks, "Well a coin can't be both head and tail at the same time." Because the term mutually exclusive had been introduced the day before, Mr. Willoughby responds, "What do we call that kind of relation between two events?"

When raising a question, you are more likely to get the whole class to listen to the question if you don't use the name of the student you call on until after the question is articulated. Consider the next vignette.

❏ **VIGNETTE 6.15**
Ms. Wilford asks, "Paul, what is the inverse of the sine function called?" When Riva heard Paul's name, she knew she wouldn't be called on, so she didn't think about the answer. Later Ms. Wilford asks, "What's the ratio of these two sides of this right triangle called? . . . Okay, Martina." This time, Riva paid attention to the question longer and even took time to think of an answer before Mr. Wilford called on Martina.

Calling on students in a sequence they can't predict tends to enhance their attention to questions. This idea works for the same reason as does withholding the student's name until after a question is asked. To achieve an unpredictable sequence, all students must feel they have an equal opportunity to be called on for each question. This means that

(1) over the course of several sessions, students have been called on about an equal number of times and (2) students who have just responded are still candidates for the next question.

Although the length of the wait time between when you ask a knowledge-level question and when a student addresses it aloud does not need to be as long as for intellectual-level questions, students still need time to recall a response before they're interrupted by someone telling them the answer.

Although large-group recitation sessions are poor sources of data for summative evaluations of student achievement, they inherently provide formative feedback that should be used in regulating the session.

ENGAGING STUDENTS IN SMALL TASK-GROUP SESSIONS

Appropriate Uses of Small Task-Group Sessions

For some learning activities, it may be more efficient for you to organize your class into several subgroups rather than a single large group. Intraclass grouping arrangements in which students in each group work on a common task provide greater opportunities than whole-class activities for students to interact with one another, tasks to be tailored to special interests or needs, and a wide variety of tasks to be addressed during class.

Cooperative learning activities in which students learn from one another have proven to be quite successful (Joyce and Weil 1986, 215–305). Students can engage in cooperative learning activities in large-group settings, but small-task-group sessions are particularly well suited for students teaching one another.

Peer Instruction Groups

In a peer instruction group, one student teaches others, either presenting a brief lesson, tutoring, or providing help with a particular exercise. Traditionally, this type of activity involves a student who is advanced relative to achievement of a particular objective working with students who need special help in achieving that objective. Consider Vignette 6.16.

❏ **VIGNETTE 6.16**

Mr. Jackson notes the following from the results of a unit test he's recently administered his 21-member advanced algebra class:

Regarding test items 3, 7, 8, and 16, all of which are relevant to students' comprehension of the central

limit theorem, Anita responded correctly to all four, whereas none of the following students got more than two of those items: Bernie, Deborah, Amalya, Francine, and Jay.

Regarding test items 5, 6, and 11, all of which are relevant to students' conceptualization of a normal distribution, Benju responded correctly to all three items, whereas none of the following students got any of those three items: Bernie, Amalya, Don, Steve, and Malcom.

Mr. Jackson thinks that (1) Anita and Benju's insights into the content would be enhanced by experiences teaching their peers, (2) the other eight aforementioned students will not succeed in the next unit until they better achieve certain objectives from this unit, and (3) Bernie and Amalya need to conceptualize normal distributions before they can comprehend the central limit theorem. Thus, he decides to conduct a session in which the class is subdivided into three groups:

Group 1, in which Anita explains the central limit theorem and how she worked test items 3, 7, 8, and 16 to Deborah, Francine, and Jay.

Group 2, in which Benju explains normal distributions and how he worked test items 5, 6, and 11 to Bernie, Amalya, Don, Steve, and Malcom.

Group 3, in which the other 11 students work on an individual assignment.

But peer instruction does not have to involve mentor students who display more advanced achievement levels than their peers. Consider the idea demonstrated by the following vignette.

❏ **VIGNETTE 6.17**

Ms. Harris integrates historical topics into most of the units for her algebra class of 25 students. As part of a unit on numbers and numeration, she subdivides the students into five groups of five, with groups assigned to historical topics as follows:

Group A

Topic: Origins of the Hindu-Arabic numeration system
Students: Oprey, Byron, Bryce, Chris, Nadine

Group B

Topic: The origins of our beliefs about prime numbers
Students: Marion, Joe, Charlene, Jennifer, Dominica

Group C

Topic: The discovery of π

Students: Patti, Scott, Jan, Chen-Pai, Garth

Group D

Topic: The history of perfect, deficient, and abundant numbers

Students: Crystal, Henry, Cinny, Jason A., Jason T.

Group E

Topic: Karl Friedrich Gauss and the theory of numbers

Students: Julie, Eian, John, Rich, Willie

She then conducts an hour-long small-task-group session, in which each of these five groups studies and discusses its topic using references from Ms. Harris' resource library. For homework, each student prepares a 15-minute lesson on his or her group's topic to be presented to four students from the other groups.

Over the next 2 days, Ms. Harris conducts additional small-task-group sessions in which the five students from each group concurrently present their 15-minute lessons to groups of four students from other groups. For example, Oprey presents her lesson on origins of Hindu-Arabic numbers to Marion, Patti, Crystal, and Julie. Marion presents his on the origins of our beliefs about prime numbers to Oprey, Patti, Crystal, and Julie. Patti presents hers on the discovery of π to Oprey, Marion, Crystal, and Julie. Crystal presents hers on the history of perfect, deficient, and abundant numbers to Oprey, Marion, Patti, and Julie. And Julie presents hers on Gauss and the theory of numbers to Oprey, Marion, Patti, and Crystal.

The other four groups for the rounds of lessons are

❏ Byron, Joe, Scott, Henry, Eian
❏ Bryce, Charlene, Jan, Cinny, John
❏ Chris, Jennifer, Chen-Pai, Jason A., Rich
❏ Nadine, Dominica, Garth, Jason T., Willie

Practice Groups

Large-group recitation sessions (e.g., those in Vignettes 6.4, 6.12, and 6.13) do not always provide the most efficient ways for students to review, drill, and receive feedback for knowledge-level objectives. With small-group arrangements, several or more students can recite concurrently. For example,

❏ Students work in groups of three. One student reads questions about vocabulary, symbols, and relations from a pack of cards. Feedback is provided after each response. The role of questioner rotates.

❏ Students play mathematics memory games (e.g., one patterned after the board game Trivial Pursuit) in groups of five.

Interest or Achievement-Level Groups

Intraclass groups may be organized around interests (as in the first of the following two vignettes) or achievement levels (as in the second vignette).

❏ VIGNETTE 6.18

Mr. Frank sometimes groups his geometry students according to their varied areas of interest. Throughout a unit on similarity between geometric figures, he uses four different interest groups: sports, pets, partying, and music. For the unit's conceptualization lesson, each of the four groups works within its interest area during the *task confrontation* and *task work* stages (as explained on page 83). Reports from the four groups are then used in subsequent lesson stages in large-group sessions.

The four-subgroup arrangement is further utilized in other lessons, such as one for an application-level objective. In general, the small-interest-group sessions are used for students to confront tasks in their respective areas of interests; these are followed by large-group sessions, in which the mathematics commonly used by all four groups is discussed and analyzed.

❏ VIGNETTE 6.19

To help her deal with the wide range of student achievement levels in her eighth-grade general mathematics class, Ms. Goldberg conducts virtually the whole course with the 32 students partitioned into three groups:

❏ The *green* group, consisting of eight students who average about 3.5 weeks per teaching unit.
❏ The *blue* group, consisting of 15 students who average about 2.5 weeks per teaching unit.
❏ The *gray* group, consisting of nine students who average about 1 week per teaching unit.

For all practical purposes, she conducts three courses in one. She is able to manage such a configuration by staggering large-group, small-group, and individualized sessions among the groups.

Problem-Solving Groups

Small-task-group sessions can facilitate students' concurrently working on a variety of problems that are subsequently used in large-group activities. Here is an example of such a session being used within an application-level lesson.

❑ **VIGNETTE 6.20**

Mr. Breland has his 23 prealgebra students working in four groups, A, B, C, and D, in the arrangement illustrated by Exhibit 6.11 as part of a lesson for the following objective:

> When confronted with a real-life problem, determines whether or not computing a ratio will facilitate solution of the problem *(application)*.

As directed by Mr. Breland, each group has 18 minutes to answer the questions listed on its task sheet and prepare a 6-minute oral report of its work to the class as a whole. The four task sheets are depicted in Exhibit 6.12.

As the groups complete their tasks, Mr. Breland circulates about the room, monitoring each group and cuing students on-task as the need arises.

After the session, a designated member of each group reports its findings. Mr. Breland then conducts a large-group intellectual-level questioning/discussion session for the *rule articulation phase* (see page 111) of the

Exhibit 6.11

Arrangement of Mr. Breland's class for a small-task-group problem-solving session.

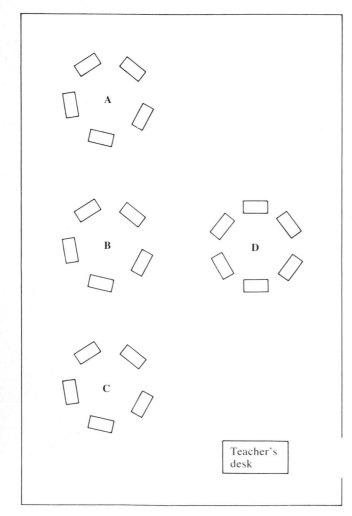

application-level lesson. Prompted by Mr. Breland's deductive questions, students examine and compare the four group reports to articulate the rules for applying ratios to real-life problems.

Common Misuses of Small-Task-Group Sessions

Research studies examining how students spend their time in classrooms indicate that students tend to have poor engagement levels in small-group learning activities unless the teacher is actively involved in the session (Fisher et al. 1980). But a teacher cannot be in the middle of several groups at once, so subgroups often fail to address their tasks due to a lack of guidance. For example:

❑ **VIGNETTE 6.21**

Ms. Clay has her prealgebra students organized into four subgroups similar to the arrangement in Exhibit 6.11. She directs them, "I want each group to discuss when we use ratios to solve real-life problems. . . . Okay, go ahead and get started."

After 6 minutes discussing what they're supposed to be doing, the students in one group no longer bother with ratios and socialize with one another. Ms. Clay hardly notices that they're off-task because she is busy explaining to another group what she meant for them be doing. A third group becomes quite noisy, and Ms. Clay raises her voice from her position with the second group and announces, "Better keep it down in here. You won't learn how to apply ratios unless you get on the stick and get your discussion going." In the fourth group, Magdalina dominates the first 5 minutes telling the others about ratios. She stimulates Ann's interest and the two of them engage in conversation in which Magdalina reviews what Ms. Clay explained in a previous session about computing ratios. The other three members of the group are doing other things unrelated to the topic.

After managing to get the second group on track, Ms. Clay moves to the noisy third group, saying, "You people aren't following directions; you're supposed to be discussing problems that use ratios." She then tells the group what she had hoped they'd discover for themselves.

After spending 9 minutes with the second group, Ms. Clay calls a halt to the activity and announces, "Okay, class let's rearrange our desks back. . . . Now that you understand when to apply ratios, I want to move on to . . . ."

Ms. Clay failed to initiate student engagement because her directions did not spell out the tasks each subgroup was to address and just how to go about completing the tasks. Without an advanced organizer (e.g., similar to Mr. Breland's in Exhibit

Exhibit 6.12 (pp. 183–186)
Four task sheets for groups A, B, C, and D in Mr. Breland's prealgebra class

Group A

DIRECTIONS: Answer the questions based on the box score from Tuesday's Flyers-Tigers basketball game. Prepare a 5-minute oral report to the class that explains what problem-solving strategies you used to answer the questions.

Flyers 79, Tigers 75

Flyers	min.	fgm–fga	ftm–fta	reb.	ass.	pf	tp
Champagne	23	4– 7	2– 2	8	1	4	10
Noto	28	9–19	6– 8	4	2	2	26
Kora	21	3– 4	4– 9	11	3	4	10
Guillory, K.	15	2– 7	2– 3	2	0	0	8
Demouy	32	4– 6	0– 0	3	10	3	8
Guillory, T.	11	0– 3	0– 0	0	2	1	0
Miller	20	7–13	1– 1	1	1	0	15
Knight	5	0– 0	0– 0	0	0	2	0
Losavio	5	1– 3	0– 0	0	0	0	2
Totals	160	30–62	15–23	29	19	16	79

Tigers	min.	fgm–fga	ftm–fta	reb.	ass.	pf	tp
Cassano	32	11–19	0– 0	4	3	4	22
Silva	30	2– 9	5– 8	7	0	4	9
Burke	14	0– 6	1– 2	2	1	2	1
Parino	32	12–27	5– 5	9	7	3	29
Price	22	4– 5	0– 0	4	7	5	8
Weimer	19	3– 6	0– 4	6	2	1	6
Bowman	11	0– 4	0– 1	1	1	0	0
Totals	160	32–76	11–20	33	21	19	75

1. By how much did the Flyers win?
2. Which team made the most 3-point field goals?
3. Who made more field goals, Noto or Parino?
4. Who was the more accurate field goal shooter, Noto or Parino?
5. Who scored more points for the amount of time they played in the game, Noto or Parino?
6. Since the Tigers made more field goals than the Flyers, how did the Flyers manage to score 4 more points than the Tigers?
7. If Kora had played the whole game and rebounded at the same rate he did for the time he was in the game, what would his rebound total have been?
8. For which of the preceding seven questions did you use ratios to help you determine your answers?

6.12) for focusing students' attention, it was difficult for her to provide guidance efficiently to one group while still monitoring the others. Furthermore, her students are less likely to engage diligently in her next small-task-group session because they failed to achieve closure in this one and Ms. Clay did not follow up on the work they did in the subgroups. Unlike Mr. Breland (Vignette 6.20), she did not take what the subgroups did and use it in a subsequent activity.

Ms. Clay also illustrated another common misuse of small-task-group sessions by stepping in and doing the second group's work for it. Some teachers get so frustrated with subgroups failing to maintain their focus that they break into lectures when they should simply ask a leading question or two and let the students do their own work. Otherwise, a large-group session would be more efficient.

Whereas the failure of Ms. Clay's session was due at least in part to a lack of structure, sometimes intraclass grouping is misused because of inflexible structure. Recall Vignette 6.19, in which Ms. Goldberg's class is subdivided into three achievement levels—the *green, blue,* and *gray* groups. Although

Exhibit 6.12 continued

Group B

DIRECTIONS: Answer the questions based on the labels from the two soup cans. Prepare a 5-minute oral report to the class that explains what problem-solving strategies you used to answer the questions.

CHICKEN WITH LETTERS

Size: 10.6 oz (298 g)   *Price:* 58¢

Nutritional Information

Serving size (condensed) .... 4 oz
Serving size (prepared) .... 8 oz
Per serving:
    Calories 60
    Protein (grams) 3
    Simple sugars (grams) 1
    Complex carbohydrates (grams) 6
    Fat (grams) 2
    Cholesterol (mg) 10
    Sodium (mg) 870
Percentage of U.S. Recommended Daily Requirement:

Protein	4	Riboflavin	2
Vitamin A	8	Niacin	4
Vitamin C	*	Calcium	*
Thiamine	2	Iron	2

*Contains less than 2% of the US RDA of this nutrient.

NOODLES AND CHICKEN

Size: 10.6 oz (298 g)   *Price:* 61¢

Nutritional Information

Serving size (condensed) .... 4 oz
Serving size (prepared) .... 8 oz
Per serving:
    Calories 80
    Protein (grams) 3
    Simple sugars (grams) 1
    Complex carbohydrates (grams) 8
    Fat (grams) 3
    Cholesterol (mg) 15
    Sodium (mg) 960
Percentage of U.S. Recommended Daily Requirement:

Protein	4	Riboflavin	2
Vitamin A	25	Niacin	6
Vitamin C	*	Calcium	*
Thiamine	4	Iron	4

*Contains less than 2% of the US RDA of this nutrient.

1. With which soup do you get more grams for the money?
2. Which soup has more vitamins?
3. Which soup has more cholesterol?
4. Which soup has more vitamins per calorie?
5. Which soup is the best buy considering only the amount of iron it provides?
6. What appears to be more expensive, calories or complex carbohydrates?
7. How many grams of sodium are contained in the entire can of Noodles and Chicken?
8. For which of the seven preceding questions did you use ratios to help you determine your answers?

Exhibit 6.12 continued

Group C

DIRECTIONS: Answer the questions based on the lists of songs from audio tape albums. Prepare a 5-minute oral report to the class that explains what problem-solving strategies you used to answer the questions.

RABID DOG IN CONCERT

Price: $9.98

Side One	*Side Two*
Every Rose Ain't a Flower (2:55)	Feelin' Too Much Pain (3:06)
Three-Woman Dog (4:20)	Too Fine To Be Mine (2:30)
After the Pigs Come Home (3:01)	Too Young (3:11)
Smilin' 'stead of Cryin' (4:44)	Lucy the Lucky One (2:05)
My Kind of Party (3:15)	It Lasts Forever (8:09)
Allison (2:02)	

THE SENSATIONAL SCREAMERS ONE MORE TIME

Price: $8.79

Side One	*Side Two*
Who Likes to Kill Animals? (5:17)	Reasons to Live (3:11)
Help Is on the Way (2:10)	Not Much More to Say (5:12)
Casey the Drum-Man (2:14)	Not too Much Longer (2:09)
Momma Said It's Okay (3:29)	No-Mo-Dough (2:45)
Comfort (4:04)	Not Much Help (3:00)
One More Time (3:35)	Mindy, Mindy (1:55)

1. Which of the two tapes has more songs?
2. Which of the two tapes has more songs for the money?
3. Which of the two tapes has the more minutes of music?
4. Which of the two tapes has the more minutes of music for the money?
5. Which of the two tapes do you like better?
6. On the average, how long does one side of these two tapes play?
7. What's the difference between the longest and shortest songs on the two tapes?
8. For which of the seven preceding questions did you use ratios to help you determine your answers?

---

this type of organization can compensate for some differences in student learning rates, it—as most other messy teaching functions—should carry a warning label:

❏ Subdividing a class into achievement-level groups does not result in "homogeneous" subgroups. Thus, it is important to remember that any one subgroup varies considerably on each of a multitude of student variables (Cangelosi 1974).
❏ Care must be taken that students do not get "locked" into an achievement-level group and become labeled "bright," "average," or "dull" (Cali-

fornia State Department of Education 1987, 55–70; Ginott 1972).

Initiating and Maintaining Student Engagement in Small-Task-Group Sessions

Here are some suggestions for designing and conducting small-task-group sessions:

Have a clearly defined task with a specific objective in mind for the session. The *Standards* (NCTM 1989, 6–11) emphasizes the need for students to interact about mathematics with one another. Small-group discussions provide for that need. However, to

Exhibit 6.12 continued

Group D

DIRECTIONS: Answer the questions based on the data given about crime in our city during the years 1990 and 1991. Prepare a 5-minute oral report to the class that explains what problem-solving strategies you used to answer the questions.

	1990	1991
Population	320,000	323,000
Murders	34	37
Rapes	99	112
Robberies	704	691
Aggravated assaults	1,001	1,120
Burglaries	3,092	3,212
Thefts by larceny	7,344	7,360
Motor vehicle thefts	1,611	1,786

1. Did crime increase or decrease from 1990 to 1991?
2. Which type of crime is the most common?
3. Relative to the size of the population, did the rate of murders go up or down from 1990 to 1991?
4. Relative to the size of the population, did the rate of burglaries go up or down from 1990 to 1991?
5. The rate relative to population of what type of crime increased the least?
6. The rate relative to population of what type of crime increased the most?
7. By how much did the population grow over the course of 1 year?
8. For which of the preceding seven questions did you use ratios to help you determine your answers?

keep students engaged in learning activities that not only facilitate interactions but also help them achieve specified objectives, the groups need to be focused on clearly defined tasks.

Utilize efficient and routine procedures for making transitions into and out of small-group activities. To avoid the time-wasting chaos often following a direction (such as "Let's move our desks so that we have four groups of five or six each.") establish procedures whereby students efficiently move from one classroom arrangement to another. For example:

❑ VIGNETTE 6.22

Prominently displayed on the front wall of Ms. Bringhurst's classroom is the brightly colored, 2-foot by 3.5-foot poster depicted in Exhibit 6.13. She moves the arrow to the symbol on the poster to indicate if students should be working alone (1), in pairs (2), . . . , groups of five (5), . . . , or in a single large group (whole class).

In Vignette 4.9 Ms. Smith uses an especially efficient and attention-getting method for getting students into a small-task-group session.

Prepare an advanced organizer for such sessions. Task sheets, such as the ones in Exhibit 6.12, direct

Exhibit 6.13
The poster Ms. Bringhurst displays to indicate grouping arrangements.

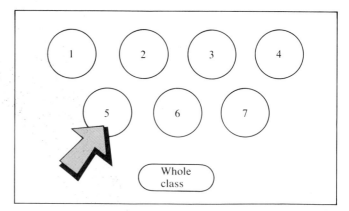

students' focus and provide them with an overall picture of what they are expected to accomplish in their groups.

Specify directions and the task before attempting to engage students. It's far more efficient to make directions clear to everyone before students have turned their attention to their individual subgroups. Avoid having to interrupt small-group work to clarify directions that the whole class should hear.

Monitor groups' activities, providing guidance as needed without usurping subgroups' responsibilities for the designated task. You should move from one group to another, cuing students on-task without actually becoming a member of any one group. Consider the following vignette.

❏ **VIGNETTE 6.23**

Mr. Breland stops to sit in with group C as they struggle with Question 4 from Exhibit 6.12. One student tells him, "I like the Sensational Screamers better. Doesn't that make a difference?" Mr. Breland turns to the group, "What does *more* minutes of music mean?" Noticing the discussion is on track, he moves over to group B, continuing to keep an eye on all the groups.

Model active listening techniques. Students do not automatically know how to listen to one another without being shown. From classes they take with teachers other than you, they may unfortunately have learned that anything of academic importance (i.e., will be on the test) is said by teachers, not peers. Thus, you should demonstrate that you intently listen to them and make use of what they say. For example:

❏ **VIGNETTE 6.24**

Mr. Breland stops to sit in with group B as they struggle with Question 6 from Exhibit 6.12. As Emily is commenting, John attempts to engage Mr. Breland with his own private question, "Mr. Breland, this doesn't make—" But Mr. Breland uses a frown and hand motion to cue John to be quiet and then says to the group, "Excuse me, Emily, would you repeat that last part about adding the two prices? I missed what you said about that." Emily repeats and finishes her comment. Mr. Breland says, "Thank you. That should shed some light on John's concern. John, raise your concern with the group." John: "To me, the question ought to be. . . ."

Later in the large-group session, Mr. Breland uses different comments students made in their subgroups as a basis for discussion.

Use formative feedback to regulate activities. Engaged behaviors during small-task-group sessions are observable because students should be involved in discussions and working on a specified task. Thus, formative feedback for regulating the activities is relatively easy to obtain.

Plan for closure points, especially for lengthy sessions. As with other types of sessions, students need to experience climactic moments to positively reinforce engagement. Having a sequence of questions on the task sheets of Exhibit 6.12 rather than just one overall question to answer helped Mr. Breland achieve this.

Follow up on subgroup work by utilizing it in subsequent learning activities. In Vignette 6.21, the students' work was left hanging, not seeming to make any impact on whatever else went on in class. Mr. Breland's students (Vignette 6.24) put the outcomes of their efforts to productive use.

ENGAGING STUDENTS IN INDEPENDENT WORK SESSIONS
Appropriate Uses of Independent Work Sessions

A major share of mathematical activity is solitary; discovering relations, computing, and problem solving are behaviors for which people generally need quiet "think" time. Traditionally, the most common way allocated time is spent in mathematics classrooms is in independent work sessions in which students quietly sit at their desks or in front of computers working on exercises. Such sessions are appropriately used in a variety of ways:

As an integral part of an inquiry lesson, students work independently on tasks that were previously defined during a large-group interactive lecture or questioning/discussion session. The work from the independent session is subsequently used in follow up activities. In Vignette 4.8, Mr. Citerelli used an independent work session for students to perform a test on a list of examples and nonexamples of arithmetic sequences that was just developed in a large-group session. The results of students' independent work was then used in formulating relations in a follow-up large-group activity.

As an integral part of direct instruction, students independently practice what has just been explained to them in a large-group activity. The teacher provides individual guidance during the independent work session. Students receive feedback on what they practiced either in a subsequent large-group session or by the teacher collecting and then annotating their work. After explaining an algorithm for differentiating algebraic functions in Vignette 4.17, Ms. Allen directed her students to complete a related exercise as she circulated about the room monitoring work and providing help as needed. She used her observations of their work as formative feedback to regulate the remainder of the lesson.

Students use part of a class period to begin a homework assignment in an independent work session. This practice allows them to start the assignment while the teacher is still available to provide guidance.

Independent work sessions are essential to most teaching units. However, they need to be integrated with other types of learning activities, monitored, and guided. Rosenshine (1987, 261) states

Studies have shown that when students are working alone during seatwork they are less engaged than when they are being given instruction by the teacher. Therefore, the question of how to manage students during seatwork, in order to maintain their engagement, becomes of primary interest.

One consistent finding has been the importance of a teacher (or another adult) monitoring the students during seatwork. Fisher et al. (1980) found that the amount of substantive teacher interaction with students during seatwork was positively related to achievement and that when students have contacts with the teacher during seatwork their engagement rate increases by about 10 percent. Thus it seems important that teachers not only monitor seatwork, but that they also provide academic feedback and explanation to students during their independent practice. However, the research suggests that these contacts should be relatively short, averaging 30 seconds or less. Longer contacts would appear to pose two difficulties: the need for a long contact suggests that the initial explanation was not complete and the more time a teacher spends with one student, the less time there is to monitor and help other students.

Another finding of Fisher et al. was that the teachers who had more questions and answers during group work had more engagement during seatwork. That is, another way to increase engagement during seatwork was to have more teacher-led practice during group work so that students could be more successful during seatwork.

A third finding (Fisher et al. 1980) was that when teachers had to give a good deal of explanation during seatwork, then student error rates were higher. Having to give a good deal of explanation during seatwork suggests that the initial explanation was not sufficient or that there was not sufficient practice and correction before seatwork.

Another effective procedure for increasing engagement during seatwork was to break the instruction into smaller segments and have two or three segments of instruction and seatwork during a single period.

Common Misuses of Independent Work Sessions

The more common misuses of independent work sessions stem from teachers failing to consider the suggestions implied by Rosenshine's report. The consequences of imprecise directions, inadequate preparation for the task, and inefficiently administered teacher help include the massive time-wasting

Jones (1979) identified in his classroom observations of independent-work sessions. Jones reported teachers perceived spending an average of between 1 and 2 minutes per conference with individual students during the sessions. His observations indicated the actual average to be about 4 minutes for a single conference. Even in a mathematics class with as few as 15 students, devoting more than 45 seconds to any one conference is inefficient. For example, consider Vignette 6.25.

❑ VIGNETTE 6.25

Mr. Fife's 24 students are individually working at their desks on an exercise involving factoring algebraic polynomials. Ruth and 11 other students have their hands up for help. He goes to Ruth, who says, "I don't know how to do these."

Mr. Fife: What is it you don't know how to do?
Ruth: I don't understand enough to know what I don't know!
Mr. Fife: Let's look at this second one here. Are there any common factors you could take out?
Ruth: I guess so. . . . Is 3 common?
Mr. Fife: Yes.
Ruth: So what do I do next?
Mr. Fife: Since 3 is common, you should. . . .

In the meantime, other students are waiting, feeling they cannot continue the exercise until Mr. Fife gets to them. But he doesn't get to most who request help. While waiting, students find ways to entertain themselves.

Initiating and Maintaining Student Engagement in Independent Work Sessions

Here are some ideas to consider when designing and conducting independent work sessions:

By providing explicit directions, clearly defining the task, you avoid many of the nagging questions about what to do. The idea is to devote the time you spend conferring with individual students guiding them on *how* to complete the task, not reiterating directions in response to questions such as, "What are we supposed to be doing?"

Having artifacts (e.g., notes, a sample exercise, and a list of steps in an algorithm) from the preceding group-learning activity still visible to students (e.g., on the chalkboard or in their notebooks) during an independent work session provides a reference that facilitates the efficiency with which students receive help. For example, consider Vignette 6.26.

❑ VIGNETTE 6.26

Ms. Towers has just conducted a large-group interactive lecture session that included an explanation of an algorithm for factoring algebraic polynomials, a demonstration of the algorithm with an example, and the class working through an example with Ms. Towers' guidance.

Leaving the two completed examples and the step-by-step outline of the algorithm on the chalkboard, Ms. Towers directs the students into an independent work session in which they are to practice the algorithm on six exercises from the textbook.

In a few minutes, Phyllis and Juaquin raise their hands. Silently acknowledging Juaquin with a wink and hand gesture, Ms. Towers moves to Phyllis' desk; Phyllis says, "I don't know where to start." Ms. Towers, seeing that Phyllis has nothing written on her paper, says, "Read the first two steps from the board and then look at what we did first for the example on the right. I'll be back within 30 seconds." She moves directly to Juaquin's desk and Juaquin says, "Is this right?" Detecting that he's begun the first exercise by factoring out only 2 when he could have factored out 6, she responds, "It's not wrong, but you could make it easier on yourself if you repeat step 2 before continuing— see if there's still another factor that's common." She walks back to Phyllis as Juaquin blurts out, "Oh, yeah! The 3 —" Realizing he's being disruptive, Juaquin grabs his mouth, muffling the rest of his sentence.

Back at Phyllis' desk, Ms. Towers sees that Phyllis is now started and softly tells her, "Just keep following the steps on the board and checking how that example is worked—one step at a time. I'll check with you every few minutes." By this time three others have their hands up. By referring to the outline and examples and raising pointed questions, Ms. Towers has all three students back on track within a minute. She continues moving about the room, responding to students' requests for help and volunteering guidance as she sees fit from observing their work. At no time does she spend more than 20 seconds at a time with any one student.

———————

You can provide efficient individual guidance and help to students, but only if you organize for it prior to the session and communicate assertively during the session. Both Ms. Towers in the previous vignette and Ms. Strickland in the next one illustrate this point.

Cooperative learning activities can be incorporated into independent work sessions to increase opportunities for students to receive help. For example, consider the next vignette.

❑ VIGNETTE 6.27

At the beginning of the school year, Ms. Strickland fashions from a towel rack the "flag-raising" device pictured in Exhibit 6.14. She then produces enough such devices to install them on the corners of the students' desks in her classroom. Each is supplied with a yellow, red, and green flag, which can be raised one at a time.

She then establishes a procedure for independent work sessions by which students display a

❑ Yellow flag as long as they are progressing with the work and do not feel a need for help,
❑ Red flag to indicate a request for help,

Exhibit 6.14
Ms. Strickland installs "flag raisers" on students' desks.

❏ Green flag to indicate that they've finished the work and are willing to help others.

As Ms. Strickland monitors a session, she responds to a red flag by either helping the student herself or by signaling to a student with a green-flag display to provide the help (Exhibit 6.15).

Ms. Strickland believes her system has four distinct advantages over more conventional hand-raising procedures:

❏ Cooperative learning among students is encouraged.
❏ When waiting for help, students can continue doing some work without having to be burdened with holding up a hand.
❏ Students who finish the task before others have something to do that will not only help their peers but will be a learning experience for them also.
❏ The systematic air of the procedure enhances the businesslike environment of the classroom.

———————

To avoid having students who finish early idly waiting for others to complete a task, you can sequence independent work sessions so they are followed by individual activities with flexible beginning and ending times. Students do not work at the same pace. Unless the task can be completed by all in less than 10 minutes, you need to manage independent work sessions to accommodate students' finishing at varying times. One solution is to schedule a subsequent activity that early finishers can start (e.g., begin the homework assignment) but that can be conveniently interrupted when you are ready to halt

the independent work session (e.g., when almost all students have completed the task). Here is an example.

❏ VIGNETTE 6.28

Ms. Wharton has established a routine in which each teaching unit includes a long-range assignment that students must use microcomputers to complete. The assignment is given at the beginning of the unit and is not due until the day of the summative unit test. Ordinarily it involves either completing some programmed exercises related to the unit's objectives or writing programs for executing algorithms learned during the unit.

Ms. Wharton's classroom is equipped with 9 microcomputers, but she has no fewer than 21 students in any one of her classes.

For independent work sessions she has established a routine in which students who finish the task before the session is completed are to work on their unit-long computer assignment. Those who may have already completed the computer assignment have the option of either beginning their homework assignment or utilizing the computers in other ways (e.g., playing games).

———————

As with other types of learning activities, students need feedback to correct errors, reinforce correct responses, and positively reinforce engagement. You need formative feedback to regulate the lesson. Formative feedback is facilitated during independent work sessions because each student's efforts are reflected by a product (e.g., written responses to exercises). Note how Ms. Allen utilized formative feed-

Exhibit 6.15
Flag raising during one of Ms. Strickland's independent work sessions.

back during the independent work session she conducted near the end of Vignette 4.17.

ENGAGING STUDENTS IN MEANINGFUL HOMEWORK
Appropriate Uses of Homework

Homework provides students with opportunities for solitary work at their own pace. The crowded social setting of a classroom is not particularly conducive to the concentrated, undisturbed thinking that is essential for achievement of intellectual-level objectives. Furthermore, school schedules often do not permit adequate classroom time to be allocated for practice exercises that are essential for achievement of knowledge-level objectives. Posamentier and Stepelman (1990, 48) suggest that for many students, classroom instruction serves as a forum for exposure to new material, whereas the genuine learning experiences occur while they are engaged in homework. Learning activities via homework assignments complement classroom activities in three ways: (1) as preparations for classroom activities, (2) as extensions of classroom activities, and (3) as follow-ups to classroom activities.

Use of Homework as Preparation for Classroom Activities

One way you help students associate mathematics with their own real worlds is to engage them in learning activities utilizing numbers and other mathematical variables (e.g., geometric figures) from students' outside-of-school environments. Rather than always working with textbook numerals or data you bring into class, occasionally assign homework in which *students collect data or other information for use in classroom activities.* For example:

❑ **VIGNETTE 6.29**

Mr. Greene directs his students near the end of a class period, "As part of your homework assignment, locate three circles defined by objects in or near your home. Anything that determines a circle will be fine—the base of a light, a bicycle wheel, a dinner plate, the top of your little brother's head. After locating each of your three circles, measure its diameter and circumference. Write the measurements down and bring in the three pairs of numbers to class tomorrow." (See Exhibit 6.16.)

The next day, Mr. Greene displays Exhibit 6.17 on the overhead projector and directs students, one at a time, to call out circumference/diameter pairs. Each student contributes one of his or her pairs as Mr. Greene completes the form, as shown in Exhibit 6.18.

Exhibit 6.16
One of Mr. Greene's students engaged in a homework assignment.

Mr. Greene then conducts an inductive questioning/discussion session leading students to discover that the ratio of the circumference of any circle to its diameter is a constant that is slightly greater than 3.

You may sometimes initiate a lesson with a homework assignment *exposing students to a problem or task that stimulates them to direct their thoughts toward a topic you plan to introduce during the next classroom session.* Here are two examples.

❑ **VIGNETTE 6.30**

Ms. McKnight conducts an inductive lesson on permutations, followed by a direct lesson on using the formula $_nP_r = n!/(n - r)!$. For homework she assigns nine word problems. The first eight problems can be solved using the permutation formula; to solve the ninth a *combination* formula is applicable. Ms. McKnight doesn't plan a lesson on combinations until the next day, after the homework is due.

The following day, the homework is reviewed in class. Some students mindlessly used the permutation formula for the ninth problem. Others realized that this problem was different from the others but didn't devise a solution. One student correctly solved the ninth problem via a tedious examination of all possible cases. Students complain

Exhibit 6.17
The form Mr. Greene used on an overhead transparency to record data students collected for homework.

Person	Object	Circumference C	Diameter D	C/D

Exhibit 6.18
Mr. Greene records one pair of measurements from each student.

Person	Object	Circumference C	Diameter D	C/D
Barbara	ring	6.8 cm	2.2 cm	3.09
Andrea	barrel bottom	32"	10"	3.20
Jerry	jar	19"	6"	3.17
Oral	base of light fixture	18.74 cm	25 cm	3.15
Glenn	wheel	81.5"	26"	3.13
Karel	top of head	7.75"	2.94"	2.94

to Ms. McKnight that the ninth was a "trick" problem. Acknowledging her "error," Ms. McKnight uses their discussion of that problem as a springboard into the day's lesson, which is about *combinations*.

❏ VIGNETTE 6.31

Mr. Cooper's students know how to plot points of an algebraic function in a Cartesian plane. However, except for linear functions they are unaware of any methods for sketching a graph without plotting numerous points.

The day before he plans to introduce shortcuts for finding key features of graphs of quadratic functions (such as the vertex and line of symmetry), Mr. Cooper includes three quadratic functions to be graphed as homework.

The next day, students, with varying accuracy, have the graphs for class. Some complain about how boring it was to plot so many points. Mr. Cooper jumps on the students' expressed need for some shortcuts and embarks on his planned inductive lesson to discover some useful relations.

Some skills or knowledge needed for participation in an upcoming classroom activity may be effi- *ciently acquired during a homework assignment.* For example, consider Vignette 6.32.

❏ VIGNETTE 6.32

Mr. Triche assigns some background reading on the Pythagoreans for homework. The next day, he draws on that knowledge of mathematical history in a lesson on polyhedra.

❏ VIGNETTE 6.33

Ms. Clarion distributes a list of words and symbols she plans to use in a large-group interactive lecture session the next day. For homework, the students are to look up and memorize the definitions for those words and symbols.

Traditionally, students depend on time allocated for homework to study for in-class tests. Assignments to study for tests need to be specific; students do not naturally know how or what to study without specific instruction from you.

Students can be assigned take-home tests for purposes of formative feedback that you utilize to regulate classroom activities. Consider Vignette 6.34.

Unsure of just how ambitious objectives should be for an upcoming unit on systems of linear equations, Mr. Title assigns a test over tentative unit objectives for homework. The next day he reviews the test and has students do "think-aloud" exercises to indicate just how they approached different test items. He uses the information gained from this activity to determine what the unit's objectives should be.

Use of Homework as an Extension of Classroom Activities

One of the disadvantages of independent work sessions is that students complete assigned tasks at different times. Often, there is inadequate class time allocated for all students to complete independent work. Also, practice exercises to polish algorithmic skills may be too time-consuming to schedule within class. Homework assignments relieve at least some of the pressure of trying to squeeze necessary work into class periods.

Use of Homework as a Follow-Up to Classroom Activities

For some objectives, students need time alone, analyzing content at their own pace. For example:

❑ VIGNETTE 6.35
Ms. Hundley designs a lesson for helping students use a problem-solving strategy in which they consciously and systematically move through the nine stages listed on pages 75–76. She believes that students will learn to apply the strategy only with experience trying it out *on their own* with numerous problems. Many students, she's noted, lack the confidence to depend on their own thinking; they would rather be told a solution than devise one. Consequently, she wants them to experience their initial success with this problem-solving strategy by themselves, not in a social setting.

Thus, she structures the lessons so that she spends nearly an entire class period in a large-group interactive lecture session explaining how to do a homework assignment. She begins by saying, "Your homework assignment for tonight will be to solve three problems that I will distribute on a worksheet at the end of today's period. When you solve these problems, I want you to follow a procedure that is outlined on this *solution blueprint form*—I'll give you copies of it now."

She distributes three copies of a form quite similar to the one appearing in Exhibit 4.21 used by Mr. Wilson in Vignette 4.20.

She then spends the next 45 minutes explaining how to use the form and the nine-stage strategy for solving a problem. The day's classroom activities present the strat-

egy to the students, but the homework is the activity leading them to learn to apply the strategy.

A more common type of homework assignment that, like Ms. Hundley's, is a follow-up to classroom activities is homework that is used to provide formative feedback on what was learned in class. A lesson is presented in class and students are assigned exercises that serve as a formative test over the day's objectives. The results are used to reinforce what was learned and identify areas in need of remediation.

Common Misuses of Homework

The benefits of homework are widely debated in educational literature (Coulter 1987). Arguments against assigning homework focus not on whether homework *can* be an effective learning activity but on how it is routinely misused by some teachers. Misuses include the following:

Teachers mindlessly assign homework out of tradition and habit with little attention to purpose or selection of exercises. "Do the odd-numbered exercises for Section 7-4 in the textbook," is echoed in mathematics classrooms day after day, with only the section designation varying (Farrell and Farmer 1988, 6–5; Jesunathadas 1990). Such assignments typically degenerate into unnecessarily repetitious drudgery that colors students' perceptions of mathematics. It is quite common for middle and secondary mathematics students to work only the first couple of exercises in a lengthy assignment, reasoning that "All the rest will work the same. If I can do the first few, then I can do them all. If I can't, then I can't do any of them." In situations where teachers award points for homework, these students often copy work from friends for the missing exercises (Cangelosi 1985).

Homework assignments are not connected to classroom activities. In such cases, students' only motivation for doing homework is to receive points toward grades or to avoid their teachers' wrath. What they learn about mathematics and how well they do on tests appears unrelated to whether or not they complete homework assignments. Homework is perceived as "in addition" to learning because it is assigned as neither a preparation for, extension of, nor follow-up to classroom activities.

Homework either is assigned as a punishment for misbehavior or failure to achieve or is not assigned as a reward for cooperative behavior or achievement. "If you don't quiet down right now, there will be a few extra problems added to your homework assignment!" "Because you've worked so hard today, you can enjoy your evening—no homework! [cheers] . . .

But be ready to get back to work tomorrow!" For years, such utterances have managed to perpetuate the idea that mathematics is an unpleasant, unrewarding activity to be avoided. Although the threat of homework or anticipation of getting out of homework may sometimes discourage misbehaviors, it also devalues homework as a learning activity (Cangelosi 1988a, 36–41).

Initiating and Maintaining Engagement in Homework Activities

Engagement in a homework assignment usually requires students to (1) understand directions for the assignment, (2) schedule time outside of class for the work, (3) resist distractions in a relatively unsupervised setting, and (4) complete the work by a specified deadline. To motivate your students to engage in homework you assign, consider the following suggestions:

Every day for the first few weeks of a course, assign clearly defined, specific tasks for homework. Spend class time during that early stage of the course in teaching students to schedule time for homework and efficient ways of completing it. Follow up on every assignment. Until you make a concerted effort to teach them, your students are unlikely to:

❏ know how to schedule time for homework, especially considering that they have assignments from other courses besides yours
❏ discriminate whether content relative to an assignment should be memorized, figured out by themselves, or found out from an outside source
❏ know how to study
❏ know how you expect results of their homework to be reported.

Besides actually conducting a lesson in how to do homework, you should keep initial assignments relatively simple and highly structured. Directions should be explicit and feedback should be descriptive. Your extra efforts along these lines during the first few weeks of a course will pay dividends in time saved and completed assignments once students learn your routine and expectations. Students will develop a *behavior pattern* of engaging in homework if their efforts are positively reinforced.

Positively reinforce engagement in homework and punish failure to attempt homework by designing units so that success in classroom activities, especially tests, depends on homework efforts. Students can be motivated to engage in homework faithfully without you resorting to awarding points toward grades for turning in assignments. Recall the system Ms. Goldberg (Vignette 5.28) initiated.

Beginning class periods with a short test that includes items similar to exercises from the previous homework assignment teaches students the importance of doing homework far better than preaching to them about the importance of homework or threatening to lower grades if they don't do it. Here's an example of a teacher demonstrating a businesslike attitude to motivate students to do homework.

❏ **VIGNETTE 6.36**

Mr. Heidingsfelder carefully examines the 30 algebraic inequalities from the exercises on page 188 of his textbook. From the 30, he selects the 13 exercises he thinks will provide students with the most useful practice for the different problem-solving situations they'll be encountering in a subsequent lesson.

The day after the assignment, he collects the work and performs a quick error-pattern analysis (Ashlock 1990) and returns the papers with a clear indication of exactly those steps in the algorithm they did correctly and those they did not. Because he had carefully selected the exercises, he was able to do the analysis more efficiently than if they had been selected with less thought.

While the rest of the students are correcting their work and beginning an independent work session, he calls aside the five students, Angela, Donna, Pruitt, Pam, and Carl, who did not complete the homework and says, "I'm sorry you didn't give me an opportunity to provide you with feedback on how to solve the inequalities we had for homework."

Pam: "I would've done it but—" Mr. Heidingsfelder interrupts, saying, "It doesn't make any difference why you didn't do it. I've just got to figure out when you can get this done so I can get my analysis back to you before you leave school today. You need that from me before you're able to go on to our next lesson." Pruitt: "I forgot—" Mr. Heidingsfelder: "Please let me think how to help you. . . . I've got it! Here's what we'll do. I'll meet you in here as soon as final announcements are completed this afternoon. As soon as you've finished the 13 exercises, I'll give you my analysis."

Keep in mind that students have other assignments besides yours. Fewer well-chosen exercises tend to be more productive than a lengthy assignment that is more time-consuming for you and the students. Long-range assignments that students are expected to take days to complete should be broken out in a sequence of shorter assignments with due dates that serve as progress points toward completion. Consistently heeding this suggestion in the early stages of a course encourages students to get into a routine of doing homework. Otherwise, they tend to be overwhelmed by lengthy assignments or delay starting long-range assignments until just before they are due.

To elicit parents' cooperation in encouraging and supervising homework, utilize ideas from the section, "Communicating with Parents" beginning on page 139. What you gain from taking this suggestion varies considerably, depending on students' home situations. Some students do not even live with responsible guardians. But whenever you do elicit parental support, students' engagement in homework activities tends to increase remarkably.

❏❏❏❏❏❏❏❏❏❏❏❏❏❏❏❏❏❏❏❏

SELF-ASSESSMENT EXERCISES

1. Analyze the cognitive process a person would use to answer the following questions; classify each question as either *knowledge-level* or *intellectual-level:*
   a. According to Kennedy (1969), the "supply-and-demand" relationship between trigonometry and another field of study was so intimate prior to the thirteenth century that the two were indistinguishable. What is that other field?
   b. What is a polyhedron?
   c. Would it be better to weigh this box in kilograms or grams?
   d. Should I set up a quadratic equation to solve this problem?
   e. Have you ever written a computer program in BASIC?
   f. How long would it take me to write a BASIC program for solving systems of n linear equations with n variables?
   g. Does $x^2 + 4x = 18$ have rational roots?
   h. Why are there so few women mentioned in historical accounts of mathematics prior to the twentieth century?
   i. Who was Maria Gaetana Agnesi?
   Compare your responses to these: Knowledge-level: a, b, e, and i; Intellectual-level: c, d, f, g, and h.
2. Design a *cooperative learning* activity in which students learn from one another for one of the objectives listed on pages 58–60 (Exhibit 3.2 identifies the learning levels for those objectives). Compare your work on this exercise to someone else's.
3. Compare Mr. Smart's method of engaging students in intellectual questioning sessions (Vignette 6.10) to that of Ms. Cramer (Vignette 6.11). Which of the two methods do you expect to use more? Explain why. Exchange your work on this exercise with someone and discuss similarities and differences between the two.

4. Observe a mathematics class in a middle, junior high, or high school. For each allocated time period, classify the type of learning activity as either a(n) (a) *large-group interactive lecture,* (b) *large-group recitation,* (c) *large-group intellectual-level questioning/discussion,* or (d) *independent work* session. Select one of the sessions and design an alternate type of learning activity. Explain the relative advantages and disadvantages of the two approaches for the given circumstances. Compare your work on this exercise to someone else's.
5. Devise a game for students to play in small groups that would help them achieve knowledge-level mathematics objectives. Now, modify the game so that it can be used in a large-group session. Exchange your game designs with those of a colleague who also completed this exercise.
6. On pages 176–177, four ways of responding to student-initiated intellectual-level questions and five ways of responding to their knowledge-level questions are listed. Discuss with a colleague the relative advantages and disadvantages of those different response styles.
7. Retrieve the work you did in responding to Exercise 4 of Chapter 4 and Exercise 10 of Chapter 5. Classify the different learning activities identified by your lesson designs as (a) *large-group interactive lecture,* (b) *large-group recitation,* (c) *large-group intellectual level questioning/discussion,* and (d) *independent work* sessions. In light of thoughts you've had since you last worked on these lesson designs, would you now modify the designs? Explain why or why not.

❏❏❏❏❏❏❏❏❏❏❏❏❏❏❏❏❏❏❏❏

TAKING WHAT YOU'VE LEARNED TO THE NEXT LEVEL

Having examined how to (1) define learning goals (Chapter 3), (2) design lessons for achieving those goals (Chapter 4), and (3) manage student behaviors and keep them engaged during those lessons (Chapters 5–6), it is time to turn your attention to the business of how to assess student achievement. Assessments of student achievement of *specific objectives* are needed for obtaining formative feedback during the course of a teaching unit. Assessments of student achievement of *learning goals* are needed for summative evaluations used to determine students' grades.

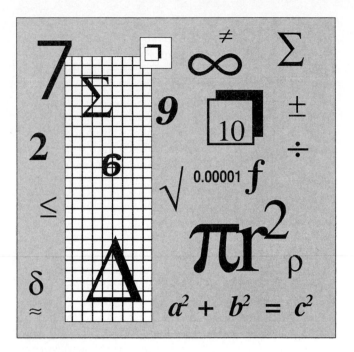

CHAPTER 7
Assessing Student Achievement

This chapter introduces fundamental measurement and evaluation principles and explains how to develop and use tests for assessing student achievement of your learning goals. Chapter 7 will help you:

1. Distinguish between the measurements and evaluations you make and clarify the role each plays in assessing student achievement (*conceptualization*).
2. Explain why a measurement's validity depends on its relevance and reliability (*conceptualization*).
3. Explain why the value of a measurement depends on its validity and usability (*conceptualization*).
4. Describe the common uses of three types of measurements of student achievement: teacher-produced tests, commercially produced tests, and standardized tests (*simple knowledge*).
5. List and explain the following steps in the process for designing and constructing a valid achievement test: (a) clarify the learning goal, (b) develop a test blueprint, (c) obtain relevant item pools, and (d) synthesize the test (*comprehension*).
6. Organize a system for maintaining item pools that enhances your capability of producing valid and usable tests (*application*).
7. Design items relevant to any objective you include in a teaching unit, whether the objective's learning level is (a) affective, (b) conceptualization, (c) simple knowledge, (d) comprehension, (e) knowledge of a process, (f) application, or (g) creativity (*application*).

DIFFICULT DECISIONS
Formative Evaluations

Consider a sample of the complex questions you face as you orchestrate teaching units:

❑ Who in the class has conceptualized the laws for multiplying signed numbers? Is the class ready to move on to my knowledge-level and application-level lessons on those laws or should I extend this conceptualization lesson?
❑ Are these students following my explanation of this algorithm for computing compound interest? Should I go back and review the steps, push on, or stop and have them practice the steps up to this point?
❑ Should I introduce this activity with a problem on dirt bikes, health, or music videos? Which will be more motivating for the class as a whole?
❑ Unless these students have achieved the goal of this unit on limits of algebraic functions, they're not ready to start the one on the derivative. Who is ready to move on and who isn't?

By answering such questions, you make *formative evaluations* that are necessary for designing and regulating lessons. However, the accuracy of your answers depends on how well you solve for variables such as (1) the degree to which each student has *conceptualized* the laws for multiplying signed numbers, (2) which steps in an algorithm for compound interest students *know* how to execute, (3) how *interested* students are in using mathematics to solve problems involving dirt bikes, health, and music videos, and (4) how well each student has *achieved* the goal of the unit on limits of algebraic functions. But, as suggested in Chapter 1, teaching involves messy functions, and variables such as these are not directly measurable—as are the variables that are more conventionally dealt with in formal mathematics (e.g., height, weight, frequencies, area, volume, density, wave length, age, air pressure, and cardinality).

Your empirical senses (sight, hearing, touch, smell, and taste) are incapable of directly observing what is in students' minds to determine the degree with which they achieved or are achieving mathematical learning objectives. Thus, you must set up situations that evoke students to make observable responses that provide you with indirect evidence of their learning. Doing this so that the evidence, though indirect, reflects students' actual achievement of learning objectives is no trivial task. It requires you to apply a sophisticated understanding of your learning goals (including the mathematical content and the learning levels specified by the objectives), how your students think, and fundamental principles and techniques for assessing student achievement.

Summative Evaluations

There are also complex questions for you to answer at the conclusions of teaching units, such as the following:

❏ What letter grade should I assign Louise for this unit?
❏ Rosita's father wants a report on her progress in mathematics. What should I tell him?
❏ Did Grayson achieve this goal well enough to receive at least a B?

You make *summative* evaluations of how well students achieved learning goals so that you can determine individual grades and periodically report on students' achievements to the students themselves, their parents, and to authorized professionals (e.g., your school's principal). As a teacher, you make far more formative than summative evaluations be-

cause your instructional behaviors are continually being influenced by formative feedback. However, because students and parents tend to be so grade-conscious, you are likely to find them keenly interested in your periodic summative evaluations but barely aware of your ongoing formative evaluations.

In any case, you are responsible for both types of evaluations, and summative evaluations—like formative—require access to data that reflect how well your students have achieved learning goals and objectives.

COMMON MALPRACTICE

Tests and observations provide the data bases for teachers' evaluations of student achievement. Unfortunately, studies examining the validities of tests commonly used in schools (both commercially prepared and teacher-prepared) and the evaluation methods of many teachers suggest that testing malpractice and inaccurate evaluations are widespread (Stiggins, Conklin, and Bridgeford 1986). Too often, faith is placed in poorly designed tests that tax students' test-taking skills but don't reflect actual achievement of the teachers' learning goals (Cangelosi 1990b, 3).

Of particular concern are incongruencies between learning levels specified by objectives and the actual learning levels measured by the tests. It is quite common for mathematics teachers to include intellectual-level learning objectives for their units but then to test their students for achievement only at the knowledge level. The consequence of this practice is pointed out by Stiggins (1988, 365):

> Teacher-developed paper and pencil tests and many tests and quizzes provided by textbook publishers are currently dominated by questions that ask students to recall facts and information. Although instructional objectives and even instructional activities may seek to develop thinking skills, classroom assessments often fail to match these aspirations. Students who use tests to try to understand the teacher's expectations can see the priority placed on memorizing, and they respond accordingly. Thus poor quality assessments that fail to tap and reward higher-order thinking skills will inhibit the development of those skills.

RESEARCH-BASED PRACTICE

Although testing is widely malpracticed, you *can*, as do many teachers, manage to collect valid data and accurately evaluate students' achievement of your learning objectives—the intellectual and affective ones as well as those at the knowledge level. To do this, you must:

❑ Heed Evaluation Standards 1–10 of the NCTM (1989, 189–237), which are listed in Appendix D.
❑ Apply research-based measurement and evaluation principles and techniques for assessing student achievement.

A table accompanying Evaluation Standard 3 (Appropriate Assessment Methods and Uses) (NCTM 1989, 198–201) is reproduced here as Exhibit 7.1. Fundamental research-based principles and techniques for measuring students' achievement of mathematical learning goals are dealt with in the remainder of this chapter. Other references provide more comprehensive treatises of these principles and techniques across all content areas (i.e., not only mathematics) (e.g., Cangelosi 1982, 1990b; Ebel and Frisbie 1986; Gronlund and Linn 1990; Hopkins, Stanley, and Hopkins 1990; Kubiszyn and Borich 1987; Linn 1989b; Popham 1990; Tuckman 1988).

MEASUREMENTS

A *measurement is a process by which data are gathered through empirical observations.* Teachers measure by reading what students write, hearing what they say, and seeing their behaviors. What they remember or record from those observations provides the data for the teachers' formative and summative evaluations of students' achievements.

Typically, mathematics teachers depend on *tests* for the data they use in evaluations. Tests are *planned measurements by which teachers attempt to create opportunities for students to display their achievements relative to specified learning goals.* Appendix F contains an example of a mathematics test.

Tests are composed of *items*. Each item of a test (1) confronts students with a task and (2) provides a means for observing and quantifying their responses to the task. Here is a sample of four different types of test items relevant to a variety of learning objectives:

Task Presented to the Student
Express the following number of stars as a base three numeral:

* * * * * * * * * *

Answer: _____
Scoring Key. +1 for "102;" otherwise +0

Task Presented to the Student
Using only the space provided, prove that subtraction of integers is *not* commutative.

Scoring Key. 3 points maximum scored according to the following:

❑ +3 for either a counterexample (e.g., $3 - 7 = -4$, but $7 - 3 = 4$) or for a tenable abstract argument (e.g., If $a, b \in$ {integers} such that $a > b$, then $a - b$ is positive, but $b - a$ is negative.).
❑ +1 if the response indicates the student knows what "subtraction is not commutative" means but doesn't prove it (e.g., $a - b \neq b - a$ for some integers a and b).
❑ +0 otherwise

Task Presented to the Student
Multiple Choice.   Circle the letter in front of the response that either correctly answers the question or completes the given statement so that it is true.

A history test and a science test are given to the same class of students. Which one of the following statistics would be an indication of whether or not students who do better in history also tend to do better in science?

A. The difference in the arithmetic mean of the history test scores and the arithmetic mean of the science test scores.
B. The pooled variance from both the history and science test scores.
C. The standard deviation of the history test scores minus the standard deviation of the science test scores.
D. A correlation coefficient computed from both the history and science test scores.

Scoring Key.   +1 for circling D only; +0 otherwise

Task Presented to the Student
While on a 55-kilometer journey, a car traveled along a 10-kilometer stretch where the road had a steady 8° angle of inclination. How much altitude did the car gain while traveling along that particular stretch of road? Express your answer in kilometers so that it is accurate to two decimal places. Please clearly display your work, including a diagram illustrating the problem.
Display of work:

Answer: _____
Scoring Key.   5 points maximum scored according to the following:

❑ +5 for an answer of 1.39 with an appropriate equation and diagram displayed. For example,

$$\sin 8° = x/10 \Rightarrow x = (10)(0.1392) = 1.392$$

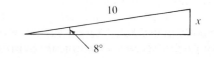

Exhibit 7.1
''Purposes and Methods of Assessment'' from Evaluation Standard 3 (NCTM 1989, 200–201)
(used with permission).

Purpose (Examples of Questions Asked)	For Whose Use	Unit of Assessment	Type of Assessment	Assessment Methods
Diagnostic ❑ What does this student understand about the concept or procedure? ❑ What aspects of problem solving are causing difficulty? ❑ What accounts for this student's unwillingness to attempt new problems or see the application of previously learned materials?	Individual teacher Individual student	Individual student	❑ Tasks that focus on a specific skill, type of procedure, concept, strategy, or a type of reasoning ❑ Each student evaluated	❑ Observation ❑ Oral questions that ask students to explain their procedures ❑ Focused written tasks ❑ Directed test items
Instructional Feedback ❑ What do students know about the material presented? ❑ Can students apply their learning to new situations? ❑ Do students understand the connections among ideas? ❑ How shall I pace instruction? ❑ Does the class need more intensive review or more challenging material?	Individual teacher	Class	❑ Tasks that require an integration of knowledge ❑ Tasks that cover a range of skills, concepts, and procedures ❑ Tasks that require the application of learning to new contexts ❑ Problem-solving and reasoning tasks ❑ Tasks that vary the format and context in which the material is presented ❑ Matrix-sampling test situations	❑ Written tests, including those that require differential methods for solutions to problems ❑ Class presentations ❑ Extended problem-solving projects ❑ Observation of class discussion ❑ Take-home tests ❑ Homework, journals ❑ Group work and projects

❑ If the response doesn't qualify for the full 5-point maximum, then distribute from 0 to 4 points as follows:

+1 for correctly identifying the unknown to be solved.
+1 for a correct diagram.
+1 for a correct equation.
+1 for an answer that is conceptually correct but is not expressed in kilometers accurate to two decimal places (e.g., 1.4 or 1392 m).

Note that what is labeled as Task Presented to the Student is the aspect of the item that students see on a test. The item's scoring key provides the rules the teacher uses to observe and quantify students' responses to the item. A student's *test score* is the sum of the scores he or she receives on the items comprising the test.

EVALUATIONS

An *evaluation,* whether formative or summative, is a *value judgment.* You cannot solve for a qualitative variable such as how well one of your students achieved a learning goal without making a value

Exhibit 7.1 continued

Purpose (Examples of Questions Asked)	For Whose Use	Unit of Assessment	Type of Assessment	Assessment Methods
Grading ❏ How well has this student understood and integrated the material? ❏ Can this student apply his or her learning in other contexts? ❏ How prepared is this student to proceed to the next grade or level?	Individual student Parents School	Individual student	❏ Tasks that demand the integration of material that was taught ❏ Tasks that are intrinsically interesting and challenging to the student ❏ Tasks that require the student to structure the material and generate solutions, in the context of the real world, as well as in mathematics	❏ Extended problem-solving projects ❏ Papers or written arguments that demand thoughtful inquiry about a mathematical topic ❏ Written tests that present problems with a range of difficulty based on expectations for course ❏ Oral presentations
Generalized Mathematical Achievement ❏ How does the general mathematical capability of this student compare with others or with a national norm?	Parents Teachers Administrators	Individual student	❏ Tasks organized in highly reliable tests designed for maximum discrimination among students	❏ Standardized achievement tests
Program Evaluation ❏ How effective is this instructional program in achieving our goals for mathematical learning?	Teachers Administrators Other decision makers	Class School	❏ Tasks that reflect the intent of the curriculum goals ❏ Tasks that are aligned to the instructional methods and content of the curriculum (see Standards 12 and 13) ❏ Matrix-sampling test situations	❏ Student interviews ❏ Performance tests ❏ Criterion-referenced tests ❏ Observation of class discussions ❏ Success of students who have completed the program

judgment (i.e., evaluation). Such evaluations are necessarily dependent on measurement results (e.g., students' test scores). However, do not make the mistake of equating measurement results or test scores with student achievement. An assessment of a student's achievement of a unit's learning goal involves two distinct steps:

1. Measurement results are obtained relative to a *quantitative* variable (e.g., the score the student obtained on the unit test).

2. An evaluation is made relative to a *qualitative* variable (i.e., the student's achievement of the learning goal) in light of the measurement results.

Measurement results provide only evidence of, not a definitive reflection of, student achievement. How well the results or scores reflect actual achievement depends on the *validity* of the measurement. Thus, how much one of your evaluations is influenced by test scores should be a function of the test's *validity.*

MEASUREMENT VALIDITY

The validity of a measurement depends on its *relevance* and *reliability*.

Relevance to Student Achievement of the Stated Learning Goal

A test is *relevant* to the same degree that

1. Its items pertain to the content and the learning levels specified by the objectives that define the learning goal.
2. It is designed so that emphases are placed on objectives according to their importance to goal achievement.

Pertinence of Items to the Content and Learning Levels of Objectives

A test item pertains to the content and learning level specified by an objective if students must operate at the specified learning level with the specified content in order to respond successfully to the item. How well do the three test items designed by the teacher in the following vignette (adapted from Cangelosi 1990b, 28) pertain to her objective?

❏ **VIGNETTE 7.1**

To help her evaluate her seventh-graders' achievement of the learning goal for a unit on surface areas, Ms. Curry is designing a test. The unit has nine objectives. The ninth objective is:

> When confronted with a real-life problem, determines whether or not computing the area of a surface will help solve the problem (*application*).

She constructs three tasks to present to the students intended to be relevant to that ninth objective:

1. Task Presented to the Student

Multiple Choice. Computing a surface area will help you solve one of these three problems. Which one is it?

A. We have a large bookcase we want to bring into our classroom. Our problem is to determine if the bookcase can fit through the doorway.
B. As part of a project to fix up our classroom, we want to put stripping all along the crack where the walls meet the floor. Our problem is to figure how much stripping to buy.
C. As part of a project to fix up our classroom, we want to put carpet down on the floor. Our problem is to figure how much carpet to buy.

Scoring Key. +1 for C only; +0 otherwise.

2. Task Presented to the Student

Multiple Choice. What is the surface area of one side of this sheet of paper you are now reading? (Use your ruler to help you make your choice.)

A. 93.5 square inches
B. 93.5 inches
C. 20.5 square inches
D. 20.5 inches
E. 41 square inches
F. 41 inches

Scoring Key. +1 for A only; otherwise +0

3. Task Presented to the Student

Multiple Choice. As part of our project for fixing up the classroom, we need to buy some paint for the walls. The paint we want comes in two different size cans. A 5 liter can costs $16.85 and a 2 liter can costs $6.55. Which one of the following would help us decide which can is the best buy?

A. Compare 5 × $16.85 to 2 × $6.55
B. Compare $16.85 ÷ 5 to $6.55 ÷ 2
C. Compare $16.85 − $6.55 to 2/5

Scoring Key. +1 for B only; otherwise +0

How well do Ms. Curry's items match the stated objective? The first one appears relevant because it requires students to *apply* (the objective's learning level) their understanding of *surface areas* (the objective's content). Of course students might select C for Item 1 just by guessing, but to increase one's chances from $\frac{1}{3}$ based on random guessing, one must reason deductively about surface area.

Item 2 does not seem to match the objective very well. The correct response of A can be selected simply by remembering how to compute a surface area without having to decide *when* surface area should be computed. Thus, whereas Item 2 appears to pertain to the *content* of the objective—namely, *surface area*—its learning level is *knowledge of a process* instead of *application*. Item 2 fails to be relevant to the objective because it pertains to the wrong learning level.

Item 3 requires students to operate at the application level as specified by the objective. However, the item fails to match the objective because its content is not surface area.

Emphasis on Objectives According to Relative Importance

For a test to be relevant to a stated learning goal, not only must each of its items match one of the objectives, but various objectives must be represented on the test according to their importance to goal achievement. Suppose, for example, that you wanted to design a test relevant to your students' achievement of the following learning goal:

> Understands that $\pi = C/d$ for any circle and utilizes that relation in the solution of real-life problems.

Further suppose that you define this goal with the following objectives:

A. Provides an inductive argument for concluding that the ratio of the circumference of any circle to its diameter is π (*conceptualization*).
B. Displays a willingness to attempt to develop a method for obtaining a rational approximation of π (*willingness to try*).
C. Explains at least three methods for obtaining rational approximations of π: (1) a method for averaging measurements that the students themselves invent, (2) an ancient method (e.g., one listed by von Baravalle (1969)), and (3) a computer-based method (*conceptualization*).
D. States the following: (1) π is the ratio of the circumference of any circle to its diameter, (2) π is an irrational number, (3) $\pi \approx 3.1415929$ (*simple knowledge*).
E. Explains why $C = \pi d = 2\pi r$ for a circle with circumference C, diameter d, and radius r (*conceptualization*).
F. Solves for the circumference of a circle given either its radius or diameter (*knowledge of a process*).
G. Solves for the diameter and radius of a circle given its circumference (*knowledge of a process*).
H. Given a real-life problem, determines how, if at all, a solution to that problem is facilitated by using the relation $\pi = C/d$ (*application*).

There are eight objectives defining the goal. In your opinion, are some of the objectives more important to goal attainment than others? If not, then your test should reflect students' achievement of any one objective by $\frac{1}{8}$, or 12.5 percent. Thus, for the case in which you believe each objective is equally important, then 12.5 percent of the test points should match Objective A, 12.5 percent for Objective B, . . . and 12.5 percent for Objective H.

On the other hand, suppose you had these thoughts: "Objectives A and H are more important than the others. Objective A because if students conceptualize that ratio, they can always discover the related formulas. H is the culminating objective of the unit. Students who achieve H can put it all together. On the other hand, objectives B and C, though important, are less important than the rest.

I included those mainly as interest builders. All the rest seem about equally important."

If you really thought like that, you might decide to design the test so that the relative weights you place on the objectives are as indicated in Exhibit 7.2.

Thus, to design a relevant test in this case you would need to select items and distribute the points according to the values of Exhibit 7.2. If, for example, 50 is the maximum possible score a student could attain on the test, then approximately 10 of those points should pertain to Objective A, 3 to B, 3 to C, 6 to D, 6 to E, 6 to F, 6 to G, and 10 to H.

Measurement Reliability

For a test to produce valid results, it must not only be relevant to the intended learning goal, it must also be *reliable*. A measurement is *reliable to the same degree that it can be depended on to yield consistent, noncontradictory results*. To be reliable a test must have both *internal consistency* and *scorer consistency*.

Internal Consistency

Suppose a friend tells you, "Math is so boring; I don't know how you can bear studying it!" You respond, "You find mathematics pretty dry, eh?" Your friend: "Absolutely! Of course I love using numbers to solve problems—and, of course, geometry has a real beauty." Does your friend like mathematics or not? His or her comments are contradictory. Thus, the results of the informal measurement based on what you heard the friend say lack *internal consistency*.

Consider the internal consistency of partial test results Ms. Curry obtained in the following example (adapted from Cangelosi 1990b, 30):

❑ **VIGNETTE 7.2**

Ms. Curry administers a 22-item test to help her evaluate students' achievement of the learning goal for a unit on

Exhibit 7.2
Hypothetical way you weighted eight objectives.

Objective	Relative Weight
A	20%
B	6%
C	6%
D	12%
E	12%
F	12%
G	12%
H	20%

surface area. Two of the test's items, 7 and 19, are intended to measure the sixth of the unit's nine objectives. The sixth objective is:

Given the dimensions of a right triangle, computes its area (*knowledge of a process*).

Items 7 and 19 are as follows.

7. Task Presented to the Students
What is the area bounded by a right triangle with dimensions 5 centimeters, 4 centimeters, and 3 centimeters? (Display your computations and place your answer in the blank.)

Answer: _____

Scoring Key. 4 points maximum score distributed as follows:

+1 if $A = \frac{1}{2}bh$ is used.

+1 if 4 and 3 are used in a computation but not 5.

+1 if 6 (irrespective of the units) is given as the area.

+1 if the answer is expressed in square centimeters.

19. Task Presented to the Students
What is the area of the interior of $\triangle ABC$ if $m \angle B = 90°$, $AB = 6$ centimeters, $BC = 8$ centimeters, and $AC = 10$ centimeters? (Display your computations and place your answer in the blank.)

Answer: _____

Scoring Key. 4 points maximum score distributed as follows:

+1 if $A = \frac{1}{2}bh$ is used.

+1 if 6 and 8 are used in a computation but not 10.

+1 if 24 (irrespective of the units) is given as the area.

+1 if the answer is expressed in square centimeters.

Curious about how well her students achieved the sixth objective, Ms. Curry notes five students' performances on items 7 and 19:

Student	Points on Item 7	Points on Item 19
Roxanne	4	4
Luanne	1	0
Izar	0	4
Mel	3	2
Jan	4	1

Relative to the sixth objective, the data suggest that Roxanne's level of achievement is high, Luanne's is low, and Mel's may be somewhere in between. However, Ms. Curry is perplexed by the performances of Izar and Jan on these two items. Does Izar know how to compute areas of right triangles? Item 7 suggests not, whereas item 19 indicates yes.

———————

Relative to the sixth objective, Ms. Curry's test yielded contradictory results, at least for Izar and Jan. If the test results are dominated by such inconsistencies, the test lacks *internal consistency* and is, therefore, unreliable. On the other hand, if the results do not contain a significant proportion of contradictions and are more in line with what Ms. Curry obtained for Roxanne, Luanne, and Mel, the test is internally consistent (Cangelosi 1990b, 29–31).

To design a test that is likely to produce internally consistent results, the following factors must be afforded attention:

How clearly the tasks presented by items are specified for students. For students to respond consistently to items, they must clearly understand the task required by each item. Directions need to be unambiguously communicated. Consider the following vignette.

❑ VIGNETTE 7.3
One of Mr. Cotrell's teaching units includes the following objective:

Interprets the meanings of expressions using the language of sets (*comprehension*).

Among the items on his unit test are the following two, both designed to measure that objective:

Task Presented to the Student
How many elements in {8, −9, 0, 11.3, 77}?_____

Scoring Key. +1 for "5," otherwise +0

Task Presented to the Student
How many elements in {a, b, c, d}? _____

Scoring Key. +1 for "4," otherwise +0

Confronted with the first of the two items on the unit test, one student, Robin, counts the five elements and writes "5" in the blank. For the next one she thinks, "One, 2, 3, 4—the answer is 4. . . . Oh! Maybe not. *a, b, c,* and *d* could be variables and maybe two or more are equal to one another. If *a* = *b,* that'd make no more than 3 in the set. . . . The answer could be 1, 2, 3, or 4. So, it's got to be 1, because I know there's at least one element, but I can't tell if there's more."

———————

To fix the item, Mr. Cotrell needs to replace {a, b, c, d} with an unambiguous expression (e.g., {Wilt Chamberlain, Martin Luther King, Marie Curie, Richard Pryor} or {letters a, b, c, d}). It's easy to understand how ambiguity crept into Mr. Cotrell's item. Ideally, when he reviews the test results with the class, Robin will explain her reasoning and Mr. Cotrell will turn his "mistake" into a productive learning experience.

The number of items on the test. A test with a large number of items provides a greater opportunity for consistent student response patterns to emerge than a test with only a few items. If, for example, Mr. Cotrell's test included 10 items similar to the first in Vignette 7.3 and 10 "ambiguous" ones similar to the second, then a consistent pattern to Robin's responses would likely surface. There would be a clear distinction between her responses to items with well-defined sets (e.g., {8, −9, 0, 11.3, 77} and {Wilt Chamberlain, Martin Luther King, Marie Curie, Richard Pryor}) and those with ambiguously defined sets (e.g., {a, b, c, d} and {tall people in the classroom}).

Furthermore, the more items on a test, the less affected are the test's results by fortuitous factors. Suppose, for example, that one of a test's objectives is measured by only two true/false items. By random guess, a student has a 25 percent chance of scoring 0, 50 percent of scoring 1, and 25 percent chance of scoring 2. Results of the two items are unlikely to discriminate consistently between students who

have and have not achieved the objective. However, if there were 10 such true/false items, then random guessing is less of a factor, with 0.1 percent chance of scoring 0, 1.0 percent of scoring 1, 4.4 percent of scoring 2, 11.7 percent of scoring 3, 20.5 percent of scoring 4, 24.6 percent of scoring 5, 20.5 percent of scoring 6, 11.7 percent of scoring 7, 4.4 percent of scoring 8, 1.0 percent of scoring 9, and 0.1 percent of scoring 10.

The conditions under which the test is administered. A scientific experiment is the application of systematic procedures for the purpose of uncovering evidence that helps answer a specified question. An achievement test is a type of scientific experiment in which the question to be answered is how well students have achieved a particular learning goal. The experimental conditions need to be controlled to minimize distractions to students and assure directions are followed. Internal consistency is threatened anytime students' thoughts during testing are interrupted or student cheating is allowed. References are available that suggest how to prevent student cheating without threatening the businesslike, cooperative environment of your classroom (e.g., Cangelosi 1982, 237–238; 1988a, 259–265; 1990b, 63–69).

Scorer Consistency
Exhibit 7.3 contains two items as they appeared on a test that Eugene took. Eugene's responses are included. The maximum possible score on item 1 is 1

Exhibit 7.3
Eugene's responses to two test items.

Name Eugene Ibavuri

1. (1 pt.) Is the sum of any two odd integers odd or even?

even

2. (4 pts.) Either prove or disprove that the sum of any two odd integers is even.

a+b is even for any a, b, ε Odds because:
if a and b are odd, then they can
be written as 2i+1 for a and 2i−1 for b
so that i ε Integers
Then a+b =
(2i+1) + (2i−1) = 2i+2i +1 −1
= 4i + 0 = 4i
and 4i is even.   QED

point; that of item 2 is 4 points. Score Eugene's responses now.

Obviously, Eugene's response to item 1 merits the full point. But how many points out of 4 did you award for his response to item 2? Surely Eugene's response indicates he's captured the conceptual spirit of a proof, but his "proof" is flawed. For one thing, he's demonstrated the theorem to be true only for consecutive odd integers, not any two odd integers. How do you compare Eugene's response to Shirley's and Lydia's in Exhibit 7.4?

How would you rank the quality of the three proofs? Shirley's proof by example seems the least complete. But her examples are relevant, so should not some of the 4 points be awarded? Eugene provides a general proof but only for consecutive odds. Do you think his response merits more points than Shirley's? Lydia's response seems complete and clear. I assume you would award the full complement of points for it.

If you asked a colleague who also teaches mathematics to score Eugene's responses from Exhibit 7.3, would the two of you agree? You would agree on Item 1, but there might be discrepancies in how you scored Item 2.

A test has *scorer consistency* to the same degree that:

1. The teacher (or whoever scores the test) faithfully follows the item's scoring keys so that the test results are not influenced by when the test is scored.

2. Two different mathematics teachers, both familiar with the test's content, agree on the score warranted by each item response so that the tests results are not influenced by the person scoring the test.

A test's scorer consistency will be poor if the test is dominated by items that do not have clearly specified scoring keys. There is only one correct response to item 1 of Exhibit 7.3. Thus, consistently scoring it poses no difficulty. Item 2, on the other hand, requires the scorer to make judgments about responses. To build scorer consistency into such items, scoring keys must specifically indicate just how points are to be distributed. Formulating scoring keys is a major aspect of test item design.

Scoring keys for the items appearing on pages 199–200 are specified. Of course, for an item to be relevant, both the *task-to-be-presented-to-students* component and the *scoring-key* component must be developed in light of the objective the item is intended to measure.

MEASUREMENT USABILITY

No matter how valid a test might be for measuring student achievement, it is of no value to you if it is

Exhibit 7.4
Shirley's and Lydia's responses to item 2 from Exhibit 7.3.

Shirley

2. (4pts.) Either prove or disprove that the sum of any two odd integers is even.

Two odds are even because 7 + 7 = 14, 3 + 1 = 4, 9 + 1 = 10, ...

Lydia

2. (4 pts.) Either prove or disprove that the sum of any two odd integers is even.

$a + b \in \{even\}$ for any $a, b \in \{odd\}$ because:
$a, b \in \{odd\} \Rightarrow$ There exist $i, j \in \{integers\}$ such that $a = 2i + 1$ and $b = 2j + 1$.
So, $a + b = (2i + 1) + (2j + 1) = 2i + 2j + 2$
Thus, $a + b = 2(i + j + 1)$. And since integers are closed under addition $i + j + 1 \in \{integers\}$ and so $a + b$ is twice sum integer which makes $a + b$ even by definition.

too time-consuming to administer or score, is too costly to purchase, or threatens the well-being of your students. It must be practical for your needs. Whenever designing or selecting a test to help you assess student achievement, you need to consider the measurement's *usability* as well as its *validity*. A test is *usable to the degree that it is inexpensive, is brief, is easy to administer and score and does not interfere with other activities.*

Exhibit 7.5 depicts the variables you should take into consideration whenever selecting or designing a test.

TYPES OF TESTS
Commercially Produced Tests

Mathematical achievement tests can be purchased from commercial publishers. Ordinarily, each set of student textbooks is accompanied by a package of materials for the teacher that includes tests— usually one test per chapter. Most such tests emphasize knowledge-level learning, especially algorithmic skills. Because they are hardly relevant to intellectual-level objectives, it's rarely advisable to use them for unit tests. However, tests that accompany textbooks provide a source of individual items for knowledge-level learning, especially algorithmic skills, that you may well incorporate into tests you design yourself. Pools of individual items are available from some commercial outlets. Advertisements for such products are sent to practicing mathematics teachers and members of NCTM; they are also found in professional journals (e.g., *Mathematics Teacher*) and displayed at annual meetings of professional societies (e.g., NCTM).

Unlike tests that are packaged as part of a textbook series, some commercially produced tests are administered on a schoolwide basis once or twice a year. These are the "big-event" tests that some people *naively* think of as true measures of students' intellectual achievements. Although capable of providing some evidence of an *average* achievement level of a *group* of students regarding some broad general areas, big-event, commercially produced tests do not yield data relative to the specific achievement of individual students (Cangelosi 1990b, 26).

Standardized Tests

The more familiar, big-event, commercially produced tests (e.g., *Sequential Tests of Educational Progress End-of-Course Tests: Algebra/Geometry, grades 9–12* (Floden 1985), *SRA Survival Skills in Reading and Mathematics* (Chase 1985), *Stanford Achievement Test: Mathematics Tests* (Aleamoni 1985), and *Stanford Diagnostic Mathematics Test* (Rogers 1985)) are *standardized*. A standardized test is one that has been field-tested for the purpose of assessing its reliability and establishing normative standards to be used in interpreting scores.

Unfortunately, misuses and overuses of standardized tests are quite common, especially in school districts where evaluations of teaching success are untenably linked to students' scores on these tests (Archibald and Newman 1988; Cangelosi 1982, 343–349; 1991, 104–105; Houts 1977; McClaren 1989, 13; Popham 1988, 129–149). However, numerous sources on how to use standardized tests appropriately are available (e.g., Cangelosi 1990b, 178–195; Hills 1986; Hopkins, Stanley, and Hopkins 1990, 389–481).

Teacher-Produced Tests

Standardized achievement tests, as do other commercially produced achievement tests, almost always emphasize knowledge-level learning. Thus, it is imperative for you to design and construct most of your tests yourself. *Teacher-produced* tests provide the most common data for formative and summative evaluations. The remainder of this chapter is devoted to methods for you to use in designing and constructing usable tests that provide valid indicators of how well students achieve your particular learning goals.

DESIGNING AND CONSTRUCTING TESTS
A Systematic Approach
The Haphazard Method
Vignette 7.4 is an example of how one teacher goes about designing and constructing a unit test.

❑ **VIGNETTE 7.4**
Ms. Houlahan begins the task of developing a test she plans to administer to her geometry class tomorrow. She thinks, "Let's see, . . . this unit was on π and using $\pi =$

Exhibit 7.5
Test-quality variables.

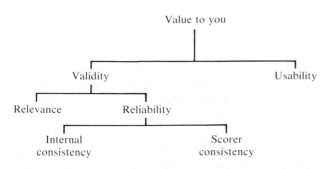

c/d in problem-solving. I'll start with an easy item—one about the value of π.... I could just ask, What is π? But that'd be ambiguous; they wouldn't know if I meant for them to put '3.14 something' or 'circumference ÷ diameter.'... Hmmm, okay, first two items." She writes:

1. π is between what two whole numbers? _____ and _____ .
2. For any circle with diameter *d* and circumference *c*,
   c/d = _____ .

"Now, what should I do for item 3?" she thinks, "I'd better grab some of these problems out of the book, and just change some of the numbers around. Anyone who has been paying attention and keeping up with the homework shouldn't have any trouble with them. Okay, . . . page, ahh . . . ."

Ms. Houlahan continues in this vein until her test is ready.

————————————

Ms. Houlahan's haphazard method is unlikely to produce a very relevant test for her learning goal. For one thing, she's not paying attention to the objectives that define the goal (if she has even defined it at all). This procedure of thinking up items in the same order they'll appear on the test typically results in tests that overemphasize easy-to-measure objectives and neglects the more difficult-to-measure objectives. Consequently, the tests stress knowledge-level learning; thus, students bother to learn only at the knowledge level (Stiggins 1988; Stiggins, Conklin, and Bridgeford 1986).

A more systematic approach is needed, one with the following advantages over the haphazard approach:

❑ You have a system for designing tests that reflect objectives according to your judgment of their relative importance to goal attainment. You consciously control the content and learning levels to which the test is relevant rather than them being a function of default.
❑ You establish a system that facilitates both the validity of tests and the ease with which you produce tests.

The Research-Based Method

There are four phases to the systematic research-based method: (1) clarifying the learning goal, (2) developing a test blueprint, (3) obtaining relevant item pools, and (4) synthesizing the test.

Clarify the Learning Goal

Eavesdrop on the following faculty room conversation:

❑ **VIGNETTE 7.5**

Mr. Coco: Hey, Eva, would you take a look at this test for me? Do you think it's any good?
Ms. Scott: Good for what?
Mr. Coco: For my algebra II class; it's the first draft of my midterm.
Ms. Scott: I can't judge the validity of this test without knowing what you want to evaluate.
Mr. Coco: What my students learned.
Ms. Scott: What did you intend for them to learn?
Mr. Coco: Algebra.
Ms. Scott: You've got to be more specific than that. A test's validity depends on how relevant it is to exactly what it's being used to evaluate. Unless you have the learning goal you want to evaluate clearly spelled out, there's no way to judge how relevant a test is. If this test is reliable—and from the looks of it, it should be—then it's relevant to something. The question is whether or not that something is what *you* want.

————————————

You can hardly be expected to create an achievement test until you've answered the question, Achievement of what? Thus, the first step in the test design and construction process is to clarify the learning goal to which the test is supposed to be relevant. Fortunately, you already defined your learning goal with a set of objectives when you initially developed the teaching unit. All that needs to be done for this step is to weight each objective according to its relative importance to goal achievement.

For example, suppose that the goal of the unit is the one on the relation $\pi = C/d$ given on page 203 and defined by Objectives A through H. Further suppose that you think those objectives should be weighted as indicated in Exhibit 7.2. Having weighted the objectives, the learning goal is clarified and you are prepared to move to the second stage of test design and construction.

Develop a Test Blueprint

After the learning goal is clarified with a list of *weighted* objectives, the next step is to develop a *blueprint* listing the features you want to build into the test. You need to make decisions regarding (1) the complexity of the test, (2) how much class time you'll devote to administering it, (3) how much of your time you'll devote to scoring it, (4) types of items comprising the test, (5) number of items, (6) difficulty of the items, (7) maximum number of points, (8) number of points for each objective, (9) method for determining cutoff scores, and (10) the outline for the test.

The Complexity of the Test Design

Whether your test blueprint should describe a complex or simple test design depends on how sophisticated your students are in taking tests and the nature of the learning goal. Test directions need to be simple enough so that students don't exert greater effort comprehending how to take the test than they do thinking about the relevant mathematics. Ordinarily tests emphasizing knowledge-level objectives can be designed much more simply than those emphasizing intellectual or affective objectives.

Administration Time

Generally speaking, students need more time to respond to intellectual-level items than to knowledge-level ones. Also, tests with many items tend to be more reliable than those with fewer items (Cangelosi 1982, 229–236). The catch-22 in this is the more items you include, the less time is available per item. Traditionally, the number of items and time allotted for mathematics tests are such that students must rush through each item without time for intellectual-level thinking.

By allotting adequate time for administering a reliable test that is relevant to intellectual-level as well as knowledge-level objectives, you enhance validity while reducing usability. How you decide to resolve compromises between validity and usability considerations determines the length of the test and administration time. For some situations, consider administering a test in a number of short sessions over several days. Do not limit your test plans by thinking each test must be confined to a single class period.

Scoring Time

Just as you schedule class time for administering tests, so you must also schedule professional time for scoring the tests. The amount of time you are willing and able to devote to this task influences the number of and types of test items (e.g., of the four items on pages 199–200, the two "right-or-wrong," 1-point items can be scored much more quickly than the two with the more complex scoring keys). In estimating scoring times for test blueprints, keep in mind that your students' learning is enhanced if you can provide them with feedback on their test responses sooner rather than later (Beyer 1987, 71–73, 148).

Types of Items

The variety of test items is literally limitless. Written-response, computerized, oral-response, or demonstration items can be multiple choice, essay, short answer, display (e.g., a proof), true-false, completion, matching, or a myriad of other types you invent yourself. The NCTM's (1989, 189–243) evaluation standards emphasize the need for measuring student achievement in a variety of ways using innovative and unconventional test items. The types of items you specify in a test blueprint are functions of five variables: (1) content of objectives, (2) learning level of objectives, (3) relative weights assigned to objectives, (4) time allotted for test administration, and (5) time allotted for scoring.

Number of Items

The test blueprint should include an estimate of the number of items you'll need. The estimate depends on time allotted for administration and scoring, the weighting of the objectives, types of items, and learning levels of the items (e.g., more time is needed for intellectual-level than for knowledge-level items).

Difficulty of Items

A major concern of item-response theory is the relations between how difficult various test items are for students to answer and exactly what the test measures (Linn 1989a; Millman and Greene 1989). In designing a test, you should be concerned with the roles played by items relative to their difficulty levels (Cangelosi 1990b, 53–54):

❑ *Easy items.* An item is *easy* if at least 75% of the students for whom it is intended respond to it correctly. A test needs a number of *easy* items to measure relatively low levels of achievement. Such items provide information about what students with less than average achievement of the goal have learned.
❑ *Moderate items.* An item is *moderately difficult* if between 25% and 75% of the students respond to it correctly. Moderate items are valuable for measuring the achievement levels of the majority of students for whom the test is designed.
❑ *Hard items.* An item is *hard* if no more than 25% of the students respond to it correctly. A test needs a number of *hard* items to measure relatively advanced levels of achievement. Unless a test has some hard items to challenge students with advanced goal attainment, the extent of those students' achievement levels is not detected.

Compare the three items in the following vignette (adapted from Cangelosi 1990b, 53):

❑ VIGNETTE 7.6

Objective 9 of Ms. Curry's sixth-grade math unit on surface area reads:

When confronted with a real-life problem, determines whether or not computing the area of a surface will help solve the problem *(application)*.

Three of the items Ms. Curry has constructed for that objective are as follows.

1. Task Presented to the Student

Multiple Choice.   Carpet is to be bought for the rectangular-shaped floor of a room. The room is 8 feet high, 12 feet wide, and 15 feet long. Which of the following computations would be the most helpful in deciding how much carpet to buy?

A. 12 feet + 8 feet + 15 feet
B. 2 × (12 feet + 15 feet)
C. 12 feet × 8 feet × 15 feet
D. 12 feet × 15 feet

Scoring Key.   +1 for D only; +0 otherwise.

2. Task Presented to the Student

Multiple Choice.   Suppose we want to build bookshelves across one wall of our classroom. The shelves are to be 18 inches apart. Which one of the following numbers would be most helpful in figuring how many shelves we can fit on the wall?

A. The area of the wall
B. The width of the wall
C. The height of the wall
D. The perimeter of the wall

Scoring Key.   +1 for C only; +0 otherwise.

3. Task Presented to the Student

Multiple Choice.   The 13 steps of a staircase are to be painted. Each step is 36 inches wide, 12 inches deep, and 7 inches high. Which of the following computations would be most helpful in determining how much paint will be needed?

A. [(12 inches × 13) × (7 inches × 13)] ÷ 2
B. 36 inches × [13 × (12 inches × 7 inches)]
C. (13 × 7 inches) × (36 inches + 12 inches)
D. 13 × [(36 inches × 7 inches) + (36 inches × 12 inches)]

Scoring Key.   +1 for D only; +0 otherwise.

Which of the three items do you think will be easiest for Ms. Curry's students? Which one will be the hardest? She needs items like the first to help her detect the lower bound of her students' achievement of the objective. The third item should help her detect the upper bound.

Commercially produced standardized tests are dominated by moderate items and designed so that the average of students' scores is about 50% of the maximum possible score. Typical teacher-produced tests are dominated by easy items with the average score about 80 to 85 percent of the maximum. Your tests will produce more detailed feedback on student achievement (especially for formative evaluations) than typical teacher-produced tests if you include easy, moderate, and hard items and design the test so that the average score is about 50 percent of the maximum (Cangelosi 1982, 309–339; Hoffmann 1975). Of course, if you apply this suggestion to tests you use to make summative evaluations for determining students' grades, then you should not use traditional percentage grading (in which 70 percent is typically required for passing and 93 percent is needed for an A). A method for converting scores to grades that can tolerate unconventionally difficult tests is explained in a subsequent section of this chapter; it is referred to as the *compromise method* (Cangelosi 1990b, 208–210).

Estimate of the Maximum Number of Points on the Test

Many teachers arbitrarily set the total number of points for each test at 100. Educational measurement specialists tend to discourage this practice, arguing that the maximum point total should be a function of the number and complexity of the items (Cangelosi 1990b, 47–48). If all items have scoring keys stipulating either +1 or +0, as would be appropriate for a right-or-wrong type of item, the maximum number of points equals the number of items. However, some types of items (e.g., display of a proof or show-your-work type) provide for responses that are not simply right or wrong. Such items have more complex scoring keys and cause the maximum points possible on the test to exceed the number of items.

While developing the test blueprint, you should estimate the maximum possible score by multiplying the number of items planned for the test by an approximation of the average maximum score per item. A more accurate estimate is unnecessary for purposes of the blueprint.

Number of Points for Each Objective

To distribute the maximum number of points on a test according to relative importance of objectives, multiply the weight of each objective by that maximum. This yields an estimate of the number of points that should be devoted to items relevant to that objective. For example, if you weighted the eight objectives A–H listed as indicated in Exhibit 7.2 and if you estimated your test to have 60 points, then include Exhibit 7.6 in the blueprint for a test of students' achievement of the goal those objectives define.

Exhibit 7.6
Point distribution for a 60-point test based on the weights of Exhibit 7.2.

Objective	Weight	Computation	Test Points
A	20%	0.20 × 60	12
B	6%	0.06 × 60	3 or 4
C	6%	0.06 × 60	3 or 4
D	12%	0.12 × 60	7 or 8
E	12%	0.12 × 60	7 or 8
F	12%	0.12 × 60	7 or 8
G	12%	0.12 × 60	7 or 8
H	20%	0.20 × 60	12
	100%		About 60

Method for Determining Cutoff Scores

Suppose you plan to use the 60-point test to make summative evaluations of how well your students achieved the goal about the relation $\pi = C/d$ given on page 203. You're faced with the decision of how to convert the test scores (e.g., 44, 51, 44, 9, 39, . . .) to letter grades (e.g., A, B, C, D, and F). The need to make such a decision raises issues regarding how *cutoff scores* should be identified.

A subsequent section of this chapter deals with setting cutoff scores for determining grades. The task is mentioned here to indicate that the method of determining cutoff scores should be listed in the test blueprint.

Test Outline

Finally, the test blueprint should contain an outline indicating the sections and subsections of the tests. Exhibit 7.7 is an example of a test blueprint.

Obtain and Maintain Relevant Item Pools

After clarifying the learning goal and developing a test blueprint, you need to have an *item pool* for each objective. An item pool is a *collection of test items that are all designed to be relevant to the same learning objective.* This is the most difficult phase of the test design/construction process if the test you're creating is to be relevant to objectives that you've never before measured. However, once you have built a collection of items for each objective, you may need only to retrieve preexisting item pools.

The Advantages of Item Pools

There are five reasons to utilize item pools:

❑ Building item pools focuses your attention on one objective at a time, stimulating you to expand your ideas on how student achievement of each objective can be demonstrated.

❑ Each item in a pool is designed to focus on the content and learning level specified by the objective. Thus, a test synthesized from items drawn from item pools is more likely to be relevant than one with items designed as the test is being put together (as Ms. Houlahan did in Vignette 7.4).

❑ Having access to an item pool for each objective before items are actually selected for a test makes it easier to construct the test according to the relative weights assigned to objectives.

❑ Being able to associate each item with a particular objective provides a means for assessing *which specific objectives* were achieved, not just general goal achievement. This facilitates access to *diagnostic* information needed for formative evaluations.

❑ It is much easier and efficient to create and refine tests once a system for maintaining and expanding item pools is in place.

Desirable Characteristics of Item Pools

To take full advantage of having item pools, build them so that the following occur:

❑ Each item contains both a *task for students to confront* and a *scoring key.*

❑ Each pool contains a variety of types of items (e.g., brief essay and display problem solution).

❑ Each pool contains easy, moderate, and difficult items.

❑ Data relative to each item's performance (once it's used) are filed (e.g., item analysis data indicating how difficult the item proved to be and how well students' performance on it correlated with their test scores) (Cangelosi 1982, 309–340; Ebel and Frisbie 1986, 223–242).

❑ The item pool system is organized and maintained so that retrieving existing items, constructing tests, creating new items, modifying existing items, and gaining access to information about items are executed efficiently.

The system should be organized so that each item is filed according to the scheme depicted in Exhibit 7.8.

Computerized Item Pools

A decade ago, teachers organized and managed item pools in file boxes on index cards. Today, microcomputers allow you to organize and manage item pools so efficiently that you can concentrate your energies on the creative aspect of the process—designing the items. Computer programs developed especially for setting up and utilizing item pools are readily avail-

Exhibit 7.7 (pp. 212–213)
Sample test blueprint.

UNIT 16: Circumferences, diameters, and π

ADMINISTRATION TIME In 2 sessions:
1. Parts I, II, III, and IV on Wed., Jan. 22, 1:10–2:00.
2. Parts V & VI on Thurs., Jan. 23, 1:10–1:45.

SCORING TIME
1. Part I to be scored by aide Wed. between 2:45 and 3:15
2. Part IV to be scored by me as administered
3. Parts II and III scored by me Wednesday between 3:15 and 5:00
4. Parts V and VI scored by me Thursday between 3:15 and 5:00

ITEM FORMATS

Objective	Format of Items
A	Essay
B	Interview
C	Brief essay and display computation
D	Multiple choice and completion
E	Multiple choice and brief essay
F	Multiple choice, display computation, and completion
G	Multiple choice, display computation, and completion
H	Multiple choice and display problem solution

NUMBER OF ITEMS About 60.

DIFFICULTY OF ITEMS Average test score should be slightly greater than half the maximum total with approximately 30% of the items easy, 50% moderate, and 20% hard. These ratios should be nearly consistent across all 8 objectives.

MAXIMUM NUMBER OF POINTS 60

MAXIMUM NUMBER OF POINTS FOR EACH OBJECTIVE

Objective	Points
A	12
B	3 or 4
C	3 or 4
D	7 or 8
E	7 or 8
F	7 or 8
G	7 or 8
H	12

---

able from both commercial and noncommercial sources. Computer software catalogues, computer retail stores, computer magazines, professional journals for teachers, and school district resource and media centers have information on how to obtain the software for such programs. Of course, you don't have to have special software to maintain and manage item pools efficiently with a computer. Many teachers use standard word-processing programs, storing each pool in a document file. Others prefer to write their own programs.

These programs free you from the time-consuming clerical aspects of expanding pools, modifying items, retrieving items in accordance with test blueprints, synthesizing tests, and printing tests. You can then focus more on intellectual tasks.

The teacher in Vignette 7.7 is using a commercially produced program to add a new item she's just designed to one of her item pools.

❏ **VIGNETTE 7.7**

Ms. Castillo accesses her item pool program and engages the computer in the following exchange (see Exhibit 7.9):

Computer: What function do you want?

1 Review table of contents
2 Review existing pool
3 Modify existing pool
4 Begin new pool
? Help

Exhibit 7.7 continued

METHOD FOR DETERMINING CUTOFF SCORES   The *compromise method* (Cangelosi 1990b, 208–210) will be used to convert test scores to letter grades with the following midpoints for criterion intervals:

25% (approx. 15 pts.) for F
40% (approx. 24 pts.) for D
55% (approx. 33 pts.) for C
70% (approx. 42 pts.) for B
85% (approx. 51 pts.) for A

TEST OUTLINE

First Session

Part I: 24 multiple-choice items, 1 point each. Directions given orally to the group as a whole. Items distributed among the 8 objectives as follows:

D— 7, E— 5, F— 5, G— 5, H— 2.

Part II: Three display-computation items

One 2-point item on C, one 3-point item on F, one 3-point item on G.

Part III: Two brief essay items

One 2-point item on C, one 2-point item on E.

Part IV: One 4-point interview item relevant to Objective B, individually administered one-to-one while group takes parts I, II, and III.

Second Session

Part V: Two display-problem-solution items

Each item 5 points on H.

Part VI: One 12-point essay item, relevant to Objective A

Exhibit 7.8
Organizational scheme for filing test items.

Course
   Learning goal
     Objective
       Difficulty level
         Type of item

Ms. Castillo: 3
Computer: What pool? Enter code for course/learning goal.
    If you need a list of the codes, enter LIST instead.

Ms. Castillo: ALG2/11.
Computer: What subfunction do you want?

1   Review table of contents for ALG2/11
2   Add new item
3   Modify existing item
4   Delete item
5   Modify existing ALG2/11 parameters
?   Help

Ms. Castillo: 2.
Computer: What objective? Enter code. If you need a listing of the objectives and codes, enter LIST instead.
Ms. Castillo: 4.
Computer: What is the difficulty level of the item (e, m, or h)?
Ms. Castillo: m.

Exhibit 7.9
Ms. Castillo adds to her item pools.

Computer: What type of item?

1	multiple choice	5	essay	8	performance
2	matching	6	brief essay		observation
3	completion	7	display work	9	other
4	true/false			?	help

Ms. Castillo: 7.

Computer: Enter the task you want presented to the student.

Ms. Castillo: Simple interest on a certain amount of money for one year was $30. If the interest rate had been 1% lower, $250 more would have had to be invested to produce the same amount of interest. What was the amount invested? What was the rate of interest? Please clearly display your work on this problem.

Display of work:

Answer for amount invested: _____
Answer for interest rate: _____

Computer: Enter the scoring key.

Ms. Castillo: 6 points possible, distributed as follows:

+ 1 if there is some open sentence that includes principal and interest rate as variables.

+ 1 if the relation interest = rate × time × principal is used somewhere in the response.

+ 1 if appropriate simultaneous equations with rate and principal as the only variables appears somewhere in the response. Example:

$$30 = RP$$
$$30 = (R - 0.01)(P + 250)$$

+ 1 if 750 is given as a solution for the principal.

+ 1 if 4% is given as a solution for the interest rate.

+ 1 if no other solutions are included (e.g., − 1000 for the principal).

Computer: Do you have any notes to add about this item?

Ms. Castillo: n.

Computer: Your new item has been stored in the ALG2/11 pool. Do you want to add another item to this pool?

Ms. Castillo: n.

Synthesize the Test

The final step in the test design/construction process is to select, organize, and compile the items into a test, as indicated by the test blueprint. The blueprint indicates the number of items to be selected from each pool, their formats, and the difficulty levels. This phase can be efficiently handled using a computer and printer.

DEVELOPING ITEMS

Creating test items that are relevant to your objectives is no trivial task. Organizing and managing item pools with a computer relieves you from most of the tedious work associated with test construction. However, the quality of your test items is dependent on your creativity.

The next seven sections suggest principles for creating mathematics test items for each of the following types of objectives: affective, conceptualization, simple knowledge, comprehension, knowledge of a process, application, and creativity.

ITEMS RELEVANT TO ACHIEVEMENT OF AFFECTIVE OBJECTIVES
A Matter of Choice, Not Ability or Skill

Reread the section "Affective Objectives," in Chapter 3. An item is relevant to achievement of a cognitive objective when students who have achieved that objective can perform the task presented by the item with a higher success rate than those who have not achieved the objective. On the other hand, affective objectives are not concerned with students being able to do anything. Achievement of an *appreciation* objective is the acquisition of a belief in the value of something. Achievement of a *willingness-to-try* objective is the acquisition of a tendency to attempt something.

The scoring key for an affective item does not address whether students' responses indicate if they *can* perform the task presented, but rather how they *choose* to respond to the task. Consider the problem of designing an item for the following objective:

> Attempts to formulate algebraic open sentences himself or herself when solving word problems before turning to someone else to set them up for him or her (*willingness to try*).

To be relevant to this objective, an item must present students not with the task of formulating an open sentence for a word problem, but instead with the task of choosing between attempting to formulate open sentences themselves or having it done for them.

The Self-Report Approach

One option is to use the *self-report* approach by simply asking students what they would do. Here's an example of an item for the aforementioned objective based on this approach:

Task Presented to the Students
Multiple Choice.   Suppose while thumbing through a magazine, you come across one of those brain-teaser-type sections in which there is a word problem to solve. You read the problem and think that with some effort you might be able to solve it by setting up an algebraic equation. You are not sure if you can solve it, but there is a note telling you that a solution is worked out on another page of the magazine. Which one of the following actions are you most likely to take?

A. Work on the solution yourself until you come up with a solution. Only after you come up with a solution (if at all) do you check with the one given on the other page.
B. You go directly to the solution on the other page rather than try to solve the problem yourself.
C. You neither try to solve the problem yourself nor look at the solution on the other page.
D. You see if it is a kind of problem you already know how to solve and, if so, solve it yourself before checking with the other page. If it isn't one you already know how to solve, you don't pay any more attention to the problem.
E. You see if it is the kind of problem you already know how to solve and, if so, solve it yourself before checking with the other page. If it isn't one you already know how to solve, you don't try to solve it yourself, but you check with the other page to learn how.
F. You attempt to solve it yourself before checking with the other page. However, if after about 5 minutes you don't make much progress, you find out how to solve it from the other page.

Scoring Key.   3 points maximum scored according to the following:

+3 for selecting A only
+2 for selecting F only
+1 for selecting D or E only
+0 for selecting B or C only

The value of the self-report approach is generally limited to situations in which students are confident that they risk nothing by answering honestly. Fortunately, you may want to measure your students' achievements of affective objectives only for formative, not summative, evaluations. Assessments of both their progress relative to appreciating mathematics and willingness to work at mathematics provides you with critical formative feedback for regulating lessons. However, you may be well advised to base grades only on evaluations of their cognitive mathematical achievements.

The Direct Observational Approach

An alternative to self-reporting is directly observing students' behavior in situation where they are free to make choices that reflect appreciation or willingness to try. Here, for example, is an item designed to measure the same willingness-to-try objective as the previous multiple-choice item:

> Attempts to formulate algebraic open sentences himself or herself when solving word problems before turning to someone else to set them up for him or her (*willingness to try*).

Description of the Task Presented to One Student at a Time

(Computer-administered Item). From a bank of word problems, the teacher selects one that he or she believes the student is capable of solving with some degree of effort (i.e., the equation to formulate isn't immediately obvious). The word problem is presented on the computer screen to the student with the following instructions:

> Enter an algebraic equation for solving the given problem. First label your variable. You may request help in setting up an equation anytime in the process by accessing HELP MODE. You ask for help mode by typing HELP. After you've received help, the computer will automatically return you to SOLUTION MODE, but you can return to HELP MODE by again typing HELP. Good luck!

Scoring Key. The teacher observes the student at work, recording the number of seconds spent in SOLUTION MODE and the number of seconds spent in HELP MODE. The score for the item is $S \div H$, where S = number of seconds in SOLUTION MODE and H = number of seconds in HELP MODE. See Exhibit 7.10.

ITEMS RELEVANT TO ACHIEVEMENT OF CONCEPTUALIZATION OBJECTIVES
Grouping Examples and Explaining Why

Reread Chapter 3's section entitled "Conceptualization." An item relevant to a conceptualization objective that specifies a *concept* for content presents students with the task of discriminating between examples and nonexamples of the concept. An item relevant to a conceptualization objective that specifies a *relation* for content presents students with the task of explaining why the relation exists.

When designing conceptualization-level items, you are confronted with some interesting problems. Consider the following vignette.

❑ VIGNETTE 7.8

Mr. Krisbaum conducts a seven-stage conceptualization lesson (as explained in the section "Inductive Learning Activities" of Chapter 4) for the following objective:

> Partitions a set of relations into functions and nonfunctions and for each of the given relations explains why it was so classified (*conceptualization*).

Cornell is one of about 10 students who fail to conceptualize the concept of a *function* during the lesson. However, during the subsequent direct instructional lesson, Cornell and some of these other students do achieve the following objective:

> Given a relation *r* from *X* to *Y*, where *X* and *Y* are subsets of {real numbers}, determines if *r* is a

Exhibit 7.10
Measuring affective objectives via computer-administered items.

function or not by using the following rule: If it is impossible for a vertical line to pass through more than one point of the graph of *r*, then *r* is a function. (*knowledge of a process*).

After conducting lessons on subsequent objectives, Mr. Krisbaum administers a unit test that includes the following item in an attempt to measure the conceptualization objective on functions.

Task Presented to the Student
Write Yes by the relations that are functions and No by those that are not:

_____ **A.** $\{(3, 4), (5, 6), (-2, 6), (-2, 1)\}$
_____ **B.** $\{(0, 0), (-2, 6), (6, -2), (2, 3)\}$
_____ **C.** $4x = 7y$
_____ **D.** $3x^2 + 2y^2 = 7$

Scoring Key. 4 points maximum with +1 for each of the following: A, no; B, yes; C, yes; D, no.

When Cornell gets to that item on the test, he quickly graphs each relation, does the vertical line test, and records the correct response. He gets four out of four points on the item, although he hasn't conceptualized functions. For Cornell, the item actually reflected his achievement of the knowledge-of-a-process objective, not the conceptualization one.

Items for Formative Feedback

Once inductive phases of a conceptualization lesson are completed and either the concept is defined or the relation is stated, students can depend on their memories to respond to items such as the one Mr. Krisbaum used. Thus, for purposes of formative feedback during a conceptualization lesson, it is critical for you to assess students' progress toward conceptualization during the inductive phases to determine readiness for the *articulation* phase. You do this by confronting students with a fresh set of examples and nonexamples to classify or explain. In Vignette 4.8, Mr. Citerelli utilized the form shown in Exhibit 4.7 during the inductive phases of his conceptualization lesson on arithmetic sequences. Before moving to the articulation phase, he might have been well advised to administer an item such as the following to the class:

Task Presented to the Student
Analyze the following four sequences. For each, decide whether it belongs under the "Example" column of your worksheet (Exhibit 4.7) or the "Nonexample" column. Display your choice by circling either EXAMPLE or NONEXAMPLE. In two or three sentences explain why you classified the sequence as you did.

A. 3, 9, 27, 81, 243
EXAMPLE or NONEXAMPLE (circle one only)
Explanation: _____
_____
_____

B. Your age at midnight of every Halloween since you've been born
EXAMPLE or NONEXAMPLE (circle one only)
Explanation: _____
_____
_____

C. $-6, -6.5, -7, -7.5, -8, -8.5, \ldots$
EXAMPLE or NONEXAMPLE (circle one only)
Explanation: _____
_____
_____

D. $-2, -2.4, -3, -3.4, -4, -4.4, \ldots$
EXAMPLE or NONEXAMPLE (circle one only)
Explanation: _____
_____
_____

Scoring Key. 12 points possible distributed as follows:

❑ +1 for each correctly circled (A, NONEXAMPLE; B, EXAMPLE; C, EXAMPLE; D, NONEXAMPLE).
❑ Each of the four explanations scored on the following 2-point scale:
   +2 if the explanation clearly indicates an understanding of arithmetic sequences.
   +1 if the explanation does not clearly indicate an understanding but doesn't display a lack of understanding either.
   +0 if the explanation indicates a lack of understanding of arithmetic sequences.

Items for Tests Used to Make Summative Evaluations

Assessing students' achievement of conceptualization objectives prior to completion of the respective conceptualization lessons is necessary for formative feedback. However, summative evaluations need to be made near the end of units. Thus, for constructing unit tests, you are faced with the problem of designing conceptualization items for concepts and relations that students have already learned to deal with at the knowledge level. You solve this problem by designing items that *confront students with tasks grouping or explaining examples that differ considerably from those to which rules during knowledge-level lessons were learned.*

Mr. Krisbaum (Vignette 7.8) could have selected relations that Cornell and other students would not be likely to graph unless they'd actually conceptualized functions. Here's a possible item.

Task Presented to the Student
Write Yes by the relations that are functions and No by those that are not:

_____ **A.** The relation *is the biological sister of* from the set of females in this class to the set of all living females
_____ **B.** The relation *is the biological son of* from the set of all males in this class to the set of all females who have ever lived
_____ **C.** {(*p*, *b*), where *p* is the present population of a city and *b* is its present birthrate}
_____ **D.** {(*s*, *m*), where *s* is a student in this class and *m* is a musical number he or she enjoys hearing}

Scoring Key. 4 points maximum, with +1 for each of the following: A, no; B, yes; C, yes; D, no.

One weakness of this particular item is it taxes students' comprehension of the notation as well as their conceptualization of functions. Students correctly responding to the item apparently comprehended the notation. For those that failed to perform well on the item, you may want to check how well they did with items designed to be relevant to comprehension-level objectives. If they responded well to those, then failure on this item indicates a lack of conceptualization.

Controlling the Difficulty Levels of Conceptualization Items

You can design a conceptualization-level item to be *easy, moderate,* or *hard* by *manipulating the psychological noise of examples and nonexamples,* as illustrated by Exhibits 4.4, 4.5, and 4.6. In the previous item, the similarities in relations A and B (e.g., wording is similar and both deal with family) make it easier for students to recognize how they differ— one being a function, the other not. These similarities in noise make the differences between the example and nonexample more apparent. To create a more difficult item, select relations with dissimilar noise.

Item difficulty can also be controlled by *how the item is structured.* Conceptualization items require students to reason systematically. More highly structured items tend to help students organize their thoughts more easily than items in which students must create their own structure. For example, two items are designed to measure the following objective:

> Explains why the lateral surface area of a right cylinder equals 2π*rh* (*conceptualization*).

Which of the following two items do you think would be easier for students?

1. Task Presented to the Student
Suppose you wanted to find how much paint would be needed to cover the outside of the tube pictured (it's open at both ends). Use from one-half to one page to explain why the size of the surface to be painted can be found by the following computation:

$$2 \times 3.14 \times 3.98 \times 15$$

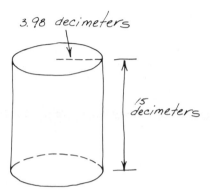

3.98 decimeters

15 decimeters

Scoring Key. 8 points maximum, distributed according to four 2-point scales, each with +2 for clearly explaining the point, +1 if there is some doubt if the point is explained, and +0 if the point is not explained. The four points are

☐ The cylinder can be reformed into a rectangle without changing the lateral surface area.
☐ The circumference of the right cylinder is associated with one side of the rectangle.
☐ The height of the right cylinder is associated with the other side of the rectangle.
☐ The computation is associated with 2π*rh*.

2. Task Presented to the Student
Suppose you wanted to find how much paint would be needed to cover the outside of the tube pictured (it's open at both ends). You can find the size of the surface to be painted with the following computation:

$$2 \times 3.14 \times 3.98 \times 15$$

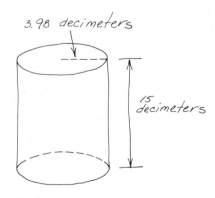

3.98 decimeters

15 decimeters

State the formula on which that computation is based.

_____

Why does that formula work for the tube in this problem? Explain why in a paragraph. Include a drawing showing how the tube has the same-sized surface as another, more familiar figure (Exhibit 7.11).

In the computation, $2 \times 3.14 \times 3.98 \times 15$, why is there a 2?

_____

In the computation, why is there a 3.14?

_____

In the computation, why is there a 3.98?

_____

In the computation, why is there a 15?

_____

Scoring Key. 8 points maximum, distributed according to four 2-point scales, each with +2 for clearly explaining the point, +1 if there is some doubt about the explanation, and +0 if the point is not explained. The four points are

❏ The cylinder can be reformed into a rectangle without changing the lateral surface area.
❏ The circumference of the right cylinder is associated with one side of the rectangle.
❏ The height of the right cylinder is associated with the other side of the rectangle.
❏ The computation is associated with $2\pi rh$.

The second item is structured so that some of the cognitive work is done for students. Unlike the first item, the task is begun for them—they need only to complete it. Keep in mind that conceptualization, like other learning levels, is achieved in varying degrees. Assessing achievement of mathematical objectives is not a matter of whether a student absolutely achieved an objective but rather _how well_ he or she achieved the objective.

ITEMS RELEVANT TO ACHIEVEMENT OF SIMPLE-KNOWLEDGE OBJECTIVES
Stimulus-Response

Reread Chapter 3's section entitled "Simple Knowledge." Note that students achieve a simple-knowledge objective by remembering the desired response to a particular stimulus. Identify the _response_ students are to remember and the _stimulus_ to which they are to make that response for the following objective:

> States the Pythagorean theorem (_simple knowledge_).

When presented with the stimulus "Pythagorean theorem," students who achieve this objective remember a response equivalent to: "For any right triangle, the square of the length of the hypotenuse equals the sum of the squares of the lengths of the two legs." Now, examine the following four test items and judge how relevant each is to the aforementioned objective:

1. Task Presented to the Student
State the Pythagorean theorem. _____

_____

Scoring Key. 2 points maximum, with +1 for indicating that the theorem is about right triangles and +1 if the relation $h^2 = a^2 + b^2$ is clearly implied

2. Task Presented to the Student
Multiple Choice.   Given $\triangle ABC$ with $m\angle B = 90°$, the Pythagorean theorem states that:

A. $(AB + BC)^2 = AC^2$
B. $AB = BC^2 + AC^2$
C. $AB^2 + C^2 = AC^2$

Exhibit 7.11

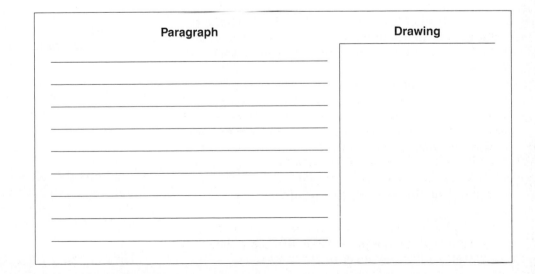

Paragraph	Drawing

D. $AC^2 + AB^2 = BC^2$
E. $(AC + AB)^2 = BC^2$

Scoring Key. +1 for C only; otherwise +0.

3. Task Presented to the Student

What is the name of the following theorem?

For any right triangle, the square of the length of the hypotenuse equals the sum of the squares of the lengths of the two legs.

Scoring Key. +1 for "Pythagorean" (spelling need not be exact as long as it is clear what the student meant); otherwise, +0.

4. Task Presented to the Student

Multiple Choice. If $\angle B$ of $\triangle ABC$ is a right angle, then $AB^2 + BC^2 = AC^2$. The name of that statement is

_____ .

A. Euclid's fifth postulate
B. The fundamental theorem of geometry
C. Archimedes' principle of right triangles
D. Fermat's last theorem
E. The Pythagorean theorem

Scoring Key. +1 for E only; otherwise +0.

All four items appear to have reasonable relevance for the given objective. However, if your principal purpose for including this objective is for students to remember the Pythagorean relation so that they can comprehend messages that use the expression Pythagorean theorem, then test items for the objective should maintain the stimulus-response order. Items 1 and 2 do that, but items 3 and 4 don't. Unlike items 1 and 2, items 3 and 4 present tasks requiring students to remember the name Pythagorean theorem in response to the statement of the relation. Thus, those items require a task different from the task students confront when reading or hearing the expression "Pythagorean theorem."

On the other hand, if you also want students to refer to the relation as the "Pythagorean theorem" in communications they send, then items that reverse the stimulus-response order of the objective (e.g., 3 and 4) should also be used. The critical point here is for you to understand the objective well enough so that you design items that present students with tasks remembering appropriate responses to appropriate stimuli.

Controlling the Difficulty Levels of Simple-Knowledge Items

As you design a simple-knowledge item, you can manipulate its difficulty level in three ways:

❏ *By how much of the response you require students to recall.* Item 2 of the previous four items gives the hypothesis of the Pythagorean theorem, leaving students with the task of recalling its conclusion. Item 1, on the other hand, requires recall of the entire theorem.

❏ *For multiple-choice items, by how distinguishable you make alternatives.* Compare the following Item 5 to Item 2 of the previous set of four items:

5. Task Presented to the Student

Multiple Choice. Given $\triangle ABC$ with $m\angle B = 90°$, the Pythagorean theorem states that

A. $AC > AB + BC$
B. $\triangle ABC$ is isosceles.
C. $AB^2 + BC^2 = AC^2$
D. $m\angle A + m\angle C = 90°$
E. $AB \geq BC$

Scoring Key. +1 for C only; otherwise +0.

Do you not agree that Item 5 would be easier for students than Item 2? The distractors (i.e., the incorrect alternatives) differ more from the correct alternative (C) for Item 5 than they do for Item 2.

❏ *For objectives with multiple stimulus-response pairs, by what pairs you select for the item.* If, for example, the objective is for students to state the six trigonometric functions, an item asking only for the sine function is probably easier for most students than one asking for the secant function.

ITEMS RELEVANT TO ACHIEVEMENT OF COMPREHENSION OBJECTIVES
Deriving Meaning from Expressions

Reread Chapter 3's section entitled "Comprehension." Note the two types of comprehension objectives: *comprehension of a message* and *comprehension of a communications mode.*

Comprehension-of-a-Message Items

An item relevant to a comprehension objective specifying a particular message as content presents students with the task of translating or interpreting meanings from the message. What, for example, might be an item relevant to the following objective?

Explains the following definition of *rational number*: r is a rational number if and only if there exist two integers p and q such that $p/q = r (q \neq 0)$ (*comprehension*).

Here is one possibility:

Task Presented to the Student
Write *Yes* in the blank in front of each one of the following statements that can be implied from the definition of rational number as given in the textbook's glossary; write *No* in front of each of the other statements:

_____ **A.** If a number cannot be expressed as a fraction with an integer for the denominator and an integer for the numerator, then the number is *not* rational.
_____ **B.** A whole number is not rational unless it is in the form of a fraction.
_____ **C.** If $z = x/y$, where x are y real numbers such that $y \neq 0$, then z is rational.
_____ **D.** The quotient of two counting numbers is rational.
_____ **E.** If a number is rational, then it is positive.

Scoring Key. 5 points maximum, with +1 for each answer as follows: A, yes; B, no; C, no; D, yes; and E, no.

Comprehension-of-a-Communication-Mode Items

An item relevant to a comprehension objective specifying a type of communication mode as content presents students with the task of translating messages from the specified communication mode into another mode (usually a more familiar mode). What, for example, might be an item relevant to the following objective?

> Explains the meaning of expressions using the summation notation (i.e., $\sum_{i=a}^{k} f(i)$) (*comprehension*).

Here is one possibility:

Task Presented to the Student
Answer each of the following questions using the space provided:

A. Why is the following statement false?

$$\sum_{i=1}^{3} (i^2 - 1) = (1 - 1) + (4 - 2) + (9 - 3)$$

_____
_____

B. Why can't the following expression be translated?

$$\sum_{j=1/2}^{5} 3j$$

_____
_____

C. Why is the following statement false?

$$\sum_{n=2}^{3} 3^n = 3^2 + 3^3 + 3^4$$

_____
_____

Scoring Key. 6 points maximum, distributed as follows:

For A, +1 for clearly indicating that consecutive integers 1, 2, and 3 should be substituted for the index variable only, not for constants; +1 if the answer includes nothing false or irrelevant to the question.

For B, +1 for clearly indicating that the function is defined only for integer values for the index variable; +1 if the answer includes nothing false or irrelevant to the question.

For C, +1 for clearly indicating that the index variable should go from 2 to 3, not 2 to 4; +1 if the answer includes nothing false or irrelevant to the question.

Novelty

Comprehension is an intellectual-level cognitive behavior. Thus, it involves reasoning and judgment that goes beyond what is simply remembered. Unlike knowledge-level items, comprehension items present students with tasks that are not identical to ones they've previously encountered. The item's task needs to have at least some aspect that is novel for the students. The five statements (A through E) used in the aforementioned item for comprehension of the definition of rational number should be statements to which students have no prior exposure. The questions used in the next item on the summation notation should not have been previously answered in class. Of course, during learning activities for the objectives, it's expected that students analyzed similar but different statements about rational numbers and answered similar but different questions about summations.

Controlling the Difficulty Level of Comprehension Items

Three variables influencing the difficulty levels of comprehension items you design include the following:

For a comprehension-of-a-message objective, whether the item is relevant to literal or interpretive understanding. Reread Chapter 4's section entitled "Literal and Interpretive Understanding." Items that tap only literal understanding of a message tend to be easier than ones that involve students in interpretive understanding. The next two items are both relevant to how well students comprehend the proof presented in Exhibit 4.13. However, the first is limited to literal understanding; the second relates to interpretive understanding:

1. Task Presented to the Student
(The student is provided with a copy of Exhibit 4.13.)

What supposed relation between *p* and *q* is ultimately contradicted near the end of the proof? Express your answer using as little of the exact terminology from the proof as you can.

_____

_____

Scoring Key. 3 points maximum, distributed as follows:

+1 for indicating that p and q are relatively prime in words other than just repeating (p, q) = 1.

+1 for not only expressing relatively prime differently from (p, q) = 1 but also adding some explanation as to what relatively prime means.

+1 for *not* including errors or irrelevant remarks in the answer.

2. Task Presented to the Student

(The student is provided with a copy of Exhibit 4.13.)

Explain why under the initial supposition of the proof, p and q could not both be even numbers. Express your answer using as little of the exact terminology from the proof as you can.

_____

_____

_____

Scoring Key. 2 points maximum, based on the following scale:

+2 if the response clearly indicates why two even numbers cannot be relatively prime.

+1 if it is unclear as to whether or not the response indicates why two even numbers cannot be relatively prime.

+1 if the response clearly fails to explain why two even numbers cannot be relatively prime.

For a comprehension-of-a-message objective, from what aspects of the message the item requires students to extract information. The complexity of the message specified by a comprehension objective is inherent in that message. So, you cannot manipulate the complexity of the message to control item difficulty without threatening the relevance of the item. However, what students are asked to derive from the message can be manipulated to control item difficulty. Suppose, for example, you are designing an item to measure the following objective:

Explains the following definition of limit of a function: $\lim_{x \to 2} f(x) = b$ if for every number $\epsilon > 0$ there exists a number $\delta > 0$ such that $|f(x) - b| < \epsilon$ for every x (in the domain of f) satisfying the inequality $0 < |x - a| < \delta$ (*comprehension*).

An item presenting students with the task of explaining the relation between ϵ and δ would probably be harder for students than one asking about the relation between x and a.

For a comprehension-of-a-communication-mode objective, the complexity of the mathematical expression or message used in the item. Unlike comprehension-of-a-message objectives, the message used in items for comprehension-of-a-communication-mode objectives can vary. Suppose, for example, you are designing an item for the following objective:

Given a textbook word problem, identifies the principal variable or variables to be solved (*comprehension*).

Here are two possible items:

1. Task Presented to the Student

Multiple Choice.   What is the main variable to be solved for in the following problem?

Hill's laundry dryers cost 25¢ for 7 minutes. How many dimes will be needed to run the dryer for 30 minutes?

A. The number of dimes needed to run the dryer for 30 minutes.
B. The rate Hill's laundry charges for running the dryers.
C. How much it will cost to finish drying the clothes.
D. The cost of 25¢ to run the dryers for 7 minutes.

Scoring Key.   +1 for A only; otherwise +0.

2. Task Presented to the Student

Multiple Choice.   What is the main variable to be solved for in the following problem?

Alma is shopping for a personal computer. There are two models she likes; both have 640K RAM, but the less expensive one is faster, whereas the other comes with a more attractive software package. She decides that if the cost of additional software she wants is no greater than the difference in the costs of the two models, she'll buy the faster one.

A. The difference between the number of kilobytes of RAM for the two models.
B. The cost of the additional software less the difference in the cost of the two models.
C. The difference in speed of the two models.
D. How much the software package that comes with the slower model actually costs.

Scoring Key.   +1 for B only; otherwise +0.

Although the two items are relevant to the same objective, the second one requires students to sift through more information to extract the principal variable.

ITEMS RELEVANT TO ACHIEVEMENT OF KNOWLEDGE-OF-A-PROCESS OBJECTIVES
Emphasis on the Process, Not the Outcome

Reread Chapter 3's section entitled "Knowledge of a Process." Students achieve a knowledge-of-a-process objective by remembering how to carry out a procedure or execute an algorithm. Thus, a knowledge-of-a-process item should present students with the task of recalling or effecting the process step by step. The nature of algorithms and other processes is such that they are remembered via a *sequence* of responses. The first step of the process is triggered by an initial stimulus. Then the first step serves as the stimulus for the second step, the second for the third, and so on. Thus, the accuracy of subsequent steps in the process depends on the accuracy of previous steps. Because of this phenomenon, knowledge-of-a-process items should be designed to identify which steps in the process are accurately remembered or executed and which are not. Unlike, simple-knowledge items, more than the final outcome to the initial stimulus needs to be considered. Consider the next vignette.

❑ **VIGNETTE 7.9**
Ms. Comaneci's students complete a set of exercises to practice and provide formative feedback relative to the following objective:

> Simplifies algebraic polynomials with nested parentheses (*knowledge of a process*).

She examines Angel's work on one exercise as it appears in Exhibit 7.12 and thinks to herself: "Let's see, . . . his answer is off. It should be $-8x^2 + 24x + 104$. What did he do? . . . He's working inside out; he remembered that. Good! . . . Okay, here's one misstep. He missed distributing the negative sign to the 2. But, if that's the only mistake then he'd have $+16$ there, not $+2$. . . . Oh, I see

Exhibit 7.12
Angel's responses to an exercise simplifying polynomials.

Simplify:

$$8(3(x + 5) - (x^2 + 2))$$

$$8(3x + 15) - x^2 + 2$$

$$24x + 120 - x^2 + 2$$

$$-x^2 + 24x + 122$$

what else he did; he dropped that outside right parenthesis. That was just careless. Okay, I need to remind him of those two things."

___

Just as Ms. Comaneci analyzes Angel's work to identify which steps in the algorithm were remembered and which were not, knowledge-of-a-process test items need to be designed so that the following occur:

The items' tasks are selected so that what students are remembering about the process becomes apparent by their responses. Had Ms. Comaneci looked only at Angel's answer rather than a display of his work, she would not have detected what he did right and what he did wrong—only that he did something wrong. Furthermore, had the exercise not included an example in which the negative sign was to be distributed, Angel's lack of attention to that task would not have surfaced. That particular error in which a negative sign is to be distributed is far more common than one in which a negative coefficient other than 1 is to be distributed (Cangelosi 1984c). In other words, Angel may not have made that mistake with this polynomial:

$$8(3(x + 5) - 4(x^2 + 2))$$

The point is that items need to sample a variety of situations to which the process is evoked.

The items' scoring keys reflect the degree to which the process is remembered, not simply whether or not the final outcome is right or wrong. Reread Vignette 4.15. Note that Mr. Champagne analyzed the algorithm and broke it down into specific steps for students to remember. Such an analysis provides the basis for scoring keys for items relevant to knowledge-of-a-process objectives.

Here's an example of an item relevant to Ms. Comaneci's objective.

Task Presented to the Student
Simplify (display your work):

$$\frac{1}{3}(c - (c - 3c) - 6(2c + c))$$

Scoring Key. 12 points maximum, distributed according to six 2-point scales, with a criterion for each scale so that $+2$ is awarded if the criterion is met in all phases of the work, $+1$ if it is met only some of the time, and $+0$ if it is never met. The six criteria are as follows:

❑ Computations proceed from inside out relative to parentheses.

❑ Associative properties are properly applied.
❑ Distributive properties are properly applied.
❑ Numerical computations are accurate.
❑ Final answer is simplified completely.
❑ Final answer is equivalent to $-5c$.

Error-Pattern Analysis

Some mistakes students make in executing algorithms are careless oversights that inconsistently occur in their work. Angel's failure to distribute the -1 and to attend to the outside right parenthesis in the previous example may not be recurring types of errors. To determine if each was an isolated incidence of carelessness or evidence of a learned error pattern, Ms. Comaneci needs to examine his work on additional exercises. It is not at all uncommon for students to develop consistent error patterns while attempting to learn algorithms (Ashlock 1990, 3–9; Schoenfeld, 1985 61–67). Unless these patterns are identified and corrected soon after they are learned, they become solidified through practice and overlearning. Thus, it is critical for you to devise knowledge-of-a-process items that help identify possible error patterns students might be learning during lessons on algorithms.

The next vignette illustrates a teacher taking advantage of her experiences observing students' work to devise an item.

❑ VIGNETTE 7.10

As she did for Angel, Ms. Comaneci looks at Cindy's work, shown in Exhibit 7.13. She engages Cindy in the following conversation:

Ms. Comaneci: How did you get from $-8x^2 + 24x + 104$ to $x^2 - 3x - 13$?
Cindy: We're supposed to simplify these all the way— right?
Ms. Comaneci: Right.
Cindy: So, I divided both sides by -8 to get rid of it in front of the x^2.
Ms. Comaneci: But I see only *one* side.

Exhibit 7.13
Cindy's responses to an exercise simplifying polynomials.

Simplify:

$$8(3(x + 5) - (x^2 + 2))$$
$$8(3x + 15 - x^2 - 2)$$
$$8(3x + 13 - x^2)$$
$$24x + 104 - 8x^2$$
$$-8x^2 + 24x + 104$$
$$x^2 - 3x - 13$$

Cindy: Can't you just factor the -8 out of the equation?
Ms. Comaneci: What equation?
Cindy: (Pointing to the polynomial $-8x^2 + 24x + 104$) This one.
Ms. Comaneci: That's not an equation.
Cindy: It isn't?
Ms. Comaneci: Read this and tell me if . . . .

From numerous exchanges similar to this one with Cindy, Ms. Comaneci has developed a wealth of knowledge about incorrect variants of algorithms students accidentally master. Her experiences debugging student error patterns have taught her some recurring ways students attempt algorithms. She uses this knowledge to devise test items for knowledge-of-a-process objectives that cause some of the more common error patterns to surface. Here she designs one such item for students' knowledge of an algorithm for finding the distance between two points in a Cartesian plane. She thinks to herself, "Okay, this item is to help me see how they use the distance formula:

$$\text{Distance between } (x_1, y_1) \text{ and } (x_2, y_2)$$
$$= \sqrt{(x_1 - x_2)^2 + (y_1 - y_2)^2}$$

. . . I'll make this one multiple-choice with alternatives being answers resulting from commonly made errors. First, I'd better come up with a stem for the item. . . ."

She develops the following stem:

What is the length AB for $A(7, -2)$ and $B(0, 3)$?

Next, she computes the correct alternative, writing out the work and examining it:

$$AB = \sqrt{(x_1 - x_2)^2 + (y_1 - y_2)^2}$$
$$= \sqrt{(7 - 0)^2 + (-2 - 3)^2}$$
$$= \sqrt{7^2 + (-5)^2}$$
$$= \sqrt{49 + 25}$$
$$= \sqrt{74}$$
$$\approx 8.60$$

Seeing her answer leads her to rethink the stem, and she says to herself, "Should the answer be exact or in decimal form? Since they'll be using calculators, I'll use the decimal form and indicate to the nearest one-hundredth in the directions."

Reexamining the computation, she thinks about error patterns she's noted students making in the past; they include the following:

❑ Computing AB as $\sqrt{(x_1 - y_1)^2 + (x_2 - y_2)^2}$, which, if other errors aren't made, leads to an answer of 9.49.

❑ Computing AB as $\sqrt{(x_1 + x_2)^2 - (y_1 + y_2)^2}$, which, if other errors aren't made, leads to an answer of 6.93.

❑ Computing AB as $\sqrt{(x_1 + x_2^2) - (y_1 + y_2^2)}$, which, if other errors aren't made, leads to an answer of 0 or other possibilities, depending on which values are substituted for (x_1, y_1) and (x_2, y_2), respectively.

❑ The correct formula is remembered but computed as if it were $\sqrt{(x_1^2 - x_2^2) + (y_1^2 - y_2^2)}$, yielding 6.63 as the answer.

❑ $\sqrt{(7-0)^2 + (-2-3)^2}$ is simplified as follows:
$\sqrt{7^2 + (-5)^2} = 7 - 5 = 2$.

❑ $\sqrt{(7-0)^2 + (-2-3)^2}$ is simplified as follows: $\sqrt{7^2} + \sqrt{(-5)^2} = 7 + 5 = 12$.

She enters the following item into her computerized item pool:

Task Presented to the Student
To the nearest hundredth, what is the length AB for $A(7, -2)$ and $B(0, 3)$?

A. 9.49	**B.** 8.60	**C.** 6.63	**D.** 2.00
E. 12.00	**F.** 6.93	**G.** 0.00	**H.** 10.07

Scoring Key. +1 for B only; otherwise +0.

She also enters a note indicating the error pattern suggested by each of the item's distractors.

_____

To help you begin gaining the kind of experience Ms. Comaneci used to design her item, examine the work with algorithms students displayed in Exhibit 7.14. For each, describe any error pattern the student might have displayed.

John's work suggests he's skillful in factoring, but he doesn't seem to differentiate between $ab = 0$ and $ab = c$, where $c \neq 0$. He blindly uses the algorithm without paying attention to the underlying relation upon which it is based.

Jane doesn't seem to discriminate among $a^n a^m$, $a^n b^m$, and $(a^n)^m$.

Pat's work displays two error patterns. First, he seems to think that the value of a fraction is unchanged by raising both the numerator and the denominator to the same power. Second, he has some notion of some sort of cross-multiplication process for finding common denominators. He's probably confusing the following relations, the first used in adding fractions, the second in reforming equations:

$$\frac{a}{c} + \frac{b}{d} = \frac{ad + bc}{cd}$$

$$\frac{a}{c} = \frac{b}{d} \Rightarrow ad = bc$$

Pete appears to add virtually everything in sight to compute perimeters.

Test items in which students must display work or multiple-choice items in which distractors reflect common error patterns are invaluable for formative feedback during knowledge-of-a-process lessons.

Controlling the Difficulty Levels of Knowledge-of-a-Process Items

Since a knowledge-of-a-process objective specifies the process to be learned, you don't control the difficulty of relevant items by making the process more or less difficult. That is, you control the difficulty level of such items not by varying how easy or hard it is to remember the steps in the process but by how hard or easy the steps are to execute. For example, design two items, one more difficult than the other, that are relevant to the following objective:

> Factors algebraic polynomials that can be expressed as $Ax^2 + Bx + C$, where x is a real-number variable and A, B, and C are integer constants (_knowledge of a process_).

Here are two possibilities, the first being easier than the second for most students:

1. Task Presented to the Student
Factor completely:

$$x^2 + 5x + 6$$

Scoring Key. +1 for $(x + 3)(x + 2)$; otherwise +0.

2. Task Presented to the Student
Factor completely:

$$21x^2 - 31x - 42$$

Scoring Key. +1 for $(3x - 7)(7x + 6)$; otherwise +0.

ITEMS RELEVANT TO ACHIEVEMENT OF APPLICATION OBJECTIVES
Deciding How to Solve Problems

Reread the sections entitled "Application," in Chapter 3, and from Chapter 4, "Problem-Solving" and "Deductive Reasoning." An application item presents students with a problem and the task of deducing whether or not the content specified by the objective (e.g., relation or algorithm) is useful in solving that problem.

Exhibit 7.14
A sample of students' work misexecuting algorithms.

Name _John_

Solve for all real values of x:

1. $x^2 - 6x - 7 = 0$

$(x-7)(x+1) = 0$

$x-7 = 0$ or $x+1 = 0$

$x = 7$ or $x = -1$

2. $x^2 - 4x - 5 = 16$

$(x-5)(x+1) = 16$

$x-5 = 16$ or $x+1 = 16$

$x = 21$ or $x = 15$

3. $2x^2 - 9x + 7 = 25$

$(2x-7)(x-1) = 25$

$2x-7 = 25$ or $x-1 = 25$

$2x = 32$ or $x = 26$

$x = 16$ or $x = 26$

4. $3x^2 - 23x - 36 = 0$

$(3x+4)(x-9) = 0$

$3x+4 = 0$ or $x-9 = 0$

$3x = -4$ or $x = 9$

$x = -\frac{4}{3}$

Name _Jane_

Simplify:

1. $(c^2)^2 = \underline{c^4}$

2. $a^2 a^4 = \underline{a^6}$

3. $(b^3)^2 = \underline{b^5}$

4. $(x^3 y^5)^0 = \underline{x^8 y^8}$

5. $b^5 b^6 = \underline{b^{11}}$

6. $(w^1 q^2)r^4 = \underline{w^3 q^7 r^7}$

Name _Pat_

Add:

1. $\dfrac{x+3}{7x} + \dfrac{2x-8}{7x} = \dfrac{x+3+2x-8}{7x} = \dfrac{3x-5}{7x}$

2. $\dfrac{2x+1}{x-1} + \dfrac{5}{\sqrt{x-1}} = \dfrac{2x+1}{x-1} + \dfrac{25}{x-1} = \dfrac{2x+26}{x-1}$

Avoiding "Giveaway" Words

Design an item to be relevant to the following objective:

Given a real-life problem, decides if the solution requires determining a combination of n things taken r at a time and, if so, determines how to find that combination (*application*).

Here is the item result of one person's attempt to develop a relevant item:

Task Presented to the Student
A group of three musicians has six instruments that they all can play (a synthesizer, a piano, two different acoustical guitars, a bass guitar, and an electric guitar). How many different instrument combinations can the group play together? Display your work.

Scoring Key. 2 points maximum, distributed as follows:

+1 for using $_nC_r = (n!)/[(n-r)!r!]$ with $n = 6$ and $r = 3$.

+1 for answering 20.

Exhibit 7.14 continued

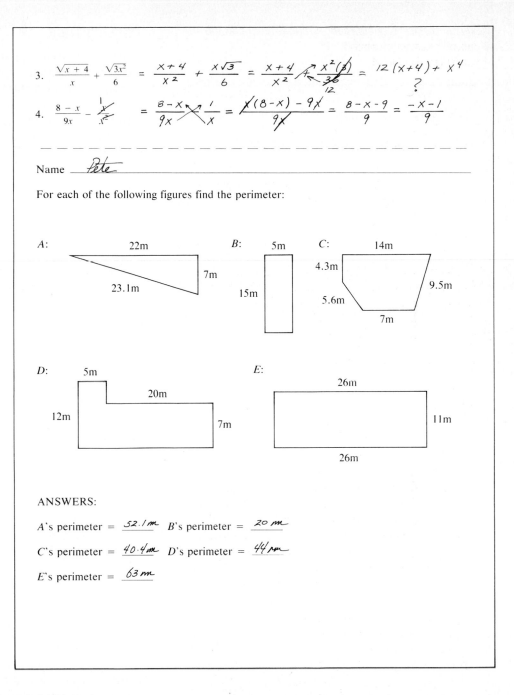

3. $\frac{\sqrt{x+4}}{x} + \frac{\sqrt{3x^2}}{6} = \frac{x+4}{x^2} + \frac{x\sqrt{3}}{6} = \frac{x+4}{x^2} \diagup \frac{x^2(3)}{\frac{36}{12}} = \frac{12(x+4) + x^4}{?}$

4. $\frac{8-x}{9x} - \frac{\cancel{x}}{x^2}\cancel{^1} = \frac{8-x}{9x} \diagdown \frac{1}{x} = \frac{\cancel{x}(8-x) - 9\cancel{x}}{9\cancel{x}} = \frac{8-x-9}{9} = \frac{-x-1}{9}$

Name _Pete_

For each of the following figures find the perimeter:

A: 22m   B: 5m   C: 14m

7m   4.3m

23.1m   15m   9.5m

5.6m

7m

D: 5m   E:

20m   26m

12m   7m   11m

26m

ANSWERS:

A's perimeter = _52.1m_   B's perimeter = _20 m_

C's perimeter = _40.4m_   D's perimeter = _44 m_

E's perimeter = _63 m_

Duane, a student, obtained a full 2-point score on this item with the following thoughts: "How many different instrument *combinations* can . . . . Oh, so this is a combination problem. Let's see, what are the numbers to plug in, ahh . . . there's a 3 and a 6. The rule is the bigger one is *n*, the smaller one *r*—so it's 6! over . . . which gives me 20."

Duane keyed in on the word *combination*, remembered the formula, and simply substituted the only data available. He demonstrated knowledge of a process relative to combinations, but he did not have to think deductively to respond correctly to the item. Thus, the item doesn't appear relevant to the

application-level objective for which it was designed.

Here's an item that is more likely to tax students' achievement at the application level:

Task Presented to the Student

Aaron, Art, Mindy, and Van have a musical group with seven instruments available to them (a synthesizer, a piano, two different acoustical guitars, a bass guitar, electric guitar, and a drum set). Aaron, Art, and Mindy can play any of the instruments except for the drums. Van can play only drums.

The group refers to any set of four instruments they can be playing together as an instrument arrangement.

How many different *instrument arrangements* can the group play during a concert?

Display your work.

Scoring Key. 2 points maximum, distributed as follows:

+1 for using $_nC_r = (n!)/[(n - r)!r!]$ with $n = 6$ and $r = 3$.

+1 for answering 20.

Luanda, a student, obtained a full 2-point score on this item with the following thoughts: "How many different instrument arrangements can the group play . . . so, what's this instrument arrangement thing? Let's see, it says any set of four instruments they can be playing at once. So, that's like bass guitar, two acoustical guitars, and the piano—that's an instrument arrangement. How many of those are possible? . . . Aaron is playing piano and Art a guitar, and they switch, does that change the instrument arrangement? . . . No. It's what is being played that counts. So, this isn't a permutation problem. It's a combination. So, okay, how many instruments can they play at once? Seven? No, it's the number of people that count—that's Aaron, Art, Mindy, and Van—4 possible out of 7 instruments. So, it's a combination of 7 instruments taken 4 at a time, which is . . . 35. Okay, is that right? Oh, no! Van's the only one that plays the drum. So, drums are in every arrangement of 4. I can just ignore them, so, it's really a combination of 6 instruments taken 3 at a time, which is . . . 20."

Avoiding the word combination increases the chances that students will have to reason deductively, as Luanda did, in order to respond correctly. Note, however, that the latter item also taxes students' reading-comprehension skills to a greater degree than the former one. Because of this unfortunate necessity, it's important to include comprehension-level objectives in units and test for achievement of them separately from application-level objectives.

Extraneous Data

Regarding the previous two items, note that the "improved" version is not only void of a giveaway word (*combination*), but it also includes extraneous information. Having 4 members and 7 instruments in a problem that requires a combination of 6 things 3 at a time taxes students' abilities to deduce what data are to be used in the formula. If the wording of the problem is such that only exactly what is needed is given, then the item is less likely to be at the application level. After all, with a real-world problem, a person is inundated with information, most of which is irrelevant to solving the problem.

Missing Data

Another strategy for designing application items is to confront students with problems without supplying them with all the information for effecting solutions. Such items help test how well they can deduce what data need be collected. Keep in mind that in the real world, one must decide what data to collect to solve problems; data aren't always conveniently presented as numerals on a printed page.

Design a *missing-data* item for the following objective:

Given a real-life problem, determines how, if at all, a solution to that problem is facilitated by using the following relation for computing accumulated dollar amount (A) in compound interest savings plan: $A = P(1 + r/k)kn$, *where P = the principal, r = the annual rate, k = the number of times a year the interest is compounded, and n = the number of years (application)*.

Here is one possibility.

Task Presented to the Student

Several years ago Riley was shopping for a bicycle. There were two that interested him, one for $350 and the other for $150. His dad advised him at the time to buy the one for $150 and put the difference in a savings account. He liked the more expensive one so much more that he bought it anyway. Now, he wonders how much he would now have in the bank if he had originally taken his dad's advice.

Write a one-half page letter to Riley explaining how to figure out how much he would have in the bank today if he had bought the less expensive bicycle and left the difference in a savings account. Be as detailed as reasonably possible.

Scoring Key. 18 points maximum, distributed according to nine 2-point scales, with a criterion for each scale so that +2 is awarded if the criterion is clearly met, +1 if it is unclear whether or not it is met, and +0 if it is clearly not met. The nine criteria are as follows:

❑ The principal is set at $200.
❑ The question of whether the interest is simple or compounded is raised.
❑ The question of the number of times per year interest is compounded is raised.
❑ The process for finding out how often the interest is compounded is explained (e.g., calling the bank or reading bank documentation).
❑ The question of how long it has been since the bicycle was purchased is raised.

❑ The process for finding out when the bicycle was purchased is explained (e.g., by looking up the receipt).
❑ The question of what is the rate of interest is raised.
❑ The process for finding out the interest rate is explained.
❑ A formula equivalent to the one stated in the objective is suggested.

Mixing Example and Nonexample Problems

To test students' ability to discriminate between problems to which an objective's content applies and problems to which it doesn't, both example and nonexample problems need to be included on the same test. As a nonexample problem relative to the application objective on combinations listed on page 226, the following problem might be used:

> Robbie can play the piano and harmonica, Amanda can play the piano, bass guitar, and lead guitar, and Amy can play the piano, harmonica, and lead guitar. The only two instruments that can be played by one person simultaneously are the harmonica and guitar. If the three musicians are to play four different kinds of instruments at the same time, what instrument must Amanda play?

Controlling the Difficulty Levels of Application Items

Application items confront students with problems to solve. If the nonmathematical aspects of the problem presented by an item are familiar to students, the students tend to find that item easier than an item relevant to the same application objective but relative to a less familiar subject. For example, students familiar with football will have an easier time visualizing the following problem than students who rarely watch or participate in football:

> At the rate of 9 yards per second, how long will it take a football player to run 10 yards straight downfield? At that rate how long would it take that same player to run from his or her team's 5-yard line to his or her team's 15-yard line if he or she runs a straight route that makes a 20° angle with the sidelines?

Because you want your application-level items to discriminate on the basis of how well students achieved the mathematical objective, not how familiar they are with topics such as football, you need to select topics that are about equally familiar or unfamiliar to almost everyone in the class.

To design an easy application item, select a problem to which the applicability of the objective's content is made obvious via very simple deductive logic. Harder items confront students with problems in which more complex deductive reasoning is used to determine if the content applies. Design two items to be relevant to the following objective; the first should be easier than the second:

> Given a word problem, determines if formulating a one-variable quadratic equation will help solve the problem, and, if so, formulates the equation and solves the problem (*application*).

Both of the following two items are designed to be relevant to the objective, but the first is intended to be the easier of the two (problems used in the items are adapted from Keedy, Bittinger, Smith, and Orfan (1986, pp. 493–494)):

1. Task Presented to the Student
A picture frame measures 20 centimeters by 14 centimeters. 160 square centimeters of picture shows. See the diagram. Find the width of the frame. Display your work.

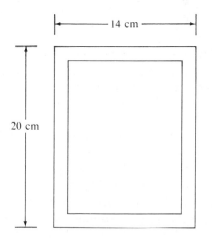

Scoring Key. 2 points maximum, distributed as follows:

> +1 for formulating an equation equivalent to $4x^2 - 68x + 120 = 0$, where x = width of the frame.
>
> +1 for a final answer of 2 centimeters.

2. Task Presented to the Student
The current in a stream moves at a speed of 2 kilometers per hour. A boat travels 24 kilometers upstream and 24 kilometers downstream in a total time of 5 hours. What is the speed of the boat in still water? Display your work.

Scoring Key. 2 points maximum, distributed as follows:

+1 for formulating an equation equivalent to $5x^2 - 48x - 20 = 0$, where $x =$ the speed of the boat in still water.

+1 for a final answer of 10 kilometers per hour.

ITEMS RELEVANT TO MATHEMATICAL CREATIVITY

Reread two sections, "Creativity" in Chapter 3, and "Some Thoughts on Creativity" in Chapter 4.

Unless you devise very unusual curricula for students, relatively few of your objectives specify *creativity* for the learning level. Lessons fostering mathematical creativity tend to be integrated with other lessons and extend beyond the confines of a single teaching unit. You may, for example, include short learning activities based on *synectics* within most teaching units but may detect an increase in students' creative mathematical activities only over the course of several or more units. Consequently, assessing achievement at the creativity level may be more of a long-range endeavor than assessing achievement of other types of cognitive objectives.

Items for creativity objectives consist primarily of the following:

1. Presenting students with tasks relative to the specified content that can be accomplished via divergent thinking.
2. Scoring students' responses in ways that reflect divergent rather than convergent thinking.

Note that the scoring keys for simple-knowledge, knowledge-of-a-process, comprehension, conceptualization, and application objectives tend to reward convergent thinking (i.e., responses that match previously conceived responses).

Following are two examples of creativity objectives, each accompanied by an item designed to be relevant to it:

Objective. Categorizes numbers in unconventional ways and formulates a rule for each category (*creativity*).

Item.

Task Presented to the Student
Given $A = \{-\sqrt{3}, \sqrt{-3}, 27, 3, 3.333\ldots\}$, compose five *distinct* (i.e., no two are equal) subsets of A so that each subset contains exactly three elements. For each of the five subsets, write a rule that defines set membership.

Write the rule without actually naming any of the three elements.

1st subset: _____
1st rule: _____
_____
_____

2nd subset: _____
2nd rule: _____
_____
_____

3rd subset: _____
3rd rule: _____
_____
_____

4th subset: _____
4th rule: _____
_____
_____

5th subset: _____
5th rule: _____
_____
_____

Scoring Key. 5 points maximum, with +1 for each subset-rule pair that fits the criterion established in the directions.

Objective. Formulates and proves theorems about subsets of whole numbers (*creativity*).

Item.

Task Presented to the Student
The number of dots in each of the following arrays is called a *triangular number:*

The set of triangular numbers is infinite. Take at least 15 minutes examining triangular numbers. Then, make three different statements you think are true about all triangular numbers. These statements should be hypotheses that are not immediately apparent (e.g., all triangular numbers are positive integers) from just glancing at the numbers. Try to prove one of your statements. Display your work on the proof or attempt at a proof.

1st statement: _____
_____
_____

2nd statement: _____

_____

3rd statement: _____

_____

Proof or work toward a proof:

Scoring Key. The rules are based on comparing responses to those of others. First of all, any blatantly obvious statement (e.g., no triangular number is imaginary) is eliminated. Then each of the remaining statements is compared to a list of statements compiled from other students who have responded to this item. Comparison statements are sequenced from the most frequently occurring to the least frequently occurring. The statement from this student is then ranked in the sequence and given a number of points equal to its rank. Thus, if there are 50 comparison statements, 20 of which have been made more than once, then if the statement is equivalent to one of those first 20, it receives a score from 1 to 20, inclusive. If the statement is equivalent to one of the previously unique 30 comparison statements, it receives a score of 21. If the statement is not equivalent to any of the 50 statements, it receives a score of 36 (i.e., a three-way tie for 21st place). If the display of the work on the proof demonstrates a discernible line of thought, the statement score is multiplied by 4. If the statement is actually proved, that score is then doubled.

USING TEST RESULTS
Formative Feedback

Obviously, you and your students depend on achievement-test results as indicators of how you should regulate your teaching and they should regulate their studying. Reviewing results from a recently taken test is a prime learning activity that provides students with formative feedback. Annotated and scored tests should be returned to students as soon as reasonably possible; ordinarily, students are primed for corrective feedback the day after a test. "Why didn't you teach us this *before* we took the test?" is an oft-heard question in sessions in which recently tested mathematical content is reviewed. The answer, of course, is, "The experience of working with this content under test conditions made you more receptive to my teaching."

Here's a routine some teachers have found successful during the class period when tests are returned:

1. Tests are returned with *descriptive* comments. *Descriptive* comments provide students with spe-cific information about their performance (e.g., "Your drawing made it easier for me to follow your logic" or "Squaring both the numerator and denominator changed the value of this fraction"), as opposed to *judgmental* comments (e.g., "good" or "poor").

2. In a brief large-group session, the teacher makes general comments about the test and, if necessary (e.g., for the first few tests) explains how to interpret scores and comments.

3. A small-task-group session is held, with each group of about six students going through the test item by item and answering one another's questions.

4. A large-group interactive lecture session is held in which the teacher (a) reviews matters that test results indicate need reviewing and (b) responds to students' questions that were either not answered in the small-group session or arose as a result of that session.

Such sessions are particularly effective when students realize that subsequent tests will contain items relevant to objectives from prior tests. Test-review sessions should be conducted with the clear understanding that the purpose is for students to learn mathematics, not simply to be provided with a summative evaluation of their performance.

Converting Test Scores to Grades
Grading

Test-review sessions are used to provide students with formative feedback. Grades are the primary means for communicating your summative evaluations of their achievement of learning goals. Periodically assigning grades (e.g., A, B, C, D, or F) to students' achievements is a responsibility faced by practically all middle and secondary school mathematics teachers. Data from tests are the primary bases for grades.

Many methods for converting test scores to grades are used; none appear completely tenable (Cangelosi 1990b, 196–212; Gronlund and Linn 1990, 427–452; Hopkins, Stanley, and Hopkins 1990, 319–338). How to establish suitable cutoff scores for grades is a question that has been addressed by evaluation specialists but which has not been satisfactorily answered (Cangelosi 1984a; Livingston and Zieky 1982). Research studies of grading methods have been more successful demonstrating the weaknesses of common practice than in providing practical and effective models.

Traditional Percentage Method

The most commonly practiced and familiar method of converting test scores to grades is *traditional per-*

centage grading. With the traditional percentage method, a percentage of a test's maximum possible score is associated with a cutoff score for each grade; for example, 94%–100% for an A, 86%–93% for a B, 78%–85% for a C, 70%–77% for a D, and 0%–69% for an F. Traditional percentage grading has two major flaws:

❏ The percentages are set so high that teachers must either give tests dominated by easy items or else plan to fail the majority of their students.

As explained in the section "Difficulty of Items," to measure a wide range of achievement levels in a class of students, tests should be designed so that the average score is about 50% of the maximum.

❏ Inflexible cutoff points lead teachers to associate different grades with scores that are not significantly different. Consider the following vignette (adapted from Cangelosi 1990b, 206):

❏ VIGNETTE 7.11

Mr. Nelson administers a test consisting of 25 four-point items. Joyce, Albin, and Winthrop score 93, 86, and 84, respectively. With Mr. Nelson's traditional percentage grading scale, Joyce receives a B for being correct on 23.25 items (93/4 = 23.25). Albin also receives a B for being correct on 21.5 items (86/4 = 21.5). But Winthrop receives a C for correctly answering only one-half item less than Albin (84/4 = 21). (See Exhibit 7.15.)

The Visual Inspection Method

Smith and Adams (1972, 237–239) suggest that the aforementioned flaws of the traditional percentage method are not a weakness of the *visual inspection method.* With the visual inspection method, test scores are converted to letter grades as follows:

1. A number line is drawn that encompasses the range of the test scores. For example, if the lowest test score is 5 and the highest is 44, the number line given in Exhibit 7.16 would suffice.
2. The frequency distribution of the test scores is graphed onto the line. Exhibit 7.17 provides an example.
3. Gaps or significant breaks in the distribution are identified.

4. A letter grade is assigned to each cluster of scores appearing between gaps.

If, for example, C is defined as average, the cluster containing the middle score might be given the grade C. Or the teacher may choose to sample some of the test papers from a particular cluster and decide the grade for that cluster based on the quality of the sample. Every score within the same cluster is assigned the same letter grade. Exhibit 7.18 depicts one possible assignment of grades from Exhibit 7.17.

The Compromise Method

Cangelosi (1990b, 208–210) raises concerns about the visual inspection method and suggests the *compromise method* as an alternative:

A Conflict Between Theory and Practice. Teachers who are introduced to the visual inspection method readily recognize the following advantages it has over the traditional percentage method:

1. Tests can include appropriate proportions of easy, moderate, and hard items without fear that too many students will receive low grades. The difficulty of the test can be factored into the grading scheme.
2. Scores that are not markedly different from one another are not assigned different grades; the error of the measurement is recognized.

However, teachers tend to reject the visual inspection method because

1. Establishing criteria for A, B, C, D, and F *after* a test has been administered does not appear as objective as having predetermined cutoff scores (e.g., 70% for passing), of which students can be aware *prior* to taking the test.
2. Norm-referenced methods [i.e., in which students' scores are compared to one another] encourage an unhealthy competition among students for grades more than do criterion-referenced methods [i.e., in which no score is interpreted in light of others' scores but only in relation to a set standard (e.g., 70%)].
3. Test scores don't always fall into convenient clusters with significantly large enough gaps to distinguish between different grades according to the visual inspection method. The distribution of Exhibit 7.19 is possible.

Exhibit 7.15
Comparison of three grades determined by the traditional percentage method.

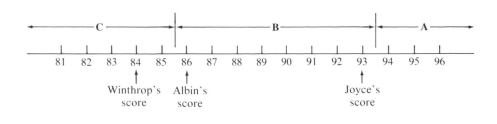

Exhibit 7.16
Number line for use with visual inspection grading.

Exhibit 7.17
Sample score distribution.

Exhibit 7.18
Example of grades assigned via visual inspection.

Exhibit 7.19
Inconvenient score distribution for use with visual inspection grading.

Exhibit 7.20
Sample letter grade cutoff scores.

Exhibit 7.21
Sample letter grade cutoff scores with grey in-between scores.

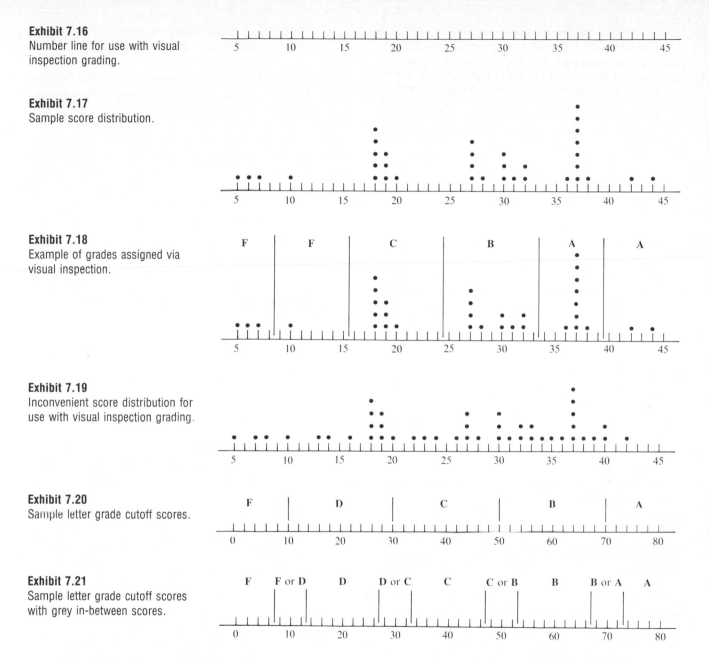

A Resolution. The method suggested here realizes the principal advantages of the visual inspection method while obviating the three weaknesses mentioned above. This method is a *compromise* between the traditional percentage and the visual inspection methods and is implemented as follows:

1. As with traditional percentage grading, establish cutoff scores for each letter grade before the administration of the test. However, there are two differences:
    a. To allow for the use of a test that includes hard and moderate as well as easy items, the percentage of points that a student must score to obtain a certain grade is set unconventionally low. Exhibit 7.20, for example, presents possible criteria for a test designed to produce an average score of 40 out of a possible 80.

b. The cutoff score for each letter grade is established with the understanding that there be a buffer, or "grey," zone between each letter grade category. In Exhibit 7.21, for example, to be assigned a *definite* B, a score would have to be at least three points above the B cutoff score of 50 and no greater than three points below the A cutoff score of 70. For those familiar with the *standard-error-of-measurement* statistic (SEM), a SEM would be an ideal determiner of the length of this buffer zone (Cangelosi 1982, 292–300). However, simply "backing off" several points in both directions around each cutoff point is sufficient.

2. Assign in-between grades to scores that fall within cutoff score intervals. For example, a score of 51 might convert to a grade of B or C. Final determination of whether the higher or lower grade pre-

vails in any of these in-between cases depends on data collected from other sources (e.g., an abbreviated retest or an interview that requires the student to expatiate on his or her responses). You also have the option of simply letting the grade for that test remain in limbo between two letter grades and then factoring in the in-between grade into your final determination of the specific report card grade.

Point and Counterpoint. The compromise method is likely to be criticized on two accounts:

1. Some teachers are uncomfortable with scores falling within the buffer zones. There *should* be clear lines of demarcation between grades.
2. Unconventionally difficult tests, replete with moderate and hard items, may lead to greater student frustration, since the students will miss more items than on more commonly used easier tests.

There *should* be clear lines of demarcation between letter grades, and it isn't always convenient for a score to fall within a buffer zone. However, the state of the art of measuring student achievement is not advanced to the point that definite lines of demarcation, discriminating between levels of achievement, are tenable. The educational community needs to recognize this fact.

Regarding the second criticism, there are some distinct pedagogical disadvantages to using unconventionally difficult tests. However, once students become accustomed to struggling with challenging test items, a teacher can utilize such tests as tools to help students achieve higher cognitive (e.g., application-level) learning objectives (Bloom, Madaus, and Hastings 1981).

Evaluating Instructional Effectiveness

In your efforts to teach as well as you reasonably can, you continually use formative feedback in carrying out instructional responsibilities of developing curricula, designing and conducting lessons, managing student behavior, and assessing their achievements. No doubt you are also interested in obtaining summative evaluations of your teaching performance. Sometimes teachers and their supervisors factor assessments of students' achievement of learning goals into their evaluations of teaching performance. They reason: "Schools are established to serve students. The success of a school depends on what students learn. Student achievement is the goal of instruction. Thus, logic dictates that summative evaluations of teaching should depend on how well students achieve learning goals."

However, the complexities of the teaching/learning process and the realities of today's schools renders that logic inapplicable to evaluations of teaching performance. Too many factors teachers cannot control (e.g., students' prior achievements, aptitudes, and home environment) affect learning for assessments of student achievement to be the primary factor in evaluations of teachers' effectiveness (Cangelosi 1986, 1991, 11–12; Soar, Medley, and Coker, 1983).

How to evaluate your teaching effectiveness is an extremely complex question few understand how to answer. A number of references are available when you decide to delve into the question (e.g., Braskamp, Brandenburg, and Ory 1984; Cangelosi 1991; Medley, Coker, and Soar 1984; Stanley and Popham 1988b).

❏ ❏ ❏ ❏ ❏ ❏ ❏ ❏ ❏ ❏ ❏ ❏ ❏ ❏ ❏ ❏ ❏ ❏ ❏

SELF-ASSESSMENT EXERCISES

1. Examine each of the following teacher activities and categorize it as either a *formative evaluation, summative evaluation,* or *measurement:*
   a. During an independent work session, Mr. Romano sees that Marion does not use a calculator as he completes word problem exercises.
   b. Mr. Romano decides to allocate 15 minutes of class time in an intellectual-level question/discussion session in which two students simultaneously work the same word problem at the chalkboard, one using a calculator and the other doing hand calculations, and the relative advantages of the two methods are discussed.
   c. Mr. Romano uses the compromise method to assign letter grades to test scores.
   d. Mr. Romano compiles Charlene's score on a test by adding her item scores.
   e. While conducting an inductive lesson, Mr. Romano decides against using a particular example he had planned to use.
   f. Mr. Romano becomes disappointed in Elaine's progress to this point in the geometry course.
   Compare your answers to these: b and e are examples of formative evaluations, c and f are summative evaluations, and a and d are measurements.
2. Select the one response to each of the following multiple-choice items that either completes the statement so that it is true or accurately answers the question:
   a. Any time teachers evaluate student achievement, they _____ .
      i. Make value judgments.
      ii. Use valid measurements.
      iii. Base results on unit test results.
      iv. Determine better ways of teaching.

b. According to the quote beginning on page 198, Stiggins suggests that _____ .

   i. All tests emphasize knowledge-level achievement.

   ii. The cognitive levels at which students are tested tend to limit the cognitive levels at which they learn.

   iii. Commercially produced tests are superior to teacher-produced tests.

   iv. Valid and usable measures of student achievement are virtually impossible to design.

c. The NCTM (1989, pp. 189–237) Evaluation Standards (see Appendix D) _____ .

   i. Emphasize the need for more written tests while de-emphasizing testing with computers.

   ii. Emphasize isolating skills in testing while de-emphasizing using standardized achievement testing.

   iii. Emphasize the clear distinction between testing and teaching.

   iv. Emphasize the use of a wide variety of test items while de-emphasizing dependence on only one or two types of tests.

   v. Emphasize the need to standardize the types of items used so that assessment of achievement is more equitable across diverse cultural groups.

d. Which one of the following is *not* a measurement?

   i. Seeing what a student writes on the board.

   ii. Administering a unit test.

   iii. Seeing that Kay is unable to solve one of the problems in an exercise.

   iv. Hearing Kay say, "I can't solve this problem."

   v. Seeing that Kay does not have the correct answer to an exercise written on her paper.

e. The set of students' scores from a test of mathematical achievement is _____ .

   i. A qualitative variable.

   ii. A quantitative variable.

   iii. A constant.

   iv. Unreliable unless the test is relevant to the learning goal.

   v. Invalid unless the test is usable.

f. Which one of the following is a *necessary* condition for measurement relevance?

   i. Usability

   ii. Validity

   iii. Pertinence to the stated learning levels

   iv. Internal consistency

g. Which one of the following is a *sufficient* condition for measurement relevance?

h. Which one of the following is a *necessary* condition for measurement reliability?

   i. Pertinence to the intended mathematical content

   ii. Relevance

   iii. Usability

   iv. Scorer consistency

i. Which one of the following is a *sufficient* condition for measurement reliability?

   i. Internal and scorer consistency

   ii. Internal or scorer consistency

   iii. Usability and relevance

   iv. Usability or relevance

j. Which one of the following is a *sufficient* condition for a measurement to be a valuable data gathering tool?

   i. Relevance, reliability, and validity

   ii. Relevance, reliability, and usability

   iii. Usability, internal consistency, and pertinence to the intended mathematical content

k. Which one of the following modifications to an item is most likely to increase the item's scorer consistency?

   i. Provide greater latitude for the scorer to use professional judgment.

   ii. Change the format from multiple choice to brief essay.

   iii. Make the rules in the scoring key more specific.

   iv. Raise the learning level to which the item is relevant from knowledge to intellectual.

l. If a test has been *standardized*, then _____ .

   i. It is valid but may not be usable because of its cost.

   ii. Its reliability has been assessed.

   iii. It is reliable.

   iv. It can be depended on only to measure knowledge-level achievement.

m. Which one of the following measurement variables depends on the stated purpose of the measurement?

   i. Internal consistency

   ii. Scorer consistency

   iii. Relevance

   iv. Usability

n. Which one of the following measurement variables depends on the time it takes to administer a test?

   i. Internal consistency

   ii. Scorer consistency

iii. Relevance
iv. Usability

o. The purpose of weighting objectives to be measured by a test is to increase the chances that _____ .
    i. Test results will reflect more important objectives to a greater degree than less important objectives.
    ii. Intellectual-level objectives will be emphasized on the test more than knowledge-level objectives.
    iii. The test will be internally consistent.
    iv. The test will be usable.

p. The value of having *hard* items on a test is to measure the achievement of _____ .
    i. Less advanced students
    ii. More advanced students
    iii. Intellectual-level objectives
    iv. Knowledge-level objectives
    v. Affective objectives

q. The value of having *easy* items on a test is to measure the achievement of _____ .
    i. Less advanced students
    ii. More advanced students
    iii. Intellectual-level objectives
    iv. Knowledge-level objectives
    v. Affective objectives

r. It takes an effort to organize and computerize item pools, but once an item pool file is established _____ .
    i. Test validity is assured.
    ii. Item design requires less creativity on the part of the teacher.
    iii. All test items are selected randomly, thus decreasing item bias.
    iv. Test construction is less time-consuming for the teacher.

s. Generally speaking, designing items for affective objectives is easiest for which one of the following situations?
    i. Students realize their achievement of the objectives is to be assessed for formative feedback only—not for summative evaluations.
    ii. Students realize their achievement of the objectives is to be assessed for summative evaluations only—not for formative feedback.
    iii. The objectives are at the *appreciation* rather than at the *willingness-to-try* level.

t. Ms. Oldham-Jones has just inserted a moderately difficult item into her pool for a particular comprehension-level objective. Now, as she attempts to design a hard item for that objective, she thinks, "I'll make this one more difficult by putting in a task that'll require inductive thinking." What reminder do you think Ms. Oldham-Jones needs to hear?
    i. Items requiring inductive reasoning are difficult to design.
    ii. Items requiring inductive reasoning are not necessarily more difficult than items requiring only comprehension; the mathematical content also makes a difference.
    iii. Items requiring inductive reasoning are normally relevant to conceptualization objectives, not comprehension objectives.

u. Out of her concern for her students' abilities to read books and articles about mathematics, Ms. Oldham-Jones includes an objective for her students to remember definitions of certain mathematical terms in most of her teaching units. During the course she plans to build their reading vocabulary of mathematical words. One item she intends to be relevant to one of those objectives is the following:

Task Presented to the Student
Fill in the missing word: _____ refers to an equation that states two ratios are equal.

Scoring Key. +1 for *proportion;* otherwise +0.

Which one of the following is a weakness of the item?
    i. *Proportion* is not a mathematical term.
    ii. The item reverses the stimulus-response order of the objective.
    iii. The item requires only simple-knowledge cognition.

v. An item with a scoring key designed to reflect those steps in an algorithm students remember and those they don't is most likely to be relevant to which one of the following types of objectives?
    i. Simple knowledge
    ii. Knowledge of a process
    iii. Application
    iv. Willingness to try

w. According to the section "Items Relevant to Achievement of Application Objectives," why should at least some items designed to test students' achievement of an *application* objective that specifies formulas for computing volumes confront students with problems that are solvable by computing areas—not volumes?
    i. Area is a subconcept of volume.
    ii. Area is at least as important to goal achievement as volume.
    iii. Application-level achievement is concerned with real-world problem-solving

for any mathematical content, not just one isolated topic.

    iv. Achievement of an application objective requires students to discriminate between problems to which the specified content applies and those to which it doesn't.

x. For items to be relevant to a *creativity* objective, they must _____ .

    i. Have a scoring key that discriminates between atypical and typical responses.

    ii. Require students to produce a novel product.

    iii. Present students with tasks never previously accomplished.

    iv. Provide students with opportunities for convergent thinking.

y. Which one of the following methods for converting test scores to grades is based on the assumption that the test is dominated by easy items?

    i. Visual inspection

    ii. Compromise

    iii. Traditional percentage

    iv. Normal curve

z. On a 40-point test, Wanda scores 35 and Darnell scores 34. Wanda receives a B but Darnell receives a C. What method for converting scores to grades does it appear the teacher used?

    i. Visual inspection

    ii. Compromise

    iii. Traditional percentage

Compare your responses to the following: a. (i); b. (ii); c. (iv); d. (iii); e. (ii); f. (iii); g. (ii); h. (iv); i. (i); j. (ii); k. (iii); l. (ii); m. (iii); n. (iv); o. (i); p. (ii); q. (i); r. (iv); s. (i); t. (iii); u. (ii); v. (ii); w. (iv); x. (i); y. (iii); z. (iii).

3. Organize a system for maintaining item pools. Either set the file up from existing software, write the program yourself, or utilize word-processing files to set it up.

4. In your response to exercises 2 and 4 of the self-assessment exercises for Chapters 3 and 4, respectively, you defined a learning goal with a set of objectives. Design and construct a unit test for student achievement of that goal. Make sure to follow the procedure explained in the section "Designing and Constructing Tests." This includes

(a) weighting the objectives, (b) developing a test blueprint (see Exhibit 7.7 for an example), (c) developing and inserting an adequate number of items into your item pool file, and (d) synthesizing the test.

5. Visit a mathematics class. Identify an algorithm students are learning or have recently learned. Devise a brief diagnostic test for the purpose of identifying students' error patterns relative to that algorithm. Explain what you've done to the teacher and ask him or her if you may administer the test to the class.

❑ ❑

TAKING WHAT YOU'VE LEARNED TO THE NEXT LEVEL

From your work with Chapter 1 you reflected on the complex art and science of teaching mathematics to adolescents and preadolescents. The conflict between traditional and research-based mathematics curricula is an issue raised in Chapter 2. You developed ideas for developing mathematics curricula consistent with research-based principles articulated in the NCTM (1989) *Standards*. In Chapter 3, you learned how to establish the target for your lessons by defining learning goals with objectives. In Chapter 4 you learned how to apply research-based principles for designing lessons according to the particular mathematical content and the learning level specified by a given objective. You examined ways of managing student behavior and engaging students in various types of learning activities from your work in Chapters 5 and 6. In Chapter 7, you gained ideas and techniques for assessing what students learned from your lessons.

Now, to help you put all this together into a coherent package that is practical in the reality of today's schools, turn to Chapter 8. Chapter 8 follows the experiences, thoughts, practices, disappointments, and successes of Casey Rudd as he embarks upon, engages in, and completes his first year as a mathematics teacher at a high school. Like you, Casey studied Chapters 1–7 of this text, and now he is discovering how to put what he learned into practice during his initial year in a difficult, but exciting, profession.

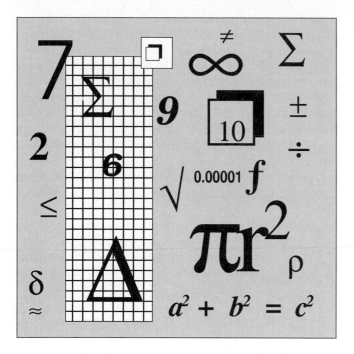

This chapter takes you through Casey Rudd's first year as a mathematics teacher as he learns to put research-based principles and techniques into practice. Chapter 8 will help you:

1. Given a realistic role description for a mathematics teacher in a school, formulate and explain alternative ways of fulfilling that role in a manner consistent with the suggestions in Chapters 1–7 of this text (*application*).
2. Explain how to integrate the various aspects of teaching mathematics (i.e., designing courses, organizing for a school year, managing a classroom, developing teaching units, managing student behavior, engaging students in learning activities, evaluating student achievement, and relating as a professional) into the role of a mathematics teacher during the course of a school year (*application*).
3. Anticipate and describe examples of the types of events and problems you are likely to confront while meeting your responsibilities as a mathematics teacher in a school (*conceptualization*).

CHAPTER 8

Theory into Practice: Casey Rudd, First-Year Mathematics Teacher

CASEY RUDD AND HIS FIRST TEACHING POSITION

Preservice Preparation

Casey Rudd, pictured in Exhibit 8.1, is embarking on his initial year as a professional mathematics teacher. Having recently graduated from college with a major in the teaching of mathematics at the secondary and middle school levels, he successfully completed more than a dozen college mathematics courses (including courses in calculus, analysis, abstract algebra, geometry, number theory, discrete structures, and statistics). However, hardly any of his college mathematics instructors employed the kind of teaching strategies that were recommended in his methods of teaching mathematics course—a course that used this textbook. Although confident in his ability to *do* mathematics, he worries that he lacks the conceptual and application levels of understanding necessary to generate the real-life examples and nonexamples that will engage his students in the kind of learning activities explained in Chapter 4 of this textbook.

A semester-long student-teaching experience provided some opportunities to try out many of the ideas from the mathematics methods course—primarily those from Chapter 6. However, in student teaching, Casey tailored his teaching style to the curriculum already established by his cooperating teacher. The cooperating teacher was very supportive of his efforts and immensely helpful in providing

Exhibit 8.1
Casey Rudd.

Exhibit 8.1
Casey Rudd.

as salary, teaching assignment, location, reputation, philosophy, personnel, and administrative style. To assess these variables, he had carefully read literature provided by school district personnel offices, read curriculum guides, counseled with trusted faculty from his college, carefully listened and raised questions at formal interviews with district personnel officials and school administrators, and sought out and conversed informally with potential faculty colleagues.

Among his reasons for favoring Malaker High were the following:

❏ He was impressed by the apparent competence and dedication of some of the mathematics teachers he met, especially Vanessa Castillo, who appeared willing to work cooperatively with him.
❏ Mathematics department chairperson Armond Ziegler, principal Harriet Adkins, and associate principal Jack Breaux all spoke as if the welfare of students were their first priority and the opinions of the faculty were both sought and utilized. They portrayed the attitude reflected in Ms. Adkins' words, "Teachers are here to help students. Administrators and supervisors are here to help teachers help students."
❏ His first-year assignment at Malaker High would include the teaching of a precalculus course each semester. At most of the other schools where he interviewed, such choice courses were the exclusive domain of the veteran teachers.

The Assignment

The Teaching Load

Exhibit 8.2 reflects Casey's year-long teaching load. Casey was somewhat concerned that his teaching assignment at Malaker included four different courses in a five-period load. The assignment at some of the other schools included multiple sections of the same course, so that he might have taught two sections of consumer mathematics and three sections of geometry. However, the precalculus assignment was especially appealing and he thought to himself, "It's unrealistic to expect to keep all the sections of the same course at the same level throughout the year. I still have to prepare differently for two different sections of the same course. Besides, it's the total number of students that influences workload far more than the number of courses."

Other Responsibilities

Besides teaching five classes per semester, Casey is expected to do the following:

learning materials and with her suggestions on managing behavior and organizing lessons. But opportunities to design complete units were quite limited as he was not involved in planning the courses prior to the opening of the school year.

Although enthusiastic about embarking on his professional career, Casey is understandably nervous about succeeding with a full complement of mathematics classes for which he is solely responsible.

Selecting a Position at Malaker High School

Even before graduation, Casey discovered that there was quite a demand for people with his qualifications to teach mathematics, and opportunities for positions in many school systems of virtually every variety were open to him. After interviewing for nine positions and being offered seven, he decided to accept an offer to join the faculty of Malaker High School. The decision was a function of variables such

Exhibit 8.2
Casey Rudd's first-year teaching schedule.

				Course Credits
First- and Second-Semester Schedule				
Class Period		**Assignment**	**Room**	**Per Semester**
Homeroom	8:10–8:25	10th grade—B	213	—
1st	8:30–9:25	Algebra I*	213	0.5
2nd	9:30–10:25	Preparation	—	—
3rd	10:30–11:25	Geometry*	213	0.5
4th	11:30–12:25	Geometry*	108	0.5
Lunch A	12:30–12:55	Lunch supervision	Lunch Room	—
Lunch B	1:00–1:25	Free	—	—
5th	1:30–2:25	Consumer math*	213	0.5
6th	2:30–3:25	Precalculus**	213	0.5
Announce-ments	3:25–3:30	—	213	—

*Two-semester course (one group of students both semesters)

**One-semester course (different group of students each semester)

❑ Serve as homeroom monitor and administrator to a group of 24 tenth graders.

❑ Serve as a general supervisor of students during school hours, enforcing school rules.

❑ Although free to eat lunch during the A lunch period, serve as a lunch room monitor during that time.

❑ Assist in the governance of the school by responding to administrators' requests for input and participating in both general faculty and mathematics department meetings.

❑ Cooperate in the school's system for both administrative supervision and instructional supervision of his own teaching and that of other teachers. (See Cangelosi (1991) for an extensive treatise on evaluating classroom instruction for purposes of both administrative and instructional supervision.)

❑ Participate in professional development activities (e.g., by attending in-service workshops, taking college courses, and being involved in organizations such as the local affiliate of NCTM).

❑ Represent Malaker High as a professional in the community.

In conversations with Armond Ziegler and Vanessa Castillo, Casey discussed the possibility of organizing a student mathematics club.

ORGANIZING FOR THE YEAR
The Situation as of July 15

With the opening day of school about 5 weeks away, Casey is given keys for the building and his home-base classroom (Room 213), a faculty handbook, a copy of the State Education Office's *Curriculum Guide for Mathematics,* the schedule in Exhibit 8.2, and for each of the assigned courses, a teacher's edition of the textbook. As part of his preservice experiences in college, Casey had conducted numerous mathematics lessons, but never before has he been responsible for organizing and preparing entire courses and a classroom for conducting business. He begins by surveying Room 213, for which he will be responsible, and then Room 108, the home base for a biology teacher and the classroom for his fourth-period geometry class. Exhibits 8.3 and 8.4 depict what he sees. He thinks: "Twelve computers available in my room; that leaves 11 for students if I reserve 1 exclusively for me. But there're none in Room 108, and with those fixed lab tables, 108 is just too inflexible for me to operate in there! . . . Why can't I use my own room for fourth period? I'll ask Armond if he can work something out and get that switched for me. For now, I should get my room arranged like I want. . . . But how do I want it arranged? I guess that depends on how I organize the

Exhibit 8.3
Room 213 when Casey first sees it.

Exhibit 8.4
Room 108.

courses—how much students need to use the computers and so forth—and how many students each period. Harriet said we won't get class rolls until the first week of school but that my classes should run between 20 and 25.

"So, I really need to get a better idea of how I want to organize the courses before worrying much more about the room. Of course, the room will also influence the courses—if there's no computers available for fourth period and I'm in an inflexible lab, that's going to limit what I can do for that geometry class.

"Armond said the textbooks are chosen for this year, but I'd have a say in the choice of some of the texts next year when there's supposed to be a turnover. . . . Might as well start going through these four texts and see what I've got to work with. . . ."

Over the next few days, Casey familiarizes himself with the textbooks and state curriculum guide, taking notes to be used in planning the courses. The curriculum guide simply lists goals to be covered in each course; the goals are quite consistent with the topics listed in the textbooks. He judges that the textbooks should be quite useful sources of exercises, examples, and definitions. But he notes that for most topics he won't be able to depend on them for conceptualization or application objectives. Overall, he's pleased that they seem to be more in line with the *Standards*-based approach he wants to implement than most other texts he's seen. His text for algebra I is titled *Merrill Algebra One* (Foster, Rath, and Winters 1986); for geometry, it's *Geometry with Applications and Problem Solving* (Clemens, O'Daffer, and Cooney 1984); for consumer mathematics, it's *Applying Mathematics: A Consumer/Career Approach* (Keedy, Smith, and Anderson 1986); and for precalculus, it's *Precalculus* (Elich and Cannon 1989).

Valuable Help from Colleagues

Discovering the Computer Lab

With Armond Ziegler, Casey raises the issue of scheduling his fourth-period geometry class in Room 213 instead of 108. Understanding of Casey's plight, Armond checks on the matter and finds out that 213 is the only room available fourth period that is large enough to accommodate a health science class. It seems that due to a new state-mandated health science requirement, a double section of more than 40 students will be using room 213, with extra desks brought in just for fourth period. Room 108 is too inflexible for extra desks to be brought in. Casey's panicky feelings over thoughts of this fourth-period onslaught on his home-base classroom are somewhat tempered during this conversation with Armond:

Armond: Why don't you have your students use the computer lab for some of your activities?

Casey: What computer lab?

Armond: I didn't realize no one told you about it. We have a room with 35 microcomputer stations and a dozen or so printers. It's available for student use from 7 to 8 in the mornings and 3:30 to 8 at night. During the school day, you can schedule a whole class in there on a first-come-first-serve basis. But no one class can use it more than one time in a week.

Casey: Really? I can't believe I missed it when I toured the school!

Armond: I should have made a point of showing it to you—it's in the basement. Most teachers don't even think about it, but a few— especially in business education—think of it as their exclusive domain.

Casey: What about the computer science classes? Don't they tie it up all day?

Armond: No, there's a special computer science classroom for most of their classes. You can arrange to hold a class in the lab with Mr. Tramonte in the library.

Casey: I'd better get my courses organized and decide what days I'll need it. You did say first come, first serve, didn't you?

Armond: Yes, but he won't put you on the schedule before August 10, the day the faculty is officially supposed to arrive. But it wouldn't be a bad idea at all to apprise him of your intentions to schedule classes periodically.

Casey: Thanks.

Discouraging Advice from Don Delaney

Buoyed by thoughts of how he might take advantage of the computer lab, Casey pursues the task of organizing his courses. He is sitting on the floor of his classroom with a box of odds and ends (e.g., pipes, wheels, measuring devices, dice, playing cards, string, and a barrel) thinking about introducing various teaching units with conceptual-level activities as Vanessa Castillo and Don Delaney enter. See Exhibit 8.5.

Vanessa: Casey, I'd like you to meet Don Delaney, another member of our mathematics department with whom you'll enjoy working.

Casey: Hello, Don, very nice to meet you.

Exhibit 8.5
Casey about to hear some discouraging advice from Don.

Don: So, you're the new man on the block! Welcome to Malaker High—glad to have you.

Vanessa: Don teaches algebra II and trigonometry—and I guess you've also got an algebra I like Casey this year.

Don: Right. . . . But what's all this stuff you've got here? Looks more like you teach shop than mathematics, Casey!

Casey: These are things I've been collecting to use as manipulatives for my conceptualization lessons.

Don: So you're another eager-beaver, fresh-out-of-college type who's going to try that discovery stuff! Look, take some advice from this veteran. I've been in this business for 9 years, and all that discovery stuff just wastes time and gets you in trouble.

Casey: What do you mean?

Don: Look, you don't need to know how a car works to be able to drive it. Mathematics works the same way. Students can learn how to do mathematics correctly without knowing why it works. You spend all that time trying to get them to discover and you never get around to covering the material. Only the really smart kids are capable of understanding why, and they'll learn that when they get to college.

Casey: So that's why you think this 'discovery stuff' wastes time. But how can it get me in trouble?

Don: In two ways. One, ever try to manage a class of students when they're all disorganized, running around measuring things and stuff? I've got perfect control of my classes; they stay in their seats with book, paper, pencil, and calculator—that's all they need!

Casey: And the second way?

Don: Look what you've got here—cards, dice, and a wine barrel . . . bring that into a mathematics class and you'll have parents coming down on you for encouraging their children to gamble and drink. You might have gotten away with that 15 years ago when teachers had some respect and authority—but now everything you do is questioned, so it's best not to try anything radical. Remember, this is a litigious society; there's a lawyer out there waiting to pick your pocket!

Casey: Ouch! I didn't think about that.

Don: Hey, we've got a close-knit department here; we look out for one another. All of us love the students and we love mathematics.

Casey: Well, thanks for the advice.

Don: Like, I said, welcome aboard. You'll really like it here. . . . You coming, Vanessa?

Vanessa: I'll meet you in the workroom in 15 minutes, I need to talk with Casey about a few things first.

Progressive but Pragmatic Advice from Vanessa Castillo

After Don leaves, Vanessa continues the conversation with Casey.

Vanessa: What'd you think about Don's advice to you?

Casey: He's a bit skeptical about how I think mathematics should be taught.

Vanessa: That's an understatement! Don's a super guy who loves to work with kids, but he's dead wrong about how to teach mathematics. I gave up trying to argue with him years ago—he'll never change because he lacks the conceptual basis for teaching any way other than to mimic his own teachers, some of whom he idolized. If I had said anything while he was giving you his standard line, we would have gotten into a useless debate, and I thought it was more important for you to hear what he had to say.

Casey: That I shouldn't teach for conceptualization?

Vanessa: Of course you should teach for conceptualization—as well as for simple knowledge, algorithmic skill, comprehension, application, creativity, and even at the affective level. But Don does have a message we should heed.

Casey: Which is?

Vanessa: Which is to start off conservatively. Discovery, inductive, and deductive lessons and all those other methods you and I know about *do* work—in fact, they're absolutely essential if mathematics is ever to be meaningful for our students. But, as a beginning teacher, you should not try to deviate too quickly from what these students are used to until you've had time to gain experiences trying out different strategies and seeing what works best for you and your students. In other words, don't try to teach every lesson with every class the 'right' way. For the first month or so of school, stick mostly to the textbooks, deviating from them and experimenting with your more progressive ideas more and more as you build upon your experiences. Before you know it, you'll have built a growing arsenal of ideas and materials and be teaching confidently as you know you should. Just give yourself time; don't expect too much of yourself too soon or you'll set yourself up for failure.

Casey: That's pretty heavy stuff you're laying on me!

Vanessa: Advice is cheap, even by the pound!

Casey: Then, I'll ask for a bit more. . . . I'm having a terrible time getting my courses planned and organized. I've gone through the books, looked at the available materials and facilities, and all that, but I just can't get a handle on the courses from A to Z. I can put together individual lessons, but I have trouble fitting the pieces together.

Vanessa: I know just what you mean, and I have a very definitive suggestion. For each course, begin writing a syllabus. Write it for the students to read. Being forced to describe the purposes and organization of a course for students' understanding will get you to organize your thoughts into a coherent whole. Not only do syllabi lend a businesslike air to your courses and serve as guides for students, but trying to write them lends structure to the process of organizing and planning the courses.

Planning and Organizing the Courses by Writing Syllabi

First-Period Algebra I

Taking Vanessa's advice, Casey sits at his computer outlining the course syllabus for his algebra I course with the aid of a word-processing program. He thinks: "This syllabus needs to be designed so that it sends the students the message that this class is serious business, and I'm serious enough about it to have it well organized and planned out. The syllabi my college instructors used tended to be full of formal-looking lists of reading references, content, deadlines, and grading criteria. I need some of that here, but I can't be too specific about dates and deadlines until I get into the course and see how things go. In college, there were also a couple of paragraphs providing a rationale for the course. I should have something like that, but I've got to keep in mind that I'm dealing with ninth and tenth graders here—there's the matter of reading level and the danger of turning them off with a long narrative.

"I need to think more about the purposes. . . . First, the syllabus should provide a guide for the course. Second, it needs to give them some idea about expectations—that includes things such as classroom rules—I don't want to forget that. Then, there's the business of getting the class off to a good start—set a businesslike tone, build some enthusiasm for algebra. And fourth, give them the impression I know what I'm doing—seeing a well-organized syllabus will give them that idea a lot better than me preaching to them about how important and organized this course is!

"I'll start with an outline of what to include: name of course, basic information such as my name and the room number, a rationale, what the course is all about, a listing of materials they need, classroom rules, an idea of what they'll be doing, goals of the course, and the bases for their grades. . . . Vanessa was right, writing this thing is going to force me to make some hard decisions that'll get me organizing this course!"

Further thought about how to format the syllabus leads Casey to an innovative idea. He decides to organize the syllabus around the questions that the document should answer for students—questions he would expect them to raise about the course. After another hour and a few false starts, he works with the following list of questions that will become the headings in the syllabus:

1. What is this course all about?
2. What is algebra?
3. Why should you learn algebra?
4. Are you ready to learn algebra?
5. With whom will you be working in this course?
6. Where will you be learning algebra?
7. How will you be expected to behave in this class?
8. What materials will you need for class?
9. What will you be doing for this class?
10. What will you learn from this class?
11. How will you know when you've learned algebra?
12. How will your grades for the course be determined?

Casey spends the next 2 days determining how to answer these 12 questions for his students and how to express the answers in the syllabus. The most taxing task is to address the tenth question, for which he has to determine the sequence of teaching units for the course and formulate a learning goal for each. He finds the "Teacher's Guide Supplement" to the textbook quite helpful in determining the units and in estimating the number of days and lessons for each. The 17 units about which he ultimately organizes the course correspond to but do not completely follow 15 of the textbook's 16 chapters.

Once Casey completes the syllabus, much of his anxiety about teaching algebra I evaporates and his enthusiasm for the school year intensifies. He feels prepared to go to work. The entire algebra I syllabus with the 17 unit titles is given in Appendix E. Please examine it now.

Third-Period Geometry

Pleased with the format of the algebra I syllabus appearing in Appendix E, Casey writes the geometry syllabus for his third-period class in a similar manner. As with the algebra I syllabus, Casey cannot include some details until arrangements such as scheduling the computer lab can be worked out. For example,

❏ He plans to assign ongoing, unit-long assignments that utilize computers. But the efficacy of such plans depend on the accessibility to computers. He's considering designating one day a week in which the class meets in the computer lab.

❏ After working out the sequence of teaching units, he notes a number of topics conducive to being taught in coordination with topics from other courses (e.g., a geometry unit on similarity with an art unit on perspective drawing). However, at this point, the syllabus cannot reflect such an effort until he can make arrangements with other teachers who also teach a major share of his students.

Fourth-Period Geometry

Because Casey uses word processing, it's a trivial matter to modify the geometry syllabus he wrote for third period so that it is personalized for the fourth period.

Fifth-Period Consumer Mathematics

Unlike the textbook for his other three courses, the consumer mathematics text is not generally organized around mathematical topics (e.g., applications of addition on rational numbers and applications of solving open sentences) but rather around consumer and career topics (e.g., earning money, housing, and taxes and insurance). He considers this arrangement inconsistent with the recommendations of the NCTM *Standards* and the way he thinks the course should be organized. However, being less comfortable with the content of the consumer mathematics course than he is with the other three courses, he doesn't want to organize the course so that he cannot depend on the textbook for examples and exercises.

Using advice from Vanessa, he patterns the teaching units so that the course will generally follow the book's sequence. However, he plans to build upon mathematical abilities, skills, and attitudes using the consumer and career topic headings primarily as motivation for learning the mathematics rather than as ends in themselves. The textbook's supplement for teachers includes a "Guide to Mathematical Skills" that Casey finds quite helpful in resolving the conflict between his ideal course orga-

nization and the organization of the book. The guide is somewhat similar to the "Guide to Integrated Topics" that accompanies the table of contents of this text you are now reading.

Casey plans for students to be working with computers and calculators in every unit.

Sixth-Period Precalculus

Casey expects that all his students for the one-semester precalculus course are planning to attend college and will have already completed courses in algebra I, geometry, algebra II, and trigonometry. Thus, he is not as concerned about using applications to real-life problems as a motivational strategy for engaging them in lessons as he is for students in the other courses. Compared with the other courses, he enjoys greater freedom in selecting content for the units for the following reasons:

❏ Topics listed in the district's curriculum guide for precalculus (e.g., exponential and logarithmic functions) are included in other Malaker High mathematics courses, primarily algebra II and trigonometry.

❏ From their experiences in previous courses, students should be familiar with the contents of the textbook's first three chapters. Those chapters are the only ones in the textbook upon which subsequent chapters depend. Thus, Casey does not feel bound to sequence units in the same order as the text's chapters.

❏ The text is designed for a year-long course. This allows Casey to select topics from a textbook menu that is larger than he needs.

As with geometry and consumer mathematics, Casey follows the same 12-question outline to write the precalculus syllabus he used in the algebra I syllabus (Appendix E). Unencumbered by many restrictions, Casey plans the course so that students will not only discover and invent mathematics within well-defined content areas (as will also be the case in the other courses) but will also have ample opportunities to pursue unanticipated mathematical topics. Inserted throughout the textbook are exercises entitled "Explore and Discover." Casey believes these and other activities he plans will interest students in problems leading them into areas of mathematics students choose for themselves. Here is an example of one of the Explore and Discover exercises (Elich and Cannon 1989, 127):

Suppose function f is given by $f(n) = \sqrt{24n + 1}$, where the domain of f is the set of positive integers. Make a table of values of $f(n)$ for several values of n. From the numbers in your table arrive at a guess for each of the following.

a. For what n is $f(n)$ an integer?

b. For those values of $f(n)$ that are integers, is $f(n)$ always a prime number?

c. Except for 2 and 3, does every prime number occur somewhere in the listing of $f(n)$?

d. State any other guesses about $f(n)$ you might observe.

Believing that the key to understanding calculus is the conceptualization and application of the concept of *limit of a function,* Casey feels that this course should provide students with a conceptual basis for understanding limits, which they'll need before being introduced to the formal definition of a limit when they take calculus. Casey knows that most calculus courses have an *algorithmic* rather than a *conceptual* focus, so he wants to make sure students get conceptual-level and application-level experiences working with limits at least informally. Noting that the textbook does not include a formal treatise on limits, avoiding the term *limit* altogether, Casey decides to select topics from the textbook for the units (e.g., partial sums of sequences) that will involve students in conceptualizing and applying limits without needing to define the term *limit* formally in the conventional ϵ, δ sense.

Organizing the Classroom

With his course syllabi in hand, Casey is anxious for the opening day of school still 2 weeks away. To begin organizing his classroom and working out a management plan for the year, he retrieves the textbook from the mathematics teaching methods course he took in college (the book you are now reading). Turning to page 131, he carefully responds to each of the 15 questions under "Classroom Organization and Ongoing Routines," to the nine questions under "One-Time Only Tasks," and to the three questions under "Reminders for the First Week's Learning Activities."

After a week of planning and organizing, he has those questions resolved and room 213 now appears very similar to Mr. Haimowitz's room depicted in Exhibit 2.20. Unfortunately, he doesn't control room 108, and it still appears as indicated by Exhibit 8.4.

Setting Up the System of Item Pool Files

Casey sets up his system for maintaining item pool files on his computer. He begins with one disk per course, with a file for each unit and a subfile for each objective. He can begin writing items only for the

first two units of each course because, at this point, those are the only units for which he has formulated objectives. However, he has the system ready to accept new objectives and new items for every unit as he develops them during the course of the school year. Casey is pleased to see that he will be able to draw many of the knowledge-of-a-process and, with some minor modifications (e.g., adding extraneous data), application-level items from tests contained in the teacher's supplements accompanying his textbooks. However, he realizes he will have to originate the vast majority of items for the conceptualization objectives.

Arrangements and Acquisitions

Although he spends much of the week before classes begin in meetings (e.g., a 5-hour orientation meeting for all new teachers in the district and meetings of the school faculty and the mathematics department), Casey finds time to do the following:

❏ Visit with Mr. Tramonte, working out schedules and procedures for using the computer lab. Casey reserves the lab for his fourth-period geometry class every Wednesday during the year. Mr. Tramonte also gives him a schedule of times each week during which Casey can send as many as six students into the lab to do independent work during class time. As Armond had indicated, the lab is open to students and faculty for an hour before school and from 3:30 to 8 after school.

❏ Learn the "ropes" for obtaining supplies and equipment for his classroom at Malaker High. Surprising as it may seem, one of the more frustrating hindrances to classroom effectiveness faced by first-year teachers is the inability to obtain equipment and supplies for their classrooms (Duke, Cangelosi, and Knight 1988). Each school seems to have a unique process to expedite such matters as obtaining colored chalk, replacing a burned-out lamp in an overhead projector, gaining access to a video recorder, and replacing lost books. Usually, it's a matter of identifying and befriending the right secretary or other staff member who knows how to get things done. Veteran teachers take such matters for granted and don't usually think to inform beginning teachers of this informal network. Fortunately, Casey asked Vanessa about the process before wasting time going through formal channels.

❏ Coordinate plans with other teachers, including the following:

Mr. Bosnick, an art teacher, agrees to have students apply geometric principles they learn from Casey to art projects.

Ms. Deere, an English teacher, and Casey plan a joint project in which students will use skills and principles developed in both consumer mathematics and communications classes to produce videotape presentations.

Casey shows some of the other mathematics teachers how to set up a computerized item pool system, and they agree to share test items.

THE BEGINNING OF AN EVENTFUL SCHOOL YEAR

Opening Day

Casey bases plans for the first day's classes on the model exemplified by Mr. Krebs in Vignette 5.4. However, unlike Mr. Krebs, Casey does not prepare videotape presentations. For each class, he prepares name cards and a questionnaire–task sheet for students to work on as soon as they are seated in the classroom. The questionnaire–task sheets for the four courses are shown in Exhibits 8.6–8.9.

Casey designed the questionnaire–task sheets with the following purposes in mind:

❑ The students will immediately get busy working with mathematics while he takes care of some administrative chores (e.g., distributing textbooks). This, he feels, will help to establish the businesslike classroom learning environment that he read about in Chapter 5 of this text.

❑ The students will be both successful and challenged by the tasks. The algebra students, for example, already know how to add simple fractions, but they've never before had to describe the process they use. Also, most of the items involve expressing opinions, describing observations, and reporting about themselves—things everyone *can* do, but which require thinking.

❑ The students will begin to get the following impressions about the course they're starting under Mr. Rudd's direction:

The mathematics they will learn is related to their own individual interests.

They are expected to make judgments, and those judgments are valued.

They are expected to write about mathematics.

Their experiences in this course will be different from those they've had in previous courses.

❑ Students will pursue tasks that they will learn to accomplish more efficiently via mathematics that's planned for subsequent lessons in the course.

❑ Casey will be able to utilize students' responses to the items in sessions for helping students understand the nature of the course's mathematical content. This will be done in two ways:

As he discusses the course syllabus with the class, he will pick up on their responses as he addresses the question, What is algebra (geometry, consumer mathematics, precalculus)?

In subsequent lessons, he will occasionally make reference to their responses to this questionnaire–task sheet.

❑ Casey will make use of information gained from responses to the last item in planning lessons (e.g., to select topics for problems that are of interest to students).

Just before each class, Casey places a name card and a questionnaire–task sheet on each student's desk. The 55-minute period is spent as follows:

1. He greets students at the door as they enter and directs each to locate the desk with his or her name card and to begin completing the questionnaire–task sheet.
2. As students answer the questions and work on the tasks, Casey distributes textbooks and course syllabi and takes roll.
3. All students have an opportunity to work on the tasks, but no one completes them before Casey interrupts the work and goes through the course syllabus (see Appendix E). He uses the sections of the syllabus as an advanced organizer for an interactive lecture session in which he communicates expectations, introduces some classroom procedures, and discusses the nature of mathematics. The students' work on the questionnaire–task sheet is utilized in discussions stimulated by the second section of the syllabus (i.e., what is algebra, geometry, consumer mathematics, or precalculus?). For example:

❑ In the algebra class, he uses students' responses to set the stage for working with variables and generalizing rules of arithmetic.
❑ Modifying an idea he picked up from reading Vignette 5.4, Casey uses students' descriptions of figures in the photographs of Exhibit 8.7 to explain the focus of geometry.
❑ He raises the types of personalized problems the consumer mathematics students will be learning to solve throughout the course.
❑ With the precalculus class, he uses the peeking-through-a-keyhole tasks to explain

Exhibit 8.6
Questionnaire–task sheet Casey
uses with his algebra I class on the
first day of school.

1. What is your name? _____

2. How many minutes does it take to listen to a Rock Top-40–type song from beginning to end?

_____

3. How many minutes does it take to listen to a Rock Top-40–type song six times from beginning to end?

_____

4. How many minutes does it take to listen to six different Rock Top-40–type songs from beginning to end?

_____

5. Simplify each of the following (showing two steps along the way):

$\frac{3}{7} + \frac{2}{3}$ _____ _____ _____

$\frac{2}{5} + \frac{1}{3}$ _____ _____ _____

$\frac{1}{5} + \frac{3}{4}$ _____ _____ _____

Now, use the space just below to write a *description* of the process you used to find the three simplified sums of fractions just given. Do *not* use the names of any specific numbers (such as 3/7, 3, or 7) in your description. Describe the *general* process you use for adding any two fractions like the ones above.

> Your description of the process:
>
>
>
>
>
>

6. Fill in the blank with one of the numbers that makes the following statement true:

$$7 - \underline{\hspace{2cm}} > 3$$

The number you put in the blank is not the *only* one that will work. But not just any number will work. Make up a rule for choosing a number for the blank that makes the statement true. Write the rule in here:

> Your rule for picking a number that works:
>
>
>
>
>

7. Make a list of 10 important questions about which you're going to have to make a decision during the next 9 months:

a. _____

b. _____

c. _____

d. _____

e. _____

f. _____

g. _____

h. _____

i. _____

j. _____

Exhibit 8.7
Questionnaire–task sheet Casey uses with his geometry class on the first day of school.

1. What is your name? _____

2. Carefully look at the photograph of the two trees. Write a *description* of how one tree looks different from the other.

_____
_____
_____

Write a *description* of how the two trees look the same.

_____
_____
_____
_____

3. Carefully look at the photograph of the two people. Write a *description* of how one of the people looks different from the other.

_____
_____
_____

Write a *description* of how the two people look the same.

_____
_____
_____
_____

what he terms the "keyhole logic" of mathematics, in which we use our intellects to expand what we know beyond what we empirically observe.

4. Casey assigns homework that includes the completion of the questionnaire–task sheet.

Casey is generally pleased with how the first day goes. The students seem willing to cooperate, the vast majority of them acting friendly and trying to follow his directions. After the first few minutes of each period, his nervousness disappears and he surprises himself with his own glibness—fluently speaking and making the "right" responses to students' questions and behaviors. His energy level and enthusiasm peaks in the second half of each class.

Because many students are reluctant to fill out the questionnaire–task sheets on their own without seemingly constant explanations and feedback from

Exhibit 8.7 continued

4. Carefully look at the photograph of the two balls. Write a *description* of how one ball looks different from the other.

_____
_____
_____

Write a *description* of how the two balls look the same.

_____
_____
_____
_____

5. Carefully look at the photograph of the two kites. Write a *description* of how one of the kites looks different from the other.

_____
_____
_____

Write a *description* of how the two kites look the same.

_____
_____
_____

6. Make a list of 10 important questions about which you're going to have to make a decision during the next 9 months.

a. _____
b. _____
c. _____
d. _____
e. _____
f. _____
g. _____
h. _____
i. _____
j. _____

Casey, in every class the administrative duties take longer than he had planned. Thus, no class gets through its syllabus and Casey fears that the students are left "hanging" at the end of the period without understanding course expectations and the meaning of algebra, geometry, consumer mathematics, or precalculus. He is especially anxious to meet with them on the second day to finish explaining the syllabi and get back on schedule.

Casey concludes that teaching in Room 108 won't be so bad after all. Fourth period goes especially well. However, after supervising lunch and arriving back in his own room just prior to fifth period, he discovers that the fourth-period health science class left the room in disarray. The consumer mathematics class gets off to a rough start and he appears flustered because he is unable to get the room back in order and the materials laid out by 1:30. The students don't appear surprised by the disorder nor do they seem to mind it. In fact, some of the students in his other classes are surprised by how well he has things organized.

Exhibit 8.8
Questionnaire–task sheet Casey uses with his consumer mathematics class on the first day of school.

1. What is your name? _____

2. What is something you bought during the month of August?

   _____

   Where did you buy it? _____
   About how much did it cost? _____
   Why did you make this purchase? _____

   When you decided to buy this thing, did you consider other options (like buying something else or another brand or not buying anything at all)? Describe the options.

   _____
   _____
   _____

   How do you know whether or not you selected the best option?

   _____
   _____
   _____

3. When people are deciding on objects to buy, what are some of the things they can do to figure out how to get the most for their money?

   _____
   _____
   _____
   _____

4. Suppose you're thinking about taking a job selling clothes in a store. Would you rather earn a salary that pays you by the number of hours you work or a salary based on the amount of sales you make?

   _____
   _____

   How would you go about finding out which way you would make more money?

   _____
   _____
   _____
   _____

Learning from Experiences

Becoming More Assertive

The ensuing weeks provide Casey with the richest learning experiences of his life. Possibly the most important lesson is that he must be *assertive* to be successful.

Casey discovers early on the need to be assertive with his colleagues. For example, just before the second day's homeroom period, Casey visits with Ms. Bomgars, who teaches the fourth-period health science class in Room 213. Casey wants to discuss the problem her class created for him yesterday, but he would rather discuss it out of earshot of her homeroom students, who are now milling around the room.

Casey: Hello, Ms. Bomgars, do you have a minute to talk?

Ms. Bomgars: Of course, Mr. Rudd—always glad to meet with a colleague! What can I do for you?

Casey: It's about your fourth-period class using Room 213. Could we step away from these students to discuss a problem I had yesterday with the room?

Ms. Bomgars: Oh, don't worry about these kids; they're not interested in what we're saying. What's your problem?

Casey: Well, it took me a long time to get the room ready yesterday for my fifth-period consumer mathematics class.

Ms. Bomgars: I thought all you math guys needed was a piece of chalk and you're ready!

Casey: (Laughing with Ms. Bomgars) That's a common misconception, but really, I'd appreciate if you could—

A student comes up, interrupting Casey by asking Ms. Bomgars a question. She answers the student and they briefly converse as Casey waits.

Ms. Bomgars: Excuse me, Mr. Rudd—it's always something. You were saying?

Exhibit 8.8 continued

5. In your opinion, who is currently the most successful singer in the world?

_____

Name another popular singer who one of your friends might argue with you should have been named in the above blank:

_____

Defend why you think the singer you chose is more successful than your friend's choice. Write out your argument in the blanks below:

_____
_____
_____
_____

6. Suppose you are going to be saving money over the next few years to buy something really expensive (like a CD player, motorcycle, or car). Where should you keep the money you save until you're ready to make the purchase—in a savings account, checking account, secure safe, in a bank at your home, in U.S. bonds, or where? Describe how you might go about making this decision for yourself.

_____
_____
_____
_____
_____

7. Make a list of 10 important questions about which you're going to have to make a decision during the next 9 months.
   a. _____
   b. _____
   c. _____
   d. _____
   e. _____
   f. _____
   g. _____
   h. _____
   i. _____
   j. _____

Casey: I'd really appreciate it if you could have your students put things back as they were when they came into the room.

Ms. Bomgars: We took all the extra chairs we brought in with us when we left. Were some left in?

Casey: No, that was great. It's just that—

Another student interrupts; because the bell is about to ring, Casey interrupts the student to say, "Excuse me, Ms. Bomgars, I've got to get to my homeroom."

Ms. Bomgars: Thanks for coming by—I'm glad to help you out any way I can.

Casey: Thank you, I appreciate it.

The room is in no better shape when Casey arrives for fifth period than it was the first day; the problem persists for the remainder of the week. Realizing that he failed to tell Ms. Bomgars what he wanted out of fear of stimulating ill feelings, Casey is angry at himself for not communicating assertively.

Over the weekend he phones Ms. Bomgars:

Ms. Bomgars: Hello.

Casey: Hello, Marilyn, this is Casey Rudd. We spoke just before your homeroom Tuesday.

Ms. Bomgars: Oh, hi, Casey. How are things going?

Casey: Some things are going very well, others aren't. We still have a problem to solve regarding sharing my classroom. I'd really like to meet with you in the room so we can work out a solution.

Ms. Bomgars: What's the matter?

Casey: It would be best if we met in the classroom where I can show you exactly.

Ms. Bomgars: You want to meet on Monday?

Casey: It has to be at a time when students won't be there to interrupt us. I can give you a

Exhibit 8.9 (pp. 254–256)
Questionnaire–task sheet Casey uses with his precalculus class on the first day of school.

1. What is your name? _____

2. Suppose that you are by yourself in this unfamiliar building. You're in a hallway and come to a door. Before opening the door, you want to know what's on the other side. Fortunately, it's one of those old doors with the kind of keyholes you can look through. You peek through the keyhole and you see what appears in the picture below. *Describe* exactly what you *see* through the keyhole—and only what you can actually see.

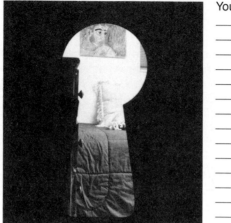

Your description: _____

_____

_____

_____

_____

_____

_____

_____

_____

_____

_____

_____

_____

Now, *describe* what you would *infer* the room behind the door looks like based on the limited view you had through the keyhole.

_____

_____

_____

_____

3. Now you've arrived at the outside of another door. Again, you look through the keyhole. *Describe* exactly what you *see* through this keyhole as pictured below.

Your description: _____

_____

_____

_____

_____

_____

_____

_____

_____

_____

_____

_____

_____

ride to school if you want to meet today or tomorrow—or Monday at 7:30 would be okay too.

Ms. Bomgars: You seem pretty serious, I'd better meet you today. But, you don't need to pick me up, I might as well stay a while and get some work done while I'm there. Would an hour from now be okay?

Casey: That would be great. See you in my room in an hour. Thank you very much.

Ms. Bomgars: Good-bye, Casey.

Casey: Good-bye, Marilyn.

Now that Ms. Bomgars understands that Casey is serious about the two of them solving what she now perceives as her problem as well as his, she is

Exhibit 8.9 continued

Now, *describe* what you would *infer* the room behind the door looks like based on the limited view you had through the keyhole:

_____

_____

_____

_____

4. According to a particular hospital's records, the number of people treated in the emergency room for drug-induced traumas were as follows for the year 1991:

Jan: 31	Apr: 40	Jul: NA	Oct: 37
Feb: 33	May: 39	Aug: 48	Nov: 35
Mar: NA	Jun: 45	Sep: NA	Dec: 34

("NA" indicates records not available for that month)

Does the given data suggest any possible pattern relative to the relation between frequency of drug-induced traumas and the time of the year? Explain your answer:

_____

_____

_____

Based on the data, what would you guess the records for March, July, and September would show if the records for those months were available? Explain the reasons for your answer.

_____

_____

_____

Estimate the total number of drug-induced traumas treated at that hospital's emergency room during 1991. Explain how you arrived at your estimate.

_____

_____

_____

5. Estimate the area of the rectangular region in terms of the number of ☐ units:

Your estimate: _____

---

very receptive to Casey's explanations of just how the room should be left after fourth period. In the classroom, Casey readily points out exactly what he expects. Casey is pleased with the agreed-to arrangement and the way Ms. Bomgars leaves the room for the rest of the semester.

Casey also learns to communicate assertively with parents. After school one day in the hallway, Casey passes one of his algebra students, Alphonse, walking with his father:

Casey: Hello, Alphonse.
Alphonse: Hi, Mr. Rudd. Mr. Rudd, this is my dad.
Casey: Hello, Mr. Oldham, I'm Casey Rudd, very nice to meet you.

Exhibit 8.9 continued

6. Estimate the area of the rectangular region below in terms of the number of ☐ units:

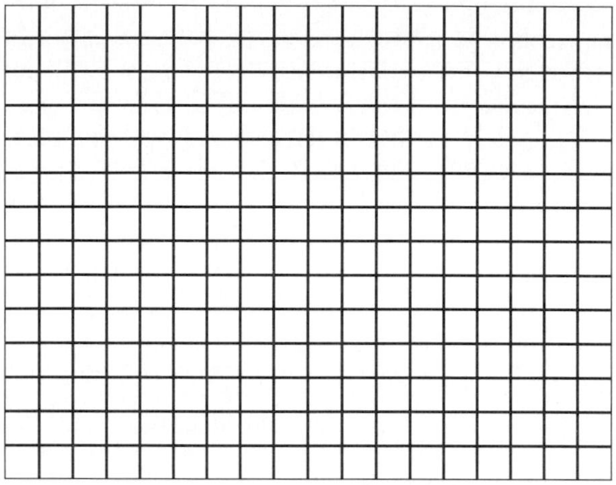

Your estimate:_____

7. Estimate the area of the region below in terms of the number of ☐ units:

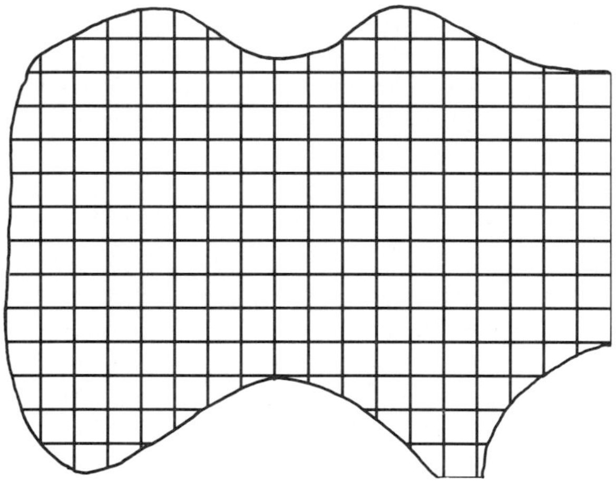

Your estimate:_____

8. Make a list of 10 important questions you're going to have to make a decision about during the next nine months:
a. _____
b. _____
c. _____
d. _____
e. _____
f. _____
g. _____
h. _____
i. _____
j. _____

Mr. Oldham: So you're Alphonse's algebra teacher. You know, I tell my kids all the time . . . subjects like algebra and Latin—where you have to memorize—those are the subjects where you discipline the mind. Study algebra, and you can make yourself do anything. Just because you don't use it much, they don't want to learn it like the frilly subjects—but a man needs to discipline his mind with stuff like algebra. It does for the mind what football does for the body! Isn't that right, Mr. Rudd; you tell him.

Smiling broadly at Mr. Oldham but quickly thinking to himself, "If only I had stayed in my room another 20 seconds, I would have avoided this dilemma. On one hand, Mr. Oldham has the best of intentions and I'm happy he's encouraging Alphonse to study algebra. He's trying to support my efforts and I really appreciate that. On the other hand, he's sending all the wrong signals about the value of algebra. I don't want Alphonse to believe what he's saying, but then I hate to contradict what a father says in front of his child!" Not wanting to appear insulting, Casey only continues to smile and says, "I agree that algebra is surely important for everyone to learn. It's a pleasure meeting you, Mr. Oldham. Thank you for introducing me to your father, Alphonse."

The next day in algebra class, during a discussion about using open sentences to solve real-life problems, Alphonse says, "Yeah, but the real purpose of algebra is to train your memory. That's what my dad says, and Mr. Rudd agreed with him yesterday."

After diplomatically attempting to correct the record about his beliefs relative to the purpose of algebra, Casey resolves to be more assertive in communicating with parents and in responding to misconceived statements about mathematics.

Fortunately, Casey's resolve is still fresh in his mind as he meets with Ms. Minnifield about her daughter Melinda's work in geometry:

Ms. Minnifield: You know, Melinda really has a lot of respect for you, she raves about your class. That's why I thought you should be the one to help me with this problem.

Casey: What problem?

Ms. Minnifield: Well, Melinda's got herself involved with this boy, who's much too old for her. She keeps seeing him even though she knows I don't like it.

Casey: I can see you're concerned.

Ms. Minnifield: I thought since she likes geometry so much, I could use that to get her to break it off.

Casey: I'm not following you.

Ms. Minnifield: Well, you know how math is harder for girls than boys. I told her if she kept spending time with this boy, she was going to do bad in geometry. That's why girls don't do good in math because they get all goo-goo over boys. . . . Do you see what I mean?

Casey: Not really, ma'am, but please go on.

Ms. Minnifield: Well, I thought you could back me up on this—tell her she's going to flunk if she doesn't spend more time studying geometry and less time fooling around with the boy.

Casey: Ms. Minnifield, I really appreciate you sharing your idea with me, and I appreciate your concern for Melinda's welfare. . . . You, being Melinda's parent, know far more about this situation than I. I'll confine my remarks to what I do know about. First of all, research studies clearly point out that girls do *not* have any more trouble learning mathematics than boys. It's a common misconception that they do, but they absolutely don't.

Ms. Minnifield: But I had always heard that.

Casey: If you're interested, I can give you some articles that explain the facts about girls and women in mathematics.

Ms. Minnifield: Oh, that would be nice of you.

Casey: Second, and more to the point here, my job is to teach Melinda and the other students mathematics as professionally and responsibly as possible. I cannot in good conscience base Melinda's grade on anything other than how well she achieves the goals of the geometry course.

Ms. Minnifield: Well, I thought if you just told her, she'd listen.

Casey: I'm flattered that Melinda would have that much confidence in what I say. But if I start lying to her, I'll lose her confidence.

Ms. Minnifield: I don't mean for you to lie to her.

Casey: I know, Ms. Minnifield. You want what's best for your daughter.

In his classroom, Casey encourages more interaction about mathematics than his students had been used to previously. Early in the year, some students tended to take advantage of their "freedom of expression" by drifting off the current topic. Casey, not wanting to alienate students or to discourage communications about mathematics, allowed some of the discussions to waste valuable class time. For instance, during a precalculus class, the difference between "negative x" and "x is negative" is being discussed.

Opal: If x is negative, then x has to be less than 0. But negative x could be a positive number.

Bernie: That's too picky. It's like in Spanish class, what's the difference between *temar* and *temer*? Mr. Waiters makes such a big deal over whether you say *ar* or *er*! Who cares?

Rita: It gives him something to grade you on!

Bernie: It's not fair that we have to . . . .

The discussion continues in this vein for several more minutes, with Casey worrying about the appropriateness of Mr. Waiters being the topic of conversation and about time needing to be spent on the topic at hand.

After a few similar experiences, Casey resolves to be more assertive in such situations, and in subsequent weeks he is more likely to respond as he does in the following instance. During a geometry lesson about applying triangle congruence theorems to real-life situations, this conversation takes place:

Eric: In basketball, there's a strategy you call the three-person game, in which you form a triangle. The triangle should be equilateral.

Casey: Yes, Damien.

Damien: Who cares about basketball? Eric's always got to talk about basketball. It's stupid!

Casey: Eric?

Eric: You've got to be better to play basketball than to—

Casey: Do not debate your opinions about basketball in here today. Even those that don't like basketball can learn something about equilateral triangles from Eric's example of the three-person strategy. Please repeat your example, Eric, without defending your opinion about basketball.

Addressing Behavior-Management Problems

It is in meeting his most challenging responsibilities of keeping students on-task and responding to off-task behaviors that Casey finds the greatest need to be assertive. At times he resents having constantly to work to maintain students' interest and teach students who tend to get off-task to be on-task. He begins what turns out to be a productive conversation with Vanessa with an expression of his frustration.

Casey: Some days, I'd just love to walk into class and just discuss mathematics without having to worry about Frankie over in the corner, who is going to fall asleep unless I'm either right on top of her or we're discussing a problem that strikes within the limited range of what she fancies! Or just once, getting through a lesson without having to deal with Brad's showing off or Christi's yakking with anyone who'll listen to her—wouldn't that be nice?

Vanessa: Obviously, you've had one of *those* days!

Casey: It's just that we were getting into our first formal proof in third period today, and they seemed so enthusiastic. But then they started to get a little noisy—some off-task talking. I let it go at first because I didn't want to put a damper on their enthusiasm. Then, it was real obvious that Christi and Livonia's conversation had nothing to do with

geometry—right in the middle of my explanation!

Vanessa: What did you do?

Casey: I kept on explaining the theorem, and just moved over to them and caught their eyes—that usually works for me.

Vanessa: And it didn't this time?

Casey: Oh, the two of them stopped as long as I stood there, but then other conversations broke out, and Christi and Livonia started up again as soon as I moved away. . . . Five minutes later, I'd had enough and made the mistake of threatening the class.

Vanessa: What'd you say?

Casey: I told them if they didn't pipe down, they'd be sorry when the test came around. I knew that wasn't the best thing to say, but the noise just got to me, and I reacted.

Vanessa: Did they quiet down?

Casey: Yes, but then Brad whispered something to Lin-Tau, who started giggling. That's when I jumped on them calling Brad a show-off. . . . In other words, I handled it all wrong and made matters worse.

Vanessa: So, you weren't Mr. Perfect. You let things go too far and reacted with hostility instead of assertiveness—the way most of us react when things go too far.

Casey: But I know better. I applied none of the stuff that's worked for me in the past—assertiveness, descriptive language, reinforcement principles all out the window!

Vanessa: I don't think you threw your principles out of the window; I think you waited too long to respond decisively. Most teachers wait until they are too near their threshold for tolerating noise or other annoyances before dealing with students being off-task.

Casey: You're saying I should have stepped in and dealt with the early minor incidences before things escalated. I was passive in the beginning instead of being assertive. Then things got out of hand.

Vanessa: And when things get out of hand, it's natural to be hostile.

Casey: And that's really why I'm upset—at my own hostile behavior. I'm afraid I've lost some of the control and good will I've worked to build up to this point. I don't have much enthusiasm for tomorrow's class.

Vanessa: What do you have planned?

Casey: Before this, I was going to continue the session on proofs.

Vanessa: I think you have two choices. You either go on with your original plan and conduct the class as if none of this had happened—but have an alternate plan ready to go to as soon as they become uncooperative—you know, one where they have to work on their own while you monitor their every move.

Casey: Yeah, I know what you mean. There was an example of that in my mathematics methods book from college. [See Vignette 5.27.]

Vanessa: The second choice is to start the period off expressing your feelings about what happened, even indicating that you're disappointed in your own behavior for letting things go too far and then acting with hostility as a result. But if you use this tactic, make sure assertively to demand their cooperation. If it turns out you don't get it even after clearing the air, then go immediately to the alternative lesson plan.

Throughout the year, Vanessa and Casey regularly share ideas on handling discipline problems as well as on other aspects of teaching. They even work out a plan by which Casey can send a student who behaves uncooperatively to Vanessa for custodial care until the end of the class period. Casey reciprocates by providing the same service for Vanessa.

Benefiting from Instructional Supervision

Instructional supervision is the art of helping teachers improve their teaching performances (Cangelosi 1991, 6–7; Cooper 1984, 1–2). Vanessa serves as an instructional supervisor for Casey by sharing ideas on planning, managing student behavior, and other aspects of instruction. Working with Casey not only helps his classroom effectiveness, it also benefits Vanessa's teaching because conferring with Casey forces her to analyze problem situations and reflect on instructional activities more than she would otherwise. As the year progresses and Casey's confidence soars, Casey more and more serves as an instructional supervisor for Vanessa as well. Consistent with research findings relative to instructional supervisory practices, Casey and Vanessa's cooperative partnership provides them with the most effective type of help with their teaching (Bang-Jensen 1986; Brandt 1989).

Accustomed to sharing ideas with Vanessa from his first day at Malaker, Casey seeks and listens comfortably to suggestions from other instructional supervisors as well (e.g., other teachers, his department head, principal, and the district mathematics teaching supervisor). Casey does not always agree with or take suggestions he receives; however, every one stimulates ideas he uses for everything from coping with individual differences among students to eliciting parents' cooperation on back-to-school night.

Casey's most frustrating problem is finding enough time to do what he considers necessary for optimal classroom effectiveness. The following exchange with Armond Ziegler, mathematics department head, helps.

Casey: There are so many things I ought to be doing but never get around to!

Armond: Like what?

Casey: I need to develop enrichment materials for some students who are ahead of the rest of the class. And there are parents I should be contacting. I haven't been entering items into my item pool file as regularly as I should. I—

Armond: Okay, slow down! I hear you. You have to realize that it's impossible to do everything you want to or should do. Make some difficult decision and partition your time. Prioritize from what you *must* do—like sleep, eat, and show up for class—to what's critical, down to what you really want to do but could put off, and then finally to what isn't all that important. Put a high priority on things that will help you save time down the road—like keeping up with that item pool file. Neglect something else instead.

Casey: I try to keep to a schedule, but then students come in for tutoring, and then—wham!—time I scheduled for formulating examples for class is used up!

Armond: Don't allow it to happen; take control. You wouldn't drop in on a lawyer or doctor without an appointment. Don't let your clients do that to you.

Casey: What clients?

Armond: Your students are your clients, but don't let parents, colleagues, or administrators abuse your schedule either.

Casey: What about you? Should I tell you to buzz off when you ask me to turn in my supply order while I'm in the midst of scoring tests?

Armond: (Laughing with Casey) You're welcome to tell me to buzz off, but I'd be less hostile and more assertive when you send Harriet [the principal] packing—actually, she'll respect your businesslike approach, seeing how you've got your time scheduled.

Casey: But everything can't be scheduled. Unanticipated things have to be taken care of.

Armond: Of course they do, but get a calendar anyway and use it as an organizational tool for your convenience—not something you blindly follow.

Casey: Today is a case in point. I planned to phone a couple of parents during the B lunch period, but then we were short a supervisor, so

I had to stay that period besides my usual A lunch period.

Armond: Those are times when I take a 'triage' approach. I decide where my time can be most efficiently spent. Some crises are beyond our reasonable control and others can wait.

Casey: So now, I have to find the time to schedule my time!

Preparing for Administrative Supervision

Instructional supervision is concerned solely with improving classroom practice. On the other hand, *administrative supervision* is concerned with quality control (Cangelosi 1991, 163–173). Malaker High and school district administrators are responsible for determining whether or not Casey teaches well enough to be retained as a teacher and given incentives to remain on Malaker High's faculty. The district has an administrative supervisory program, in which the classroom instructional practices of each beginning teacher are evaluated three times a year. The outcomes of these evaluations hinge primarily on observational data gathered by a team composed of the school principal, the district subject supervisor, and a same-subject teacher from another school.

Vanessa helps Casey prepare for the scheduled visits from his observational team by doing the following:

❑ Advising him to use preobservational conferences to apprise team members of the instructional strategies they can anticipate seeing him employ.
❑ Suggesting that it is appropriate to utilize postobservational conferences not only for learning from the team's report but also to express his own needs regarding support services from the administration.
❑ Simulating a team visit, with Vanessa playing the role of the team in a preobservational conference, an in-class observation (during one of her nonteaching periods), and in a postobservational conference.

In anticipation of the team's visits, Casey is quite nervous. However, after the first few minutes of the first in-class observation, he relaxes and learns to enjoy the attention. It helps that he thinks of his visitors as colleagues whose goals of helping students learn mathematics are the same as his own. Although he feels the team never sees him at his best, his performances receive better than satisfactory ratings and his confidence continues to rise.

SAMPLE ALGEBRA I TEACHING UNIT
Designing a Unit on Factoring Polynomials

Ten weeks have elapsed since the opening day of school. Casey's algebra I class is in the early stages of Unit 6, "Polynomials." Casey anticipates the class beginning Unit 7, "Factoring Polynomials," in 2 weeks. He starts designing Unit 7.

It's nearly 10 P.M. as Casey sits in front of his computer. Strewn about are the algebra I course syllabus, algebra I textbook, reference books, a calculator, paper, pens, pencils, and his teaching notebook. Since August, as ideas occur to him that might be useful in future lessons, he jots them down in this teaching notebook. He reads the goal of Unit 7:

> Understands why certain factoring algorithms work and can use them in problem solving.

He thinks: "I need to define this goal with objectives. . . . Let's see, why do I want to teach them about factoring polynomials in the first place? . . . Primarily because they need to know how to factor and why factoring works in order to learn how to find roots of higher-degree equations, inequalities, and functions. . . . So this unit should really emphasize conceptualization of why certain algorithms work and development of skills with the algorithm. The real application comes in units 8, 9, and so forth. . . . But I better build at least one application objective in here, or I'll lose them before they even get to Unit 8.

"Okay, so I'll end with an application objective, but where do I start? . . . Better first get them to conceptualize the role of factoring in problem solving—the value of undoing multiplication. This'll almost be like an affective objective—but, I'll stick with conceptualization."

In a few minutes, Casey has listed Objective A, as given in Exhibit 8.10. He then reviews pages 210–243 of the textbook, which will be the primary reference for this unit. He plans to cover the same four principal factoring algorithms included in those pages with two objectives each—one conceptualization objective for the students to understand why the algorithm works and one knowledge-of-a-process objective for the students to execute it efficiently. After coming up with those eight objectives (listed as C, D, E, F, G, H, I, and J in Exhibit 8.10), he decides he should include an objective involving comprehension of the language related to factoring polynomials. He feels it's important to list it to guard against just assuming students follow and use communica-

Exhibit 8.10 (pp. 261–262)
Casey's plan for the algebra I unit on factoring polynomials.

Course: Algebra I

Unit no.: 7 out of 17

Title: Factoring Polynomials

Goal: Understands why certain factoring algorithms work and can use them in problem solving.

Weighted objectives:

(06%) A. Explains how factoring polynomials can facilitate problem-solving (*conceptualization*).

(06%) B. Translates the meaning of the following terms in the context of communications relative to algebraic polynomial expressions: factor, prime factorization, greatest common factor, difference of squares, perfect square trinomial, and prime polynomial (*comprehension*).

(09%) C. Explains why the distributive property of multiplication over addition can be used to express a polynomial in factored form (*conceptualization*).

(09%) D. Factors polynomials expressible in the form $ax + ay$ (*knowledge of a process*).

(09%) E. Explains why polynomials expressible in the form $a^2 - b^2$ can be expressed in factored form as $(a + b)(a - b)$ (*conceptualization*).

(09%) F. Factors polynomials expressible in the form $a^2 - b^2$ (*knowledge of a process*).

(09%) G. Explains why polynomials expressible in the form $a^2 + 2ab + b^2$ can be expressed in factored form as $(a + b)^2$ (*conceptualization*).

(09%) H. Factors polynomials expressible in the form $a^2 + 2ab + b^2$ (*knowledge of a process*).

(10%) I. Explains why some polynomials expressible in the form $ax^2 + bx + c$ (where x is a real variable and $a, b,$ and c are rational constants) can be expressed in factored form as $(dx + e)(fx + g)$ (where $d, e, f,$ and g are rational constants) and others cannot (*conceptualization*).

(10%) J. Given a polynomial expressible in the form $ax^2 + bx + c$ (where x is a real variable and $a, b,$ and c are rational constants), determines if it can be expressed in factored form as $(dx + e)(fx + g)$ (where $d, e, f,$ and g are rational constants) and, if so, expresses it in that form (*knowledge of a process*).

(04%) K. Writes and uses computer programs to execute the algorithms alluded to in the preceding objectives (*comprehension*).

(10%) L. Given a real-life problem, explains how, if at all, factoring polynomials can be utilized in solving that problem (*application*).

Estimated number of class periods: 12

Textbook page references: 210–243 (unless otherwise indicated, page numbers referred to in the overall lesson plan are from the course textbook (by Foster, Rath, and Winters 1986)

Overall plan for lessons: I will confront students with a problem either in class or as part of a homework assignment that will be designed to set the stage for an inductive lesson relative to **Objective A.** That inductive lesson should be designed to stimulate students to discover the need to "undo" multiplication and to generalize from constant expressions in factored form to variable expressions in factored form. I'll need to design examples and nonexample problems for the lesson, but some useful follow-up practice exercises, as well as needed definitions, are given in the text on pp. 211–213. (Estimated time needed: *1.5 class periods plus homework.*)

For **Objective B,** direct instructional and comprehension-level activities will be integrated within lessons for the other objectives to help students utilize the vocabulary terms in communications. (Estimated time needed: *2–10 intermittent minutes each class period plus homework.*)

Exhibit 8.10 continued

For **Objective C,** I will conduct a relatively brief inductive lesson to help students discover the algorithm using their understanding of the distributive property. Examples on p. 214, the geometric paradigm on p. 216, and the "Excursions in Algebra" on p. 215 of the text should prove useful. (Estimated time needed: *0.5 class period plus homework.*)

I will conduct a direct instructional lesson for **Objective D** as a natural extension to the previous lesson. Adequate practice exercises are on p. 215. (Estimated time needed: *0.4 class period plus homework.*)

For **Objective K,** direct instructional and comprehension-level activities will be integrated within lessons for Objectives D, F, H, & J to help students write programs and utilize computers in executing algorithms. (Estimated time needed: *Homework plus a total of 40 minutes intermittently distributed among different class periods.*)

A brief test on Objectives A and C and parts of Objectives B and K will be given and reviewed with the class for purposes of formative feedback. Using the test review as a lead-in, lessons for **Objectives E** and **F** will be conducted following a design similar to that for Objectives C and D. The geometric model and the examples explained on pp. 217–218 will be utilized in the inductive activities along with the "Excursions in Algebra" section on p. 220. The paper-folding and cutting-up-squares experiments from pp. 172–173 in Sobel and Maletsky (1988) may also be incorporated. For the direct instructional lesson, exercises on p. 219 as well as the "Using Calculator" section should prove useful. (Estimated time needed: *1.75 class periods plus homework.*)

For **Objectives G** and **H,** I will follow a similar inductive–direct instruction sequence as for prior conceptualization/knowledge-of-a-process pairs. Examples explained on pp. 224–226 as well as the paper-folding experiment on p. 171 from Sobel and Maletsky (1988) will be utilized in the inductive lesson and exercises & examples from p. 223 for the direct lesson. (Estimated time needed: *1.75 class periods plus homework.*)

A brief test on Objectives A, C, D, E, F, G, and H and parts of Objectives B and K will be given and reviewed with the class for purposes of formative feedback. (Estimated time needed: *0.5 class period.*)

Again, the inductive–direct instruction sequence will be used but this time for **Objectives I** and **J.** Cardboard models from Sobel and Maletsky (1988, 174–175) for factoring trinomials will be utilized for the inductive lesson. Examples and exercises (including the "Using Calculator" sections) from pp. 224–234 will be used in both lessons. (Estimated time needed: *2.5 class periods plus homework.*)

I will conduct a deductive lesson for **Objective L,** drawing example and non-example problems from a variety of sources, including prior units, reference sources (e.g., Bushaw et al. 1980; Krulik and Reys 1980), and my head. (Estimated time needed: *0.75 class period plus homework.*)

Using a practice test, I'll conduct a review session for the unit test over Objectives A–L. (Estimated time needed: *0.5 class period plus homework.*)

A unit test over objectives A–L will be administered and the results reviewed with the class. (Estimated time needed: *1.5 class periods.*)

Extraordinary learning materials and equipment needed: Cardboard for cardboard cutout models, as explained in Sobel and Maletsky (1988, 173–174).

tion conventions about the topic—a mistake he made with previous units. Consequently, he formulates Objective B, as listed in Exhibit 8.10. He notes that the terms specified as content for Objective B are all terms to which students were previously exposed—but only in the context of working with integer constants, not polynomials.

Like Objective B, Objective K is not a central objective of the unit, but computer programming is something he's trying to build into most units.

Achievement of the application objective, L, is to be the climax of the unit.

For purposes of the blueprint for the unit test, Casey weights the objectives. It is past midnight when Casey completes his plan for Unit 7 as it appears in Exhibit 8.10.

Day −1: Reviewing the Unit Test on Polynomials and Setting the Stage for the Unit on Factoring

It's a Monday, the last day the algebra I class devotes to Unit 6. After reviewing the unit test, Casey calls students' attention to one of the items from the test—an item Casey had planted on the test just for this moment. The item—as most students worked it out—appears in Exhibit 8.11.

Casey engages the students in a brief intellectual-level questioning/discussion session:

Casey: I'm just looking at the −3*ab* and wondering what it means. What is it? . . . Juaquin.

Juaquin: It's a number.

Casey: I agree. But what kind of number—large, small, what? . . . Dustin.

Dustin: It's negative.

Casey: Okay, what do you want to say, Kevin?

Kevin: It wouldn't be negative if *ab* is negative or zero.

Casey: Raise your hand if you disagree with Kevin. . . . So, everyone agrees that −3*ab* could be negative, zero, or positive depending on *a* and *b*. . . . Give us a number, Cassandra.

Cassandra: 24.

Casey: If −3*ab* is 24, what would *a* and *b* be? . . . Mary.

Mary: You still don't know, because the value of one would affect the other.

Casey: Negative three times *what* equals 24? . . . Dustin.

Dustin: Eight—no! I mean negative eight.

Casey: So, what's *ab* if −3*ab* is 24? . . . Mary.

Mary: −8.

Exhibit 8.11
Item, including one student's response, planted by Casey on the Unit 6 test to help him set the stage for Unit 7.

Simplify the following polynomial:

$$21a + 3a(b − 2b − 7)$$
$$21a + 3a(−b − 7)$$
$$21a − 3ab − 21a$$
$$−3ab$$

Casey: If *ab* is −8, what is *a*? . . . Omar.

Omar: You don't know unless you know *b*. If *b* were 2, *a*'d be −4.

Casey: Thank you. . . . I see quite a few of you still have something to contribute to this matter, but we're nearly out of time, so I'll explain the homework assignment and we'll start Unit 7 tomorrow.

Casey distributes the worksheet shown in Exhibit 8.12, except, initially, the numerals 24, 24, 10 and 0 are not written in the blanks. He gives them directions for completing the sheet for homework:

Casey: Look at item 1 of the worksheet. Fill in the blank with the number Cassandra chose for us. What was it again, Russell?

Russell: 24.

Casey: Thank you. . . . Now, plug the 24 into the two blanks of item 2. For the first item you need to find all possible integer *pairs* for *a* and *b* that make the statement true. That's really only one table, I split it up into two parts just to conserve the area. For item 2, you find three more pairs that work, but this time you aren't restricted to integers—yes, Mary?

Mary: We have to use fractions?

Casey: Try fractions if you like—as long as they're real numbers. Now, since Cassandra got to choose the number for the blank in the first two items, I'm going to choose numbers for the third and fourth. Put 10 in the blank for item 3 and put 0 in for item 4. . . . Yes, Blair?

Blair: That's not fair, we only got to pick one number—you get two!

Casey: (Laughing with Blair and most of the other students) You're absolutely right, it isn't fair. That's one of the many great things about being a teacher—it's not always necessary to be fair!

Planning for Day 1

After school, Casey works on lessons for Tuesday's five classes. He starts with plans for the first day of Unit 7 for algebra I. Casey thinks: "I hope that little homework assignment will turn their thoughts toward undoing multiplication. But for this first lesson on Objective A, I really need a grabber-type real-life problem that'll stimulate them thinking why we ever want to look at factors."

He checks his unit plan (Exhibit 8.10) and rereads the part pertaining to teaching for Objective A. Struggling to come up with that "grabber" prob-

Exhibit 8.12
Homework worksheet Casey
assigned for the first day of Unit 7.

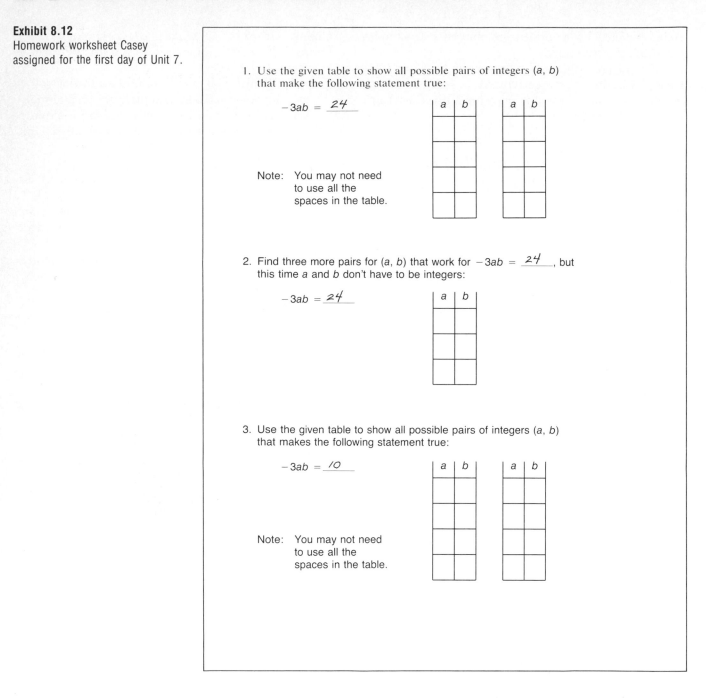

1. Use the given table to show all possible pairs of integers (*a*, *b*)
   that make the following statement true:

   $-3ab =$ ___24___

   Note: You may not need
   to use all the
   spaces in the table.

2. Find three more pairs for (*a*, *b*) that work for $-3ab =$ ___24___, but
   this time *a* and *b* don't have to be integers:

   $-3ab =$ ___24___

3. Use the given table to show all possible pairs of integers (*a*, *b*)
   that makes the following statement true:

   $-3ab =$ ___10___

   Note: You may not need
   to use all the
   spaces in the table.

lem to open the lesson, he considers using a bank interest problem in which interest earned is a given and questions are raised about possibilities for the variables principal and interest rate. Trying to use that same idea but shifting it to a more interesting topic, he thinks about a situation in which a politician brags that she has funneled so many thousands of dollars into a project that helps crime victims; he then could have the students figure how that translates into help for individuals in terms of the number of crime victims needing the help. He likes that idea but continues to think in hope of coming up with something easier to illustrate.

Problems involving finding possible dimensions of figures given the areas of their interiors are considered along with travel problems in which rate and time vary but distance is constant. Thinking about travel problems leads to the problem he finally decides to use for the opening lesson on Objective A. He selects it because it involves the mathematical content of Objective A and it involves a topic in which many students have shown an interest—namely, solving crimes. The problem is explained in Exhibit 8.13.

With the paramount problem for the day determined, Casey designs and schedules the activities;

Exhibit 8.12 continued

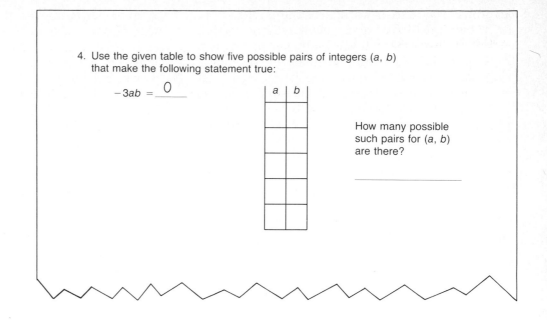

4. Use the given table to show five possible pairs of integers (a, b) that make the following statement true:

$$-3ab = \underline{\hspace{0.3cm}0\hspace{0.3cm}}$$

a	b

How many possible such pairs for (a, b) are there?

_____

Exhibit 8.13
Problem Casey uses in the first lesson of Unit 6.

One witness testifies seeing suspect in drugstore at 3:35 p.m.

2nd witness testifies masked woman burglarizing garage at 3:50 p.m.

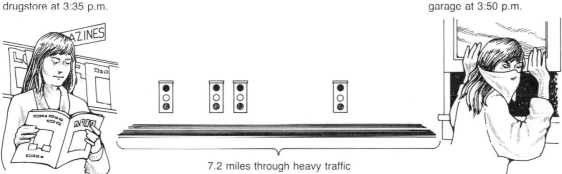

7.2 miles through heavy traffic

A woman is accused of burglarizing a garage at approximately 3:50 p.m. on a Tuesday. At 3:35 p.m. that day, she was seen in a drugstore 7.2 miles west of the garage. The direct route between the two locations is congested with traffic at that time and has four traffic lights.

A traffic engineer testifies that:

Between 2 p.m. and 4 p.m. on the day of the crime, the fastest average rate a vehicle could travel from a point near the drugstore to the crime scene would be 30 mph. The average rate at which traffic travels there at that time is 20 mph. Unless there is an extraordinary event (e.g., an accident) stopping traffic on that road, traffic will move at 15 mph at the very least. On that day, there was no such traffic stoppage.

The woman's defense attorney claims she could not possibly have been at the crime scene at 3:50 since she was in the drugstore at 3:35.

The question:

Is it possible for her to have been in the drugstore at 3:35 and be burglarizing the garage at 3:50? If so, is it likely she was able to travel the 7.2 miles in the available time?

he thinks: "I want them working on the problem right away, but I also have to somehow respond to that homework assignment. It was really just to get them thinking about isolating and analyzing factors. I don't want to spend too much time discussing it, just enough to reinforce engaging in homework—and also to plant a few seeds that'll eventually help them conceptualize some relations down the road. 24, 10, and 0 are going to turn out to be great choices!

"We'll begin with an independent work session in which they deal with the problem I'll have written for them on a worksheet while I go around and check their homework. Then, I can make comments about what I learned from reading the homework before we discuss the problem. . . . But that won't work—some will finish the problem before I could possibly look through all their homework papers, and then they'd be ready to discuss the problem, not hear about the homework. I need another plan. . . .

"I've got it! After quickly going over the homework, we'll deal with the problem in a large-group session. . . . Oh—an even better idea! I'll introduce the problem by having them role-play the characters in the problem. It'll be easy for me to make out a script, pass that out, and assign the parts. As they go through the script, I'll put this diagram on the overhead [see Exhibit 8.13]. After the problem is presented, should I have them discuss and solve it as a group or put them into the independent work session? Maybe I should have those who don't get to read parts make the judgment; I don't know. . . . Okay, I'm going to go with the independent work session, but I'll make it a writing exercise—they'll have to explain and argue for what they decide. That way, everybody will have a chance to at least put some thought into the problem before the fast ones with the answers get restless. I should probably give them about a 12-minute writing assignment on the problem, and then we discuss it. . . ."

For the in-class writing assignment, Casey develops the worksheet given in Exhibit 8.14.

He thinks: "There won't be much class time left after that—just time to do some summing up, vocabulary reviewing—the ones in Objective B—and make an assignment. . . . Better get the script written."

Within 10 minutes, Casey has the script written; as it and the worksheet are being printed and then duplicated, he writes the agenda for Tuesday's class. Exhibit 8.15 contains the script; Exhibit 8.16 shows the agenda.

Day 1

Tuesday, 24 of Casey's 26 algebra I students are in class. Four minutes into the class period, the students have their homework sheets (see Exhibit 8.12)

Exhibit 8.14

Casey's worksheet for the independent work session to solve the problem given in Exhibit 8.13.

Your mission is to solve the problem by answering the following questions:

1. Based on the evidence, was it possible for the suspect to have been in the drugstore at 3:35 P.M. on the day in question and also to be burglarizing the garage at 3:50 P.M.?

Yes _____ No _____. Explain exactly how the evidence supports your conclusion in the space provided.

2. If you answered Yes to the first question, was it likely or probable that she was able to travel the 7.2 miles in the available time?

Yes _____ No _____. Explain exactly how the evidence supports your conclusion in the space provided.

3. If you answered No to the second question, how high would the fastest average rate given by the traffic engineer have to be before you would conclude that it is likely or probable to travel the 7.2 miles in the available time?

_____ mi/h. Defend your answer with an explanation.

Exhibit 8.15
Script for students to follow in role-playing the problem situation given in Exhibit 8.13.

Prosecutor Wilma Jones: (To witness Alvin Smith) Mr. Smith, at approximately 3:50 P.M. on Tuesday, January 26, tell us what you saw just outside the garage located at 821 North Street.

Alvin Smith: I saw a woman in a ski mask enter the garage. A couple of minutes later she came out the garage carrying a television set and a small box. She put them into a car parked just outside the door. Then she made two more trips, taking what looked like auto equipment—like speakers and tools and stuff.

Wilma Jones: And what kind of car was the suspect—ah, excuse me, I mean the person you observed—using?

Alvin Smith: A light green hatchback of some kind—maybe a Dodge or something.

Wilma Jones: (To suspect Alice Brown) Ms. Brown, what kind of car do you drive?

Alice Brown: A green 1987 Dodge hatchback, but I didn't—

Wilma Jones: That's all Ms. Brown; thank you.

Defense Attorney Willie Adams: (To witness Irene Johnson) Ms. Johnson, where do you work?

Irene Johnson: At Sitman's Drugstore on 5980 North Street.

Willie Adams: Ms. Brown, please stand up so this witness can take a good look at you. Thank you. Now Ms. Johnson, have you ever seen this person at any time before today?

Irene Johnson: Only once, and that was at Sitman's Drugstore where I work. She bought some gloves and I rang up the sale for her.

Willie Adams: And at what time and on what day did this occur?

Irene Johnson: At exactly 3:35 P.M. on January 26 of this year.

Willie Adams: You seem so sure of the date and time. How can you be so sure?

Irene Johnson: The date and time are right here on this cash register slip.

Willie Adams: (To traffic engineer Bob Moore) Mr. Moore, what position do you hold with our great city?

Bob Moore: I'm a traffic engineer. I study traffic patterns and basically work to keep traffic on our city streets flowing as smoothly as possible.

Willie Adams: Mr. Moore, how far is it between Sitman's Drugstore at 5980 North and the garage, allegedly burglarized at 821 North?

Bob Moore: 7.2 miles.

Willie Adams: Please tell us, based on your scientific studies, how long it would take someone to travel those 7.2 mi between 3:35 and 4 o'clock on Tuesday, January 26, a workday.

Bob Moore: The average rate at which traffic travels between those two points on a Tuesday at that time is 20 mi/h. It's quite congested and there are four major traffic lights.

Willie Adams: That's the average. What's the fastest a car could average over that 7.2 mi?

Bob Moore: 30 mi/h max.

Willie Adams: You say that's the most. Is it realistic to expect someone to average as high as 30 mi/h over that 7.2-mi stretch at that time of day on a Tuesday?

Bob Moore: It would be a rare occurrence, to say the least.

in front of them as Casey conducts the planned intellectual-level questioning/discussion session.

Casey: How many pairs did you come up with for the first one, Alphonse?

Alphonse: 16.

Casey: Quickly, list them on the board for us—and while Alphonse is doing that, let's have

Cassandra list hers for number 2, Kyle for number 3, and Abdul, 4.

Exhibit 8.17 displays what the students write.

Casey: Let's turn our attention to Alphonse's entries for the first one. . . . Where are the rest of them, Alphonse?

lot**Exhibit 8.16**
Casey's agenda for the first day of the algebra I unit on factoring polynomials.

1. Transition period, starting class and directing students to take out the worksheets they completed for homework (see Exhibit 8.13).
2. Intellectual-level questioning/discussion session in which students share homework responses leading to the idea of undoing multiplication.
3. Transition period, in which crime-solver problem scripts are distributed and roles are appointed.
4. Interactive lecture session, in which designated students play their characters from the crime-solver script and the problem is clarified.
5. Transition period giving directions and handing out worksheet for the independent work session.
6. Independent work session with students completing the worksheet (see Exhibit 8.14) and the teacher reading and selecting sample responses to be read in the follow-up questioning/discussion session.
7. Transition period into questioning/discussion session.
8. Intellectual-level questioning/discussion session in which
   ❑ Selected contrasting responses are read aloud and analyzed,
   ❑ Strategies for solving the problem are articulated,
   ❑ Types of problems with solutions requiring the undoing of multiplication are characterized,
   ❑ Additional example problems are compared to nonexample problems.
9. Transition period, in which students are directed to open the textbook to p. 210.
10. Interactive lecture session:
    ❑ Review the textbook's and notebook glossary's definitions of factoring, prime number, composite number, and greatest common factor.
    ❑ Explain the examples and directions for the textbook exercises on pp. 212–213.
11. Transition period, assigning homework:
    ❑ Think up and write out a real-life problem. Make it one that has a solution that requires the undoing of multiplication (such as the crime-solver problem we worked on in class today).
    ❑ Work the following exercises from p. 213: 11, 15, 19, 20, 21, 25, 28, 33, 49, 53, 54, 55.
12. Independent work session beginning homework.
13. Transition period into the second period.

Alphonse: What do you mean?
Casey: You said you had 16; I only see 8 pairs.
Alphonse: That's what I meant—I was counting numbers, not pairs.
Casey: Okay, any comments or questions for Alphonse? Do his entries match your own? . . . Go ahead, Dick.
Dick: Did we have to repeat them like he did? 4 and −2 is the same as −2 and 4.
Casey: Direct your questions to Alphonse. He can either answer you himself or call on a volunteer.
Alphonse: I don't know. . . . Okay, Dustin.
Dustin: You've got to do them both, because if like, ah, a equals 4, then b's got to be −2. But if a's −2, b's got to be 4. What I did was to solve for all the a's; then b had to be whatever it had to be.
Casey: Do you have a response to Dustin's explanation, Dick? . . . No? . . . Okay. Anybody else? Put your hand up if you don't understand why

Alphonse's eight pairs are all possible ordered pairs of integers a, b in the case where $-3ab = 24$. . . . In that case, we move to the second one. . . . Questions or comments for Cassandra? . . . Ron?
Ron: You've only got two pairs up there, not three.
Cassandra: What do you mean—see, one, two, three?
Ron: The first and the second one are the same one. $-\frac{1}{2}$ is −0.5!
Cassandra: Oh! Sorry, just switch the two—make the second row 16, −0.5 instead. . . . Edwin.
Edwin: I thought they all had to be fractions.
Cassandra: Here, does this make you happy? . . .

Cassandra modifies her entries so that they now appear as in Exhibit 8.18.

Exhibit 8.17
Students' initial chalkboard entries for the activity reviewing the homework assignment with the worksheet of Exhibit 8.12.

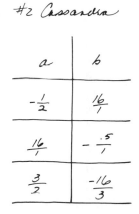

(Chalkboard)

#1 Alphonse

4	-2	-4	2
-2	4	2	-4
-8	1	8	-1
1	-8	-1	8

#2 Cassandra

a	b
$-\frac{1}{2}$	16
$-.5$	16
$\frac{3}{2}$	$-\frac{16}{3}$

#3 Kyle

a	b

#4 Abdul

a	b
0	0
0	1
0	20
0	37
-4	0

Exhibit 8.18
Cassandra's modification to her entry shown in Exhibit 8.17.

#2 Cassandra

a	b
$-\frac{1}{2}$	$\frac{16}{1}$
$\frac{16}{1}$	$-\frac{.5}{1}$
$\frac{3}{2}$	$-\frac{16}{3}$

Casey: We'll allow any pair that works as long as they both aren't integers. All the numbers Cassandra has can be expressed as fractions, but she doesn't have to express them as fractions. . . . Marlene?

Marlene: Are her answers right or not? None of mine agree with hers.

Casey: Raise your hand if you have exactly the same entries as Cassandra. . . . Nobody agrees with Cassandra! But her answers are exactly correct; so nobody else did this right. I'm shocked! Read yours, Sid.

Sid: $\frac{8}{7}$ and 7, $\frac{8}{9}$ and 9, and $\frac{8}{10}$ and 10.

Casey: Well that would be right if Sid sticks in some negative signs here and there, but then it still wouldn't be the same as Cassandra's. Read yours, Omar.

Omar: 32 and $-\frac{1}{4}$, $-\frac{1}{4}$ and 32, and 16 and $-\frac{1}{2}$.

Casey: Well that's surely right, but it's different from Cassandra's. . . . Marlene?

Marlene: So, you're really saying that there's more than one correct answer to this one.

Casey: How many possible *a, b* pairs will work if we don't say *a* and *b* both have to be integers, Xavier?

Xavier: I don't know.

Casey: What three pairs did you put down for number 2, Xavier?

Xavier: I didn't do it.

As Casey redirects his initial question for Xavier to another student, he quickly jots down, "Xavier, please check with me later on in class today right after I assign the homework for tomorrow. I want to speak with you briefly." He hands the note to Xavier as he continues.

Casey: How many possible *a, b* pairs will work if we don't say *a* and *b* both have to be integers, Juaquin?

Juaquin: There's no limit; you can keep going.

Casey: Let's go on to item 3 and look at what Kyle put. . . . Blanks! All blanks! You were supposed to fill in the blanks, not leave them, Kyle! What do you have to say about this?

Kyle: There are no answers.

Casey: Do you think I'd give you an exercise with no answers?

Kyle: You do it to us all the time.

Casey: Explain to the class why this one has no answers.

Kyle: Three doesn't go into 10, so there's no integer times 3 that'll give you 10. . . . Mary?

Mary: But you could put in fractions, right?

Kyle: But we weren't supposed to for this one.

Casey: If nonintegers were allowed, how many answers would there be, Juaquin?

Juaquin: You could keep going and going.

Casey: Okay. That brings us to the last one. . . . Do you agree with Abdul's entries?

Alena: I agree, but they're not the same as mine.

Casey: Super quick, write yours on the board, and while she's doing that, write yours also, Terri. . . . Okay, does anybody want to quarrel with anything that's on the board? How many possible correct pairs could we have? . . . Salvador.

Salvador: Infinite.

Casey: Describe what must be true for a pair to work. You tell us, Salvador.

Salvador: You've got to have a zero.

Casey: We're going to be okay as long as a or b is zero. If a is zero, then b—what about b if a is zero, Mary?

Mary: It can be anything. And if b is zero, a can be anything.

Casey distributes copies of the crime-solver script and appoints individuals to play the roles. With the diagram from Exhibit 8.13 displayed on the overhead, the students read through the parts. As planned, they then complete the worksheet shown in Exhibit 8.14 as Casey circulates about the room selecting sample responses to use in the follow-up questioning/discussion session. Students enthusiastically engage in that session (listed as item 8 in Exhibit 8.16) until there are only 7 minutes left in the period, at which time Casey terminates the discussion. Thinking quickly, he tries to summarize points made during the session, explaining that the type of problem on which they will be focusing in this unit involves situations in which they already have a product and want to look at different factor combinations that could have resulted in that product.

Lacking time to get to item 10 on the agenda (see Exhibit 8.16), Casey shifts to item 11, explaining and assigning the part of the homework in which they think up and write out a sample real-life prob-

lem. He postpones the part of the assignment from the textbook.

Planning for Day 2

It's 4:30 when Casey gets around to reflecting on the day's classes. Regarding algebra I, he thinks: "I like the way they got into the two inductive activities today. The trouble is, we didn't leave time to really get things summed up at the end and to go through the vocabulary. I'm sorry I didn't get to work in at least two more example-type problems and at least one nonexample problem. My attempt to tie things up at the end didn't work because we only had the one problem to think about. . . . They loved that crime-solver business—think I'll try that in the geometry classes. I'm glad I came up with that idea. . . . I wonder if it was a mistake to postpone the textbook assignment. Earlier in the year, I would've assigned it even though I hadn't gone through the vocabulary, but I've learned that usually doesn't work for most of this group—they see a word they don't know and just fold up the tent.

"Okay, so where do I go with this tomorrow? That'll be Wednesday, so 3 more days this week, and . . . oh, we've got plenty of time; the extra time spent on the conceptualization objective will make the rest of the unit go smoother. Okay, back to tomorrow. . . . We need to get to the vocabulary—oh, but first I need to hit them with example and nonexample problems and then try to do a better job of summing things up. Better jot down those problems I thought of at the end of class. . . . Let's see, one was on area, the other on money spent by the politician on—oh! It would be even better if I used the problems they bring into class from the homework assignment. I almost forgot about that. Some are bound to come up with super examples; others won't actually involve factoring—I can use some of those for the nonexamples. I'm glad I made that assignment—that'll work out well. Then, we tie up Objective A and go straight to the textbook and the vocabulary stuff planned for today." [See Exhibit 8.19.]

With the unit plan (Exhibit 8.10), Tuesday's agenda (Exhibit 8.16), and page 212 of the textbook in front of him, Casey calls up the computer file with Tuesday's agenda and begins modifying it into Wednesday's agenda (see Exhibit 8.20). As Casey looks at it, he thinks, "We probably won't get through this one either, but I'd much rather have too much planned than not enough and be left with dead time."

When Casey first begins writing the agenda, he doesn't plan for the activities relative to Objective A to be as elaborate as agenda items 1–4 suggest. Initially, he thinks of just quickly tying together the

Exhibit 8.19
Casey planning class agendas.

Exhibit 8.20
Casey's agenda for the second day of the algebra I unit on factoring polynomials.

1. Transition period, in which I start class and distribute an overhead transparency and transparency (erasable) pen to each student and direct them to take out the problems they formulated for homework.
2. Independent work session, in which each student quickly copies her or his homework problem onto the transparency (make sure they display their names).
3. Transition period, in which I collect completed transparencies and the pens.
4. Interactive lecture session, in which
   ❑ I quickly display each transparency on the overhead as the student who wrote it reads the problem aloud.
   ❑ After each problem is shown, the students independently and quietly classify the problem on their worksheet as either an example or a nonexample.
   ❑ After all the problems are shown, I select two example problems and two nonexample problems (assuming they exist in the sample—if not, use my own (as a last resort)) and use the contrast between the two types to sum up the need to undo multiplication to solve some types of problems.
5. Transition period, in which students are directed to open the textbook to p. 210.
6. Interactive lecture session:
   ❑ Review the textbook's and notebook glossary's definitions of factoring, prime number, composite number, and greatest common factor.
   ❑ Explain the examples and directions for the textbook exercises on pp. 212–213.
   ❑ Call their attention to the purpose of the textbook section "Factoring Using the Distributive Property" on p. 214.
7. Transition period, assigning the following homework:
   ❑ Work the following exercises from p. 213: 11, 15, 19, 20, 21, 25, 28, 33, 49, 53, 54, and 55.
   ❑ Study page 214, working through the four examples with the authors.
   ❑ Work the following exploratory exercises from p. 215: 1, 2, 3, and 9.
   ❑ Work the following written exercises from p. 215: 1, 2, 3, 5, 9, and 15.
8. Independent work session for beginning homework.
9. Transition period into the second period.

end of Tuesday's lesson for that objective. However, as he thinks of how to make efficient use of their homework and the need to involve more problems than just the crime-solver one, he ends up with a more elaborate plan. This, he thinks, should provide a stimulating start to the period but will not leave him with enough time to do all the following:

1. Go through the vocabulary and set the stage for the textbook activities.
2. Provide students with needed exposure to and practice factoring constant and variable expressions from p. 213 (e.g., find the prime factorization of 112 and find the greatest common factor of $18a^2b^2$, $6b$, $42a^2b^3$).
3. Conduct the brief inductive lesson relative to Objective C as suggested in his unit plan (see Exhibit 8.10) and the follow-up lesson for Objective D.

He estimates that stopping with only the first two of the three tasks completed will leave too much class time unused but not enough available to complete the third. The agenda of Exhibit 8.20 represents a compromise in which he plans to have the students get a jump on objectives C and D by reading ahead in the textbook (i.e., p. 214, which is reproduced in Exhibit 8.21). He doesn't really like the idea of students being introduced to the steps in an algorithm before experiencing a conceptualization lesson on why it works, but he goes ahead with the agenda of Exhibit 8.20 because it seems to be the most efficient way to use the available time. Besides, he doesn't consider this particular algorithm based on the familiar distributive property to be conceptually complex for the students.

Day 2 and Planning for Day 3

Wednesday's algebra I class smoothly followed the agenda of Exhibit 8.20. Casey reflects on the day's events and plans for Thursday's classes. He thinks to himself: "That first part of algebra really went well. Flashing every one of their problems on the

Exhibit 8.21

Page 214 of Casey's algebra I textbook (Foster, Rath, and Winters 1986).

Examples

1 **Use the distributive property to write $10y^2 + 15y$ in factored form.**

First, find the greatest common factor of $10y^2$ and $15y$.

$10y^2 = 2 \cdot \circledb{5} \cdot \circledb{y} \cdot y$
$15y = 3 \cdot \circledb{5} \cdot \circledb{y}$ *The GCF is 5y.*

Then, express each term as a product of the GCF and its remaining factors.

$10y^2 + 15y = 5y(2y) + 5y(3)$
$= 5y(2y + 3)$ *Use the distributive property.*

2 **Factor: $21ab^2 - 33a^2bc$**

$21ab^2 = \circledb{3} \cdot 7 \cdot \circledb{a} \cdot \circledb{b} \cdot b$
$33a^2bc = \circledb{3} \cdot 11 \cdot \circledb{a} \cdot a \cdot \circledb{b} \cdot c$ *The GCF is 3ab.*

Express the terms as products.

$21ab^2 - 33a^2bc = 3ab(7b) - 3ab(11ac)$
$= 3ab(7b - 11ac)$ *Use the distributive property.*

3 **Factor: $12a^5b + 8a^3 - 24a^3c$**

$12a^5b = 2 \cdot 2 \cdot 3 \cdot a \cdot a \cdot a \cdot a \cdot a \cdot b$
$8a^3 = 2 \cdot 2 \cdot 2 \cdot a \cdot a \cdot a$
$24a^3c = 2 \cdot 2 \cdot 2 \cdot 3 \cdot a \cdot a \cdot a \cdot c$ *The GCF is $4a^3$.*

$12a^5b + 8a^3 - 24a^3c = 4a^3(3a^2b) + 4a^3(2) - 4a^3(6c)$
$= 4a^3(3a^2b + 2 - 6c)$

4 **Factor: $6x^3y^2 + 14x^2y + 2x^2$**

$6x^3y^2 = 2 \cdot 3 \cdot x \cdot x \cdot x \cdot y \cdot y$
$14x^2y = 2 \cdot 7 \cdot x \cdot x \cdot y$
$2x^2 = 2 \cdot x \cdot x$ *The GCF is $2x^2$.*

$6x^3y^2 + 14x^2y + 2x^2 = 2x^2(3xy^2 + 7y + 1)$

Source: From *Merrill Algebra One* (p. 214) by A. G. Foster, J. N. Rath, and L. J. Winters, 1986, Columbus, OH: Merrill. Copyright 1986 by Merrill Publishing Company. Reprinted by permission.

overhead screen reinforced their engagement in homework and exposed them to a variety of problems—examples and nonexamples—with them both seeing and hearing the problems. I'm going to use that tactic more often—but next time I need to think of it before I assign the homework. That way they can take the transparencies home and have them prepared before coming into class, saving class time.

"Even agenda item 6 went well—switching to direct instruction using the textbook was a nice change after all the lively inquiry activities. They can take only so much inquiry before needing some old-fashioned, straightforward here's-something-to-memorize teaching. . . . But I wonder just how much they got from studying page 214. I'd better start off tomorrow with a brief test to get some formative feedback on where they are and also to reinforce their working on the assignments. . . . The test shouldn't take more than 20 minutes, but I ought to have one or two items on Objective A, items for the vocabulary we went over today, and some items similar to the textbook exercises relative to Objective D. A pretty easy item on Objective C should tell me if that little explanation at the top of page 214 [see Exhibit 8.21] helped them understand that the distributive property in reverse is the basis for the algorithm. . . . I'm afraid this brief test may not be as brief as I'd like!"

Casey spends nearly an hour entering items for objectives A, B, C, and D into his item pool file. He longs for the day when he won't have to create new items every time he puts together a test—the second year of teaching should be easier than this one. Af-

ter synthesizing the test, Casey works out the agenda given in Exhibit 8.22.

Day 3 and Planning for Day 4

Feedback from the brief test suggests to Casey that most students failed to achieve objectives C and D well enough to be ready to learn objectives E and F. Thus, he spends the majority of the class period on item 4 of the agenda (see Exhibit 8.22). Because he needs to have them complete the worksheet of Exhibit 8.23 before he spends class time on objectives E and F, he postpones agenda items 5 and 6 and begins explaining and assigning the worksheet immediately after item 4. He does not give any other homework assignment, since there is no time at the end of the period for item 8.

For Friday, he plans quick coverage of items 5 and 6 from Thursday's agenda and then to utilize the results of the homework (see Exhibit 8.23) to get them to discover that $a^2 - b^2 = (a + b)(a - b)$. He expects them to bring in a variety of square and rectangular regions, from which he'll use inductive questioning strategies to get them to generalize from their own examples to the general relation for factoring difference of squares. He'll then assign written and calculator exercises from pages 215 and 218–219 in which they practice the factoring algorithms from both objectives D and F.

Day 4 and Planning for Day 5

On Friday, Casey spends more time with the computer programming activities than he had planned.

Exhibit 8.22
Casey's agenda for the third day of the algebra I unit on factoring polynomials.

1. Transition period starting class and initiating a brief test.
2. Brief test relevant to objectives A, B, C, and D.
3. Transition period from the test to the review of the results.
4. Interactive lecture and questioning/discussion session in which
   ❑ I call out the scoring key for each test item while students check and score their own responses.
   ❑ Items about which students raise questions are discussed.
   ❑ I explain any topics the test results suggest need to be explained.
5. Transition period, in which students are directed to take out their homework papers, open textbooks to p. 214, and open their notebooks to Part 3 where they keep computer programs and flowcharts developed during the course.
6. Interactive lecture session, in which I "walk" the students through writing a basic program for factoring using the distributive property.
7. Transition period, distributing the homework worksheet (see Exhibit 8.23), explaining the worksheet, and assigning the homework to
   ❑ Complete the tasks for the worksheet.
   ❑ _____ (to be determined in class, depending on feedback from brief test).
8. Independent work session for beginning homework.
9. Transition period into the second period.

Exhibit 8.23
Worksheet assigned for homework as part of a lesson for Objective E (See Exhibit 8.10).

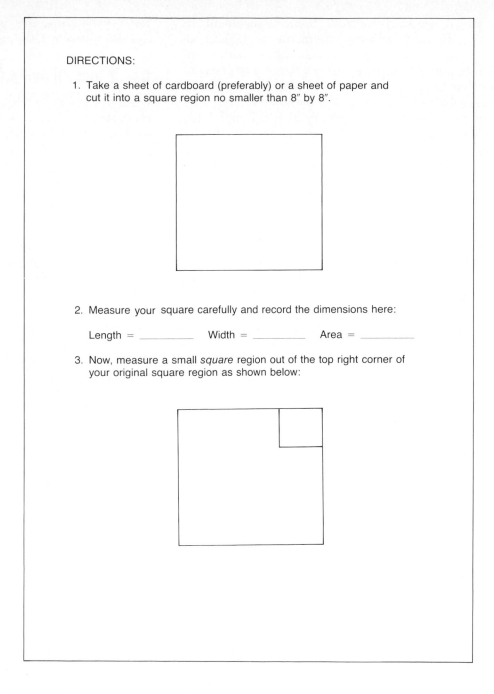

DIRECTIONS:

1. Take a sheet of cardboard (preferably) or a sheet of paper and cut it into a square region no smaller than 8″ by 8″.

2. Measure your square carefully and record the dimensions here:

Length = _____   Width = _____   Area = _____

3. Now, measure a small *square* region out of the top right corner of your original square region as shown below:

The intellectual-level questioning/discussion session is quite lively, with students abstracting the general relation for factoring the difference of two squares (see Exhibit 8.24) from the examples produced in the homework assignment (see Exhibit 8.23). However, Casey is able to complete only the first four of the seven stages for the conceptualization lesson (i.e., (1) task confrontation, (2) task work, (3) reflection on work, (4) generalization, (5) articulation, (6) verification, and (7) refinement, as explained in the section "Inductive Learning Activities" in chapter 4). He's unhappy that he has to stop the lesson with just enough time remaining to give the planned homework assignment. Most

students appear disappointed the class period is over.

The high point on which the first period ends leaves Casey so energized that he begins planning for Monday's algebra class during second period (see Exhibit 8.2 for his class schedule) instead of collecting his thoughts for periods 3 and 4, as he does on most days.

He locks his classroom door, gathers the unit plan and the day's agenda, sits at his computer, and thinks to himself: "I should've given them a computer assignment to follow up that programming session. They could've handled it with the weekend break. . . . Wow! They really got into discovering

Exhibit 8.23 continued

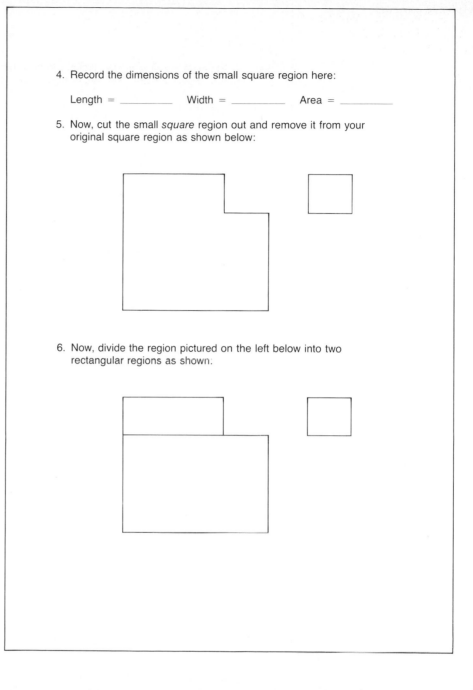

4. Record the dimensions of the small square region here:

   Length = _____ Width = _____ Area = _____

5. Now, cut the small *square* region out and remove it from your original square region as shown below:

6. Now, divide the region pictured on the left below into two rectangular regions as shown:

why $a^2 - b^2 = (a + b)(a - b)$—I sure hate to wait until Monday to tie it all down. . . . Let's see, page 217 gives them a pretty good explanation of a geometric model that's isomorphic to the one we discovered in class. Not many of them would understand it if I hadn't put them through the worksheet experience first [see Exhibit 8.23]. Page 218 lays out the algorithm quite clearly with five examples and a variety of coefficients. Then the written and calculator exercises I assigned give them skill work for this and the previous algorithm. . . . I shouldn't feel so bad about having had to cut the lesson short. It'll come together for those who put an effort into this homework assignment. That means I'd better start

Monday's class off with a brief test and reinforce those who did."

Casey develops Monday's agenda shown in Exhibit 8.25, but he doesn't get the brief test completed until Friday evening.

Day 5

Monday's first period follows the schedule of Exhibit 8.25. Twelve minutes into the period, 6 of the 25 students present have completed the test shown in Exhibit 8.27 and are waiting at their places for the others to finish. Casey regrets not having made accommodations (e.g., with an assignment) for stu-

Exhibit 8.23 continued

7. Carefully measure the two rectangular regions, both the top one and the bottom one. Record the dimensions here:

Top rectangle:

Length = _____   Width = _____   Area = _____

Bottom rectangle:

Length = _____   Width = _____   Area = _____

8. Carefully cut off the top rectangular region as shown below:

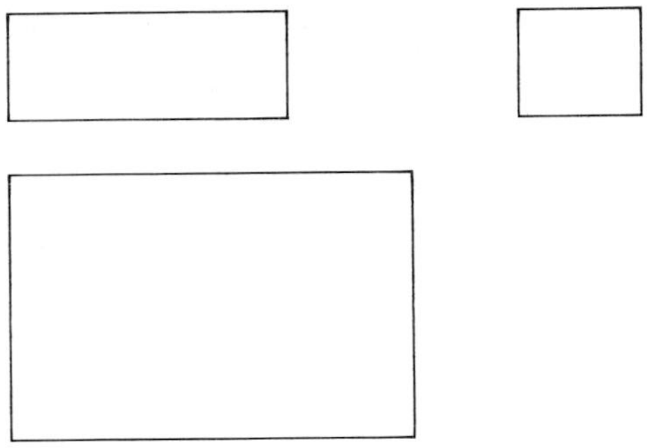

9. Now rotate the top rectangular region and attach it to the left side of the bottom rectangular region as shown below (it should fit exactly):

10. Carefully measure the rectangular region you just formed. Record the dimensions here:

Length = _____   Width = _____   Area = _____

Exhibit 8.24
General model for $a^2 - b^2 = (a + b)(a - b)$ that Casey's algebra students abstracted from their examples based on the worksheet of Exhibit 8.23.

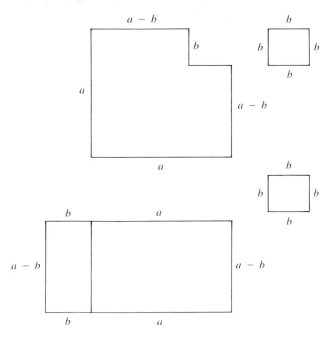

dents finishing at different times. Seven minutes later, most students are finished, and Casey halts the test and begins calling out the key to the items:

Casey: Number 1, $6x(3x - 2)$—to prove that answer, let $a = 6x$, $b = 3x$, and $c = -2$. Number 2, the greatest common factor is $7a$. Number 3, $3xy(x^2y + 3y + 12)$. Number 4, $(5w + 9q^2)(5w - 9q^2)$. Number 5, $\frac{2}{3}(x + 2)(x - 2)$. And for number 6, your dimensions and rectangle might look something like this.

He displays the following on the overhead:

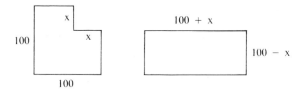

Students raise questions about a few of the test items and the homework exercises. Here's one episode:

Sid: I don't get number 5 on the test.
Casey: When you see 'factor $\frac{2}{3}x^2 - \frac{8}{3}$,' what's the first thing you think of doing, Sid?
Sid: Look for common terms, but first I got rid of the numbers at the bottom.

Casey: How?
Sid: By multiplying through by 3—that gives me $2x^2 - 8$ and now 2 is common—
Casey: Hold on, doesn't multiplying by 3 change the value of the expression?
Sid: It's okay to do it to both sides.
Casey: Both sides of what?
Sid: The equation.
Casey: I don't see an equation, just an expression standing for a number.
Sid: Oh, yeah.
Casey: What did Sid tell us he thinks about first when factoring an expression like this, Charlene?
Charlene: Look for a common term.
Casey: And is there a common term in this case, Sid?
Sid: They both have 3s on the bottom.
Casey: Divided by 3 is the same as multiplied by what, Sid?
Sid: $\frac{1}{3}$.
Casey: So, what's common?
Sid: $\frac{1}{3}$.
Casey: Using the distributive property, you take $\frac{1}{3}$ out and you have $\frac{1}{3}$ times what?
Sid: $2x^2 - 8$. . . . And now, 2 is common also, so you get $\frac{2}{3}(x^2 - 4)$. But that's not the answer you gave us.
Casey: Okay, Juaquin, you've been waiting to tell us something for a long time. You're up.
Juaquin: $(x^2 - 4)$ is the difference of two perfect squares, so you can factor that too, and you end up with your answer.
Sid: I see. Thank you.

Twelve minutes later, Casey has just talked the class through the paper-folding experiment (see Exhibit 8.26) and completes agenda item 6 (see Exhibit 8.25) by listing the steps in the algorithm for factoring expressions of the form $a^2 + 2ab + b^2$. He talks the students through two examples and then assigns the homework. He leaves the algorithm's steps and illustrative examples displayed on the board as the students begin their homework (agenda item 8). Although only 7 minutes are left for the independent work session, Casey efficiently provides individual help to 12 students by applying techniques suggested in this book's section "Initiating and Maintaining Student Engagement in Independent Work Session" in Chapter 6. For example, he responds to Mary's request for help to Exploratory Exercise 5 from page 222 of the textbook:

Determine if each trinomial is a perfect square trinomial. If it is, state its factors.
5. $n^2 - 13n + 36$

Exhibit 8.25
Casey's agenda for the fifth day of the algebra I unit on factoring polynomials.

1. Transition period starting class and initiating a brief test.
2. Brief test relevant to objectives C, D, E, and F.
3. Transition period from the test to the review of the results.
4. Interactive lecture and questioning/discussion session in which
   ❑ I call out the scoring key for each test item while students check and score their own responses.
   ❑ Items and homework exercises about which students raise questions are discussed.
   ❑ I explain any topics the test results and questions suggest need to be explained (this may well require a direct instructional learning activity on the algorithm for factoring the difference of perfect squares).
5. Transition period, in which a 10-in. by 10-in. square-shaped sheet of colored paper is distributed to each student.
6. Interactive lecture session in which I
   ❑ Demonstrate and work through the paper-folding experiment (see Exhibit 8.26) illustrating why $a^2 + 2ab + b^2$ can be expressed as $(a + b)^2$.
   ❑ Use direct instruction to explain and provide practice with the algorithm for factoring $a^2 + 2ab + b^2$.
7. Transition period, assigning the following homework:
   ❑ Read the textbook section "Perfect Squares and Factoring," pp. 221–222, and work through the accompanying examples.
   ❑ Complete the following Exploratory Exercises from p. 222: 1–6 and 9–12.
   ❑ Complete the following Written Exercises from p. 223: 5, 7, 9, 10, 12, 25, 34, 36, 39, 41, 42, 47, and 48.
8. Independent work session for beginning homework.
9. Transition period into the second period.

Exhibit 8.26
Paper-folding experiment in which Casey engages students during the fifth class meeting of Unit 7 (Excerpted from Sobel and Maletsky 1988, 171–172).

Paper Folding for $(a + b)^2 = a^2 + 2ab + b^2$

Material

One square piece of paper per student.

Directions

1. Fold one edge over at a point E to form a vertical crease parallel to the edge. Label the longer and shorter dimensions a and b.

2. Fold the upper right-hand corner over onto the crease to locate point F. Folding this way, point F will be the same distance from the corner as point E.

3. Now fold a horizontal crease through F and label all outside dimensions.

4. Find the areas of the two squares formed. Find the areas of the two rectangles formed. Show that these four areas together must equal $(a + b)^2$.

Mary: Mr. Rudd, I can't do this one.
Casey: Is the expression written in standard form?
Mary: Yes.
Casey: Are the first and third terms perfect squares?

Mary: Yes.
Casey: Then that means you are on which step on the board?
Mary: Ahh, 5.
Casey: Okay, go with step 5. I'll be back in 33 seconds.

Exhibit 8.27
Brief test for objectives C, D, E, and F (see Exhibit 8.10) Casey uses on the fifth day of the algebra I Unit 7.

Algebra I — Brief Test 7–2

1. Write $18x^2 - 12x$ in factored form;

   $18x^2 - 12x =$ _____

   Prove your answer with the distributive property $ab + ac = a(b + c)$ by indicating what you let a, b, and c equal:

   $a =$ _____ , $b =$ _____ , $c =$ _____

2. What is the GCF of $14ac + 21a^3$?

   _____

3. Factor $3x^3y^2 + 9xy^2 + 36xy$

   _____

4. Factor $25w^2 - 81q^4$

   _____

5. Factor $\frac{2}{3}x^2 - \frac{8}{3}$

   _____

6. Illustrate why $100 - x^2 = (10 + x)(10 - x)$ for $x < 10$ by writing in dimensions for the region shown below and then by drawing a rectangle with the same area:

Casey returns just in time:

Mary: So, this middle term has to be $2ab$. But I still don't get it.
Casey: What's a in this case?
Mary: n.
Casey: n or $-n$, and what's b in this case?
Mary: 6 or -6.
Casey: Is there any way $-13n$ could be $2ab$ for any of those values of a and b?

Casey moves to another student as Mary completes the exercise and moves on to number 6.

Planning for Day 6

That evening, Casey plans for Tuesday's classes. He thinks about the algebra class: "So up to this point, all of them—with the possible exception of Dick, Blair, and Delia—seem to be just fine as far as conceptualizing the three algorithms we've covered. Skillwise most of them are coming along. . . . Let's see, next, we go to the biggie—factoring $ax^2 + bx^2 + c$—objectives I and J. I'd better wait on those until they've had more practice with the distributive one, the difference of squares, and perfect-square trinomials. Also, we haven't hit on any kind of real-life problem-solving since the second day. I shouldn't go any longer without some application work, or else they'll lose that real-world connection. Okay, better build in some applications for tomorrow for the three algorithms—that means we'll begin working on parts of Objective L before getting to objectives I and J. . . . Also, I should work computer utilization into the practice and review lessons. . . ."

As Casey develops the detailed plan, he gets quite frustrated attempting to formulate or locate real-life problems in which the three factoring algorithms apply. Any problem he thinks will interest students and in which factoring is truly useful requires the upcoming algorithm for $ax^2 + bx + c$. He avoids problems solvable by finding roots to equations such as $x^2 - 25 = 0$ because he would rather students use common sense to reason that x^2 is 25, so x can only be 5 or -5 rather than blindly adhering to a factoring algorithm for solving such an equation. Consequently, he reluctantly uses contrived rather than actual real-life problems for his lesson (e.g., the two word problems in the worksheet of Exhibit 8.28).

The agenda Casey develops is displayed as Exhibit 8.29.

Day 6

Twenty-five minutes into the class period, the class has completed the first five agenda items and Casey initiates the interactive lecture session in item 6. Casey displays the same transparency (see Exhibit 8.13) he used one week ago when the class discussed the crime-solver problem.

Casey: I'd like for someone to come up here and quickly summarize the problem this reminds you of. . . . Marlene.

Marlene: This woman was accused of stealing stuff from this garage here. . . . But she was seen at the drugstore over here just before that. The problem was, did she have enough time to get from the drugstore to the garage to have committed the crime.

Casey: How far would she have had to travel?

Marlene: 7.2 miles.

Casey: Thank you. The day after we solved that problem we classified problems you people came up with for homework as either solvable by factoring or not. . . . Here's a sample of those problems.

Casey begins showing a few problems from those transparencies, one at a time:

Casey: This one was a factoring problem. . . . This one, not. . . . This one, yes. . . . This one,

yes. . . . This one, no. . . . This one, yes. . . . Now, what is special about the problems where the solution required the undoing of multiplication, or factoring? . . . Omar.

Omar: In all those we were given some product, like 7.2, and we had to find out different combinations that got you to it.

Casey: So, if I knew the dimensions of a polygon and I wanted to find the area, would I have one of those factoring problems? . . . Megan.

Megan: Yes, sir.

Casey: Why would it be?

Megan: I don't know.

Casey: What did Omar tell us we're given in one of those kinds of problems?

Megan: I don't remember.

Casey: Thanks for waiting; go ahead, Kyle.

Kyle: It wouldn't be a factoring problem, because you have to multiply—not undo multiplying.

Casey: Turn it around so that it would be a factoring problem, Kyle.

Kyle: You want to find the dimensions and you know the area.

Casey: How did I originally describe the type of problem, Megan?

Megan: Something about a polygon.

Casey: Cassandra?

Cassandra: You wanted the polygon's area, and you knew its dimensions. Kyle reversed it, where you had the area but not the dimensions.

Casey: Write your statement on the upper right corner of the board, Omar—the one about describing the kind of problems that are solvable using factoring. We're now going to discuss using factoring to solve equations. We aren't switching topics; we're still going to be dealing with the kind of problem Omar's statement described. What we'll be doing is developing a more systematic approach to solving those kind of problems. To get us started, turn your attention to the homework worksheet for the first day of this unit—it looks like this. . . . You don't have yours, Xavier? . . . Magnolia, would you mind if Xavier looks on with you? Thank you. Everybody, look at what you have for item 4. . . . Read yours, giving us one a, b pair at a time, Magnolia.

Magnolia: 0, 7; 7, 0; 0, 0; 11, 0; 1, 0.

Casey: How is yours different than Magnolia's, and how is it the same, Alena?

Alena: Well, I had 1, 0 and then—

Casey: I didn't say what I meant. Don't give us your list. *Describe* how yours differs and how it's the same without actually listing your pairs.

Exhibit 8.28

Homework worksheet Casey plans to assign on day 6 of the algebra I unit on factoring polynomials.

1. Answer the following questions assuming that a and b are two numbers such that $ab = 0$.

   If a is 19, what is b?_____

   If b is -3.74, what is a?_____

   If a is positive, what must be true about b?_____

   If b is negative, what must be true about a?_____

   If $a = 0$, what must be true about a?_____

2. Answer the following questions assuming that c and d are two numbers such that $cd \neq 0$.

   What can you conclude about c?_____

   What can you conclude about d?_____

3. There are two numbers for which the following statement is true:

   Seven times the square of the number equals 14 times the number.

   For what two numbers is that statement true? Display your work and write the numbers in the blanks.

   _____ and _____

4. Sam's age times itself is the same as 30 times his age less 225. How old is Sam? Display your work and write Sam's age in the blank.

   _____

5. According to a principle of physics:

   If an object is launched from the ground into the air and allowed to fall back to the ground, its height above the ground during the trip is governed by the following formula:

   $$h = vt - 16t^2$$

   where h is the number of feet above the ground the object is t seconds after launch and v is the velocity at which it left the ground in feet per second.

   Use this formula to assess how many seconds a golf ball will be in flight if it is hit so that it leaves the ground at a velocity of 64 feet per second.

   Hint: First solve for h by answering the following question: How high off the ground is the ball when it lands after being hit?

   Draw a picture illustrating the path of the ball, display your work and write your answer in the blank.

   _____

6. Enter, debug, and save on a disk the computer programs for factoring polynomials that we wrote in class.

7. For each of the following, use the programs to determine if the polynomial can be expressed in factored form with integer coefficients; if so, factor it and print out the results.

   $$3a + 54a^2 + 81a$$

   $$70x^2 - 7x^2 - 2y(500y + 4y)$$

   $$9b^2 + 16c^2 + 24bc$$

   $$5x^2 - 24x + 10$$

Exhibit 8.29
Casey's agenda for the sixth day of the algebra I unit on factoring polynomials.

1. Transition period, during which I start class and direct the students to do the following:
   ❑ Take out their homework and display it on their desktops.
   ❑ Begin working the mini-review exercise on p. 223 [a short exercise on topics from prior units].
2. Independent work session on the mini-review as I quickly check homework and direct some students to display selected homework exercises on the chalkboard.
3. Transition period, in which the work on the mini-review is halted and attention is directed to the completed homework exercises now displayed on the board.
4. Interactive lecture and questioning/discussion session in which
   ❑ Students individually explain to the class how they completed the homework exercises displayed on the board.
   ❑ Homework and mini-review exercises about which students raise questions are discussed.
5. Transition period directing students to put away homework and to
   ❑ Turn their notebooks to the pages relating to the first two days of the unit in which we worked on the crime-solver problem and in which they developed problems and displayed them on transparencies.
   ❑ Retrieve their completed homework worksheet for the first day (see Exhibit 8.12).
6. Interactive lecture session in which I
   ❑ Play upon their previous work on the first 2 days of the unit to get them to deduce how factoring can be used in solving open sentences.
   ❑ Walk them through writing computer programs for factoring differences of perfect squares and perfect square trinomials.
7. Transition period for distributing and assigning the homework worksheet (see Exhibit 8.28).
8. Independent work session for beginning homework.
9. Transition period into the second period.

Alena: Okay, ahh . . . just a minute, let me think. . . . This is hard. . . . Mine's different because my numbers aren't all the same as hers. But mine's the same because, like Magnolia, every pair has at least one 0 — it's got to!

Casey: Why does it have to, Megan?

Megan: You're picking on me today?

Casey: Possibly. Why does either a or b have to be zero if $-3ab = 0$?

Megan: Because the only thing you can multiply 3 by to get 0 is 0. So, ab is 0, and 0 times anything is 0.

Casey: Now, Megan makes an important point for us. Zero times any number is 0, alright. For our purposes, let's turn that around. Okay, Salvador.

Salvador: The only way the product of two numbers can be 0 is if one of the numbers is 0.

Casey: Write that down for us under Omar's statement. . . . Consider how we might solve his equation.

Casey displays $3x(x - 8) = 0$ with the overhead.

Casey: Jot down the solution. . . . What did you put, Alphonse?

Alphonse: 0.

Casey: If $x = 0$ as Alphonse indicates, what is $x - 8$? . . . Delia.

Delia: I don't know.

Casey: Look at this equation. . . .

Casey writes $ab = 0$ right under $3x(x - 8) = 0$.

Casey: What is b if a is zero, Delia?

Delia: It can be any number.

Casey: So, let $b = x - 8$. . . . Go back to the original equation. . . . $3x = 0$, so what about $x - 8$? . . . Delia.

Delia: Any number.

Casey: But if $3x = 0$, then what's x? Megan.

Megan: 0.

Casey: If $x = 0$ as Megan and Alphonse said, what is $x - 8$? Delia.

Delia: Anyth—. . . Oh! Then $x - 8$ is $0 - 8$, which is just -8! I get it!

Casey: So for $3x(x - 8) = 0$, we have numbers multiplied together giving a product of what, Xavier?

Xavier: 0.

Casey: So, for the equation to be true . . . Juaquin?

Juaquin: One of the factors has to be 0. So, either $3x = 0$, which means $x = 0$ or the other one can be zero.

Casey: Keep going. What's true if the other one is zero—that is, if $x - 8 = 0$?

Juaquin: Then $x = 8$.

Casey: Dustin.

Dustin: I don't get it. How can $x = 0$ and $x = -8$?

Casey: Dustin, it can't. . . . But x can equal 0 *or* x can equal -8. This equation happens to have two solutions. . . . Kyle.

Kyle: I get it. It's like $ab = 0$. a is $3x$ and b is $x - 8$. The x in the $3x$ equals 0; the x in the $x - 8$ equals 8. . . . Right?

Casey: You've got the idea, but technically what you said is not exactly right. And I'm not sure how to help you clear it up in the amount of time we have left. . . . Let me try something. I don't know if it's going to help, but it's worth a try. We didn't run into this problem with $ab = 0$ because we were dealing with two different variables. So when we took the case that $a = 0$, b could be anything. Now, as Kyle pointed out to us, $(3x)(x - 8) = 0$ works the same way with one difference. . . . $3x$ and $x - 8$ are related, so the value of one affects the value of the other. So in the case of $3x = 0$, x must $= 0$ and there's only one number x—it's the same x. . . .

Looking at the sea of blank faces, Casey feels ambivalent. He feels that some of the students who tend to struggle in mathematics are on the threshold of conceptual-level understanding, but on the other hand, he realizes that the subtleties of what he is trying to explain are not coming across to them. Noticing that there are only 14 minutes remaining, he continues:

Casey: We have a point of confusion that we have yet to clear up. But instead of me rattling on about it, I think we should look at two more equations and then assign the homework. The experience should help the explanations make more sense tomorrow. Look at this equation.

Casey displays $x^2 - 7x = 0$.

Casey: Let's find what if any values for x make this statement true. With the previous equation, $3x(x - 8) = 0$, we had a polynomial in factored form equal to 0. So, we knew that the

equation held for any x-value where one of the factors equaled 0. . . . But with this one, we have a binomial equal to 0. We're looking at the difference of two terms, not the product. . . . Any suggestions? . . . Does anyone see a way we could rewrite this binomial so that it's in factored form? Then we could find solutions by finding values of x that make a factor equal 0. . . . Okay, Mary.

Mary: Just factor the polynomial.

Casey: Everybody, take Mary's suggestion— quietly, on the paper in front of you. Shhh, just do it please. . . . Tell us what the equation looks like on your paper, Edwin.

Edwin: I took the x out and got $x(x - 7)$.

Casey: Read the whole equation please.

Edwin: $x(x - 7) = 0$.

Casey: If one of two things is true, the statement is true. What are those two things, Magnolia?

Magnolia: If $x = 0$ or if $x - 7 = 0$.

Casey: And if $x - 7 = 0$, what's x in that case, Sid?

Sid: 7.

Casey: We've got time for one or two more quick ones.

Casey writes and displays $12x^2 = 4x$.

Casey: How about this one? . . . Okay, Juaquin.

Juaquin: Just divide both sides by $4x$ and you get $3x = 0$. So x has to be zero.

Casey writes and displays the following:

$$12x^2 = 4x$$
$$\frac{12x^2}{4x} = \frac{4x}{4x}$$
$$3x = ?$$

Casey: What's $4x$ over $4x$?

Juaquin: Oh, yeah, it's 1, not 0. . . . So then, $3x = 1$, and $x = \frac{1}{3}$.

Casey: Everybody, quickly try $\frac{1}{3}$ for x in the original equation and see if it works. Put your hand up if and when you find that it does. . . . Okay, so $x = \frac{1}{3}$ works. Does any other value for x? . . . Sid.

Sid: $x = 0$.

Casey: Everybody, try it. Raise your hand if and when you find it works. . . . Okay. So we've got two cases for x that work. Let me just raise a little caution flag about solving equations like this. Be careful dividing through by the unknown variable for two reasons: One, you might lose a solution, and two, you need to watch that you don't try to divide by 0. By the way, we did nicely on that one, but I was surprised because I expected we'd do this.

Casey writes and displays the following:

$$12x^2 = 4x$$
$$12x^2 - 4x = 0$$
$$4x(3x - 1) = 0$$
Either $4x = 0$ or $3x - 1 = 0$.
If $4x = 0$, then $x = 0$.
If $3x - 1 = 0$, then $x = \frac{1}{3}$.

Casey: Let's squeeze in one more. I'm just going to write it out quickly; you copy it and think about it as part of homework.

Casey writes and displays:

$$x^2 + 25 = 10x$$
$$x^2 + 25 - 10x = 0$$
$$x^2 - 10x + 25 = 0$$
$$(x - 5)^2 = 0$$
$$x = 5$$

He then distributes the homework worksheet (see Exhibit 8.28) but assigns only items 1–5 because he did not get to the computer programming part of the day's agenda (i.e., the second part of item 6 of Exhibit 8.29). The bell sounds, and Casey is left pondering what happened in the class. However, he quickly turns his thoughts to the business at hand—third-period geometry.

Reflecting on Day 6 and Planning for Day 7

After school, Casey thinks about the day's algebra class and plans for Wednesday's. He thinks: "That session was exciting, but it sure went a bit haywire when I tried to parallel $3x(x - 8) = 0$ with $ab = 0$. . . . Next time, I'll anticipate some of them thinking the x in $3x$ stands for something different than the x in $x - 8$. I learn something every day! Anyway, I don't think there's any way I can explain that nuance to them until they pick up more experiences factoring to solve real-life problems. Then they'll be able to make the connections. That's why I wanted to get into applications before we got to the really useful stuff—$ax^2 + bx + c = 0$—but I hate waiting too long without touching real-life situations. As things went, my planned *application* lesson turned out to be more of a *conceptualization* lesson!

"I hadn't realized that the little business we did with that homework worksheet [see item 4 of Exhibit 8.12] on the first day didn't do the conceptual-

ization trick for most of them. It seems like such a straightforward idea—if $ab = 0$, then a or b must be 0! But I've got to remember these kids are just being introduced to this stuff; I've been using that relation for years.

"The unit is going to work out fine. Even though I didn't spend enough time with conceptualization in the beginning, I'm making up for it now. There's still time to work on application—especially after we get through Objective J. Maybe today's lesson coupled with some review and practice tomorrow will provide them with enough of a hint that factoring has real-world applicability. Of course, part of the difficulty is that the algorithms we've covered to this point in the unit are included because they lead to something that's useful, not necessarily because they are all that useful themselves. At least, they seem to be hanging in with me, and I've already given them more real-life applications of mathematics than I ever had in any six mathematics courses I ever took!

"I'd better stop trying to make myself feel better and start deciding where we go with the rest of this unit. . . . First of all, I need to follow up with this homework assignment and use their work on that to further the conceptualization stuff and give them more of an idea about applications of factoring. . . . Most everybody will have done okay with items 1 and 2 [see Exhibit 8.28]. Work with item 3 will help clear up that business about x being one number *and* another rather than one number *or* another. . . . I doubt if too many of them will really understand item 5, but it gets us into application. Actually, there's a nice progression in that worksheet from the conceptualization stuff of items 1 and 2 to the thought problems of 3 and 4 and then the heavy application word problem of 5. Not bad, Casey!

"After we get through the homework, I've simply got to walk them through writing the computer programs as planned for today. . . . Then I should give them practice with the algorithms to this point and wait until Friday or so to go on to the conceptualization lesson on factoring trinomials. If things go well tomorrow, we could get to that Thursday, but if I try to do that, we probably wouldn't start until the latter part of the period, then maybe run out of class time and not reach closure. . . . This unit may go a day or two longer than planned, but if I rush things, it'll just create difficulties in Unit 8 and on down the line. . . ."

Days 7 to 14

Day 7

On Wednesday, Casey reviews the homework and then completes the computer program–writing activity previously planned for Tuesday (i.e., the second part of agenda item 6 of Exhibit 8.29). For homework, he assigns items 6 and 7 from Exhibit 8.28, several word problems similar to items 3–5 in Exhibit 8.28, and textbook exercises practicing the factoring algorithms.

Day 8
After reviewing the homework on Thursday, Casey divides the class into three independent work groups. Some students go to the computer lab to complete factoring exercises using the programs they entered and debugged for homework. Another group utilizes the classroom computers to work on the same exercise. The remaining students engage in small-task-group sessions, working on word problems similar to item 5 in Exhibit 8.28.

Day 9
Casey finally gets to conduct the lesson on Objective I (see Exhibit 8.10) that he's been anticipating since the unit began. In an intellectual-level questioning/discussion session, he takes advantage of students' prior understanding of the FOIL method for multiplying binomials (i.e., the two first terms are multiplied, then the two outer terms, followed by the two inside terms, and then the two last terms) to lead them to formulate the algorithm for factoring trinomials.

A small-task-group session follows, in which four subgroups of about six students each work with cardboard rectangular regions developing geometric models for factoring different trinomials (e.g., $2x^2 + 3x + 1 = (x + 1)(2x + 1)$). The activity, the idea for which Casey picked up from Sobel and Maletsky (1988, 174–175), is illustrated in Exhibit 8.30.

The Weekend
Over the weekend, Casey uses procedures explained in the section "Designing and Constructing Tests" in Chapter 7 to develop the unit test for Objectives A–L listed in Exhibit 8.10. Appendix F contains a copy of the test resulting from his effort. He also synthesizes a practice test to use in a review session he'll conduct the day before the unit test is scheduled.

Day 10
Monday's class is devoted to direct instructional activities on the algorithm for factoring trinomials (i.e., Objective J from Exhibit 8.10). In Vignette 4.15 is a list of the steps in the algorithm Casey explains during this session. An independent work session and a homework assignment provide students with skill-level practice with the algorithm.

Day 11
On Tuesday, Casey guides the students through the writing of a computer program for factoring trino-

mials, as he has done for previous algorithms. He then distributes a worksheet containing word problems to be solved. As suggested in the section "Learning Activities for Application-Level Objectives" in Chapter 4, the worksheet contains both example problems solvable via factoring and non-example problems solvable via methods from prior units. Assigning the worksheet is Casey's first step in conducting a deductive lesson for Objective L (see Exhibit 8.10).

During the remainder of the period, the class engages in an independent work session in which some students work with classroom computers to enter and debug their programs and others begin working on the worksheet. All students are directed to complete both tasks for homework.

Day 12
On Wednesday, Casey conducts an intellectual-level questioning/discussion session relative to Objective L. His deductive questions focus on the problems students addressed for homework and lead them through the first three of the four stages of an application lesson (i.e., (1) initial problem confrontation and analysis, (2) subsequent problem confrontation and analysis, (3) rule articulation, and (4) extension into subsequent lessons) as explained in "Facilitating Application-Level Learning" in Chapter 4.

For homework, Casey assigns the practice test he developed over the weekend.

Day 13
Thursday is review day. The practice test that students were directed to complete for homework is reviewed and questions relative to any of the unit's topics raised by the review are addressed.

Day 14
Friday, the students take the unit test.

Scoring and Interpreting the Test
Casey scores the test and, with the aid of his computer, generates the detailed results shown in Exhibit 8.31. Using the compromise method explained in Chapter 7, he converts the scores to grades for the unit with scores greater than or equal to 74 assigned A's, scores between 65 and 70 assigned B's, scores between 40 and 60 assigned C's, the scores 22 and 24 assigned D's, and the score of 15 assigned an F.

The following are among the conclusions he draws from his analysis of the item-by-item results:

❏ In general, students tended to have more trouble expressing themselves about mathematics than executing mathematics.

Exhibit 8.30

Casey uses an experiment for factoring a trinomial (excerpted from Sobel and Maletsky 1988, 174–175).

Factoring a Trinomial

Material

A set of large squares measuring x by x, labeled by their areas as $x \times x$ or simply x^2.

A set of small squares measuring 1 by 1, labeled by their areas as 1×1 or simply 1.

A set of rectangles measuring x by 1, labeled by their areas as $x \times 1$ or simply x.

Directions

Monomials, binomials, and trinomials in x can now be represented by the appropriate geometric figures.

In factoring a trinomial, the various monomial parts are arranged in a rectangular shape. The dimensions of the rectangle give the factors.

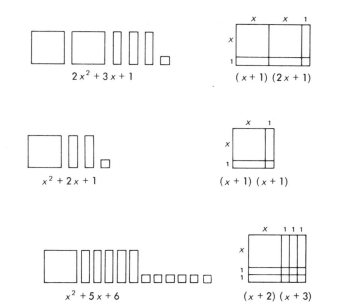

1. Show how to factor $3x^2 + 4x + 1$ using a model.
2. Show how to factor $4x^2 + 8x + 3$ using a model.
3. Show some other trinomials that can be factored using a model. Show some that cannot be factored.
4. Imagine a rectangular array of these pieces measuring $5x + 1$ by $2x + 3$. How many pieces are in it? How many of each size are there? What trinomial factorization does it represent?

Source: Max A. Sobel/Evan M. Maletsky, TEACHING MATHEMATICS: A Sourcebook of Aids, Activities, & Strategies, 2e, © 1988, pp. 174–175. Reprinted by permission of Prentice Hall, Inc., Englewood Cliffs, New Jersey.

❑ Overall, students achieved at the application level (i.e., Objective L) better than he had expected.

❑ Students in general—but especially those who scored below 60—tended to have difficulty with Item II, which was designed to be relevant to Objective A.

❑ He should think about developing and using strategies for:

Providing Magnolia and Juaquin with more advanced work;

Keeping Delia and Xavier engaged in learning activities, because their lack of attention and effort probably lead to their failure to achieve this unit's goal satisfactorily;

Remediating what appears to be significant learning gaps in Dick's understanding of mathematics.

Casey notes individual students' responses to certain items that he wants shared with the class on Monday when the test is reviewed. Since he plans to

Exhibit 8.31
Detailed results from Casey's Unit 7
test from Appendix F.

Item (Max. Points)	II (8)	III (3)	IV (3)	V (3)	VI (8)	VII (12)	VIII (28)	IX (8)	X (8)	Test Score (81)
Magnolia	8	3	3	3	8	12	28	8	8	81
Juaquin	8	2	3	3	8	12	27	8	8	80
Marlene	6	3	3	3	8	10	28	8	8	77
Alena	7	2	1	3	8	12	28	8	8	77
Cassandra	6	3	3	2	8	12	25	8	8	75
Kevin	5	3	2	3	7	10	28	8	8	74
Omar	3	3	3	3	3	10	28	8	8	69
Tawny	8	3	3	3	8	2	28	6	8	69
Edwin	7	1	3	3	8	12	20	6	8	68
Megan	4	3	3	3	8	12	28	3	4	68
Sid	5	3	2	3	4	9	26	8	8	68
Chevron	8	2	3	3	8	12	19	5	8	68
Salvador	8	3	3	3	4	10	24	6	6	67
Dustin	8	3	3	3	8	4	25	6	6	66
Mary	6	1	2	2	4	7	28	8	8	66
Kyle	4	3	3	1	6	10	22	4	6	59
Mylinn	1	1	1	0	8	10	22	8	8	59
Amad	2	2	2	2	7	10	19	6	6	56
Ron	3	3	3	3	8	10	15	4	6	55
Alphonse	2	3	3	3	4	6	26	4	4	55
Russell	6	3	3	3	8	2	12	4	5	46
Blair	5	3	3	3	4	4	13	4	5	44
Delia	2	2	3	0	1	6	5	2	3	24
Xavier	4	2	3	0	3	1	7	1	1	22
Dick	2	1	0	1	2	3	4	1	1	15
Ann	Has not taken test									—

$n = 25$ $\mu = 60.32$ $\sigma = 17.51$ $r = 0.78$ SEM $= 8.21$

utilize small task groups as part of the review session, he determines the composition of the subgroups so each subgroup has at least two students with high scores.

Day 15

Casey reviews the test results with the class by following the four stages explained in the section "Formative Feedback," in Chapter 7. In the latter part of the class, Casey uses the discussion of items IX and X to lead into Unit 8, "Quadratic Equations."

SAMPLE GEOMETRY TEACHING UNIT

Although preparing for, conducting, and evaluating outcomes from his algebra I class alone could keep Casey busy every day, Casey must split his time among five classes. While preparing and orchestrating the algebra I unit on factoring polynomials, he is also busy with a third-period geometry unit on polygonal similarity. Exhibit 8.32 displays the overall plan Casey follows for that unit.

SAMPLE CONSUMER MATHEMATICS TEACHING UNIT

Reread the section "Fifth-Period Consumer Mathematics," in this chapter. Casey designed the consumer mathematics course with 16 units in mind:

1. Using mathematics to make decisions
2. Measurements and numbers
3. Calculating, organizing data, and using formulas
4. Using statistics
5. Using computers
6. Saving and investing money
7. Borrowing
8. Spending wisely
9. Acquiring a place to live
10. Maintaining a home
11. Construction and trades
12. Taxes
13. Insurance
14. Transportation and travel
15. Sports, hobbies, and recreation
16. Occupations and employment

Exhibit 8.32
Casey's plan for the unit on polygonal similarity.

Course: Geometry

Unit no.: 10 out of 18

Title: Polygonal Similarity

Goal: Discovers and proves certain similarity relations and uses them in problem solving.

Weighted objectives:

(15%) A. Distinguishes between examples and nonexamples of similarity relations between two polygons *(conceptualization)*.

(05%) B. Defines the following terms: *similar polygons, proportion,* and *geometric mean* (*simple knowledge*).

(05%) C. Explains how the algebra of proportions relates to similarity between polygons *(comprehension)*.

(33%) D. Explains why each of the following relations holds:
   1. Side-splitting theorem.
   2. Converse of the side-splitting theorem.
   3. AAA similarity postulate.
   4. AA similarity theorem.
   5. Two right triangles are similar if an acute angle of one triangle is congruent to an acute angle of the other triangle.
   6. In a right triangle, the length of the altitude to the hypotenuse is the geometric mean between the lengths of the two segments of the hypotenuse.
   7. Given a right triangle and the altitude to the hypotenuse, each leg is the geometric mean between the length of the hypotenuse and the length of the segment of the hypotenuse adjacent to the leg.
   8. SSS similarity theorem.
   9. SAS similarity theorem.
   (conceptualization).

(20%) E. Proves similarity theorems *(application)*.

(02%) F. Writes and uses computer programs to execute algorithms used in applying similarity relations to the solutions of problems *(comprehension)*.

(20%) G. Given a real-life problem, determines how, if at all, a solution to that problem is facilitated by using relations derived from the AAA similarity postulate or theorems listed for Objective D *(application)*.

Estimated number of class periods: 14

Textbook page references: 304–329 and 336–339 (unless otherwise indicated, page numbers referred to in the overall lesson plan are from the course textbook (Clemens, O'Daffer, and Cooney 1984).

Overall plan for lessons: Throughout the unit, the students who are in both this class and Mr. Bosnick's art class (12 out of 23 students) will be applying what they learn about polygonal similarity to a perspective art project. Those students will be reporting the progress of their project in class. (Estimated time needed: *A total of 1.5 class periods intermittently distributed over about 7 days.*)

After completing the first 12 units, he is pleased with how the course has gone. However, he is concerned that virtually no new mathematics is introduced in units 6–12, as those units focus on applying previously learned mathematics to new situations. He is now planning for Unit 14, "Transportation and Travel."

Chapter 8 of the course's textbook (Keedy, Smith, and Anderson 1986, 263–301) is the principal reference for the unit. Casey rereads the chapter's section headings: "Buying a Car," "Buying a Motorcycle," "Financing Your Purchase," "Maintenance and Repair," "Highway Safety," "Planning a Trip," "Renting a Car," "Recreational Vehicles," and "Air Travel."

He thinks: "If I follow the book, there are nine topics, or situations, to apply the same mathematics we've been applying for the last eight units. I'd like

Exhibit 8.32 continued

For **Objective A,** I will conduct a seven-stage inductive lesson [as explained in this book's section "Inductive Learning Activities" in Chapter 4] using examples and nonexamples of similar pairs in the task-confrontation stage. (Estimated time needed: *1 class period plus homework.*)

For **Objective B,** direct instructional and exposure to word usage will be integrated within lessons for the other objectives to help students utilize the vocabulary terms in communications. (Estimated time needed: *1–3 intermittent minutes each class period plus homework.*)

For **Objective C,** direct instruction will be used to help students comprehend the explanation and examples in the section "Proportions" on pp. 304–305. Exercises from pp. 306–307 will be assigned for an independent work session and homework. (Estimated time needed: *1 class period plus homework.*)

Relative to the first two relations listed under Objective D (the side-splitting theorem and its converse), lessons for **Objectives D, E,** and **G** will be conducted according to the following pattern:

1. Inductive learning activities leading to the discovery of the relations
2. Deductive learning activities leading to proofs of theorems deduced from the relations
3. Deductive learning activities leading to application of the relations to problem solving
4. Exercises assigned from pp. 310–311
5. A brief test for formative feedback

(Estimated time needed: *1.5 class periods plus homework.*)

Relative to the third, fourth, and fifth relations listed under Objective D (AAA similarity postulate, AA similarity theorem, and the theorem on similarity of two right triangles), lessons for **Objectives D, E,** and **G** will follow the same five-step pattern but with the exercises being assigned from pp. 318–321. (Estimated time needed: *2.25 class periods plus homework.*)

Relative to the sixth and seventh relations listed under Objective D (the two relative to geometric means), lessons for **Objectives D, E,** and **G** will follow the same five-step pattern but with the exercises being assigned from pp. 324–325. (Estimated time needed: *2 class periods plus homework.*)

Relative to the eighth and ninth relations listed under Objective D (SSS and SAS similarity theorems), lessons for **Objectives D, E,** and **G** will follow the same five-step pattern but with the exercises being assigned from pp. 328–329. (Estimated time needed: *2.25 class periods plus homework.*)

For **Objective F,** I'll conduct a direct instructional lesson, guiding students through writing a single program and having them enter, debug, and utilize it for homework. (Estimated time needed: *0.75 class period plus homework.*)

Using a practice test, I'll conduct a review session for the unit test over objectives A–G. (Estimated time needed: *0.75 class period plus homework.*)

A unit test over objectives A–G will be administered and the results reviewed with the class. (Estimated time needed: *1.75 class periods*)

Extraordinary learning materials and equipment needed: No materials are needed that have not already been used in previous units.

to break the monotony of the pattern I set for Units 6–13.

"Let's see, 28 students in the class—if I farm out these nine topics to cooperative small task groups, that'd give us eight groups of three and one group of four—maybe make the group responsible for searching out information on how to apply the mathematics to the type of situation and teach the rest of the class. . . . It would really be nice to spice it up somehow, turn it into some sort of project. But what?

"I've got it! They love to perform in front of the video camera, and almost all of them are interested in television and videos. What if I assigned each group a topic for them to develop a short how-to-do-something—like plan a trip—videotape program? . . . I'd have to set some tight parameters—making sure they get to the application of the relevant

Exhibit 8.33
Casey's plan for the consumer mathematics unit on transportation and travel.

Course: Consumer Mathematics

Unit no.: 14 out of 16

Title: Transportation and Travel   Note: For purposes of this unit transportation/ travel includes buying a car, buying a motorcycle, financing your purchase, maintenance and repair, highway safety, planning a trip, renting a car, recreational vehicles, air travel.

Goal: Applies fundamental relations from arithmetic, algebra, and statistics to solve problems related to transportation and travel.

Weighted objectives:

(10%) A. Translates the meaning of the following terms in the context of transportation/travel-related situations: Cash price of a vehicle, base price of a vehicle, sticker price of a vehicle, down payment, amount financed, finance charge, deferred payment price, parts and materials costs, labor charges, taxable items, stopping distance, drag factors, nomogram, base air fare, discount air fare, special rate air fare, and excess baggage fare *(comprehension).*

(25%) B. Explains the rationale underlying fundamental formulas used in solving transportation/travel-related problems *(conceptualization).*

(10%) C. Executes algorithms based on fundamental formulas used in solving transportation/travel-related problems *(knowledge of a process).*

(55%) D. Given a transportation/travel-related problem, explains how, if at all, mathematical relations and algorithms learned in Units 1–5 can be used to solve the problem *(application).*

Estimated number of class periods: 16

Textbook page references: 263–301 & 336–339 (Keedy, Smith, and Anderson 1986)

General approach for conducting the unit: The class will be subdivided into nine groups of three or four each, with each group being assigned one of the nine transportation/travel topics listed in the objectives. Each group is to undertake a project in which they produce a videotape program (approximately 25 minutes long) designed to help the rest of the class achieve the four objectives of the unit relative to the assigned topic. I will supervise each group's project from design through production and presentation.

---

mathematics, limit the length of the programs, clearly define the audience—that stuff."

Deciding to try out the idea, Casey develops the overall unit plan shown in Exhibit 8.33.

At the conclusion of the unit, Casey judges that the cooperative group videotape program projects worked so well that he should use the approach more in the future and also in other courses.

SAMPLE PRECALCULUS TEACHING UNIT

Reread the section "Sixth Period Precalculus" in this chapter. Exhibit 8.34 displays the overall plan for one of Casey's precalculus units. Note that the format Casey uses to capture his plans for achieving the objectives differs from those in Exhibits 8.10,

8.32, and 8.33. He modifies his planning methods as he learns what works best for him and according to his purposes at the time.

INSERVICE OPPORTUNITIES AND THE NCTM CONFERENCE

Throughout the school year, Casey avails himself of opportunities to improve his teaching performances. Meetings of the local affiliate of NCTM provide opportunities to share ideas with colleagues and hear presentations on mathematics and on teaching mathematics. Although they rarely address his particular teaching situation, his creative thinking about teaching is stimulated by a college graduate course he manages to attend one night a week and

Exhibit 8.33 continued

Overall plan for lessons: In an interactive lecture session, I'll (1) provide the class with an overview of the plans for the unit, (2) organize the nine subgroups (based on selections I make prior to class—ideally, each group will have a student who has a relatively easy time with mathematics and one who does not but who is knowledgeable about the travel/transportation area), (3) distribute resources, and (4) explain and have them begin the initial assignment for each group (which will involve reading the relevant section of the textbook and gathering background information). (Estimated time needed: *1 class period plus homework.*)

Each group will report results of the initial assignment to the class and then I will specify the parameters for the projects, explaining what is to be included and outlining each of the following phases: information-gathering, analyzing, designing, script-writing, evaluating/refining, and video-program production. (Estimated time needed: *1.75 class periods plus homework.*)

In small-task-group sessions, each group will develop, evaluate, and refine a data-gathering, development, and production plan and have it critiqued and approved by me. (Estimated time needed: *1.5 class sessions plus homework.*)

Students will engage in data-gathering activities, including visiting off-campus sites as necessary and practical. (Estimated time needed: *1 class period plus homework.*)

In small-task-group sessions, each group will complete their production according to its approved plan. Productions are scheduled and presented to the class as a whole as soon as reasonably possible upon completion. Students observing a production are responsible for learning from the presentations in order to achieve the unit's objectives. I will conduct a questioning/discussion session on each of the nine topics after it is presented. Brief tests will be intermittently scheduled for formative feedback. (Estimated time needed: *10 class periods plus homework.*)

A unit test will be administered and the results reviewed with the class. (Estimated time needed: *1.5 class periods.*)

Extraordinary learning materials, equipment, and arrangement needed: (1) Informational resources (e.g., travel and buyers' guides), (2) arrangements for students to visit automobile dealers, motorcycle dealers, recreational vehicle dealers, travel bureaus, auto-rental outlets, and motor vehicle safety office, and (3) equipment and supplies for videotaping in the classroom over a 2-week period.

by several inservice workshops sponsored by the school district. Although he had enjoyed the journal *Mathematics Teacher* for a number of years, he finds the articles even more meaningful now that he has real students and actual courses to teach. His continuous struggle to come up with meaningful examples and real-world problems for his conceptualization and application lessons motivates him to read about mathematics more than ever before. The almost constant need to respond to students' queries and thoughts causes him to gain insights into mathematics and into human behavior that he never before imagined.

He learns from interacting with colleagues and they learn from him. Vanessa Castillo's help is invaluable; even teachers with whom he disagrees on most pedagogical issues (e.g., Don Delaney) stimulate productive thoughts.

In April, Casey takes three professional leave days to attend the annual NCTM conference. There, he interacts with colleagues from around the world, whose goals, problems, frustrations, and successes appear remarkably familiar after 8 months in the profession. Although the school year is winding down, Casey is energized by the professional associations as well as the conference sessions. Some sessions include hands-on activities; others have speakers presenting ideas or research findings. The quality of the sessions varies considerably from very boring to very exciting, but all leave Casey with thoughts that will improve his classroom effectiveness. At the conference, Casey

Exhibit 8.34 (pp. 292–294)
Casey's plan for the precalculus
unit on sequences.

Course: Precalculus

Unit no.: 6 out of 9

Title: Sequences

Goal: Understands the language of discrete mathematics; discovers, proves, and applies certain theorems about sequences; explores the idea of the limit of a sequence; and associates discrete mathematics with some of its history.

Weighted objectives:

(10%) A. Interprets and uses the following terms, notation, and media in communications about discrete mathematics: *function on the set of natural numbers, sequence, infinite sequence, finite sequence,* sequence notation (e.g., *(tᵢ)*), recursive definition, factorial notation, *partial sum,* summation notation, *sequence of partial sums, arithmetic sequence, geometric sequence, common difference of an arithmetic sequence, common ratio of a geometric sequence, convergent sequence,* and *divergent sequence (comprehension).*

(10%) B. Distinguishes between examples and nonexamples of each of the following concepts: (a) sequence, (b) finite sequence, (c) infinite sequence, (d) convergent sequence, (e) divergent sequence, (f) arithmetic sequence, (g) geometric sequence, and (h) partial sum of a sequence *(conceptualization).*

(20%) C. Explains why each of the following relations holds:
   1. $a_n = a_1 + (n - 1)(a_2 - a_1)$, where a_n is the nth term of an arithmetic sequence $(a_1, a_2, a_3, \ldots)$;
   2. $\sum_{i=1}^{n} (a_i) = (n/2)(a_1 + a_n)$, where $(a_1, a_2, a_3, \ldots)$ is an arithmetic sequence;
   3. $a_n = a_1(a_2/a_1)^{n-1}$, where, a_n is the nth term of a geometric sequence $(a_1, a_2, a_3, \ldots)$;
   4. $\sum_{i=1}^{n} (a_i) = [a_1(1 - (a_2/a_1)^n)]/[1 - (a_2/a_1)]$, where $(a_1, a_2, a_3, \ldots)$ is a geometric sequence;
   5. $\sum_{i=1}^{\infty} (a_i) = a_1/[1 - (a_2/a_1)]$, where $(a_1, a_2, a_3, \ldots)$ is an infinite geometric sequence such that $-1 < (a_2/a_1) < 1$;
   (conceptualization).

(10%) D. Explains proofs for the five theorems listed in Objective C *(comprehension).*

(20%) E. Formulates hypotheses based on the five theorems listed in Objective C and explores relations relative to limits of sequences *(conceptualization).*

(10%) F. Proves corollaries to the five theorems listed in Objective C (e.g., 0.999 . . . = 1) *(application).*

(02%) G. Writes and uses computer programs to execute algorithms used in applying relations listed in Objective C *(comprehension).*

(05%) H. Explains some episodes in the historical development of discrete mathematics *(comprehension).*

(13%) I. Given a problem, determines how, if at all, a solution to that problem is facilitated by using relations derived from the theorems listed for Objective C *(application).*

Estimated number of class periods: 15.5

Textbook page references: 406–430 and 335–437 (unless otherwise indicated, page numbers referred to in the overall lesson plan are from the course textbook (Elich and Cannon 1989).

Exhibit 8.34 continued

General day-by-day plans:

Day 1:
1. Interactive lecture session defining discrete mathematics and setting the stage for the unit.
2. Independent work session reviewing needed definitions, notation, and special functions.
3. Questioning/discussion session reviewing results of the independent work session.
4. Homework assignment continuing the review (reference pages 406–416).

Day 2:
1. Brief test for formative feedback relative to parts of Objective A.
2. Interactive lecture session reviewing the test results.
3. Questioning/discussion session discovering the concepts of convergent and divergent sequences.
4. Homework and computer laboratory assignment examining properties of various sequences.

Day 3:
1. Questioning/discussion session reviewing results of the homework and computer laboratory assignment.
2. Questioning/discussion session discovering relations 1 and 3 listed in Objective C.
3. Homework assignment from pages 414–419.
4. Independent work session beginning the homework.

Day 4:
1. Small-task-group session reviewing the results of the homework.
2. Questioning/discussion session discovering relation 2 listed in Objective C.
3. Interactive lecture session proving relation 2 listed in Objective C.
4. Homework assignment computing partial sums and making conjectures about partial sums of special sequences.
5. Independent work session beginning the homework.

Day 5:
1. Brief test for formative feedback relative to parts of Objectives A, B, C, D, and E.
2. Interactive lecture session reviewing the test results.
3. Questioning/discussion session discovering relation 4 listed in Objective C.
4. Interactive lecture session proving relation 4 listed in Objective C.
5. Homework assignment computing partial sums and making conjectures about partial sums of special sequences.

Day 6:
1. Small-task-group session reviewing the results of the homework.
2. Interactive lecture session on writing computer programs for computing partial sums of arithmetic and geometric sequences.
3. Interactive lecture session organizing and scheduling small task groups for studying and reporting on the history of some special sequences.
4. Homework and computer laboratory assignment (a) entering and debugging programs for computing partial sums and (b) reading references relative to small-task-group reports on history of certain sequences.
5. Small-task-group and independent work sessions beginning the homework.

Day 7:
1. Deductive-level questioning/discussion session relative to applications of the first four relations listed in Objective C to (a) proofs of theorems and (b) problem-solving.
2. Application-level homework assignment.
3. Small-task-group and independent work sessions beginning the homework.

Exhibit 8.34 continued

Day 8: **1.** Brief test for formative feedback relative to parts of Objectives A, B, C, D, E, F, and I.
2. Interactive lecture session reviewing results of the test.
3. Homework assignment dependent on results of the test; students also continue to work on historical reports according to the previously determined schedule.

Day 9: **1.** Questioning/discussion session reviewing homework as necessary.
2. First group's historical report.
3. Questioning/discussion session reviewing the report.
4. Second group's historical report.
5. Questioning/discussion session reviewing the report.

Day 10: **1.** Brief test for formative feedback relative to part of Objective H.
2. Interactive lecture session reviewing results of the test.
3. Questioning/discussion session discovering relation 5 listed in Objective C.
4. Interactive lecture session proving relation 5 listed in Objective C.
5. Homework assignment selected from exercises on pages 425–427.

Day 11: **1.** Small-task-group session reviewing homework results.
2. Deductive-level questioning/discussion session relative to applications of the fifth relation listed in Objective C to (a) proofs of theorems and (b) problem-solving.
3. Homework assignment relative to applications of the fifth relation listed in Objective C.
4. Independent work session beginning the homework.

Day 12: **1.** Brief test for formative feedback relative to Objective I.
2. Interactive lecture session reviewing results of the test.
3. Third group's historical report.
4. Fourth group's historical report.
5. Homework assignment dependent on the results of the test.

Day 13: **1.** Inductive/deductive questioning session exploring the concept of limits of sequences.
2. Independent work session dependent on the outcome of the exploration activities.
3. Homework assignment completing the practice test in preparation for the unit test.

Day 14: **1.** Interactive lecture session reviewing the practice test results.
2. Fifth group's historical report.
3. Homework assignment preparing for the unit test.

Day 15: Unit test.

Day 16: **1.** Review the results of the unit test.
2. Set the stage for Unit 7 beginning with binomial distributions.

reviews exhibits of instructional resources, technology, and publications for mathematics teachers.

WINDING DOWN THE SCHOOL YEAR AND ANTICIPATING NEXT YEAR

The end of May is filled with clerical tasks (e.g., retrieving textbooks and completing scores of year-end forms and reports required by the district school board). Though feeling exhausted, Casey is already anticipating his second year. He thinks to himself: "If I had known in August what I know now, my students would've learned so much more! I can't wait until next year to do it right! Now, I know what to expect and for what to prepare. This year, I started from scratch. Now, I have a wealth of resources— lesson plans, item pools, examples, nonexamples, real-world problems, contrived problems—all neatly stored on computer disks, quite a bit to build on. I know I can succeed in this profession. Even with all my mistakes, the vast majority of my students developed conceptual-level understandings, comprehension and communication skills, algorithmic skills, real-world problem-solving abilities, and healthy attitudes about mathematics."

❑❑❑❑❑❑❑❑❑❑❑❑❑❑❑❑❑❑❑

SELF-ASSESSMENT EXERCISES

1. With a group of your colleagues who have also read Chapters 1–8, engage in a discussion relative to the following questions or tasks:

   a. How important to his success was Casey's assertive behavior? What might have gone differently if he had not learned to be more assertive?

   b. Critique Casey's syllabus in Appendix E with respect to readability for the algebra I students, completeness, format, and inclusion of unnecessary material.

   c. The *Standards* (NCTM 1989, 127) suggests that the use of factoring to solve equations should receive less attention in algebra courses than it has in the past. In what ways does Casey's Unit 7, described in the section "Sample Algebra I Teaching Unit," depart from this suggestion? In what ways is it consistent with this suggestion?

   d. As indicated by Exhibits 8.10, 8.32, 8.33, and 8.34, each of Casey's four sample units included several "brief tests" prior to the unit test. Besides providing him and the students with formative feedback, how do you suppose these brief tests enhanced the unit?

   e. What are the advantages and disadvantages of Casey's use of a practice test for purposes of review just before the unit test? Contrast this strategy to reviewing simply by fielding students' questions and summarizing salient points about each of the unit's topics.

   f. In the example on page 278, Casey is conducting an independent work session when he tells Mary, "Okay, go with step 5. I'll be back in 33 seconds." Why do you suppose Casey chose to say 33 seconds rather than "in a minute" or "right away" or even "half a minute"?

   g. Rather than using a factoring algorithm, Casey prefers students to solve equations such as $x^2 - 25 = 0$ by reasoning, "25 from what number is 0? Obviously, 25. What number squared is 25? Either 5 or -5." Why do you suppose he feels this way?

   h. In the example on page 280, Casey directs Xavier, who doesn't have his own worksheet, to look on Magnolia's. What are some of the possible repercussions of that action by Casey?

   i. Later in the same example alluded to in (h), Megan appears unprepared and unwilling to get involved in the questioning/discussion session. What are the advantages and disadvantages of the manner in which Casey attempted to help her be engaged?

   j. Later in the same example alluded to in (i), Casey writes $ab = 0$ under $3x(x - 8) = 0$. How did this move backfire? How did it help? In the long run, do you think the strategy will turn out to be more helpful or more hurtful to the students' understanding of mathematics?

   k. From the examples of the questioning/discussion session described in the section "Sample Algebra I Teaching Unit," does it appear that Casey managed to involve a satisfactory number of students in the lessons? Compare his tactics to those of Mr. Grimes, Mr. Smart, and Ms. Cramer in Vignettes 6.9, 6.10, and 6.11, respectively.

   l. In the example on page 283, Juaquin simplifies the equation $12x^2 = 4x$ to be $3x = 0$. Critique the way Casey responded to the mistake.

   m. Critique the homework sheet of Exhibit 8.28 in light of Casey's purpose for assigning it.

   n. No examples of Casey using games (as suggested in the section "Initiating and Maintaining Student Engagement in Recitation Sessions," in Chapter 6) are included in this chapter. In light of the sample unit plans shown in Exhibits 8.10, 8.32, 8.33, and 8.34, where do you think Casey might have appropriately incorporated games in his lessons?

   o. How consistently do Casey's four sample unit plans follow the suggestions in Chapter 4 for designing lessons?

   p. What are the advantages and disadvantages of Casey guiding students through writing computer programs for executing algorithms he taught in the four sample units?

   q. What are the advantages and disadvantages of centering the transportation and travel unit on the videotaping projects (as indicated in the section "Sample Consumer Mathematics Teaching Unit")?

   r. In what ways did Casey depend on a computer to get things done? What things would he have not accomplished efficiently without ready access to a computer?

2. In light of the number of points per item indicated in Exhibit 8.31 and the weights assigned to his objectives in Exhibit 8.10, critique the unit test (Appendix F) that Casey constructed.

3. Develop a course syllabus for a given mathematics course with a given textbook. Also, devise a unit plan for that course.

4. Formulate two example problems Casey may have been able to utilize in a lesson for Objective G of Exhibit 8.32. Do the same for Objective D of Exhibit 8.33 and for Objective I of Exhibit 8.34.

5. Interview a first-year mathematics teacher. Include the following questions: (a) What are some

of the more prominent things you've learned since you've started teaching? (b) To this point in your career, what has been the most satisfying surprise? (c) To this point, what has been the most frustrating surprise?

❑ ❑

TAKING WHAT YOU'VE LEARNED TO THE NEXT LEVEL

By vicariously experiencing Casey's first year of teaching, you should gain a step in learning from your direct experiences as you embark on your own teaching career. What is the outlook for your career? You, of course, are the principal factor influencing the answer to that question. Of less but still significant importance is how certain issues presently confronting the mathematics teaching profession are resolved over the next decade. Those issues are raised in Chapter 9.

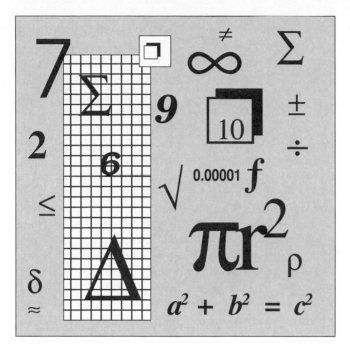

CHAPTER 9
Looking Ahead

This chapter is intended to stimulate your thinking about the current movement to reform the way mathematics is typically taught in schools and to reflect on your own professional role in that movement.

A MIXED HISTORY

Exemplary mathematics teaching consistent with research-based principles and the *Standards* (NCTM 1989) has been successfully practiced at least since the time of Socrates. The merits of teaching methods based on these principles were extolled in literary works as early as 1791, when Johann Pestalozzi wrote *Leonard and Gertrude* (Cubberley 1962, 394–397; Wilds and Lottich 1961, 292–293). In Skemp's (1973) classic *The Psychology of Learning Mathematics,* the fundamental principles by which students conceptualize mathematical concepts and relations are explicated. The efficacy of the model by which inductive lessons lead students to discover mathematics, direct instruction helps them remember mathematics and improve their algorithmic skills, comprehension lessons help them communicate about mathematics, and deductive lessons help them apply mathematics is supported by a myriad of research findings (see, for example, Driscoll 1982; NCTM, 1988–1989, in press; Suydam 1989). Many mathematics teachers, like Casey Rudd, continue to practice these research-based methods successfully within the entire spectrum of middle, junior high, and senior high school mathematics classrooms.

However, such exemplary mathematics teaching has never been typical (Jesunathadas 1990; NCTM, in press). With nearly 200,000 teachers estimated to be teaching mathematics courses in the middle and secondary schools of the United States, most students never have the opportunity to learn mathematics from a teacher like Casey Rudd. Consequently, the history of mathematics education is mixed, marked by the crowning achievements of relatively few and missed opportunities for the masses.

AN IMPENDING REFORMATION

In the minds of some teachers, a question still exists as to whether they should attempt to follow the research-based approaches recommended by the mathematics education literature (e.g., the *Standards* and this text). They argue that although inquiry instruction may work in theory, it is simply too difficult to implement in realistic classroom situations. Although agreeing that their own traditional approaches are unsuccessful with the majority of students, they contend that most people need only fundamental skills and that conceptual and application learning is possible only for the "gifted" few. They point to the successful mathematicians, engineers, and scientists who profited from traditional instruction.

In the minds both of teachers who have successfully implemented research-based approaches and mathematics education specialists (e.g., the authors of the *Standards* (NCTM 1989)), the research-based approaches are clearly superior to the traditional approaches, not only in theory but also in practice with every type of student. At this point, the most critical issue facing mathematics education specialists is not how mathematics should be taught but rather how to increase the number of mathematics teachers who break from tradition and begin applying the research-based approaches. Because teaching is a complex of messy functions successfully executed only by professionals astute in pedagogy, cognitive science, mathematics, behavior management, and evaluation of student achievement, reformation of the practices of the majority of mathematics teachers is an ambitious goal to say the least.

As indicated on page 27, a century of efforts to reform the teaching of mathematics has failed to have an impact on the majority of practitioners. What, if anything, would lead anyone to believe that the current movement under the banner of the *Standards* would be any more successful than those in the past? First of all, on the heels of highly publicized reports of widespread mathematical illiteracy (e.g., Dossey et al. 1988; "U.S. Students Again Rank Near Bottom in Math and Science" 1989), the political climate seems ripe to support a reformation. The greatest challenge for mathematics education professionals may not be to stimulate the reformation as much as to guide the direction of the movement.

There is cause for optimism regarding impending reform. The *Standards* are being afforded a high profile supported by a solid coalition of learned and professional societies of educators (e.g., American Federation of Teachers and National Education Association), mathematicians (e.g., American Mathematical Society and Mathematical Association of America), scientists (e.g., American Chemical Society and Council of Scientific Society Presidents), engineers and other technical professionals (e.g., Institute of Management Sciences and National Society of Professional Engineers), school administrators (American Association of School Administrators and National School Boards Association), and instructional supervisors (e.g., Association for Supervision and Curriculum Development and National Council

of Supervisors of Mathematics). Following the *Standards,* which spells out guidelines for curriculum and evaluation reform, the NCTM (in press) published the *Professional Standards for Teaching Mathematics,* which describes the competencies and practices of teachers who implement *Standards*-based curricula (i.e., utilize the research-based approaches suggested in Chapter 4 of this text). By combining a strong preparation in mathematics and pedagogy with achievement of the objectives listed for Chapters 1–8, you meet these professional standards for teaching mathematics. This assumes, of course, that through actual classroom teaching experiences you are about to develop your abilities to implement what you now understand.

Recent widespread agreement on resolutions to some previously controversial issues should also hasten the reformation in a direction favorable to *Standards*-based curricula. Although in some influential circles resistance to the resolutions still exists, the following is generally accepted:

Virtually everyone needs to be able to use mathematics creatively to solve real-life problems and is quite capable of learning to do so. Some people (e.g., Don Delaney in the section "Discouraging Advice from Don Delaney," in Chapter 8) continue to perceive mathematics as a mystical sequence of rules that most people can learn to follow but only the gifted can understand. Such an erroneous perception, coupled with prejudiced attitudes about the capabilities of women and various ethnic groups to learn mathematics, flies in the face of overwhelming evidence to the contrary (e.g., Friedman 1989). Fortunately, naivete and prejudice can hardly stand up to the current movement favoring meaningful mathematics for all students (e.g., California State Department of Education 1987; Johnson and Ferrini-Mundy 1989; National Research Council 1989).

A wealth of proven instructional strategies, techniques, resources, and technologies are now available to help teachers implement research-based approaches that heretofore were either unavailable or untested. As illustrated throughout this text, there are now effective strategies for (1) integrating mathematical history to demystify topics, (2) utilizing reading, writing, and speaking activities to facilitate intellectual learning of mathematics, (3) integrating mathematical topics with each other and with those from other disciplines to facilitate application-level learning, (4) using cooperative learning activities to tap the vast wealth of experiences and teaching potential among students, (5) using computers, calculators, and other technologies to relieve much of the tedium of executing algorithms, generate examples, generate and manipulate models, make quality presentations, manage and maintain files, and facilitate experimentation, (6) managing student behavior, and (7) evaluating student achievement for both formative and summative purposes.

Teachers need in-depth preparation in both mathematics and teaching methods (which includes cognitive science, behavior management, pedagogical principles, and evaluation of student achievement). In some naive circles, people still contend that to teach mathematics, one needs only to be very knowledgeable in mathematics and that there is no value in wasting time with teaching methods. Others, in equally naive circles, argue that teachers do not need to know mathematics beyond the levels they teach to be effective—as long as they practice sound teaching methods (e.g., to teach algebra, you don't need to understand calculus). Such uninformed opinions have been recently countered by the joining of forces of professional societies of both mathematicians and educators. For example, *Guidelines for the Continuing Mathematical Education of Teachers* (The Mathematical Association of America 1988) and *Professional Standards for Teaching Mathematics* (NCTM, in press) both emphasize the necessity of teachers having advanced work in mathematics as well as in instructional methods. Mathematics and the teaching of mathematics are inextricably related. In mathematics education, the two are inseparable.

Teachers should no longer be expected to succeed without appropriate support services of administrators, without competent instructional supervision, and without continuing inservice education. With nearly 200,000 teachers estimated to be conducting mathematics courses in the nation's middle and secondary schools, the reformation can hardly succeed unless inservice as well as preservice teachers are affected. The outmoded model by which teachers collected the tools of their profession (e.g., understanding of mathematics and instructional methods) from their preservice preparation programs in college and then were left unattended to learn how to use the tools during their first inservice years in the classroom has proven ineffectual at worse and inefficient at best (Duke, Cangelosi, and Knight 1988). In response to such findings, promising models for providing inservice teachers with necessary instructional supervisory support services have been developed and validated (Cangelosi 1991, 119–159; Harris 1989, 1–28). With the influence of the Association for Supervision and Curriculum Development, there is considerable hope that the inservice support and education so desperately needed by teachers will become widely available through im-

plementation of these models. Wherever such services are available, they could become a vehicle for guiding mathematics teachers toward research-based practices.

YOUR ROLE

Clearly, the most important variable in determining the future of mathematics education is *you* and your colleagues who are also embarking on careers as mathematics teachers. How do you influence the success of the profession and the course of the reformation? You begin by teaching as well as you reasonably can. How you execute your messy teaching functions impacts the students fortunate enough to be in your tutelage. Sometimes teachers complain, "My students just aren't capable of learning mathematics at this level. With a more capable group, I could succeed, but not with this bunch!" But the capabilities of your students do not influence the success of your teaching performance. Your teaching success depends on how well you lead your students to extend their grasp of mathematics within their own capabilities. In other words, evaluate how far they reach not where they reach.

Avail yourself of inservice education opportunities. Mathematics and pedagogical discoveries and inventions occur every day. How well you execute your messy teaching functions depends on continuing to learn from experiences as well as staying abreast of current research findings. Your NCTM membership will serve you well in this area.

Our profession is represented by dedicated, highly competent teachers as well as by fools. As a member of the former category, be a protagonist in the reformation of the profession.

❑ ❑ ❑ ❑ ❑ ❑ ❑ ❑ ❑ ❑ ❑ ❑ ❑ ❑ ❑ ❑ ❑ ❑ ❑ ❑

SELF-ASSESSMENT EXERCISES

1. Interview two currently active mathematics teachers. Include the following items:
   a. Have you read the NCTM *Standards*?
   b. If so, what is your opinion of the points it makes and how do you think it has and will impact what actually goes on in classrooms?
   c. I would like to compare the preservice college preparation programs that you had with my own. I'm interested in how, if at all, they compare relative to mathematical content and teaching methods—especially mathematics teaching methods, field-based experiences, learning theory or educational psychology,

classroom management, and evaluation of student achievement. Please describe your program and let's compare the similarities and differences between yours and mine.

d. What did you learn in your preservice college preparation program that has helped you succeed as a mathematics teacher?

e. What aspects of your preservice college preparation program have not been helpful to you as a teacher?

f. In what inservice education programs have you participated? In what ways have they been helpful to you?

g. What advice do you have for me as I start my own career as a mathematics teacher?

❏ ❏ ❏ ❏ ❏ ❏ ❏ ❏ ❏ ❏ ❏ ❏ ❏ ❏ ❏ ❏ ❏ ❏ ❏

TAKING WHAT YOU'VE LEARNED TO THE NEXT LEVEL

The ball is in your court.

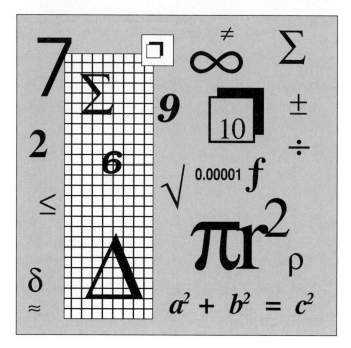

APPENDIX A

Topics from the Table of Contents of a Prealgebra Textbook*

*Source: Table of Contents from PRE-ALGEBRA: SKILLS, PROBLEM SOLVING, APPLICATIONS by V. Brumfiel, Golden, Heins, Copyright © 1986 Harcourt Brace Jovanovich, Inc., reprinted by permission of the publisher.

I. Essential skills and applications
  1. Whole numbers and applications
    A. Formulas and whole numbers
      a. Using formulas: addition
      b. Using formulas: subtraction
      c. Using formulas: multiplication
      d. Using formulas: division
      e. Problem solving and applications: estimating with whole numbers
    B. Using whole numbers and variables
      a. Numerical expressions
      b. Using variables
  2. Decimals and applications
    A. Operations with decimals and applications
      a. Decimals and place value
      b. Addition and subtraction
      c. Multiplication
      d. Division
    B. Decimals and applications
      a. Problem-solving and applications: estimating with decimals
      b. Metric units of measurement
      c. Problem-solving and applications: scientific notation
  3. Number properties and expressions
    A. Number properties and applications
      a. The special numbers 0 and 1
      b. Simplifying algebraic expressions
      c. Problem-solving and applications: formulas—area
    B. Algebraic expressions and applications
      a. Like terms
      b. Combining like terms
      c. Problem-solving and applications: formulas—perimeter
  4. Number theory
    A. Factors and divisibility
      a. Factors, multiples, and divisibility
      b. Divisibility tests
    B. Properties of prime numbers
      a. Prime numbers
      b. Prime factorization
      c. Least common multiple
      d. Greatest common factor
  5. Fractions: multiplication and division
    A. Fractions and applications
      a. Writing fractions in lowest terms
      b. Customary measures
      c. Multiplying fractions
      d. Problem-solving and applications: formulas—temperature
    B. Mixed numerals and applications
      a. Multiplying mixed numerals
      b. Problem-solving and applications: area—parallelograms and triangles

c. Problem-solving and applications: volume—rectangular prisms

d. Dividing fractions

6. Fractions: addition and subtraction
   - **A.** Fractions and mixed numerals
     - **a.** Addition and subtraction: like denominators
     - **b.** Addition and subtraction: unlike denominators
     - **c.** Addition and subtraction: mixed numerals
   - **B.** Applications of addition and subtraction
     - **a.** Problem-solving and applications: time cards
     - **b.** Fractions and decimals
     - **c.** Problem-solving and applications: circles—circumference and area

II. Percent and application
   7. Solving equations
      - **A.** Equations: subtraction and addition
        - **a.** Solving equations by subtraction
        - **b.** Solving equations by addition
        - **c.** Problem-solving and applications: Using equations—multiplication and division
   8. Ratio, proportion, and percent
      - **A.** Ratio and proportions
        - **a.** Ratio
        - **b.** Proportions
        - **c.** Problem-solving and applications: using proportions
      - **B.** Introduction to percent
        - **a.** Meaning of percent
        - **b.** Percents and decimals
        - **c.** Finding a percent of a number
        - **d.** Problem-solving and applications: formulas—simple interest
        - **e.** Problem-solving and applications: formulas—discount
   9. Percent and applications
      - **A.** More on percent
        - **a.** Finding what percent one number is of another
        - **b.** Problem-solving and applications: percent of increase or decrease
        - **c.** Finding a number given a percent
        - **d.** Using proportions to solve percent problems
      - **B.** Graphs and estimation
        - **a.** Bar graphs
        - **b.** Circle graphs
        - **c.** Problem-solving and applications: using estimation

III. Integers and rational numbers
   10. Rational numbers: addition and subtraction
      - **A.** Integers and rational numbers

   - **a.** Integers
   - **b.** Rational numbers
   - **c.** Addition on the number line
   - **B.** Addition and subtraction
     - **a.** Adding rational numbers
     - **b.** Subtracting rational numbers
     - **c.** Properties of addition
     - **d.** Adding polynomials
   11. Equations: addition and subtraction
      - **A.** Addition and subtraction properties
        - **a.** Equations: addition and subtraction
        - **b.** Like terms—more than one equation
        - **c.** Variables on both sides
      - **B.** Applications of equations
        - **a.** Problem-solving and applications: words to symbols—addition and subtraction
        - **b.** Inequalities on the number line
        - **c.** Using addition and subtraction to solve inequalities
   12. Rational numbers: multiplication and division
      - **A.** Multiplication
        - **a.** Multiplication: unlike signs
        - **b.** Multiplication: like signs
        - **c.** Properties of multiplication
      - **B.** Division
        - **a.** Dividing rational numbers
        - **b.** Factoring
   13. Equations: multiplication and division
      - **A.** Multiplication and division properties
        - **a.** Equations: multiplication and division
        - **b.** Problem-solving and application: words to symbols—multiplication and division
        - **c.** Combined operations
        - **d.** Equations with parentheses
      - **B.** Applications of equations
        - **a.** Problem-solving and applications: more than one unknown—angles in a triangle
        - **b.** Problem-solving and applications: more than one unknown—consecutive numbers
        - **c.** Inequalities: multiplication and division
        - **d.** Problem-solving and applications: using inequalities

IV. Real numbers
   14. Graphing and equations
      - **A.** The coordinate plane
        - **a.** Graphing ordered pairs
        - **b.** Graphing equations
        - **c.** Problem-solving and applications: broken line graphs
        - **d.** Slope of a line

B. Using graphs
  a. Intercepts
  b. Direct and indirect variation
  c. Solving a system of equations by graphing
  d. Graphing linear inequalities
15. Special triangles
  A. Squares and square roots
    a. Meaning of square root
    b. Irrational numbers
    c. Table of squares and square roots
    d. Problem-solving and applications: formulas—using square roots
  B. Pythagorean theorem and special triangles
    a. Pythagorean theorem and applications
    b. Tangent ratio and applications
V. Other applications
  16. Statistics and probability
    A. Statistics

      a. Mean, median, and mode
      b. Histograms
    B. Probability
      a. Probability
      b. Probability and tables
      c. Tree diagrams
      d. Multiplying probabilities
17. Geometry
  A. Introduction to geometry
    a. Introduction to geometry
    b. Angles
    c. Properties of triangles
    d. Problem-solving and applications: using similar triangles
    e. Perpendicular and parallel lines
    f. Properties of quadrilaterals
  B. Surface area and volume
    a. Problem-solving and applications: surface area and rectangular prisms
    b. Volume: cylinders
    c. Volume: pyramids and cones

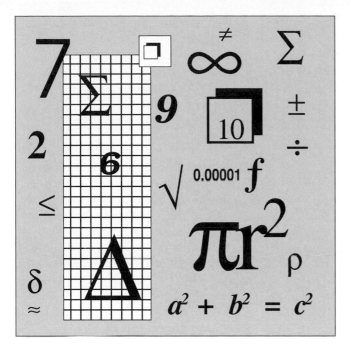

APPENDIX B
Excerpt from *Mathematics Core Curriculum: Grades 7–12* Relative to the Teaching of Elementary Algebra*

Course Title	Unit of Credit	Prerequisite
Elementary Algebra	1.0	Mastery of Math Level 8 or Algebra Preparation

E	L	E	M		A	L	G	E	B	R	A

SIS COURSE NUMBER: 5250
SIS CODE: MO

COURSE DESCRIPTION

The Elementary Algebra course of study consists of three principal parts:

1. Review of previously learned mathematics concepts including maintaining the previous mathematics core standards.
2. Introduction of new concepts and skills outlined in A Course of Study for Mathematics in Utah, district curriculum guides, and textbooks.
3. Mastery of core standards and objectives for Elementary Algebra.

Students in Elementary Algebra explore a mathematical model for the real number system involving the study of straight lines and numerical relationships. The properties of the real number system are used to solve linear equations and inequalities. Simple operations with polynomials are introduced and the laws of exponents are studied.

CORE STANDARDS FOR THE COURSE

Standard 5250–01	The students will demonstrate knowledge of the properties of equalities.

OBJECTIVES

5250–0101.	Know that for any "a," then a = a, (reflexive property of equality). (116–411)
5250–0102.	Know that for any "a" and "b," if a = b then b = a (symmetric property of equality). (116–412)
5250–0103.	Know that for any "a," "b," and "c" if a = b and b = c, then a = c (transitive property of equality). (116–413)

*Source: From "Mathematics Core Curriculum: Grades 7–12" by Utah State Office of Education, 1987, Relative to the Teaching of Elementary Algebra, pp. E:49–E:53. Reprinted by permission.

5250-0104. Know that adding or subtracting the same numbers to both members (sides) of an equation yields an equivalent equation. (116–416)

5250-0105. Know that multiplying or dividing (divisor not zero) both members (sides) of an equation by the same number yields an equivalent equation. (116–417)

| Standard 5250-02 | The students will demonstrate knowledge of real numbers. |

OBJECTIVES

5250-0201. Define the set of real numbers.

5250-0202. Define closure for addition, subtraction, multiplication, and division in the set of real numbers. (116–418)

5250-0203. Know that in the set of real numbers, the operations of addition and multiplication are commutative and associative, but subtraction and division are neither commutative nor associative. (116–419)

5250-0204. Know that multiplication is distributive over addition and subtraction in the set of real numbers. (116–420)

5250-0205. Know that zero is the additive identity for the set of real numbers. (116–421)

5250-0206. Know that the number one is the multiplicative identity for the set of real numbers. (116–422)

5250-0207. Know that the sum of a real number and its additive inverse (opposite) is zero. (116–423)

5250-0208. Know that zero is its own additive inverse in the set of real numbers. (116–424)

5250-0209. Know that the product of a non-zero real number and its multiplicative inverse (reciprocal) is the number one. (116–425)

5250-0210. Know that zero does not have a multiplicative inverse. (116–426)

5250-0211. Know that the product of real numbers is zero if and only if at least one of its factors is zero.

5250-0212. Define absolute value.

5250-0213. Define prime number.

5250-0214. Define composite number. (116–429)

5250-0215. Define relatively prime. (116–432)

5250-0216. Know that every natural number, except the number one, has a unique prime factorization. (116–433)

5250-0217. Find the least common multiple (LCM) of two or more given natural numbers. (116–430)

5250-0218. Find the greatest common factor (GCF) of two or more given natural numbers. (116–431)

5250-0219. Add, subtract, multiply, and divide real numbers.

5250-0220. Know that a natural number exponent indicates how many times the base is used as a factor.

| Standard 5250-03 | The students will demonstrate knowledge of polynomial and other algebraic expressions. |

OBJECTIVES

5250-0301. Identify an algebraic term. (116–434)

5250-0302. Identify an algebraic expression. (116–435)

5250-0303. Classify polynomials by the number of terms or by degree. (116–436)

5250-0304. Know the order of operations. (116–437)

5250-0305. Add, subtract, and multiply polynomials, and divide a polynomial by a monomial. (116–438)

5250-0306. Factor first- and second-degree polynomials.

5250-0307. Simplify rational algebraic expressions. (116–440)

5250-0308. Know that rational algebraic expressions are reduced when the greatest common factor of both the numerator and the denominator is one. (116–441)

5250-0309. Know that a number can be written in exponential form "a^n" where "a" is the base and "n" is the exponent.

Standard 5250–04	**The students will demonstrate ability to solve simple linear equalities and inequalities.**

OBJECTIVES

5250–0401. Recognize algebraic sentences (equalities and inequalities).

5250–0402. Solve simple rational algebraic equations.

5250–0403. Define root (solution).

5250–0404. Find the solution set. (116–447)

5250–0405. Know that equivalent open sentences have the same solution set. (116–446)

5250–0406. Know that if the same number is added to or subtracted from each member of an inequality, the sense of the inequality is preserved. (116–442)

5250–0407. Know that if each member of an inequality is multiplied or divided by the same positive number, the sense of the inequality is preserved. (116–443)

5250–0408. Know that if each member of an inequality is multiplied or divided by the same negative number, the sense of the inequality is reversed. (116–444)

5250–0409. Solve simple systems of linear equations containing two equations and two variables.

5250–0410. Solve simple word problems. (116–448)

Standard 5250–05	**The students will demonstrate knowledge of graphing.**

OBJECTIVES

5250–0501. Know that the axes of a rectangular (Cartesian) coordinate system separate a plane into quadrants.

5250–0502. Know that the rectangular coordinate system establishes a "one-to-one" correspondence between the set of all ordered pairs of real numbers and the set of points in a plane.

5250–0503. Define a relation. (116–450)

5250–0504. Define abscissa and ordinate (x − coordinate and y − coordinate). (116–451)

5250–0505. Define the domain and range of a relation. (116–452)

5250–0506. Define and determine slope of a line. (116–459)

5250–0507. Know that when a line rises from left to right, its slope is a positive number. (116–460)

5250–0508. Know that when a line falls from left to right, its slope is a negative number. (116–461)

5250–0509. Know that the slope of a horizontal line is zero. (116–462)

5250–0510. Know that the slope of a vertical line is undefined. (116–463)

5250–0511. Know that the graph of a first-degree polynomial equation in one or two variables on the Cartesian Coordinate System is a straight line. (116–455)

5250–0512. Know that the graph of a linear inequality in one variable on the real number line is a subset of a straight line. (116–456)

5250–0513. Graph the solution set of a linear equation in one or two variables.

Standard 5250–06	**The students will select three objectives from this course and apply each of these objectives in a job or work setting.**

OBJECTIVES

5250–0601. Describe how each of three selected objectives is applied or used in a job or work setting.

5250–0602. Select a job or work setting and show how the mathematics of this course has changed the manner in which work has been done in that job or setting.

5250–0603. Solve a problem applied to a job or work setting for each of three objectives from this course.

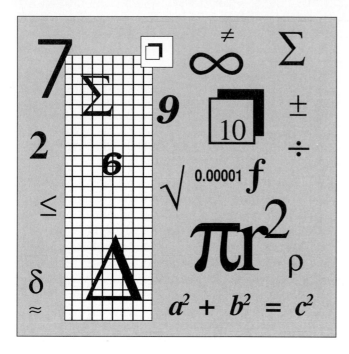

APPENDIX C

"An Application of Quadratic Equations to Baseball"*

In baseball, the primary objective of each team is to have the greatest winning percentage in its division at the end of the season. During the season, daily standings list the teams in order of decreasing winning percentages. Beside each team's percentage is the number of games it is behind, a measure of how many games that a team trails the team with the greatest winning percentage. For example, consider the standings of National League teams on the morning of 8 August 1984, as shown in table 1.

The number of games behind (GB) is calculated as follows: Suppose that the leading team has a won-lost record of (A, B) and the trailing team has a won-lost record of (a, b), where

$$\frac{A}{A + B} > \frac{a}{a + b}$$

Then the trailing team is $A - a$ wins behind (or "games behind in the win column") and $b - B$ losses behind (or "games behind in the loss column"). The number of games behind, *GB*, is calculated as the mean of these two quantities:

$$GB = \frac{(A - a) + (b - B)}{2}$$

Baseball fans and players know that "games behind" is not always a good measure of the deficit between the trailing team and the leading team. A New York Mets fan would look at the standings and think: *We're 3.5 games behind the Cubs but only 2 in the loss column.* That is, if the Cubs lose 2 games, the Mets can catch them by winning as many as the Cubs do over the rest of the season (to use a baseball cliche, the Mets would "control their own destiny"), so the Mets' deficit appears to be *less than* 3.5 games. In contrast, the Atlanta Braves trail the San Diego Padres by 10 in the loss column, although they are only 9.5 games behind. This means that San Diego must lose 10 more games than Atlanta over the rest of the season for the Braves to have a chance, so the Braves' deficit appears to be *greater than* 9.5 games.

Strangely, it is even possible for the leading team to be "behind" the trailing team in games. For example, consider the following standings:

Team	W	L	Pct.	GB
Leaders	18	13	.581	0.5
Trailers	22	16	.579	0.0

Because of the difference in the number of games played, the Leaders are 0.5 games behind the Trailers.

Let's define the deficit D of a trailing team as the number of times the trailing team would have to

***Source:** From "An Application of Quadratic Equations to Baseball" by M. P. Eisner, 1986, Mathematics Teacher, 79, pp. 327–330. Copyright 1986 by National Council of Teachers of Mathematics. Reprinted by permission.

Table 1

	Eastern Division					Western Division				
Team	W	L	Pct.	*GB*	Team	W	L	Pct.	*GB*
Chicago	67	45	.598	—	San Diego	67	44	.604	—
New York	62	47	.569	3.5	Atlanta	58	54	.518	9.5
Philadelphia	60	51	.541	6.5	Los Angeles	55	58	.487	13
St. Louis	56	56	.500	11	Houston	52	61	.460	16
Montreal	53	58	.477	13.5	Cincinnati	47	65	.420	20.5
Pittsburgh	48	65	.425	19.5	San Francisco	44	65	.404	22

beat the leading team for them to be tied in the standings. If the two teams have played the same number of games (i.e., $A + B = a + b$), then *GB* is equal to D. However, if they haven't played the same number of games, *GB* and D are not equal. To illustrate, consider the standings of 8 August 1984 given in table 1.

Chicago and St. Louis have both played 112 games. St. Louis is 11 wins behind Chicago and 11 losses behind Chicago. If St. Louis beat Chicago 11 times, both teams would have records of 67–56 and they would be tied. Thus St. Louis has a deficit of 11 games, which is equal to the number of games behind listed in the standings.

In contrast, New York has played 109 games. New York is 5 wins behind Chicago and 2 losses behind Chicago. The mean of these, 3.5, is New York's games behind. But if New York beat Chicago 3.5 times (assuming that such a thing is possible), then New York would have a record of 65.5–47, whereas Chicago would have a record of 67–48.5. New York's winning percentage would be .582, whereas Chicago's would be .580, so New York would be ahead of Chicago rather than tied. Thus, the deficit between New York and Chicago is actually *less than* 3.5 games, confirming our intuitive judgment that was based on the loss column.

Now look at the situation in the Western Division between San Diego and Atlanta. Atlanta is 9 wins behind and 10 losses behind, which are averaged to give 9.5 games behind. But if Atlanta beat San Diego 9.5 times (again, assuming it's possible), then Atlanta would have a record of 67.5–54 and San Diego would have a record of 67–53.5. Atlanta's winning percentage would be .5556, but San Diego's percentage would be .5560, so Atlanta would still be behind. Thus, Atlanta's deficit is actually *greater than* 9.5 games, again confirming our intuition that was based on the loss column.

The examples of New York and Atlanta suggest that the relationship between a team's games behind and its deficit is this: *The direction of the inequality between the deficit and the games behind is the same as the direction of the inequality between losses behind and wins behind.* That is, if a team's losses behind are fewer than its wins behind, its def-

icit is less than its games behind, whereas if its losses behind are greater than its wins behind, its deficit is greater than its games behind.

Having established that games behind does not accurately describe the deficit between teams, we are faced with two mathematical questions: (1) How can we calculate the deficit between teams? (2) Can we use the answer to question (1) to *prove* the relationship between games behind and the deficit just described?

Earlier we said that a team's deficit is the number of times it would have to beat the leading team to become tied in the standings. (The two teams may not actually play that number of games in the remaining schedule.) Returning to the standings, suppose the New York Mets trail the Chicago Cubs by a deficit of D games. Then if the Mets had D more wins (and no more losses) and the Cubs D more losses (and no more wins), they would be tied, that is,

$$\frac{62 + D}{109 + D} = \frac{67}{112 + D}$$

Solving this proportion, we obtain the following:

$$(62 + D)(112 + D) = 67(109 + D)$$
$$6944 + 174D + D^2 = 7303 + 67D$$
$$D^2 + 107D - 359 = 0$$

Thus, the number of games by which the Mets really trail the Cubs is the solution of a quadratic equation. Solving by the quadratic formula, we have (ignore the negative root)

$$D \approx \frac{-107 + 113.512}{2} \approx 3.26.$$

Thus, the Mets trail the Cubs by 3.26 games. The result confirms that the Mets are actually closer to the Cubs than their 3.5 games behind would indicate.

Similarly, if the Atlanta Braves have a deficit of D games with respect to the San Diego Padres, then

$$\frac{58 + D}{112 + D} = \frac{67}{111 + D},$$

or

$$(58 + D)(111 + D) = 67(112 + D),$$

$$D^2 + 102D - 1066 = 0,$$

and

$$D \approx \frac{-102 + 121.11}{2} \approx 9.56.$$

So the Padres lead the Braves by 9.56 games. The result confirms that the Padres' lead is greater than the Braves' 9.5 games behind would indicate.

These two examples should whet any mathematician's appetite for a proof. Let us restate the relationship in the form of a proposition and try to prove it.

Proposition. *The direction of the inequality between a team's deficit and its games behind is the same as the direction of the inequality between its losses behind and its wins behind.*

Let's define some variables so we can express the proposition with algebraic inequalities. As before, let the leading team have A wins and B losses. Suppose the trailing team is x wins behind and y losses behind. Then its record is $a = A - x$ wins and $b = B + y$ losses. The proposition states that if $x > y$, then the team's deficit D is less than $(x + y)/2$, whereas if $x < y$, D is greater than $(x + y)/2$.

Now by definition, D is the solution to the equation

$$\frac{A - x + D}{A - x + B + y + D} = \frac{A}{A + B + D},$$

which simplifies to

$$D^2 + (A + B - x)D - (Ay + Bx) = 0.$$

Using the quadratic formula and ignoring the negative root, we have

$$D = \frac{\sqrt{(A + B - x)^2 + 4(Ay + Bx)} - (A + B - x)}{2},$$

so

$$D < G = \frac{x + y}{2}$$

if and only if

$$\sqrt{(A + B - x)^2 + 4(Ay + Bx)} - (A + B - x) < x + y,$$

$$\sqrt{(A + B - x)^2 + 4(Ay + Bx)} < A + B + y,$$

$$(A + B - x)^2 + 4(Ay + Bx) < (A + B + y)^2,$$

and

$$x^2 - 2(A - B)x < y^2 - 2(A - B)y.$$

Now let $f(t) = t^2 - 2(A - B)t$. The proposition is equivalent to the following statement: If $x > y$, then $f(x) < f(y)$, and if $x < y$, then $f(x) > f(y)$. That is, the proposition is true if x and y belong to an interval on which $f(t)$ is a decreasing function. But $f(t)$ is a quadratic function; it is decreasing on the interval $t \leq A - B$ and increasing everywhere else. Hence, the proposition is true if both x and y are less than or equal to $A - B$, the difference between the leading team's wins and losses. So we can restate the proposition as a theorem:

Theorem. *Suppose the numbers of games by which a team trails the leading team in the win and in the loss columns are both fewer than or equal to the difference between the leading team's wins and losses. Then the direction of the inequality between the team's deficit and its games behind is the same as the direction of the inequality between its losses behind and its wins behind.*

In most pennant races, this condition will hold. In major league baseball, the leading team usually has a percentage near .600, as both leading teams do in the example. That means that late in the season, the difference between the leading team's wins and losses will be greater than 20. So the relationship will hold for any team that is fewer than 20 games behind in both the win and loss columns. Looking back to the league standings, we see that Chicago's win difference is 22, so that for any team whose wins behind and losses behind are both fewer than or equal to 22, the conclusion of the theorem will apply. For San Diego, the corresponding number is 23.

A final note: If the deficit rather than the games behind is used as the measure of the distance between teams, the anomaly at the beginning of this article—a team trailing the leader by a negative number of games—cannot occur. The calculation of the deficit between the Trailers and the Leaders requires us to solve the equation

$$\frac{22 + D}{38 + D} = \frac{18}{31 + D},$$

or $D^2 + 35D - 2 = 0$, yielding $D \approx 0.06$, so the Trailers trail by 0.06 games.

In fact, it is easy to prove that D is always positive. Recall that D is the greater of the two solutions (the lesser solution is always negative) of the quadratic equation

$$D^2 + (A + B - x)D - (Ay + Bx) = 0.$$

Replacing x by $A - a$ and y by $b - B$ yields the equivalent equation

$$D^2 + (B + a)D - (Ab - Ba) = 0.$$

This equation has a positive solution if and only if

$$\sqrt{(B + a)^2 + 4(Ab - Ba)} > B + a,$$

that is, $Ab > Ba$. But the relationship of the two teams' winning percentages is

$$\frac{A}{A + B} > \frac{a}{a + b},$$

which is equivalent to $Ab > Ba$. Thus, D is always positive for a team with a lower winning percentage than the leader. We can conclude that a team's deficit D is a better measure of its distance from the leader than its games behind.

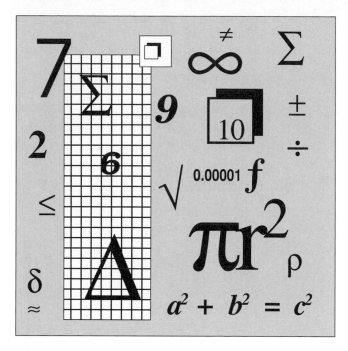

APPENDIX D

List of Standards from *Curriculum and Evaluation Standards for School Mathematics**

***Source:** From "List of Standards" by National Council of Teachers of Mathematics, 1989, Curriculum and Evaluation Standards for School Mathematics. Copyright 1989 by NCTM. Reprinted by permission.

CURRICULUM STANDARDS FOR GRADES K–4

Standard 1: Mathematics as Problem Solving

In grades K–4, the study of mathematics should emphasize problem-solving so that students can—

❑ Use problem-solving approaches to investigate and understand mathematical content;
❑ Formulate problems from everyday and mathematical situations;
❑ Develop and apply strategies to solve a wide variety of problems;
❑ Verify and interpret results with respect to the original problem;
❑ Acquire confidence in using mathematics meaningfully.

Standard 2: Mathematics as Communications

In grades K–4, the study of mathematics should include numerous opportunities for communication so that students can—

❑ Relate physical materials, pictures, and diagrams to mathematical ideas;
❑ Reflect on and clarify their thinking about mathematical ideas and situations;
❑ Relate their everyday language to mathematical language and symbols;
❑ Realize that representing, discussing, reading, writing, and listening to mathematics are a vital part of learning and using mathematics.

Standard 3: Mathematics as Reasoning

In grades K–4, the study of mathematics should emphasize reasoning so that students can—

❑ Draw logical conclusions about mathematics;
❑ Use models, known facts, properties, and relationships to explain their thinking;
❑ Justify their answers and solution processes;
❑ Use patterns and relationships to analyze mathematical situations;
❑ Believe that mathematics makes sense.

Standard 4: Mathematical Connections

In grades K–4, the study of mathematics should include opportunities to make connections so that students can—

❑ Link conceptual and procedural knowledge;
❑ Relate various representations of concepts or procedures to one another;
❑ Recognize relationships among different topics in mathematics;
❑ Use mathematics in other curriculum areas;
❑ Use mathematics in their daily lives.

Standard 5: Estimation

In grades K–4, the curriculum should include estimation so students can—

❑ Explore estimation strategies;
❑ Recognize when an estimate is appropriate;
❑ Determine the reasonableness of results;
❑ Apply estimation in working with quantities, measurement, computation, and problem solving.

Standard 6: Number Sense and Numeration

In grades K–4, the mathematics curriculum should include whole-number concepts and skills so that students can—

❑ Construct number meanings through real-world experiences and the use of physical materials;
❑ Understand our numeration system by relating counting, grouping, and place-value concepts;
❑ Develop number sense;
❑ Interpret the multiple uses of numbers encountered in the real world.

Standard 7: Concepts of Whole-Number Operations

In grades K–4, the mathematics curriculum should include concepts of addition, subtraction, multiplication, and division of whole numbers so that students can—

❑ Develop meaning for the operations by modeling and discussing a rich variety of problem situations;
❑ Relate any mathematical language and symbolism of operations to problem situations and informal language;
❑ Recognize that a wide variety of problem structures can be represented by a single operation;
❑ Develop operation sense.

Standard 8: Whole Number Computation

In grades K–4, the mathematics curriculum should develop whole-number computation so that students can—

❑ Model, explain, and develop reasonable proficiency with basic facts and algorithms;
❑ Use a variety of mental computation and estimation techniques;
❑ Use calculators in appropriate computational situations;
❑ Select and use computation techniques appropriate to specific problems and determine whether the results are reasonable.

Standard 9: Geometry and Spatial Sense

In grades K–4, the mathematics curriculum should include two- and three-dimensional geometry so that students can—

❑ Describe model, draw, and classify shapes;
❑ Investigate and predict results of combining, subdividing, and changing shapes;
❑ Develop spatial sense;
❑ Relate geometric ideas to number and measurement ideas;
❑ Recognize and appreciate geometry in their world.

Standard 10: Measurement

In grades K–4, the mathematics curriculum should include measurement so that students can—

❑ Understand the attributes of length, capacity, weight, area, volume, time, temperature, and angle;
❑ Develop the process of measuring and concepts related to units of measurement;
❑ Make and use estimates of measurement;
❑ Make and use measurements in problem and everyday situations.

Standard 11: Statistics and Probability

In grades K–4, the mathematics curriculum should include experiences with data analysis and probability so that students can—

❑ Collect, organize, and describe data;
❑ Construct, read, and interpret displays of data;
❑ Formulate and solve problems that involve collecting and analyzing data;
❑ Explore concepts of chance.

Standard 12: Fractions and Decimals

In grades K–4, the mathematics curriculum should include fractions and decimals so that students can—

❏ Develop concepts of fractions, mixed numbers, and decimals;
❏ Develop number sense for fractions and decimals;
❏ Use models to relate fractions to decimals to find equivalent fractions;
❏ Use models to explore operations on fractions and decimals;
❏ Apply fractions and decimals to problem situations.

Standard 13: Patterns and Relationships

In grades K–4, the mathematics curriculum should include the study of patterns and relationships so that students can—

❏ Recognize, describe, extend, and create a wide variety of patterns;
❏ Represent and describe mathematical relationships;
❏ Explore the use of variables and open sentences to express relationships.

CURRICULUM STANDARDS FOR GRADES 5–8

Standard 1: Mathematics as Problem-Solving

In grades 5–8, the mathematics curriculum should include numerous and varied experiences with problem-solving as a method of inquiry and application so that students can—

❏ Use problem-solving approaches to investigate and understand mathematical content;
❏ Formulate problems from situations within and outside mathematics;
❏ Develop and apply a variety of strategies to solve problems, with emphasis on multistep and non-routine problems;
❏ Verify and interpret results with respect to the original problem situation;
❏ Generalize solutions and strategies to new problem situations;
❏ Acquire confidence in using mathematics meaningfully.

Standard 2: Mathematics as Communications

In grades 5–8, the mathematics curriculum should include opportunities to communicate so that students can—

❏ Model situations using oral, written, concrete, pictorial, graphical, and algebraic methods;

❏ Reflect on and clarify their own thinking about mathematical ideas and situations;
❏ Develop common understandings of mathematical ideas, including the role of definitions;
❏ Use the skills of reading, listening, and viewing to interpret and evaluate mathematical ideas;
❏ Discuss mathematical ideas and make conjectures and convincing arguments;
❏ Appreciate the value of mathematical notation and its role in the development of mathematical ideas.

Standard 3: Mathematics as Reasoning

In grades 5–8, reasoning shall permeate the mathematics curriculum so that students can—

❏ Recognize and apply deductive and inductive reasoning;
❏ Understand and apply reasoning processes, with special attention to spatial reasoning and reasoning with proportions and graphs;
❏ Make and evaluate mathematical conjectures and arguments;
❏ Validate their own thinking;
❏ Appreciate the pervasive use and power of reasoning as part of mathematics.

Standard 4: Mathematical Connections

In grades 5–8, the mathematics curriculum should include the investigation of mathematical connections so that students can—

❏ See mathematics as an integrated whole;
❏ Explore problems and describe results using graphical, numerical, physical, algebraic, and verbal mathematical models or representations;
❏ Use a mathematical idea to further their understanding of other mathematical ideas;
❏ Apply mathematical thinking and modeling to solve problems that arise in other disciplines, such as art, music, psychology, sciences, and business;
❏ Value the role of mathematics in our culture and society.

Standard 5: Number and Number Relationships

In grades 5–8, the mathematics curriculum should include the continued development of number and number relationships so that students can—

❏ Understand, represent, and use numbers in a variety of equivalent forms (integer, fraction, decimal, percent, exponential, and scientific notation) in real-world and mathematical problem situations;

❏ Develop number sense for whole numbers, fractions, decimals, integers, and rational numbers;
❏ Understand and apply ratios, proportions, and percents in a wide variety of situations;
❏ Investigate relationships among fractions, decimals, and percents;
❏ Represent numerical relationships in one- and two-dimensional graphs.

Standard 6: Number Systems and Number Theory

In grades 5–8, the mathematics curriculum should include the study of number systems and number theory so that students can—

❏ Understand and appreciate the need for numbers beyond the whole numbers;
❏ Develop and use order relations for whole numbers, fractions, decimals, integers, and rational numbers;
❏ Extend their understanding of whole-number operations to fractions, decimals, integers, and rational numbers;
❏ Understand how the basic arithmetic operations are related to one another;
❏ Develop and apply number theory concepts (e.g., primes, factors, and multiples) in real-world and mathematical problem situations.

Standard 7: Computation and Estimation

In grades 5–8, the mathematics curriculum should develop the concepts underlying computations and estimations in various contexts so that students can—

❏ Compute with whole numbers, fractions, decimals, integers, and rational numbers;
❏ Develop, analyze, and explain procedures for computation and techniques for estimation;
❏ Develop, analyze, and explain methods for solving proportions;
❏ Select and use an appropriate method for computing from among mental arithmetic, paper-and-pencil, calculator, and computer methods;
❏ Use computation, estimation, and proportions to solve problems;
❏ Use estimation to check the reasonableness of results.

Standard 8: Patterns and Functions

In grades 5–8, the mathematics curriculum should include exploration of patterns and functions so that students can—

❏ Describe, extend, analyze, and create a wide variety of patterns;
❏ Describe and represent relationships with tables, graphs, and rules;
❏ Analyze functional relationships to explain how a change in one quantity results in a change in another;
❏ Use patterns and functions to represent and solve problems.

Standard 9: Algebra

In grades 5–8, the mathematics curriculum should include explorations of algebraic concepts and processes so that students can—

❏ Understand the concepts of variable, expression, and equation;
❏ Represent situations and number patterns with tables, graphs, verbal rules, and equations and explore the interrelationships of these representations;
❏ Analyze tables and graphs to identify properties and relationships;
❏ Develop confidence in solving linear equations using concrete, informal, and formal methods;
❏ Investigate inequalities and nonlinear equations informally;
❏ Apply algebraic methods to solve a variety of real-world and mathematical problems.

Standard 10: Statistics

In grades 5–8, the mathematics curriculum should include exploration of statistics in real-world situations so that students can—

❏ Systematically collect, organize, and describe data;
❏ Construct, read, and interpret tables, charts, and graphs;
❏ Make inferences and convincing arguments that are based on data analysis;
❏ Evaluate arguments that are based on data analysis;
❏ Develop an appreciation for statistical methods as powerful means for decision making.

Standard 11: Probability

In grades 5–8, the mathematics curriculum should include explorations of probability in real-world situations so that students can—

❏ Model situations by devising and carrying out experiments or simulations to determine probabilities;
❏ Model situations by constructing a sample space to determine probabilities;

❑ Appreciate the power of using a probability model by comparing experimental results with mathematical expectations;

❑ Make predictions that are based on experimental or theoretical probabilities;

❑ Develop an appreciation for the pervasive use of probability in the real world.

Standard 12: Geometry

In grades 5–8, the mathematics curriculum should include the study of geometry of one, two, and three dimensions in a variety of situations so that students can—

❑ Identify, describe, compare, and classify geometric figures;

❑ Visualize and represent geometric figures with special attention to developing spatial sense;

❑ Explore transformations of geometric figures;

❑ Represent and solve problems using geometric models;

❑ Understand and apply geometric properties and relationships;

❑ Develop an appreciation of geometry as a means of describing the physical world.

Standard 13: Measurement

In grades 5–8, the mathematics curriculum should include extensive concrete experiences using measurement so that students can—

❑ Extend their understanding of the process of measurement;

❑ Estimate, make, and use measurements to describe and compare phenomena;

❑ Select appropriate units and tools to measure to the degree of accuracy required in a particular situation;

❑ Understand the structure and use of systems of measurement;

❑ Extend their understanding of the concepts of perimeter, area, volume, angle measure, capacity, and weight and mass;

❑ Develop the concepts of rates and other derived and indirect measurements;

❑ Develop formulas and procedures for determining measures to solve problems.

CURRICULUM STANDARDS FOR GRADES 9–12
Standard 1: Mathematics as Problem-Solving

In grades 9–12, the mathematics curriculum should include the refinement and extension of methods of mathematical problem-solving so that all students can—

❑ Use, with increasing confidence, problem-solving approaches to investigate and understand mathematical content;

❑ Apply integrated mathematical problem-solving strategies to solve problems from within and outside of mathematics;

❑ Recognize and formulate problems from situations within and outside of mathematics;

❑ Apply the process of mathematical modeling to real-world problem situations.

Standard 2: Mathematics as Communication

In grades 9–12, the mathematics curriculum should include the continued development of language and symbolism to communicate mathematical ideas so that all students can—

❑ Reflect upon and clarify their thinking about mathematical ideas and relationships;

❑ Formulate mathematical definitions and express generalizations discovered through investigations;

❑ Express mathematical ideas orally and in writing;

❑ Read written presentations of mathematics with understanding;

❑ Ask clarifying and extending questions related to mathematics they have read or heard about;

❑ Appreciate the economy, power, and elegance of mathematical notation and its role in the development of mathematical ideas.

Standard 3: Mathematics as Reasoning

In grades 9–12, the mathematics curriculum should include numerous and varied experiences that reinforce and extend logical reasoning skills so that all students can—

❑ Make and test conjectures;
❑ Formulate counterexamples;
❑ Follow logical arguments;
❑ Judge the validity of arguments;
❑ Construct simple valid arguments;

and so that, in addition, college-intending students can—

❑ Construct proofs by mathematical assertions, including indirect proofs and proofs by mathematical induction.

Standard 4: Mathematical Connections

In grades 9–12, the mathematics curriculum should include investigation of the connections and interplay among various mathematical topics and their applications so that all students can—

❏ Recognize equivalent representations of the same concept;
❏ Relate procedures in one representation to procedures in an equivalent representation;
❏ Use and value the connections among mathematical topics;
❏ Use and value the connections between mathematics and other disciplines.

Standard 5: Algebra

In grades 9–12, the mathematics curriculum should include the continued study of algebraic concepts and methods so that all students can—

❏ Represent situations that involve variable quantities with expressions, equations, inequalities, and matrices;
❏ Use tables and graphs as tools to interpret expressions, equations, and inequalities;
❏ Operate on expressions and matrices, and solve equations and inequalities;
❏ Appreciate the power of mathematical abstraction and symbolism;

and so that, in addition, college-intending students can—

❏ Use matrices to solve linear systems;
❏ Demonstrate technical facility with algebraic transformations, including techniques based on the theory of equations.

Standard 6: Functions

In grades 9–12, the mathematics curriculum should include the continued study of functions so that all students can—

❏ Model real-world phenomena with a variety of functions;
❏ Represent and analyze relationships using tables, verbal rules, equations, and graphs;
❏ Translate among tabular, symbolic, and graphical representations of functions;
❏ Recognize that a variety of problem situations can be modeled by the same type of function;
❏ Analyze the effects of parameter changes on the graphs of functions;

and so that, in addition, college-intending students can—

❏ Understand operations on, and the general properties and behavior of, classes of functions.

Standard 7: Geometry from a Synthetic Perspective

In grades 9–12, the mathematics curriculum should include the continued study of geometry of two and three dimensions so that all students can—

❏ Interpret and draw three-dimensional objects;
❏ Represent problem situations with geometric models and apply properties of figures;
❏ Classify figures in terms of congruence and similarity and apply these relationships;

and so that, in addition, college-intending students can—

❏ Develop an understanding of an axiomatic system through investigating and comparing various geometries.

Standard 8: Geometry from an Algebraic Perspective

In grades 9–12, the mathematics curriculum should include the study of the geometry of two and three dimensions from an algebraic point of view so that all students can—

❏ Translate between synthetic and coordinate representations;
❏ Deduce properties of figures using transformations and using coordinates;
❏ Identify congruent and similar figures using transformations;
❏ Analyze properties of Euclidean transformations and relate translations to vectors;

and so that, in addition, college-intending students can—

❏ Apply transformations, coordinates, and vectors in problem-solving.

Standard 9: Trigonometry

In grades 9–12, the mathematics curriculum should include the study of trigonometry so that all students can—

❏ Apply trigonometry to problem situations involving triangles;

❏ Explore periodic real-world phenomena using the sine and cosine functions;

and so that, in addition, college-intending students can—

❏ Understand the connection between trigonometric and circular functions;

❏ Apply general graphing techniques to trigonometric functions;

❏ Solve trigonometric equations and verify trigonometric identities;

❏ Understand the connections between trigonometric functions and polar coordinates, complex numbers, and series.

Standard 10: Statistics

In grades 9–12, the mathematics curriculum should include the continued study of data analysis and statistics so that all students can—

❏ Construct and draw inferences from charts, tables, and graphs that summarize data from real-world situations;

❏ Use curve-fitting to predict from data;

❏ Understand and apply measures of central tendency, variability, and correlation;

❏ Understand sampling and recognize its role in statistical claims;

❏ Design a statistical experiment to study a problem, conduct the experiment, and interpret and communicate the outcomes;

❏ Analyze the effects of data transformations on measures of central tendency and variability;

and so that, in addition, college-intending students can—

❏ Transform data to aid in data interpretation and prediction;

❏ Test hypotheses using appropriate statistics.

Standard 11: Probability

In grades 9–12, the mathematics curriculum should include the continued study of probability so that all students can—

❏ Use experimental or theoretical probability, as appropriate, to represent and solve problems involving uncertainty;

❏ Use simulations to estimate probabilities;

❏ Understand the concept of random variable;

❏ Create and interpret discrete probability distributions;

❏ Describe, in general terms, the normal curve and use its properties to answer questions about sets of data that are assumed to be normally distributed;

and so that, in addition, college-intending students can—

❏ Apply the concept of random variable to generate and interpret probability distributions, including binomial, uniform, normal, and chi-square.

Standard 12: Discrete Mathematics

In grades 9–12, the mathematics curriculum should include topics from discrete mathematics so that all students can—

❏ Represent problem situations using discrete structures such as finite graphs, matrices, sequences, and recurrence relations;

❏ Represent and analyze finite graphs using matrices;

❏ Develop and analyze algorithms;

❏ Solve enumeration and finite probability problems;

and so that, in addition, the college-intending students can—

❏ Represent and solve problems using linear programming and difference equations;

❏ Investigate problem situations that arise in connection with computer validation and the application of algorithms.

Standard 13: Conceptual Underpinnings of Calculus

In grades 9–12, the mathematics curriculum should include the informal exploration of calculus concepts from both a graphical and a numerical perspective so that all students can—

❏ Determine maximum and minimum points of a graph and interpret the results in problem situations;

❏ Investigate limiting processes by examining infinite sequences and series and areas under curves;

and so that, in addition, college-intending students can—

❏ Understand the conceptual foundations of limit, the area under a curve, the rate of change, and the slope of a tangent line and their applications to other disciplines;
❏ Analyze the graphs of polynomials, rational, radical, and transcendental functions.

Standard 14: Mathematical Structure

In grades 9–12, the mathematics curriculum should include the study of mathematical structure so that all students can—

❏ Compare and contrast the real number system and its various subsystems with regard to their structural characteristics;
❏ Understand the logic of algebraic procedures;
❏ Appreciate that seemingly different mathematical systems may be essentially the same;

and so that, in addition, college-intending students can—

❏ Develop the complex-number system and demonstrate facility with its operations;
❏ Prove elementary theorems within various mathematical structures, such as groups and fields;
❏ Develop an understanding of the nature and purpose of axiomatic systems.

EVALUATION STANDARDS
Standard 1: Alignment

Methods and tasks for assessing students' learning should be aligned with the curriculum's—

❏ Goals, objectives, and mathematical content;
❏ Relative emphases given to various topics and processes and their relationships;
❏ Instructional approaches and activities, including use of calculators, computers, and manipulatives.

Standard 2: Multiple Sources of Information

Decisions concerning students' learning should be made on the basis of a convergence of information obtained from a variety of sources. These sources should encompass tasks that—

❏ Demand different kinds of mathematical thinking;
❏ Present the same mathematical concept or procedure in different contexts, formats, and problem situations.

Standard 3: Appropriate Assessment Methods and Uses

Assessment methods and instruments should be selected on the basis of—

❏ The type of information sought;
❏ The use to which the information will be put;
❏ The development level and maturity of the student.

The use of assessment data for purposes other than those intended is inappropriate.

Standard 4: Mathematical Power

The assessment of students' mathematical knowledge should yield information about their—

❏ Ability to apply their knowledge to solve problems within mathematics and other disciplines;
❏ Ability to use mathematical language to communicate ideas;
❏ Ability to reason and analyze;
❏ Knowledge and understanding of concepts and procedures;
❏ Disposition toward mathematics;
❏ Understanding of the nature of mathematics;
❏ Integration of these aspects of mathematical knowledge.

Standard 5: Problem Solving

The assessment of students' ability to use mathematics in solving problems should provide evidence that they can—

❏ Formulate problems;
❏ Apply a variety of strategies to solve problems;
❏ Solve problems;
❏ Verify and interpret results;
❏ Generalize solutions.

Standard 6: Communication

The assessment of students' ability to communicate mathematics should provide evidence that they can—

❏ Express mathematical ideas by speaking, writing, demonstrating, and depicting them visually;
❏ Understand, interpret, and evaluate mathematical ideas that are presented in written, oral, or visual form;

❑ Use mathematical vocabulary, notation, and structure to represent ideas, describe relationships, and model situations.

Standard 7: Reasoning

The assessment of students' ability to reason mathematically should provide evidence that they can—

❑ Use inductive reasoning to recognize patterns and form conjectures;
❑ Use reasoning to develop plausible arguments for mathematical statements;
❑ Use proportional and spatial reasoning to solve problems;
❑ Use deductive reasoning to verify conclusions, judge the validity of arguments, and construct valid arguments;
❑ Analyze situations to determine common properties and structures;
❑ Appreciate the axiomatic nature of mathematics.

Standard 8: Mathematical Concepts

The assessment of students' knowledge and understanding of mathematical concepts should provide evidence that they can—

❑ Label, verbalize, and define concepts;
❑ Identify and generate examples and nonexamples;
❑ Use models, diagrams, and symbols to represent concepts;
❑ Translate from one mode of representation to another;
❑ Recognize the various meanings and interpretation of concepts;
❑ Identify properties of a given concept and recognize conditions that determine a particular concept;
❑ Compare and contrast concepts.

In addition, assessment should provide evidence of the extent to which students have integrated their knowledge of various concepts.

Standard 9: Mathematical Procedures

The assessment of students' knowledge of procedures should provide evidence that they can—

❑ Recognize when a procedure is appropriate;
❑ Give reasons for the steps in a procedure;
❑ Reliably and efficiently execute procedures;
❑ Verify the results of procedures empirically (e.g., using models) or analytically;

❑ Recognize correct and incorrect procedures;
❑ Generate new procedures and extend or modify familiar ones;
❑ Appreciate the nature and role of procedures in mathematics.

Standard 10: Mathematical Disposition

The assessment of students' mathematical disposition should seek information about their—

❑ Confidence in using mathematics to solve problems, to communicate ideas, and to reason;
❑ Flexibility in exploring mathematical ideas and trying alternative methods in solving problems;
❑ Willingness to persevere in mathematical tasks;
❑ Interest, curiosity, and inventiveness in doing mathematics;
❑ Inclination to monitor and reflect on their own thinking and performance;
❑ Valuing of the application of mathematics to situations arising in other disciplines and everyday experiences;
❑ Appreciation of the role of mathematics in our culture and its value as a tool and as a language.

Standard 11: Indicators for Program Evaluation

Indicators of mathematics program's consistency with *Standards* should include—

❑ Student outcomes;
❑ Program expectations and support;
❑ Equity for all students;
❑ Curriculum review and change.

In addition, indicators of the program's match to the *Standards* should be collected in the areas of curriculum, instructional resources, and forms of instruction.

Standard 12: Curriculum and Instructional Resources

In an evaluation of a mathematics program's consistency with the *Curriculum Standards,* the examination of curriculum and instructional resources should focus on—

❑ Goals, objectives, and mathematical content;
❑ Relative emphases of various topics and processes and their relationships;
❑ Instructional approaches and activities;
❑ Articulation across grades;

❏ Assessment methods and instruments;
❏ Availability of technological tools and support materials.

Standard 13: Instruction

In an evaluation of a mathematics program's consistency with the *Curriculum Standards,* instruction and the environment in which it takes place should be examined, with special attention to—

❏ Mathematical content and its treatment;
❏ Relative emphases assigned to various topics and processes and the relationships among them;
❏ Opportunities to learn;
❏ Instructional resources and classroom climate;

❏ Assessment methods and instruments;
❏ The articulation of instruction across grades.

Standard 14: Evaluation Team

Program evaluations should be planned and conducted by—

❏ Individuals with expertise and training in mathematics education;
❏ Individuals with expertise and training in program evaluation;
❏ Individuals who make decisions about the mathematics program;
❏ Users of the information from the evaluation.

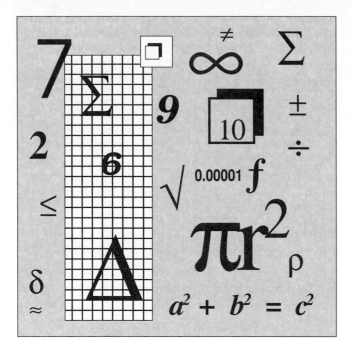

APPENDIX E

Casey Rudd's Syllabus for His First-Period Algebra I Course

**Course Syllabus
for
First-Period Algebra I**

WHAT IS THIS COURSE ALL ABOUT?

The course is all about *algebra:*

❑ Understanding how algebra is used to solve problems
❑ Discovering and inventing ways to use algebra to solve your own problems

WHAT IS ALGEBRA?

When you learned arithmetic, you learned how to work with specific numbers. For example, you learned how to divide 3.45 by 0.82.

In algebra you learn to work with what are called *variables*. Being able to work with variables allows you to extend what you learn in one situation to countless other situations.

The question What is algebra? will be answered during the first few weeks of the course.

WHY SHOULD YOU LEARN ALGEBRA?

You should learn algebra because:

❑ Using algebra will help you solve many of the problems you face right now as well as later on in your life
❑ Without algebra you cannot continue to advance in school for two reasons:

Your success in other courses you take in high school as well as in any vocational school, technical school, or college you might attend depends on your understanding of algebra.

A full year credit in algebra is required for a high school diploma in this state.

❑ An understanding of at least some algebra is expected of literate citizens in today's society and is needed in many occupations.

ARE YOU READY TO LEARN ALGEBRA?

Absolutely yes, as long as

❑ You can do fundamental arithmetic.
❑ You want to solve problems that life tosses your way.

WITH WHOM WILL YOU BE WORKING IN THIS COURSE?

You will be working with Casey Rudd, who is responsible for helping you and your classmates learn algebra. You will also be working with your classmates, each of whom will be making a unique contribution to what you get out of this course. In turn, you will contribute to what they learn by sharing your ideas, problems, discoveries, inventions and solutions.

WHERE WILL YOU BE LEARNING ALGEBRA?

You will draw your understanding of algebra from your entire environment, whether at home, school, or anywhere else. Your classroom, Room 213 at Malaker High, is the place where ideas about algebra are brought together and formalized. Room 213 is a place of business for learning algebra.

HOW WILL YOU BE EXPECTED TO BEHAVE IN THIS CLASS?

You and your classmates have the right to go about the business of learning algebra free from fear of being harmed, intimidated, or embarrassed. Mr. Rudd has the right to go about the business of helping you and your classmates learn algebra without disruption or interference. Thus, you are expected to follow five rules of conduct:

1. Give yourself a complete opportunity to learn algebra.
2. Do not interfere with the opportunities of your classmates to learn algebra.
3. Respect the rights of all members of this class (they include you, your classmates, and Mr. Rudd).
4. Follow Mr. Rudd's directions for lessons and classroom procedures.
5. Adhere to the rules and policies of Malaker High as listed on pages 12–14 of the *Student Handbook*.

WHAT MATERIALS WILL YOU NEED FOR CLASS?

Bring the following with you to every class meeting:

❑ The course textbook:
   Foster, A. G., Rath, J. N., and Winters, L. J. (1986). *Merrill Algebra One.* Columbus, Ohio: Merrill.
❑ A four-part notebook:
   1. Part 1 is for class notes.
   2. Part 2 is for homework and class assignments.
   3. Part 3 is for saving computer programs and flowcharts developed during the course.
   4. Part 4 is for definitions of vocabulary and symbols.
❑ A scratch pad
❑ Pencils, pens, and an eraser
❑ A hand-held, battery-operated calculator that includes the following features: (a) at least two memories, (b) x^n function key, (c) $\sqrt{}$ function key, (d) (−) function key, (e) (function key, (f)) function key, and (g) π function key.
❑ A ruler (at least 12 inches but not more than 15 inches long)

You will also need five 5.25-inch computer diskettes in a storage case. You will not have to bring these to class every day, but have them available at school (e.g., in your locker).

   A textbook has been checked out to you for the school year. You are responsible for maintaining it in good condition and returning it to Mr. Rudd on the last day of class. The other materials can be purchased at the Malaker High Bookstore or at other retail outlets.

WHAT WILL YOU BE DOING FOR THIS CLASS?

The course is organized into 17 units of about two weeks each. During each unit you will be:

❑ Participating in class meetings. Depending on the agenda for the meetings you will be:
   Listening to Mr. Rudd speak and seeing his illustrations as you take notes on what is being explained
   Listening to a classmate speak and seeing his or her illustrations as you take notes on what is being explained
   Explaining things to the class as your classmates take notes on what you say and show them
   Asking questions, answering questions, and discussing issues with members of the class during questioning/discussion sessions
   Working closely with your classmates as part of small task groups
   Working independently on assigned exercises
   Taking brief tests
❑ Completing homework assignments

❏ Completing computer laboratory assignments
❏ Taking a unit test

WHAT WILL YOU LEARN FROM THIS CLASS?

Each unit will either introduce you to a new algebraic topic or extend your understanding of a previous topic. During the unit you will:

❏ Discover an idea or relationship
❏ Add to your ability to use the language of algebra
❏ Acquire a new skill or polish previously acquired skills
❏ Extend your ability to solve problems

Here are the titles of the 17 units:

1. Algebra and Its Language
2. Types of Numbers and Arithmetic Operations
3. Operations on Rational Numbers
4. Algebraic Inequalities
5. Powers
6. Polynomials
7. Factoring Polynomials
8. Quadratic Equations
9. Algebraic Functions
10. Extending Functions
11. Systems of Open Sentences
12. Extending Powers and Radicals
13. Extending Quadratic Functions
14. Operations with Rational Polynomials
15. Extending Work with Rational Polynomials
16. Special Functions with Natural Numbers
17. Extending What You've Learned

Units 1–8 are planned for the first semester; units 9–17 are planned for the second semester.

HOW WILL YOU KNOW WHEN YOU'VE LEARNED ALGEBRA?

Everyone knows at least some algebra, but no one ever learns algebra completely. Algebra is being discovered and invented every day. You will use what you learn in this course to develop further your ability to use algebra to solve problems.

The question is not whether or not you've learned algebra but how well you are learning it. During this course, you will be given feedback on your progress through comments Mr. Rudd makes about work you complete, scores you achieve on brief tests, and the grades you achieve based on unit, midsemester, and semester tests.

HOW WILL YOUR GRADES FOR THE COURSE BE DETERMINED?

Your grade for the first semester will be based on eight unit tests, a midsemester test scheduled between the fifth and sixth units, and a semester test. Your scores on these tests will influence your first-semester grade according to the following scale:

❏ The eight unit tests .... 60% (7.5% each)
❏ The midsemester test 15%
❏ The semester test 25%

Your grade for the second semester will be based on nine unit tests, a midsemester test scheduled between the 12th and 13th units, and a semester test. Your scores on these tests will influence your second semester grade according to the following scale:

❏ The nine unit tests .... 60% (6.7% each)
❏ The midsemester test 15%
❏ The semester test 25%

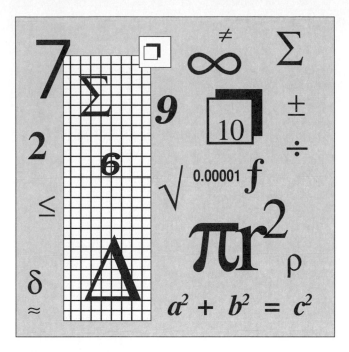

APPENDIX F

Test Casey Rudd Constructed for Unit 7 of His First-Period Algebra I Course*

*See Exhibit 8.10 for the goal and objectives.

Algebra I ** 1st Period ** Unit 7 Test

1. What is your name?_____

2. Following is a list of questions. For each, determine whether or not analyzing the factors of a number would help one to answer the question. If so, write Yes in the blank. If not, write No. Write one sentence explaining the reason for your answer.

    _____ $5,378 was donated for the cause. How many people donated to the cause and what was the average donation?

    Reason: _____

    _____

    _____ How large an area can I enclose with 60 meters of fencing?

    Reason: _____

    _____

    _____ If I save $175 in a bank at an interest rate of 6% compounded per month for a year, how much interest will I have earned after 2 years?

    Reason: _____

    _____

    _____ How long will it take me to travel 300 miles by car?

    Reason: _____

    _____

3. List all the factors of -18 that are integers.

    _____

4. Express 72 in a factored form using only prime numbers.

    _____

5. Which of the following two expressions represents a prime polynomial? Put an X in the blank in front of the prime polynomial and then use the space provided to explain why it is prime and the other one is not.

    _____ $80a^3b - 4ab^2$ _____ $80a + 17b$

    _____

    _____

6. Write $21x^3 + 6x$ in factored form. _____
    Prove your answer with the distributive property $ab + ac = a(b + c)$ by indicating what you let a, b, and c equal:
    $a =$ _____ , $b =$ _____ , $c =$ _____

7. Illustrate that $x^2 + 4x + 3$ can be expressed in factored form as $(x + 3)(x + 1)$ by drawing a puzzle constructed from the following eight puzzle pieces:

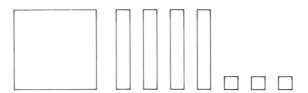

    Label your finished puzzle to indicate the dimensions of the two-dimensional region it forms:

8. For each of the following that is factorable, factor completely; write Not factorable under the others:

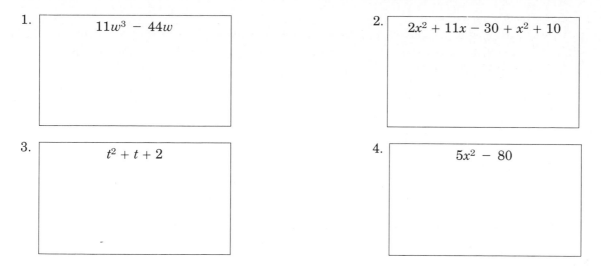

1.
$$11w^3 - 44w$$

2.
$$2x^2 + 11x - 30 + x^2 + 10$$

3.
$$t^2 + t + 2$$

4.
$$5x^2 - 80$$

9. A rectangle is 4 meters wide and 7 meters long. If the length and the width are increased by the same amount, the area is increased by 26 square meters. What are the dimensions of the new rectangle? Display your work and write your final answer in the blank.

_____

10. The difference between the square of a particular whole number and itself is 12. What is that whole number? Display your work and write your final answer in the blank.

_____

11. Smile.

REFERENCES

Aaboe, A. (1964). *Episodes from the early history of mathematics.* Washington, DC: The Mathematical Association of America.

Activity Resources Company: 1989. (1989). Haywood, CA: Activity Resources Co., Inc.

Aleamoni, L. M. (1985). Review of *Stanford Achievement Test: Mathematics Tests.* In J. V. Mitchell (Ed.), *The ninth mental measurement yearbook* (pp. 1453–1455). Lincoln, NE: The Buros Institute of Mental Measurements and the University of Nebraska Press.

Allen, R. R. (1988, April). *Mathematics, reform, and excellence—Japan and the U.S.* A presentation at the annual meeting of the National Council of Teachers of Mathematics, Chicago.

Allen, R. R., Davidson, T., Hering, W., and **Jesunathadas, J.** (1984). *A study of the conditions of secondary mathematics teacher education.* San Francisco: Far West Laboratory.

Ames, C., and **Ames, R.** (Eds.). (1984). *Research on motivation in education: Vol. 1. Student motivation.* New York: Academic Press.

Ames, C., and **Ames, R.** (Eds.). (1985). *Research on motivation in education: Vol. 21. The classroom milieu.* Orlando, FL: Academic Press.

Amundson, H. E. (1969). Percent. In the National Council of Teachers of Mathematics *Historical topics for the mathematics classroom: Thirty-first Yearbook* (pp. 146–147). Washington, DC: NCTM.

Archibald, D. A., and **Newman, F. M.** (1988). *Beyond standardized testing: Assessing academic achievement in the secondary school.* Reston, VA: National Association of Secondary School Principals.

Arends, R. I. (1988). *Learning to teach.* New York: Random House.

Arnold, D., Atwood, R., and **Rogers, V.** (1974). Question and response levels and lapse time intervals. *Journal of Experimental Education, 43,* 11–15.

Artino, R. A., Gaglione, A. M., and **Shell, N.** (1983). *The contest problem book IV: Annual high school mathematics examinations 1973–1982.* Washington, DC: Mathematical Association of America.

Ashlock, R. B. (1990). *Error patterns in computation: A semiprogrammed approach* (5th ed.). Columbus, OH: Merrill.

Azrin, N. H., Hake, D. G., and **Hutchinson, R. R.** (1965). Motivational aspects of escape from punishment. *Journal of Experimental Analysis of Behavior, 8,* 31–44.

Azrin, N. H., Hutchinson, R. R., and **Sallery, R. D.** (1964). Pain-aggression toward inanimate objects. *Journal of Experimental Analysis of Behavior, 7,* 223–228.

Ball, D. L. (1988a). *The subject matter preparation of prospective mathematics teachers: Challenging the myths* (Research Report 88-3). East Lansing: Michigan State University, National Center for Research on Teacher Education.

Ball, D. L. (1988b). *Unlearning to teach mathematics* (Issue Paper 88-1). East Lansing: Michigan State University, National Center for Research on Teacher Education.

Bandura, A. (1965). Behavior modification through modeling procedures. In L. Krasner and L. P. Ullman (Eds.), *Research in behavior modification* (pp. 310–340). New York: Holt, Rinehart and Winston.

Bang-Jensen, V. (1986). The view from next door: A look at peer "supervision." In K. K. Zumwalt (Ed.), *Improving teaching* (pp. 51–62). Alexandria, VA: Association for Supervision and Curriculum Development.

Baroody, A. J. (1989). Kindergartners' mental addition with single-digit combinations. *Journal of Research in Mathematics Education, 20,* 159–172.

Begle, E. G. (1958). The School Mathematics Study Group. *The Mathematics Teacher, 51,* 616–618.

Behle, J. H. (1985). The nature of problem solving instruction in seventh grade mathematics classrooms. *Dissertation Abstracts International, 45*(08), 2428A.

Berg, F. S. (1987). *Facilitating classroom listening.* Boston: College-Hill Press.

Berliner, D. C. (1986). In pursuit of the expert pedagogue. *Educational Researcher, 15,* 5–13.

Beskin, N. M. (1986). *Fascinating fractions.* Moscow, Russia: Mir Publishers.

Beyer, B. K. (1987). *Practical strategies for the teaching of thinking.* Boston: Allyn & Bacon.

Beyer, W. H. (Ed.). (1987) *CRC standard mathematical tables* (28th ed.). Boca Raton, FL: CRC Press.

Bloom, B. S. (Ed.). (1984). *Taxonomy of educational objectives: The classification of educational goals, book I: Cognitive domain.* New York: Longman.

Bloom, B. S., Madaus, G. F., and **Hastings, J. T.** (1981). *Evaluation to improve learning.* New York: McGraw-Hill.

Bongiovanni, A. F. (1979). An analysis of research on punishment and its relation to the use of corporal punishment in schools. In I. A. Hyman and J. Wise (Eds.), *Corporal punishment in American education* (pp. 351–372). Philadelphia: Temple University Press.

Bourne, L. E., Dominowski, R. L., Loftus, E. F., and **Healy, A. F.** (1986). *Cognitive processes* (2d ed.). Englewood Cliffs, NJ: Prentice Hall.

Bowden, R. (1991). *Precision teaching in algebra.* Unpublished doctoral dissertation, Utah State University, Logan.

Bowers, J. (1988). *Invitation to mathematics.* Oxford, England: Basil Blackwell.

Brandt, R. (1989). A changed professional culture. *Educational Leadership, 46,* 2.

Braskamp, L. A., Brandenburg, D. C., and **Ory, J. C.** (1984). *Evaluating teaching effectiveness: A practical guide.* Beverly Hills, CA: Sage.

Bridges, E. M. (1986). *The incompetent teacher.* Philadelphia, PA: The Falmer Press.

Brissenden, T. H. F. (1980). *Mathematics teaching: Theory in practice.* London, England: Harper & Row.

Brophy, J. (1986). Teaching and learning mathematics: Where research should be going. *Journal of Research in Mathematics Education, 17,* 323–346.

Brubaker, D. L. (1982). *Curriculum planning: The dynamics of theory and practice.* Glenview, IL: Scott, Foresman.

Brumfiel, V., Golden, N., and **Heins, M.** (1986). *Pre-algebra: Skills, problem solving, applications.* Orlando, FL: Harcourt Brace Jovanovich.

Bushaw, D., Bell, M., Pollack, H. O., Thompson, M., and **Usiskin, Z.** (1980). *A sourcebook of applications of school mathematics.* Reston, VA: NCTM.

Cajori, F. (1985). *A history of mathematics.* New York: Chelsea Publishing.

California State Department of Education. (1987). *Caught in the middle: Educational reform for young adolescents in California public schools.* Sacramento, CA: Author.

Callahan, L. G. (1985). Pressing problems in primary mathematics programs: Time, texts, and tests. *Arithmetic Teacher, 33, 2.*

Cangelosi, J. S. (1974). Competency based teacher education: A cautionary note. *Contemporary Education, 46,* 124–126.

Cangelosi, J. S. (1980). Four steps to teaching for mathematical application. *Mathematics and Computer Education, 14,* 54–59.

Cangelosi, J. S. (1982). *Measurement and evaluation: An inductive approach for teachers.* Dubuque, IA: W. C. Brown.

Cangelosi, J. S. (1984a). Another answer to the cut-off score question. *Educational Measurement Issues and Practice, 3,* 23–25.

Cangelosi, J. S. (1984b). Increasing student engagement during questioning strategy sessions. *Mathematics Teacher, 77,* 469–472.

Cangelosi, J. S. (1984c, May). *Teaching students to apply mathematics.* Paper presented at the meeting of the

Research Council for Diagnostic and Prescriptive Mathematics, San Francisco, CA.

Cangelosi, J. S. (1985, October). *Problem-solving and school mathematics textbooks.* Invited paper presented at the annual Conference of the Utah Education Association, Salt Lake City, UT.

Cangelosi, J. S. (1986). Evaluating teaching within a teacher advancement plan. *The Clearing House, 59,* 405–409.

Cangelosi, J. S. (1988a). *Classroom management strategies: Gaining and maintaining students' cooperation.* New York: Longman.

Cangelosi, J. S. (1988b). Development and validation of the underprepared mathematics teacher assessment. *Journal for Research in Mathematics Education, 19,* 233–245.

Cangelosi, J. S. (1988c). Language activities that promote awareness of mathematics. *Arithmetic Teacher, 36,* 6–9.

Cangelosi, J. S. (1989a). *Demystifying school mathematics.* A videotape program. Logan, UT: National Science Foundation and Utah State University Telecommunications Division.

Cangelosi, J. S. (1989b, April). *A video inservice program for underprepared mathematics teachers.* A presentation at the annual meeting of the National Council of Teachers of Mathematics, Orlando, FL.

Cangelosi, J. S. (1990a). *Cooperation in the classroom: Students and teachers together* (2d ed.). Washington: National Education Association.

Cangelosi, J. S. (1990b). *Designing tests for evaluating student achievement.* New York: Longman.

Cangelosi, J. S. (1990c). *Using mathematics to solve real-life problems.* A videotape program. Logan, UT: National Science Foundation and Utah State University Telecommunications Division.

Cangelosi, J. S. (1991). *Evaluating classroom instruction.* New York: Longman.

Cangelosi, J. S., Struyk, L. R., Grimes, M. L., and **Duke, C.** (1988, April). *Classroom management needs of beginning teachers.* Presented at the American Educational Research Association annual meeting, New Orleans.

Canter, L., and **Canter, M.** (1976). *Assertive discipline: A take-charge approach for today's educator.* Seal Beach, CA: Canter and Canter Associates.

Carnegie Forum on Education and the Economy. (1986). *A nation prepared: Teachers for the 21st century: The report of the Task Force on Teaching as a Profession.* Washington, DC: Author.

Carpenter, T. P., Lindquist, M. M., Brown, C. A., Kouba, V. L., Silver, E. A., and **Swafford, J. O.** (1988). Results of the fourth NAEP assessment of mathematics: Trends and conclusions. *Arithmetic Teacher, 36,* 38–43.

Chance, P. (1988). *Learning and behavior* (2d ed.). Belmont, CA: Wadsworth.

Charles, C. M. (1989). *Building classroom discipline: From models to practice* (3d ed.). New York: Longman.

Chase, A., and **Wolfe, P.** (1989). Off to a good start in peer coaching. *Educational Leadership, 46,* 37.

Chase, C. I. (1985). Review of *SRA Survival Skills in Reading and Mathematics.* In J. V. Mitchell (Ed.), *The ninth mental measurement yearbook* (pp. 1438–1439). Lincoln, NE: The Buros Institute of Mental Measurements and the University of Nebraska Press.

Chrisco, I. M. (1989). Peer assistance works. *Educational Leadership, 46,* 31–32.

Clemens, S. R., O'Daffer, P. G., and **Cooney, T. J.** (1984). *Geometry with applications and problem solving.* Menlo Park, CA: Addison-Wesley.

Cobb, P. (1988). The tension between theories of learning and instruction in mathematics education. *Educational Psychologists, 23,* 87–103.

College Board Publication. (1990). *Advanced placement course descriptions in mathematics.* Princeton, NJ: Author.

Collins, A. F. (1987). *Rapid math without a calculator.* Secaucus, NJ: Citadel Press.

Conference Board of the Mathematical Sciences. (1983a). *The mathematical sciences curriculum K–12: What is still fundamental and what is not.* Report to the National Science Board Commission on Precollege Education in Mathematics, Sciences, and Technology. Washington, DC: Author.

Conference Board of the Mathematical Sciences. (1983b, November). *New goals for mathematical sciences education.* Report. Washington, DC: Author.

Cooney, T. J., Davis, E. J., and **Henderson, K. B.** (1983). *Dynamics of teaching secondary school mathematics.* Prospect Heights, IL: Waveland Press.

Cooper, J. M. (1984). Introduction and overview. In J. M. Cooper (Ed.), *Developing skills for instructional supervision* (pp. 1–9). New York: Longman.

Coulter, F. (1987). Homework. In M. J. Dunkin (Ed.), *The international encyclopedia of teaching and teacher education* (pp. 272–277). Oxford, England: Pergamon Press.

Court, N. A. (1961). *Mathematics in fun and earnest.* New York: Mentor Books.

Coxford, A. F., and **Payne, J. N.** (1987). *HBJ algebra* (rev. ed.). Orlando, FL: Harcourt Brace Jovanovich.

Cubberley, E. P. (1962). *Public education in the United States* (rev. ed.). Cambridge, MA: Riverside Press.

Curwin, R., and **Mendler, A.** (1980). *The discipline book: A comprehensive guide to school and classroom management.* Reston, VA: Reston Publishing Co.

Delgado, J. M. R. (1963). Cerebral heterostimulation in a monkey colony. *Science, 141,* 161–163.

Devaney, R. L. (1990). *Chaos, fractals, and dynamics: Computer experiments in mathematics.* Menlo Park, CA: Addison-Wesley.

Dossey, J. A. (1987). National efforts in curricular reform take shape. *NCTM News Bulletin, 24*(2), 1.

Dossey, J. A., Mullis, I. V. S., Lindquist, M. M., and **Chambers, D. L.** (1988). *The mathematics report card: Are we measuring up? Trends and achievement based on the 1986 National Assessment.* Princeton, NJ: Educational Testing Service.

Doyle, W. (1986). Classroom organization and management. In M. C. Wittrock (Ed.), *Handbook of research on teaching* (3d ed.) (pp. 392–431). New York: Macmillan.

Dreikurs, R. (1968). *Psychology in the classroom* (2d ed.). New York: Harper & Row.

Driscoll, M. (1982). *Research within reach: A research-guided response to the concerns of educators.* Reston, VA: National Council of Teachers of Mathematics.

Dubelle, S. T., and **Hoffman, C. M.** (1986). *Misbehavin' II.* Lancaster, PA: Technomic Publishing.

Dudeney, H. E. (1958). *Amusements in mathematics.* New York: Dover.

Duke, C. R., Cangelosi, J. S., and **Knight, R. S.** (1988, February). *The Mellon Project: A collaborative effort.* Colloquium presentation at the annual meeting of the American Association of Colleges for Teacher Education, New Orleans, LA.

Easterday, K. E., Henry, L. L., and **Simpson, F. M.** (Eds.). (1981). *Activities for junior high school and middle school mathematics: Readings from the Arithmetic Teacher and the Mathematics Teacher.* Reston, VA: NCTM.

Ebel, R. L., and **Frisbie, D. A.** (1986). *Essentials of educational measurement* (4th ed.). Englewood Cliffs, NJ: Prentice Hall.

Eisner, M. P. (1986). An application of quadratic equations to baseball. *Mathematics Teacher, 79,* 327–30.

Elam, S. M. (1989). The second Gallup Phi Delta Kappa poll of teachers' attitudes toward the public school. *Phi Delta Kappan, 70,* 785–798.

Elich, J., and **Cannon, L. O.** (1989). *Precalculus.* Glenview, IL: Scott, Foresman.

Ellis, H. C., and **Hunt, R. R.** (1983). *Fundamentals of human memory and cognition* (3d ed.). Dubuque, IA: W. C. Brown.

Emmer, E. T., Evertson, C. M., Sanford, J. P., Clements, B. S., and **Worsham, M. E.** (1989). *Classroom management for secondary teachers*

(2d ed.). Englewood Cliffs, NJ: Prentice Hall.

Emphasize application of math skills. *Education USA, 31,* 218ff.

Engelmann, S. (1977). Does the Piagetian approach imply instruction? In D. R. Thomas, M. P. Ford, and G. P. Flammer (Eds.), *Measurement and Piaget.* New York: McGraw-Hill.

Evertson, C. M. (1989). Classroom organization and management. In M. C. Reynolds (Ed.), *Knowledge base for the beginning teacher* (pp. 59–70). Oxford, England: Pergamon Press.

Eves, H. (1983a). *Great moments in mathematics after 1650.* Washington, DC: Mathematical Association of America.

Eves, H. (1983b). *Great moments in mathematics before 1650.* Washington, DC: Mathematical Association of America.

Farrell, M. A., and **Farmer, W. A.** (1988). *Secondary mathematics instruction: An integrated approach.* Providence, RI: Janson.

Fennell, F., and **Ammon, R.** (1985). Writing techniques for problem solvers. *Arithmetic Teacher, 33,* 24–25.

Fisher, C. W., Berliner, D. C., Filby, N. N., Marliave, R., Cahen, L. S., and **Dishaw, M. M.** (1980). Teaching behaviors, academic learning time, and student achievement: An overview. In C. Denham and A. Lieberman (Eds.), *Time to learn* (pp. 7–32). Washington, DC: National Institute of Education.

Floden, R. E. (1985). Review of *Sequential Tests of Educational Progress, Series III.* In J. V. Mitchell (Ed.), *The ninth mental measurement yearbook* (pp. 1363–1364). Lincoln, NE: The Buros Institute of Mental Measurements and the University of Nebraska Press.

Foster, A. G., Rath, J. N., and **Winters, L. J.** (1986). *Merrill algebra one.* Columbus, OH: Merrill.

Friedman, L. (1989). Mathematics and the gender gap: A meta-analysis of recent studies of sex differences in mathematical tasks. *Review of Educational Research, 59,* 185–213.

Frye, S. M. (1989a). The NCTM *Standards*—Challenges for all classrooms. *Arithmetic Teacher, 36,* 4–7.

Frye, S. M. (1989b). The NCTM *Standards*—Challenges for all classrooms. *Mathematics Teacher, 82,* 312–317.

Furth, H. G., and **Wachs, H.** (1974). *Thinking goes to school.* New York: Oxford University Press.

Gardner, M. (1986). *The unexpected hanging and other mathematical diversions.* New York: Simon & Schuster.

Ginott, H. G. (1965). *Parent and child.* New York: Avon Books.

Ginott, H. G. (1972). *Teacher and child.* New York: Avon Books.

Ginsburg, H. (1977). *Children's arithmetic: The learning process.* New York: D. Van Nostrand.

Glasser, W. (1986). *Control theory in the classroom.* New York: Harper & Row.

Gnanadesikan, M., Landwehr, J. M., Newman, C. M., Obremski, T. E., Scheaffer, R. L., Swift, J., and **Watkins, A. E.** (1986). *Quantitative literacy series.* Palo Alto, CA: Seymour.

Good, T. L. (1984, April). *Recent studies of teaching implications for research and policy education.* Paper presented at the annual meeting of the American Educational Research Association, New Orleans.

Good, T. L., Grouws, D. A., and **Ebmeier, H.** (1983). *Active mathematics teaching.* New York: Longman.

Gordon, W. J. J. (1961). *Synectics.* New York: Harper & Row.

Gowan, J. C., Demos, G. D., and **Torrance, E. P.** (1967). *Creativity: Its educational implications.* New York: John Wiley.

Gronlund, N. E., and **Linn, R. L.** (1990). *Measurement and evaluation in teaching* (6th ed.). New York: Macmillan.

Guilford, J. P. (1959). *Personality.* New York: McGraw-Hill.

Harris, B. M. (1989). *Inservice education for staff development.* Boston: Allyn and Bacon.

Harris, T. A. (1969). *I'm OK—you're OK: A practical guide to transactional analysis.* New York: Harper & Row.

Hills, J. R. (1986). *All of Hill's handy hints.* Washington: National Council on Measurement in Education.

Hirsch, C. R. (Ed.). (1986). *Activities for implementing curricular themes from the Agenda for Action.* Reston, VA: NCTM.

Hirsch, C. R., and **Zweng, M. J.** (1985). *The secondary school mathematics curriculum: 1985 yearbook.* Reston, VA: National Council of Teachers of Mathematics.

Hoffman, P. (1988). *Archimedes' revenge: The joys and perils of mathematics.* New York: Fawcett Crest.

Hoffmann, R. J. (1975). Concept of efficiency in item analysis. *Educational and psychological measurement, 35,* 621–640.

Holden, C. (1989). Big changes urged for precollege math. *Science, 243,* 1655.

Honsberger, R. (1973). *Mathematical gems I.* Washington, DC: Mathematical Association of America.

Honsberger, R. (1976). *Mathematical gems II.* Washington, DC: Mathematics Association of America.

Honsberger, R. (Ed.). (1979). *Mathematical plums.* Washington, DC: Mathematical Association of America.

Hopkins, K. D., Stanley, J. C., and **Hopkins, B. R.** (1990). *Educational and psychological measurement and evaluation* (7th ed.). Englewood Cliffs, NJ: Prentice Hall.

Houts, P. L. (Ed.). (1977). *The myth of measurability.* New York: Hart Publishing.

Hunkins, F. P. (1989). *Teaching thinking through effective questioning.* Boston: Christopher-Gordon Publishers.

Hyman, I. A., and **Wise, J. H.** (Eds.). (1979). *Corporal punishment in American education.* Philadelphia: Temple University Press.

Illinois Council of Teachers of Mathematics. (1989). *Mathematics teaching in Japanese elementary and secondary schools: A report of the ICTM Japan Mathematics Delegation*

(1988). Carbondale, IL: Southern Illinois University.

Jacobsen, D., Eggen, P., and **Kauchak, D.** (1989). *Methods for teaching: A skills approach* (3d ed.). Columbus, OH: Merrill.

James, W. (1890). *The principles of psychology,* Vol I and II. New York: Holt, Rinehart and Winston.

Jesunathadas, J. (1990). *Mathematics teachers' instructional activities as a function of academic preparation.* Unpublished doctoral dissertation, Utah State University, Logan.

Johnson, D. R. (1982). *Every minute counts: Making your math class work.* Palo Alto, CA: Seymour.

Johnson, D. R. (1986). *Making every minute count even more: A sequel to every minute counts.* Palo Alto, CA: Seymour.

Johnson, M. L., and **Ferrini-Mundy, J.** (1989). The mathematical education of the underserved and underrepresented groups: A continuing challenge. *Journal of Research in Mathematics Education, 20,* 371–375.

Jones, F. H. (1979). The gentle art of classroom discipline. *Principal, 58,* 26–32.

Joyce, B., and **Weil, M.** (1986). *Models of teaching* (3d ed.). Englewood Cliffs, NJ: Prentice Hall.

Kane, R. B., Byrne, M. A., and **Hater, M. A.** (1974). *Helping children read mathematics.* New York: American Book Company.

Kansky, B. (1986). Utilizing appropriate technology in the learning and teaching of mathematics. In R. Lodholz (Ed.), *A change in emphasis: Mathematics for the transition years, grades 7 & 8.* St. Louis, MO: Monsanto Corporation and Parkway School District.

Karush, W. (1989). *Webster's new world dictionary of mathematics.* New York: Simon & Schuster.

Kasner, E., and **Newman, J. R.** (1989). *Mathematics and the imagination.* Redmond, WA: Tempus Books.

Keedy, M. L., Bittinger, M. L., Smith, S. A., and **Orfan, L. J.** (1986). *Algebra.* Menlo Park, CA: Addison-Wesley.

Keedy, M. L., Smith, S. A., and **Anderson, P. A.** (1986). *Applying mathematics: A consumer/career approach.* Reading, MA: Addison-Wesley.

Keeves, J. P. (Ed.). (1988). *Educational research, methodology, and measurement: An international handbook.* Oxford, England: Pergamon Press.

Kennedy, E. S. (1969). The history of trigonometry: An overview. In the National Council of Teachers of Mathematics *Historical topics for the mathematics classroom: Thirty-first yearbook* (pp. 333–359). Washington, DC: NCTM.

Kidder, R. M. (1985). How a high-schooler discovered a new math theorem. *The Christian Science Monitor, 75,* 19–20.

Kinney, L. B., and **Purdy, C. R.** (1952). *Teaching mathematics in the secondary schools.* New York: Holt, Rinehart and Winston.

Kogelman, S., and **Heller, B. R.** (1986). *The only math book you'll ever need.* New York: Dell Books.

Kohut, S., and **Range, D. G.** (1979). *Classroom discipline: Case studies and viewpoints.* Washington, DC: National Education Association.

Kouba, V. L. (1989). Children's solutions strategies for equivalent set multiplication and division word problems. *Journal of Research in Mathematics Education, 20,* 147–158.

Kounin, J. (1977). *Discipline and group management in classrooms.* New York: Holt, Rinehart and Winston.

Krathwohl, D., Bloom, B. S., and **Masia, B.** (1964). *Taxonomy of educational objectives, the classification of educational goals, handbook 2: Affective domain.* New York: Longman.

Krulik, S., and **Reys, R. E.** (Eds.). (1980). *Problem solving in school mathematics: 1980 yearbook.* Reston, VA: NCTM.

Kubiszyn, T., and **Borich, G.** (1987). *Educational testing and measurement: Classroom application and practice* (2d ed.). Glenview, IL: Scott, Foresman.

Leinhardt, G., and **Greeno, J. G.** (1986). The cognitive skill of teaching. *Journal of Educational Psychology, 78,* 75–95.

Levine, J. M. (1989). *Secondary instruction: A manual for classroom teaching.* Boston: Allyn & Bacon.

Linn, M. C. (1986). Science. In R. F. Dillon and R. J. Sternberg (Eds.), *Cognition and Instruction* (pp. 155–204). San Diego, CA: Academic Press.

Linn, R. L. (1989a). Current perspectives and future directions. In R. L. Linn (Ed.), *Educational measurement* (3d ed.) (pp. 1–10). New York: American Council on Education & Macmillan.

Linn, R. L. (Ed.). (1989b). *Educational Measurement* (3d ed.). New York: American Council on Education & Macmillan Publishing Company.

Livingston, S. A., and **Zieky, M. J.** (1982). *Passing scores: A manual for setting standards of performance on educational and occupational tests.* Princeton, NJ: Educational Testing Service.

Mathematical Association of America. (1988). *Guidelines for the continuing mathematical education of teachers.* Washington, DC: Author.

McLaren, P. (1989). *Life in schools: An introduction to critical pedagogy in the foundations of education.* New York: Longman.

Medley, D. M., Coker, H., and **Soar, R. S.** (1984). *Measurement-based evaluation of teacher performance: An empirical approach.* New York: Longman.

Merriam-Webster Inc. (1986). *Webster's Third New International Dictionary.* Chicago: Author.

Miller, L. (1969). Radical symbol. In the National Council of Teachers of Mathematics, *Historical topics for the mathematics classroom: Thirty-first yearbook* (pp. 147–148). Washington, DC: NCTM.

Millman, J., and **Greene, J.** (1989). The specification and development of tests of achievement and ability. In R. L. Linn (Ed.), *Educational measurement* (3d ed.) (pp. 335–336). New York: American Council on Education and Macmillan.

Nahrgang, C. L., and **Petersen, B. T.** (1986). Using writing to learn mathematics. *Mathematics Teacher, 79,* 461–465.

National Council of Teachers of Mathematics. (1940). *Fifteenth yearbook: The place of mathematics in general education.* New York: Teachers College, Columbia University.

National Council of Teachers of Mathematics (1969). *Historical topics for the mathematics classroom: Thirty-first yearbook.* Reston, VA: Author.

National Council of Teachers of Mathematics. (1980). *An agenda for action: Recommendations for school mathematics of the 1980s.* Reston, VA: Author.

National Council of Teachers of Mathematics. (1988–1989). *Research agenda for mathematics education* (Volumes 1–5). Reston, VA: NCTM and Hillsdale, NJ: Laurence Erlbaum Associates.

National Council of Teachers of Mathematics. (1989). *Curriculum and evaluation standards for school mathematics.* Reston, VA: Author.

National Council of Teachers of Mathematics. (in press). *Professional standards for teaching mathematics.* Reston, VA: Author.

National Education Association. (1972). *Report of the task force on corporal punishment.* Washington, DC: Author.

National Research Council. (1989). *Everybody counts: A report on the future of mathematics education.* Washington: National Academy Press.

National Science Board Commission on Precollege Education in Mathematics, Science, and Education. (1983). *Educating Americans for the twenty-first century: A plan for action for improving the mathematics, science, and technology education for all American elementary and secondary students so that their achievement is the best in the world by 1995.* Washington, DC: National Science Foundation.

Nelson, D., and **Reys, R. E.** (Eds.). (1976). *Measurement in school mathematics: 1976 yearbook.* Reston, VA: NCTM.

Nielsen, K. L. (1962). *Mathematics for practical use.* New York: Barnes & Noble.

Niven, I. (1961). *Numbers: Rational and irrational.* Washington, DC: Mathematical Association of America.

Niven, I. (1965). *Mathematics of choice: How to count without counting.* Washington, DC: Mathematical Association of America.

Niven, I. (1981). *Maxima and minima without calculus.* Washington, DC: Mathematical Association of America.

Packel, E. (1981). *The mathematics of games and gambling.* Washington, DC: Mathematical Association of America.

Péter, R. (1961). *Playing with infinity: Mathematical explorations and excursions.* New York: Dover.

Peterson, I. (1988). *The mathematical tourist: Snapshots of modern mathematics.* New York: W. H. Freeman.

Phye, G. D. (1986). Practice and skilled classroom performance. In G. D. Phye and T. Andre (Eds.), *Cognitive classroom learning* (pp. 141–168). San Diego, CA: Academic Press.

Pòlya, G. (1977). *Mathematical methods in science.* Washington, DC: Mathematical Association of America.

Pòlya, G. (1985). *How to solve it: A new aspect of mathematical method,* (2d ed.). Princeton, NJ: Princeton University Press.

Popham, W. J. (1988). *Educational evaluation* (2d ed.). Englewood Cliffs, NJ: Prentice Hall.

Popham, W. J. (1990). *Modern educational measurement: A practitioner's perspective* (2d ed.). Englewood Cliffs, NJ: Prentice Hall.

Posamentier, A. S., and **Stepelman, J.** (1990). *Teaching secondary school mathematics: Techniques and enrichment units* (3d ed.). Columbus, OH: Merrill.

Post, T. R., and **Cramer, K. A.** (1989). Knowledge, representation, and quantitative thinking. In M. C. Reynolds (Ed.), *Knowledge base for the beginning teacher* (pp. 221–231). Oxford, England: Pergamon Press.

Quina, J. (1989). *Effective secondary teaching: Going beyond the bell curve.* New York: Harper & Row.

Raney, P., and **Robbins, P.** (1989). Professional growth and support through peer coaching. *Educational Leadership, 46,* 35–38.

Reardon, F. J., and **Reynolds, R. N.** (1979). A survey of attitudes toward corporal punishment in Pennsylvania schools. In I. A. Hyman and J. H. Wise (Eds.), *Corporal punishment in American education.* Philadelphia: Temple University Press.

Robbins, A. (1987, May). *Skills of power seminar.* Seminar presentation of the Robbins Research Institute, Detroit, MI.

Roe, B. D., Stoodt, B. D., and **Burns, P. C.** (1987). *Secondary reading instruction: The content areas* (3d ed.). Boston: Houghton-Mifflin.

Rogers, B. G. (1985). Review of *Stanford Diagnostic Mathematics Test.* In J. V. Mitchell (Ed.), *The ninth mental measurement yearbook* (pp. 1457–1462). Lincoln, NE: The Buros Institute of Mental Measurements and the University of Nebraska Press.

Rogers, R. L., and **McMillin, S. C.** (1989). *Freeing someone you love from alcohol and other drugs: A step-by-step plan starting today!* Los Angeles: The Body Press.

Romberg, T. A., and **Carpenter, T. P.** (1986). Research on teaching and learning mathematics: Two disciplines of scientific inquiry. In M. C. Wittrock (Ed.), *Handbook of research on teaching* (3d ed.) (pp. 850–873).

Rose, T. L. (1984). Current uses of corporal punishment in American public schools. *Journal of Educational Psychology, 76,* 427–441.

Rosenshine, B. (1987). Direct instruction. In M. J. Dunkin (Ed.), *The international encyclopedia of teaching and teacher education* (pp. 257–262). Oxford, England: Pergamon Press.

Rust, J. O., and **Kinnard, K. Q.** (1983). Personality characteristics of the users of corporal punishment in the schools. *Journal of School Psychology, 21,* 91–105.

Ryan, K., and **Cooper, J. M.** (1988). *Those who can, teach* (5th ed.). Boston: Houghton-Mifflin.

Salkind, C. T., and Earl, J. M. (1973). *The contest problem book III: Annual high school contests 1966–1972.* Washington, DC: Mathematical Association of America.

Santrock, J. W. (1984). *Adolescence* (2d ed.). Dubuque, IA: W. C. Brown.

Saunders, H. (1981). *When are we ever gonna have to use this?* Palo Alto, CA: Seymour.

Schiffer, N. M., and Bowden, L. (1984). *The role of mathematics in science.* Washington, DC: Mathematical Association of America.

Schoenfeld, A. H. (1985). *Mathematical problem solving.* San Diego, CA: Academic Press.

Schoenfeld, A. H. (1988). When good teaching leads to bad results: The disasters of "well-taught" mathematics courses. *Educational Psychologist, 23,* 145–166.

Schoenfeld, A. II. (1989). Teaching mathematical thinking and problem solving. In L. B. Resnick and L. E. Klopfer (Eds.), *Toward the thinking curriculum: Current cognitive research: 1989 Yearbook of the Association for Supervision and Curriculum Development* (pp. 83–103). Alexandria, VA: ASCD

Schulman, L. S. (1987). Knowledge and teaching: Foundations of the new reform. *Harvard Educational Review, 57,* 1–22.

Shapiro, M. S. (Ed.). (1977). *Mathematics encyclopedia.* Garden City, NY: Doubleday.

Sharron, S., and Reys, R. E. (Eds.). *Applications in school mathematics: 1979 yearbook.* Reston, VA: NCTM.

Skemp, R. R. (1973). *The psychology of learning mathematics.* Middlesex, England: Penguin Books.

Smedslund, J. (1977). Symposium: Practical and theoretical issues in Piagetian psychology III—Piaget's psychology in practice. *British Journal of Educational Psychology, 47,* 1–6.

Smith, F., and Adams, S. (1972). *Educational measurement for the classroom teacher* (2d ed.). New York: Harper & Row.

Soar, R. S., Medley, D. M., and Coker, H. (1983). Teacher evaluation: A critique of currently used methods. *Phi Delta Kappan, 65,* 239–246.

Sobel, M. A., and Maletsky, E. M. (1988). *Teaching mathematics: A sourcebook of aids, activities, and strategies,* (2d ed.). Englewood Cliffs, NJ: Prentice Hall.

Souviney, R. J. (1981). *Solving problems kids care about.* Santa Monica, CA: Goodyear Publishing.

Stallion, B. K. (1988, April). *Classroom management intervention: The effects of mentoring relationships on the inductee teacher's behavior.* Paper presented at the annual meeting of the American Educational Research Association, New Orleans, LA.

Stanley, S. J., and Popham, W. J. (1988a). Introduction: A dismal day in court. In S. J. Stanley and W. J. Popham (Eds.), *Teacher evaluation: Six prescriptions for success.* (pp. xi–xii). Alexandria, VA: Association for Curriculum and Supervision.

Stanley, S. J., and Popham, W. J. (Eds.). (1988b) *Teacher evaluation: Six prescriptions for success.* Alexandria, VA: Association for Curriculum and Supervision.

Steen, L. A. (1987). Mathematics education: A predictor of scientific competitiveness. *Science, 237,* 251ff.

Steen, L. A. (1988). Out from underachievement. *Issues in Science and Technology, 10,* 88–93.

Steere, B. F. (1988). *Becoming an effective classroom manager: A resource for teachers.* Albany, NY: State University of New York Press.

Stiggins, R. J. (1988). Revitalizing classroom assessment: The highest instructional priority. *Phi Delta Kappan, 69,* 363–368.

Stiggins, R. J., Conklin, N. F., and Bridgeford, N. J. (1986). Classroom assessment: A key to effective education. *Educational Measurement: Issues and Practices, 5,* 5–17.

Stiggins, R. J., and Duke, D. (1988). *The case for commitment to teacher growth: Research on teacher evaluation.* Albany: State University of New York Press.

Strike, K. and Soltis, J. (1986). Who broke the fish tank? And other ethical dilemmas. *Instructor, 95,* 36–39.

Strom, R. D. (1969). *Psychology for the classroom.* Englewood Cliffs, NJ: Prentice Hall.

Sulzer-Azaroff, B. and Mayer, G. R. (1977). *Applying behavior analysis procedures with children and youth.* New York: Holt, Rinehart and Winston.

Suydam, M. N. (1989). Research in mathematics education reported in 1988. *Journal for Research in Mathematics Education, 20,* 371–426.

Thorndike, E. L. (1904). *An interpretation of the theory of mental and social measurements.* New York: Teachers College, Columbia University.

Thorndike, E. L., and Woodworth, R. S. (1901). The influence of improvement in one mental function upon the efficacy of other functions. *Psychological Review, 8,* 247–256.

Torrance, E. P. (1962). *Guiding creative talent.* Englewood Cliffs, NJ: Prentice Hall.

Torrance, E. P. (1966). Fostering creative behavior. In R. D. Strom (Ed.). *The inner-city classroom: Teacher behavior* (pp. 57–74). Columbus, OH: Merrill.

Towers, R. L. (1987). *How schools can help combat student drug and alcohol abuse.* Washington, DC: National Education Association.

Towers, R. L. (in press). *Children of alcoholics/addicts.* Washington, DC: National Education Association.

Tuckman, B. W. (1988). *Testing for teachers* (2d ed.). San Diego, CA: Harcourt Brace Jovanovich.

Ulrich, R. E., and Azrin, N. H. (1962). Reflexive fighting in response to aversive stimulation. *Journal of Experimental Analysis of Behavior, 5,* 511–520.

U.S. students again rank near bottom in math and science. (1989). *Report on Educational Research, 23*(2), 1–4.

U.S. teens lag behind in math, science. (1989). *Education USA, 31,* 161+.

Use new standards to upgrade math. (1989). *Education USA, 31,* 153+.

Usiskin, Z. (1985). We need another revolution in secondary school mathematics. In C. R. Hirsch and M. J. Zweng (Eds.), *The secondary school mathematics curriculum: 1985 Yearbook*. Reston, VA: National Council of Teachers of Mathematics.

Utah State Board of Education. (1987). *Mathematics core curriculum: Grades 7–12*. Salt Lake City, UT: Author.

Van Dyke, H. T. (1984). Corporal punishment in our schools. *The Clearing House, 57*, 296–300.

Van Horn, K. L. (1982, April). *The Utah pupil/teacher self-concept program: Teacher strategies that invite improvement of pupil and teacher self-concept*. Paper presented at the annual meeting of the American Educational Research Association, New York.

von Baravalle, H. (1969). The number π. In the National Council of Teachers of Mathematics, *Historical topics for the mathematics classroom: Thirty-first yearbook* (pp. 148–154). Washington, DC: NCTM.

Wadsworth, B. J. (1979). *Piaget's theory of cognitive development* (2d ed.). New York: Longman.

Weber, W. A. (1986). Classroom management. In J. M. Cooper (Ed.), *Classroom teaching skills* (3d ed.). (pp. 271–357). Lexington, MA: D. C. Heath.

Weinstein, C. E., Goetz, E. T., and **Alexander, P. A.** (Eds.). (1988). *Learning and study strategies: Issues in assessment, instruction, and evaluation*. San Diego, CA: Academic Press.

Welsh, R. S. (1985). Spanking: A grand old American tradition? *Children Today, 14*, 25–29.

Wilds, E. H., and **Lottich, K. V.** (1961). *The foundations of modern education* (3d ed.). New York: Holt, Rinehart and Winston.

Wolpe, J., and **Lazarus, A. A.** (1966). *Behavior therapy techniques: A guide to the treatment of neuroses*. Oxford, England: Pergamon.

Wood, F. H. (1982). The influence of public opinion and social custom on the use of corporal punishment in schools. In F. H. Wood and K. C. Lakin (Eds.), *Punishment and aversive stimulation in special education: Legal, theoretical and practical issues in their use with emotionally disturbed children and youth* (pp. 29–30). Reston, VA: Council for Exceptional Children.

Yaglom, I. M. (1978). *An unusual algebra*. Moscow, Russia: Mir Publishers.

Zippin, L. (1975). *Uses of infinity*. Washington, DC: Mathematical Association of America.

Zumwalt, K. (1989). Beginning professional teachers: The need for a curricular vision of teaching. In M. C. Reynolds (Ed.), *Knowledge base for the beginning teacher* (pp. 173–184). Oxford, England: Pergamon Press.

INDEX

Aaboe, A., 14, 43, 333

Adams, S., 232, 339

Administrative and non-instructional responsibilities of mathematics teachers, 133, 240–241, 247, 294

Affective teaching and learning. *See also* Attitudes about mathematics.
  appreciation level, 65–66, 78–82, 215–216
  willingness-to-try level, 65–66, 78–79, 82, 215–216

Agnesi, M. G., 195

Aleamoni, L. M., 207, 333

Alexander, P. A., 10, 340

Algebra and prealgebra
  curricula, 24–40, 58–60, 245, 260–263, 303–307, 317–331
  sample lessons, 7–8, 17–18, 22–23, 45, 47, 79–82, 85–95, 102–104, 116, 119–123, 126–127, 146, 157, 167, 170–175, 178–179, 182–185, 188–189, 192, 248–252, 260–287, 309–312

Algorithms, 63
  sample lessons, 17–18, 33–34, 104–108, 178, 188–189, 260–287
  strategies for teaching, 17–18, 25, 29–30, 45, 49, 76–79, 103–108, 223–227

Allen, R. R., 10, 42, 333

American Association of School Administrators, 298

American Chemical Society, 298

American Federation of Teachers (AFT), 42, 151, 298

American Mathematical Society, 28, 298

American Psychological Association, 151

Ames, C., 5, 9, 333

Ames, R., 5, 9, 333

Ammon, R., 18, 336

Amundson, H. E., 14, 333

Anderson, P. A., 243, 288, 290, 337

Andre, T., 338

Application-level teaching and learning, 7–8, 67, 75–79, 109–114, 202, 209–210, 225–230. *See also* Problem solving.

Aptitude for learning mathematics, 6–10, 76–78

Archibald, D. A., 207, 333

Archimedes, 13–14, 16, 18

Arends, R. I., 2, 5, 333

Arithmetic
  curricula, 24–40, 63, 313–317
  sample lessons, 30, 32, 80, 84–85

Arnold, D., 173, 333

Artino, R. A., 42, 333

Ashlock, R. B., 16, 29, 42, 194, 224, 333

Assertiveness, 132–133, 138–139, 252–269. *See also* Communicating with students, parents, colleagues and administrators.

Assessing student achievement, 197–237
  blueprint, test, 208–213
  formative evaluation and feedback, 38, 147–148, 167, 172, 180, 187, 190–193, 197–198, 200–201, 215, 217, 231, 266–285
  item pools and measurement items, 199–206, 209–231, 247
  reliability, measurement, 203–207
  summative evaluation and grading, 38, 150, 178, 198, 200–201, 215, 217–218, 231–234, 285–287
  tests and measurements, 199–231, 279, 329–332
  usability, measurement, 206–207
  validity, measurement, 198, 202–208

Assessing teaching performance, 207, 234. *See also* Supervision for mathematics teachers.

Association for Supervision and Curriculum Development (ASCD), 25, 298–299

Association for Women in Mathematics, 28

Attitudes about Mathematics, 3–18, 30–33, 75–76, 191, 224–25, 298. *See also* Affective teaching and learning.
Atwood, R., 173, 333
Azrin, N. H., 151, 333, 339

Ball, D. L., 3, 5, 83, 333
Bandura, A., 151, 333
Bang-Jensen, V., 150, 259, 333
Baroody, A. J., 7, 333
Beginning or first-year teachers, 6, 122, 239–296, 299
Beginning the school year, 127–132, 245–252
Begle, E. G., 27, 333
Behle, J. H., 5, 333
Bell, M., 334
Berg, F. S., 9, 334
Berliner, D. C., 5, 334, 336
Beskin, N. M., 43, 334
Beyer, B. K., 2, 3, 109, 115, 209, 334
Beyer, W. H., 334
Bittinger, M. L., 229, 337
Bloom, B. S., 334, 337
Bongiovanni, A. F., 151, 334
Borich, G., 199, 337
Bourne, L. E., 83, 96, 115, 334
Bowden, L., 43, 339
Bowden, R., 16, 49, 156, 334
Bowers, J., 43, 334
Brandenburg, D. C., 234, 334
Brandt, R., 259, 334
Braskamp, L. A., 234, 334
Bridgeford, N. J., 198, 208, 339
Bridges, E. M., 122, 334
Brissenden, T. H. F., 42–43, 334
Brophy, J., 5, 7, 26, 334
Brown, C. A., 335
Brubaker, D. L., 21, 334
Brumfiel, V., 13, 41, 301, 334
Burns, P. C., 8, 16, 338
Bushaw, D., 42, 262, 334
Business mathematics. *See* General, business, and consumer mathematics courses.
Byrne, M. A., 8, 16, 337

Cahen, L. S., 336
Cajori, F., 43, 334
California State Department of Education, 185, 198, 334
Calculators, 10, 30–34, 49–50
Calculus and precalculus
  curricula, 13, 24–40, 246–247, 290, 292–294, 317–322
  sample lessons, 33–34, 106–108, 248–252, 292–294
Callahan, L. G., 9, 334
Cangelosi, J. S., 3, 5–7, 9–10, 13, 18, 21, 25, 38, 40–42, 48, 63, 65, 75, 79, 84, 103, 112, 115, 118, 122, 127, 131, 133, 135–137, 141–143, 146, 149, 150–151, 156, 170–171, 178, 185, 193–194, 198–199, 202–205, 207, 209–211, 223, 231–234, 241, 247, 259–260, 299, 334–335
Cannon, L. O., 41, 243, 246, 292, 335
Canter, L., 138, 150, 335
Canter, M., 138, 150, 335

Carnegie Forum on Education and the Economy, 335
Carpenter, T. P., 5, 9, 30, 170, 335, 338
Chambers, D. L., 335
Chance, P., 16, 97, 335
Charles, C. M., 10, 335
Chase, A., 207, 335
Chase, C. I., 42, 335
Chrisco, I. M., 42, 335
Churchill, W., 40
Classroom management. *See* Management of student behavior.
Classroom organization and equipment, 40–55, 131–135, 186–190, 241–248. *See also* Management of student behavior.
Clemens, S. R., 66, 243, 288, 335
Clements, B. S., 335
Cobb, P., 5, 8, 335
Coker, H., 234, 337, 339
Collins, A. F., 43, 335
Committee of Fifteen on the Geometry Syllabus, 27
Communicating with students, parents, colleagues and administrators, 125–143, 149–150, 182–183, 185–187, 194, 231, 240–247, 252–260
Comprehension-level teaching and learning, 66–67, 78–79, 98–103, 220–223
Computations. *See* Algorithms.
Computers, 44–49, 144–145, 156, 190, 211–214, 216, 241–243, 247, 260–287
Concepts, Mathematical, 60–63, 67, 76–79, 82–92, 98–100, 109
Conceptualization-level teaching and learning, 61–62, 67, 78–79, 82–95, 216–219, 262–273
Conference Board of the Mathematical Sciences, 28, 335
Conklin, N. F., 198, 208, 339
Constants, Mathematical, 62–63, 83–84, 109
Consumer mathematics. *See* General, business, and consumer mathematics courses.
Conventions, Mathematical, 64, 170
Convergent thinking. *See* Creativity-level teaching and learning.
Cooney, T. J., 5, 66, 243, 288, 335
Cooper, J. M., 9, 259, 335, 338, 340
Cooperative learning, 175, 180–187, 189–190, 298. *See also* Small task-group sessions.
Coulter, F., 193, 335
Council of Scientific Society Presidents, 298
Court, N. A., 43, 335
Coxford, A. F., 41, 335
Cramer, K. A., 5, 13, 338
Creativity-Level Teaching and Learning, 67–68, 78–79, 114–116, 230–231
Cubberley, E. P., 156, 297, 335
Curricula, Mathematics, 5, 21–68, 77–116, 245–247, 260–294, 297–299, 301–307, 313–327
Curwin, R., 151, 335

Davidson, T., 333
Davis, E. J., 5, 335
Deductive lessons. *See* Application-Level Teaching and Learning.
Deductive reasoning, 109–110

Delgado, J. M. R., 151, 335
Demos, G. D., 336
Descriptive language, 136–137, 231. *See also*
    Communicating with students, parents,
    colleagues, and administrators.
Devaney, R. L., 43, 335
Dillon, R. F., 337
Direct instruction
    principles and applications, 2–3, 26–27, 76–79,
        96–108, 155–157, 170–172, 177–178, 188, 192
    sample lessons, 2–3, 22–23, 96–98, 104–108,
        126–127, 157–158, 167–168, 188–189, 260–287
Discoveries, Mathematical, 16–19, 47, 62–64
Discrete mathematics
    curricula, 24–40, 319–322
    sample lessons, 79–82, 85–92, 112–114, 158–161,
        167–169, 191–192
Dishaw, M. M., 336
Divergent thinking. *See* Creativity-level teaching and
    learning.
Dominowski, R. L., 334
Dossey, J. A., 6, 25, 29–31, 49, 82, 170, 298, 335
Doyle, W., 10, 118, 335
Dreikurs, R., 10, 137, 335
Driscoll, M., 297, 335
Dubelle, S. T., 335
Dudeney, H. E., 43, 335
Duke, C. R., 42, 247, 299, 334, 335
Duke, D., 150, 339
Dunkin, M. J., 335, 338

Earl, J. M., 43, 339
Easterday, K. E., 42, 335
Ebel, R. L., 199, 211, 335
Ebmeier, H., 3, 5, 336
Eggen, P., 3, 337
Eisner, M. P., 309, 335
Elam, S. M., 10, 335
Elementary school mathematics, 29–31, 313–317
Elich, J., 41, 243, 292, 335
Ellis, H. C., 3, 335
Emmer, E. T., 143, 335
Engelmann, S., 7, 336
Error analysis, 8, 16–17, 29–30, 45, 105–108, 194,
    224–227, 295
Euclid, 12
Evaluation. *See* Assessing student achievement;
    Assessing teaching performance.
Evertson, C. M., 122, 335, 336
Eves, H., 14, 43, 336

Farmer, W. A., 193, 336
Farrell, M. A., 193, 336
Far West Laboratory, 43
Fennell, M. A., 18, 336
Ferrini-Mundy, J., 298, 337
Fibonacci, L., 96
Filby, N. N., 336
Fisher, C. W., 188, 336
Flammer, G. P., 336
Floden, R. E., 207, 336
Ford, M. P., 336

Foster, A. G., 243, 261, 272, 336
Friedman, L., 298, 336
Frisbie, D. A., 199, 211, 335
Frye, S. M., 30–31, 336
Furth, H. G., 7, 336

Gaglione, A. M., 42, 333
Games and Puzzles, Mathematical, 39, 43–44, 104,
    146–147, 178–181
Gardner, M., 43, 336
Gauss, C. F., 12
General, business, and consumer mathematics courses
    curricula, 22–40, 59, 246, 287–291, 317–322
    sample lessons, 144, 209–210, 248–252, 290–291
Geometry
    curricula, 22–40, 58–59, 246, 287–289, 317–322
    sample lessons, 2–5, 51–53, 80, 105, 110–111,
        128–131, 191, 202, 248–252, 288–289
Ginott, H. G., 136–137, 185, 336
Ginsburg, H., 29, 336
Glaisher, J. W. L., 43
Glasser, W., 10, 336
Gnanadesikan, M., 43, 336
Goals, Learning. *See* Objectives, Learning.
Goetz, E. T., 10, 340
Golden, N., 13, 41, 301, 334
Good, T. L., 3, 5, 336
Gordon, W. J. J., 14–16, 336
Gowan, J. C., 115, 336
Grading student achievement. *See* Assessing student
    achievement: summative evaluation and grading.
Greene, J., 209, 337
Greeno, J. G., 5, 337
Grimes, M. L., 334
Gronlund, N. E., 199, 231, 336
Grouws, D. A., 3, 5, 336
Guilford, J. P., 65, 336

Hake, D. G., 151, 333
Harris, B. M., 299, 336
Harris, T. A., 137, 336
Hastings, J. T., 234, 334
Hater, M. A., 8, 16, 337
Healy, A. F., 334
Heins, M., 13, 41, 301, 334
Heller, B. R., 43, 337
Henderson, K. B., 5, 335
Henry, L. L., 42, 335
Herring, W., 333
Hills, J. R., 207, 336
Hirsch, C. R., 35, 42, 336, 340
History of mathematics
    curricula, 12–16, 18–19, 43, 170, 317–322
    sample lessons, 96, 180–181, 192
Hoffman, C. M., 335
Hoffman, P., 43, 336
Hoffmann, R. J., 210, 336
Holden, C., 29, 336
Homework
    principles and applications, 9–10, 138, 150, 191–195
    sample assignments, 33–34, 81, 83, 90–92, 96, 98,
        126, 191–194, 248–252, 260–287

Honsberger, R., 43, 336
Hopkins, B. R., 199, 207, 231, 336
Hopkins, K. D., 199, 231, 297, 336
Houts, P. L., 199, 207, 336
Hunkins, E. P., 3, 42, 336
Hunt, R. R., 3, 335
Hutchinson, R. R., 151, 333
Hyman, I. A., 151, 334, 336, 338

Illinois Council of Teachers of Mathematics, 10, 336
Independent work sessions
    principles and applications, 187–191
    sample sessions, 106–108, 136, 148, 187–190,
        248–252, 260–287
Inductive lessons. *See* Conceptualization-level teaching
        and learning.
Inductive reasoning, 83–84
Inquiry teaching
    principles and applications, 2–5, 18, 47, 76–95,
        109–116, 155–157, 169–172
    sample lessons, 2–5, 22–23, 39, 47, 51–53, 83–95,
        99–103, 110–114, 119–123, 128–131, 158–161,
        168–169, 172–177, 182–185, 191–193, 260–287
Inservice education for teachers. *See* Supervision of
        mathematics teachers: Instructional supervision.
Institute of Management Sciences, 298
Integrating mathematics with other subject areas,
        247–248, 287–290
Intellectual-level questions, 167–177. *See also*
        Questioning/discussion sessions.
Intellectual-level teaching and learning. *See*
        Comprehension-level teaching and learning;
        Conceptualization-level teaching and learning;
        Application-level teaching and learning;
        Creativity-level teaching and learning.
Inventions, Mathematical, 16–19, 47, 63–64

Jacobsen, D., 3, 337
James, W., 26, 337
Jesunathadas, J., 11, 26, 83, 152, 170, 193, 297, 333, 337
Johnson, D. R., 42, 337
Johnson, M. L., 298, 337
Joint Commission to Study the Place of Mathematics in
        Secondary Education, 27
Jones, F. H., 127, 133, 135, 188, 337
Joyce, B., 2, 5, 16, 96, 114, 116, 180, 337
Judgmental language, 136–137, 231. *See also,*
        Communicating with students, parents,
        colleagues, and administrators.

Kane, R. B., 8, 16, 337
Kansky, B., 30, 49, 337
Karmarker, N., 15
Karush, W., 43, 337
Kasner, E., 43, 337
Kauchak, D., 3, 337
Keedy, M. L., 41, 229, 243, 288, 290, 337
Keeves, J. P., 15, 337
Kennedy, E. S., 195, 337
Kidder, R. M., 15, 337
Kinnard, K. Q., 151, 338
Kinney, L. B., 27, 337

Klopfer, L. E., 339
Knight, R. S., 42, 247, 299, 335
Knowledge-level questions, 169–170, 177–180. *See also*
        Questioning/discussion sessions.
Knowledge-level teaching and learning
    knowledge-of-a-process level, 66, 78–79, 103–108,
        223–225
    simple knowledge level, 66, 78–79, 96–98, 219–220
Kogelman, S., 43, 337
Kohut, S., 151, 337
Kouba, V. L., 7, 335, 337
Kounin, J., 127, 337
Krasner, L., 333
Krathwohl, D., 65, 337
Krulik, S., 43, 262, 337
Kubiszyn, T., 199, 337

Lakin, K. C., 340
Landwehr, J. M., 336
Language of mathematics, 8, 12–14, 16, 64, 98–103,
        220–223
Lazarus, A. A., 138, 340
Lecture Sessions, Interactive
    principles and applications, 156–167
    sample sessions, 22–23, 51–53, 97–98, 106–108,
        157–161, 260–287
Leinhardt, G., 5, 337
Levine, J. M., 337
Lindquist, M. M., 335
Linn, M. C., 3, 337
Linn, R. L., 15, 199, 209, 231, 336, 337
Listening, Student, 9. *See also* Management of student
        behavior; Reading, listening, writing, and
        speaking about mathematics.
Livingston, S. A., 231, 337
Lodholtz, R., 337
Loftus, E. F., 334
Lottich, K. V., 297, 340

Madaus, G. F., 234, 334
Maletsky, E. M., 39, 43–44, 262, 278, 285–286, 339
Management of student behavior, 10–11, 43–44, 51–53,
        118–195, 205, 258–259. *See also* Beginning the
        school year. *See also,* Classroom organization and
        equipment.
    allocated time, 122–124
    behavior patterns, 124–125
    businesslike climate for learning mathematics, 127–135
    classroom rules of conduct and procedures, 143–145,
        161, 186–190
    corporal punishment, 150–151
    off-task and disruptive behaviors, 124–125, 141,
        145–151
    on-task and engaged behaviors, 124–125, 127,
        155–195
    transition time, 122–124, 133–135, 186
Mann, H., 15
Marliave, R., 336
Masia, B., 65, 337
Math COUNTS, 42
Mathematical Association of America (MAA), 28, 42,
        298–299, 337

Mathematics Teacher Inservice Project, 42
Mayer, G. R., 151, 339
McLaren, P., 135, 207, 337
McMillin, S. C., 10, 338
Measurement of student achievement. *See* Assessing student achievement.
Measurements, 50–51, 63
Medley, D. M., 234, 337, 339
Mendler, A., 151, 335
Miller, L., 170, 337
Millman, J., 209, 337
Mitchell, J. V., 333, 335, 336, 338
Mnemonics, 96–98, 170
Möbius strip, 44
Motivating students to learn mathematics, 5–11, 25–26, 39–40, 44. *See also* Attitudes about mathematics; Management of student behavior.
Mullis, I. V. S., 335

Nahrgang, C. L., 18, 338
National Assessment of Educational Progress, 49
National Center for Research in Education, 42
National Council of Supervisors of Mathematics, 298
National Council of Teachers of Mathematics (NCTM), 10, 24, 26–28, 30–32, 34, 38, 40–43, 55–56, 64–65, 74, 83, 112, 115, 170, 185, 199–201, 207, 209, 235, 237, 241, 246, 290–291, 295, 297–299, 309, 313, 333, 338. *See also, Standards, NCTM.*
National Education Association (NEA), 42, 151, 298, 338
National Research Council, 298, 338
National School Boards Association, 298
National Science Board Commission on Precollege Education in Mathematics, Science, and Technology, 28, 338
National Science Foundation, 42
National Society of Professional Engineers, 298
Nelson, D., 43, 338
Newman, C. M., 336
Newman, F. M., 207, 333
Newman, J. R., 43, 207, 337
Nielsen, K. L., 43, 338
Niven, I., 43, 338
Number theory
    curricula, 24–40, 317–322
    sample lessons, 39, 47, 96–97, 99–101, 180–181

Objectives, Learning, 11–12, 36–38, 57–71, 78–79, 202–203, 208, 215–231, 260–262
Obremski, T. E., 336
O'Daffer, P. G., 66, 243, 288, 335
Orfan, L. J., 229, 337
Ory, J. C., 234, 334
Overlearning, 96–98

Packel, E., 43, 338
Parents, Working with, 10, 139–143, 255–258. *See also* Communicating with students, parents, colleagues, and administrators.
Payne, J. N., 41, 335
Pestalozzi, J., 297
Pèter, R., 43, 338

Petersen, B. T., 18, 338
Peterson, I., 15, 43, 338
Phye, G. D., 3, 338
Piaget, J., 7
Pollack, H. O., 334
Pòlya, G., 43, 338
Popham, W. J., 150, 199, 207, 234, 338, 339
Posamentier, A. S., 39, 43, 47–48, 191, 338
Post, T. R., 5, 13, 338
Probability and statistics
    curricula, 22–40, 59–60, 317–322
    sample lessons, 79–82, 112–114, 158–161, 167–169, 175–177, 180–181, 191–192
Problem solving, 7–9, 24–26, 30, 39–40, 44, 47, 74–78, 102–103, 109–110, 181–182, 225–231, 260–286, 298, 317–322, 329–332. *See also* Application-level teaching and learning.
Professional teacher behavior, 141–143, 148–151, 239–241, 291, 294, 299
Proofs, Mathematical, 47, 64, 99–101, 205–206, 230–231
Psychological noise, 84–95, 172, 218
Purdy, C. R., 27, 337
Pythagoras, 12

Questioning/discussion sessions
    principles and applications, 167–180
    sample sessions, 4–5, 22–23, 84–92, 99–103, 109–114, 116, 167–175, 260–287
Questions, Responding to students', 175–177. *See also* Intellectual-level questions. *See also* Knowledge-level questions.
Quina, J., 3, 7, 156, 162, 167, 338

Raney, P., 42, 150, 338
Range, D. G., 151, 337
Rath, J. N., 243, 261, 272, 336
Reading, listening, writing, and speaking about mathematics, 8, 40–43, 64, 98–103, 220–223. *See also* Comprehension-level teaching and learning. *See also, Language of mathematics.*
Reardon, F. J., 151, 338
Relations, Mathematical, 47, 63–64, 67, 76–79, 82–84, 92–95, 98–99
Resnick, L. B., 339
Reynolds, M. C., 336, 340
Reynolds, R. N., 151, 338
Reys, R. E., 43, 262, 337, 338, 339
Robbins, A., 156, 338
Robbins, P., 42, 150, 338
Roe, B. D., 8, 16, 338
Rogers, B. G., 207, 338
Rogers, R. L., 10, 338
Rogers, V., 173, 333
Romberg, T. A., 5, 9, 338
Rose, T. L., 151, 338
Rosenshine, B., 188, 338
Rust, J. O., 151, 338
Ryan, K., 9, 338

Salkind, C. T., 43, 339
Sallery, R. D., 151, 333
Sanford, J. P., 335

Santrock, J. W., 7, 25, 339
Saunders, H., 43, 339
Scheaffer, R. L., 336
Schiffer, N. M., 43, 339
Schoenfeld, A. H., 3, 6–7, 18, 25, 30, 43, 75, 104, 224, 339
School Mathematics Study Group, 27
School Science and Mathematics Association, 28
Schulman, L. S., 5, 339
Shapiro, M. S., 43, 339
Sharron, S., 43, 339
Shell, N., 42, 333
Simpson, F. M., 42, 335
Silver, E. A., 335
Skemp, R. R., 43, 297, 339
Small task-group sessions
    principles and applications, 180–187
    sample sessions, 93–95, 146, 180–185, 260–287
Smedslund, J., 7, 339
Smith, F., 232, 339
Smith, S. A., 229, 243, 288, 290, 337
Soar, R. S., 234, 337, 339
Sobel, M. A., 39, 43–44, 262, 278, 285–286, 339
Socrates, 297
Soltis, J., 151, 339
Souviney, R. J., 43, 339
Speaking about mathematics. *See* Reading, listening, writing, and speaking about mathematics.
Special Needs of Students, 5–11, 48, 147–148
Stallion, B. K., 42, 339
Standardized Tests, 207
Standards, NCTM, 10, 26–35, 38, 40, 43, 55–56, 64–65, 74, 115, 185, 199, 201, 235, 237, 246, 297–299, 313–322, 338
Stanley, J. C., 199, 336
Stanley, S. J., 207, 231, 234, 339
Steen, L. A., 24, 339
Steere, B. F., 10, 118, 339
Stepelman, J., 39, 43, 47–48, 191, 338
Sternberg, R. J., 337
Stiggins, R. J., 150, 198, 208, 235, 339
Stoodt, B. D., 8, 16, 338
Strike, K., 151, 339
Stringer, R., 15
Strom, R. D., 15, 26, 114–115, 339
Struyk, L. R., 334
Sulzer-Azaroff, B., 151, 339
Supervision of mathematics teachers
    administrative supervision, 241, 260
    instructional supervision, 41–42, 241, 259–260, 290–294, 299
Supportive replies, 137–138. *See also* Communicating with students, parents, colleagues, and administrators.
Suydam, M. N., 297, 339
Swafford, J. O., 335
Swift, J., 336
Syllabus, Course, 128–131, 245–248, 323–327

Syllogism, 109–110
Synectics, 116

Teaching as a set of messy functions, 1–12, 197
Technology in the classroom, 43–55, 128–131, 166, 289–290, 298, 317–322. *See also* Calculators. *See also* Computers.
Textbooks, Mathematics, 7–8, 13, 38–41, 102–103, 207, 242–247, 260–290, 301–303
Thomas, D. R., 336
Thompson, M., 334
Thorndike, E. L., 15, 26, 339
Torrance, E. P., 114–115, 336, 339
Towers, R. L., 10, 339
Trigonometry
    curricula, 22–40, 318–322
    sample lessons, 97–98, 109, 179
Tuckman, B. W., 199, 339

Ullman, L. P., 333
Ulrich, R. E., 151, 339
Units, Teaching, 22, 36–40, 57–60, 78–79, 181, 197–199, 245–247, 260–290
Usiskin, Z., 40, 334, 339
Utah State Board of Education, 340
Utah State Office of Education, 305

Van Dyke, H. T., 151, 340
Van Horn, K. L., 136, 340
Variables, 41, 50–51, 61, 126–127, 172–175
von Baravalle, H., 58, 340

Wachs, H., 7, 336
Wadsworth, B. J., 3, 5, 340
Watkins, A. E., 336
Weber, W. A., 10, 118, 340
Weil, M., 2, 5, 16, 96, 114, 116, 180, 337
Weinstein, C. E., 10, 340
Welsh, R. S., 151, 340
Wilds, E. H., 297, 340
Winters, L. J., 243, 261, 272, 336
Wise, J. H., 151, 334, 336, 338
Withitness, 128, 152
Wittrock, M. C., 335, 338
Wolfe, P., 42, 138, 335
Wolpe, J., 340
Wood, F. H., 151, 340
Woodworth, R. S., 26, 339
Worsham, M. E., 335
Writing mathematics. *See* Reading, listening, writing, and speaking about Mathematics.

Yaglom, L., 43, 340

Zieky, M. J., 231, 337
Zippin, L., 43, 340
Zumwalt, K. K., 21, 333, 340
Zweng, M. J., 35, 42, 336, 340

ABOUT THE AUTHOR

With extensive experience teaching mathematics at the middle school, high school, and university levels, James S. Cangelosi (Ph.D., Louisiana State University, 1972) serves as a professor at Utah State University specializing in mathematics education, data collection, assessment of student achievement, and behavior management. Among his publications are articles in journals such as *Mathematics Teacher, Arithmetic Teacher, Journal for Research in Mathematics Education, Phi Delta Kappan, Mathematics and Computer Education, Educational Measurement Issues and Practices, Contemporary Education, The Clearing House, NASSP Bulletin,* and *Delta Pi Epsilon Journal,* books including *Measurement and Evaluation: An Inductive Approach for Teachers* (1982), *Classroom Management Strategies: Gaining and Maintaining Students' Cooperation* (1988), *Cooperation in the Classroom: Students and Teachers Together* (1990), *Designing Tests for Evaluating Student Achievement* (1990), *Evaluating Classroom Instruction* (1991), and *Systematic Teaching Strategies* (in press), and videotape programs for mathematics teachers such as "Demystifying School Mathematics" and "Using Mathematics to Solve Real-Life Problems." Recent research and development efforts (e.g., the Mathematics Teacher Inservice Project) reflect Dr. Cangelosi's concern for narrowing the gap between typical teaching practices and research-based teaching practices.